THE DIARY
OF
COLONEL PETER HAWKER

1893

Republished
with a new introduction
by
The Richmond Publishing Co. Ltd. 1971

BIBLIOGRAPHIC NOTE

The original copy of this diary was produced in two volumes. This is a facsimile of both volumes bound into one.

S.B.N. 85546 010 5

Republished in 1971 by The Richmond Publishing Co. Ltd.

Printed in Offset by Kingprint Limited
Richmond, Surrey, England.

INTRODUCTORY NOTE

Like Sir Ralph Payne-Gallwey before me I am keenly conscious of the honour of being asked to write an introduction to this work. Unlike Sir Ralph I have not the advantage of being one of the finest shots of my generation. The passage of nearly eighty years has, however, given one a new appreciation of Hawker and his *Diary*.

In the 1890's the great encroachment of the towns upon the countryside had little effect. Shooting was for the most part in the hands of the nobility and gentry. Pheasants were reared on a vast scale. Today the cost of such rearing is quite beyond the purses of most shoots be they private or syndicated. Although there are far more pheasants about than in Hawker's time, a result of this great increase in cost is that many of the guns of today have to work to find their sport. This would have happened to few game shots of the late nineteenth century. The cycle of change has not, of course, taken us so far as the American position where driving is almost unheard of. Nonetheless, the great increase in the numbers of those who want to shoot has brought us back in many instances to a kind of sport not unlike that which the Colonel would have enjoyed.

Just as Palmerston was said to be the last eighteenth century statesman, so Hawker must have been, in turn, one of the last examples of the eighteenth century's soldiers, inventors and sportsmen. A fascination of the diaries is the way in which the various facets of his life were all set out, all completely naturally, and with no thought of publication. If one takes any one of them one sees the extraordinary ability of the man. Above all he had that exclusively eighteenth century quality of *bottom.*

Of Hawker the soldier there is but little. Having in a thoroughly eighteenth century way sought the assistance of a royal duke in his candidature for command of the Hampshire Yeomanry he obtained that post despite the lack of the riches that were normally necessary for a commanding officer of a yeomanry regiment of that time. It was no accident that his duke wrote to him whilst the appointment was pending, urging him for the good of the county to accept the post of second in command if the colonelcy was denied him for lack of wealth (in those days a commanding officer was expected to equip his regiment largely out of his own pocket. This continued to be true of cadet battalions even until the 1920's when this writer's father maintained a cadet battalion on five shillings per boy per year!) In the Penninsular Hawker showed that gallantry and bloodcurdling courage which marked so many of those who fought that campaign. A gauge of this comes in the fact that by 1812 he had still not recovered from the wounds he had received in 1809 at Talavera. The pain in his shattered hip was something which dogged him until the end of his days.

Of particular interest is the operation of the old game laws, well illustrated by Hawker's shooting travels. The attempt to warn him off by Squire Jones was something of a flop. Nonetheless, the system of gun control based upon heraldic qualifications seems in very general terms to have succeeded. For an account of the old game laws see Hawker's *Instructions to young Sportsmen* (1824).

Those with interest in gun-collecting will be delighted by the passages dealing with the great men of the London gun trade. Here the great names of the past come alive again – whether one's hero is Joe Manton, 'Old Egg', or any of those whose job was that most exacting trade at its most exacting period Hawker gives us new insight into their trade and their ways. He himself was never a gunmaker but the *Diary* tells of his exhibits for the Great Exhibition. His design for a musket he believed in passionately – even to the extent of having a long interview with the Prince Consort upon the subject. He was an amateur exhibitor at the Exhibition and had to work hard to get his exhibits (Birmingham made) as he wished. By this time the poor Colonel was nearing the end of his life – he died twentyseven months later in 1853. The lameness which had long troubled him actually prevented his presence at the opening by the Queen (the *Diary* shows a lot of the less glittering aspects of the Exhibition too). Despite his illness December 1st 1851 again saw Hawker in the field – his first outing that season. He was 'too weak and unwell to shoot as I have always done' and he consequently missed four shots that 'I ought to have killed; but I managed to bag 2 teal and 6 snipes'. What a man!

One aspect of this remarkable diarist, which is well worthy of thought, is that he never seems to have fought a duel. Every gentleman of the period was skilled in the use of the pistol. Hawker was no coward by any stretch of the imagination, yet there is no known mention of duel or even of duelling pistols in the diaries. It is possible that such an incident might have been expurgated (as, Parker tells us, were the references to Mrs. Hawker's presence on many shooting trips). Equally he may have shared the views of Colonel Ross who was without dispute the finest pistol shot of his time, and who would not duel. The explanation which appeals most to the writer is that history has been over-influenced by the romantic view of the duel which was perpetuated in the pages of Lever and denegrated by the writings of the anti-duelling journalists. We know that Squire Jones tried to call him out. In reply he got a letter that was a far greater insult (saying he was no gentleman and so could not call Hawker to answer for his conduct). The Squire was a person of substance and probably bore arms. Hawker, though not, was still in the Royals, one of the smartest cavalry regiments. By today's standards he behaved outrageously. At that time it would have seemed far worse. Nonetheless, there seems to have been no duel. Can it be that the strict code of the Clonmell rules was in reality only for the Fireaters and their English equivalents? Such a view is hard to reconcile with the Wellington/Winchelsea encounter but it seems a tenable explanation.

Many shooters are accused of being bores. In his introduction Sir Ralph sets out Hawker's literary achievements. When one considers his music, his fishing and his shooting one can only imagine how full of interest the man must have been for his contemporaries.

These thoughts are by way of introduction. If at the end the reader has an additional appreciation or understanding of this greatest of our shooting writers I will have served my humble purpose. If at the same time the immense and timeless enjoyment of reading the diaries in the 1970's is enhanced even a little I have served it well.

W.W.

COLONEL PETER HAWKER'S

DIARY

VOL. I.

Painted by A.E. Chalon R.A.
Engraved by H. Adlard

THE DIARY

OF

COLONEL PETER HAWKER

AUTHOR OF 'INSTRUCTIONS TO YOUNG SPORTSMEN'

1802—1853

WITH AN INTRODUCTION

BY SIR RALPH PAYNE-GALLWEY, BART.

IN TWO VOLUMES—VOL. I.

WITH ILLUSTRATIONS

LONDON

LONGMANS, GREEN, AND CO

AND NEW YORK: 15 EAST 16th STREET

1893

INTRODUCTION

I HAVE GREAT PLEASURE in acceding to the request that I should write a short introductory notice of Colonel PETER HAWKER, the Author of this Diary and of the well-known 'Instructions to Young Sportsmen.' Colonel Hawker's position among sportsmen and writers on sport is mainly owing to the great reputation he achieved with reference to the art of killing wild fowl, and he may most justly be termed the father of wild-fowling, for he brought this sport to such perfection that his name will always suggest itself wherever duck shooting is practised in our Islands.

Although Colonel Hawker's present reputation is mainly based on his proficiency in this one branch of sport, it must not be forgotten that he was equally celebrated in his own day for his knowledge of and success in game shooting.

The immense popularity of Colonel Hawker's book 'Instructions to Young Sportsmen' was due to the large amount of original information it contained, and to the terseness, accuracy, and common sense with which it was written; it is in fact a work every line of which was evidently penned from actual personal experience and nothing else. It is true that 'Instructions to Young Sportsmen' may not seem original in these days, but this is because almost every writer on shooting since the first edition of the book was published has so freely borrowed from it.

There is no doubt the Colonel's book stood unrivalled for quite fifty years as a manual on guns and shooting, and on all connected with killing game and especially wild fowl, and in many respects its contents are, with possibly a few alterations, such as the substitution of breech-loaders for muzzle-loaders, just as useful to the present generation as they were to the last and to the one before that, particularly in regard to all details of coast fowling.

The steel illustrations in the later editions of Colonel Hawker's book are splendid examples of sporting pictures, and some of them are reproduced in this Diary. I consider the one facing page 146 is the best. The best edition of 'Instructions to Young Sportsmen' is the ninth (1844), which was dedicated to the Prince Consort. The tenth was brought out ten years later, and the eleventh in 1859. The two latter, being somewhat abridged by the Colonel's son, are not so interesting as the last published in the Author's lifetime, i.e. the one of 1844. The first edition was printed in 1814, the last (the eleventh) in 1859.

This Diary only contains extracts from its original, the whole of which if given intact would fill several more volumes. In it the Author was in the habit of setting down almost everything he did, thought, and said during fifty years, adding comments on nearly every shot he fired, how he killed, and why he missed. The Diary bears the impress of truth and close observation from beginning to end, and contains numerous quaint and highly original remarks very characteristic of the Colonel. There are some very interesting accounts of its writer's journeys to the Continent both before and after the fall of Napoleon, and of his expeditions to the North to shoot moor game. These latter records will doubtless entertain sportsmen of the present time when they read of the Colonel's delight at bagging a few brace of grouse at places where now hundreds are killed in one day. I should say, after perusing this Diary, that Colonel Hawker was the keenest and most hardworking shooter ever known; such entries as—'breakfasted by candlelight, walked hard all day in a deluge of rain, bagged 3 cock pheasants; gloriously outmanœuvred all the other shooters, came home very satisfied and dined off one of the birds'—will show the thorough sportsman he was. That the Colonel was a marvellous shot there can be no doubt whatever, and in the style of game shooting he pursued has probably no equal in these days; as a snipe shot he has never been, and perhaps never will be, equalled—fourteen to fifteen snipe without a miss in as many single shots, and with a flint gun, speaks volumes as to his skill. My idea of the Author of this Diary has always been that he was the 'hardest' man, in regard to health, that could be imagined; but it will be seen that he was continually fighting against illness, and frequently incapacitated by his severe Peninsular wound[1]; and the way in which he was, to use his words, wont to 'quack himself up,' to enable him to take the field with his gun, is worthy of admiration as an example of British pluck. Colonel Hawker was, it may easily be seen, a man of vast energy, and a very shrewd observer. Nothing, apparently, could escape him, whether on his travels abroad or in pursuit of game and wild fowl at home. He was, besides, a most accomplished musician and musical critic, and was intimately acquainted with many of the celebrated pianists and operatic singers of his day.

Longparish House and its water meadows, so often alluded to by the Author of this Diary, and the river Test, in which he caught literally thousands of trout (when trout could be caught therein without first crawling for them like stalking a stag, and then throwing a floating fly), are just as of yore. So is Keyhaven near Lymington, save that there are few or no ducks and geese to be seen there now. The cottage which Colonel Hawker built is still standing, and is the large one shown facing in the view on page 146.

I must not omit to record that the Colonel served with the greatest bravery and distinction under Wellington, and when

[1] A bullet went clean through his thigh, the bone of which it severely shattered.

merely a boy led his squadron, and won the word 'Douro' for the colours of his regiment, the then 14th Light Dragoons. The recognition of this gallantry by his old corps is feelingly alluded to in the note on page 163, vol. ii.

In figure Colonel Hawker was over six feet and strikingly handsome, and up to the end of his life was very erect. He was, no doubt, somewhat of an egotist, but it was in a good-natured way, and a confirmed but amusing grumbler against his personal ill-luck, and his constant enemy the weather; he was, however, an instructive and witty companion, and a conversationalist who always commanded attention, particularly when he related his long and varied experiences of sport, the adventures of his younger days in the Peninsular war, or conversed on music, literature, and travel.

Colonel Peter Hawker was born in London, December 24, 1786. He was the son of Colonel Peter Ryves Hawker, who died in 1790, by Mary Wilson Yonge, a daughter of an Irish family. His great-grandfather, Colonel Peter Hawker (who died 1732), was Governor of Portsmouth in 1717, and his father commanded the 1st Regiment of Horse. It is worthy of note that his ancestors served in the British army without a break from the days of Elizabeth.

Colonel Hawker was gazetted cornet to the 1st Royal Dragoons in 1801, lieutenant 1802, and then reduced to half-pay by the peace of Amiens; he exchanged into the 14th Light Dragoons in 1803, and obtained his troop in 1804; with this regiment he served in Portugal and Spain, and in 1813 retired from active service in consequence of a severe wound received at the battle of Talavera in 1809. In 1815 he was appointed major of the North Hampshire Militia, and in 1821 was made its lieutenant-colonel by the Duke of Wellington, and afterwards a deputy lieutenant for his county.

Colonel Peter Hawker first married, at Lisbon in 1811, Julia, only daughter of Major Hooker Barttelot.

In 1844 he married (secondly) Helen Susan, widow of Captain John Symonds, R.N., and daughter of Major Chatterton. Colonel Peter Hawker died in London at No. 2 Dorset Place, August 7, 1853, and is buried at Marylebone Church.

Colonel Hawker had by his first marriage two sons,—Richard, who died young, and Peter William Lanoe, for some time a captain in the 74th Highlanders (who married in 1847 Elizabeth, daughter of John Fraser, of Stirling, N.B.); and two daughters,—Mary, who married Mr. Charles Rhodes in 1842, and Sophy, married in 1843 to the Rev. Lewis Playters Hird.

The late Captain Hawker, of the 74th Highlanders, left a son and a daughter. His son, Mr. Peter Hawker, formerly of the Royal Navy, the present owner of Longparish House, married in 1883 the eldest daughter of Colonel Alfred Tippinge, late Grenadier Guards; and his sister, Miss Hawker, is the talented authoress of 'Mademoiselle Ixe.'

Besides his celebrated 'Instructions to Young Sportsmen' Colonel (then Captain) Peter Hawker published anonymously, in 1810, 'The Journal of a Regimental Officer during the Recent Campaign in Portugal and Spain;'[1]

'Instructions for the best Position on the Pianoforte;'

'An Abridgment of the New Game Laws, with Observations and Suggestions for Improvement,' an appendix to the sixth edition of 'Instructions to Young Sportsmen,' which was dedicated to William the Fourth.

In 1820 Colonel Peter Hawker patented his very ingenious hand-moulds for use on the pianoforte.

RALPH PAYNE-GALLWEY.

THIRKLEBY PARK, THIRSK: *August* 1893.

[1] Very scarce; if any reader of this could kindly lend me a copy, I should feel extremely indebted.—R. P.-G.

LIST OF PLATES

IN

THE FIRST VOLUME

THE DIARY

OF

COLONEL PETER HAWKER

CHAPTER I

1802 [1]

June 27th.—Arrived at Longparish House.

September.—Altogether killed 200 head of game this month.

Instances of uncertainty in killing jack snipes: The first thirteen shots I had at these birds this year I killed without missing one; have since fired eight shots at one jack and missed them all.

1803

January 26th.—Sketch of a bad day's sport: Being in want of a couple of wild fowl, I went out with my man this morning about ten o'clock. The moment we arrived at the river 5 ducks and 1 wigeon flew up; we marked the former down, and just as we arrived near the place it began to snow very hard, which obliged us to secure our gunlocks with the skirts of our coats. No sooner had we done this than a mallard rose within three yards of me. I uncovered my gun and made all possible haste, and contrived to shoot before it had gone twenty yards, but missed it, which I imputed to the sight of

[1] My second season of sporting (age 16½ years).

my gun being hid by the snow. My man fired and brought it down, but we never could find it; and another mallard coming by me, I fired and struck him, insomuch that before he had flown a gunshot, he dropped apparently dead, but we were again equally unfortunate notwithstanding our dogs were with us. While we were loading, the 3 remaining ducks came by, a fair shot. Having reloaded, we went in search of them, but could not succeed. On our road home, coming through the meadow, the wigeon rose in the same place as before. I shot at it, and wounded it very much; we marked it down and sprung it again; it could hardly fly, from its wounds. Unluckily, my gun missed fire, and my man was unprepared, thinking it had fallen dead. We marked it into a hedge; before we had reached the place we spied a hawk that had followed it; from the same place the hawk was, the wigeon flew out of the hedge close under my feet. I fired at it, but, owing to agitation, had not taken a proper aim; however, a chance shot brought it to the ground; my dogs ran at it; it flew up again, but could not rise to any height, but continued to clear the hedges, and we never could find it again. To add to our misfortunes, we both tumbled into deep water.

June 4th.—Left Longparish House to join the 14th Light Dragoons on the march at Hythe.

September 1st.—Folkestone. 4 partridges and 1 landrail. I went with Major Talbot and his brother: we were out from half-past four in the morning till eight at night, and walked above five hours before we saw the first brace of birds. Major Talbot killed a brace, and his brother 1 bird; a brace of birds and 1 rabbit were shot between us by means of firing at the same instant.

1804

February 18th.—Left Folkestone to be quartered at Dover, till further orders.

March 6th.—Left Dover for Romney.

May 3rd.—Romney. Went out in the evening, saw several very large shoals of curlews, but could not get near them ; just as it grew dusk I laid myself down flat on the sands: every flock assembled into one prodigious large flight, and pitched within ten yards of me. I put them up with the expectation of killing not less than twenty, and my gun missed fire.

June 14th.—Romney. Shot an avoset (swimming). This is a bird rarely to be met with but on the Kentish coast. The above is its name in natural history ; it is here known by the name of cobbler's awl, owing to the form of the beak, which turns up at the end like the awl.

September 1st.—Romney. In a bad country we had never been in before Major Pigot and I bagged nine brace and a half of birds, exclusive of several we lost. We sprung one covey too small to fire at ; Major Pigot picked out the old hen and I the cock, and bagged them both. There were sportsmen in almost every field. In the course of the day, my old dog Dick caught 8 hedgehogs.

November 23rd.—Marched from Romney to be quartered at Guildford.

December 23rd.—Left Guildford to stay a week at home at Longparish House.

1805

May 28th.—Marched from Guildford to Chertsey.

June 11th.—Marched from Chertsey to Wandsworth.

17th.—Marched from Wandsworth to Hounslow Barracks.

26th.—11 brace of carp with a draw net, average weight one pound.

27th.—21 brace of carp and 3 dozen dace (casting net).

October 17th.—My new gun, No. 4536, arrived from Manton.

31st.—I followed a teal for near four hours before I could get a shot at it, and after I fired it flew almost out of sight and dropped within a few yards of my servant John, who happened to be riding by and who picked it up.

December 27th.—Marched into the town of Hounslow. As we were getting close to the town, a mallard flew up and came round several times within shot of the troops. I rode on to the Colonel's, borrowed his long gun and returned to where the bird had dropped, which was within thirty yards of the turnpike road, in a large pond. After looking for him for some time I heard him fly up behind me from the very place I had been beating, therefore it appeared I must have gone within a few yards of him; I had, however, a tolerably fair shot, but the gun, being very foul, hung fire, and I missed him.

1806

February 10th.—1 jack snipe, 1 rabbit, and 2 hares. The hares ran out of a hedge together. I killed them right and left immediately in front of Lord Berkeley's house at Hounslow; and while I was hiding under the hedge, fearing a keeper might be on the look-out at hearing the gun, a dragoon ran and picked up both the hares, gave a view hollow, and held one up in each hand in order to be seen from the windows of his Lordship's mansion. Of course I retreated immediately, and luckily got off unseen.

Game killed by me up to February 1st, 1806 (at Hounslow): 46½ brace of partridges, 12 brace of hares, 4 brace of pheasants.

Fowl, rabbits, and snipe, killed up to April 1st, 1806 (at Hounslow): 8 brace of rabbits, 23½ couple of snipes, 1 couple of teal. A wild duck, ox-eyes, rails, fieldfares, redwings, herons, larks, &c.

June 22nd.—Went a gudgeon fishing at Walton-on-Thames with a party; had good sport and returned in the evening.

29th.—Went a gudgeon fishing at Walton; had indifferent sport. In the evening tried for barbel, and killed 2; the one small, the other 6 lb.

July 4th.—Went a fishing at Walton; in the morning killed 2 dozen gudgeon; in the evening 4 barbel. Their weights were: (1) 9¾ lb., (2) 3 lb., (3) 1 lb., (4) ½ lb.

17th.—Marched from Hounslow Barracks to Alton in Hampshire, to remain with my troop till further orders.

31st.—Marched to Winchester, to remain till further orders.

August 1st.—Rode over to my home at Longparish and killed 8 trout (fly fishing), and returned in the evening to Winchester.

12th.—At Longparish. 7 trout.

21st.—At Longparish. 8 trout, and shot 1 heron, 1 snipe and 1 green sandpiper. Received my new double gun, No. 4699, from Manton.

September 1st.—Longparish. 30 partridges and 2 hares. N.B.—3 brace shot and lost besides.

Altogether I killed in September 53½ brace of partridges, 5½ brace of hares, 1 brace of quails, and 1 landrail (at Longparish).

22nd.—Marched to Fareham, for the purpose of conveying the horses of the 17th Light Dragoons to Salisbury.

25th.—Marched to Romsey.

26th.—Marched into Sarum.

30th.—Received an order to join at Winchester.

October 12th.—Marched from Winchester to Romsey, on our way to Dorchester.

13th.—Marched from Romsey to Ringwood. N.B.—Drove over in the morning before the troops and killed 6 partridges, 1 pheasant, 1 teal (flying), and 1 rabbit.

14th.—Marched to Blandford; remained there till the 18th, when we marched into Dorchester Barracks.

November 5th.—Marched to Sturminster, to remain during the election at Dorchester.

24th.—3 woodcocks, 2 rabbits, and 1 pheasant.

Previous to killing the last woodcock I missed both barrels at him, and followed him for near two hours.

25th.—4 cock pheasants.

It rained incessantly during the time I was beating for them, which obliged me to secure the lock of my gun under my jacket, and consequently lost much time in firing; yet, although the wind was high and the covers thick, I missed but one shot.

December 14th.—Went on leave to Longparish.

1807

January 1st.—Returned to the regiment at Dorchester.

22nd.—4 pheasants, 1 hare, 1 woodcock, and 1 wood pigeon.

Notwithstanding it blew a hurricane, and rained almost the whole time I was out, I only discharged once without bagging; I had then a shot going rapidly down the wind, and greatly intercepted by trees. It was at a pheasant, which I marked down and killed afterwards. I saw but 5 pheasants, 1 cock, and 1 hare all day; so (with the exception of 1 pheasant which rose out of shot) I brought home all I sprung up.

24th.—In the morning, going past a lake, I saw 5 tufted ducks, which I fired at on the water with the long gun at about 70 yards, and winged one of them. Old Dick immediately dashed in after it, and on getting near it some tame ducks fluttered from under the banks of an island, which he sprang at, and in consequence lost the bird I so much wished to have brought home. On my return by the same place, a mallard flew over my head, which I winged (a very long shot) and lost. While beating the ditches for snipes I spied a very fine trout, which, with a piece of whipcord and a stick, I instantly snared; and he proved, when dressed, to be very well in season.

Game killed up to February 1st: 182 partridges, 33 pheasants, 43 hares, 2 quails, and 2 landrails. Total, 262 head.

March 9th.—Marched with my troop to Blandford, to remain during the assizes at Dorchester.

May 10*th.*—Left Dorchester to remain at Longparish during the Hampshire election.

11*th.*—The election began and ended in favour of Sir H. Mildmay and Mr. Chute.

27*th.*—Longparish. Killed 20 brace of trout with a fly in three hours.

31*st.*—Joined the regiment at Dorchester again.

June 29*th.*—Marched to Weymouth.

July 10*th.*—Received orders for the regiment to march from Dorchester, Weymouth &c. to Guildford and Basingstoke.

12*th.*—Marched to Blandford.

13*th.*—To Salisbury.

14*th.*—To Andover. Went over to Longparish: had some indifferent sport fly fishing.

17*th.*—Joined my troop at Basingstoke.

22*nd.*—Marched away from Basingstoke to Bagshot.

23*rd.*—Marched from Bagshot to Hounslow.

27*th.*—The regiment were reviewed.

29*th.*—The regiment marched on their way to the east coast of Sussex. I went on leave to London.

August 1*st.*—Went to Lord Bridgewater's at Ashridge Park. (Killed a number of rabbits here.)

7*th.*—Returned to London.

10*th.*—Left town on my way to Sussex.

11*th.*—Joined the regiment at Blatchington.

12*th.*—Went over to my troop at Bexhill.

14*th.*—Went on leave of absence to Longparish.

September 1*st.*—Longparish. 40 partridges and 2 hares. I had only one gun, and shot with the same three dogs the whole day. Rested two hours in the forenoon, and left off shooting by six o'clock.

Game bagged the first week: 91 partridges and 3 hares.

October 26*th.*—A woodcock. I found him in some very low wood where cocks seldom resorted, and taking him for a nightjar, did not think it worth while to disturb the cover by firing, and refused an excellent shot at him; but soon discovering my mistake, I followed and flushed him again, and fired twice at him, and although the wood was not four acres he escaped, and completely defeated us. But being the first that had been seen here this year I was so unwilling to give him up, that I went home and returned with all the rabble I could muster, and placed Buffin in a tree to mark. We began with beating where he first sprang from; we had not gone thirty yards before one of Siney's terriers flushed him, and I brought him down.

November 20th.—Received a new double gun from Mr. Joseph Manton, No. 4326.

1808

Game bagged from September 1st, 1807, to February 1st, 1808: 217 partridges, 11 pheasants, and 31 hares. Total, 259 head.

February 5th.—Received an order to join the regiment.

7th.—Left Longparish and joined at Eastbourne to-day.

10th.—Went to Bexhill Barracks.

March 17th.—Went up to London. I rode the fat mare to Tonbridge (above 35 miles) in three hours and ten minutes, from whence I took the young mare to Westminster Bridge (30 miles) in two hours and forty-five minutes.

20th.—Returned (on horseback) to Bexhill in a little more than eight hours.

Wild fowl, rabbits &c. bagged up to April 1st, 1808: 72 snipes, 5 wild ducks, 5 woodcocks and 14 rabbits. Total, 96 head; adding game, total 355 head; exclusive of herons, wood pigeons, moorhens, fieldfares, rails, &c.

May 14th.—Marched from Bexhill to Pleydon Barracks.

16th.—Went a fishing with a casting net and stop net, and killed 11 tench (average weight above 1 lb.), 5 jack, 1 eel, and a large quantity of roach.

17th.—Went with the same nets to the canal, where we killed a large basketful, consisting of bream, jack, perch, eels, roach and dace.

July 6th.—Marched away from Pleydon Barracks to Cranbrook.

20th.—Arrived at Ipswich with my troop.

29th.—Arrived at Norwich Barracks.

September 3rd.—Returned to Ipswich; while on the road tried some stubbles and killed 1 partridge, and 2 more shot and lost in the corn.

8th.—18 partridges, besides a brace shot and lost. Notwithstanding the weather was very stormy I only fired three shots the whole day without killing, two of which were decidedly too far off. I took three double shots, and bagged both birds each time; and one brace I took while it was raining, and had to take my gun from under my coat before I fired right and left.

10th.—13 partridges, 4 French partridges, and 1 turtle dove.

13th.—9 partridges and 1 rabbit, with 2 partridges shot and lost in fourteen shots.

N.B.—One of the two shots missed was a long random one.

14th.—Went out round the barracks for two hours after the field day and had three single shots, and one right and left, and bagged 5 partridges.

15th.—12 partridges, 1 French partridge, and 1 turtle dove. In eighteen shots, though a wild windy day, and most of them long ones (fired right and left twice; bagged both birds each time).

17th.—14 partridges and 2 rabbits, besides a brace shot and lost, in twenty-one shots. On going out I met with a farmer who (having the deputation) told me I was welcome to shoot wherever I pleased provided I would not disturb his pheasants. After having beat the whole manor we went down to some rushy ground, where Dido came to a dead point. This farmer (who was then in an adjoining field with his labourers) came to the hedge to see the result of Toho! Five partridges rose at the same instant, all flying different ways and excessively rapid; I killed first to the left, and then (turning round) to the right; and Pearson, who was with me, killed also a bird with each barrel. The farmer judging of our shooting by what he had seen, and appearing to think us dangerous fellows to invade a manor, went up to Pearson in a violent rage desiring him immediately to leave the grounds; assigning no other reason than that 'he did not choose we should shoot any more.' He then made up to me, but I ran through the river; and he (not being willing to wet his toes) relinquished his pursuit, and stood bawling and beckoning for me to stop, which I of course pretended not to hear, and escaped without being warned off. Before I was out of his sight the dogs ran into a bog, and put up an immense number of snipes, and by making haste up, I got six shots and bagged 4 snipes, besides a fifth, shot and lost. The farmer soon disappeared; and I beat my way to the alehouse, reserving his manor for another day's sport.

21st.—8 partridges and 1 red-legged partridge.

One of the partridges which I killed was found by Don in a hedge, who caught it, and after I had forced it from him by opening his mouth with one hand, and taking the bird in the other, it fluttered from me, and then flew up; and went off so strong that it was with difficulty I could fire quick enough to bring it again to hand.

22nd.—16 snipes, two of them jacks; and a redshank.

The last day I had been shooting here I found these snipes and avoided the farmer (who had the deputation) by running through the water, in order to save my warning, and secure a well-prepared attack on them. As the whole ground they occupied consisted only of a few small bogs, my only chance was to lose no time, for which I had a second double gun. The commencement of my attack was a bird with each barrel; and then taking the other gun from my man John, killed with that also with each barrel. As I fired so many random and unfair shots, I did not keep account of my missing, but my markers said they thought I could not have killed more than four more shots. I brought home the greater part of what I found; and picked up the snipe which I lost the other day. Finding the snipes I had left were completely driven away, I went (with snipe shot) over some turnip fields &c. and bagged 6 partridges. I had two doublets; the other shots were single, and some very long ones; yet I only fired once without bagging, and then I broke both the legs of the bird, which dropped apparently dead in the next field.

27th.—12 partridges.

Calculating that I wanted six brace to make up my 200 head of game, and knowing I should not be able to have another day's shooting in September, I fagged till nearly dark, and could only make up five brace and a half; it then got so late I gave it up and drove towards home. On going along the road I spied a covey feeding; to which I immediately ran down under the hedge, and when I thought I was nearly opposite to them, stopped; but before I could discern them, they flew up. I let fly at one (an immense distance) which I brought down dead, and completed my number.

N.B.—In looking over my book I find I might have saved myself all this trouble, as I had miscalculated; and have now made up 203 head of game, which are as follows:

Game bagged in the month of September 1808: 177 partridges (three brace of which were the red-legged French birds), 2 hares, 3 rabbits, and 21 snipes. Total, 203 head of game.

October 1st.—6 pheasants, 2 partridges, 1 rabbit, and 1 jay. Besides 2 fine cock pheasants which I shot and lost in the underwood, almost every pheasant I fired at was a snap shot among the high cover; notwithstanding which, I am glad to say I missed but twice all day, making my 8 out of 10.

3rd.—Went from Ipswich with a party amounting to near twenty, beside markers and beaters, to storm a preserved cover belonging to a Parson Bond, because he never allowed anyone a day's shooting, and had man traps and dog gins all over his wood. I had made out a regular plan of attack and line of march, but our precision was frustrated by the first man we saw on reaching the ground, who was the keeper; we therefore had no time to hold a council of war, but rushed into cover like a pack of foxhounds before his face. Away he went, naming every one he could, and we all joined him in the hue and cry of 'Where is Parson Bond?'

In the meantime our *feu de joie* was going on most rapidly. At last up came the parson, almost choked with rage. The two first people he warned off were Pearson and myself; having been served with notices, we kept him in tow while the others rallied his covers and serenaded him with an incessant bombardment in every direction. The confused rector did not know which way to run. The scene of confusion was ridiculous beyond anything, and the invasion of an army could scarcely exceed the noise. Not a word could be heard for the cries of 'Mark!' 'Dead!' and 'Well done!' interspersed every moment with bang, bang, and the yelping of barrack curs. The parson at last mustered his whole establishment to act as patriots against the marauders, footboys running one way, ploughmen mounted on carthorses galloping the other, and everyone from the village that could be mustered was collected to repel the mighty shock. At last we retreated, and about half-past four those who had escaped being entered in his doomsday book renewed the attack. The parson having eased himself by a vomit, began to speak more coherently, and addressed himself to those who, being liable to an action of trespass, were obliged to stand in the footpath and take the birds as they flew over; at last so many were caught that the battle ceased. Though a large number of pheasants were

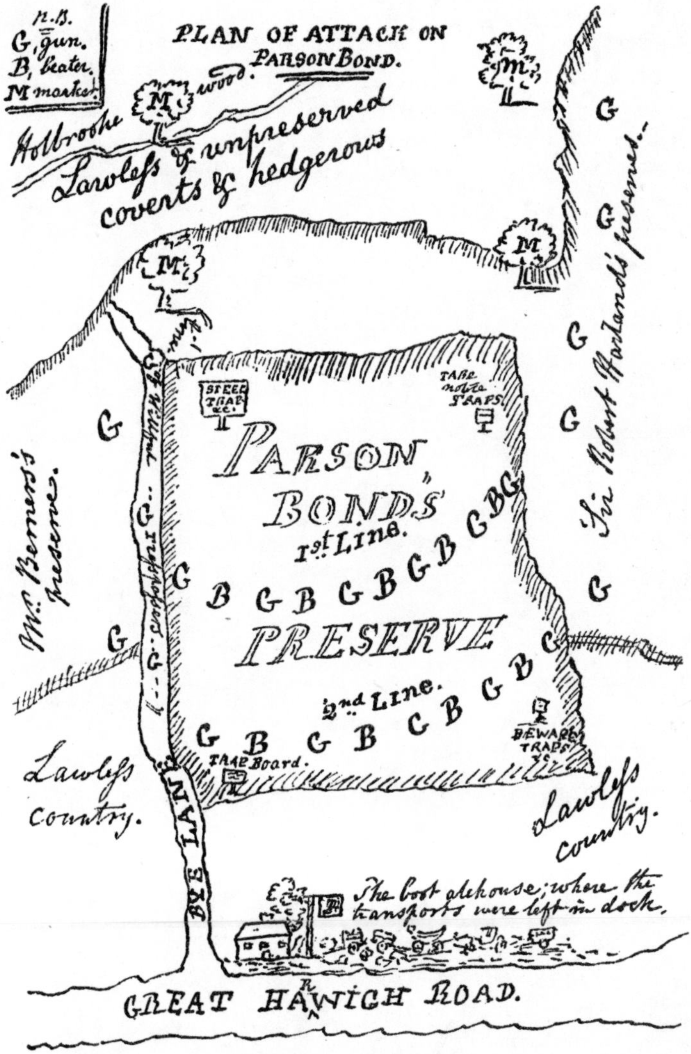
N.B.
G, gun.
B, beater.
M marker.
PLAN OF ATTACK ON PARSON BOND.
Holbrooke wood.
Lawless & unpreserved coverts & hedgerows
Sir Robert Harland's preserves.
Mr. Berners's preserve.
STEEL TRAP &c.
TAKE notice TRAPS
PARSON BOND'S PRESERVE
1st Line.
B G B G B G B G B G
2nd Line.
G B G B G B G B G
BEWARE TRAPS &c.
TRAP Board.
Lawless country.
Lawless country.
BYE LANE
The boot alehouse; where the transports were left in dock.
GREAT HARWICH ROAD.

destroyed, the chase did not end in such aggregate slaughter as we expected, and not more than one-third of those brought down were bagged, in consequence of our being afraid to turn off our best dogs ; we brought away some of the parson's traps, one of which was a most terrific engine, and now hangs in the mess-room for public exhibition. Only one dog was caught the whole day, and whose should that be but Parson Bond's! After leaving the cover I killed 2 partridges and 1 hare.

5th.—4 partridges.

6th.—Went to Woolpit for two days' shooting.

7th.—8 pheasants, 3 partridges, and 1 hare.

8th.—5 pheasants and 8 partridges, and returned to Ipswich (23 miles) by four in the afternoon. In one of the covers I fired five shots at pheasants and only bagged one, though I brought down my bird every shot. In both days I lost a number of pheasants, owing to the brambles being so strong the pointers would not face them ; I scarcely bagged a bird except those killed dead, and to the best of my recollection out of all the pheasants I winged only one was bagged. As it was, with what Pearson and I killed we were literally obliged to buy a sack to bring them home, which we nearly filled ; and what with the addition of some hares and rabbits caught by the dogs it was nearly as much as I could lift. What then would our sport have been, had we bagged all those we lost ? I scarcely missed a shot in the two days, and certainly never let a fair shot escape.

19th.—4 partridges. I went on horseback from Ipswich about three in the afternoon purposely to get a shot at some French partridges, in hopes of getting the old cock to have stuffed. I went into a piece of potatoes (where they always laid) without a dog ; at last I trod up the whole covey, which I forbore shooting at, and singled out the old cock, which I winged and lost ; coming home I killed the above 4 birds.

Game bagged by myself up to leaving Ipswich: 231 partridges, 9 of which were French red-legged, 29 pheasants, 8 hares, 4 rabbits, 21 snipes. Total, 293 head of game.

24th.—The regiment commenced its march for Romford, preparative to going on foreign service.

26th.—The first division arrived at Romford (to remain till further orders).

November 4th.—The first division marched from Romford on their way to Exeter.

7th.—Marched to Reading.

8th.—Marched to Newbury, from whence I went over to Longparish on leave.

17th.—Left Longparish for Dorchester on my way to Falmouth for embarkation to Spain.

CHAPTER II

1809

September 28th.—Arrived once more home again at Longparish House, having returned from Spain and Portugal, in consequence of my wound received at Talavera, on July 28.

(All memorandums of my military service and my journal abroad are put by themselves in another book,[1] and published.)

Shooting abroad.—N.B. I had scarcely any shooting in Portugal, and the only birds I killed there which I had never shot before were 2 storks and a Portuguese owl.

On finding the shooting so bad in this country, I despaired of getting any in Spain, and left my gun with the heavy baggage, which I had afterwards reason to regret, as I found that Spain not only abounded with game, but curious foreign birds of every description. While there, I sometimes borrowed an old gun, with which I never failed to have sport, particularly with red-legged partridges, wild pigeons, &c.

October 3rd.—Went to London to be under the care of Mr. Home for my wound, which on the 4th he examined, and having discovered that the ball had gone through and shattered my hip bone, advised me to continue in London under his care.

1810

Mr. Home having daily attended me, extracted two splinters, and instructed John how to pass the setons, which were deemed necessary to be used for a length of time, gave

[1] *Journal of a Regimental Officer during the recent Campaign in Portugal and Spain.* (London, 1810.)

me leave to return to the country for a few weeks for change of air, as my lungs were in a very bad state, and I had in consequence been dangerously ill.

January 13th.—Left town and arrived at home at Longparish House.

25th.—While we were sitting at dinner a woodcock flew up the lawn and dropped under the parlour window. All jumped up, and I hobbled to see him as well as I could. My servant seized a loaded gun, and began opening the window; while he was doing this, I eagerly snatched the gun from him and killed the woodcock. The three following circumstances make this occurrence still more remarkable: the first, that woodcocks are so scarce in this country, I have but rarely killed three in a whole season's shooting; secondly, that when I shot this bird I was confined a perfect cripple, and could not venture out even to the garden; and, thirdly, that a friend of mine had laid a bet that I was well enough to shoot a cock before this season was over.

February 3rd.—Went out in my mother's chaise. Except being conveyed from place to place, this was the first time I had been outside the house for six months and three weeks.

I took the gun with me, and, among other things shot from the chaise, I killed a sea-gull and a rook, right and left.

10th.—I adopted the plan of driving the phaeton down the banks of the river and firing from it at what few snipes I could find. They, however, rose too wild to give me a fair chance.

17th.—Have continued to drive out almost every day, taking my gun, and killing (from the carriage) redwings, fieldfares, blackbirds, larks, &c. To-day, among other things, I killed several snipes.

27th.—Being a fine day for fishing, I was taken in the chaise to the river side, where with the assistance of a stick I contrived to support myself so as to be able to throw a fly, with which I killed 5 brace of trout.

I continued by the river for about an hour, when I became so faint, and my wound so painful, I could fish no longer and returned home. After resting on the sofa, I got again in the carriage, and was driven to the common, where I killed a snipe, and should have got several more had the bitch behaved well and stood them. I came home to dinner about four o'clock; and dined on trout and fieldfares of my own killing.

March 12th.—Left Longparish for London. I took a chaise and pair at Whitchurch, from which place I started after four o'clock; and, notwithstanding I was detained near half an hour at Westfordbridge, and the roads were execrably bad, I reached Staines (42 miles) by thirty-five minutes past eight.

13th.—Proceeded from Staines to town. In the evening I hobbled to the new Covent Garden Theatre.

14th.—Mr. Home inspected and probed my wound, and was of opinion that the setons should be continued several months longer, and therefore advised me to return to the country.

20th.—Dined out and went to the opera, from whence I had to crawl all the way up the Haymarket without being able to get a conveyance home; and then had to sit in a house while a fellow with a wooden leg went in search of a Jarvey.

21st.—Left town at one o'clock (with chaise and pair), reached Longparish at ten minutes before eight. I was driven one eight-mile stage, namely, from Basingstoke to Overton, within forty minutes.

24th.—Received my leave of absence till November 24th in consequence of Mr. Home's sick certificate.

June 16th.—At about four in the morning my mother's accident happened. She was dreadfully burnt, and lost her right hand by endeavouring to light her fire with the paper from a canister of powder.

July 13.—2½ brace of trout (largest fish 1½ lb. weight), besides many thrown in, not wanting.

N.B.—Caught fish by throwing the fly as I sat in the phaeton.

19th.—Received a letter from Mr. Home desiring me to close my wounds by discontinuing the operation of the seton.

N.B.—They have now been kept open twelve calendar months all but eight days.

August 6th.—Went fly fishing and caught a number of small trout, which I threw in. Coming home I saw two woodpeckers on the lawn, got a gun, and, at one shot, killed one of them, wounded the other, and winged a swallow which was flying by at the time.

7th.—Went fly fishing to Hurstbourne Park; caught 2 brace of trout (about 1½ lb. each), besides small ones thrown in. Afterwards hobbled after a shooting party and killed 1 leveret and 1 jay.

CHAPTER III

1810

September.—Longparish. My wound having sufficiently recovered to enable me to go out for a few hours a day on horseback, I took out my certificate for killing game, and on the 1st I killed 36 partridges and 2 hares, besides 1 brace of birds lost. We sprung a covey near Furgo Farm, out of which I killed a brace with each barrel, and several of those that flew off pitched, and ran on the thatch of Furgo barn. In the evening I killed and bagged five successive double shots.

N.B.—The most I heard of being killed in our neighbourhood by anyone else was seven brace by Captain Haffendon. Some parties from Longparish have been out and killed nothing.

30*th.*—N.B. My wounds are now so far healed, that I am able to walk as sound as ever I did in my life, but have yet to recruit myself in general health, being at present very nervous and weak.

Game bagged in the month of September 1810: 210 partridges, 6 hares, 4 quails, 3 landrails, 2 snipes, 2 wild ducks. Total, 227 head.

October 26*th.*—Went to shoot with Mr. Wakeford, at Tytherley House, and killed 3 hares, 2 pheasants, and 1 partridge. We shot with spaniels, and soon after we began were joined by a sheep dog, who forsook his flock to spend the day with us, and rendered us more service than any one of the cry; he kept well in bounds while we were beating; ran the pheasants off their legs the moment we found them, and pressed the hares so hard that he obliged most of them to leave the hedgerows within shot.

29th.—4 partridges, 1 woodcock, and 1 pheasant, besides 2 snipe at one shot. The cock was the first I had seen or heard of this season. I killed him a snap shot in high covert, and never knew that he fell till John found him dead. In addition to my day's shooting I had famous sport with the harriers, which I met in the field, and followed with my old shooting pony. I found them two hares sitting, one of which I started, was in at the death of, and brought home in my game bag.

November 2nd.—4 snipes and 1 jack snipe. I was extremely ill and nervous, and shot infamously bad, or I should have killed ten couple.

3rd.—2 snipes, besides 2 which I fired at with Captain Haffendon (who also killed a couple).

N.B.—We beat Bramsbury Moor (the very ground where I yesterday found such an immense number of snipes) and only saw a couple, one of which I got a shot at and killed. In the other places we found but very few more than we killed.

7th.—5 snipes. I returned home by some fens which were literally swarming with starlings, of which I killed a large number. These birds cared so little for being shot at, that (the moment I had fired both barrels) they returned and pitched within twenty yards of me. They literally darkened the air, and the noise they made was not to be described.

12th.—1 pheasant and 10 snipe (one a jack snipe, besides another shot and lost), and (excepting two long random shots, which, I believe, I fired accurately on the birds) I only missed 2, one of which I secured with my second barrel, so that, out of the 12 snipes I fired at (within range of my gun) I brought down 11.

16th.—Saw Mr. Home in London, who inspected my wound, and gave me a certificate to extend my leave, and advised my remaining in England for at least two months.

21st.—Received my leave (from the Adjutant-General) till January 24, 1811.

26th.—Wrote to Lord Bridgewater, offering to relinquish my leave, and volunteer out with the detachment which was under orders for Portugal.

30th.—Saw Lord Bridgewater, who approved of my going out, and gave me leave to remain at Longparish till the detachment marched by on their way from Coventry to Portsmouth.

December 2nd.—Having again equipped myself with chargers and appointments for foreign service, I returned to Longparish. Walked the whole day in the Clatford and Abbot's Ann marshes, and only got three shots at snipes. One of the two I killed, I first wounded, and he flew up in a high elm tree, and there sat till we pelted him out. He then flew off so strong that I was forced to stop him with a second shot.

17th.—Went to shoot at Longstock and killed 2 ducks, 2 snipes, 1 red-headed curre, and 3 bald coots, besides 1 snipe, 1 duck, and 2 coots, which I could not get out of the water for want of a good dog. In the evening went on to Houghton Lodge, where I dined and slept.

18th.—Got up by candlelight, breakfasted at break of day, and sallied forth for a grand *chasse* at Longstock, in which we were sadly disappointed, for, after being detained there, wet through, for four hours, waiting for the rain to blow off, it came on such a stormy day, that the punt could not be managed, and the boatman (who was a very sulky, stupid fellow) got me bogged among the rushes on the middle of the lake, there broke his punt pole and told me we should most likely spend the evening out. Luckily, however, the blockhead was mistaken, and my day was finished with only being wet through, never getting a shot, losing my ammunition out of the bag, and coming home as sulky as a bear.

20th.—Went to shoot at Collingbourne Wood; got wet

through, and never fired off my gun. In the evening went to Clanville Lodge to shoot the next day.

21st.—A wet day.

22nd.—Was out all day, and only fired twice. Killed 1 pheasant and 1 partridge.

23rd.—Returned to Longparish.

1811

January.—Game killed up to leaving Longparish for Portugal: 249 partridges, 13 hares, 24 pheasants, 5 rabbits, 3 woodcocks, 68 snipes, 4 quails, and 3 landrails. Total, 369 head of game. Besides 5 ducks, 1 curre, coots, wood pigeons, moorhens, water rails, fieldfares, &c.

6th.—Left Longparish to go (per mail) to Exeter, and from thence to Plymouth, to embark once more for Portugal.

N.B.—My wound is not yet healed.

7th.—At four in the morning got into the mail, and at eleven at night reached Exeter. Had a delightfully jolly party, and, not being post day, the mail stopped whenever we saw game, and during the journey I killed 4 partridges. When it was too dark to shoot, our party mounted the roof, and sang choruses (while I joined them and drove), and in which the guard and coachman took a very able part.

9th.—At one in the morning got into the mail, and at nine reached Plymouth.

12th.—The detachment and baggage were embarked.

15th.—Went (although far from well) to the Hangings near Mavey (about eight miles from Plymouth), and killed 1 snipe and 3 woodcocks, including one which I knocked down, apparently dead, and had in my hand above five minutes, when it suddenly sprang from me, and after fluttering for a few seconds on the ground, flew away as strong as if it never had been fired at, and I stopped it with a second shot.

N.B.—Only saw 8 cocks (very wild) the whole day, 3 of which were killed by those who were with me. Consequently, we only left a couple behind, at which, by the way, we never got shots.

Specimen of what a bag of game in a sortie from garrison usually costs. Chaise and postboy, *29s.*; refreshment at ale-houses, *13s.*; paid man for his dogs, *7s.*; gates, *6d.* Total, *2l. 9s. 6d.* With the comfort of getting wet through, and sitting benumbed in the chaise for nearly three hours while crawling over (and often being lost on) the cross roads.

16th.—Found myself extremely unwell, and was confined for the day.

In consequence of seeing a letter from Lord Bridgewater wherein he thought that I had embarked for the command of the remount, I wrote to his Lordship explaining why I had not, which was my having, for several days, been very unwell.

23rd.—Received a letter from Lord Bridgewater to countermand my going to Portugal, and apprising me that he, of his own accord, had applied to the Adjutant-General for an extension of my leave. In consequence of this I disembarked my horses and baggage.

24th.—The convoy sailed, and I proceeded home again to Longparish.

27th.—This day, finding myself considerably better, I began to regret that I had not gone abroad, and, contrary both to orders and advice, resolved on going to Portsmouth, from whence twelve ships of the line were on the point of sailing. Accordingly, in the night (or, rather, on the morning of the 28th), I posted off to the above place, where I saw Sir Joseph Yorke, of whom I got a passage in the 'Victory,' and re-embarked on the 29th. This ship, in addition to her own crew, being stowed with the whole of the 36th Regiment besides several other military men, was so crowded that all those on board were in perfect misery. The only berth that could be got for me was in the surgeon's medicine closet, off the cockpit, in total darkness, where the air was so foul that in several parts a candle could not be kept alight, and the extinguished snuff of it was literally a relief from the infernal stench of the place. Our mess in the ward room, consisting of above sixty, was so crammed that comfort of any kind was out of the question, and we were the whole time sick, and far more from this circumstance than the motion of the ship. Our living was the worst we had seen on board any ship whatever.

Contemplating on what I had to go through, how little I was able to bear it, and the chance of giving great displeasure to Lord Bridgewater, for going away in direct disobedience to his orders and advice, I got into the long-boat, which was going ashore in the evening, and took my portmanteau, with some thoughts of not returning, and on my arrival at Portsmouth I was so much at a loss how to act for the best, and so whimsically undecided, that I actually tossed up whether I would return to the ship or not. The toss coming in favour of my going again on board, I returned in the long-boat.

30th.—At about eight in the morning, got under way with a fine breeze from the eastward.

31st.—The wind shifted directly against us, but, it not blowing very hard, we continued to lay our course, and nearly reached the mouth of the Channel.

February 1st.—There came on a severe gale of wind, and the fleet was so blown about that some damage was done, and we, among others, broke a mizen-topmast. We were at last obliged to put about, and sail into Torbay, where we arrived just as night set in. During the four days I was on board I ate scarcely a morsel; was so weak that I fainted several times, and my wound discharged considerably more than it had done for a length of time. I was in consequence told by all the officers on board that I was a madman if I continued in the ship, and this suggestion being strongly repeated by the surgeons induced me, once more, to relinquish the attempt of joining the army in Portugal, and I was taken on shore to a little fishing town called Brixham. Here I slept the night, and in the morning took a chaise, and proceeded to Exeter, on my road to which place I was overtaken by a man who told me that the fleet had again sailed.

4th.—Home again to Longparish House.

10th.—Went per mail to London.

15th.—Went down to Lord Bridgewater's in Hertfordshire.

16th.—Walked out with the keeper's gun and killed 4 hares, 5 rabbits, and 1 wood pigeon.

17th.—Returned to London, and took places in the mail of Tuesday night for Falmouth, to proceed once more to Portugal, having given up my six weeks' leave and decided on a passage by the first Lisbon packet! Arrived in Falmouth on the 21st.

24th.—Took my passage for Lisbon in the 'Princess Charlotte' packet, and in the evening went on board.

25th.—Sailed early in the morning, and after being all day at sea and nearly clearing Channel, we were driven back by contrary winds, and obliged to return to Falmouth Roads, where we dropped anchor about four o'clock. We then went on shore, leaving nearly all our baggage packed up on board.

March 1st.—The wind having shifted to the north, the signals were fired, and we were routed up soon after daylight; and no sooner had we discharged our bills, given up our lodgings, and were on the point of going on board, than the wind returned to its old quarter, and the preparations for sailing were of no avail.

8th.—The wind came again to the north, and we were called up at break of day, but it blew such a violent hurricane that it was impossible for the boats to get off till evening, when, about six o'clock, we returned to our ship.

9th.—Soon after eight in the morning we got under way with a gentle breeze from the N.N.E. accompanied by the whole convoy, which had so long remained windbound in Falmouth harbour.

Number of miles travelled in my three attempts to rejoin the army in Portugal, notwithstanding I have been the whole time in a bad state of health: From London to Longparish, 61; from Longparish to Plymouth, 155; back again, 155; from Longparish to Portsmouth, 39; from Brixham to Exeter, 32; from Exeter to Longparish, 112; from Longparish to London, 61; from London to Ashridge, 29; back again, 29; from London to Longparish, 61; and from Longparish to Falmouth, 204. Total miles, 938. Besides four days' hard beating in Channel, being imprisoned, at anchor, in three different ships, and costing me about 200*l.*

16th.—Came in full view of the rock of Lisbon early in the morning, and were beating to windward all day and night.

17th.—After beating the whole morning off the bar, we got a fair wind, and sailed into the Tagus; where we anchored by four o'clock, and I went on shore to Madame de Silva's.

N.B.—A very comfortable passage of nine days.

27th.—Went to see the cork convent, which is about a league from Cintra, and inhabited by twelve friars. The whole of this little monastery is cut through solid rocks, which are beautifully interspersed with the gardens and temples of the monks, and command a full view of the sea and town of Colaris. The inside of this convent is entirely constructed with cork, and from being detached among the most solitary mountains, and having scarcely a light but the glimmering lamps of the altars, it has a sepulchral appearance truly calculated for the retirement of its holy fathers. On our return, we inspected the house, which was built by Mr. Beckford, and is now in a state of ruin. This fine quinta stands in a forest of cork trees, overlooking Mafra (with the whole vale around it), the sea, and the stupendous heights of Cintra, from a foreground of cork trees and orange groves.

28th.—We were shown over the Prince Regent's palace, which stands in the town of Cintra, commanding the whole country around it. This edifice is very large, and contains one immense hall richly gilded and decorated with painted swans; a second with magpies; and a third with deer, which are yoked with divers coats of arms, containing the heraldry of all the noblemen in Portugal. The fountains here are very fine, and among them is the principal curiosity of this palace, namely, a large temple lined with Dutch tiles which spout forth water from every side, above and below, by the mere touch of a small engine in an adjoining room, and thus form a sudden and continued shower bath, resembling torrents of rain.

29th.—Walked out with my dog and gun accompanied by a captain in the 2nd Portuguese Foot; killed 2 red-legged partridges, some Portuguese larks, some of which are like ours only of a redder tint, from the high coloured sand of this country, others considerably larger, more the colour of ours, and with a black ring round their necks, and 1 snipe. The latter was considered a curiosity at this time of the year, and the partridges are now so scarce that I saw but three all day.

April 2nd.—Found myself considerably better from a severe illness, which I brought on by my exertions in the few hours' shooting.

4th.—Hired asses and went round the environs of Cintra, having that place and the rock in every point of view. In our ride we passed the town of Colaris, from whence come the greater part of the oranges for exportation. The beauty of the road to this place is scarcely to be described; it first goes through an immense forest of cork trees lying under stupendous rocks, and is covered with the most beautiful shrubs and flowers, and contains the quinta of the Duc de Cadaval; and then it goes through a most extensive range of orange and lemon orchards, where the trees are breaking down with fruit, with which you may load yourself without dismounting.

7th.—Returned to Belarra, and took up our abode at Madame Silva's in Jonqueira.

N.B.—Our bill at Cintra came to near *70l.* for nine days' plain living, and no visitors.

12th.—Having received a letter authorising me to return to England (as well as a sanction to the same from General Peacocke), and not wishing to avail myself of this without being fully justified in so doing, I had my wound inspected by Dr. Hosack, the staff surgeon, and voluntarily appeared before the Medical Board, who pronounced me 'totally unfit for field duty' and gave me a certificate accordingly.

May 5th.—Appeared again before the Medical Board (for a final decision), and was ordered 'to return to England for the recovery of my health,' &c.

10th.—Embarked on board the 'Sally' transport, which (with a fleet of 58 sail) was bound for England, under convoy of the 'Abercrombie.'

13th.—Soon after daylight we got under way, but with such an unfavourable wind that we were obliged to work the direct contrary course for England so far as to be past St. Ube's, and halfway to Cape St. Vincent, before we could get a favourable offing.

19th.—Passed a turtle sleeping on the water. A boat was immediately sent after him, and when, with great caution, the crew had rowed close to him, he was taken up and brought on board.

21st.—Having neither aldermen's cooks nor London recipes on board, we were so hard run for dressing our turtle, that I was the man honoured with that appointment; and, as my receipt was most highly approved, I have made a memorandum of the way precisely in which I dressed it, viz.: Having the turtle killed, boned, and well cleaned with scalding water over night, it was put in the saucepan about half-past nine in the morning, with more than twice as much water as would cover it, and then left to keep boiling. At eleven I put in two onions (cut in quarters), a piece of butter half the size of an orange mixed with flour (and a teaspoonful of fine sugar), and a crust of burnt bread. At twelve I added half a pint of Madeira, a small teaspoonful of cayenne, a tablespoonful of anchovy essence, two ditto of Coratch sauce; some allspice, cloves, cinnamon, and peppercorns; some pickled samphire, and capsicorn, with all the juice and half the rind of a large lemon. At two I added another squeeze of lemon, with two glasses more Madeira, and (after it had boiled with these a few minutes) it was served up.

N.B.—About half an hour before we sat down to dinner, the wind at last came fair for England. We had, till then, been (ever since we left Portugal) working to westward for a fair wind, and instead of being any nearer to home in our nine days' sail, we were this day (at twelve o'clock) 125 miles farther from England than we were when in the river Tagus, viz. 37 degrees 27 miles north latitude; 14 degrees 20 miles west longitude; the Land's End bearing N.N.E. 850 miles.

25*th.*—Entered the Bay of Biscay, the wind continuing very fair.

28*th.*—Opened the Channel.

29*th.*—Saw the Start Point (which was the first land discovered, in consequence of the weather being too thick to distinguish the Lizard), and continued up Channel with a beautiful wind.

30*th.*—Passed the Needles, and dropped anchor a little beyond Hurst Castle. We were here destined to remain the night, having a contrary wind, the tide against us, and being above 30 miles from Spithead. As we were nearly opposite Lymington, it luckily occurred to me that I had better (if possible) get put ashore there; I accordingly gave the pilot a guinea who put me across, by which I saved at least 30 miles by sea and 4 miles by land. After taking some tea at

Lymington, I proceeded to Romsey, where I passed the night, and on the morning of the 31st arrived once more at Longparish.

I must observe that the miseries I encountered on the voyage (from being without a soul to attend me, except occasional assistance from a cabin boy, and an Italian steward that would turn the stomach of a hog) were adequately compensated for by the master of the ship, who (I think it but justice to say) was one of the most civil, agreeable, and accommodating men I ever saw, and (it may be unnecessary to add) very far superior to his bearlike brethren. We were (as it is but fair to expect and customary) poisoned to death with putrid water, rancid salt butter, fleas and other dirt (added to having our brains nearly beat out between decks); but I had no time to grumble or complain, having been every day busily employed in taking care of my things, cooking my dinner, looking after my sheep, &c. We were luckily tolerably well the whole three weeks we were on board, and not at all seasick.

The following is the diary of our passage from the log-book: Monday, May 13th, 52 miles; Tuesday, 14th, 50 miles; Wednesday, 15th, 50 miles; Thursday, 16th, 50 miles; Friday, 17th, 54 miles; Saturday, 18th, 39 miles; Sunday, 19th, 47 miles; Monday, 20th, 58 miles; Tuesday, 21st, 85 miles; Wednesday, 22nd, 104 miles; Thursday, 23rd, 142 miles; Friday, 24th, 112 miles; Saturday, 25th, 122 miles; Sunday, 26th, 122 miles; Monday, 27th, 128 miles; Tuesday, 28th, 120 miles; Wednesday, 29th, 120 miles; Thursday, 30th, not worked off when we left the ship, but said to be about 100 miles. Total made good: 1,555 miles.

July 9th.—Went in a boat to the Needles for rock shooting, and killed among other birds a cormorant. My killing the latter bird was considered great sport; as the boatman and other people informed me that it was the first they had seen dead the whole season; for, although every shooting party had tried every way for them, the cormorants were so difficult of access, and (even when within reach) carried away so much shot, that none had been killed.

The plan I adopted was, being put on the extreme point of the Needles, and then climbing part of the way up them, and there waiting till these birds came over from behind me.

It is unnecessary for me to remark the terrific grandeur and majestic appearance of the rocks, when these (as well as every other beauty we surveyed in the island) are so well known, and have been so often described.

The shooting here is most excellent practice, and well calculated to teach a person to fire quick, and divest himself of that bungling trick of what is called 'covering my bird,' as you have not only the rapid flight of these fowls to encounter, but the incessant motion of the boat, as the bays with which these rock birds abound are seldom without a great swell of sea: you have, therefore, your object to catch in a moment, and unless you put the very centre of your shot on to the birds, they will very rarely fall, as the blow they take is scarcely to be credited. They dive so quick that if you fire at one on the water, he will generally be down at the flash, and particularly if wing-broken. I was told by the boatmen that a man completely outmanœuvred them (a few days since) by one of Forsyth's patent locks, which never failed to kill them on the water.

Coming home I went ashore to see the white sand pit, and the coloured chalk height, in Alum Bay, and in my walk killed a rabbit.

The only objection to this excursion was that (from my having been ill and nervous) it gave me a severe headache, which is little to be wondered at, when we consider the incessant firing of heavy loaded guns, the constant confusion and scramble in the boat, and the continual view of the chalk precipices, added to the intense heat of a broiling sun, and the repeated (though irresistible) application of a beer bottle to one's mouth.

10*th.*—After having surveyed Freshwater Bay, the cave,

and everything else within our morning's sail, I again paid my respects to my friends the cormorants, which, by the way, are provincially called the 'Isle of Wight parsons.'

I was landed again on the point of the Needles, and this day, not having Mrs. Hawker with me, I had no one to be alarmed, and therefore climbed a considerable way up the rock, and there took a position in ambush, directing the boatmen to put to sea at some distance behind the rock, and prepare me, by the blowing of a post horn, for the approach of the 'reverend devourers.' At last there came three of them suddenly upon me, and I killed 2 cormorants, right and left.

The first I brought down by putting small snipe shot through his head, and the second bird I shot in the body and wings with No. 3, and though, I suppose, forty yards from me, my Joe Manton broke both his wing bones short off from the body, and killed him dead. It may be proper to observe that this bird fell quite lifeless, whereas the first-barrel bird, through whose head I put the small shot, paused for some time before he fell.

I found that my plan of the horn answered extremely well.

I then went to have a few hours' pastime under the rocks, but found the birds so very wild that I despaired of getting shots, but by dint of perseverance killed 5 puffins, 2 razorbills, and 3 willocks. We then went and amused ourselves taking up the lobster pots, and in lieu of what we took out, fastened a paper with some money in it to the wickers of the pots, and then sank them again.

28th.—This day being the anniversary of the battle of Talavera, makes it exactly two years since I got my wound, from which I may now consider myself just recovered, though it has not completely healed up.

August 8th.—Went with Lord Hinton, who had never fished with a minnow before, and the trout ran so remarkably well that he caught 7 brace of the largest fish we had seen for the season in the space of an hour and half. I killed also one trout, while instructing him how to troll, which was the largest caught this year, weighing 2 lb.

Lord Hinton hooked a trout with a minnow, which was so large as to require nearly twenty minutes to get him to the top of the water; and while we were in the very act of landing him, we had the sad mortification to see him break the tackle and swim away. He was the largest trout I ever saw, and has defeated all the fishermen. I should guess his weight at about 7 lb.

19*th*.—Attended the carpenters and fishermen at the taking up the weir wherein we thought that the enormous trout, hooked by Lord Hinton, must have concealed himself, as he clearly went there on breaking the tackle. We, of course, caught every fish that it contained, but saw nothing of him, our largest fish being but little more than 2 lb.

CHAPTER IV

1811

September 1*st.*—Longparish. Sunday.

2*nd.*—18 partridges, 4 hares, and 1 quail. Little as this may appear in comparison with our sport some years, it is more than we have ever done in proportion to the extreme scarcity of birds. There never was so bad a breed of, or so few, partridges since the memory of the oldest men in our village. What we got was by downright slavery.

3*rd.*—Walked out with lame dogs after a three o'clock dinner, and killed 10 partridges. (I missed but one shot.)

4*th.*—9 partridges, 1 hare, 1 landrail, 1 rabbit, 1 wood pigeon, and 1 teal.

N.B.—Killed everything I fired at, except two partridges, one of which was a long distance from me, and at the other the gun hung fire.

5*th.*—7 partridges, 1 quail, and 1 hare. Shot at Enham, where the extreme scarcity of birds prevails, as well as in every other place.

6*th.*—5 partridges, 2 snipes, and 1 hare.

7*th.*—4 partridges and 1 hare. Found but one covey the whole day, out of which I killed a double shot; I had but six shots with fagging all the morning; luckily, however, I killed them all, one being at a bird which I knocked down and lost; and all (except the double shot) single birds.

Received an order from Lord Bridgewater to take charge of a recruiting party about to be stationed at Newbury.

12*th.*—2 partridges.

N.B.—Fagged the whole morning, and got but two fair shots: never was the game so scarce.

13*th.*—7 partridges.

14*th.*—Went over to take up my recruiting party at Newbury.

16*th.*—12 snipes and 1 water crake (or spotted gallinule). Besides another water-crake and 3 snipes shot and lost in the high reeds. With the exception of some random shots which I fired towards evening, when the snipes became very wild, and once when I lost my bird by the gun hanging fire, I missed but one shot the whole day, so that (with these exceptions) I knocked down 15 snipes and 2 water crakes out of 18 shots. We found three couple of the latter birds, which I consider a great curiosity, as I never saw but three before in my life, and all of these were in different years and different countries. I never met with any in Hampshire before, although the water rails here are very numerous.

Game killed in the month of September: 73 partridges, 8 hares, 3 quails, 1 landrail, 18 snipes, 1 rabbit. Total, 104 head.

N.B.—Never was game so scarce as this year.

October 1*st.*—7 pheasants and 2 partridges. It was a very wet day, and I got my game partly at the expense of a tenacious old farmer, who (leaving his own covers behind for his private preservation) sallied forth to the annoyance of every poor little farmer in the neighbourhood, when I enticed him on by a feint to cross his beat, and then tipped him the double and hung upon his rear; had the weather been fine I should have played the devil with his pheasants, as every bird I shot quite dead on the spot.

14*th.*—Went to Weyhill Fair, where the principal curiosity was a creature (shown under the name of a mermaid) that was caught and brought alive from the Southampton river.

November 3*rd.*—Went to Lord Bridgewater's at Ashridge.

4*th.*—Walked out (in my Bond Street dress, and, in short, completely unprepared for shooting) with the keeper's old gun, which was stocked so different from my own, that I missed a third of what I fired at; notwithstanding this (and the day being showery), I bagged 10 partridges, 4 hares, 1 pheasant, 1 rabbit, and 1 woodcock, besides a quantity of game that I only wounded from the gun not coming well to my shoulder. The birds here were so wild that we could scarcely get into the fields before they were up, and even in high turnips and cover they sprung out of shot; but their numbers I could compare to nothing but swarms of bees; seven and eight coveys in a field was quite common, and through a tract of country for ten miles; I am confident that had I been prepared to go out at Ashridge and taken my own gun, had a fine day, and plenty of ammunition, I could have filled a sack. As to hares, you kill as many as you want, and then leave off; fifty in a field are sometimes found, and all this clear of the preserves.

1812

Recapitulation of game killed up to February 1812: 119 partridges, 20 hares, 3 quails, 1 landrail, 41 pheasants, 13 rabbits, 2 woodcocks, 48 snipes, 7 wild ducks, 1 teal, 1 wigeon. Total, 256 head. Besides adding herons, wood pigeons, fieldfares, &c.

March 1st.—After being tortured for three days and three nights with the toothache, I had a tooth drawn and driven in again, by which severe operation you effectually remove all pain (by destroying the nerve), and at the same time restore the tooth for mastication.

April 16th.—After having made up my mind to return to the army in Portugal, I was this evening taken with a slight cold in my loins, and on Sunday I completely lost the use of my limbs. I went to Mr. Home for something to give me relief, and on seeing how far from being recovered I was, he decidedly forbid my going abroad, and advised me to leave the army, on the annexed certificate:

(*Copy.*)

'This is to certify that Captain Peter Hawker's general health is so much impaired by the wound in his hip, and the parts so liable to inflame and swell upon slight exertions, that he is, and will continue to be, unfit for actual service for a considerable time.

(Signed) 'EVERARD HOME.

'London, Sackville Street:
'*May 17th*, 1812.'

June 26th.—Received a letter from Lord Bridgewater giving me choice either to join the depot, take a recruiting party (in a district where the new system was not yet established), or remain at Longparish on the strength of my sick certificate.

Having declined the latter, I wrote to Lord Bridgewater to request his orders for my doing whatever would be, in his opinion, most for the good of his regiment, &c.

July 1st.—Went fly fishing and killed 10 trout.

August 11th.—This evening received a new double gun from Mr. Joseph Manton, No. 5802.

12th.—After trying my gun at paper, and finding that it shot tolerably close and remarkably strong, I rode over to Leckford and killed about a dozen coots and moorhens, with two ducks; and (as far as I could then judge) think the gun will suit me.

19th.—Fished (with a fly) at Wherwell, and killed 22 large trout.

24th.—Agreeably to an order received the preceding day, I left Longparish to take up a recruiting party at Bradford, Wilts, where, on my arrival, the place was so full (owing to the fair) that I was obliged to take my tired horses out of the dog cart and feed them in the back way to the inn; and after riding the leader all over the town (which is roughly paved, and up and down tremendous hills), and then galloping two miles to the fair ground in search of my party, I heard that the men had marched from Bath back to Weymouth, instead of to Bradford, owing to a mistake in the route. I then proceeded to Bath (in order to get a bed, &c.), and on my arrival found this to be the case.

25th.—Having (till my party could arrive) nothing to do, I started soon after nine o'clock for Bristol, and having spent an hour in seeing the 'lions' of that place, I mounted the box of the Welsh mail, and went to the New Passage (in Gloucestershire), and crossed the Severn to the Black Rock (in Monmouthshire), where, after dining on plenty of Severn salmon and an excellent leg of Welsh mutton (for 3*s.* 2*d.*), I recrossed the water, in a vessel with 119 Irish pigs and 4 Tipperary hog drivers, and then went back to Bristol by the return mail, into which I bundled with three old women from Glamorgan ; and, what with the incessant roar of the herd of swine and the everlasting clack of the Taffys, my ears were for hours recovering. To recover my nerves I got some tea and coffee with Charley Langford, of the Middlesex Militia, and after sitting with a party there till half-past nine, I returned in a hack chaise to Bath, where I arrived at 11 o'clock and went to bed.

30th.—Having got leave to be absent, I went to Longparish to meet Lord Hinton, for a week's shooting.

CHAPTER V

1812

September 1st.—So much corn was standing, and so execrably bad was the prospect of sport for this year, that many first-rate sportsmen declined going out, and several of those who did came home with empty bags. Lord Hinton and I started between ten and eleven. I killed 11 partridges and 1 hare.

4th.—Was out all the morning, and never got a shot.

5th.—5 partridges.

N.B.—All we found the whole day was one covey of 15, out of which Lord Hinton and I bagged 12.

7th.—5 partridges and 2 hares. Killed some birds besides, which I lost in the corn. Excepting long random shots, I never missed a bird the whole week. With the exception of one which towered, all my birds fell dead to the gun.

Game bagged the first week: 33 partridges and 3 hares. Total, 36 head of game.

N.B.—Though (without picking my shots) I never missed a fair shot the whole week, and I had five brace of good dogs to shoot with, yet the above is all I killed, so infamously bad, in every respect, is the shooting this year.

8th.—Having hired a house for my family at Bradford, Wiltshire, I was on the point of starting for that place, bag and baggage, at seven in the morning, when Woollard (who had been riding all night) arrived to inform me that I was to give up the recruiting party on the 24th inst.

I was, however, obliged to go to Bradford to settle some accounts, &c., and I arrived there by about three o'clock, in time for the post.

9th.—After a wet morning I started for Atworth, about 4 miles from Bradford, to shoot with Mr. Robert Webb. We did not start till near four in the afternoon, and I bagged 9 partridges, besides one knocked down and lost in the corn, in ten shots. I had two double and six single shots, and every bird fell dead to the gun. Shooting and sport of this kind being voted a rarity in Atworth, my success was the talk of the whole village.

10th.—After getting up very early I visited Mr. Coltatt, of Wraxall, who is keeper over all these manors, and landlord of the 'Plough' inn; consequently, by putting up there, you have his good-will to shoot. Owing to bad weather, however, and trusting to his dogs, I got but four shots, and bagged 3 partridges.

11th.—Never got a shot. It is singular that the only two blank days I had were on the two Fridays, and that on each of those days I found nothing but a pair of barren birds, although in two different counties.

12th.—Drove my tandem to a heath (between Lord Lansdowne's and Colonel Thornton's), where I killed 5 rabbits, 3 partridges, and 1 wood pigeon.

14th.—4 partridges; and (owing to being baulked by the dogs chasing) I missed within fair distance 1 hare; I, however, secured her with the second barrel.

N.B.—With the exception of some random shots out of reach and three snap shots at rabbits in high grass, the above first-barrel shot at the hare is the first miss I have made this season, making sixty shots in succession without missing, besides some birds killed and lost in the standing corn, &c.

N.B.—I never picked my shots to seek the reputation of never missing; and I invariably fired both barrels when opportunity offered.

16th.—2 partridges. Went in search of a leash of birds, which has been seen (the previous day) by the butcher, and although—so intensely hot and dry—there was scarcely any scent I found them, and killed a double shot; the third bird got off to covert, and we could not find him.

17th.—2 partridges. Went out near the town, and as I arrived at a stubble the farmer came up; and with his damning and swearing, frightened up the above brace of birds, which I killed right and left before his face, put them in my pocket, and wished him 'good evening.'

18th.—Walked out, never was more than a mile from the town all day, and bagged 12 partridges (besides two shot and lost). I killed every bird I fired at, and made good the only three double shots I fired. We only found 19 birds all day, and on my return I found a note from Squire Jones to request I would desist from sporting in these fields or near Bradford Wood as they were preserved, and telling me he was authorised to 'forbid all trespassers,' notwithstanding the whole town shot constantly over them, and he had previously given his approbation to my shooting, and I had even robbed myself to supply him with game.

My Answer.

'Dear Sir,—As to my certain knowledge every fellow in this town shoots in the neighbourhood of Bradford Wood, I am almost induced to think you are joking when you call it a preserve. I regret, however, that you were not a day sooner in your application, as I have this moment returned with the only remaining birds (fourteen) in my bag; four brace of which I was on the point of sending you when I received your note, and consequently disposed of them otherwise.

'I am, &c.

'P.S.—I have also countermanded the sending for a capital

pointer bitch of which I had promised myself the pleasure of making you a present!'

The squire sent a verbal message that 'I was no gentleman!'

'Sir,—I am surprised that you should aggravate your uncivil conduct by saying I am "no gentleman." I beg to observe that did I consider you as worthy the name of one I should not hesitate to take up your message in a proper light.

'I am, &c.'

I received the squire's message when getting into my tandem for Longparish, and had to turn back to make the above acknowledgment of its receipt.

23rd.—On my return from Longparish I received the following epistle from the squire:

'Woolley: September 18th, 1812.

'Sir,—As to my knowledge there has not been any fellow who has sported on the estate at Bradford Wood, I hereby give you notice that you are forbidden to shoot (or otherwise sport) on the several estates of Earl Manvers, in the hundred of Bradford, or the liberty of Trowbridge, and I am at the same time to bring to your remembrance that any officer sporting on the estates of persons without leave is contrary to law; you are also forbidden to shoot on the manor of Trowle, or on any of the estates of Earl Manvers, as well as on my own lands, subject to a report to the Commander-in-Chief.

'I am, Sir,

'Your obedient servant,

'JOHN JONES.

'To Captain P. Hawker, 14 L.D.'

The squire being the most unrelenting tyrant and nefarious sinner, the annexed is what I returned him.

I should observe that the whole town of Bradford, and all the poor fellows he had persecuted, were quite in an uproar of joy about it, and ready to eat me up.

'Bradford, Wiltshire: September 24th.

'Captain Hawker begs to inform Squire Jones that he is always a day after the fair with his insignificant revenge. Captain Hawker having only this night received his polite notice, and being obliged to take his farewell of Bradford early to-morrow, he is prevented beating the remainder of the manor, which he otherwise, upon his honour, most assuredly would have done. He feels particularly obliged to the squire for his civil information, as the article of war wherein "an officer who has leave from the landholder can be prosecuted by the lord of a manor," has not yet appeared before the public! Whatever manors Squire Jones may hold for others, he is about as deficient in manners of his own as he is of popularity, good nature, or capacity for a magistrate; and as, therefore, the squire has even got the start of the articles of war and even of the law itself, the Captain most strongly recommends him to study Blair's Sermons, Lord Chesterfield, and the Bible; and, in bidding him adieu, sincerely wishes him a sound and permanent reformation both of mind and body, and that he may have time to repent his sins, and prepare himself for that day when "every man shall be judged according to his works!" (the text given last Sunday at Bradford church, where Jones never goes).'

Out of the twelve double shots which I have fired since Sept. 1st I have killed both birds eleven times, and bagged them all but one, which I bungled at, and did not kill dead. This makes seventy-seven out of seventy-eight fair shots.

Having been only from a quarter past eleven till three to-day filling my bag, I returned to Bradford at the latter hour, in good time to despatch some birds to town. Every other bird, except one brace, I gave away to the natives, so they could not call me a pot hunter.

Having got my dinner I started for Longparish (in the tandem) at a quarter before eight, and arrived home, 45 miles, by two in the morning; having only stopped for a short time to feed my horses, and they arrived quite fresh and tolerably cool.

Game bagged the month of September 1812: 78 partridges, 7 hares, 7 rabbits, 3 snipes. Total, 95 head of game.

October 7th.—3 partridges, 3 snipes, 1 pheasant, and 1 jay.

I sprung a single snipe, and after seeing it fall, I observed another going away, which, in a few seconds, towered and fell in the river, so that I bagged two with firing but once: the latter bird, therefore, was evidently killed by accident, on the ground.

10*th.*—Left Longparish for Weymouth. I took a gun in the carriage, and in three shots going along the road, I got 3 pheasants which I much wanted.

13*th.*—Went over, with Lords Poulett and Hinton, to Hinton St. George Park.

14*th.*—After viewing the beauties of Hinton House I rode out and killed 2 snipes and 2 jack snipes, which were all that could be got, as the immense swarms seen the preceding days were driven away by a change of weather.

16*th.*—Returned to Longparish. Carried a loaded gun in the carriage to flank the road occasionally, and bagged 5 pheasants and 3 rabbits.

20*th.*—Having, on the 19th, received orders to join a recruiting party at Glasgow, I left Longparish and arrived in London this day.

24*th.*—After the post came in, I started for Ashbridge Park; and, having dined with Lord Bridgewater, returned to town, where I arrived soon after twelve at night.

As we passed Lord Bridgewater's grounds we observed

his people at oat cart, and his Lordship informed us that 'he was this day to finish his harvest.' This shows what a late season we have had.

26th.—Left London for Scotland.

Having taken places for Ferrybridge, I left the 'Bull and Mouth' inn, per Glasgow mail, at a little before eight, and, after taking up the bags in Lombard Street, at the General Post Office, we proceeded for the North.

N.B.—On passing the Duke of Newcastle's, on the right going down, between Ollerton and Worksop, the enormous quantity of pheasants, which were within twenty yards of the road, is scarcely to be credited; there were nearly 100 of them all close together like a flock of pigeons. Unluckily for me, and luckily for his Grace, it poured so hard with rain that I never could have unpacked my gun, otherwise the guard and coachman would readily have brought to for action.

I had intended to stop at Ferrybridge to have taken a day at Methley Park with Lord Pollington; but finding the roads so bad, and that his seat was nine miles out of the highway, I had not sufficient spare time.

While passing through Lincolnshire &c. we saw the people at harvest, and in a few hours after, the mail was so covered with snow, that, in spite of all coats, 'toggerys and upper benjamins,' the whole of the outside crew were wet to the skin, and almost frozen with cold. I kept my myrmidons well, with the never failing remedy of cold gin and beer.

I arrived at Mr. Thompson's inn, 'The Old George and Morritt's Arms,' at Greta Bridge about half-past six o'clock on the morning of the 28th.

N.B.—I think the north roads, as far as possible, inferior to the western. They are mended with large soft quarry stones, which, at first, are like brickbats, and afterwards like sand. Indeed, what with the wet weather and other circumstances, it would have been misery to have travelled in anything but the mail.

The posting is 1*s.* 9*d.* per mile, and very inferior to that of the western road at 1*s.* 6*d.* The people of this mail, and particularly the ruffians at the 'Bull and Mouth' office, are in general a dissatisfied, grumbling set of fellows. Their 'turns-out' of horses and harness are beggarly.

In Lincolnshire there are many gentlemen's parks, fenced with walls of loose quarry stone; ricks made upon raised sheds, and the carts put under their cover; second storeys, of many houses, of spear reed, cemented over and under with plaister; bread either very white or very brown, no medium; fires very large and a profuse waste of coals, which, I learnt, are 5*s.* 6*d.* a cartload, free of gates and everything. In Hants, they would be 30*s.*

Table of mail-coach expenses to the Grouse Moors

	£	s.
My place inside to Ferrybridge	4	16
Outside places for two servants at 2*l.* 10*s.* each	5	0
To a dog brought per mail	1	5
To extra luggage	1	10
Ferrybridge to Greta Bridge	3	17
Six coachmen and four guards, at 4*s.* each .	2	0
Total . .	£ 18	8

I usually gave the coachmen and guards 2*s.* for myself and 1*s.* each for my servants, though generally more if they were civil and obliging. The above, however, is the common price on this road.

28th.—Having learnt that the grouse were become so wild and scarce that a man who had, a few days ago, killed a brace was spoken of as having done wonders, I despaired of getting any; but, having travelled till I had scarcely strength from my Peninsular wound to go farther (in order to secure a day or two), I was resolved, at all events, to look at the moors and, if possible, see a live grouse, which I had all my life been longing to do. This evening, therefore, I proceeded (in a post-chaise) on the high road for Glasgow &c. and stopped at Bowes (a small place 6 miles from Greta Bridge), where I bought some shot, and drove on to a public-house (3 miles further) kept by one Kitty Lockey, who horses the mail.

Never was there a more admirable situation than this public-house. It stands in the very best part of the moor (this is Strathmoor, and from it we had a fine view of Durham); and, being an isolated place, the grouse are as likely to be found close to the house as anywhere farther, and indeed the landlord informed me that he this very morning saw a grouse sitting within a fair shot of his door, and that these birds often come close to it. I was, of course, not a little 'on my metal' at hearing this.

The public-house here is in every respect remarkably good. The place where it stands is known by the name of Spittle.

It was curious, on passing to this place (or rather to Bowes) to observe the quantity of standing corn; two-thirds of the fields, in every direction, not being yet reaped or mowed. Common wheat, oats, and barley standing all over the country.

After supping (so my landlord chose to call it, though it was a six o'clock dinner) on a roast duck, Yorkshire ham, and preserve tarts, which (to my astonishment) I had in perfection at this hut, I went to bed with every inducement to rise early, except the weather, which had been very snowy and wet, and was still very stormy—all much against the chance of my getting a grouse.

N.B.—It should be remembered that one brace of moor game now is equal to 15 (or more) in August, both for value and difficulty of shooting them.

29th.—The weather having suddenly changed to a very hard frost, with sharp winds, I, after getting some breakfast, started with my one dog and Kitty Lockey for a pilot. Within 250 yards of my bedroom window, and directly in front of the alehouse, Nero found 3 grouse, then 2 more, and 7 more (I looked at my watch, and found that we had seen these six brace within nine minutes from our leaving the door). Within twenty-five minutes from our throwing off we found two packs, of about 10 or 12 each; and, in short, saw about forty brace during our walk, all within one mile, and two-thirds of them within less than half a mile from the public-house and some close to the road, where the mail and other coaches pass. But the certainty of finding them was sadly counterbalanced by the utter impossibility of getting at them; in spite of every manœuvre, I could scarcely get even so near as 150 yards to them, and it was only two or three times that the dog could come within that distance. I contrived, however (by creeping, with my hat off, behind hillocks and ridges which I thought likely) to get within sixty yards of some pairs, and single ones, three of which I fired at, but with no other hopes of killing than a chance shot taking a vital part. At last (after I had voted it impossible to get a grouse in such weather, and so late in the season) Nero came to a point, and (as luck would have it) the brow of a hill was between him and his bird, and I by creeping up 'took him on the hop,' fired directly he rose (at about 45 yards) and down I knocked him, in the act of crowing at me—a fine old cock grouse. Bagged also 1 teal, 1 jack snipe, and 1 snipe, which (with another wild snipe and a flock of golden plover) were all I saw except grouse.

On my return to the inn, I met a Mr. George Edwards (of Barnard Castle, Durham), who, on my complaining at not being able to make up a brace of moor game, said that (with such a day &c.) he should not have credited my having killed one, had I not produced the bird.

This gentleman (as well as the landlord) informed me that anyone who had a freehold (even under 40*s.*) had a right (if qualified &c.) to sport over the whole of these moors (for 10 or 12 miles). Thus, here is no lord of the manor; but every freeholder has an equal right to sport. Their plan to prevent poachers, and serve notices, is (or rather ought to be) carried on by a committee; but so little attention is paid to the matter, that a stranger may shoot a whole season, with little or no opposition, and a gentleman would have no trouble in getting a month's leave.

In August it is common for a bungler to bag his eight brace.

30*th.*—Left Spittle for Penrith, but was obliged to leave one of my men behind, in consequence of the guard being unable to take on my luggage. I should observe that nothing creates more disputes on this road than a gun case, as it will go nowhere but the outside of the coach, where the guards are forbid to put anything; and, from the wretched horses driven, the coachmen have so much difficulty in keeping their time, that they in general are very tenacious of taking anything more than they are obliged to do. They are, however, much more civil here than farther upwards.

As you enter Westmoreland, the scenery becomes very romantic, and the approach to Appleby, which you enter down a steep hill, presents a magnificent landscape.

My reason for stopping at Penrith was to see Ulswater, one of the finest of the lakes, and the only one I could reach without going nearly forty miles out of my way. I hired a gig, and got a weaver's boy for a pilot; and, in six miles, reached the village of Pooley, at the foot of the lake. Nothing can be more romantically beautiful than the richly wooded hills that form the side scenery, and the majestic heights which compose the background of this landscape; in a word, the view creates a sort of sensation which we feel on hearing Mozart's music, seeing Shakespeare's tragedies, hearing Braham sing, or seeing ourselves surrounded by a good evening flight of wild fowl.

After driving a considerable way on the road, which is on the edge of the lake, I returned to Pooley to make inquiries for sport, and found that a Mr. Russel had, as he termed it, the farming of the fishery, and that by putting up at his house, you insured yourself the liberty of angling on the lake for nine miles. The following are the fish it produces: grey trout, running up to 35 lb.; common trout; charre; perch; skilly, or fresh-water herrings, which are caught by thousands at a draught; chub; eels, and brandlings.

No wild fowl to speak of, but good partridge shooting round the lake.

On my return to Penrith about 5 P.M. I got a brace of trout dressed, some good gravy soup, a roast chicken, cranberry tarts, jellies, &c., all elegantly served up, and with great civility, for *6s. 8d.*, which I thought much better bestowed than on a lawyer's letter.

After dinner, about half-past six, I got a lift on to Carlisle, by the Manchester mail.

31*st.*—Saw the whole of Carlisle, and the only thing I observed to be worthy of remark is the excellent architecture, and construction of the two new courthouses, which give a grand effect to the entrance of this town. Carlisle is well paved with quarry stone of a reddish brown colour, with which the cathedral, castle, and other edifices are built. The former has a fine window and some good oak carving; the latter has arms for 10,000 men; though neither of these is anything beyond mediocrity.

I should observe that the inns are so small and bad, in proportion to the numbers who travel through this town, that it is but seldom you can be accommodated with a sitting room to yourself, and you are, consequently, obliged to live at the same table with persons of every description.

At half-past three this evening, I left Carlisle for Moffat, where I arrived about half-past ten. When you have passed the river Sarke, 3½ miles beyond Longtown, you enter Dumfriesshire in Scotland, where the country soon appears barren, and the little cabins of stones, poorly thatched and only on a ground floor, contribute to its wild appearance.

After getting nearly two miles into Scotland you go through Springfield, which is now the grand receptacle for enamoured fugitives; the hymeneal business being now carried on by one David Ling, a *ci-devant* coachman, who married the niece of the late old man, commonly called 'the Blacksmith,' and thereby succeeded him in his property and business. Priest Ling resides in a tenement, or rather hovel, among a small row of slated cabins, on the left as you pass down; and a little farther, on the opposite side of the street, is a pothouse called 'The Maxwell's Arms,' and kept by one Jemmy Reade, where the nuptial ceremony has, of late, been performed. This temple, however, was formerly kept at Gretna Hall, on the green, which joins the hamlet of Springfield, but the house being since bought for a private residence, the impatient lovers have now only to direct their flight to the place before mentioned, by which they will be accommodated with having 500 yards less distance to reach their asylum of security; unhappily, however, the roads in this poor country are ill calculated for the wings of love.

I should mention that the old man, who officiated for nearly forty years, at 40*l.*, 50*l.* and sometimes 100*l.* a job, never was a blacksmith, but, merely so called because his pairs were welded together in heat. Old Joe Parsley, for that was his name, was by trade a tobacconist. He was a very large, heavy man, and might have died worth a great deal of money; but from being an intolerable drunkard and a very unsteady fellow, his money went as lightly as it came, and after he had solemnised the marriages, and dismissed his 'couple of fools' from the forge, they could not possibly be more eager to follow their avocations than his reverence was to trudge off to a whisky house.

The roads and horses in this country are so bad and ill attended to, that even the mails get on but slowly and in a very slovenly manner; the harness being generally second-hand, one horse in plated, another in brass harness, and, in short, all of a piece; and when they do have new harness (which is very seldom) it is put on like a labourer's leather breeches on a Sunday, and worn till it rots, without being cleaned. The coachmen are like a set of dirty gipsies; they drive but one stage each, and then look after their own horses. The mails are (from London) exactly the same as all others.

November 1st.—I was prevented surveying this country by an incessant pour of rain, which lasted the whole day. The town of Moffat has nothing to make mention of, except the wild country in which it lies, and the mineral waters for which it is frequented in the summer, one of the springs being similar to that of Cheltenham, and the other considered good for consumption.

2nd.—Went out in hopes of getting a blackcock, for which this place has the name of being good; but, after slaving till I could scarcely get one leg after the other, I found but one pack, two single cocks, and a grey hen, all of which were too wild to give me the least chance. Indeed, getting at them in this country (after August or September) appears impossible, as they occupy the open heights, where they generally sit like cormorants, with a sentry, either on a rock or in a tree, to give the alarm. In my walk, however, I killed 2 woodcocks, which were all I saw, and 3 partridges, and should have had a brace more, and a couple of snipes, but the only shot I could buy was so large that it was quite by chance that I bagged what I did with it.

My walk gave me a full view of this place, which lies in a fine valley among small rivers, and is surrounded by a perfect amphitheatre of mountains. The oats and barley were standing in every direction, and some quite green.

My guide was one David Dinwoodie, who gave me an excellent account of Moffat as a sporting place; and, among other information, corroborated what I had before heard here, that in June and July the salmon trout fry were so plentiful that the boys would go out with an artificial fly and bring in 400 of a day. They are, however, small; as they run about the size of a smelt; but they are most delicious eating, and as red as any salmon.

In consequence of having seen at a distance a great many ducks, I, tired as I was, after getting my grouse, and a cranberry tart for my dinner, poured a flask of whisky into my boots, whipped on a box coat, and posted off to the side of the stream, but only saw 5 ducks, which were too far from me to fire at.

I went to bed with my loins in such pain from walking that I was fearful my wound would break out again; but luckily, by taking something warm, I soon recovered.

3rd.—Being told that the only possible way to get black-cocks was to creep after them in the morning by daylight, I started off with my friend David Dinwoodie, and after despairing of seeing any, we espied a pack at feed; but the moment we stopped they flew up, although they were on the opposite side of an immense valley from the hill on which we were. After taking a long flight like ducks they perched on a plantation of high larch firs, among some stone walls; accordingly, I began to creep when about 500 yards from them, but having got to the end of my ambush, I found the distance too far; I then, in preference to firing at random, crept over the wall, and succeeded in getting to another, where I had a safe march to a breach within forty yards of an old cock, who was the vidette, and after crawling on all fours, with my heart in my mouth, for about 100 yards, I gained the point, and down I knocked him, a fine old black-cock. I was thus lucky in getting both specimens of the grouse so fine for stuffing.

N.B.—It is somewhat remarkable that in the very act of getting over this wall I found on it a shilling, which inspired me with confidence of success.

The place where I was being near 'Moffat Springs,' which is where the sulphur waters are drunk, I took a look in and tasted them, and they were quite sparkling and very cold, though of a strong brimstone flavour. They are under a lock-up shed, in a rock close to the mountains; their distance from Moffat is nearly two miles, and that of the consumption waters nearly seven, both lying to the north-east of the town.

I must do David Dinwoodie the justice to say he was one of the most obliging men I ever met with—not with an object in his civility, as is often the case in the North, for he was absolutely affronted when I offered to reward him for his attendance. Not so with Kitty Lockey, for he not only took care to ask for money directly he had attended me, but made the most imposing charges in his bill. It is, indeed, too often the case that when they get a gentleman in an alehouse, they take good care to make him 'pay his footing.'

I got back to Moffat about half-past nine, where after taking my breakfast I proceeded in a chaise for Douglas-mill, which is about halfway to Glasgow. I took my gun, ready loaded, in the chaise; and after killing 1 magpie out of the window, while going on, to test the barrel that I feared would hang fire, I was prepared for anything I might see on the road.

I bagged 3 partridges, and should have had 2, if not 3,[1] more, had I not laboured under the disadvantage of the large shot, which to so small a quantity of powder, and in such little charges, as a double gun holds, has neither velocity enough to cut through the feathers of a bird, nor compression sufficient to avoid his escaping very often among the intervals. The difference between large and small shot in a gun is, that the former goes in like the back of a knife, and occasionally only; and the other like a razor, with unerring certainty. No. 7 is best for everything, unless you take a duck gun.

I should make a memorandum of the posting in this country, which, as well as the inns where you change horses, more forcibly depicts misery than even the travelling in Spain. The horses are scarcely good enough for dog's meat, being

[1] Round Moffat is a most admirable beat for partridges.

half starved, and kept in sheds of loose stones; the chaises are of the very worst description; and the travelling, on an average, I found to be about 4 miles an hour.

The road from Moffat to Douglas-mill has nothing for remark, except that it is one of the most wretched deserts I ever passed. There are several small rivers in this wild country, which the postboy, or rather the ragamuffin, who drove me, said were full of trout. No coach whatever, excep the mail, makes it worth while to pass this road to Glasgow; but all the carriages of conveyance go round by Dumfries.

I reached Douglas-mill between seven and eight at night.

4th.—I started on my journey soon after six in the morning, having got an excellent chaise with a decent driver; and having found everything at and from Douglas passable except the roads, I flashed them occasionally, and bagged 1 snipe and 4 partridges. I am sure, had I time, dogs, and small shot, I could kill a hamperful of partridges in this neighbourhood; as, from the country being so little inhabited they are in great abundance, and you may shoot unmolested; and from the corn being out in the fields, and some of it standing, the birds lie nearly as well as in September. I tried the grouse as I passed the heath, but getting anywhere near them proved impossible. I reached the town of Hamilton soon after twelve, and there found the posting nearly as good as in parts of England. I arrived in Glasgow between two and three o'clock this day.

The post arrives at Glasgow from London on the fourth day; for instance, if a letter be put in on Monday it arrives on Thursday morning. The mail leaves London Monday evening at eight, and gets into Glasgow Thursday morning before eight; it leaves Glasgow soon after two on Monday afternoon, and arrives in London very early Thursday morning; and so on through the week, except that no post comes into Glasgow on Wednesday, nor goes out of it on Thursday. You have 3 hours, from half-past ten to half-past one, sometimes more, in which you may answer letters by return of post.

Table in order to show for how much a gentleman and his servant, the former inside with 14 lb. of luggage, the latter outside with 7 lb. of luggage, may go from London to Glasgow, with two breakfasts, two dinners, and two suppers:

	£ s. d.	£ s. d.
Inside to Ferrybridge from London	4 16 0	
" Greta Bridge	1 12 6	
" Carlisle	1 9 6	
" Glasgow	2 10 0	
		10 8 0
Outside to Ferrybridge	2 10 0	
" Greta Bridge	1 2 0	
" Carlisle	1 0 0	
" Glasgow	1 13 0	
		6 5 0
Inside, seven guards at 2*s.* each		0 14 0
" six long-stage coachmen at ditto		0 12 0
" twelve short-stage coachmen at half ditto . .		0 12 0
Outside, for man, half price of the above		0 19 0
Grand total		£19 10 0

9th.—Went per mail to Edinburgh.

10th.—Having spent the whole of the previous afternoon in seeing this fine city, I got up very early in the morning and went all over Leith, from whence, after buying 100 oysters and a live codfish of 24 lb. weight for 3*s.* 6*d.*, I returned to Edinburgh, two miles, saw the remainder of the town, and, at twelve, started by the heavy coach to return to Glasgow. Although this machine carries six in and ten outside, yet it goes the 42, or rather 45, miles, including the suburbs, in six hours and a half. The horses, and indeed the whole concern of this coach, are superior to the mail; and it performs the journey in the same number of hours, as do also, I am told, the five or six other coaches which start every day to and from Glasgow. From the extreme roughness of the Scotch roads, and consequently the stiffness of the springs, and strength with which they are obliged to build these coaches, we found the noise so great inside, that the passengers could scarcely hear each other speak.

On passing Bathgate (in the second stage, where we stopped to water) we were saluted by two old women, or rather fairies, one sixty-eight, the other a few years younger, and each very little more than three feet high. These Lilliputians are not related to each other, except in their occupation, which entirely consists in presenting themselves to the different coaches, and the diversion and novelty which their appearance affords the passengers generally produces them plenty of halfpence, and by this means alone they gain their livelihood.

The road by which I returned from Edinburgh to Glasgow in this coach lies nearly parallel to that which I came by the mail; the two roads are often within a mile, and never more than four, from each other; they are about the same in point of goodness and distance, and unite in one at about a mile from Glasgow, and somewhat more than a mile from Edinburgh.

N.B.—I found Edinburgh full as dear as London; for example, 2*s.* for fire and 7*s.* for lodgings, 2*s.* a mile for a hackney coach, &c.; without a tenth part of its comforts.

The castle (built on a stupendous rock) is one of the strongest fortifications, and the finest thing of the kind I ever beheld; but with regard to everything else in this town, the high expectations I had raised were sadly disappointed.

11*th.*—Walked out from the town of Glasgow (after twelve o'clock), and bagged 4 partridges and 1 pheasant—a very old cock bird. The latter was spoken of as an extraordinary circumstance in this country, and from what I heard, it appears to be one that several people had been a long time in pursuit of.

I got a random shot at a woodcock, which I could see nothing of at the moment of firing, and, as the lairds of this country take especial good care to turn their timber into money before it is large enough to bear a man's weight, I was prevented being able to 'mount my marker' in a tree, which is of course the sure way to secure a woodcock for the bag.

I fired but five times; I killed the pheasant full sixty yards, and a partridge at nearly the same distance; and, indeed, all my shots were extraordinary lucky ones.

N.B.—I shot with No. 8, and Butts's Hounslow cylinder powder, which I found superior to Manton's. I see every day more and more the consummate stupidity of people who abuse small shot.

16*th.*—After having passed the morning in going to the College, and seeing the invaluable collection in Hunter's Museum, I started for Dumbarton, on my way to Loch Lomond, and slept at the 'Elephant and Castle' inn, which is kept by a Mr. McNicol, and far superior to any I had met with in Scotland; I had an excellent bed, a good accommodation, with a moderate bill, and great civility.

17*th.*—Proceeded in a hack chaise to Luss inn, thirteen miles farther. The last eight miles of this road are on the 'indescribably beautiful Lake of Loch Lomond,' and present a magnificent view of wooded islands and mountainous scenery, together with the tremendous 'Ben Lomond,' and other snow-capped mountains.

On arriving at Luss inn, which is close to the lake, I set out partly to sketch and partly to shoot, and was far better repaid my journey by the landscapes than the sport, as the game was so very scarce that, although with leave over the whole of Mr. McLaughlin's grounds, and with the attendance of his man, I killed but 3 snipes and 1 woodcock, which were all I shot at, and all I saw.

18*th.*—Having heard that there were several roe deer on Sir James Cohoun's property, I obtained his permission to sport for a few hours, but could not succeed in finding any, at which his keeper, a respectable man who attended me, seemed rather surprised; the only shooting I got was firing both barrels at a hare. After getting an early dinner I set off, escorted by one Donald on my way to ascend Ben Lomond ; and after going nearly four miles by land and one by the lake ferry, reached the inn at Row Ardenan, which is a real Highland whisky house. I here sat down by a peat fire with some whisky toddy, till a bed-in-a-hole (like the berth of a transport) was prepared, and then retired to rest.

N.B.—Previously to reaching the ferry we passed a stone, on which there is an inscription relative to Colonel Lascelles' regiment having cut this road through the rock in 1745, about the time of the rebellion.

19*th.*—After getting some boiled bread and milk, which, with a basket of peat to make a fire, I secured previously to going to bed, I started with a guide at daybreak to ascend Ben Lomond, and within three hours we barely reached the shoulder of the summit ; but getting to the most elevated part of it was impossible, as we found the last fifty yards a solid sheet of ice ; and, indeed, for more than the last half-mile we travelled in perfect misery and imminent danger ; we were literally obliged to take knives to cut footsteps in the frozen snow, and, of course, obliged to crawl all the way on our hands, knees, and toes, all of which were benumbed with cold, and were repeatedly in danger of slipping in places where one false step would have been certain destruction. The going up, however, was comparatively a mere nothing to the coming down, in which our posteriors and heels relieved the duty performed by our toes and knees. My man John Buffin, as well as myself and the guide, had some very providential escapes, and on our getting below this frozen atmosphere and again in safety, the latter told us that 'had we slipped nothing could have stopped us ; ' and, indeed, we had proof of this by my dropping a stick, which soon went rapidly out of sight.

The inn where we slept stands at the foot of, and is called five miles from the summit of, Ben Lomond. We were lucky in having a clear day to present us with the grand amphitheatre of mountains in which this one stands. I of course took my dog and gun; but the latter we were obliged to leave behind on a rock, after crawling with it strapped to the back as far as possible; we found no ptarmigans; indeed, they are now become very scarce.

The killing of these birds is, from what I was told, no merit beyond the labour of traversing the frozen pyramids, and the novelty of getting them, as they will sit on an open stone as tame as chickens, and suffer themselves to be pelted before they will move, and are very frequently killed with stones. Ben Lomond has on it some white hares, but we saw none.

The ascent to the summit of this mountain is, even in winter, sometimes very passable; and in summer so much so, that ladies very commonly go up, and sometimes take with them a piper, and other apparatus for dancing. The summer may, perhaps, have a different effect; but, for my own part, I was so exhausted that, being unable to walk home from the inn, I hired a boat and returned by water.

In several of the most solitary glens we saw the caves where the smugglers manufacture the famous Highland whisky, which is so far superior to the ordinary by being distilled from the pure malt and smoked with the peat. They usually do this work in the dead of night. There are various opinions about where the Highlands begin, in consequence of the English language having within these few years extended itself to where the Gaelic was spoken; but, as that language appears still familiar to most of the old people, even as far as Luss, we may safely say that Luss is in the Highlands; at all events they unquestionably begin a few miles beyond that place. After getting my dinner at Luss inn I returned to Dumbarton, where I went to bed very unwell.

20th.—Having had every comfort the preceding night, I found myself better; and returned, by the Dumbarton coach, to Glasgow.

21st.—Removed from the filthy lodging of Mrs. Sheddon, 94 George Street, to the cleanest house I had seen since I left England, a Mrs. Watson's in Clyde Buildings.

Mrs. Sheddon having swore that I had engaged her lodgings for two months, when I particularly expressed, before witness, that I would not even engage them for more than a week, I was the previous evening served with the letter of a lawyer, which was brought me by a most assassin-like-looking fellow, with a hare lip, cut-throat face, and in a beadle's livery. Mrs. Sheddon having this day refused to go before a magistrate (which in this country is optional), and she having preferred 'a suit at law,' to increase my trouble and expense, I was obliged to employ a Mr. Donald, to enter on a regular lawsuit; and Mr. Provost Hamilton was so kind as to stand bail, in order to get a certificate for the removal of my baggage, which had remained all the morning under quarantine. The action is of course going on.

This is a common species of imposition in Glasgow, Mr. Donald having had many similar cases in hand.

27th.—Partly from illness, and partly from seven days' rain (with scarcely any intermission), I have been prevented using my gun till this day, when I went in Mr. Mackintosh's chariot—accompanied by his son and Mr. Horrocks—to Keiss' estate, belonging to Mr. Sterling; but only fired my gun twice the whole day.

December 8th.—As before, I have (partly from illness, and partly from bad weather) been deprived of shooting till this day, when I walked out of this execrable town; and all the game to be found was 2 hares, 1 of which I fired at and killed.

10th.—Walked out for a few hours near the town; fired my gun five times and bagged 2 hares, 2 partridges, and 1 fieldfare.

13th.—The weather having for nearly a fortnight been intensely severe, I went by the evening mail to Greenock, to try for wild fowl.

14*th.*—Hired a boat, and found several flocks of barnacle and other fowl; but getting even near enough to fire ball at them proved impossible. Indeed, as far as can be judged from what I have seen, no coast can be worse than this for water shooting, as here are scarcely any rivers but what freeze; and the lakes being also susceptible of frost, the fowl daily frequent the open Clyde, where no device whatever will succeed in getting at them; and, by night, they usually feed on the mud, in which you must walk and stand up to your knees to get a bad evening flight.

15*th.*—Crossed the Clyde to Dumbarton, within three miles of which (opposite Craig-end ferry, where there are good boats) the wild fowl are in myriads, and the solid squares of barnacle have the appearance of black islands. We found it, however, impossible to come within even a quarter of a mile of them.

I took my dinner at Dumbarton, and went to a place, called 'the meadow,' for evening flight. Saw nothing but ten wild fowl, which dropped in, one at a time (by moonlight), within sixty yards of me. I fired at them, all in a cluster (with a huge gun), and literally swept the pool where they were, but they all escaped by diving at the flash. On my return to the inn I sent for one Reade, a blacksmith (the head shooter), who informed me that two couple of fowl here were reckoned a good day's sport, and that with the many tons of ammunition that were every year fired in the Clyde not fifty barnacles were killed. It appears that even the punt-shooting and cask-burying systems fail here.

16*th.*—Out for morning flight; saw but two small lots of fowl, and never fired my gun. Went, at high water, to shoot at the scaups, and was shown the best plan of getting at them, which is to keep concealed at a distance from the river, and when the birds dive, to spring up and run as fast as possible to the water, and on their coming up (perhaps within ten yards of you) they will instantly take wing, and give you a beautiful shot. I killed 5 of them.

Though the most bitter cold day that could be described, the fly fishers were, if possible, more numerous than the shooters; their tackle is quite coarse, and the trout they kill very small. From the natural propensity Scotsmen have for staring at anything new, it is highly diverting to show them any gun beyond the most common size or inferior value. On my producing a Joe Manton to the blacksmith, I had a mob, similar to one attendant on a dancing bear, or a man killed in the street.

17th.—Mrs. Hawker having come to me at Dumbarton from London the previous evening, I went to Ballock ferry to show her Loch Lomond, where I killed 2 divers, 1 wood pigeon, and 1 teal, which, with the exception of a wild duck that I knocked down and lost for want of a dog, and a water ousel that I unfortunately missed from having too large shot, were all I fired at. This evening we got back to Dumbarton, and there put fresh horses to our chaise, and returned to the vile, stinking, foggy, asthmatic town of Glasgow.

19th.—Dined on some of the best trout I ever ate, which proves that these fish are not only to be caught, but worth catching, here all the year.

N.B.—On my return received information that the lawsuit with the relentless Mrs. Sheddon was at last decided in my favour.

21st.—Went with Colonel Douglas to Dumbarton; and, through having a very clever sportsman [1] to manage the boat, we at last got within about 120 yards of a few barnacle geese, by means of getting between them and the sun, and sculling down on them. We then fired with slugs (Colonel Douglas with a Spanish barrel, and I with a huge wall gun), and killed a barnacle; besides a second one which was picked up by another shooting party.

22nd.—Out again; killed only a golden-eye duck. Fired my wall gun several times among flocks of barnacle and other

[1] One John Menzies (called Mingas), the ferryman of Craigend.

fowl, at not much more than a hundred yards, and plainly discovered that the barrel was a bad and weak shooter; had I one of my own duck guns, I should, no doubt, have astonished the natives with the bulk of my bag. No wonder these birds are wild. Not less than a dozen boats are out every day filled with shooters, who, as well as those from the shore, are incessantly firing at all distances. In the evening we returned to Glasgow.

December 31st.—Went to Dumbarton for the purpose of shooting next day; but on my arrival had reason to regret leaving Glasgow, by a discovery that it is the custom of this place for every soul who can carry arms to go out shooting on New Year's Day.

1813

January 1st.—The beginning of this day was ushered in with such incessant firing, that, what with the guns from the castle and every other explosion, down to the boys firing old pistols in the street, I could compare the town to nothing but a place besieged. And the innumerable shooting parties, in the fields and round the river, were like light infantry in confusion. I had several narrow escapes of both shot and ball, not only round the town, but in the very streets. I contrived, however, in the midst of this besieged country, to bag 3 partridges and 1 jack snipe, which, with another snipe I lost, were all I fired at. I went out merely to see whether or not I could beat this whole host of shooters, and, as far as I could learn, fully succeeded. On my return, about one in the forenoon, I saw a mob of people assembled, and was informed that they were met for a purpose of charity, namely to pay sixpence a shot with ball at a small target, for the benefit of a poor old man, who was to furnish the winner with a cheese. I repaired to the place, and gave half a crown for the poor man, and as I was informed that, although an immense number of shots had been fired, no one had touched the target,

I was induced to draw my shot, and put a pair of balls in the double gun, and, to the astonishment of the elegant company by which I was surrounded, put the said pair of balls into the target. I then left word that if I won the cheese, I would give it to the old man again, and went away. But, unluckily, about two hundred more shots were fired, and, of course, out of that number, some nearer the bull's eye than mine, though I heard none of them hit it.

Under a hope that all the shooting rabble would repair to the alehouses about dusk, I went out flight shooting ; but it appeared that those who had any powder left, still kept blazing away. In short, I had no shots, and was very near getting wrecked on my return, by being dashed by the current on the rocks under Clyde bridge, where four of us in a little cock boat were thumped like a shuttlecock, expecting every moment to go to pieces.

2nd.—Returned to Glasgow.

N.B.—I must remark the cheapness of my bill at Dumbarton. I had two excellent breakfasts ; two dinners, with soup, fish, flesh, wild fowl, sweet things, wine, and a bowl of punch each day. Soup in the middle of the day, board for a servant and a dog, also a capital bed, with fire in my bed-room, and the attendance of a waiter shooting, and my bill for all only amounted to 1*l.* 4*s.*

4th.—3 partridges and 12 snipes. I killed the 12 snipes successively. This is great luck in a place where they are so scarce, as you generally have your sport interspersed with random shots ; making allowance for these, however, I may venture to say that I have killed 30 or 40 snipes in succession.

6th.—Went with Mr. Macintosh to Dumbarton, and then proceeded to Ardencaple inn, ten miles farther, where we passed the night, with very good accommodation.

7th.—Bagged 1 sparrowhawk, 1 hare, and 5 woodcocks, which, with the exception of one fine shot that I missed, by getting a bough directly in my face, were all I fired at, and either 7 or 8 were all we saw, which, for this place, is reckoned a miserable scarcity. We then got a grouse, that, by means of my previously striking with a long random shot, sat till the dogs very near caught him. I also got a wild snap shot at a grey hen, which I hit so hard that we were much disappointed at not bagging her, and, by bad luck and our dogs going down wind, we lost shots at some more grouse and blackcock, which, to our astonishment, lay till the dogs were within a short distance of them. And, but for some showers which came on about twelve, we should have had some fair partridge shooting ; as it was, I lost a brace by my barrels hanging fire. Thus it may be seen with what a beautiful variety of game Ardencaple abounds, and how decidedly this place is the paradise of the country to a sportsman.

The little strip of wood in which I killed my first 3 cocks begins within a gunshot of the inn door. It was somewhat singular that Mr. Macintosh, although a good fag, an old sportsman, and an excellent shot, only got two chances the whole day, and only one of them at a cock which was out of reach. After getting our dinner at two o'clock, we left this beautiful place for Dumbarton, where we drank tea, as the best refreshment after fagging, and we then returned to Glasgow. We having been obliged to post all the way, and entertain some myrmidons, made our expenses for everything just ten guineas.

12*th.*—This evening I hired a buggy, and drove Mrs. Hawker over to Ardencaple, which place we reached after dining at Dumbarton.

13*th.*—We walked out shooting from about ten till one, and, finding that not a single woodcock was to be seen, I mounted the hills, and had the extraordinary luck to bag 4 grouse, as well as 1 hare and 1 partridge. Besides which I knocked down another old cock grouse with my second barrel, having secured one of the hens with my first, but he escaped in the heather.

I only discharged my gun eight times; indeed, the only shot I missed was at a grouse, quite out of fair distance. After getting a two o'clock dinner, we drove back to Glasgow.

15*th.*—In consequence of knowing that my recruiting party would be recalled on the 24th, and having urgent business, in which there was no time to be lost, I had applied for leave to return to England, which was granted, and communicated to me this day, when, after settling with the district paymaster and my party up to the 24th, I prepared for my journey to London, by way of Edinburgh, which road I chose both for variety and comfort.

16*th.*—Took leave of Glasgow at three this afternoon, and arrived in Edinburgh a quarter before ten.

17*th.*—Got into the mail a quarter before three, and (at a quarter before six) on the morning of the 20th arrived in London, after incessantly travelling in more than usual misery, I having been very ill and sick the greater part of the way; the weather having been very bad, with first snow and then rain, and the travelling companion who was bundled into the mail with Mrs. Hawker and myself having a happy mixture of the elephant, the bear, the hog, the ass, and the polecat.

20*th.*—Dined at Blake's Hotel, St. James's, on grouse, which I killed myself on the borders of the Highlands of Scotland this very day week.

February 6*th.*—Left London and arrived at Longparish on my way to the depot, where I had orders to be by the 10th.

9*th.*—Left Longparish, and arrived at Radipole Barracks.

Game &c. bagged up to February 1813: 119 partridges, 18 hares, 41 pheasants, 1 blackcock, 6 grouse, 11 rabbits, 26 snipes, 8 woodcocks, 9 wild fowl, 5 plover. Total, 244, besides wood pigeons, fieldfares, &c.

22*nd.*—A match being made between Captain Coles (of the 12th) and Mr. Bacon (of the 16th), I hired a stage coach and horses, with way bill and everything complete, and covered the expenses by taking nearly all the officers of the depot. Much as larking was in force, there had been no spree to top this since the lads had been together. We (being taken for 'the Union coach') galloped past all the gatekeepers, had repeated applications for a cast, and stopped to malt it at all the hedge alehouses. We had some prime slang on the road, and, of course, blew up every spoony fellow we could meet. After seeing the race won easy by Captain Coles's brown horse we repaired from Blandford race down to the 'Crown,' where dinner was ordered for thirty at *7s.* a head, and we having nearly drunk the landlord out of both his English and French wine, a grand attack was made on the Johnny raws of Blandford, in which were said to be captured fifteen knockers, three signs, and a barber's pole. The boys then returned to their broth, and finished the evening with some prime grub, swizzle, and singing.

On the morning of the 23rd, after my getting shaved by the barber and sounding him about his pole, and making the waiter fiddle country dances while we ate our breakfast, we returned in triumph, with Captain Coles, the winner, on the roof; and having larked all the way down the road, we took a turn up and down Weymouth, with the royal accession of two monkey-faced chimney sweepers that we had picked up on the road and made stand on the coach, the one tuning up with his brush and shovel, and the other bearing a huge Nelson handkerchief from a pole twenty feet long. Our whole crew then began cheering, screeching, and horn blowing, to the irresistible laughter of even the gravest codgers in Weymouth, and the delight of all the damsels, from those in the peerage down to beggar wenches. All the windows were full, the esplanade very gay, and what with bells ringing, children squalling, misses giggling, and dogs barking, the fun was not to be described.

Our career was finished by landing at the barracks, where we had no sooner left the coach than it was mobbed by tag rag, and bob-tail, and as quickly covered with children as a piece of meat is with crabs when thrown in the sea. No lark could possibly end with more good humour on all sides, or more liberality; as we even remunerated the fellows that we blackguarded with beer, and left every place with the name of 'nice gentlemen.' I had the honour of working the whole of the ground, and drove to the satisfaction of all my passengers, although every stage I was bothered with some proper rusty 'divils.'

March 7th.—I had agreed with Major Baker for the purchase of his majority, but was refused the recommendation for no other reason than because I had been unserviceable from the wounds I received in the service, notwithstanding I offered to go abroad forthwith, and to resign immediately if I proved unequal to do my duty. In consequence of this shameful injustice I was driven to send in my resignation, at the same time stating my reasons for so doing to the Commander-in-Chief, who (after a personal interview) most handsomely offered it back, in opposition to Lord Bridgewater. But I, having pledged my word to Mr. Foster that in the event of my not succeeding to the majority his son should have my troop, and his memorials having reached the War Office, and his money being lodged, as well as Major Baker having then hesitated to risk his resignation, I felt it right, under all circumstances, to decline his Royal Highness's kind offer, and submitted to the mortification of retiring from the regiment as eldest captain.

25*th.*—Received official information that I was gazetted out (on Tuesday, the 23rd), and that Captain Foster's commission bore date the 18th instant.

During the few months I had to remain in suspense about the final arrangement of my business, I had (what with having to go to Scotland and waiting on Lord Bridgewater &c.) 1,291 miles to travel.

Statement of the circumstances from which I left the

army: The unfortunate circumstance by which I was so unjustly driven out of the service was as follows. I (being eldest captain) had agreed to give Major Baker 2,000 guineas for his majority, and he had promised me his resignation the moment I could be recommended. I wrote to Lieutenant-Colonel Hervey (then in Spain) to ask his sanction; and he declared that he had nothing to do with any recommendations at home, and that they all went through Lord Bridgewater, at the same time informing Major Baker, and (according to Major Baker's letter to me) promising that I should have his recommendation. I then applied to Lord Bridgewater, who (though I transmitted him Colonel Hervey's answer) said that the business must be referred to Colonel Hervey. Inimical, however, to this shuffling and evasive treatment towards me, Colonel Hervey had occasion to come to England, and I (who had taken a recruiting party in Scotland till I heard of his arrival in London) lost no time in getting to town, to learn the result of his interview with Lord Bridgewater, being extremely anxious to secure my promotion and join my regiment in the Peninsula. I should observe that previously to my leaving Scotland, Major Baker wrote me word that Lord Bridgewater had signified to him that 'he would do nothing in the business till he had consulted the Lieutenant-Colonel.' And subsequent to this Lord Bridgewater refused to forward my memorial to the Commander-in-Chief under the excuse that I had therein stated the probability of a vacancy, of which he not only declared himself (both privately and officially) perfectly ignorant, but gave me his word that he thought it highly improbable, at the very time he was conferring with Major Baker on the subject.

On my arrival in London I wrote to Lord Bridgewater (who was then at Ashridge) to ask if, in the event of a vacancy, I might hope for the honour of his recommendation, as I wished to join my regiment, which I, of course, would not do as long as there existed an impediment to my promotion, and saying that if a reply to such a question was the least irregular, I should esteem it a favour if I might be allowed to speak with him (Lord Bridgewater) on the subject. And he returned an evasive answer, merely persisting that he had heard nothing of Major Baker's intention to quit, and neither giving me a word in answer to my letter, nor allowing me to speak to him. I, about the same time, received Colonel Hervey's determination (by letter), which was that if Major Baker intended to quit (which at present he much doubted), it was his determination to recommend Captain Milles to succeed him. Captain Milles was then in England, and, according to the report of his own friends, brought home purposely to supersede me, who, when he was a young cornet, was a captain in the regiment. I had, of course, made up my mind to leave the service in the event of not succeeding, and had pledged my honour to Lieutenant Foster's father, that, if I could not be recommended to the majority, he should have my troop for his son, and accordingly agreed with him for the sale of it. I had, at last, no other alternative than sending in my resignation, and previously stating to the Commander-in-Chief my reasons for so doing. Colonel Hervey (having no doubt heard of my agreement with Mr. Foster) wrote to Major Baker to request he would continue in the regiment; at least I am justified in supposing so by Major Baker's answer, which was:

'Dear Hervey, I will remain if you wish it.'

Thus being foiled at all points in the majority, I felt myself bound in honour to refuse my resignation (which his Royal Highness most handsomely offered back to me, contrary to the entreaty of Lord Bridgewater), and was driven out of the service by the Colonel and Lieutenant-Colonel, for no other reason than what ought to have been a recommendation—namely, the very severe wounds with which I had till lately been deprived from doing my duty. For (as I stated in writing to the Commander-in-Chief) 'I defied either

Lord Bridgewater or Colonel Hervey to give any other reason.'

Annexed is a list of my losses by leaving the service, viz.:

Cr. *Paid for Commissions.*

	£	s.	d.
In the 1st (or Royal Dragoons) Cornetcy	735	0	0
" Lieutenancy . . .	262	10	0
Being reduced, by the peace, in 1802, I had to pay (the regulation) for exchange to full pay in the 14th Light Dragoons	817	10	0
(In a few months after the half-pay Lieutenants were reinstated gratis.)			
Besides my other commissions paid Major Browne for troop	3,990	0	0
(Shortly after a troop went for little more than the regulation, and another without purchase.)			
Besides all this I had some heavy losses by a Quarter-Master, who misapplied money while I was on leave.			
Total . .	£5,805	0	0

Dr. *Received for Commissions.*

	£	s.	d.
Troop	1,785	0	0
Lieutenancy	262	10	0
Cornetcy, provided it is sold before there comes a peace (otherwise I lose it)	735	0	0
Privately promised by Mr. Foster	400	0	0
Lost by my commissions	2,622	10	0
Total . .	£5,805	0	0

N.B.—I was a Captain of Dragoons soon after I was seventeen years old, but paid dearer for it than anyone in the service.

April 13th.—Went to London.

May 18th.—Instead of leaving town (as intended), I was this day seized with another violent attack of my wound, which obliged me to be put to bed. I there lay in torture till the 24th, when I was greatly relieved by three small pieces of bone being cut out of my thigh. Sir Everard Home, on seeing this, considered that my life was saved by the circumstance of my being driven from the army!

30*th.*—I left London and arrived this evening at Longparish.

My reason for being so anxious to leave town was, that my little child had been at the point of death, and when given over by Sir E. Home I saved his life by strong port wine negus and nutmeg.

June 9th.—Notwithstanding my little infant (Richard Hawker) had completely recovered his health and appetite, he was this evening suddenly seized with another relapse, and died between nine and ten o'clock at night.

12*th.*—Longparish House. My wound having got so much better as to admit of my walking (with a stick) I went fly fishing, and killed (yesterday and to-day) 14 trout.

14*th.*—10 trout (average weight 1 lb. each) in three-quarters of an hour, and, had I not broke my fly rod (which obliged me to leave off), should have had extraordinary sport.

18*th.*—Having been informed that an outlying buck (for which I and, I believe, several others had been above a fortnight hunting) had been seen feeding near Budget Farm, about ten o'clock the previous night, I this evening repaired to the place, and after my lying in wait in a rickhouse, and peeping through its crevices till daylight had almost disappeared, the gentleman suddenly presented himself in a fine attitude, at a gap in the bottom of Castle field ; but, instead of advancing towards my entrenchment, he stole up very cautiously, under the hedge, till he got to the top of the field and left it again by an upper gap. From the approaching darkness it became necessary that no time should be lost, and following him (wild as he was) appeared my only chance. About five minutes after I had reached the top of the hill, I could just discern him, at a considerable distance (in our standing corn), making off at a full gallop. On this I despatched John to the farm, with directions to mount a horse, and make an immense circle at full speed, in order to outflank him, while I lay in ambush at the last gap by which he had passed. This plan succeeded so admirably well that, in a few minutes, John turned him, and up he came, bounding like a kangaroo, directly towards me. I had my best duck gun, loaded with swan shot, and an old army rifle, but being loth to depend on either the latter or my own nerves, I determined on receiving him with a volley of swandrops. In a few seconds he came up, and suddenly stopped at about fifty yards, in a place from which, had he turned either right or left, he would have been lost to my view, so I opened my fire—bang—directly in his face, but with so little good (well as I had levelled the gun) that the shot had no other effect than to drive him directly back again into the standing corn. Here John played his part well. While I, with the rifle, was following the deer, he outflanked him a second time, and drove him back. He then came across me, within forty yards, at full speed. I fired the ball directly through his neck, and he never gave a struggle. Thus after an indefatigable pursuit (in spite of my ill health) had I the fortune to bag the outlying buck. He was remarkably large and in very fair condition.

N.B.—Having previously heard of this deer, I practised with the rifle for the first time I ever fired with one, and in eight shots at a hundred yards I put six balls (two of which were immediately in the centre) into a newspaper. This, however, is but average shooting, unless it be considered that my rifle is an old one that was cast from Hornpesch's corps as being unserviceable, and given me by an officer.

27th.—Disastrous ill luck with two more deer. This morning, about six o'clock, I was hurried out of bed by being informed that two more deer were feeding in the next field but one to our house. After running up, and placing myself in a hedge, one of them was, after a little beating, started from the peas, and, being turned at a favourite gap where I had previously placed a vedette for that purpose, galloped up to within twenty yards of me, and (as the devil would have it) continued his pace inclining to the left, by which means I was obliged to fire through a bough, which so intercepted the sight of my rifle that I had the mortification to see him completely missed. He instantly bolted into an immense hedgerow, which I got the other side of just in time to give him a double shot with Joe Manton; but my chance here was bad, as I had loaded merely with two balls that were much too small for the calibre, so that my double gun was of little avail for any other purpose than to give a *coup de grâce* had I stopped him with the other gun.

The other deer was seen following him, and after a long hunt for the one at which I had fired, under an idea that, from having seen one deer come out without the other, I had wounded the former one, I returned to the pea field, and (having got two dogs, and being joined by an immense rabble that my firing had brought out) began to beat, but all to no purpose. I had loaded my double gun, to be on the safe side, should he have been found wounded.

On my purposing to return home, an old poacher expressed a wish to beat the peas again, for which everyone laughed at him, knowing that both the deer were moved. His request, however, was complied with, and, to our utter astonishment, up sprang, in the middle of the mob, the other deer, which trotted across me, at about thirty yards. I fired both barrels without being in the least nervous, and with the most accurate aim, and (to add to my bad luck) never touched him.

Had I but loaded the rifle instead, or even had I common shot in my double gun, nothing could possibly have saved him.

Thus had I (who so seldom let anything escape within fair distance) the mortification to miss one deer at twenty, and the other within thirty yards, and both from sheer ill luck and misfortune.

The damage the three deer have done in the corn is calculated at 40*l.*

N.B.—This unlucky day ended with the following truly afflicting circumstance. Poor Annesley Powell, after coming here (unexpected), and dining with a quiet sober party, was thrown from his horse, with his head on the point of a flint stone, which so fractured his skull, and occasioned such a concussion of the brain, that (melancholy to relate) he never spoke a word afterwards, and expired the following morning, sincerely regretted by the whole neighbourhood, and (what is still more to his credit) by all the poor, to whom his charities were unbounded.

July 3rd.—Attended the funeral of poor Powell, who was this day buried in Wherwell church.

7th.—1 stone curlew, which I killed (on my return from waiting for the deer) late at night, by calling it close to me with imitating its whistle.

9th.—Having been out most mornings at daybreak, and regularly every evening, in search of the deer, I this day scoured the country with old Siney and his host of terriers, but to no purpose, notwithstanding we found several places where the deer had been browsing.

21st.—One of the deer, after a long armistice, having been again seen, I this morning got up during a mizzling rain at three o'clock, and, with my rifle, sat among the branches of an oak till long after sunrise, but never saw him. What induced me to persevere, was the deer having been seen near this tree overnight by a friend who, although within two yards of him, was tantalised by hearing him eat without being able to level his gun, in consequence of the wretched interference of a huge blackthorn hedge, which to such a nicety protected the animal that my friend could occasionally see his ears, but nothing more ; had any person five inches taller been there he might have blown his skull off. It was provoking to me, who from my height could have seen his whole head, that I should have cruised past the croft but a few minutes before he came out. Such a chance may never recur, as the shyness of these deer now exceeds all description, and Lord Portsmouth's keepers have been always so completely outmanœuvred by them that they have given a general leave for their destruction.

23rd.—Started with a party and a cartful of prog &c. to amuse ourselves in Miller's pond and Netley Abbey ponds. Although equipped with rods, snares, a casting net, and plenty of cocculus indicus, we only got some small carp, an eel, and some roach ; and the greater part of the carp I killed with a worm, I having landed 3 brace.

August 5th.—Left Longparish for London, on way to the moors in Yorkshire.

8th.—Left London per mail, and after a journey with a very pleasant set, and a profusion of noise, mirth, and fun on the road, reached Ferrybridge at nine on the evening of the 9th, and then got to Methley Park, eight miles, in a chaise by ten o'clock.

11th.—Went with a party, consisting of Lord Pollington, Mr. Hawkins, and Mr. Chadwick, to Holmfirth, a wild manufacturing town among small mountains, and about four miles from the grouse moors.

12th.—We were all up at three o'clock and off by daylight, but the birds were so extremely wild that it was almost impossible to get near them, and our going quietly to work was out of the question, as the moors were swarming with disciples of General Ludd, who always allow themselves a holiday on the 12th of August purposely to see the sporting on the moors. It was chiefly by firing snap shots that I got any game, and I soon saw enough to convince me that the grouse shooting in Yorkshire is now very poor ; add to this, I had the disadvantage of being accommodated with two wild unsteady dogs only nine months old, and they never had seen a bird killed to them ; while Lord Pollington, with dogs which he offers to challenge all England, and with two guns, was working the finest part of the moor, which he had signified his positive intention of keeping quiet till after dinner, when we were able to join him.

Notwithstanding all this advantage he took in order to excel, and then I suppose to crow over, his party, he only beat me by one bird, and that one of his followers told me was a bird which some other person had wounded. I killed 10 grouse, including one which Mr. Hawkins had slightly struck before me. I killed all I could have done till the latter end of the day, when I was seized with a fit of sickness, and was so ill that I lost three birds by missing fair shots, and many others from being unable to walk up to the dogs when they did point, which was very seldom the case.

I returned from the moors very faint, and, under all circumstances, thought proper to take my departure, and sent to Huddersfield for a chaise which brought me to that place by about eleven at night.

Number of birds killed: Lord Pollington, including a doubtfully claimed bird, 5½ brace; myself, including bird hit by Mr. Hawkins, 5 brace; Mr. Hawkins, 2 brace; Mr. Chadwick, 1½ brace; gamekeeper, 1 brace. Total, 15 brace.

13*th*.—Proceeded about twelve o'clock per heavy coach to Wakefield, and, after there waiting an hour for the Sheffield coach, I found it quite full; but some bagsmen being also disappointed, I joined in a chaise and proceeded with them to Sheffield, where, after passing for a traveller, being treated as such, and, luckily for the low estate of my purse, charged as such, and buying some hardware as such, I went to bed.

I had nearly omitted to mention that on our way from Huddersfield to Wakefield we passed the village of Almondbury, noted for the following droll circumstance: A chimney sweeper being wanted in a hurry to perform the office of his profession, and at the moment unable to attend, sent a stupid boy as his *locum tenens* to make the chimney fit for use, and with a message that he would come himself on the morrow and sweep it completely. The boy got up the tunnel, and after giving the usual salute and flourish with his brush on the outside, descended by a wrong tunnel, which brought him directly into the office of a pettifogging attorney, who was alone writing by the gloomy light of evening. The quill driver had scarcely strength to support himself on seeing this fiend, and while struggling with the guilty conscience of a lawyer and this hellish appearance, the boy said in a low sepulchral tone, 'I am come for you to-day, and my master will attend you to-morrow.' Away ran the lawyer, and God knows what became of him.

I got to bed at Sheffield, having retired from the bagman's room, about eleven, and at three started by the 'Slope' heavy coach for Northampton, where, after travelling with sixteen passengers, bad wheels, and restive horses, we arrived by about ten at night. We stopped at Nottingham for breakfast, and Leicester for dinner; but neither of these meals being provided, nor even a cloth laid, we got nothing till the last moment, when bolting and pocketing were the order of the day.

I was obliged to enliven myself this tedious journey by passing for divers characters; first, a fellow who had tipped the double to some bailiffs on the York road, then for a naval officer, &c. I had a fresh character to each fresh passenger, as the travellers on this road only go a few stages, and then stop to do business.

Number of miles travelled for one very bad day's shooting: Longparish to London, 61; to Ferrybridge, 172; Methley Park, 8; to the moor town, 21 (Holmfirth); to the ground and back, 8 (mountain travelling); back direct to London, 206; through London and back, 6 (about); home to Longparish, 61; in all, 543 miles!

CHAPTER VI

1813

September 1st.—Longparish. 14 partridges. I never saw the birds so wild the first day in my life, and the scent was so infamously bad that the dogs could do nothing; and we had to shoot in a pour of rain almost all the afternoon. Lord Hinton returned home to a seven o'clock dinner. I remained out till near eight.

The bags were filled as follows: Lord Hinton, 3 brace and 1 hare; Mr. L——, 2½ brace; myself, 7 brace; dogs caught 1½ brace. Total, 14 brace and 1 hare.

All the game we could bag the first week is as follows: Lord Hinton, 12 brace of partridges and 1 hare; Mr. L——, 9½ brace of partridges, 1 hare and 1 rabbit; myself, 21½ brace of partridges and 3 snipes; divided birds 3, and dogs caught 3; in all, 46 brace of partridges, 1 brace of hares, 3 snipes, and 1 rabbit. Total, 98 head.

15th.—Went out with Siney and his troop of terriers to our home field, and killed (in six snap shots) 5 rabbits. Hinton killed 1 rabbit and 1 partridge, and Mrs. Hawker shot 1 cock pheasant out of a fir tree, for which I lent her my gun with half a charge.

23rd.—7 partridges, 1 hare, 1 snipe, and 2 wild ducks, the latter of which I had killed right and left with No. 7 shot at immense distances, after lying on my back for nearly half an hour before I could get them to pitch. I saw 10 in the air at first, but they divided, and 5 went out of sight, and the other 5 kept wheeling round till they fancied they might rest in security.

25*th.*—4 partridges, 1 hare, and 1 snipe (which was the last remaining bird of a wisp of eight that took up their abode in our fen, I having killed every one of them), and coming home I made a very long shot at a sparrowhawk, which had for some time annoyed us.

27*th.*—Went to see and made a drawing of Stonehenge, the principal information about which we got from a poor old man, aged 72, who, since losing his hand by a gun bursting when firing at a bustard, has frequented this solitary spot for the purpose of gathering mushrooms, and picking up what he can from the company who come to visit it. The stones are ninety-four in number, viz. ninety in the Druidical circle, and four detached. The absurd stories about this place are too ridiculous for remark ; suffice it to say, therefore, that the stones are one mile and three-quarters from Amesbury, and about a quarter of a mile beyond the hills where the Deptford Inn and Heytesbury roads divide. They are formed nearly in a circle, and are, I have no doubt, a composition, as they will, immediately on their being broken, dissolve in water like lump sugar.

Game bagged up to the end of September : 113 partridges, 7 hares, 5 rabbits, 12 snipes, 9 wild ducks. Total, 147 head.

30*th.*—Went to Mr. Chamberlain's farm, near Bere, in Dorsetshire.

N.B.—Chamberlain (with whom and with whose one excellent dog I shot) killed 9 pheasants, 5 partridges, 1 hare, and 2 rabbits. I saw him miss but twice, and both times much beyond fair distance. So he killed 17 out of 19, making 55 pieces of game in 59 shots between us; two of the misses quite out of reach ; a third secured with second barrel, and a fourth a long shot at the hare that I crippled.

This would be mere average shooting were it not that Chamberlain and I fired (and always do fire) long shots instead of never shooting beyond 40 yards, as so many do who have a wish never to miss, and therefore content themselves with firing only one barrel at a covey, merely from this mistaken idea of real good shooting.

October 2nd.—3 pheasants, 7 partridges, by the road on my way to Hyde, whither I went to see and pass a day or two with Mr. Knight. The only shot that I did not kill was at a hare, a long way off, which I struck so hard that she never would have escaped had not she run into forbidden ground.

In these two days, without picking my shots (which I never do), I killed 38 head of game and wounded 1 out of forty times firing, and almost everything 'died in the air.'

6th.—5 partridges and one lost, 1 jack snipe, and 1 pheasant. Went back to Hyde, saw a brace of birds, marked them down, and bagged 1 with each barrel, viz. 2 partridges. On getting near Hyde we had a narrow escape from an accident. My leader took fright, and with one prodigious spring, in spite of both rein and whip applied in due time, jumped off a terrace road into a bog, out of which I flogged him up again, and he made a second bolt into the bog, where he became restive; but luckily I kept my wheeler in, so as to hold him till the leader was taken off, and everything ended well.

Since being in Dorsetshire, I had (including a few birds lost) killed 82 head of game before I missed a fair shot.

11th.—4 rabbits; and lost a fine old cock pheasant, at which I made a very long shot.

12th.—After having spent our time very pleasantly with the Knights, Mrs. Hawker and I took our leave, and left Hyde on our way home to Longparish, by way of Wareham, by which road I travelled for the purpose of reconnoitring the country, and finding out the best coast for wild fowl, should I be disposed for an excursion in the winter. While the tandem horses were baiting I hired a post horse and surveyed the Isle of Purbeck, and went to the village of Arne, which is well situated, but so destitute of even the roughest accommodation, that I could find no plan better than resolving either to put up at Poole, or one of the passage houses, in case I should take this coast in winter. After two or three hours' hard riding on a bad day, I started with Mrs. Hawker and passed through Wimborne to Cranborne, where we put up for the night at the 'Fleur de Lis,' *alias* 'Flower de Luce,' a most desirable public-house, celebrated for civility and comfort, as well as good living and reasonable charges.

13*th.*—Returned to Longparish, and on my road bagged 1 pheasant and 1 partridge. I had the bad luck to shoot 3 more cock pheasants, and lose them all in the furze; owing to having lost my dogs at the time, these birds, being all long shots, were only winged.

Memorandum of my shooting in Dorsetshire,
with exact account of shots fired.

HITS.

(Wounded birds not included.)

Pheasants: bagged 29; lost 4	33
Partridges: bagged 20; lost 3	23
Hares (except the one wounded; all I shot at)	1
Rabbits	16
Snipes	12
In all	85

MISSES.

(Of every kind.)

Fair shots (within distance)	6
Namely: 1 pheasant, which turned at the moment I fired, and which I secured with second barrel. 1 hare, which I so crippled that nothing but her crawling into forbidden ground could have saved her. 1 partridge, by my foot slipping at the moment I fired. An unpardonable miss at a jack snipe. Two equally shameful misses at partridges.	
In all	6

20*th.*—This morning I was routed out of bed by a cry of 'The buck under the windows, and Farmer Smith's dog at his heels!' We turned out cavalry and infantry, but it was impossible to overtake him, otherwise nothing could have saved him, as Smith's dog, which must have killed him with the least assistance, literally held and struggled with him for several minutes at nearly a mile away from the inclosed country. This cursed nine-lived buck then escaped, afterwards evaded Twynam's pack of harriers, and then was seen, quite lame, going off towards Freefolk Woods.

I had given up all idea of this buck, having laid out for him since about August 30, when it was reported that he had returned to the park and been there shot, and up to which period I had been days and nights slaving after him.

4 o'clock P.M. The buck was seen close to the park near Whitchurch.

November 8th.—Posted up to London purposely to attend Joe Manton while altering and repairing three of my guns, by which means I got them in five days done right, instead of five months done wrong.

9th.—Was nearly tortured to death by a relay of three dentists, who failed in drawing a tremendous tooth, and finished with breaking my jawbone, and complimenting me for the *sang-froid* with which I braved their infernal operations.

13th.—Having secured my guns and bound up my head, I left London 'in the pains of the damned,' and, to mend the speed of my journey, got horses that had just returned from previous jobs at every stage, and was nearly eleven hours getting down.

On my arrival, had the great satisfaction to find a letter from the Secretary at War, saying that 'his Royal Highness the Prince Regent had been graciously pleased to order me the pension of one hundred a year, commencing from December 25, 1811, in consideration for the wounds which I had received in his Majesty's service.'

14th.—Lord Hinton came to us, and left us on the 19th, and during his stay he had some excellent sport; for, what with the fall of the leaf having driven out Lord Portsmouth's hares and pheasants, and a good flight of snipes having come, the shooting was far better than it usually is here in November.

I crawled out on the 15th, and killed 1 pheasant; then came home and went to bed, and here I have been laid up in torture with my jaw, with scarcely a moment's intermission from pain, and with occasional spasms that have almost taken away my senses, and my only ease has been when dozing under the influence of laudanum; my unmercifully handled jaw having defied blisters, leeches, and every other remedy that could be devised.

20th.—Was for a few hours this evening nearly free from pain; this is literally the first time I have been free from severe pain for these twelve days and twelve nights.

21st.—My pains having returned, I became again almost distracted, when, by my own wish, a leech was applied to the very nerve of my gum; it kept me for twenty minutes in great misery and continual pain, but the permanent relief I got is almost incredible.

25th.—Was well enough to walk out; so I took my gun, and killed 1 rabbit and 1 partridge.

29th.—Was able to renew my shooting, for which I believe I have to thank the leech that was applied to my gum. Killed 3 hares, 2 partridges, 2 snipes, and 1 jack snipe.

December 2nd.—3 snipes, 3 jack snipes, 2 teal, and 2 woodcocks.

I had seen some teal the previous day, when, being unable to mark them down, I was forced to give them up; and I was out all the evening, and up an hour before daylight in search of them this morning, but to no purpose; and, having returned to breakfast, I left my duck gun and went to Whitchurch, and then beat the whole river down with my double gun and snipe shot, with which I killed the above two teal (all I saw); and, coming home, I put up a couple of cocks and killed them both, after having just made a capital right and left at two jack snipes in a gale of wind. I never missed all day, and never was I better pleased with any shooting at Longparish.

4th.—4 pheasants and 4 snipes. All I fired at, except a long shot at a partridge that I wounded and lost, and another snipe which I ought to have killed.

N.B.—Since December began, I have had 34 shots, out of which I killed 31, wounded 1, and missed 2.

6th.—Left Longparish on a reconnoitre of the Dorsetshire coast, and, with a tired horse, reached Cranborne, where, in consequence of the fair, the inn was in one general scene of riot and drunkenness, and I had a thin partition only between me and rooms filled with fellows who were drumming, fifing, fiddling, dancing and screeching, till six in the morning, when nothing but threatening to shoot them prevented them from breaking into my room.

7th.—Reached Poole, and proceeded to the 'Haven Passage House,' where rooms were prepared for me, and round which the wild fowl were flying in hundreds, though too far for a shot. I could plainly see that if hard weather comes, this place will be a paradise to a shooter. I killed on the road 1 pheasant and 1 partridge.

8th.—I took the morning flight an hour before dawn, and, of course, the evening flight, but although the geese, dunbirds and wigeons were in myriads, yet none flew low enough even for swan shot. I this day surveyed every creek and corner, and although getting any good shots at fowl proved almost impossible, yet in order to be ready to receive them on the approach of proper weather (which should be either very rough or very severe), I decided on remaining here, and accordingly sent John away with my dog cart, and to return here with Mrs. Hawker; I also hired an old fisherman, with his boat and a canoe, to attend me on all occasions and go water errands, catch fish for me, &c.; and I adopted the hours of six for breakfast, two for dinner, six for tea (or pipe and grog), and nine for bed, by which means I avoid going with an empty stomach to the cold creeks and sandbanks, morning, evening and night.

9th.—Killed 3 brent geese at one shot.

N.B.—While Caleb Sturney (the old fisherman) and I were endeavouring to launch a boat, 6 geese came over at about seventy yards, and with No. 2 shot I brought down the above 3; one of them, however, floated away before my face, quite dead, and the current was so strong I dare not go in, and I had no dog. I afterwards got a shot at about 100, no farther off, and the gun missed fire.

10th.—The only shot I got was at a flock of curres an immense way off. I knocked one down and crippled some more, but they were carried off by the tide, and I had not even the luck to bag one.

I defy any wild fowl (were they in great numbers) to escape the various means which I could devise to get at them in the night; but, unfortunately, so many scores of people are every night either laid up, buried in casks, or floating in canoes, that the birds literally go out to sea at night and come in to feed in the morning, instead of *vice versâ*, and they generally fly above 100 yards high, very much scattered. General frost, however, it is to be hoped, will, as in the Russian campaign, do more than all our modern manœuvres.

Saw a very fair show of birds, but, as yet, no good shooting to be got. The novelties of the place, however, and the delightful sailing every day, make amends for the present impossibility of getting wild fowl within reach.

The harbour and coast of Poole &c. has never, since the memory of the oldest person, been so bereft of wild fowl any previous winter as it has this.

15th.—Finding I could get no birds to fly low enough in the harbour, I tried a large pond, inland, where the wigeon had been seen. I got up about four in the morning, and after some trouble in getting across the heath, I found the pond; and after creeping round by moonlight, I espied these 3 wigeon on the water, but dare not wait to get them together, as several other shooters were round the pond. I therefore got 2 in a line, knocked them both over, but lost 1; so bagged but 1 wigeon. Went out all day shooting. Killed a jack snipe, all I shot at, and, at night, lay up at the pond and killed 2 divers.

16*th*.—Attended the ponds an hour before daylight, as well as (in an incessant pour of rain) the whole afternoon, but saw no living creature except four other shooters, and, in short, never fired a gun all day.

17*th*.—Fxcept at a large diver which I knocked down and could not catch, and a gull which I discharged my gun at and killed, I never fired a shot; in the afternoon the pilot and I were overtaken by a gale of wind while paddling in a canoe, and was too happy to escape with merely getting well ducked.

20*th*.—Went in a small boat to Christchurch haven, about fourteen miles. Saw thousands of wild fowl, chiefly ducks and mallards, under the cliffs at Bourne-bottom, though never got a shot, except at a large diver, which I killed. After surveying the harbour, and finding it far inferior to our own head quarters, I tramped in water boots to the town of Christchurch, and having seen all there, I took a chaise to the public-house, commonly called 'Kay-pond,' in hopes of a flight of ducks, as this place lies directly off Bourne-bottom bay, but the swarms of birds which were there at midday never appeared, and I walked home to the 'Haven,' having left my boat at Christchurch haven to come off by the tide next morning.

21*st*.—After killing 2 partridges, 1 pheasant, 1 jack snipe, and 5 ox-birds, I was taken very ill, and obliged to return to the haven. It was obvious that what I suffered was from dining on cold boiled beef at Christchurch, as I never partook of this refreshment at inns, where boiled beef is generally ill cured, half done and stale. My case therefore required tartar emetic, and the difficulty of getting a boat against tide to Poole, and the distance there by land being above five miles, I was almost in torture till I luckily thought of sending to Brownsea Castle, where Mr. Sturt, who was fortunately at home and had some of the medicine, very kindly sent it, and, I am sure, saved me from a very serious illness.

So enthusiastic is my mania of waiting for an evening shot at wild fowl, that while under the influence of the medicine I leant on a bank by the seaside with one duck gun in my hand, and another ready loaded. Nothing, however, came within reach, and I was soon too ill to support myself, and then went to bed.

22nd and 23rd.—Having considerably recovered was out again, but, as usual, never fired a shot, and the latter day was chiefly employed in recovering my Newfoundland dog, which had decamped after a quarrel with my pointer.

24th.—Completed the twenty-seventh year of my age. This day was spent in a very pleasant sail to the two pyramids called 'Old Harry and his Wife,' of which, as well as the rocks and other curious places, I had a regular survey. I, of course, took my gun, and, among these cliffs, made an immensely long flying shot at a goshawk. I also knocked down several ox-birds, but got no shots at wild fowl except one out of reach, but the evening flight was like the roar of the sea, though not one string of birds came low enough to be fired at.

29th.—This and the two previous days I passed in sailing, shooting gulls, ox-birds, divers, &c., which were neither killed for practice nor wanton cruelty, but as tit-bits for Caleb Sturney, my fisherman and pilot, who regularly feasted on them and swore that they were 'as good as "backside fowls."' I killed, among other rubbish, a speckled diver, which I note down, being the first I have been able to secure. In the evening I buried myself in the sand, near where I observed the fowl generally flew; but owing to the unparalleled mild weather, they came over too high; my plan, however, so far succeeded, that I got a diving duck, and should have had more shots had there been cold weather, or wind, to lower the flight of the birds.

31st.—For the first day, Sundays excepted, I gave up the

morning flight, and lay in bed till daylight. We were out from ten till three after the geese, but never got a shot. I was also from five till nine at the pond without firing, and having been equally unsuccessful in a canoe from nine till twelve, we returned home to oysters, and, with a good bowl of punch, drowned the execrably bad sport of 1813, and drank in the year 1814, surrounded by a crashing chorus of jolly smugglers. This grand crew was within a thin partition of us, so I ordered them a huge bowl of punch, and had then an opportunity of partaking of their mirth without being bored by their company, and edified by a breeze from the north-east and a hope of proper weather.

Got all the guns, fired in 1814, and went to bed.

1814

January 1st.—Buried myself in an old sugar cask in the mud, where I remained from ten till two, reading, and waiting for the geese, which were coming in immense force precisely where I wished them, till some scoundrel in a canoe rowed after them to no purpose, and spoiled me a shot, which I certainly should have had with my largest 25-lb. shoulder gun. In the evening I went by moonlight to my pond, which was infested by a multitude of 'gunners.' I killed a single dunbird, and missed a heron, which is the first time I have failed killing within distance since my arrival at the haven.

3rd.—A pour of rain which turned to snow, and with a tremendous gale of wind and hard frost, continued without intermission till the night of the 5th.

6th.—Was out with every hope of sport, but literally saw no wild fowl, except one small flock of curres at an immense distance; I winged one, and after a long chase he beat the boat and escaped.

The weather was this day so severe that the small birds pitched on the boat in full sail; and when we went on shore the fieldfares were hopping under my feet. This proves that our wretched sport is not so much to be imputed to the weather, as the unparalleled scarcity of wild fowl on every part of this coast. The head shooter, in the harbour, has this year killed only three couple of fowl, and two men near here, who at 2 shillings a couple cleared 50 guineas by birds last year, have this season, with the same perseverance, got but a few couple.

8th.—The weather became so intensely severe, that the people of the house were busily employed in preparing puddings of the larks and other birds, which flocked into the house and sheds, and were not only there, but even in the furze and on the shore, easily taken with the hand. I fired at 5 geese out of reach and shot a plover, which I lost (at night). Out sailing the whole day with a strong N.E. wind, and the severest cold I ever felt, and literally never saw a flock of wild fowl. Was all over Poole harbour, and very near Wareham, where, according to report of punters from that place, the same unheard-of scarcity prevailed. Such was the intensity of the cold that I picked up pocketfuls of larks that had perished and fallen in the water, and on our return old Sturney and I had a hairbreadth escape of sharing the same fate, by getting driven on a mud bank 2 miles from land; luckily, however, by throwing our ballast overboard &c. we got afloat just in time to save the tide.

There were this day, at least, 20 canoes paddling in the creeks, but no birds killed, and very few seen.

9th.—Went to Wareham.

10th.—Proceeded to Hyde, to try for snipes, and returned on the morning of the 12th, with 1 mallard, 2 wild ducks, 3 teal, 1 woodcock, 1 wood pigeon, 28 snipes, 2 jack snipes, and 1 water rail, besides some moorhens, and my pockets full of larks, &c.

13th.—The wild fowl at last came into the haven by thousands, in one continued succession of swarms, and in a few hours, notwithstanding this was a day appointed for a general thanksgiving, an immense levy *en masse* of shooters was assembled at all points, and there was not a neck of land, bank, or standing place of any kind but what was crowded with blackguards of every description, firing at all distances, and completely annihilating the brilliant prospects of sport.

14*th.*—It blew such a tremendous hurricane that comparatively few birds would fly, as they could remain unmolested in the harbour from the impossibility of the numerous host of boats and canoes being able to follow them. Some, however, came out and would have afforded charming sport, but after I had been at the trouble and expense of making proper masked entrenchments of every kind, I had in all quarters the mortification to find myself closely surrounded by vagabonds of every description, who were standing quite exposed, firing at sea gulls, ox-birds, and even small birds, and repeatedly, as the geese were coming directly for me, like a pack of hounds full cry, I had to endure the provocation of seeing some dirty cabin boy spring up and drive them away with the paltry discharge of an old rusty popgun. Had it been possible for me to have lain peaceably in any one place, I should have filled a sack; as it was, however, I had no further satisfaction than that of killing more than all these ruffians put together. I got 3 wigeon, 2 grey plover, 2 cormorants, 1 ring dotterel, 18 ox-birds, and 1 dusky grebe. Had the coast been quiet, I should, of course, have only fired at proper wild fowl. When the rabble could not see to shoot they adjourned to the 'Haven' to drink, and when the liquor gave them fresh courage the guns were again taken out, and finding it too dark to see to fire at anything they began to amuse themselves with shooting in the air, till I was obliged to put a stop to it.

Thus do these gunners, in large bodies, from places 5, 6, and even 10 miles off, make a point of assembling for the whole time the hard weather lasts, and literally make a merit of their wasteful expenditure in ammunition.

I this day, by firing at random, contrived, as usual, to beat the sum-total of the shooters here, with 2 wigeon, and 2 curres, and John shot another wigeon, which a rabble wanted to claim, till I soon stopped their impertinence.

17th.—Finding it impossible to get within even bullet shot of the fowls, I amused myself with sailing about and shooting grebes, gulls, redshanks, ox-birds &c. and a snipe.

18th.—I fell dead lame with my right foot, from having some days ago had some boiling water thrown over my instep. I, however, hobbled to the shore, got carried over the creeks, and lay up in a barrel in an incessant pour of rain, for it this day began to thaw. The flight, as usual, was dreadfully slack: killed all the fair chances I got, 1 golden-eye and 1 curlew.

19th.– My foot became so bad that I was obliged to be carried again to my ambush, where I sat in the rain all day and got 2 brent geese.

20th.—Was called before daylight, but was in such pain with my foot that I was obliged to send John out and remain in bed. He began by getting half killed by the recoil of my large gun, and while he and the gun were lying together in the snow the geese came close over him in one grand army; this gave him fresh spirits, and he put in half a charge and knocked down four of them. I contrived to crawl out for evening flight, but the geese then took another route,[1] and I only killed a wigeon.

Birds bagged while at Haven: 6 brent geese, 3 ducks and mallards, 3 teal, 17 wigeon, dunbirds, and curres, 2 curlews, 3 plover, 31 snipes (all the latter but 3 at Hyde).

N.B.—On our leaving the haven the geese were in tens of thousands before the windows.

26th.—It began to thaw, and the weather became very mild. I this evening bagged a wild goose.

[1] A man may remain fifty nights in waiting and not have the luck to get under the grand army of geese, as their course is so very uncertain. John, it appears, this morning had that luck, and no doubt would have killed a large number but for the severe check he got at starting.

Eight of the fine large grey geese pitched in front of the house, and I had to hobble a long distance round before I could get within 100 yards from them. I therefore made an immensely long shot at this one, as well as wounding another which (after being knocked over) recovered and flew away.

April 2nd.—Returned to Longparish.

12th.—Went out fly fishing, and, notwithstanding a bright sun the whole time, I in a few hours killed 36 trout.

N.B.—My flies were (what I always use) the yellow dun at bottom, and red palmer bob.

15th.—28 trout.

16th.—24 trout (average weight above 1 lb each, and many of them weighed 1½ lb.). Also a great many fair-sized ones which I threw in.

I had all this admirable sport in less than two hours and a half, and the weight of these fish was so much that they were quite a burthen to carry home.

In the evening I was ludicrously amused with throwing a fly on horseback, which answers as well as on foot; though I then caught no fish large enough to save, owing to the wind having shifted to a cold quarter.

18th.—15 trout.

21st.—4 trout, after killing which and throwing in many small ones, was driven in by an incessant pour of rain.

23rd.—21 trout.

26th.—16 trout.

27th.—12 trout.

28th.—13 trout, average weight 1¼ lb. each fish.

29th.—14 trout.

30th.—17 trout, which make up in eleven days' angling 100 brace.

N.B.—I, of course, have reckoned only those fish which I killed; namely, such as were ¾ lb. and upwards. But had I killed all the small ones and added them to my number, it would have amounted to between 400 and 500 fish.

May 2nd.—10 trout.

June 11th.—Left Longparish for London.

16th.—I decided on remaining in town for this month to see the allied sovereigns and their suites. The influx to the metropolis for this purpose was calculated at 100,000 souls.

30th.—We have seen one continued series of state processions, been at most of the public places where the illustrious visitors were, and seen them repeatedly. We saw the Emperor (Alexander I.) of all the Russias; his brother, Prince Constantine; and his sister, the Duchess of Oldenburgh; the King and three Princes of Prussia; Marshal Blucher, Prince of Walstadt; Platoff, the 'hetman of all the Cossacks;' and Barclay de Tolle, with other great men and foreign princes out of number; which, added to our own royal family, formed an assembly of more blood royal than had perhaps ever before been in the metropolis of Great Britain. We returned to Longparish this day; and, after viewing the immense improvements which had been made in our absence, I walked out in search of the buck. Found him in some corn, out of which he sprang up, and so crippled him with two barrels of swan shot that he could only reach the third field, where Tiger pinned him in the hedgerow. He proved to be one of the finest and fattest deer we had seen for a long time.

The horse and cart (when coming up for him) were precipitated down a chalk pit, and, strange to say, no damage whatever was done.

July 3rd.—Tried two duck guns, namely—the last new one by Egg, to give strength to the shooting of which I was obliged to have it fresh bored and breeched by Joe Manton. This made it almost as good as one of his; as it shot much stronger and so close that, at 30 yards, it put in 360 grains out of 3 oz. of No. 3. The other duck gun was made (entirely under my own directions and daily inspection) by Joe Manton, No. 6364. Nothing could surpass the excellent shooting of this gun; and, although 19 lb. weight and loaded with $\frac{1}{3}$ lb. of shot, it was made to shoot so pleasant, and set up so manageable, that I killed with it 2 peewits and 2 swifts out of 5 single shots, flying.

4th.—Killed 8 trout, 1 leveret, and 2 peewits.

10th.—Mr. and Mrs. Joe Hawker, Lord Hinton, and Mr. Cudmore came to us.

11th.—9 trout, and in the evening killed a full-grown young wild duck at flight.

14th.—Mr. Cudmore never having seen a bird killed flying, I took him out to see me fire 10 shots at swifts and swallows, 2 at moorhens, 2 at sparrows, and 1 at a halfpenny thrown up. I killed every bird and handsomely marked the halfpenny.

24th.—Mr. and Mrs. J. Hawker and Mr. Cudmore left us, after our having spent a fortnight most agreeably. Music was the order of the day, and never were Mozart's works more delightfully enjoyed. Mr. Cudmore petrified the whole neighbourhood with his astonishing pianoforte playing, and convinced even the bigots of Cramer that, although perfect master of three other instruments, no man now in England could play the piano with so much taste, fire, and execution as himself.

29th.—Left Longparish, and arrived at our old winter quarters, the 'South Haven Passage House,' Poole Harbour. Arrived about dusk, and immediately went out and killed a wild duck.

30th.—Took a cruise out in harbour and killed 4 young sheldrakes and 9 ox-birds.

These sheldrakes (burrough ducks or barganders) take their young ones out to sea as soon as they are hatched, and being in this month nearly as large as the old ones, they are much followed, as (while young) sheldrakes are very good eating. The shooting, however, is tame; the flocks disperse so much on your getting near them, that you can seldom bag more than one at a shot, and that oftener swimming than flying.

August 3rd.—After having some capital sport netting and spearing large flounders, and bringing in as many as I could possibly carry, we sailed over to Poole and brought back L——, who arrived there per coach.

4th.—Inspected the castle and the whole of the island of Brownsea.

5th.—This evening anchored off the haven the 'Lord Nelson,' pilot vessel, for which I agreed to give 15*l.* for a run over to France. An incessant gale of wind, however, and that unfavourable, detained us from sailing

6th.—Got under way for France at half-past six in the evening, and, after having encountered a very heavy sea, dropped anchor in Cherbourg Roads at half-past seven on the morning of the 7th. The tide not serving sufficiently to bring our little vessel into harbour, we came ashore in a boat, by doing which we reached the quay no further observed than by the custom-house officers, who did their duty in a gentlemanlike manner.

This proved a fortunate circumstance, particularly for Mrs. Hawker, as our crew, on sailing under the quay, were attacked by the whole *canaille* of the place, and so pelted with large quarry stones that Mr. Wills, the master, who bravely stood to his helm, was severely wounded, and afterwards confined under a surgeon. This outrageous conduct originated from the determination of the French to suppress, by mutiny, the exportation of corn and cattle, for which purpose they supposed that our little party of pleasure had entered their port. The military were called out, and a mob of about two thousand were soon dispersed; and this was more done by the resolution of the colonel than any disposition for quietude on the part of the soldiers, for they are most enthusiastically devoted to Buonaparte, and their daily prayers are to have him again at their head. They abuse poor Louis to absolute treason.

Here are thousands of idlers (now unemployed) who are ripe for murder and insurrection, and the farmers are almost starved, wheat being about 6*l.* a load, and they having on hand more than enough for two years' consumption.

After having made ourselves as comfortable as being in a dirty French seaport would admit of, we lost no time to inspect the town and environs, of which I may give a brief account by the following memorandums.

Entrance of Cherbourg a very fine and formidably strong situation. On the right a dockyard for first-rate ships of war, entrenched all round. On the left in entering are two forts (La Liberté and Impérial) which were made by Buonaparte in the middle of the sea, one on a rock and the other entirely built on an artificial foundation of stone. Near these are floating buoys for the assistance of shipwrecked mariners. The town lies under an immense rocky height, which has on it a few fortifications, and which commands the town, with a fine basin or second harbour for large ships. A 74 (the 'Duquesne') is stationed to take down the names of all, who must lie to under her stem for this purpose, for which the captain goes on board her. Went to mass. Church built by English; nothing particularly fine, except that, as far as I could judge in a bad light and during service, the statuary at the altar appeared to be good.

Town much like Lisbon, with the addition of chimneys. Lamps suspended by a rope from each house to the middle of the street and about 150 yards apart. Houses built of small stone and badly slated. Three thousand infantry here, with a general noise and inclination for disturbance. Police (as in all France) remarkably good. Extensive barracks and military works on a grand scale. Town coarsely paved; views round it fine and extensive. We put up at the Hôtel de France no less from a wish to enter into the French language and customs than to avoid the risk of being insulted by the mob at the British Hotel, which we probably should have been; as, in consequence of the landlord (Mr. Robbins) having speculated in the exportations, his house was attacked, and he dare not stir out for fear of getting his head broken, as well as his windows, which were stoned to pieces. The best subject in the place is a Mr. Touchard, a merchant who was the first to mount the white cockade, and who is celebrated for his civility and attention to the English. He is on the point of removing to Havre de Grâce. Wines excellent; even in the worst inns you seldom get a bad bottle. The *vin de musquer* is more delicious than anything I ever tasted; this is six francs (that is five shillings English) a bottle, and champagne from four to five francs; but the *vin du pays*, claret or bordeaux &c. are most excellent at about from fifteen pence to two shillings the bottle. These, however, are dear prices, and only countenanced as tavern charges. Soldiers who have distinguished themselves are allowed to wear a stripe near the cuff, and many other honours; but all these are so lavishly bestowed that their value is quite depreciated. Dangerous to touch on politics or converse on anything further than commonplace subjects. I was deterred from taking sketches (for which I had prepared myself) by being told that it was dangerous to be seen thus employed.

Beds in the French fashion; people here sit in their bedrooms, and either dine privately, or at the table d'hote, where the landlady serves out every dish to all society, from a field marshal to a beggar, and where there is an abundant variety for 2 francs a head. Although this was Sunday the shops were open, the people at work, and the billiard tables, as well as a variety of other gambling places, completely crowded.

Stage coaches here enormously large and clumsy, and drawn slowly by six horses in rope harness. We had hired a carriage to spend Monday at Valognes (15 miles), but were advised to compromise the engagement, and decline our excursion, in consequence of the disturbed state of the country; while in hesitation on the matter, our determination not to go was fixed by the badness of the weather.

After having kept up our inspection of all that could be seen till dark night, we supped pleasantly at the table d'hôte and went to our beds, which, although in filthy rooms, were in themselves clean and comfortable.

7th.—Went out shopping. No stamps for receipts used here. All articles about one-third the price of what they are in England. The only taxes are on houses and windows, the latter levied by Buonaparte. Thirty francs are paid for a shooting licence; game is private property, and killed at any time that the cutting corn will admit of, but one must have a regular permission to carry firearms, which of course is granted to all respectable persons. Great civility to be met with from the police and custom-house departments; but the port charges may be avoided by anchoring out of harbour, where there are very good moorings.

This evening I was sent for by the prefect, who had reported twelve ringleaders of the mob. He was very polite to me.

9th.—Repassed the guardship and the 74 at six this morning; but, not being able to lay our course for England, were obliged to make for an eastern port, not choosing to encounter a second entry into Cherbourg. After being properly tossed off Barfleur, we put into that port, a small fishing town, where we were most hospitably taken compassion on by M. Delamare, commissaire de marine, who insisted on our being his visitors till we could put to sea, and soon after we became acquainted used every endeavour to get our promise of spending a week with his family. Barfleur and La Hogue are a few miles separate, and celebrated for the most dangerous coast in the whole Channel, and are places which are characteristic for shipwrecks. On entering Barfleur you have literally to wind between hidden rocks. You pass a superb lighthouse and the village of Gatteville.

After a dinner, at two, our good host did everything in

his power to amuse us, and took us in every direction to gratify our curiosity.

We went over his farm, gardens, and estate, and then walked to see the environs called Monfarelle. Here is a large church built of the same granite that composes the destructive rocks of Barfleur, and upwards of 600 years old. Carving extremely good, and the ceiling one well-turned arch. Near here the guns were firing for a wedding; a custom in this country, where there is also a peal of bells on such occasions. Reverting to the farm, I should observe that the land is most excellent, but the farming very bad indeed. The farmers here are poor men, who hold from 4 to 10 acres at about 4*l.* a year per acre, extremely cheap for such land, and work hard themselves, assisted only by two or three servants, and all they look to is mere existence. They carry everything here on small horses, and only thresh their corn with common sticks as fast as they want it.

10*th.*—Sailed at six, and after losing sight of land were taken in a dreadful gale of wind, and driven again into Barfleur, in sight of another vessel which went to pieces on the rocks. Our crew were all seriously alarmed.

Again we took up our excellent quarters, and in the evening directed our attention to other sights. Being then low water we first surveyed the rocks, from which we had so providentially escaped, and where so many have perished, and then went over the lighthouse, which is one of the best I ever saw. It has an excellent safeguard from lightning, which is a conductor from the very summit into a well at the bottom.

We then visited Gatteville, where the people are all red hot for Buonaparte in consequence of his having found them plenty of lucrative employment. It was from this place that he took all the stone to build the Place des Victoires at Paris.

11*th.*—Windbound again. Walked nine miles and through

two small villages to inspect the château of St. Pierre, and the park of a French nobleman, at which we arrived after having taken some luxurious refreshment at the house of a French officer. House very large, paintings in one room by Rubens and other fine masters; the others not very good: tapestry, fine: an extraordinary mixture of splendour and beggary; common deal dining tables in a room magnificently decorated. Floors set in squares and polished; grounds laid out formally; trees in avenues, &c.

Dined at the hotel, where we had an immense choice.

The town of St. Pierre is only of note for a great market, on which the conscription has made such an impression that you see about twenty women to one man, and the same proportion of mares to one horse.

We, having walked about twenty miles, got back to Barfleur by night, when the Cherbourg exportations had been heard of, and in consequence much disturbance had taken place. Here the women were the champions, and in a mob assailed our crew, and searched the vessel; but finding no corn they directed their attacks on another, being then assisted by some men, who were assembled from all parts. M. Delamare, however, soon restored order by his prompt and well-conducted interference.

12*th.*—A fair wind. Sailed at six in the morning, and reached Poole harbour after a delightful passage of eleven hours.

The custom-house officers here are the most savage set of blackguards that ever were heard of; they kept my property all night, so that I was deprived even of the comfort of cleaning myself, and this because they chose to give themselves a holiday at the office. My servant was detained in close arrest so long, that in coming home he was cast away, and left on the mud all night.

13*th.*—After getting my trunks &c. free from these infernal sharks, we set off a little before two o'clock in my carriage with four posthorses, and reached Longparish by eight o'clock, where we, thank God, found our dear child, and all, well.

25*th.*—Surveyed different improvements on the banks of the Southampton river; and, among others, a place belonging to Mr. Chamberlain, which has the appearance of being never used, and kept only for himself to look at.

26*th.*—Left Hamble and breakfasted at Lyndhurst, 18 miles, and then drove to Lymington, 8½ miles. Here my carriage and horses remained, while I walked 4 miles to Keyhaven, with which being delighted as a wild-fowl place, I there made some provisional arrangements for a future winter. I then returned to Lyndhurst, and passed the evening and night at Shrubb's Hill, the seat of Mr. Mathew, a quarter of a mile from that place.

27*th.*—Started for home, by way of Romsey, 10 miles, Stockbridge, 10 miles, and from the latter place, round the good road, 12 miles. Reached Longparish to dinner.

N.B.—I made my excursion, in the landaulet, with my own two horses, which always, without whip and with perfect ease to themselves, travelled from 8 to 9 miles an hour.

CHAPTER VII

1814

September.—The partridge shooting here deferred till the 14th inst. by mutual agreement, in consequence of the late harvest.

14th.—22 partridges. Birds nearly as wild as in November. All full grown, and the young as strong on wing as the old ones. Scent very bad; I could only fill my bag by firing at all distances.

Game bagged from 14th to 30th September: 100 partridges, 3 hares, 3 snipes, and 1 rabbit. Total, 107 head.

October 1st.—Lord Hinton left us. I walked out alone and killed 16 pheasants, 5 hares, 1 partridge, and 1 rabbit. Among the former was the celebrated white pheasant, which had been so long heard of in Wherwell great wood, and had escaped all the sportsmen; the bagging of this bird raised a general rejoicing, and I fortunately killed him very clean for stuffing. Although I have often brought home much more than 23 head of game, yet I estimate this as the best day's sport I ever had at Longparish, when I consider the following circumstances. Though it blew a tremendous gale of wind the whole day, and I only saw 19 pheasants, yet I secured 16: I bagged everything I fired at, except two partridges, one of which was quite out of reach, and the other a long shot, which I wounded, though I ought to have killed it. Except about two hours in Wherwell Wood, I beat over a country where everyone goes, and indeed knew of no other place to try without begging a favour or giving offence. I killed all my game to one steady pointer and a Newfoundland dog, and got 11 cock pheasants to 5 hens. My having found all this game where two brace is considered a very good day's sport, I impute to the wind having carried the pheasants from Lord Portsmouth's preserves, from which I was a mile or two to leeward. I only saw 5 hares all day, and 4 of them were long snap shots.

4th.—4 pheasants, 2 partridges, 1 snipe, and 1 jack snipe. Coming home with all I had fired at, I flushed a woodcock, and after working the cover till not a dog would stir from my heels, I left it and returned with every man and dog I could muster, and after a laborious task to find him again I had the mortification to miss a fair shot at him; I, however, knocked him down with my second barrel, but never could find him, though I worked till dark and half the next day.

18th.—Got intelligence of another white pheasant, which, after a hard fag in a pour of rain, I found and bagged; I got 5 shots only, and brought home 2 pheasants, 2 hares, and 1 rabbit.

20th.—I was under the painful necessity of ordering poor Tiger, my favourite Newfoundland dog, to be shot, in consequence of an unusually virulent distemper, which had defied all the doctors and every prescription, and with which the poor fellow was dying in agony. Never could there have been a more faithful creature destroyed, or a more severe and irreparable loss to a sportsman. This dog was of the real St. John's breed, quite black, with a long head, very fine action, and something of the otter skin, and not the curly-haired heavy brute that so often and so commonly disgraces the name of the Newfoundland dog. He was just in his prime, three years old, and from his sagacity, attachment, good temper, high courage, and a personal guard, as well as his excellence in shooting for the fields, for the cover, for the hedgerows, for the marshes, and above all for night work with the wild fowl, I may not disgrace the lines of our immortal poet by saying :

> Take him for all in all,
> We shall not look upon his like again.

24th.—Left Longparish for Lymington, with the intention of embarking immediately for France, having only been waiting for a fair wind to make a second excursion to that country. On arriving at Lymington, however, I found that the Order in Council,[1] from the Lords Commissioners of the Treasury, had been sent to Southampton, and I was obliged to send a man there and back, 36 miles, to request the favour of getting permission to embark here, where I had been informed my order was lying, and for which purpose I came here, 39 miles, instead of to Southampton, which is only 24. The loss of this night, however, proved an interference of Providence, as, had we sailed, we might have fallen victims to a directly contrary gale of wind, in which our vessel might have been lost off the Needles.

25th.—In consequence of the tremendous hurricane which blew last night, the mate of our vessel, whom I had sent to Southampton, was unable to recross the passage to Hythe, and therefore did not return till this afternoon, when the wind and tide were fair for our getting under way ; but instead of this I was directed to appear myself at Southampton. I then hired a most extraordinary pony, that took me with the greatest ease and without whip, stick, or spur, to Hythe, twelve miles, in three-quarters of an hour, and I was at the custom house, between three and four miles more by water, in a very little more than an hour altogether. On just saving the hours of business, I was informed that my being sent there was all a mistake, as the only person whose presence was absolutely necessary was the master of the vessel, who must appear a

[1] Without which my guns and dogs could not be embarked, or, if they were, they would be subject to very heavy duties on bringing them home.

second time with the Lymington papers &c., which could not have been made out before he had first been to Southampton, and in default of going through all this process he would be open to the penalty of 100*l.* and endangered on entering another port. I then returned, as much to the purpose as I had been sent, and got to Lymington all in about three hours. Hired a gig for the master to go over again in the morning, and after some hard fagging and bustling about the town, went to bed.

26th.—All difficulties being surmounted, we trudged to Keyhaven with our provision at our backs; there embarked at 6 P.M., and after a rough and miserable passage, dropped anchor at Barfleur about half-past nine on the morning of the 27th. Here I was rather in a trouble, and was therefore indebted to a great deal of my own management, and also the great civility of the custom-house officers, for saving my vessel from confiscation, being regularly laden with an immensity of presents from England. The astonishment of the mob on board was highly diverting at the opening of my Joe Manton gun, cases, &c. All being well got over, we landed and breakfasted, after fasting for twenty hours.

29th.—Went out to try the French shooting. Their game in Normandy is precisely the same as ours, but so scarce that I literally never saw a partridge the whole day, and only one hare at a distance. I bagged 4 snipes, 1 jack snipe, and 1 quail, the only one I saw; and as the latter bird is seldom to be met with after September, my finding this one was considered accidental. I should have killed more snipes but was interrupted by the attendance of all the idle boys of Gatteville, and annoyed by the infamous behaviour of a brute which my servant had bought by way of a Newfoundland dog. I then went to inspect a beautiful piece of water called Gattemare, where I was led to expect nothing but a quantity of coots; but, to my astonishment, I found it literally black with every description of wild fowl. While the washerwomen were beating the clothes on the stones, according to French custom, the coots were in thousands around them, but the wild fowl took care to keep in the middle of the lake, and when I fired a shot they would pitch again, and, in short, had the usual audacity peculiar to their nation. I winged some wild-fowl and some coots at long distances, but my *soi-disant* Newfoundland dog would not venture his worthless carcase so far as they fell. The lake of Gattemare[1] is half a mile broad and upwards of a mile long, and for the multiplicity of coots and wild fowl, particularly of dunbirds, it surpasses anything I ever saw. We adjourned our shooting till a boat could be conveyed overland to this place, as without it nothing can possibly be done, we having tried all day, and nearly all night, on the banks.

30*th.*—Went on some poor horses on a miserable road to a miserable place called Réville, where we went to mass and inspected the ruins of a château, and we finished the day with other excursions and visits.

31*st.*—After a great deal of trouble, a boat was carried overland to Gathemare lake, but on my arrival I found what they here called 'a little shooting canoe' was a yawl large enough for twelve people, which, of course, sprung all the fowl the moment we got to the middle of the lake. I then got set ashore on a little bank of rushes, and had some excellent diversion with the coots, which I should not have thought worth firing at singly, but to amuse the Frenchmen, whom I astonished not a little with Manton's guns; but the infamous behaviour of my water dog spoiled all my amusement; he was too sulky to bring the birds, but chopped them, and not only left them, but sulked on the islands and prevented others from coming near me. Out of 12 coots and 10 wild fowl which I brought down, I only bagged 7 coots, 2 scaup ducks, 2 wigeon, and 1 snipe.

[1] The only misery of shooting here, particularly at night, is that you have to stumble over rocks and wade through mud for three miles, and then to tramp in deep sand for above a mile more.

N.B.—I finished my day with shooting the dog, at the express desire of Mrs. Hawker, and to the great satisfaction of all who were with us.

November 1st.—Went with the *premier chasseur* of Barfleur and a large party to surround the pond, but the fowl immediately left, owing to the noise that was made; we then went to the *chasse* with this gentleman's dogs, said to be two first-rate animals. The one ran home, and the other was so slow that I preferred beating for myself. The party killed nothing; I bagged 1 hare, 2 partridges, and 1 snipe, which was considered as wonderful, and was thought more of than all the wild fowl.

2nd.—Went to Valcalville, where, as a great favour, I had permission to shoot in what was there called a 'forest;' my day, however, ended, as usual, with finding nothing the whole day but one small covey of birds. I killed 2 partridges, which were considered a *bonne chasse.* We then returned to a poor hovel, where I contrived to get some eggs and the produce of an almost barren garden, with which I knocked up a few dishes, and we contrived to dine most heartily; and I sent to the neighbouring priest to beg some wine and coffee.

3rd.—To-day I proceeded to the village of Neville, where I met a large dinner party and passed the night at the house of a jolly priest named Cruely.

6th.—After a miserable ride of about seven hours, on an execrable road (and after losing Mrs. Hawker's horse for some time in the forest), we reached the town of Valognes, 6 leagues from Barfleur, and once the winter residence of many nobility.

The following are the market prices of Barfleur:

	French. sous	English. s. d.
1 lb. of butter	20	0 10
1 lb. of veal	12	0 6
1 lb. of mutton	8	0 4
1 lb. of beef	8	0 4

	French. sous	English. s.	d.
1 lb. of salt	5	0	2½
1 lb. of common soap	24	1	0
1 lb. of pepper	64	2	8
1 dozen eggs	10 [1]	0	5
2 fowls	24	1	0
2 ducks	30	1	3
2 bushels of potatoes	15	0	7½
1 turkey	30	1	3
1 lb. of bread	3	0	1½
1 hare	40	1	8
2 partridges	20	0	10
1 bushel of oats	44 [2]	1	10
12 bottles of claret	264	11	0
6 bottles of brandy	180	7	6
2 bottles of old hollands	70	2	11

7th.—After the account we had heard of Valognes, and knowing it to be one of the first towns in Normandy, we at least expected to see something decent; but of all the filthy, ugly, dirty, imposing, miserable places I ever saw, I may name this as one of the most abominable. After a tedious crawl we got home to Barfleur by another route, which gave us a fine and picturesque view of La Hogue.

10th.—Having some business at Valognes (from whence it is seldom the custom to return the same day), I went there and back within eight hours, notwithstanding I stopped half an hour at the great cotton mill of Vast, which was established under the directions of a Mr. Orford, late of the 7th (English) Light Dragoons.

12th.—This morning we left M. Delamare's and took some excellent lodgings at the house of a Madame Apvrel, viz.: 2 sitting rooms; apartments for 3 servants and ourselves; a kitchen; stabling, yard, the whole use of a well-stocked kitchen garden; the use of a horse, plate, linen &c. for 100 francs per calendar month.

14th.—4 snipes and 5 dunbirds. I fired at 3 dunbirds

[1] Very dear now.

[2] For a bushel of English oats 1*s.* 10*d.*!

flying high over my head, and killed them all 3 dead at one shot.

18*th.*—Went to try the evening flight at the lake of Rettaville (about half the size of Gattemare), but instead of 5 we found it nearer 8 miles distant; being thus late, as well as greatly out of luck, I bagged only 1 mallard.

When the tide is going out and it blows fresh, you can seldom bag the half of what you kill; and indeed I am indebted to the purchase of a capital French poodle bitch for what I have bagged; I gave 14 francs for her.

Game &c. bagged at Barfleur: 6 partridges, 1 hare, 1 rabbit, 34 snipes, 1 mallard, 2 wigeon, 18 dunbirds, 13 curres, &c.

December 7th.—Having been almost poisoned with dirt (in reality nearly poisoned by the earthenware, which is glazed with white lead), and, in short, too happy to relinquish the few remaining days of our month at Madame Apvrel's lodgings, we, through the kind assistance of Mr. Orford, got a passage in the cotton vessel, in which we sailed from Barfleur at a quarter before three this morning, and dropped anchor in the basin at Havre de Grâce (20 leagues) at half-past four P.M. The entrance to this place is beautiful; you sail under fine fortifications all the way in, and the perspective of the town presents a really picturesque landscape. We entered the hotel of M. Justin (the great house of Havre), and had to put up with the usual dirt, misery, and confusion of a French inn; but all this, of course, is luxury compared to what we had heretofore been used to abroad. The cooking, however, was excellent.

8*th.*—Was highly gratified with a general inspection of the harbours, basins &c of this fine trading town, and passed above two hours in the celebrated snuff manufactory (the largest in France), where we had explained to us the whole process, in which about 700 men were at work. There were stacks of unprepared tobacco worth 120,000*l.*, and the snuff in much larger bins than I ever saw corn in. We took a comfortable dinner with Mr. Touchard, the merchant, and I then embarked my man and shooting apparatus in the Southampton packet, having previously secured places for Mrs. Hawker, myself and maid, for Rouen, on our way for Paris.

9th.—Being called up soon after five, and having breakfasted a little before six this morning, we tramped in the dark and in the rain to the bureau des messageries, where our voiture, the grande diligence, was prepared as follows: Two horses at wheel, and three abreast leaders; the driver, with a smock frock, pigtail, powder, and a pair of water boots,[1] was mounted on the near wheeler with strings (or small ropes) to that, and the other four horses were harnessed in a sort of raw hide leather fitted up with ropes. By the tremendous appearance of this carriage and miserable-looking horses we were led to expect that we should travel very slowly, and in constant danger, with almost every misery that could be endured; but, to our agreeable surprise and astonishment, we found the whole concern, in some respects, superior to even our own stage coaches in England. Perfectly safe, very fast,[2] very easy, very commodious, and on most excellent turnpike roads. Everything most carefully regulated, and, instead of being troubled with repeated calls at public-houses, and interruptions of guards and coachmen, you have only to settle, once for all, on reaching your destination, where you pay the fare and, in short, arrange the *tout ensemble.* There is also no danger of not being called in the morning, as there is a man regularly appointed to wait on you an hour before the coach starts, and should he neglect this, you can oblige him to pay your fare!

We reached Rouen about 4 P.M. after an unusually long journey of ten hours. The distance is 22 post leagues, rather under 66 English miles, which we should have performed in eight hours but for the incessant rain, which had made the roads particularly heavy and bad.

[1] As we got farther up the road the drivers wore shoes, and then set their legs into stupendous pairs of jack boots about the size, and more than the weight, of common butter churns.

[2] The only stoppages are for the change of horses, which is completed with most wonderful expedition.

The country which we passed was beautiful, and our journey really comfortable in spite of the rainy weather. The entrance to Rouen, where you descend a wooded hill and have in constant view the Seine winding through the valley, is really magnificent, but the town itself is more celebrated for its almost unlimited commerce and grandeur than anything to gratify the traveller. It has, however, a museum, a garden of plants, an opera, and a theatre; but our having engaged places in the diligence to proceed to Paris the next morning made it more prudent to relinquish anything beyond a view of the town, get our suppers, and go quietly to bed. We put up at the Hôtel de Vatel, where we found perfect cleanliness, good living, and civility, but, as is now the case at and everywhere near Paris, with an extravagant bill.

10*th*.—Proceeded by the grande diligence on our way for Paris, which is 28 leagues (about 84 English miles) from Rouen. We started at five this morning, and at half-past twelve reached Magny (within a league of halfway to Paris), where we stopped to dine. Instead of being served with a dirty stage coach dinner, as in England, our table was spread in a manner that would have done credit to a nobleman's house, and with everything good clean, and comfortable, silver forks, &c., for which (with wine, fruit, spirits, and ale) we paid 3 francs a head. Having thus comfortably refreshed ourselves, we proceeded on our road, which all the way from Magny to Paris (about 44 miles) was well paved and we travelled nearly as fast as a London mail coach, having entered the gates of Paris by half-past six o'clock. After waiting to sign our names at the coach office, and got our luggage, we repaired to our hotel, but from thence were sent adrift in consequence of it being full; we then deposited ourselves, goods, and chattels in the Hôtel des Sept Frères Maçons.

Paris. As the well-known 'spectacles' of this place are ably described and judgmatically criticised in almost every newspaper at this present time, I shall merely note down a memorandum of what places I may see, and (instead of writing even for the few minutes a day which I usually do) make use of every moment to see all I can, and then get out of this stinking, imposing place.

11*th.*—Finding that a passport was indispensably necessary, I was obliged to go to the Duke of Wellington's to procure one. This being done, we saw the following places: Tuileries and gardens with mythological statuary, &c., and most of the magnificent edifices in that direction. Then inspected and ascended the monument (Colonne de la Place Vendôme) which was erected by Buonaparte, and is built with the cannon taken in the battle of Austerlitz, &c., and from which you have a panorama of Paris and its environs that surpasses any description. Indeed, the unbounded magnificence of all the public buildings here is such, that one can hardly refrain from adding superfluous panegyrics to memorandums. Saw the greater part of the French cavalry (consisting of hussars, cuirasseurs, dragoons, and lancers). The cuirasseurs were infinitely the best appointed and finest looking troops. Saw statuary of the best artists out of number, and in every direction different edifices with the grandest sculpture and carving; walked in the Champs-Elysées; and after taking refreshment at a *restaurateur's*, promenaded the streets, saw the Fontaine des Innocents, Palais Royal,[1] &c.; and in the evening went to the Théâtre Comique, where we were much pleased with the opera of 'Joconde,' and in this the singing of Martin.

12*th.*—Hired a coach[2] and saw the Invalides; containing

[1] Famous for having a piazza (or cloisters) in which are all the first and (of course) the most extravagant shops, *restaurateurs*, &c., and which may be termed the Bond Street of Paris.

[2] A private carriage is 25 francs per day; a servant (out of livery) with it 4 francs, and whatever fee you choose to give the coachman. A sort of covered one-horse chaise, 15 francs. A hackney coach (with footman) 30 sous per drive (whether long or short 'tis all the same); and you generally give 4 sous more for the men. The hackney coaches and public town voitures here are much better, and infinitely faster, than in London, but the private equipages (like the private houses) are very far inferior.

depot, gardens, church, kitchen, messhouses, library, &c., all on a most stupendous scale—three thousand men now dine there every day.

'Museum Petit Augustin:' containing all the sculpture of the first masters (chiefly in monuments) from the thirteenth to the seventeenth century inclusive.

'Luxembourg.' Saw a whole room of enormous-sized pictures all by Rubens (except two of David's, Titian's, and another master's), another almost entirely filled with Lesueur's progressive paintings of St. Brunot, and a detached gallery with most extraordinary naval paintings by Vernet.

'Senate House.' Magnificent large frames containing paintings of Buonaparte's victories, &c., which are (unfortunately for the curious) covered over by green canvas, too fast nailed over for even a peep. Flags and standards taken in Austria. Spacious and elegant saloons and committee rooms, one of which is decorated with paintings on cloth, and has some furniture painted on velvet; gardens arranged with fine statuary, basins, &c., much in the superb style of those before the Tuileries.

'Ecole de Medicine,' containing a museum of everything that can possibly be selected for the amusement and instruction of surgeons, every preparation of anatomy, instruments, surgical curiosities, &c.

'Panthéon.' An immense hall of the most perfect architecture, and under which we were shown all the (locked up) vaults containing the bodies or hearts of all the great men, marshals, authors, &c. We here saw the tombs of Voltaire, Rousseau, &c., but the kings are buried at St.-Louis. We ascended the dome and enjoyed another panorama of Paris, than which nothing can be more picturesque.

'Eglise de Notre-Dame.' On one side the New, on the other the Old Testament in tapestry: fine paintings, among which is the 'Visitation' (of St. Elizabeth) by Jouvenet, who having, after beginning it, lost his right hand by palsy, finished it with his left; but, even putting this aside, the piece has

I 2

sufficient merit to stand high in Paris; wardrobes, from which were shown us the robes, canopies &c. of all the high priests, kings, &c.; the Pope's chair, his robes, and all his nonsensical apparatus; Buonaparte's crown of laurels in gold, his sceptre, and his hand of justice; ditto of Charlemagne; Maria Louisa's crown &c. and the most magnificent church plate (chiefly in massive gold set in brilliants, rubies, and emeralds); among this there is a service given by Buonaparte on his coronation; church curiosities, such as crucifixes in coral, goblets in crystal, &c.; a fine piece of statuary of our Saviour taken from the cross; superior carving in oak; the finest marble candelabras given on the birth of the little King of Rome; fine painted glass, &c.

We had just time to partake of a sumptuous dinner at the table d'hôte of our house, and drive off to the Italian Opera. We had here Paisello's delightful composition, 'Il Re Theodoro.' As far as the band was concerned, we were highly gratified, but it was vexatious to hear a *chef-d'œuvre* of such acknowledged merit murdered by the most infamous set of singers I ever heard. Excepting Crivelli and a passable comic singer, there was not one fit to exhibit on a country stage. Scenery very good; house poor and shabby; orchestra about fifty musicians.

13*th.*—After inspecting the Halle au Blé (a grand and fine-built rotunda for wheat and flour), we took breakfast and proceeded with our carriage to the spectacles. Were disappointed in being refused admission to the Gobelins tapestry, for want of an order from some baron, so proceeded to the Bicêtre, or madhouse, containing one large factory, where convalescents carry on different trades. An immense wall, where the buckets &c. weighing 2,900 lb. are worked by about fifty men to a wheel, and emptied by an iron catch as large as a ship's anchor; five minutes required for the drawing of a bucket of water, and noise like thunder—great laundry, kitchen, and other offices for lunatics, whom we saw in all classes.

'Cabinet de l'Histoire Naturelle,' containing the greatest collection in the world of beasts, birds and fish, every specimen in conchology ; fossils, precious stones &c. surpassing description ; a superior library of natural history, and, in short, everything in that study that can possibly be imagined. Garden of plants of all the rarest sorts.

Cabinet of Anatomy of the whole creation, and all valuable kinds of animal curiosities preserved in spirits, wax specimens for human anatomy, &c. Live wild beasts. Live birds of all sorts, land and water.

'Bureau d'Artillerie,' or ordnance, containing first all the stores, cannon, &c. ; and secondly, a museum for every model of arms and other implements used in war, with a most valuable collection of firearms of all countries, the armour of all the great men, standards, sidearms, &c.

After hastily dressing,[1] and dining, we re-entered our voiture, and drove off to the celebrated Opera of Paris. Found the house spacious and well built, though shabbily decorated and fitted up. The band very fine, and immensely strong, too much so for the choruses, it consisting of at least sixty professors. The singing most disgracefully infamous, and the acting nearly as bad, but the scenery, dresses, and decorations far surpassed all our English theatres in every respect. The opera was 'Les Abencérages ;' in this was introduced a Mr. Aubert, who danced and played on the guitar, and although with the addition of having to execute considerably on this, the only music to which he danced, he was decidedly superior to any in the ballet, which was 'Télémaque.' Although they could not complain for want of having a *chef-d'œuvre* to perform in, yet the dancing was far short of what I had been led to expect from the pompous account I had everywhere had of the French opera dancing. The carriages, after the opera was

[1] The French never dress for the opera, and have it, like their other public places, poorly lit up, as if to hide their dirt and dishabille ; instead of fine chandeliers all round the house, they have only a cluster of lamps suspended from the centre, and one row of stage lamps.

over, were well regulated by the horse and foot gendarmes, who act as life and foot guards do in London; and instead of allowing Mrs. Such-a-one's carriage to stop the way, every voiture was obliged to draw on as fast as it arrived, and therefore you must be ready to seize the opportunity of getting in without delay.

14*th*.—The Louvre, containing such a collection of the arts as I never supposed it possible that any one place, or even metropolis, could boast of. Fully prepared as we were to be lost in astonishment, yet the collection here far, very far, surpassed all the descriptions we had heard from those who had seen it. To inspect this grand depot of sculpture and painting[1] would require at least a month, and we were therefore obliged to content ourselves with hurrying through it in five hours, in order to see a little of the other inexhaustible sights of Paris. Here are sculpture, mosaic &c. most superior of all the great masters; paintings of the French, German, Dutch, Flemish, Italian, English, and, in short, the very best of every school in Europe. One of the rooms here is above 1,300 feet, and contains about 1,250 immense pictures of Raphael, Rubens, Titian, Carracci, Albano, Domenichino, Vinci-Leonardo, and Guido, added to many others of the first ancient and modern artists.

Inside of the Tuileries. In getting permission to enter here while the King is in Paris, it requires some trouble and interest, but we were fortunate in meeting with Colonel Athorpe, of our Royal Horse Guards, who had a card for himself and party, which he kindly invited us to join. After entering the palace and passing through very strong guards, all in full dress uniforms, and with a most stately appearance, we had some trouble, even with our printed document, to get admission, but all these difficulties were perhaps magnified by the royal servants with a view of getting a little English money; at last we entered, and saw all the magnificent apartments in this spacious and richly decorated palace, the saloons, halls, State bedrooms, billiard room, chapel, theatre, &c. Here we had an

[1] Here are three immense pieces of the finest mosaic I ever saw.

opportunity of seeing several fine paintings on the subject of Buonaparte's achievements, in which he was himself conspicuously introduced; but in the rooms which are open publicly to the French, and to the mere passports of foreigners, all paintings representing the *ci-devant* Emperor are either put away or closely covered. It may be needless to add that, for their own interest in his reign, no pains were spared by the artists to render these subjects their masterpieces.[1] We saw also many valuables in the palace; a very fine vase, an enormous solid gold box (brought from Italy), some of the finest carved, gilded, and painted ceilings in the world, &c.; also most superb tapestry by Gobelin.

15*th*.—Elysée des Bourbons, the *ci-devant* Emperor's château of repose for the months of March and April; here he remained quite *en retraite*, and amused himself with his family. Here we saw all the comfort, as well as luxury, that could be imagined. Here too we saw his writing table, which appeared to have been the only thing used in the place, and to which there was a chair or a pivot, so that he had not even the trouble of lifting his seat to write if, while sitting at the fire, he was struck with an idea worth noting down. We also saw the *ci-devant* Empress's bedroom, dressing room, and every little ornament that could be suggested, and among them some fine mosaic, and other valuables from Italy; we had also a view of the billiard table,[2] and enjoyed the novelty of playing with the Emperor's favourite cue and Maria Louisa's mace. This palace, although on a smaller scale than the others, and with scarcely any paintings, except Buonaparte's family pictures, is, for taste and elegance in the fitting up, before all the others; and, in short, a perfect lesson for the

[1] Here is one grand hall hung round with full length portraits of Buonaparte's marshals, and his eagles, bees, and the letter N are so universally distributed, that it will require some time and expense to erase them without considerable damage to the rooms.

[2] Lit up with two groups of lamps, which are each suspended so as to represent the scales of justice, an idea of the Emperor's, as an emblem of the desideratum for general peace and happiness.

man of taste in furnishing; everyone should see it, as no one can help being delighted with it. The Empress Josephine was some time here, and this is the house which Alexander chose for his residence during the two months the Russians were here; he, however, selected one of the worst rooms, and preferred his camp bed on a sofa to the luxurious beds and couches of this palace of comfort.

In going to the Bourbon Elysée we saw the two *ci-devant* palaces of the Bourbons, which are exactly alike, and are now used, one for the bureau of the Minister of Marine, and the other as the residence of dragoon officers of rank. Passed Talleyrand's house, and the Corps Législatif, &c.

Boulevards or immense streets round the town, with footpaths, and double rows of trees on each side.

National Library of Paris: contents, above 400,000 valuable books.[1] This library is formed in three-fourths of a long quadrangle; the partitions average about 100 yards long each, by a very considerable breadth.[2] Here is also another fine room, in which two stupendous globes, celestial and terrestrial, are sunk from within a large gallery that surrounds them, into a fine hall below.

In the first grand room there is a well-executed statue of Voltaire, a group in brass and copper, and a correct model of the Pyramids of Egypt.

We then descended to the hall and cloisters below, and after passing a room hung with framed plates, we entered a library of folio engravings. It may be needless to say they are perhaps, most likely, the best in the world, and of every nation where the arts are known.

Café Montacier. Our hard morning's work and glut of more novelties obliged us to finish with walking over this place, which was a large and handsome theatre, and is now

[1] This immense repository of literature is all in one room, and open to the public, who may read there, or look over folios of engravings, at six sous per day.

[2] Length 544 English feet, and breadth 128 feet.

(stage, boxes, pit, and all) converted into a magnificent coffee room, where is the grand resort in the evening of all classes of Parisian loungers.

I omitted to mention to-day my having passed nearly an hour in the morning to inspect the shops and work of the first gunmakers of Versailles and Paris, and in my life I never saw such infamous concerns by way of fowling pieces; the springs of the locks were worse than any musket I ever handled; their breechings a most bungling imitation of our old discarded patent; their touch-holes three times as thick as they had need to be, and the locks literally ready to scratch your hands for want of being let into the stock. While all these matters, which really contribute to the intrinsic value of a gun, are thus neglected, the whole study of the workman appears to be directed to the exterior ornament of the gun, and thus you see a machine worth about two guineas fitted up with 100*l.* worth of gold, silver, and even carving. In this they appear to think solely consists the perfection of a gun, and on my endeavouring to suggest (most civilly, and for their information) a few of our unquestionable improvements, their utter ignorance in argument and obstinacy were, although disgusting, really laughable.

Finding we had a few minutes before dinner would be ready, we took a sight of the baths, which are arranged on an extensive scale, one side for men, the other for women, and well built.

The moment we had dined we started off to Franconie's Olympic Theatre, which is the Astley's of Paris, and in every respect precisely on the same plan. The horsemanship was good, but, on the whole, rather inferior to England; a horse there was brought forward, who was taught to fetch and carry like a dog, and finished his exploits by marching off with an old woman's cap from the boxes. The pantomime, a sort of romance, was very well got up, and we gave it the preference to the average of those in England. The acting was good, the scenery well managed, and, on the whole, did credit to the theatre. The house is shabby for want of new doing up only, but it was better lit than the other theatres, or even their opera houses.

16*th*.—Breakfasted[1] by candlelight, and started in our voiture for Versailles, 4 leagues from Paris, but about 5 (15 miles) from our hotel. On getting out of the suburbs we drove for a very long time by the banks of the Seine, on a road which is the whole way most excellent, and nearly all on pavement.

Just beyond the 'bridge of Vienna' we had a full view of the Ecole Militaire and Champ de Mars: a place extending in a circle of 6 miles, and formed in various sorts of ground for every kind of artificial warfare. On the right, opposite, is the beginning of a palace which was intended for the little King of Rome.

'Saint-Cloud and the Palais.' A lovely place overlooking all Paris from a commanding and cheerful situation, and where the royal residence is, if possible, more grand than the others: it is, like the rest, one blaze of magnificence, with every luxury that can be devised, and the marble and many other ornaments are most valuable and exquisitely fine.

'Royal Manufactory of Porcelain.' A place as large as a palace, where there is made the most elegant china that can be conceived, and where almost everything is manufactured equal to fine sculpture; for instance, flowers, &c., and lace so

[1] If you breakfast at a coffee house you can seldom get served before nine, whereas to save our time I always get my breakfast before eight, and the difference not only in comfort, but expense, was considerable, had the value of a breakfast been my object; for instance:

Coffee house: A miserable small pot of indifferent coffee, a roll, and a little pat of butter, served without a cloth on a marble slab, cost me 36 sous.

At my own room: Two large hot French rolls, 2 sous; proportionable quantity of superior butter, 2 sous; new milk, 1 sou; as much delicious collared boar's head as I could eat, 8 sous. Total, 13 sous.

Thus, by buying your tea and coffee, you may breakfast luxuriously by your own fireside for half the price that half a breakfast would cost you at a 'café.'

N.B.—The hotels do not find breakfast, and most of them find nothing but wines and liqueurs, in which case you dine at, or have your dinner from, a *restaurateur's*.

well imitated round a figure that I, at first, would not believe it was anything but real.

'Sceaux.' Stopped here for a few minutes to refresh ourselves with a slice of collared boar's head, and some cakes for which a coffee house in this place is well known.

'Versailles.' On entering the place we were soon struck with its appearance, as being cleaner, having better looking private houses and more spacious streets than any place we had seen in France. We were a little annoyed, however, at the governor, who was absent, having left a peremptory order that no one should see the palais, as the workmen were repairing it, and all the ornaments in confusion; this we would not so much have regretted, but for the loss of seeing the opera house therein, which is said to be the finest in the world: after tormenting officers, architects, and workmen with my persevering though useless entreaties, I gave up all attempts to get even a look in here, and proceeded to see everything else (which required nothing further than a good supply of francs for the gardeners and doorkeepers), viz.: Les Affaires Etrangères, library, and antiquities.

'Orangery.' One of the finest, as a greenhouse, in Europe, containing trees planted from the year 1421 to the present day.

Gardens are laid out before the palais, standing on a commanding height and overlooking the royal woods and park of *chasse*, which latter are 60 miles round. These gardens are the most perfect paradise I ever saw; filled with every sort of sculpture; fountains, basins,[1] canals, &c.; and on one are many fine gondola boats; the avenues are most tastefully arranged, and made beautiful by every corresponding ornament that can be devised.

The Bas d'Apollon, an artificial rock, with statuary, where is introduced Louis XIV., is a wild and beautiful ornament to the retired shades in which it stands. From the

[1] Every one of the many basins played 104 fountains at a time.

centre of the gardens the groves lead off to all points, and you can see nowhere without a display of fountains before you.

Colonnade. A rotunda of 32 marble columns, and 25 fountains, with fine statuary in the centre.

Great basin with fountains, representing the chariot of Phaeton, which throw the water 55 feet high.

'Palais du Grand Trianon.' Another immense and magnificent residence of the *ci-devant* Emperor; everything here again is perfected for grandeur and luxury, and yet with comfort in no wise forgotten: this palais is entirely on a ground floor, and therefore the site is considerable. Another large collection of the finest paintings in the world, and in which Claude Lorrain, Poussin, and Vernet stand conspicuous. An immensely long gallery is here, richly fitted up; the walls hung with pictures of the best masters, and the opposite sides (from the best light for the paintings) are decorated with large and valuable models of the different ships of war.

Here are a variety of slabs, fonts &c. made from solid pieces of the production of copper mines (a sort of green like marble, I forget the name), said to be the largest specimens in existence.[1] A small piece of carving in agate of very great value. Many valuable things, nearly of the same description as those in the other palaces, or, to speak more to the purpose, of every description.

A whispering room, which has the effect of the gallery at St. Paul's, but is quite square, instead of being formed in a circle, like the latter.

'Petit Trianon.' An elegant little palace, which was occupied by the infant King of Rome and his attendants; it is very near the Grand Trianon, and is, perhaps, of all others, the situation which a private individual would prefer to live in.

Manufactory of arms on a large scale; but no good

[1] The greater part, if not all, of these were presented to Buonaparte by the Emperor Alexander.

work, except, as I before remarked, in carving and inlaying; the manufacturer was civil, and I therefore pretended to admire.

We got back to Paris by five, bolted our dinners and flew to another theatre.

'Le Théâtre du Vaudeville.' A house of comedy &c. much the same as our little theatre in the Haymarket; after seeing a little of this we found it so crowded as to be hot and uncomfortable; and having a wish to see the

Café Montacier lit up, we proceeded there and took some ice and cakes. Nothing could be more gay than the illuminated *coup d'œil* of this Bacchanalian[1] temple. The order of the day seemed to be burnt brandy and sweet cakes; but tea, coffee, and about twenty different kinds of refreshment were passing among the immense concourse here assembled. The *ci-devant* stage was filled up with groves of trees and flowers; and, on the whole, this appeared to be a perfect temple of gaiety.

We then started on foot, and took a view of the dissipations in the Palais Royal, which was crowded to excess; and notwithstanding we saw about 200 ladies of the demi-monde, there was literally not one but was worthy of being remarked for extreme ugliness. Here were coffee houses, all thronged from the garrets down to subterraneous vaults; and where, had we thought it prudent to come a little later, we might have seen the very essence of dissipation.

17th.—Having to arrange some money matters, and letters to write &c., I lost a part of this morning; we saw, however, enough to say that our time was well bestowed.

After inspecting the triumphal arch of Buonaparte and the gate of St.-Denis, both of which we had before passed, we proceeded to the Boulevard du Temple. First we saw here a fine fountain, to which the water is conveyed from the distance

[1] I may be wrong in using this term, as I believe, being a coffee house, no wine is allowed, but everything else is in abundance.

of 25 leagues, and which spouts from the mouths of eight lions, placed two and two octagonally.

'L'Abbaye St.-Martin,' a *ci-devant* convent which is now converted into a repository for models of almost every sort of manufacture, and where in one spacious range of apartments you see the process of almost every work. This is highly gratifying to a mechanic, and somewhat interesting to every one; we really found relief in seeing things of a sober colour, after being day after day so dazzled with the splendid blaze of magnificent palaces.

'Café d'Apollon.' A really good theatre, fitted up with chairs and tables instead of benches, and where, by calling for even a glass of spirits and water, you may every night see a comedy and a pantomime, with a passable orchestra. I am told they are worth seeing, but the cheapness and freedom of eating brings that sort of company which makes this place exceptionable in the evening.

We saw some inferior waxwork and many other trifling things in these Boulevards, which are entirely full of all sorts of little 'spectacles;' small theatres, temples and coffee gardens out of number, which are every night thronged with idle people of pleasure.

18*th.*—Went to the 'Tuileries' to see the Royal Family go in state to prayers; being English we were readily admitted into the saloon, through which they passed as follows: Duc de Berri, Duke of Angoulême, Monsieur Comte d'Artois, Louis XVIII., Duchesse d'Angoulême, marshals, attendants, &c. The affability and good-natured look of his Majesty could not but be admired by every honest man.

After leaving the Palais we drove through the Champs-Elysées, and passed the Barrière de Neuilly, a stately lodge with the finest avenue we had seen, and near which there is, half finished, another of the Corsican's triumphal arches, to his own memory, as usual. Then the Bois de Boulogne, a royal hunting wood, at the beginning of which are places of recreation, and for refreshment, as the avenues to and in this wood are in fine weather the Hyde Park of Paris. Here is the little Palais de Muet, once a royal villa, now a place for public amusement; also the country house of Talleyrand.

We then crossed over to the Champs de Mars for a review, which, to our disappointment, had just been countermanded; from there we drove to L'Institution des Sourds et Muets; but the deaf and dumb of the establishment being out, we had only a view of the buildings.

'Corps Législatif,' or Parliament House, which, instead of being, as ours, like a lawyer's dirty chambers, is truly magnificent. It is fitted up with every sort of comfort and ornament. The Salle where are assembled the members is, like the Luxembourg Senate Room, a half-circle, and the gallery supported by fine architecture of marble pillars; on the right of the President, or Speaker, are figures of Lycurgus, Solon, Demosthenes, and on the left, Cato, Brutus, and Cicero, all in the finest sculpture.

Among other grand saloons there is that which was the Emperor's, and still remains with decorations emblematical of his victories, and the insignia of all the different kingdoms of Europe. In the Corps Législatif are some good sculpture, paintings, tapestry, &c.

'L'Eglise de St. Sulpice.' Went here during mass, and were much more gratified by the superb architecture than the ranting of the preacher.

'Théâtre François.' We had delayed visiting this theatre till the celebrated Talma was announced to perform, and then we were obliged to conform to the French custom of profaning the Sabbath, or we should have left Paris without seeing him. He played Coriolanus, but with much more the deportment of a Whitechapel butcher than a dignified Roman; and his acting was such that we were sadly disappointed. The Roman matron was performed by a Madlle. George, a ranting woman, who is here considered a fine actress.

19th.—Cabinet of Mineralogy and Medals, and after this, having got an order from Baron Monier, we proceeded to the Gobelins tapestry, celebrated for being unquestionably the best in the world; we here saw many fine paintings which were left at this manufactory to be worked, and after being astonished with some of the finest tapestry that could be described, going through the whole process of making, we were shown a finished piece which represented the death of General Dessaix, and which astonished us (even though we supposed it was a painting) for its admirably fine colouring and spirit.

'Observatoire Royal,' a sort of obelisk from which you have a panorama of Paris, but by no means a better one than from many other edifices which we had mounted.

Dined at M. Véry's Restaurant. To have dined here is to have seen one of the 'lions' of Paris; and we therefore directed our steps to the Palais Royal for this purpose. The printed bill of fare was about the size of a newspaper, and the whole place seemed to be a temple of unbounded luxury. We dined on as many of the best dishes as we could possibly get through, and had afterwards ices, liqueurs, &c., the whole bill for which cost exactly an English guinea for Mrs. Hawker and myself; everything served up in silver, and, in short, this place is so noted for good living that the Emperor Alexander and the King of Prussia made a point of dining at Véry's while the Allies were in Paris, and since which the highly illuminated room (where we dined this day) is called the Alexandre.

20th.—'Catacombs,' subterraneous passages which extend for nine miles under the streets and boulevards, and from which the stone was taken (600 years ago) to build Paris. Here are two millions of skulls arranged with bones (like wine in a cellar), a spring of water with gold and silver fish, and an altar where mass is said once a year; several tombs &c. all nearly thirty yards below the surface of the earth, and where, had we extinguished our two glimmering candles, we should have lost our places in the coach for Calais. It luckily, however, happened that only one light went out at a time, and we got to our hotel just with time to partake of a scrambling dinner.

Paris, for public edifices, museums, and in short for splendid palaces and as a grand emporium for science and literature, may be termed the capital of the world; but so truly filthy are the streets, houses, and inhabitants, and so poor and vulgar are the almost numberless places of entertainment, that it was to us astonishing how any of the English could remain there a prey to imposition a day longer than was absolutely required to see the principal spectacles.

At two o'clock, having on a former excursion had enough of French posting (for instance, waiting while horses were taken from a plough or caught from a field a league distant), and having been much pleased with the diligence from Havre, we had taken our places at the 'Grande Messagerie' for Calais.

At twelve a dear and bad supper at Beauvais, 18 leagues from Paris.

21st.—At half-past eight breakfast at Amiens, 30 leagues from Paris; ran to look into the magnificent cathedral, than which nothing can be finer in the architecture.

At half-past five, found a most excellent dinner, with good wine, great civility and very reasonable charges, at Abbeville, 40 leagues from Paris.

22nd.—At a quarter before eight, a pretty good breakfast and things comfortable at Boulogne, 62 leagues from Paris.

Arrived by two in Calais, 70 leagues from Paris. Total, 193½ English miles.

N.B.—Tronchet in his guide book says 186½, but he is wrong, as in many other statements.

Thus we crawled for forty-eight hours at a trifle more than four miles per hour, notwithstanding the roads were in the best condition from the hard frost; add to which we were repeatedly annoyed by trifling accidents on the way. We were, however, induced to bear all with patience and even good humour, from the great civility and attention of M. Massin, the conducteur.

On our arrival we found Calais a perfect scene of confusion; the hotels were all crowded, and, in preference to starvation and sitting in the yard, we joined the table d'hôte, which I could compare to nothing but an ill-regulated kennel of foxhounds. The imposition, the misery, and the aping of the English, was at this place truly laughable.

At eight this evening went on board to sail, but it came on to blow so fresh that we all had to march back again. Being an old campaigner I took care to get a bed out of the hotel, and to offer a premium to an old woman, for which a good breakfast and hot rolls were prepared ready for us the next morning.

23rd.—Sailed at nine, and at half-past one reached Dover.

We came in a French packet, the 'Parfaite Union,' Captain Mascot, who, I suppose in consequence of his having piloted his Majesty on a day when the cabin boy might have brought in the vessel, thought his passengers (about sixty, instead of twenty which he ought to have taken) unworthy of the least civility or attention, further than to secure their money before they were fairly in sight of Dover. We had, most fortunately, an English sailor who was a passenger on board, and showed the crew how to manage the vessel.

The whole of the luggage was carelessly thrown together, and among which were the poor suffering passengers, many of them ladies, rolling in sickness and everything that was filthy, with the risk of having their brains beat out. Our getting into the boat which came alongside was so far bad that we thought it miraculous that only two passengers fell overboard. All our campaigning was a joke, for the time it lasted, to these four hours and a half. We had several women on board who suffered dreadfully, though not enough to move the assistance of Captain Mascot.

Soon after our arrival the very vessel into which we had the nearest possible escape from embarking was wrecked on the pier, the 'Henri Quatre,' Captain Benois, who refused a pilot to save expense, and whom they say was drinking with his crew instead of minding his vessel. Let these and the many late accidents be warnings to our countrymen never to trust themselves in a French packet; and let me observe that since the Peace every one has turned packet master, as money is such an object in France that every fellow will risk the life of himself and passengers to clear a few guineas; and therefore it is at all ports the order of the day to keep an ill-manned vessel.[1]

24th.—After being most strictly overhauled at the custom-house, we got off from Dover at eleven, and reached London in twelve hours by the Paris light coach.

25th.—After having been two hours only in bed, we proceeded for home, and at five o'clock we, thank God, arrived safe and found all well at Longparish, where we most heartily enjoyed our Christmas dinner.

Distance which we travelled, exclusive of excursions in and round Paris, and from Barfleur during our stay in those places, 719 miles.

The whole of this excursion, for exactly two calendar months, cost me about 120*l.* (exclusive of powder, shot, tea &c. taken out, and about 30*l.* laid out in little purchases).

27th.—1 wigeon, 1 heron, 1 jack snipe.

1815

January 2nd.—Left Longparish and arrived at Keyhaven, near Lymington.

3rd.—Keyhaven. 1 wigeon, the only one I fired at, but the flights we saw were prodigious.

[1] It was really afflicting to hear of the number of wrecks that had taken place within these ten days.

6th.—2 snipes, 1 jack snipe, and 1 partridge. In the evening, as usual, lay up in my canoe on the mud, where there were thousands of wigeon; but owing to the Christmas shooters, I never got a flock near enough to fire at.

7th.—The army of shooters had driven every fowl from the mud, except a few coots, at which I fired my capital Joe Manton duck gun with common shot and stopped 6, at the enormous distance of 132 yards, which we accurately measured with a 9-foot punt pole. Indeed, this extraordinary gun has scarcely ever failed, in a flock, at that distance.

14th.—Made a regular survey of the coast and places, as per annexed memorandum. The infamously bad sport prevailed everywhere this season.

Hasty sketch of shooting places.—'Pitt's Deep,' good creeks for canoe. 'Park,' not so many creeks, but better for the flights. Warren Farm has excellent flighting when the wind is from S. to W., as the Duke of Buccleuch stops the shore gunners; it is about a mile from Needs'oar Point, 2 from Bucklershard, and seven from Lymington. Bucklershard, eight miles from Lymington Road, good.

N.B.—All the mud is good, but everywhere equally disurbed by shooting punts and boats.

25th.—After being out all night, in a bitter cold north-east wind, with sleet, and waiting for three hours without stirring for water sufficient to approach the wigeon, which were unluckily disturbed, I was obliged to content myself with a random chance flying, and bagged only two. Last night our chance was again spoiled by fools trying to walk to the birds.

26th and 27th.—It blew and snowed so hard that going after wild fowl was impossible, and the levy *en masse* of blackguards as usual destroyed all chances for the shore; I therefore walked out inland, and killed 2 rabbits and 1 snipe, all that could be found.

28th.—A brent goose, the longest single shot I ever saw;

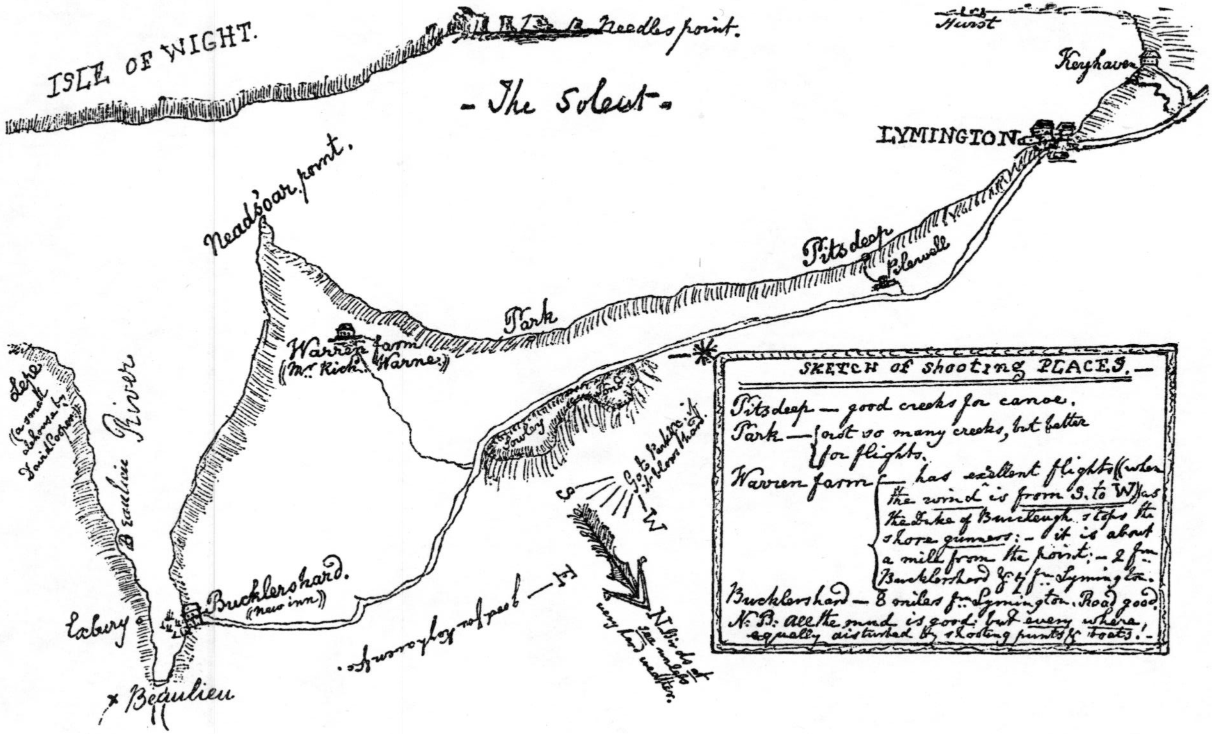
ISLE OF WIGHT.
Needles point.
Hurst
Keyhaven
- The Solent -
LYMINGTON
Pitsdeep
Pilewell
Park
Nead's oar. point.
Warren farm
(Mr. Rich. Warne.)
Bucklershard.
(new inn)
Exbury
Beaulieu River
Beaulieu
Lepe
SKETCH OF SHOOTING PLACES.—
Pitsdeep — good creeks for canoe.
Park — not so many creeks, but better for flights.
Warren farm — has excellent flights (when the wind is from S. to W.) as the Duke of Buccleugh stops the shore gunners; — it is about a mile from the point; — 2 fr. Bucklershard & 7 fr. Lymington.
Bucklershard — 8 miles fr. Lymington. Road good.
N. B: All the mud is good; but every where equally disturbed by shooting punts & boats! —

a keeper, who was present, supposed it to be 120 yards. This was with Joe Manton's famous 19-lb. gun, and the only shot I got.

I had afterwards to ride from Warren Farm (Mr. Richard Warne's) to Keyhaven, about 14 miles, and among unfrequented marshes and bogs, where I had never been before, in the most miserable night I ever weathered ; it was so dark, I literally could not see my hand before me ; and my eyes were almost blinded by hail, which was, the whole time, driven full in my face by a tremendous hurricane. I had my 19-lb. gun and an immense quantity of ammunition to carry ; and as my old blind mare would hang back when I tried to lead her, I was obliged to tie the gun to her bridle while I waded the dykes, then mount and force her through them, and afterwards anchor her with the shot belt, while I went back and groped up my gun. I had twice made up my mind to pass the night under a bank, and should have been too happy to have thus avoided the danger of being bogged or drowned, had I not been wet to the skin, and benumbed with cold.

30*th.*—Mrs. Hawker and I left Keyhaven, and luckily without having lost the use of our limbs, as Mrs. Benche's house was as damp as a church, and scarcely fit to shelter a Newfoundland dog. Mrs. Hawker went to Longparish ; and I proceeded for wild fowl shooting to Bucklershard, and got a very comfortable little lodging at the house of Joseph Beale.

February 1*st.*—'Bucklershard.' Prevented from going out till this evening by the rain, and found an immense company of wigeon, and put into a small creek at about eleven o'clock, and there lay in wait till half-past five in the morning ; we then got water, and were sitting up, with the almost certainty of half a boatful of birds, when an infernal rascal openly approached some of the straggling birds, and with the very worst management and a miserable old gun killed seven !

2nd.—More wet weather. I attempted the evening flight, but could get no chance; and the wind and tide having delayed the canoe coming for me, I had to wander over the marshes in utter darkness with wind and rain, and fell about a dozen times from the tops of the banks down into broad ditches full of water. I was almost borne down every step by the weight of my gun and ammunition. I then wandered all over the inclosures for several miles, and once lay down where some sheep had been penned, to pass the night; but the violence of the rain having somewhat abated, I made a second attempt, and after wandering in the fields for several miles more, and tearing through every hedge to keep a straight line, I found a road, which I followed till I came to a light. This luckily proved to be the house of a farmer, who gave me some beer, and put me in the road home. He said it was no wonder that I was lost, as even those who knew all the country rarely ever ventured on these marshes at night.

4th.—Rowed our canoe into a hole in the mud, where after the water had run off we remained invisible, and no sooner were the geese beginning to fly in swarms than a host of blackguards surrounded us on every side, and kept up such a fire with bullets that our prospect of sport was again annihilated; we had to remain in this hole from two in the morning till five in the evening; we got home about nine at night without having had a single chance.

5th.—Finding the sport so inferior to what it had been in other seasons, that even men who last year supported their families by wild fowl have this winter only killed two or three couple, and the weather having become quite mild and wet, I this day left Bucklershard and returned home to Longparish.

15th.—Being selected by Mr. Joseph Manton as one of the sportsmen to be examined on the advantages of his patents, I this day received a subpœna to attend his trial (*versus* his brother and others) for infringements on them.

16th.– Went to London. By the unexpected delay of other trials, the one of Mr. Manton could not be brought on, and was therefore deferred till the ensuing term.

19th.—I returned to Longparish.

The worst wild-fowl year ever known.

April 6th.—Having purchased Mr. Lee's cottage at Keyhaven, I this day went to Lymington to arrange for the rebuilding of the house.

July 1st.—'Longparish.' Went minnow fishing in the dusk of the evening, and lost all the best time by having to send home for some fresh tackle, and on its arrival the first and only fish I caught with it was the very one which had just broken my line before, and from whose mouth I pulled out my former hooks, gut, swivels, &c.

The angling this year has been so execrably bad, that, during the whole season, I have killed but 62 brace of trout.

I have in former years done nearly that in one day.

CHAPTER VIII

1815

September 1*st.*—34 partridges, besides 2 brace lost, 4 hares, and 2 quails. Every covey we found were as large as the old ones, but so unaccountably wild that I was obliged to take both single and double shots at all distances, notwithstanding which I may safely say that I only lost two head of game by bad shooting.

6th.—16 partridges and 1 hare. I also lost 2 birds, and except wounding one which I ought to have killed, and firing a random shot off my horse, I never missed. My double shots were three, and all killed.

7th.—8 partridges and 1 hare. My sport this day would have been as good as or better than yesterday, but I had only some young dogs, one of which spoiled all my best shooting by running in and chasing. This morning, an hour or two before I was prepared to start, I was called to go down to the river for two 'curious birds.' I loaded my double gun, and crawled under cover of a heap of stones near enough to bring down one sitting and the other flying with the second barrel. They proved to be a godwit and a spotted redshank, birds which I had often killed on the coast, but never before heard of in this part of the country.

I was, of course, obliged to fire kneeling, having crawled up to the birds, which, although one was a sitting shot, made the killing with the second barrel somewhat difficult, particularly as I had not an instant to spare.

Game bagged the first week: 90 partridges, 11 hares, 2 quails, 1 snipe (all I saw), 1 rabbit. Total, 105 head.

N.B.—Scarcely anyone else in this country has had good sport, by reason that the birds have been so unusually wild nothing could be done without the knack of killing them as soon as they topped the stubble. Including my 2 seabirds this morning, I have bagged every brace I fired at in my last ten double shots.

16*th.*—Till this day I have been laid up with an inflamed sore throat, and finding I could get but little better, I went out on my old mare, armed with gargle and hartshorn, to try for a few birds, as the coveys were so wild that almost all the shooters had given up doing anything. I bagged 10 partridges, lost 2 more, and missed but twice, one shot a long way off, and another in the sun.

20*th.*—From incessant dry weather, the scent became so bad that the birds were always on the run. I went out for a little airing on horseback, and killed all I could have killed, which were 1 partridge and 1 hare.

23*rd.*—5 partridges and 1 snipe. I this day, on a covey rising unawares, and in the sun, missed a first-barrel shot; at least, I only feathered the bird and killed him with the second barrel. Previous to this I had killed and bagged with both barrels fourteen times successively, without once taking down my gun from the shoulder between the two shots.

I have now completed 29 birds out of fifteen double shots. I did this with my old 22-gauge gun; last year I killed 27 birds out of fourteen double shots with a 14-gauge gun; but this last is far better, as the birds required such quick shooting.

As far as I could learn at Manton's and Egg's &c. my having this wild season bagged fourteen double shots successively is the best shooting that has been accomplished in England.

October 2nd.—Having without the slightest provocation (except being a friend of Mr. Fellowes, his brother) been uncivilly encroached on by the keeper of Lord Portsmouth, and having heard that his gang of myrmidons, who had previously been sent to annoy Mr. Fellowes through a whole day's sport, were watching to warn me off Lord Portsmouth's land, and to follow me wherever they dared, I got some men with guns and pistols to draw their attention to different parts while we attacked their grand preserve: everything was arranged agreeably to a military plan, which I regularly drew and coloured beforehand, and which answered so well that we got two hours' glut at their pheasants before the gang came up to warn us off; to my own share I bagged 28 pheasants (including 2 white ones), 3 partridges and 1 hare.

Notwithstanding we had rain for the first hour, I killed in two hours 24 pheasants in 24 shots, bagging every bird. I was determined not to fire out of distance; but among my shots were many very difficult ones and four double ones. We were taken after my 24th shot, when we finished our day on some neutral ground, to which we took care to drive a fine sprinkling of game, and where we defeated the gangs by being well mounted. We began at half-past nine in the morning, on the moderating of a heavy fall of rain, and came home to a comfortable dinner at four o'clock. We each shot with one old dog, which is always best where game is very plentiful.

7th.—Till this day I had uniformly shot, ever since the 1st of September, as well as it was possible to shoot; to-day I missed both barrels twice at partridges, which lay like stones: afterwards, however, I finished without missing, and bagged 5 partridges, 3 pheasants, and 1 hare.

8th.—I this day drove to Freefolk, where my tandem had a most extraordinary and providential escape. While I was in the house, my servant not being so attentive as he ought to have been to the horses, they suddenly galloped off, knocked him down, and drew the wheel over his arm, body and shoulder; they then charged a fastened-up gate with such violence that they broke it and burst it open, in doing which they completely bent the top bar, which was of wrought iron, thick as my wrist; tearing the dog cart after them, they flew all up the most dangerous cross road in the place, and after reaching the summit of one hill, had to go down another, which was frightfully steep, full of loose stones, and with a gate at the bottom, where this road ended with others going short to the right and left: strange to say, they cleared the turn most dexterously, and the wheeler and buggy were found overturned about a mile and a half from Freefolk House, and the leader, who had broken loose from his reins and traces, was brought back by a countryman.

Instead of finding James half killed, the road strewed with the wreck, and the horses blemished, we had the good fortune to find that the extent of all the damage done was the breaking off at the two extreme holes of the leader's traces, which we only had to buckle to the next two holes and the leading reins at the buckle which couples them. In short, all was so well got over that I afterwards proceeded ten miles, and paid two other visits.

12*th.*—Having late last evening killed some game, amidst the annoyance of Lord Portsmouth's banditti, who could not then catch the tenant to warn me off, I (knowing that a notice would be sent for my breakfast) attacked the place again this morning at sunrise, while my men diverted the gang with a little random shooting in another direction. I got 4 hares and 3 pheasants, and made a long shot flying over my head at a teal.

14*th.*—Worked Wherwell Wood all day, and got but one shot, which was at a single partridge, and that I lost in the high wood.

20*th.*—Went out while it blew a hurricane, and in eight shots killed, including a pheasant lost out of bounds, 8 head of game.

Game &c. bagged up to November 1: 149 partridges, 2 quails, 23 hares, 7 rabbits, 80 pheasants, 9 ducks and mallards, 1 teal, and 6 snipes. Total, 277 head.

November 26.—Proceeded from London to inspect the Fens; went in chaise as follows: Waltham Cross, 13 miles;

Wade's Mill, 11 miles; Royston, 15 miles; Caxton, 12 miles; Huntingdon, 9 miles; Ramsay, 12 miles. Total, 72 miles. Put up at Mrs. Belshaw's 'Crown' inn, Ramsay.

27th.—Walked nearly thirty miles in surveying the Fens, and could soon perceive that they would not answer for wild-fowl shooting: if a frost, the birds are gone; if a thaw, the greater part of them remain in the decoys; so that the breeding season (when the ague is predominant) is the only time for this infernal country.

28th.—Took a hack buggy, by way of Whittlesea, to Peterborough, 15 miles, and then a chaise to Oundle, 13 miles.

After having spent the day with Mr. Sherrard, I returned to town on the 29th per coach by Kimbolton, St. Neots, &c. As my presence in town was not required again till the morning of the 30th, I enjoyed a pleasant and cheap tour for these few spare days instead of remaining idle in London.

30th.—Having finished my business, I left town this afternoon, and reached Longparish soon after midnight per Weymouth coach. Total travelled from Thursday to Thursday, 309 miles. Killed on the road 2 partridges.

December 13th.—Left Longparish for Keyhaven, where we took Aubrey House from the 11th. I had some days before sent off my baggage, &c., but was detained by having been taken suddenly and severely ill.

15th.—Went down to Poole (21 miles) relative to building a new canoe and stanchion gun on a plan of my own invention.

16th.—Returned to Keyhaven.

19th.—1 wild duck and 1 mallard. So scarce and bad has the coast shooting yet been, that the only two shots I fired all yesterday and this evening were one at a single wigeon, and another at 4 ducks, of which I knocked down 3, though only bagged the above 2.

28th.—My gun having been loaded ever since I killed the 2 ducks (eight days), I at last got a flying shot, and killed 1 wigeon, and afterwards a second shot, with which I knocked down 2 more that I lost on the tide. There has scarcely been a bird killed by any one of the constant followers of wild fowl since we came here, so mild, wet, and unfavourable has been the weather.

29th.—Went to Poole to pay for and send off my new canoe boat, and bring away the stanchion gun &c. to be finished under my own direction.

1816

January 6th.—'Keyhaven.' After having waited in a creek for water to float from half-past eleven at night till four this morning, Tom Fowler got me in the canoe to within 40 yards of above 1,000 wigeon, just half an hour before which the morning came on suddenly so dark and wet that we could not see fifteen yards before us, and were obliged to go home. Before the next tide the birds were found out, and routed by two fellows who had heard of them ; otherwise, we should with two guns have had every chance of killing fifty at one volley.

9th.—Took a drive to Warren Farm and Need'soar Point, where I heard the same complaint as here prevails among all the punters, on the almost impossibility of getting a shot at any wild fowl.

11th.—Launched my new canoe and stanchion gun, and in the evening went out, but there was not a bird to be heard or seen in the harbour, and I could only remain afloat a few hours in consequence of a tremendous gale of wind.

12th.—Killed only 3 birds ; but so bereft of wild fowl is this coast now, that I never could get a chance for the long gun, and in the evening it came on a gale of wind with a pour of rain.

17th.—I proceeded to Poole on business, and slept two nights over at Studland, in the Isle of Purbeck. I took my gun, though could kill nothing but a few coots, as the general scarcity prevailed here like everywhere else, and I consequently got home to Longparish on the night of the 19th.

I was amply repaid for my five weeks on the coast by the benefit derived by the change, but so mild was the weather that to get any shooting was out of the question.

February 8th.—Frost and snow; out from seven in the morning till dinner, and then out all night, and so destitute was the country (like all others this year) that I never saw but two ducks and one wild wisp of snipes; and, in short, got no shooting except a roast of fieldfares, redwings, and larks.

10*th.*—A wild duck with green feet.

12*th.*—Proceeded to London on business.

14*th.*—Returned to Longparish in my carriage, with three people and luggage, in eight hours; notwithstanding we stopped three-quarters of an hour to breakfast at Staines, and a quarter of an hour at Kensington, where a posthorse threw his shoe. We had only pairs of horses all the way, and the last 15 miles my horses brought us in an hour and a half. From being constantly in the habit of guessing and calculating time on a journey, I foretold the hour of arrival within three-quarters of a minute.

Game &c. bagged up to March 1st: 164 partridges, 106 pheasants, 30 hares, 15 rabbits, 2 quails, 36 snipes, 19 wild ducks, 4 wigeon, 2 teal. Total, 378 head.

April 17*th.*—Till this day it was so cold, that we had constant frost and occasional snow storms; the weather now having become suddenly warm, I tried fly fishing for the first time this season, and killed 10 trout, besides a great many small ones thrown in.

May 29*th.*—London. Was presented by the Duke of Clarence on my appointment as Major of the North Hants Regiment.

June 9*th.*—Published my second edition of 'Instructions to Young Sportsmen' previously to leaving town.

15*th.*—10 trout. Fishing very indifferent, owing to the trout being glutted with the mayfly and small gnats.

18*th.*—Went over to fish at Stockbridge; but so innumerable was the mayfly that our sport was wretched. I killed only one large trout; we never could get a rise, or a run, the whole day.

July 4*th.*—Left Longparish on a visit to the marshes, in the east of Norfolk.

5*th.*—Proceeded from London by the mail to Norwich, where we arrived on the evening of the 6th, and proceeded in a chaise to Mr. Rising's at Horsey, 130 miles from London.

12*th.*—Went to stay with Mr. Huntingdon.

14*th.*—Went to Norwich.

15*th.*—Came up from Norwich, by way of Newmarket, 110 miles within thirteen hours, by the 'Light Telegraph' morning coach, which beat the mail by nearly five hours.

17*th.*—Returned from London to Longparish.

My object in going to Norfolk was to shoot young wild fowl, and catch pike, perch, tench, bream, &c.; but as the custom of that country is to sport in large battue parties I at last gave up attempting to reckon what I killed myself, though I had far more sport than the others. The fish were in size greatly beyond any I had before seen, and the young wild fowl shooting was most capital. We killed large numbers of almost every kind of sea and marsh birds, interspersed with occasional good shooting at leverets and rabbits, young snipes, plovers, &c. The only birds, however, that I had not killed before were the crested grebes and the shoveller ducks, with which I had, one day in particular, most excellent sport. The circumstance that makes the birds so plentiful here cancels all the pleasure of the shooting, which is that the fear of death deters strangers from hazarding their constitutions in such a pestilential climate. I came home ill, but was happy to escape as well as I did.

25*th.*—Some wild ducks having flown, I went up the

river and had a most excellent shot at five all close together; but unluckily my stool upset while I was in the act of firing. Afterwards I got a wild duck, and shot another, and a heron, which fell in Lord Portsmouth's grounds, where I would not go after them.

31*st.*—Went over to Ponton's at Stockbridge. Found the fly fishing, as it almost always is at this celebrated though infamously bad place, not worth a penny. The cockney-like amusement of bobbing with a live mayfly is all that this miserable river does for; indeed, scarcely a fish ever moves till about the last quarter of an hour that you can see to throw a line.

August 28*th.*—During the whole season I only killed 37 brace of trout with a fly, which number I have, before now, exceeded in one day. The worst fishing season ever known.

CHAPTER IX

1816

September 1st.—Longparish. Shooting the first week out of the question. From the unprecedented lateness of the harvest, owing to the incessant wet weather, the greater part of the wheat was standing, and, in most places, the sport was deferred by agreement till the 16th; but as I could not succeed in my attempt to get it postponed about here, I deferred even taking out a dog till other people had begun shooting in earnest, and then I began the second week by going round what few stubbles there were cleared. The standing corn, however, was so abundant, that sport could only be had for an hour or two in the day. The weather having now favoured fly fishing more than it had done before, I generally divided the morning by first shooting and then getting a dish of trout for dinner. My sport on the 14th was very great, and something rather novel, as I that day happened to be most lucky in both diversions; between the hours of eleven and one I killed 9 brace of partridges, with only missing one bird, and that was a long second-barrel shot, and feathered; and by three o'clock had brought home two brace of trout, besides catching smaller ones, which I threw in.

14th.—Completed, and found most fully to answer, my new invention of a portable ambush and artillery carriage for firing my stanchion gun with perfect safety on shore, by which I could get about and follow wild fowl with a gun weighing 80 lb. as well, nearly, as with a shoulder gun. The whole of the apparatus was built to my order, and admirably executed, by the ingenious Mr. Fielder, wheelwright, of Longparish.

16th.—This I considered as my first day's shooting. I went out at ten o'clock, and returned by five to dinner, having with me the same two dogs the whole morning, Nero and Comus. And, notwithstanding I have brought home more at a time, yet I never in my life had such a satisfactory day's shooting. Although the birds were rather wild than otherwise for the time of the year, and the number of coveys the Longparish fields contained were by no means considerable, yet I had the good fortune to bag 36 partridges and 1 hare, with literally never missing a single shot and without losing one bird. I had 8 doublets and bagged both my birds every time, and having once killed 2 at one shot with my first barrel, I made 37 head of game in 36 shots. Had I at all picked my shots, I should not have thought this any such very extraordinary performance; but so far from this a great number of my birds were killed at long distances, and with instantaneous rapidity of shooting. I had my favourite 14-gauge barrels of Joe Manton's, and Mr. Butts's cylinder gunpowder. The same gun all day, which was neither cleaned afresh nor even new flinted. This with Saturday makes 54 partridges and 1 hare, with only 1 miss. This with a single gun would not be worthy of much comment; but with a double gun, where I honestly and fairly worked both barrels wherever it was possible, and all at large strong birds, I consider it the best performance I ever accomplished. I have now killed 60 shots in succession and 93 birds, with only 1 miss.

Game bagged up to October: 218 partridges, 6 hares. Total, 224 head.

N.B.—Made scarcely any beginning till the 16th: had only a brace of dogs, and only shot between a half-past nine o'clock breakfast and a four o'clock dinner. Was out altogether (including three wet days, when I was driven home) but fifteen times.

Since the 14th inclusive I bagged 198 head of game, with missing only 6 fair shots. Though I never failed to use both barrels where fair opportunity offered and did not at all pick my shots, as such double-gun [1] shooting is rare, and I may not perform it again, I have noted a faithful statement of the particulars.

October 1st.—Shot in the unpreserved part of Wherwell Wood, a place free for every vagabond; and notwithstanding it blew a continued hurricane, with an almost incessant pour of rain, I killed and bagged every bird I shot at, viz. 12 pheasants, all full-grown birds, and 9 of them cocks.

Had much fun to-day in manœuvring against, and beating, other shooting parties.

2nd.—A gale of wind all day, with a drizzling rain and sometimes a heavy pour. Up at five, and, as I said would be the case, found no pheasants where I was the day before, as they seldom return the next day. Came home wet to the skin at eleven. Out again at one: went fly fishing; bagged at the same time 1 jack snipe, 1 hare, 1 cock pheasant, and 2 partridges, and had capital sport pulling out the trout. Returned (wet through again) by four o'clock with fish, flesh, and fowl in plenty.

4th.—After killing 8 partridges, 2 snipes, and 1 pheasant, which I wanted for London, and for which I had a hard fag in a rainy morning, I went fly fishing and caught 3 fine trout just in time for a four o'clock dinner.

7th.—Rode off to another neutral beat, a rendezvous for unqualified tradesmen, and bagged 8 pheasants and 4 partridges.

8th.—Walked out with a young dog, got three shots to him, and bagged three partridges. Weather fine, and birds

[1] 'I say 'double gun,' because a man by taking only one bird at a time, and selecting choice shots, might kill 100 times in succession with little merit.

lay well. Had I gone out in earnest, with double gun and broken-in dogs, I should have had a good day.

9th.—Drove to where I had such sport on the 7th, and never saw a pheasant. Weather rainy again, but it cleared up, so I shot on my way home and bagged 12 partridges and 1 rabbit by means of firing at all distances, and such long shots as I (or rather my barrels, as the credit is theirs) made, I never before saw.

19th.—Worked the river and common for miles in search of a snipe for Mrs. Hawker, and only found 1 snipe, at which I had a bad chance, though I contrived to kill it. This is the fifth snipe only I have either killed, seen, or heard of this season, which is very extraordinary, and particularly after a wet summer.

November 7th.—Went to Whitestaunton, beyond Chard in Somerset, eighty-five miles from here, per 'Auxiliary' mail.

8th.—Shot with Lord Hinton, and killed only 3 woodcocks, 1 hare, and 2 rabbits.

9th.—3 hares, 1 pheasant, and 2 partridges; so bad was the sport, that Lord Hinton's share was even less than mine, though there was nothing missed that offered a tolerable chance.

10th.—Having had enough of shooting in the wet weather, and not being very well, I returned again to Longparish per mail.

16th.—After a deep fall of snow in harvest, and in a hard frost, I went out shooting again. Bagged 6 snipes and 1 teal.

26th.—Shot a sparrow-hawk when perched on the house. In the evening killed a mallard, which I could not see, but fired by guess as he pitched. This is the first shot I have had at flight this winter, though I have waited out above a dozen nights.

December 16th.—Went up to London.

20th.—Returned to Longparish, and drove my tandem

with an immensely heavy load, notwithstanding the roads were very dead and bad, the last twelve miles in fifty-five minutes.

27th.—Went out (with Mr. Kalkbrenner, who came to me for a few days on the 25th) and killed all that could have been killed, viz. 1 partridge, 2 jack snipes, and 1 woodcock.

28th.—Mr. Kalkbrenner and I literally fagged over 25 miles of country, in my attempt to show him some sport, and he never got a fair shot, and I killed only 2 partridges.

1817

January 8th.—3 jack snipes and 1 snipe; the only four shots I got, though out all day, the wild fowl being so scarce here now that none can be seen or heard. I drove my boat on wheels 8 miles at nine o'clock this night, and stayed out till four on the morning of the 9th, but never saw or heard but one duck. I was, however, amply repaid for my trouble, as the shaking of the boat cart effectually removed a pain in my side with which I had been suffering for nearly a fortnight.

14th.—Left Longparish this morning, arrived at Poole in the afternoon, and just saved my tide to Southhaven; to do which I was obliged to get on board in such a hurry, that I had only time to scramble up (near the quay) some infamously bad bread, a few red herrings, and a little paper of salt butter. Even this was well worth exportation, as the family who occupy the only hovel I could be sheltered in at Southhaven almost entirely subsist on bad potatoes and sour beer. No sooner had I reached my quarters than the frost, as if by magic, was turned to an incessant pour of rain, which, with a foul gale of wind, kept me (cut off from Poole) a close prisoner all the 15th and nearly all the 16th with the worst of campaigner's fare, and without a book, newspaper, or anything to amuse me but a pen and ink and my own thoughts. Thus in my prison (which, by the way, was scarcely weather-tight) I sat alternately writing, thinking, and taking snuff, till a half-starved cow deprived me of the former amusement, by thrusting her horns through the window, and consequently obliging me to close the board which, I suppose, is called a 'shutter.' I had then no other resource than to brave the elements, which I did till my gun was wet, and I killed, as they flew over, 1 wigeon and 2 brent geese, also some more of each sort, that fell out upon the ebbing tide, where I dare not either send a dog or a boat. Attempted to get out in the evening, but was again driven in by rain, when I had just killed a heron, which I voted well worth my charge, in order to make me a substitute for giblet soup.

17th to 19th.—Wet weather and gales.

20th.—A tremendous hurricane all day. The communication with Poole entirely cut off, it being impossible even to cross the Channel (to get there by land); all our boats filled, our oars washed away, and the house so full of water that I was obliged to stand in water boots, and cook my dinner where there was water enough to float a boat, the house, like Noah's ark, being literally in the flood. A scarcity of provision, except red herrings and the few wild fowl we had shot. Being on the weather shore, no birds would fly over the haven, so that we had nothing to compensate for the most unmerciful misery of the weather. More rain, of course. My pilot poorly with the rheumatism, and my servant put to bed with a cold, where he could only be approached by means of water boots or a bridge of chairs.

21st.—Most miserable weather.

22nd.—Worse and worse. Contrived to weather it across to Poole in a gale of wind and pour of rain.

23rd.—Got on the 'Lord Exmouth' coach, and, having left my man and shooting things at Southhaven, went home to Longparish (of course, in a pour of rain) to wait till this pretty little shower was over.

26th.—Wet. Many people ill and dying, and everything nearly ruined by the unprecedented wetness of the season.

February 1st.--Went back again to Poole, and at night crossed over to Southhaven. Having business there I was obliged to go; and the change of scene was, of all others, the thing to do me the most good. Otherwise, even had the weather been cold enough, I was scarcely in the humour even for wild-fowl shooting after the sudden death of my little child. Weather very fine, but as mild as April.

3rd.—Real bad luck with the wild fowl. At half-past one this morning I got close up to about 40 wigeon, and had only to wait for about ten minutes' more tide to bring the swivel gun to bear, when a rascal rowed by to windward and put them all up. This was nothing to what happened an hour afterwards, viz. I got about 150 wigeon, feeding under the moon, all doubled together in a space scarcely the size of a canoe, and literally not so much as thirty yards from me. Such a chance had not been known or heard of in Poole harbour for many years. Indeed, had I chosen my ground, time, and place, and positioned the birds myself, I could not have had a more glorious opportunity for aggregate slaughter, and my swivel gun was loaded with a pound of the choicest sized shot. I levelled at the very bull's eye of the phalanx, when, to my dire annoyance and mortification, instead of seeing 50 or 60 dead and wounded, my priming, in spite of the greatest care, had got damp, and the gun flashed. Up, of course, flew the birds, like a roar of the sea, and the cursed powder kept hissing away, so that they had all flown far above the utmost level of the stanchion before the gun went off. Having been out all night, I then came in, breakfasted, and went out all day, but had no hope till the dusk of the evening, when occurred my chance for an enormous swarm of geese. Old Tom left the canoe for a few minutes, when she slipped her painter and drifted off to sea. Here I had to pay dearly for a four-oar boat and crew to go out after her, as it 'came on to blow' very hard, and my guns and everything were in her, and the whole concern was all but lost. Having luckily got her in, I went out all night again ; but the wind having shifted to the unfortunate south-west, I never saw or heard a single wild fowl, though incessantly working till five in the morning.

4th.—Out all day ; but could not, as yet, get a chance even at inferior birds, except one shot with my smallest gun, with which, at a very great distance, I got 2 grey plover and 1 knot. Could not go out to-night, as it came on wet weather again, with a strong gale of wind. Thank God that such infamous luck has been only in trifling concerns, and not in matters of consequence.

6th.—Out all night, and never heard or saw but three wigeon.

7th.—2 brent geese.

8th.—Out best part of the night, and never saw or heard a single bird.

9th.—Crossed over to Poole on my way home, and this night reached Salisbury by the conveyance of my boat on wheels, in which I never travelled more pleasantly.

10th.—Rode on from Salisbury, and arrived to dinner at Longparish.

N.B.—The shooting at Poole this year is even worse than that of the last year, or even the preceding one, and, indeed, the sport has been worse this season than ever was remembered by the oldest gunner. I never before, too, owing to the gales of wind, lost so many wild fowl in proportion to the few I bagged ; and although I was day and night at work for three weeks, I got but one shot with my swivel gun, and that was the famous one at which it missed fire. Previously to coming home I had plenty of sport at birds not worth noting, such as coots, divers, goosanders, grebes, &c.

18th.—Shrove Tuesday. Began fly fishing, and with a yellow dun and red palmer killed 16 brace of good trout in two hours.

Not only most of those killed to-day, but some which

I caught a week ago, dressed quite red, and proved in excellent season. This, of course, may be imputed to the extreme mildness of the winter.

20th.—Walked all down the river, with a large duck gun. Killed 1 snipe, which was all I saw, except 2 more snipes, which flew off very wild. Wet weather as usual.

21st.—Torrents of rain again. All of us being quite bilious for want of being able to get exercise, the never-ceasing wet weather obliged me to set up a full-sized billiard table, on which we played the first match on the 20th.

March 1st.—List of game &c. killed in the season: 308 partridges, 40 pheasants, 1 quail, 17 hares, 9 rabbits, 99 snipes, 6 ducks and mallards, 3 wigeon, 1 teal, 6 geese, 3 plover, 10 woodcocks. Total bagged, 503 head,[1] exclusive of all the young wild fowl and different birds with which I had excellent sport in the Norfolk Fens previously to September, and also exclusive of a variety of other birds, such as herons, coots, water rails, &c. The worst wild fowl season ever heard of, and the quantity that I lost in proportion to the very few I bagged, from having quartered on a weather shore in the tremendous gales of wind, is beyond all proportion. The wettest season since the memory of the oldest man.

June 11th.—Went over to Ponton's, where after two days' fishing I caught but 4 brace of trout; and so execrable is the Stockbridge fishing that this was literally called good sport. The fish are immensely large, but so flabby and soft as to be scarcely worth eating. We worked the real mayfly as well as the artificial.

25th.—Went to London for Norfolk.

28th.—Arrived with Mr. Rising at Horsey.

July 2nd.—Removed to Mr. Huntingdon's at Somerton House.

5th.—Left Norfolk.

[1] Gave away, as presents to my friends, 470 head.

6th.—Arrived at Longparish, 200 miles, without stopping, except to breakfast in town.

N.B.—While in Norfolk I had some excellent sport with perch, pike, and bream fishing; and I had the best of shooting at rabbits, flappers, shovellers, ruffs and reeves, and every kind of marsh bird. The order of the day was to sally forth with all sorts of netting, trolling, angling, and shooting tackle, so as to attack all the marshes both by land and water—as an invading enemy would march over a country—and bring in our punts laden with fish, flesh, and fowl.

August 23rd.—Longparish. The fishing has been so inferior this year that I have seldom gone out for a whole day; and, at last, I gave up keeping an account of what I caught, it being not worth it. In the whole season I killed about 50 brace of trout, which I have, in former years, often done in two days.

CHAPTER X

1817

September 1st.—Longparish. Birds greatly destroyed by an incessant rain, no barley cut, and even the greater part of the wheat standing. I tried to get the shooting deferred, but could not prevail on others to agree.

The few birds which were to be caught out of the corn were as wild as in November. I, however, did vastly well, considering all disadvantages, having bagged 20 partridges, 1 hare, 1 quail, and 1 landrail.

4th.—Mr. Sola came to us.

9th.—Killed 2 brace of trout with a fly for the amusemen of Mr. Sola.

10th.—Went out, with a double gun, which I had made up myself (barrels by Manton), and in sixteen shots killed 15 partridges and one bird lost; and Mr. Sola killed and bagged 1 partridge.

15th.—Out all day and got but seven shots. Killed 8 partridges—and another lost—and a rabbit. Mr. Sola left us for Southampton. Bad luck on the 15th, as well as poor sport. Had one of my only two dogs stuck with a scythe and severely wounded, broke my ramrod, and sprained my ankle.

20th.—My sprain being nearly well I went out on horseback, and after slaving from morning till evening I only bagged 7 partridges. Never since the memory of the oldest person here has there been such a deplorable scarcity of birds; for 1 partridge now we had 20 last year.

Game bagged in September 1817: 108 partridges, 2 hares, 3 rabbits, 3 snipes, 1 quail and 1 landrail. Total, 118 head.[1]

October 1st.—Had again to contend with many strong parties in the lawless part of Wherwell Wood, and manœuvred so that I beat them all put together with only 1 brace of pointers. Considering the very bad breed of pheasants, this was one of the best days I ever enjoyed; bagged 11 pheasants, 3 partridges, and 1 hare. Adding what Signor Vercellini shot, and two divided birds, we killed 16 pheasants, 6 partridges, and 2 hares, nearly all we saw.

N.B.—I could have killed more, but gave all the best shots up to the Signor, as he never shot before in England.

3rd.—Vercellini and I beat Wherwell Wood again, and never found anything but 1 hare and 1 pheasant, both of which we put in the bag.

20th.—3 partridges, 2 hares, and 1 teal; while a party from my house, consisting of five crack double-barrel shots, touched on Lord Portsmouth and bagged 11 brace of birds, 3 brace of hares, 1 pheasant, and 1 rabbit.

26th.—Received a detonating double gun (No. 8111), value 100 guineas, presented to me by Mr. Joseph Manton.

27th.—Went out with this elegant gun, and, notwithstanding an incessant pour of rain, I killed in fifteen shots: 9 snipes, 3 partridges, 1 spotted gallinule, and 1 water rail. The one shot that I missed was far beyond a fair distance.

November 4th.—Drove to Andover, walked from the town, down the river, and bagged 19 snipes; besides 2 shot and lost; making 10½ couple, without having missed a shot.

6th.—2 partridges and 4 snipes. Tried the effect of the detonating gun at birds which 'duck the flash,' and found it to answer admirably, by killing dabchicks swimming at a considerable distance.

[1] N.B.—Although a very poor September's shooting, yet I have every reason to be satisfied when I consider how extremely wild and scarce the game has been, and what wretched sport all other people have had here this season.

20th.—In consequence of the death of our lamented Princess Charlotte, I had laid aside my gun, and prohibited every kind of sport, till this day. Her mortal remains having been last night committed to the tomb, we may now, without indecency, endeavour to divert our minds from the universal affliction that has been produced by this severe calamity.

29th.—I have now killed 121 snipes, exclusive of those shot in the summer in Norfolk. For our river this is unusual sport before December.

December 2nd.—1 snipe, 1 jack snipe, and 3 pheasants (the first I had seen, or heard of, for a long time; I caught them feeding out of bounds, cut off their retreat, and put them all 3 in the bag in about 10 minutes).

8th.—Out all day, and bagged only 1 jack snipe.

10th.—Beat Wherwell Wood the whole day with three cries of dogs; found the game nearly extirpated; and never saw but 3 woodcocks, which were the first I had seen this season. Never saw 1 hare the whole day, and only moved 2 pheasants. I bagged 2 woodcocks.

22nd.—Beat the river for miles, to see if any snipes had arrived in my absence; only saw 3 snipes and 2 jack snipes, all of which I put in the bag on their first appearance.

29th.—2 jack snipes, 1 pheasant, and 1 mallard, the very first I have fired at this year, although up the river by day and night above thirty times.

30th.—2 hares, for which I paid pretty dearly. I went in my tandem, with four people, and dogs, to drive 16 miles, when the road was literally a sheet of ice, to one of the most deplorable deserts that ever disgraced a Christian country. I had to drive the tandem through the filthy village of Tidworth, when the waters were out 3 feet deep; and, with a broken spring and the cart tied up with a stirrup leather, had literally to traverse the ice, which was so thick that it bore up my horses (which were of course rough-shod) before it would burst to let them in. The rain came on the moment we began shooting, and I had to drive Mr. Kalkbrenner down afterwards to Everley; the buggy was broken a second time, and in this state I had to proceed. The variety of our other dangers and mishaps would fill a romance.

1818

January 12th.—9 snipes, 2 jack snipes, and 1 bittern. I have now killed 132 snipes and 74 jack snipes. Total, 206.

14th.—I began fly fishing, and in about an hour caught as many trout as I could well carry, exceeding generally a pound each, and in such perfect season that most of them dressed as firm, and as red, as a salmon, and had on them a fine curd the same as in July. This may be perhaps attributed to the mildness of the winter.

17th.—Proceeded to Norwich.

18th.—Went over to Mr. Rising's at Horsey.

20th.—Went to Mr. Huntingdon's, at Somerton Hall, to stand godfather to his son and heir; and partook of his grand fête, at which I, as well as many others, played several characters, in, and out of, the masquerade, and which was kept up most brilliantly till the

22nd.—Returned to Horsey.

30th.—Went to Yarmouth, and in the evening left that place for London per mail.

N.B.—Although I took my guns for wild-fowl shooting, yet I was so unlucky that I never got a chance all the time I was in Norfolk, though out every day, and every evening, while at Horsey. I literally never saw but one snipe during the whole time, though a week only previous to my arrival 25 couple had been killed in a day, and the quantity of wild fowl was so immense that every common fellow on the mere boundary of where I, and only I, had the full liberty of shooting, was earning his pound a week by shooting. What occasioned my unprecedented essence of bad luck was the incessant hurricane from the south-west, which blew every creature that had wings across to the Dutch coast, and where, in such a case, they usually stay till the pairing season.

I had some very fair game shooting, though with parties (as is the unpleasant custom of this county and Suffolk), I kept no account of what I killed, which I seldom do on such days. Though I have never yet been beat by anyone in any country that I have ever yet seen, still this style of shooting leads to a jealousy that I detest; and as I consider more than two guns a party for fun and society, and not a party for sport, I reckon all the game shot as much a general concern as a fox when killed by a pack of hounds, though I certainly killed far more than anyone else. I, one day in particular, got 4 brace of hares, 3 of partridges, wood pigeons, rabbits &c. in about two hours, and among my hares was a white one, the first of the kind ever killed there, and which had been before eagerly fired at and missed.

Among the trials of skill, I made some double shots at halfpence thrown up together, and finished by throwing away two halfpence with my right hand, and then shooting one with each barrel before they fell to the ground. The halfpence of my different double shots were kept as a curiosity.

February 1st.—Returned home to Longparish.

5th.—Worked the river all day, and saw but 2 jack snipes, both of which I put in the bag.

12th.—Went to Keyhaven to see about my cottage; drove down in my canoe on wheels, with my large gun. Got no chance there for wild fowl, the weather being far too mild, and the season too far gone; indeed, all I bagged was one brent goose. I had, however, capital sport with the coots, having got a great many almost every day. One night I killed 16 at a shot, at about 120 yards, with my stanchion gun.

19th.—When firing at some geese, my new stanchion gun, of 96 lb. weight, was literally blown to atoms from the breeching to near the end of the stock, and though the lock and other appendages were dealing destruction in every quarter, and I was for a considerable time on fire (with a pound of gunpowder in my pocket), thank God, I sustained not the slightest injury further than the end of one of the oars being blown off. Nothing but the kind interference of Providence and my invention for fixing this gun could possibly have saved my life. The barrel, a Birmingham one, which was to all appearance clean, proved to be scarcely better than unbeat ore or granite stone. Let this be a caution to discard all barrels that are not twisted. After my happy escape I returned in a pour of rain.

21st.—Drove home in a vile road, with one incessant torrent of rain the whole way, and after the narrow escape from being killed by the fore part of the carriage breaking when going down a steep hill, I thank God arrived safe and sound at Longparish House.

23rd.—Having purchased the celebrated fishery of Mr. Widmore, I this day bought Mr. Sutton's lease, with which it was encumbered, and became possessed in fee simple of one of the first trout rivers in the world. Shot 1 hare and 3 jack snipes; afterwards went fly fishing on my newly purchased river, and when the snow was a foot deep, I caught a dish of fish for dinner in about half an hour, which proved in capital season. At night it thawed, and we had another attack from torrents of rain.

27th.—1 jack snipe, and another shot and lost, being the last two, to the best of my knowledge, left in the country. Afterwards fly-fished for half an hour, and killed 10 very large and very well-seasoned trout.

List of game &c. bagged in the season to March 1, 1818: 178 partridges, 20 pheasants, 12 hares (nearly extirpated here), 8 rabbits, 7 woodcocks (all I saw), 230 snipes, 1 quail (all seen), 1 landrail, 2 ducks, 2 teal, 1 goose (this year even worse than the last for fowl, which I had thought impossible), 1 bittern. Total, 463 head, exclusive of coots, water rails, fieldfares &c. and also exclusive of what birds I shot in the marshes in Norfolk in the summer, and also of the game I killed there in the winter, which were not kept account of.

I gave away as presents to my friends 495 head.

March 2nd.—Went to London, and after studying harmony, musical composition &c. three months in the academy of Mr. Logier, I completed other business in town, and returned to Longparish on June 23.

June 28th.—M. and Madame Bertini came to us to study the harp and piano with Mrs. Hawker and myself.

July 10th.—In about an hour I killed with a fly before the house three large baskets of trout, which averaged $1\frac{1}{4}$ lb. each fish.

N.B.—As the whole fishery which goes through our premises was purchased by me of Mr. Widmore previous to this season, I never made a regular day's fishing, but merely went angling for a few hours before dinner, and seldom failed to kill a large dish of trout whenever we wanted them. I therefore have this year kept no account, though, were I to include nets and all, I should perhaps have to note down about a ton weight of trout, &c.; this is about the half of what the previous occupier took in a season by dragging.

CHAPTER XI

1818

September 1st.—Longparish. Our country has been entirely clear of corn for nearly a fortnight, and never do we remember having been so long without rain; not a turnip to be seen; everything completely burnt up, and the fields as bare as in December, with the ground as hard as rocks.

Started about nine o'clock (a very stormy day, and the birds as wild as hawks), and bagged 30 partridges (besides a leash shot and lost), 3 hares, and 1 snipe, all to poor old Nero, who behaved most admirably. The scent, however, was so bad, that I owe a great deal to having markers. It was impossible to make any succession of shots, for I had to fire at random three times at least to every bird that I could get within fair distance.

17th.—1 wild duck, by moonlight, a little before midnight.

Game &c. killed to September 30: 112 partridges, 7 hares, 1 rabbit, 2 landrails, 10 snipes, 14 ducks and mallards. Total, 146 head.

Birds scarcer and wilder than ever, and my sport has been more than that of all the people round the country put together, though I had no dog to shoot to that was of the smallest assistance to me but poor old invaluable Nero.

October 1st.—The pheasants here being nearly extinct, I started this morning before four o'clock, and threw off in the great woods round Cold Henley, where the whole day I never saw but 4 pheasants. I bagged 2 pheasants at very long distances, and both snap shots in the high covert, 1 hare, and 1 partridge. Shot also 3 more partridges, and, most extraordinary, lost them all, owing to their falling in high covert while it poured with rain. Mr. Vercellini killed 1 pheasant and the only one that escaped the bag was one that was travelling by as we passed a road. We drove home ducked and drenched to the skin, and had the satisfaction to learn no one had bagged a head of game but ourselves.

2nd.—Went fly fishing, and in a little more than half an hour killed 5 brace of the finest trout I had seen this year, highly in season, averaging 1½ lb. each, and the largest of them weighed 2 lb.; besides this, I threw in several more that were small.

18th.—Drove Mr. Sola (who came to us yesterday morning) in the tandem to Winchester.

N.B.—I left the parlour at twenty minutes before three, and was in it again before the clock struck five, having trotted the tandem to Winchester and back in two hours and twenty minutes, including nearly a quarter of an hour that I stopped there, and I never had occasion to use my whip the whole way, except once to punish the leader for vice.

20th.—Went to London to study music, &c.

November 28th.—Returned to Longparish.

December 26th.—Tom Fowler, my sailor, arrived from his mission to survey the wild-fowl shooting at St.-Valery, on the coast of France, of which place he gave an excellent account; and on the 28th he went off to survey Keyhaven.

31st.—Received my new stanchion gun, a first-rate high-finished piece, of, as near as possible, 1 cwt., from Mr. D. Egg, made on my own plan.

1819

January 6th.—Went down to my cottage at Keyhaven, having previously sent on my new stanchion gun &c. in order to take the opportunity of trying it.

15*th.*—At last I discharged my gun, a long shot at some coots, two of which I got with the dog, but the cripples I dare not follow, as it blew too fresh on the tide. Nothing but a pour of rain, hurricanes, thunder, and lightning, ever since our arrival at Keyhaven, and although I 'weathered it' for the whole of several nights, I have, as yet, scarcely heard a wigeon, and not one to be seen in Lymington market for some weeks.

18*th.*—A wigeon at morning flight. The first that has been killed here for some weeks.

19*th.*—Tried my stanchion gun at two flying shots, in each of which the birds were about 30 yards high, and at least 200 distant, and knocked down 2 geese with the second shot.

21*st.*—Went to morning flight, the only chance; got one shot, knocked down 3 wigeon, and lost them all in the sea, which ran mountains high.

22*nd.*—The rainy weather still continuing, I despaired of getting fowl, so attacked the coots with my large gun; they were, however, so wild that I could only get 2 very long random shots, the first of which stopped 5 and the second 11.

30*th.*—Sent away my piano which I hired, and began to prepare for leaving Keyhaven, as the scarcity and wildness of the birds, together with the wildness and almost incessant wetness of the weather, made it impossible for me or anyone else to get sport. With the coots, however, such things as they are, I had, most days, excellent diversion, by banging into them with the stanchion gun at about 100 yards, and, after setting ten or a dozen at a time sprawling on the mud, I amused myself by chasing the cripples with two Newfoundland dogs and a double gun. Save these, and a few wigeon that I shot in the windy weather, and dare not face the sea for, I had no sport or pleasure here of any description whatever. Even my sport with the coots was, at first, annihilated by fellows called 'head gunners,' who come up from eight miles off, and bully all the poor fellows here from getting a shot.

These fellows I soon made sick of coming, by hiring sailors with blank cartridges to drive them out of the harbour, and if they offered to shoot at them, to return the attack by coming to close quarters.

31st.—No sooner had we prepared for starting for Longparish than a little frost came.

February 1st.—Was induced to stay here for a day or two longer, in hopes a little white frost, which was pretty hard last night, might give me the chance of a shot this evening.

Towards night, we started with every prospect of a shot, and before the time of tide arrived, the wind shifted into its old eternal and infernal quarter, and we had to pull back against tide in a drenching pour of rain.

3rd.—Fired the great gun into the geese, with small balls, at about 300 yards flying; bagged 1 brent goose, and 2 more dropped out of the flock on the tide. At night fired a broadside into the coots, and beat down a dozen of them.

4th.—Left Keyhaven, and arrived at Longparish House.

March 9th.—Tried my largest shoulder duck gun with a detonating lock on the new plan; and with this gun, which weighs 17½ lb., I killed 2 snipes, 2 jack snipes, 1 rook, 1 moorhen, 1 dabchick, 1 fieldfare, 1 water-wagtail, and 1 pigeon, all flying, never missed but once, and then I broke the legs of one of these jack snipes, which I bagged the next shot.

List of game &c. killed in the season, to March 1819: 125 partridges, 3 pheasants (all I shot at, and, except one, all I saw the whole season), 2 landrails, 11 hares, 3 rabbits, 89 snipes, 16 ducks, 1 wigeon (but killed several more that were either lost or not bagged by myself), 1 brent goose, 2 teal. Total, 253 head.

I was in London during the best part of this shooting season, and the only good sport I had on the coast was with the coots, of which I kept no account.

18th.—After killing a wood pigeon out of a flock, I knocked down an immense goshawk, which I killed by means of lying down in the young wood over which he had been hovering for several evenings.

24th.—Lord Poulett (who came to us yesterday) and I went fishing, and, in about three hours, killed 12 brace of large trout between us, besides catching a great many that we threw in again.

25th.—12 trout.

26th.—12 trout.

27th.—12 trout in about two hours, averaging 1½ lb. each. I this day, instead of fly fishing, trolled with a minnow, to try Parson Hutchins's new 'poaching hook,' which beggars every other tackle in existence.

29th.—Lord Poulett left us. Killed 12 trout.

April 26th.—Left Longparish to spend a week with Mr. and Mrs. Chambers, in Stratford Place, London, on our way for France.

May 3rd.—Left the 'White Bear,' Piccadilly, at half-past seven this morning, and arrived at the 'London Hotel,' Dover, about half-past six; after getting an excellent dinner with a very moderate charge at the 'King's Head,' Canterbury, and, previously to going to bed, exchanged some bank notes for napoleons with Mr. Moses, who, although a Jew, is a very fair, honest-dealing man.

4th.—Embarked in the 'Lark' packet; and, after being tossed without victuals, from morning till night, among a mass of vomiting cockneys, was forced to return to Dover and pass a second night among the myriads of sharpers by whom you are every instant imposed on at that place.

5th.—Reached Calais, till my going to bed in which place I never ceased having to distribute money for one fellow or other. Put up at the Hôtel Dessein (M. Quillac), which is first-rate, clean, and superbly furnished.

6th.—Left Calais, per diligence, at ten A.M., and reached Abbeville, 70 miles, about a quarter before twelve at night. Went to the Hôtel de l'Europe, a most capital house.

7th.—Took General Hawker by surprise, having entered his room while he was drawing, and tapped him on the shoulder; he was petrified with astonishment. Inspected the church, the outside of which is magnificent.

8th.—Went with the General in a cabriolet (a machine only fit for firewood) to Bouvancourt, a little hamlet on the banks of a stream under the great forest, about 20 miles from Abbeville. Here I was led to expect most extraordinary fly fishing; but a dead calm, with a burning sun from morning till night, so ruined our chances of sport that I only killed 5 brace of small trout, and the General never hooked a single fish. Had the weather been even tolerable, we might have done very well; but, after all, the fishing at this celebrated place appears far inferior to that of Longparish.

9th.—Went with the General to inspect St.-Valery, 4 leagues from Abbeville, at the mouth of the Somme.

10th.—Hired a coach and three horses, for 5 napoleons, to take us to Paris. Were driven 6 leagues to breakfast, at a small public-house, where we only stopped half an hour. Proceeded 7 leagues farther to Granvilliers, where we dined and put the horses up to be fed &c. for scarcely more than an hour; and, at night, reached Beauvais, thus making up 56 miles with only taking the horses once from the coach. And these horses, which had performed what would have half killed many English ones, were three poor miserable-looking animals apparently worth about 12*l.* apiece. Previously to going to bed we visited the magnificent church of Beauvais, which we were prevented from doing when last in France.

11th.—Left Beauvais at half-past four this morning, and with the same horses &c. continued our journey, and at about six in the evening arrived at Paris to dinner.

N.B.—When we were in this country some time ago (while Boney was in Elba) everything was considerably cheaper than in England, even on the great roads, where imposition is always practised on strangers. But now, since the English have been in the habit of frequenting this part of the world, the charges are become so exorbitant that the travelling is scarcely to be endured; your hand nowadays in France is never out of your pocket, and you are, at almost every place, obliged to have a complete battle with the *aubergiste* to resist being literally cheated. We several times had charges in our bills so exorbitant as to provoke our remonstrance, on the making of which the people of the inn pretended that such charges were 'mistakes,' and had even the duplicity to assume an air of anger 'that the persons who were deputed to write the bill should have been so stupid.' The various attempts that were made to impose on us in the most shameful manner are too numerous, and too much beneath my notice, to be worth keeping a memorandum of; suffice it to say that from the instant you enter Dover till you have got safely clear of your hotel in Paris, you have to guard against one incessant attack of the grossest imposition. A hotel in Paris (up God knows how many flights of stairs) was always a misery; but now it is become so bad, that Newgate is a paradise when compared to it. The charge to us for being consigned to this misery for one short night is 15 francs, exclusive of everything except the beds on which we are to sleep, as well as damp sheets, filth, noise, and a concatenation of stinks will admit of.

On our way to the precious town of Paris we were diverted with the attempts that are now made to drive four in hand in the diligence. An idea of the French coachmanship may be sufficiently formed when I observe that they have literally no reins at all for the wheel horses; and that some of the diligences in this state were driven curricle fashion by a baboon-looking fellow, seated almost on the pole and with two wheels only; twelve persons inside and four outside were driven full gallop down the steepest hills, and among crowds of carriages and waggons. Nothing but the extreme docility of the French horses could save the occurrence of incessant accidents, which, to my utter astonishment, are here less frequent than in England.

13*th.*—Engaged (for a month at 200 francs) and entered a furnished lodging at No. 15 Rue de Provence. During our stay I took lessons of Mr. A. Bertini on the piano.

June 7th.—Having seen everything in Paris worth looking at, which I had not seen four years ago when there in the winter, such as Tivoli, some of the minor theatres, the *combats des animaux*,[1] the environs &c., I took the 'Malle Royale,' and started from Paris this evening at a quarter past four, and arrived at the Hôtel d'Angleterre, in Abbeville, at half-past eleven on the morning of the 8th. The conveyance by this coach is decidedly the pleasantest and most respectable in France; and, for comfort and accommodation, greatly superior to even the stage coaches in England. The price no more than that of the diligence, and with the tenfold advantage of pursuing your journey and sleeping in a clean vehicle, instead of stopping to go to a damp bed in a filthy French inn.

I had intended to proceed from Paris to Milan, by way of Geneva, for which place my passport now stands good, but the intolerable stink, filth, and extravagance of that putrid furnace, Paris, in the summer, so injured my health, and lowered my stock of cash, that I found it necessary to fall back on Abbeville,[2] which is a cheap and healthy place, and where I could enjoy tolerable sport, and Mrs. Hawker

[1] Here I went out of curiosity, and with an idea of disgust; but the hunting of the wild boar, stag, deer, wolf &c. and the baiting of the bull and the bear were the best amphitheatrical exhibitions I ever saw; and without exception I never met with anything so well calculated to raise convulsions of laughter as the hunting the jackass with about a dozen dogs and with a monkey on his back. The ass has so much the advantage that if there be cruelty in the sport it is decidedly against the dogs. But the fun the most ridiculous is the incessant screams of the affrighted monkey, who, although the greatest coward when mounted, is obliged to keep his seat through fear of being thrown among the dogs.

[2] The people in and round Abbeville are worth all the rest of the nation put together; they are civil, loyal, reasonable, and have no particular dislike to the English, rather the reverse.

could be near her father, add to which the heat of the weather made it prudent for us to withhold going to Milan. We have now, for the present, got into a tolerably good inn, which is cheap and a model of cleanliness after the indescribable filth of Paris.

9th.—Hired a rotten chariot and rotten harness, and after breaking down twice with each, arrived at Noyelle-sur-Mer, 8 leagues, and inspected the right bank of the Somme from that place to St.-Crotoi, attended by the chief gunners of the place, and directed by the mayor, Monsieur Meurice de Campy. A man named Frizez showed me all the gunning huts and straw decoy birds used on this coast, but their wild-fowl shooting is a perfect farce, they know nothing about it.

On our way back we stopped at 'Port,' where one Picarde, the 'innkeeper,' the landlord of a little *cabaret*, knew more than all the others put together. We crossed the Somme in his boat, about two leagues from Abbeville, and after gaining every information relative to the winter's *chasse*, returned to Abbeville just in time to save having the barriers shut against us, about half-past nine o'clock.

12th.—Hired the *berline* and three horses of Dalgrange, the man who drove us so well to Paris, and started this morning for Dieppe, I finding it necessary to go to England, and preferring to be there now, instead of at a time when I could perhaps have the wild-fowl shooting on the Somme. I accordingly left my servant and what sporting things I had with General Hawker, in the hope of being able to return in September. We took an early dinner at La Ville d'Eu, a little beyond halfway to Dieppe, where we inspected a fine church that was built by the English, amused ourselves on the organ, went all over the château of the Duchesse d'Orléans, which is close to the church, and then proceeded to Dieppe, where we arrived by five o'clock, and had the whole evening to inspect the town, &c.

The drivers call it fifteen leagues from Abbeville to

Dieppe, but the distance is, as near as possible, 39 English miles.

The road from Abbeville to Dieppe is most capital, and the inns here, not having been used by the English, are by no means expensive.

13*th.*—Embarked on board the 'Lord Wellington' packet, one of the finest sailing schooners I ever set eyes on (Captain Cheesman, master) at two o'clock. We were becalmed till near seven, and then it came to blow pretty fresh all night, and all the next morning directly in our teeth; but, notwithstanding, this excellent vessel lay so 'close to the wind,' that she 'fetched' but very little to leeward of her course; and at three o'clock on the afternoon of the 14th we landed,[1] in a gale of wind, after being well drenched by the breakers, and having literally fought with winds and tides all the way from Dieppe. The usual miseries and messes of sickness among our younger travellers were tenfold increased here by our having to lie so close to the wind, and by the length and roughness of the passage; but we were induced to be content, notwithstanding, because on this voyage and journey there are not those attempts at constant imposition as at Dover and Calais, and everything on both sides of the water is more reasonable, and, with a few exceptions, the civility much greater. After getting 'cleared off' at the custom house, where the duty is done in the most gentlemanly manner, and dining at the 'New Ship' inn, we took a chaise for Chichester at seven, and got there, to sleep, at eleven.

15*th.*—Left Chichester at half-past eight this morning, arrived safely at Longparish House just in time to sit down to dinner, and, thank God, found all well.

24*th.*—24 trout.

The fishing is now become very dull, owing to the trout being glutted with the mayfly.

[1] At Brighton, to which place the passage direct is 75 English miles; but the log generally runs to about 80.

July 1*st.*—Having received my new stanchion gun (after having it sent to Mr. Egg again, to be highly finished, after a winter's trial and approval of it in the rough state), I this day tried it again, at boards covered with paper, in the river. After thus trying it in the canoe, I then took the artillery carriage and mounted it on land, where I fired: 1st shot at a few straggling pigeons, and killed 1 at 120 yards; 2nd, at 12 swallows on a tree, and killed 8 of them; 3rd, at single swallows flying, and killed 2 out of 3, so nicely have I brought this machine to bear, though 88½ lb. in weight.

10*th.*—Paid the bill for my stanchion gun, as follows:

	£	*s.*	*d.*
Gun	115	10	0
Cases	6	6	0
2 ramrods	1	11	6
2 wadding punches	0	12	6
Shot pouch to fit gun	0	15	6
Carriage and packing	1	3	0
	£125	18	6

August 1*st.*—Mr. and Mrs. Logier with Mr. Donaldson and two of the pupils came to us this day, preparative to the exhibition of Messrs. Langstaff and D'Aubertin's academies, on the Logerian system of musical education, at Andover and Southampton. On the 3rd we drove to Andover, and on the 4th took a chariot and four freighted with young ladies to Southampton, at both of which places the public examinations went off admirably well.

CHAPTER XII

1819

September 1*st.*—I have now to record one of the most brilliant day's shooting I ever made in my life, when I consider the many disadvantages I had to encounter. I had but three dogs: poor old Nero, who was lame when he started; Red Hector, who was so fat and out of wind that he would scarcely hunt; and young Blucher, a puppy that never was in a field but three times before, and who till this day had never seen a shot fired. The country had been for some time clear of all corn, and the stubbles in general afforded but thin cover. The scent was so infamously bad, that at least two-thirds of the birds I killed were sprung without the dogs finding them. The wind blew quite fresh the whole day, and the coveys were wilder than ever I yet saw them in the first part of the season; and, what was unusual, in windy weather, I could scarcely get a bird into the hedges. I had four shooting parties round me, and the best half of my ground was beaten before I took the field, which I never do till after eight o'clock, because I have found, by experience, that dew is death to the dogs, and that a covey, if disturbed on the feed, is much more difficult to disperse than when left till the dew is off the ground. My list of killed and wounded was fairly and precisely as follows:

Misses: 4 very long shots, 2 of which were struck and feathered.

Kills: 45 partridges and 1 hare, bagged.

The constant succession of long shots that my favourite old Joe Manton barrels continued bringing down, surpassed anything I had before done, or seen, in my whole career of shooting.

3rd.—26 partridges and 1 hare.

4th.—Went out after dinner, and in three hours bagged 14 partridges, all I fired at. I made one extraordinary shot, viz.: a very wild pack (2 coveys) of strong birds got up and came towards me. I killed 2 at a shot with the first barrel, and 4 at a shot with the second, and among them were the 4 old birds.

7th.—Having bagged 101 birds in my first four days' shooting, to poor old Nero, who had been incurably lame in the shoulder for these ten months, I would not take him out to-day; and as I had no dog that would stir from my heel besides, I took two men with a rope about thirty yards long, and dragged the ground, being in want of birds, and I bagged 13 partridges, besides shooting 2 more which I lost.

28th.—One shot that I made to-day I cannot account for, except by the shot having adhered together. I blew a bird's head from his body (so that I could never find the head) at seventy-two paces distant.

30th.—Started, agreeably to a pressing invitation, to my friend Jack Ponton, at Upton (22 miles), preparative, as I expected, to taking the first day's pheasant shooting; but he, despairing of my coming, and my letter having reached him a few hours too late, had gone off into Kent; and, not thinking it handsome to shoot in his absence, I returned home again by way of Southampton (28 miles), which I was obliged to do in order to avoid going a vile bad road by night, and I had thus 50 miles to drive bag and baggage for nothing; which, to me, was a less disappointment than if I had missed two fair shots.

Game &c. bagged by September 28th: 204 partridges, 9 hares, 1 rabbit, 4 landrails, 18 snipes, 7 wild ducks. Total, 243 head.

Though the country was barren and the weather almost always stormy, yet (with the exception of a young dog that did more harm than good) I literally killed all to poor old Nero, who was lame from the very first day till now. Including some days in which I was driven home by rain, I only took the field seventeen days during the month of September.

October 1st.—One of the finest mornings I ever saw for covert shooting; but my disappointment in having gone to Upton made it too late for me to accept many other invitations for the first day; and, literally, not having a single pheasant on my whole estate, I was obliged, of course, to give up the idea of getting one, consequently did not go out shooting.

7th.—Heard of a cock pheasant, which nowadays is like a wild beast on my property, and in half an hour came home with 2 fine old cock pheasants, I having found another with the one reported, and bagged them both.

11th.—Was called up this morning with information that my man, who had gone off with my duck punt on wheels, containing all my baggage, for Brighton, I having engaged his passage for France to-morrow night, had met with a severe accident the other side of Winchester. The horse took fright going down Movestead Hill, three miles from the town, ran away, broke the carriage and wheels to pieces, and most severely wounded the man. I had therefore, ill as I was, to drive off, to put several coachmaker's workmen to replace the wreck, get a cart to convey the wounded man to the county hospital, and make arrangements for hiring other horses in order that my sailor and my things might not lose their passage to France.

12th.—Left Longparish for London, on our way to France.

14th.—Submitted to and had accepted by Mr. Chappell my new-invented apparatus for running over the keys of a pianoforte in a mathematically true position.

15th.—Got to Dover.

16th.—Had so good a passage to Calais that we set foot

on both English and French ground within three hours and five minutes. After being, as usual, fleeced by innumerable scoundrels, we proceeded post (the most expensive, yet by far the worst mode of conveyance in France) and stopped for the night at Boulogne. Here, as a matter of course, we had to sit up till one in the morning airing wet sheets by a fire made of green wood.

17*th.*—I was to be called at six this morning; but at near seven no one was up, and I had to alarm the whole house before I could get a soul to move; when, at last, half a dozen fellows ran out, all inquiring what was the matter. In short, after crawling like a road waggon the whole day in a pour of rain, and in a machine that was worse than open, we reached Abbeville, where, to my great mystification, I found that my man, punt, guns &c. had been neither seen nor heard of, though I could see nothing to prevent their arrival five days ago. By way of comfort, too, I learnt that the river was full of wild fowl.

18*th.*—This day, I, in constant anxiety about my man, property, and the whole of my shooting apparatus, on which the winter's pleasure depended, offered a premium to the first beggar (Abbeville swarms with these poor wretches) who should announce the arrival of my flotilla &c., and at four this afternoon, to my great joy, an old woman in wooden shoes came, in as much ecstasy at receiving the money as I was in at finding my things (which it would take years to replace) had arrived, and very narrowly escaped shipwreck, which two other vessels had lately encountered, of which I had heard, and on one of which I had reason to fear all my things were on board. I then proceeded to my little villa at 'Port' on the banks of the Somme, where I was received in procession by the populace of the village, and presented with bouquets, as is the custom for what they call the 'grand seigneur' in this country.

19*th.*—After arranging all my things &c. I went to survey the water, and although it was so hot that the air swarmed with butterflies, yet the wigeon, teal, and ducks were by hundreds and thousands on the Somme, but in some degree protected by the dreadfully dangerous currents that now run like a mill tail in spring tides all over this place; and in the evening[1] I went out for fowl (the birds, it appears, are only here by day till hard weather), but not a fowl remained in the river, for all the ducks &c. had dispersed to feed inland. I shot at some birds in the dark and stopped 9 or 10, and on sending out the dog he brought me 4 large curlews. I am delighted with my house and everything about the place, except the trouble of having always to guard against thieves.

20th.—A gale of wind from the south, and the Somme so frightfully dangerous with the spring tides that going out was impossible, and the birds were some leagues off on the opposite shore.

25th.—Mrs. Hawker and L—— this day started from Abbeville for Paris. From the 20th to this day no one could be more unpleasantly situated than I have been. Poor L——, was so ill that I expected every night he would breathe his last, and here was I, for five whole days, pacing the room with that anxiety of mind that I could enjoy, or apply to, nothing; while an incessant deluge of rain, with howling winds, was without intermission rattling against the windows of our cottage. The bad weather still continued, but, thank God, L—— was a little better, and therefore prudently struggled into a change of air, as the best possible remedy for his extreme illness. The Somme continued frightfully dangerous, and of this river some idea may be formed if I remark that when in calm weather you put your punt pole in the water, it is wrenched from your hand as if thrust into the wheel of a carriage when drawn full

[1] I never like to disturb fowl by day lest they should forsake the place; but here I suspect I shall be obliged to do so, as the river is dangerous and the fowl leave it to feed in peace and comfort.

gallop. Only at very few periods, therefore, dare we venture afloat.

26th.—After walking out with a French chasseur, and killing for him 1 snipe, 3 jack snipes, some water rails &c. I this night went off in a ship's boat belonging to a merchant. We were obliged to put into Crotoi very late at night, and then sleep in our clothes on some miserable straw and on a miserable floor, which would have been all delightful if we could have had sport; but owing to this gentleman, contrary to my advice, not taking my punt in tow, we could get at nothing to shoot, and, instead of having good sport the following day, we were imprisoned till the evening tide for want of water, while the weather and the birds were quite in favour of good sport with a proper outfit. The excursion ended, as I said it must, in getting little or nothing; and we were out six-and-twenty hours all to no purpose. We got home to 'Port' on the night of the 27th.

29th.—Being very uneasy about L——, I was resolved to follow him to Paris; and after going to Abbeville, and there waiting till two this morning, I entered a vehicle called the 'Swallow,' a hideous machine that carries tons of luggage and stows sixteen people like a freight of hogs, and goes on two wheels, in which, after being tortured worse than if in the stocks, I was dragged into Paris at ten on the night of the 30th, when, I thank God, I found L—— much recovered. I then, the next day, presented my pianoforte hand-moulds to Messrs. Ignace & Camille Pleyel, which they approved and accepted for their manufactory.

November 2nd.—L—— was taken very ill again.

6th.—We have once before taken, paid for, and forfeited the whole of the mail to Boulogne, and we even now again desired to suffer the same loss to-day; but poor L——, ill as he lay, was so crazy to escape the chance of dying in this detestable country, that he would insist on our all leaving Paris this evening, and, by the mercy of God, we brought him to Abbeville, where we arrived about midday on the 7th, but such was his disgust at the smoky stye of starvation into which we were ushered that he implored us to let him be dragged on till he should either die or reach home in time to recover; and, what distracted me, he would not permit me to accompany him, and I had even to use persuasion to make him take a servant. Mrs. Hawker and I then left Abbeville and proceeded, just before dusk, in tears of anxiety and in torture of conveyance, to 'Port,' while the rain poured down ready to break the vile tumbeil in which we were dragged; here we remained in a state of agitation enough to destroy the nerves of a Hercules or to melt the heart of a savage, while praying to God that L—— may, by the extraordinary interference of Providence, be able to reach home in time to recover.

9th.—Went over to Abbeville, with my clothes and some money, determined to follow L—— if I heard nothing further to my satisfaction. On reaching the town I met my servant Charles, whom he had sent back, L—— having got rather better and embarked last evening on board the Dover packet; consequently I returned to 'Port' trusting to God that he would reach home in safety.

N.B.—Yesterday and to-day there were such chances for sport as I may not have again, without hard weather; the ducks and teal were close to 'Port,' but I was so uneasy about L—— that I could not have the heart to load my gun or launch my punt, and felt indifferent to everything but tidings from him.

15th.—After waiting for six days in such a miserable state of suspense about L——, that I was almost distracted, I this day had the consolation to receive a letter from him, dated the 10th inst., saying that he was rather better, and purposed starting from London for home the next day. My mind being now at ease in some degree, trusting to God that L—— was at home and in comfort, I could have wished to take out my gun and boat, but, as ill luck would have it, my sailor was taken ill, and consequently I was still prevented from trying my sport.

17th.—Being half dead from anxiety and want of amusement, I this day crossed the Somme, and rode down to St.-Valery.

18th.—I rode over to Rue, where I inspected the beautiful ruins of a small church, and afterwards walked in the marshes, and killed 6 snipes, 6 jack snipes, and 1 teal, all I fired at. What with family sufferings, added to innumerable little grievances of a minor consideration, we never in our lives were so unlucky; but God send us a turn of fortune and a little comfort, after all we have endured in this abominable country. On the evening of the 19th we received a letter from L—— announcing his safe arrival at Longparish, and his amendment of health, as well as good accounts from our dear children, which gave us more ease of mind than we have for a long time experienced.

22nd.—Mrs. Hawker taken very seriously ill, and as the dirty scoundrel of whom I had hired a horse had just been here and taken him away, because I had then settled with him, and some one else had offered him a few pence more, I was obliged (late enough for the various gates to be open) to tramp through six miles of filthy mud on foot, and then hunt the town of Abbeville for the doctor. Luckily my old friend Dr. Radford (once of my regiment) was a practitioner there, otherwise God alone could have helped us. Not a horse to be got to-day in all Abbeville, and while Mrs. Hawker was suffering dreadfully for want of port wine and assistance, the doctor and I had to tramp through the mud on foot.

23rd.—Mrs. Hawker being still extremely unwell, I wished to get a little bird of some kind for her dinner; and after going a league, to Noilette, and there slaving in the marshes till my heels bled, I got one shot, and killed 1 snipe; a pretty specimen of the fine shooting in France!

25th.—While I was out to-day, Mrs. Hawker became so

dangerously ill that the servants were in the greatest alarm, thinking she could not live till I got home. Happily, however, she got better again by the evening; and we had also further satisfaction, viz. a letter from L—— saying he was so much recovered as to be able to walk, and that my dear children and all our friends at home were well.

26th.—Finding it prudent that Mrs. Hawker, who still was very ill, having again had a severe relapse, should leave 'Port,' I this day hired a coach, and removed her to the Hôtel de l'Europe, in Abbeville, for change of air.

27th.—Was taken very ill myself, but, with the assistance of Dr. Radford, I got much better by the morning of the 28th, when Mrs. Hawker and I hired the coach again, and drove to St.-Valery for an airing; and after I got back to Abbeville, I left Mrs. Hawker there, and returned once more to 'Port,' where all my shooting things were left in confusion. Charles, too, having been attacked a few days ago, and I yesterday, our whole family, dogs, cat and all (the cat died, and three of our family were in imminent danger), have been ill; and on inquiry we find that the country we are in, notwithstanding its healthy appearance, is in one of the most pestilential climates of France. Never since I was born have I been so fleeced of my money, and so bereft of all my comforts and happiness.

29th.—Still very unwell. I this day left 'Port' for the Hôtel de l'Europe at Abbeville, to escape the infernal contagion that was rapidly spreading throughout this filthy village.

30th.—Mrs. Hawker and I were both confined to our room, which, although one of the best in the very first hotel in France, is colder and more full of draughts than any English barn, a pretty situation for me with a dose of calomel in my inside; and during our illness we had to battle against the most villanous attempts at imposition relative to the disposal of our property, and settling for the occupation of the unlucky hovel at 'Port' to which we had most unfortunately transported ourselves for shooting.

December 1st.—Having found myself extremely unwell all yesterday with a kind of shivering sensation and burning heats, which the French in Abbeville consider as their prevalent disease all round there, and call 'the fever,' I thought it madness to remain any longer in their vile department, and finding myself infinitely better last night, I decided on quitting this place for Boulogne ; but, hearing that Péronne was a place better suited to me than any I could find, and being most anxious at all events to avoid repeatedly travelling the same road, I changed my route, and at six this morning drove off with a *voiturin* for the latter place, which is about sixty English miles from Abbeville, and which lies on the road from Paris to Brussels. We breakfasted at a village called Flixecourt, and were particularly well served for France. This place is halfway to Amiens. In order to arrive early at Péronne, we could only stop to bait at Amiens, and proceed four leagues beyond there to dine and sleep. We were told that at Vilaire we could be tolerably accommodated. The road after leaving Amiens became so vilely bad and in so miserable a wilderness that we could scarcely go a league an hour, and we reached Vilaire about six o'clock. I had then become so ill and exhausted I was determined to get to bed, and on the comforts I should receive depended whether the change of air should rid me of the illness, or whether I should get worse for want of the necessaries of life ; but miserable, most miserable, was the vile hornet's nest into which we were ushered, and here I met the greatest scoundrel that I ever before encountered. I was thrown, trembling with cold, on a miserable dirty bed, while laughed at and insulted the whole night by a set of waggoners and assassin-looking fellows who called themselves officers, but who were dressed *à la bourgeois* ; one in particular tried to pick a quarrel with me, and while eyeing me as I lay on the bed, put his hand on his sword, and looked at me with a most malicious grin, while the others kept laughing and quizzing. I left the bed, and lay for a time in the carriage, but was there so cold that I was forced to return to this damnable situation. Mrs. Hawker and her maid sat all the time (too frightened to sleep) in this *berline*. We would have given twenty guineas to have gone on, but our horses were dead tired, and the coachman was fearful of passing through the forest at night, as he could only go two miles an hour on the heavy road, and he said that, rare as it was in France, yet he suspected there were some *mauvais gens* (bad people) in the forest. This I did not mind, so as soon as the horses could slowly proceed we put them to, and called for the bill, which ought not to have exceeded ten sous, because all that we had, or could have, was literally one cup of bread and milk. The daughters of the house told me that for the bread and milk and for lying down I must pay ten francs, and at last they said they would take eight. I of course refused, and this alarmed the house; the father locked his doors on me, and swore I should not move till I had paid ten francs. I had, therefore, to unpack my trunk among all these villains to get more money, and let him take his demand. I then, ready to die, had to search for the mayor, but at last found a gendarme; and in short I could get no redress, because unless you make a bargain with a Frenchman he may charge you as he pleases. This was about two o'clock in the morning. We at six reached the village of Foufoucourt, where, at the sign of the 'Violin,' we met some very civil peasants, who kept this cabaret, and who gave us a very nice breakfast for fivepence each, and to whom I gave double for their honesty; at half-past ten we reached Péronne, and got such good beds at the 'Stag' inn that on the morning of the 3rd I was tolerably well. About twelve o'clock I wrapped myself up and went to inspect the lakes, but more like an old woman than a gunner, as I was stuck up in a chair instead of being seated down on straw, and equipped with an umbrella instead of a gun. The lakes of Péronne are certainly more calculated for a lover of comfort to shoot at his ease than any place I ever saw; the water is almost stagnant, and in every part about four or five feet deep, surrounded and intersected by innumerable islands and walls of rushes; the places to keep your boat are all at the back of little cottages, and therefore under private protection; and as for safety, I never saw a place more secure from dangers, even if it blew a hurricane, or came on the thickest fog; certainly, therefore, the place itself is well calculated for my shooting, but unfortunately it happens to be rented in lots by about fifty watermen, who get their livelihood by the few wild fowl they kill, and who have innumerable shooting huts all over the lakes, so that if I went afloat I should have to pass the muzzles of perhaps a dozen guns every quarter of a mile, and if I spoiled the sport of these fellows, which I should in all probability do most effectually, I should stand a chance of getting *accidentally* wounded by some jealous fellow or other. The man who escorted me was one of the chief proprietors, and his huts were the very best I ever saw; they were made, as the French huts usually are, ten times warmer than their houses, but much better concealed, and more commodious than any I had seen before. The hut (*la hutte*) is precisely like a tilted waggon inside, viz. hooped and covered; at the back of it there is a hole to creep in at, and in front are from two to four loopholes to fire through. In this country they use 12 tame ducks for decoy birds, 4 drakes in the centre and 4 ducks at each side, tied in lines to pegs at about fifteen yards distance from their masked popgunnery (I will not say battery); but in other countries the French *huttiers* (hut shooters) generally use but 3 decoy ducks, 1 male and 2 females, and place them not more than seven or eight yards from the muzzles of their miserable guns. The quantity of fowl here is nothing equal to that in the English fens, and by day you seldom see a duck, although the French coast is more plentifully supplied with wild fowl than the coast of England.

By means of swallowing plenty of Madeira and tincture

Designed & Painted by P. Hawker — Eng.d on Steel by H. Adlard.

HUT SHOOTING ON THE FRENCH SYSTEM.

London, Published by Longman & Co.

of bark I contrived to quack myself sufficiently to try for the ducks this evening; and accordingly was conducted by Monsieur Desabes (a very civil and obliging man, the proprietor of the huts I saw to-day) to his best entrenchment, where he had twelve decoy ducks all in battle array, under the light of a most beautiful moon, and within the quarter of an English gunshot of a hut that was uncomfortably warm. Here I remained, more likely to be suffocated than chilled, with the patience of Job for goodness knows how many hours, but not a wild duck ever came, though the decoy birds kept chattering like the other bipeds of the French nation; and although the place, for a league, was resounding with the quacking of tame ducks in strings, and defended by the masters of them, yet I could not have the honour to say I had seen or heard the firing of a single shot.

4*th.*—Being anxious to lose no more time at Péronne I agreed with a fellow to take me across to Arras, where I could find conveyances to any part of the north-eastern coast. He was to bring a commodious voiture, and arrived by half-past ten at the door, in order that we might reach Arras before the barrier gates would be shut, which would be at six in the evening. The fellow never came till near twelve, and then he hurried us into the most abominable two-wheeled machine that ever I saw even in France, and in which we were literally crushed by each other and our baggage; he then shut the front part with the rudeness of a bear, and accidentally struck Mrs. Hawker, when she fell into hysterics, fainted away, and was carried back to the inn and put to bed. I had then of course to unload again, to get at the medicines necessary for her, but the scoundrel would not let me have any of my baggage till I paid him the whole fare to Arras, the same as if I had gone; nor did he even offer to change the day, though I voluntarily offered him a crown to get rid of him. Instead of being able to assist Mrs. Hawker, therefore, I was obliged to leave her with the maid, while I took the villain before a justice of peace. Here he told a thousand lies as fast as he could chatter; but fortunately I met with a respectable gentleman, who, to the villain's dire mortification, awarded that I should pay 5 francs and the 4 francs duty for the posting, and be set at liberty with my baggage. I remained the rest of the day a prisoner in this town, with Mrs. Hawker of course very unwell.

5th.—We were obliged to get up an hour before daybreak in order to reach Arras (only 30 miles) before six o'clock in the evening, when the barriers are shut. We got under way about seven in a thing called a voiture, which was near tumbling to pieces and full of cobwebs, and driven by the master of it, who was the most lazy, sulky, stupid hound I ever saw. He did nothing but smoke and stuff himself the whole way, and when I begged of him to go in the light road instead of the heavy, he literally said that he preferred walking his horses through the mud, because there was 'a track, and he could enjoy his pipe and his victuals without the trouble of holding his reins;' and the villain being the only coachmaster in the place, except the scoundrel who tried to swindle us yesterday, I was forced to pay him 36 francs. We entered the barrier of Arras just in time to escape being shut out for the night, having gone 30 miles in eleven hours.

6th.—After having been well and reasonably served at the Hôtel de Messagerie in Arras, we at six o'clock this morning proceeded by the diligence for St.-Omer, and arrived there at seven in the evening, which, although but 50 miles in thirteen hours, was comparative flying after the torments of crawling that we had to endure yesterday. After we got clear of Péronne, and got into what is commonly called the Netherlands, we found ourselves less imposed upon in the bills, and more free from filth and humbug.

7th.—Proceeded at eight this morning by the relay diligence, and at three reached Calais, 30 miles. We here found out a place called the Brussels Hotel, where at last we found some comfort, as nought but an English person or an English thing was in the house. We therefore decided on remaining a few days, on a kind of forlorn hope that a little sport might be found before I decided on ordering my men home again with the shooting apparatus and heavy baggage.

8th.—Went in every direction to survey the environs of Calais, with one of the hardest frosts that ever was remembered here. The shore being one flat sand (as it is all the way to the Netherlands on the one side, and to Boulogne on the other) was quite out of the question for shooting otherwise than at flight time, and particularly as the birds do not rest there at night. Their feeding places are in the marshes, which at this moment are in one region of ice. The few birds that are now killed here are shot by the 'hutters,' who break an open place in the frozen ponds, and there keep their decoy birds, to which the wild ones are called down from about three till eight in the morning. I remained a long time in a hut this night, but not a bird ever came, and I never fired a shot the whole day, except killing 1 jack snipe while reconnoitring in the morning, when I counted about 35 shooters out besides myself.

9th.—Hired a cabriolet and went to Guines (6 miles inland from Calais), where in like manner I found the whole country frozen, and where in a space of a mile the boy who conducted me said there were about 180 huts belonging to the night shooters, who among them all had killed but 2 ducks the whole of last night. The moment I got home and swallowed a hasty dinner, I drove off for the flight 3 miles from here, and never saw or heard but 3 birds.

10th.—Mrs. Hawker and I were laid up with illness, evidently owing to the everlasting thorough draughts we sit in, and the want of good nourishing food during this unprecedentedly severe weather. The snow is now two feet deep in the streets, and we are dying to get to our own country, but not a packet has been able to reach the harbour here for these ten days. Here we are again in sickness, misery, and expense; for all the comforts of English things will not stop the thorough draughts that for ever blow through every creek and corner of a French house. God send us and our property once more in safety on the other side of the Channel.

This afternoon I was so ill that I was every moment near fainting from pain. Here am I laid on the bed, with the very frost and snow that I had been longing and watching after for these six years, in a place where not a warm corner is to be found, without medical assistance, and with a gale of wind directly foul for my emancipation from France; and, to vex me still more, I have an invitation from an English gentleman—Mr. Penton—to partake of his *hutte* and rented decoy to-morrow morning, where the flight is expected to be something very extraordinary. Mrs. Hawker, too, still very unwell; again and again do we pray that we could even be removed to the very worst house on the other side of the Channel.

11*th.*—Mrs. Hawker was taken so ill that we were forced to refuse our passage in the packet with a very fine wind, and poor I was in such pain as scarcely to be able to support myself. The hopes of a recovery to-morrow, and a second chance of a passage, somewhat cheered me up. But alas! what was my vexation to receive a letter from General Hawker to say that if I did not instantly return, through all the snow, to Abbeville, that all my property, guns and boats, was to be sold by auction to-morrow, by order of the police, because Mr. Terrier, the villain, the scoundrel, had entered a process against me 'for leaving his house at "Port" without paying the trifling remainder of the rent,' which I had by his own consent before a witness deputed General Hawker to do, and whose responsibility he accepted, and even shook hands with me on the occasion. I had, therefore, to crawl to the office, and book a place for Abbeville in to-night's mail. May the Lord support me and defend me through such cruel oppression, during my bodily afflictions and the distress I am in about my poor wife.

To add to this undeserved oppression and insult, I am under orders here to be detained from embarking by the police, had I chosen so to do.

At four o'clock Mrs. Hawker was almost lifeless from weakness and agitation about the cruel and unjust process against me, which, by getting the letter while I was seeing to her gruel below, she unfortunately heard of first. Instead of being able to attend her, I was forced to enter the mail at six o'clock, and be dragged through the deep snow at a foot pace to Abbeville. We did not reach Boulogne till near one, and here my poor aching stomach required something warm to relieve me from excruciating pain, for, in truth, I was so distracted that I took no thought about provision. A surly brute of a woman refused to warm me a little water, and I fainted on the earthen floor, at which all were callous and even laughed at me till I had just strength enough to offer a reward for something warm, and then the postillion was all mercy, and by means of procuring some coffee which literally stank, beat up with a stale egg and bad brandy, I was enabled to re-enter the mail. By this time, I had picked up a woman, and then a man, as fellow-travellers, and if ever there were brutes on earth here I met with them. They saw me trembling—ready to die—in the coldest snowy night that ever came from the heavens, and the brutes would have the windows open, and felt amused at my annoyance. I expected every moment to be frost bitten, and had no strength to rub my limbs. However, God protected me through all, and, after being in sheer starvation and torture for twenty hours, I reached Abbeville at two o'clock on the afternoon of the 12th, and got to bed at the Hôtel de l'Europe. I had scarcely got to bed, and found benefit from the medicine that Dr. Radford gave me, when I was obliged to receive my counsel for the trial to-morrow; and, after earnestly having to explain everything in *my* French, I was, of course, in more fever than ever. However, I got a tolerable night, and had sufficient strength to appear in court on the morning of the 13th, when, after the usual anxieties and trouble that attend a trial, I had the fortune to get a verdict in my favour, with double costs &c. The whole of the 14th I was employed in being obliged to face that contagious place 'Port' once more; and, what with taking inventories, battling about broken things, disposing separately of every article I had in store &c. without a soul to assist me, I was driven about like a mad dog, and in such pain that I could hardly draw my breath.

15*th.*—Got up two hours before daylight, and left Abbeville in a *berline*, followed by my punt, servants, and all my rescued property, and travelled over a sheet of ice, with hail, snow, and rain for the whole day. After having occasional stoppages as usual to mend, patch up, and rectify the little accidents that commonly attend French travelling, and repeated falls of the horses on the ice &c. we reached Dieppe at night, where we supped and went to bed.

16*th.*—Embarked my things on board the 'Independence' packet, which was to sail to-night; but at present the terrific state of the lee shore here renders it very improbable we shall start. This afternoon the wind changed directly in our favour, and a most delightful evening it was: we accordingly prepared to sail at night, but, as if the devil always got in the way of all my movements on this most infernal trip to France, the vessel in which my property and baggage had been embarked was seized and detained in consequence of some smuggling transaction of the captain, and in spite of me and others battling like barristers till our mouths were parched with anxiety, and I was fit to burst with rage, we were obliged to return to our hotels, and hope that we might have liberty to be wafted from these most diabolical, detestable shores to-morrow.

17*th.*—A most tremendous hurricane all day, in which, although fair for us, it would be madness to venture out with a lee shore before us at night.

18*th.*—Though the gale was still continuing, and the sea running mountains high, our captain was determined to sail to-night, and in a pour of rain, with the night as dark as pitch, we got under way about eleven o'clock. The case was that our captain had got into a serious scrape, and while he spread a report that he was in England, he was concealed in his ship, and quite mad to be off, through fear of being taken to prison. My friend, Mr. Parrot, too, being so situated that he had difficulty in leaving the country, I had him under the disguise of my servant; and therefore what with having to humbug the police while they boarded us &c. I was in rather a nervous situation till clear of the bar. The sea was so tremendous and the night so awfully dark, that we dare only move under close-reefed sails. The sailors were but a sorry crew, and everything contributed to a rough and most violent passage. The captain miscalculated his distance, and the heavy and thick rain had so obscured the atmosphere that when morning came we were lost for several hours; at last, we found ourselves off Brighton, but not a vessel or boat dare venture from land to us, and therefore we were forced to beat up for Shoreham, where the captain had intended to go at first, but lost his course. We were now in a very serious difficulty, for if too late to have water over the bar into Shoreham harbour, nothing remained for us but to ride upon the billows for twenty-three hours longer, till the next day's tide should serve, at the risk of being wrecked on a lee shore, which we must have been before morning had the gale come on as strong as it regularly has done every night. At last we fetched the harbour, when to our disappointment the flags, which are always flying while there is ten foot of water, were no longer up, and besides a hot tide was running out against us; we had then to choose whether, or not, we would make all sail, and literally charge at the bar, while the pilots, who dare not come to our assistance, were anxiously holloaing and making signals from the pier; at last came the awful moment, when, after being bumped several times with violence against the bar, we forced our way against the surge and sand, and in a few minutes set foot on our own dear English ground again. Everyone said that the chances were five to one against us, and that we must have all perished but for the mercy of God giving us the only spot where we could have forced our vessel through. All was for the best. The wind soon after became tremendous, and the shore was strewed with a wreck that had just taken place. After most extraordinary trouble with our things, owing to the custom house being four miles off, we could not get our clothes &c. to change till seven at night; we landed about two, and we were racing up and down the shingles in a pour of rain about our things, and without a morsel to eat till just before bedtime, when we got to the 'Ship' inn at Brighton.

19th.—Having been so short of money that I was yesterday forced to take tea instead of dinner, and also to book a place outside the coach in very wet weather, I this morning got up to start, and was in great alarm about my friend, who had gone out, and, according to French custom, locked his door. The waiters all declared the street door had not been opened, and as all the noise we raised would not make him answer, the people of the house swore he must have either died or cut his throat, and when the blacksmith was just coming up to pick the lock and enter the room, my friend Mr. Parrot came upstairs, having gone off and let himself out to see the pavilion of Brighton before breakfast. We had just time left to swallow one cup of tea, and went up to town in a pour of rain.

21st.—After another wet journey on the rostrum of the Salisbury coach I once more arrived safe, and, thank God, found all well at Longparish House, after having passed seventy-one of the most unlucky, miserable, and expensive days in France I ever passed in my life, deprived of every comfort, and with the expenditure, in sheer waste, of 335*l.*

The Lord deliver me from such another excursion.

22nd.—My sailor Williams arrived on a horse to say that, after all my things had been ducked in the harbour by the ship's boat capsizing on coming ashore the other day, he was yet again in trouble, as the cart had broken down near Winchester. I had, therefore, to go off and bring home the wreck of my rescued property before another night should elapse without my having it safely housed; and at seven this evening the team drove up with the wreck and the remainder of all my property, and this night, therefore, we got clear of all difficulties attending this most detestable expedition, and I fully hope that here will end all our almost incredible coincidence of misfortunes.

29th.—Till this day I have been too ill, owing to the effects of my abominable trip to France, to get out with my gun. We have now a severe frost, with a moon, and gladly would I be strong enough for the coast at this moment. I killed to-day, just walking out, 3 snipes, 3 jack snipes, and 1 hare, and in the evening 1 wild duck.

N.B.—I had made a French hut, on our river, with six call birds. This was the only duck that I saw or heard, and he pitched down with them directly, so that had we fowl at Longparish this system would no doubt answer here.

1820

January 15th.—The coldest day in the memory of any person I had met with. I got up this morning at three, crawled over a sheet of frozen snow to the turnpike in my cart with lamps, there got into the mail, and then proceeded from Salisbury, by coach, to Poole. The harbour was one solid plain of frozen snow, and the place so cold that my man Williams, the whale fisher, said it was quite equal to Greenland. Never was there here known so severe a frost; the birds were half starved. The gunners could scarcely venture out, and two men were this night frozen to death in their punts. Dead rooks, small birds &c. were lying about in every direction, starved to death.

16*th.*—Having left my things at my old quarters at Southhaven, near Poole, ready to use when a thaw should come, I this day went over to Wareham with my double gun and one duck gun, in order to shoot at Hyde, where Mr. Knight has kindly given me leave to sport in his absence, and where I can walk out, which better suits my very poor state of health, than venturing just yet afloat in the night.

19*th.*—When I got up this morning the whole valley was inundated; almost every bridge and weir was washed away, and the valley was more like sea than land; all shooting was consequently put an end to. I went out with my favourite 18-lb. gun (old Joe), killed 1 hare and 2 rabbits, all I shot at, having no chance for fowl. About eleven o'clock the waters lowered a little, and on sallying forth for a few ducks that appeared, away went the great weir at the moment that my boy Joe was carrying my gun Joe across it. The boy was all but drowned, but at last I saved him and brought him to life. The whole day, to no effect, was absorbed in trying to recover my gun, which was washed away in the flood, twelve feet deep at least, and with more rapidity than any mill tail. Nets, weights, grapples, and the Lord knows what, were lost in the attempt to fish it up by their adhering to the part of the broken weir under water. Towards evening, however, my old friend Benjamin, the *ci-devant* keeper, arrived with a dung prong tied to a very long pole, and, by the most extraordinary luck, hooked the gun by the scroll guard and brought it up, to my greatest delight. I gave him a guinea in presence of the other lazy brute of a keeper, who never exerted himself in the least, and as the thaw now will make Poole harbour passable, I had no time to lose in repairing to Southhaven.

20*th.*—Left Hyde at daylight this morning, and, after stocking myself with provisions, I arrived at Southhaven, the tide having served just in time for me to leave Poole when I was prepared to start ; but on my arrival I found that the late thaw had inundated the place, and that the lower part of the house had been for two days six inches deep in water. This I could have easily encountered, as I did there the last flood, when I cooked my dinner in the parlour in water boots in a foot deep of water, but unfortunately half the chimneys were so damaged by the wind and weather, that there was not one room in the house but what smoked to that degree that, in five minutes after a fire was lighted, you could neither see nor breathe. I tried with bricks, baskets, and everything, on a ladder, to quack up one of them, but, all being of no avail, I was forced to return to Poole. In the meantime there came on a torrent of snow and sleet and a gale of wind, and I had a most deplorable passage across ; but after getting a good dinner and a good fire at the 'Antelope' inn I got dry and warm. Here is the luxury of England over France ; for without such comforts I might have caught my death.

21st.—After searching the town the whole day no one could find the landlord of Southhaven, and I was therefore obliged to send bricklayers over to attempt making his hole of a house habitable, while I this day remained a prisoner at the inn in Poole, the boat and bricklayer being this evening driven on the mud in a gale of wind, and from other detentions and troubles I could not reach Southhaven till the evening of the 22nd, where (in a quarter where no common sailor would stay if he possibly could avoid it) I began, *à la bivouac*, to make myself as comfortable as possible, under an idea that if under a hedge in a campaign I might be worse off for board and lodging. Here I had to weather the 23rd, being Sunday, when I walked over Studland heath, and went to an apology for a church.

24th.—It poured with rain so that I could do nothing all day except killing a cormorant ; and I had no other amusement left than to remain within the walls of my hovel, which the wind blew through so hard that the chair fell in the fire and burned my best shooting dress to pieces. Went out, with wind and occasional rain from seven this evening till three o'clock the next morning, with James Reade, whom I with great difficulty hired, and who kills more than all the gunners in the harbour put together. No man could work more beautifully than he did, but not a wigeon did we see the whole night, though he tried every inch of the harbour. Towards morning I killed on the mud a sheldrake; we saw a small lot of these under the moon, and fired by word of command (in a low voice, the Poole custom) each man at his bird, Reade's brother and we. The guns went all together, and the 3 sheldrakes were killed.

25*th.*—Another wet day; made attempts to get about, and only got wet for our pains.

26*th.*—Cruel weather again. Imprisoned by wind and rain, and half starved owing to mishaps in getting provisions from Poole.

27*th.*—Wind and rain again; no attempting anything.

28*th.*—Better weather; out from seven at night till seven the next morning (with Reade, who worked like a slave), but owing to the swarm of gunners, it was impossible to get a shot, and not one of them killed a bird the whole night. Never was I out in a more miserable trip, a keen northerly wind with a nipping white frost. A few more such nights, debarred as I was from the exercise of rowing or even moving, would knock me up.

February 1*st.*—Having at last got a fine night I went out at two this morning, and, after remaining afloat till daylight with a full moon, I never saw nor even heard a single wigeon, which is easily accounted for, as about fifteen fellows, who are just thrown out of employ in the clay trade, have all turned floating gunners, so that not a bird can enter this part of the harbour without being frightened away. Reade was obliged to leave me in consequence of having to attend his brother, who was this morning severely wounded through carelessness with his gun, so that I decided on leaving Southhaven, and trying a day or two hard by at Poole, where, although near the town, the harbour is less infested with gunners than here. On my way there to-day I killed 7 coots under sail in the passage boat.

2nd.—Quitted the execrable hovel of Southhaven, and removed my things to a small lodging on the quay at Poole. Went out for the whole night with Richard Lock, the 'head gunner' of Poole, and never heard a bird.

3rd.—After lying down a few hours, was at it again all day, from dawn till eight at night, with no refreshment but a morsel of bread and cheese, and never got a shot. Not a gunner here has killed a bird for this week past; everything appears to be extirpated.

4th.—At it again, from before daylight till bedtime, with an infernal run of ill luck. Owing to the delay of my man, I was a few minutes too late where the most enormous swarm of geese I ever set eyes on came to feed every morning; but, as my usual bad luck would have it, though no gunner was out, yet a horrid fellow, on his way from Ham to Poole market, saw the birds, and went with his boat to them just as we were going up; he got within 60 yards of them longways, fired a popgun and never touched a feather. After slaving the whole day we fell in with this enormous phalanx again, but then another gunner got the start of us, and fired before us. I took a random shot, flying, at about 300 yards, with a pound of pistol balls in my stanchion, and knocked down 1 brent goose.

5th.—Was in full preparation to attack the geese again to-day, but it blew a hurricane and poured with rain from morning till night.

6th.—My sailor, Williams, whom I sent for a day to reconnoitre Keyhaven, returned this afternoon bringing me word that not a chance of sport remained there now, but that the shooting had been so good there this season that even the Frenchman to whom my house was unfortunately let for the winter had killed a great deal of wild fowl with his popgun, and that had I been there this season I might have done wonders. How extraordinary is, invariably, my escape from all good luck in wild-fowl shooting! Williams was this night put to bed very ill. The wigeon have totally quitted Poole harbour, but the geese still remain though very wild.

7th.—1 brent goose; was tripped up by the dog and fell overboard 5 miles from home, ducked to the skin—gun and all.

8th.—Wind and rain again; went out in a yawl boat and towed the punt astern. Got 2 brent geese, and shot and lost 2 more, as well as some wounded ones. It blows so fresh that you lose half your birds, as they are now so wild that nothing but pistol balls will reach them, and the winged birds are off at sea before you can row out to catch them.

9th.—The shooting having been so bad that I was literally the only person who killed a fowl in the whole town of Poole during the week I was there, I gave it up for this season, and returned this day to Longparish, after the worst winter's sport I ever had in my life.

11th.—3 snipes and 1 jack snipe.

N.B.—A man getting watercresses told me of these 4 snipes, and in half an hour I had them all in the bag. I then beat the rest of the day, but found nothing more whatever.

26th.—5 snipes. This evening poor old Nero died, having never recovered the French illness, with which we were all such sufferers. He was the best dog I ever had, ever saw, or ever heard of.[1]

[1] I killed during this extraordinary dog's service, and almost entirely to him, game &c. as follows:

Up to 1812, 356; 1813, 244; 1814, 402; 1815, 320; 1816, 378; 1817, 503; 1818, 463; 1819, 253; 1820, 344; to the day of his illness. Total, 3,263 head.

I almost always used him single-handed for every purpose, as he would of his

28*th*.—I drove to Keyhaven, to arrange about my cottage &c., and having a strong easterly wind took my gun; but in six hours after I left home a westerly wind came and made this unnecessary. My presence, as if like a charm, changed from good to bad the shooting.

March 1*st*.—Having finished my business at Keyhaven and Lymington, and as nothing remained for me to shoot but a quantity of geese which were too wild for the only gun I had, I got to Southampton this evening, and on the 2nd drove home to Longparish.

List of game &c. killed in the season, to March 1820: 216 partridges, 10 hares, 2 pheasants, 3 rabbits, 4 landrails, 88 snipes, 15 wild ducks, 7 geese, 1 wigeon, 3 teal, 1 sheldrake. Total, 350 head.

N.B.—I lost one of the finest winters we have had for years, by my unfortunate excursion to, and illness in, France.

April 1*st*.—Killed 5 brace of trout. This is the first tolerable day I have had, though I have killed a few for dinner most days for some time; but now, as the river is my own, I never care about taking any but the best fish, which I kill only when I want them, and therefore do not take the trouble to keep any account of the great number that I catch.

June 7*th*.—Went up to London and was presented to the King at his Levee.

13*th*.—Mrs. Hawker remained in town, and I went to Manchester by the mail, which left the Post Office at eight

own accord 'down charge' and bring the game when told. At a hedge he would stand till I came, and then, if ordered, go all the way round and drive the game to my side; for a river, for a boat, for everything, he was a perfect wild-fowl dog, although a high-bred pointer, with a cross of foxhound. The game that I calculate has been killed to this dog, including that shot by my friends as well as myself, I estimate at about 5,000 head, but to be widely under the mark, I will say 4,000; supposing then we take each head of game one with another at two shillings apiece, which would be a low price among those who deal in such thngs, I may say that the poor old dog has earned me 400*l*. besides trifling wagers &c.

o'clock, and arrived in Manchester by half-past seven (186 miles in 23½ hours) on the evening of the 14th. A transportation to this place I can compare to nothing but a man going to sleep, never to wake again, and finding himself in the very Billingsgate or St. Giles's of the infernal regions. I went on a musical excursion, which, except a wild-fowl expedition, is the only event that would have brought me here.

My object in going to Manchester was to see Mr. Cudmore (my first master in music), and if the place agreed with me, to avail myself of his offer to spend the holidays with him at his house and study the whole time; and, if not, to leave the place after seeing it, and then make a little tour, which I had long wished, through Birmingham and Oxford. I had very soon such a sickening of this most brutal town that my decision for leaving it was almost immediate. The very evening that I arrived I was made so ill by the suffocating fumes of stench and smoke which I inhaled, that I was violently sick the whole night, and it was with the greatest difficulty that I could pass the day of the 15th here, to inspect the manufactories and what few things were worth seeing in the town. At six o'clock on the morning of the 16th I left Manchester by the 'Eclipse' coach, and within 12 hours arrived at Birmingham, 86 miles, including the stoppage of half an hour to dine at Wolverhampton.

17th.—Ever since my arrival last evening, and the whole of this morning, I was busily employed by inspecting the beautiful and various manufactories of Birmingham, and to even the most superficial admirer of mechanics nothing could be a more delightful treat. The steam engines, the gun manufactories, the making of all hardwares &c. would require a volume to describe; and the extensive assortments of all sporting apparatus, at one-fourth the price charged by the shops, would really make it worth the while of a shooter or fisherman to come here on speculation. This afternoon I left Birmingham for Oxford. While the coach stayed to change horses at Stratford-on-Avon, I had plenty of time to visit the house which gave birth to our immortal Shakespeare, as luckily it was within a gunshot of the public-house at which we halted. I was shown the chair in which he sat (and of course sat myself in it), his sword, the box which contained his will, and many other trifles that are exhibited and declared to have been in his possession. The place which was once the residence of this illustrious dramatist was never better than a poor man's house, and is now occupied by a butcher, and, in part, fitted up for his shop and slaughter house. About eleven at night we reached Oxford.

18*th.*—Was occupied from the time I got up this morning till three o'clock this afternoon, with visiting the University of Oxford and inspecting the different colleges. Of all the libraries, as a building and for architecture, I preferred the Ratcliffe Library, and of all the chapels, that of 'New College.' The theatre fell far short of what I had been led to expect, but the *tout ensemble* of the colleges far exceeded my expectations, and the town is by odds the most beautiful and the neatest I ever saw. As to the libraries I had not time, nor do I profess to have learning enough, to appreciate their value. At three this afternoon I hired a gig and retraced the steps which I had last night travelled in darkness, back again to Woodstock, 8 miles, in order to pass the rest of the day at Blenheim, the Duke of Marlborough's. Little did I think there was such a palace in England. Were it in France, Italy, or even as far as Greece, everyone would be going to see it. The house, the park, the grounds, the everything, bids defiance to all the gentlemen's and noblemen's seats I have ever seen either at home or abroad. The park is 13 miles round, and all within a stone wall; the house is 1 mile round. Among the venerable and stately avenues of timber, we here see a whole army of trees planted in the exact positions of the armies of and against the great Duke of Marlborough, and, among them, a monument erected to his illustrious memory, which in its style is little inferior to the Colonne de Vendôme at Paris. The only disappointment I met with was not being able to see the valuable paintings, in consequence of the present degenerated duke being at home and at an early dinner with company. I this evening, after returning to Oxford, prepared for going home by the Southampton coach to-morrow.

N.B.—With the exceptions of Herefordshire and Shropshire, I have now been in every county in England.

19th.—Arrived again at Longparish House.

August.—Was detained in London this month on account of my new invention for playing the scales of a pianoforte by mechanical means.

CHAPTER XIII

1820

September.—I had agreed, for the purpose of attending to my musical invention and other more rational pursuits, to give up my shooting this year; but, unfortunately, from the unsettled state of the country, owing to the Queen's trial &c., I felt bound in honour to decline my leave from the militia in August, though I had even procured my passport for Brussels; and finding it unlikely that I could proceed just yet, I therefore, to avoid the expense and misery of being now in London, returned to Longparish House on September 3, but with little inclination for shooting, having prepared nothing, and having no dogs but two wild puppies. My 1st of September was rather a novelty for me, who for many seasons had been the champion; I broiling in the streets of London, and my poor old dog in his grave.

4th.—Went out, with two puppies, and bagged 24 partridges and 1 hare, without ever missing a shot, and having made six double shots. Notwithstanding I had resigned all pretensions to shooting this year, I have this day done the most that has been yet heard of in our line of country, although I was out only from ten till four, and surrounded by other shooters.

Game bagged in September: 94 partridges, 3 hares, 3 snipes. Total, 100 head.

Business and my intended absence abroad prevented me from being prepared for shooting this year. Except a quail, the only one I saw, I killed this 100 head of game without missing one fair shot.

October 24th.—Went to remain at Winchester, to command the North Hants Regiment, and previously to the 30th, when we were again disembodied, the regiment, which on the day of assembling consisted almost wholly of lads from the plough, was able to manœuvre as well as the line, and march with its band almost equal to the Guards. So admirable was the conduct of officers and men that I made reports in their favour to the Secretary of State, Lord Lieutenant, and Colonel, and came home on the night of the 30th.

November 8th.—Rode over to Winchester, to finally settle all the pay lists of my regiment, and with the chestnut horse returned to Longparish in forty minutes. I galloped nine miles on the downs in twenty-seven minutes.

11th.—7 snipes and 5 jack snipes (all I shot at), making in these last few days 20 snipes without missing a shot.

1821

January 8th.—Reached Southampton this evening, and arrived at Keyhaven on the afternoon of the 9th.

N.B.—The weather till the very day I had despatched my punts for the coast was unprecedentedly severe, but it then became as mild as April; my injured finger prevented me from being here during the most extraordinary week's shooting ever known! But *nil desperandum!* Let me hope some fowl may still be got. Out all the night of the 9th, but owing to fog and rain could not see 20 yards; fired the swivel gun by guess, and heard several birds beating on the sand, but before we could find them the tide flowed, and the fog defeated us.

11th.—Contrived this afternoon to get out in the rain; fired a shot with the stanchion gun at between 200 and 300 yards; bagged 3 brent geese (flying) and knocked down 2 more, which I dare not follow. Out till two the next morning, in a drizzling rain, very few wigeon, and too dark and too wet to get a chance.

12*th.*—Wet again; out towards sunset, and was overtaken in the most tremendous gale of wind, and the most furious pour of rain I ever yet witnessed; we set in the midst of it to a flock of geese; but, to our astonishment, even this did not prevent their rising at 200 yards. I knocked down 6.

13*th.*—Killed 3 coots, before daylight, which I mistook for wigeon: got a flying shot with stanchion gun, and bagged 2 wigeon. Afterwards 6 brent geese at a shot.

16*th.*—I got but one shot all day and all night—I killed an old cock wigeon, under the moon, out of a small trip at which I fired the swivel gun, at about 120 yards. Mild weather, and birds so scarce that no gunners but myself would go out.

23*rd.*—At Lymington all day about my gun; out all night, found a large flock of wigeon about three in the morning, and had not my boatman, over eager, prevailed on me to fire before my gun was clear enough of the mud, I should have made a great shot; whereas I cut a lane of back feathers for three yards long, without touching the body of the birds, which were feeding (of course with their heads all down) in a hollow place, that in one more hour I could have fired into point blank.

24*th.*—Up again to-night, but the fog and rain would not let us get out, though we were on the watch all night. Weather so calm and mild, that day shooting is at an end.

25*th.*—Out all night, but weathter so damp and thick we could not get a clear interval to shoot; came home at daylight; on 26th went sailing, and got a brent goose, all I shot at.

27*th.*—My man Charles, whom I sent to Poole for the unrivalled James Reade, the Mozart of all the wild-fowl men, returned this evening with this illustrious gunner and his punt in my boat cart.

The 28th being Sunday, we started at three on the morning of the 29th, when, extraordinary as it may appear, the wigeon, as if by instinct, had almost disappeared. The only little trip we met we got at about daybreak and fired a long shot at, but in so bad a light that we both missed.

30*th.*—Two ducks, out of 4 knocked down. Afloat at daybreak; no wigeon. Out all night again in wet.

31*st.*—Went out in a fresh wind and rain to attack a flock of geese, which, in spite of the weather, would not let us come nearer than 300 yards; I got 1 brent goose by means of blowing off a pound of small bullets in the stanchion gun. Wet day and night.

February 1*st.*—Out all night, but owing, no doubt, to the mild weather and strong westerly wind, we literally never found one trip of wigeon.

5*th.*—There not having been one single wigeon heard along the coast for several nights, we planned an attack on a swarm of coots near the town of Lymington, and had to row six miles round; we started at seven this evening, and about two in the morning, when we were just looking forward to bagging at least fifty, a rascal shoved over the mud and put the birds so to the rout that we never could get two together afterwards. My man lost himself, and we were forced to trust to the mercy of the waves, by going all round the main Channel, between the Hampshire coast and the Isle of Wight. and got home about six in the morning, just in time to escape a strong wind that might have been fatal to us. I was thus eleven hours in a nipping white frost, with a kind of raw rime falling that kept gradually turning to rain.

8*th.*—Left Keyhaven, or rather 'Wigeon Cottage,' which I call my little gunning place, and arrived at Longparish House.

N.B.—Since my arrival on the coast, which, owing to my bad finger, was after all good shooting was at an end, I contrived to kill about 40 couple of birds, and to bring home more than all the other gunners put together, little as the quantity I killed was in proportion to what anyone might have done during the frost.

So extremely wild were the birds, even by night, that, except one very long shot, I never killed a bird but with my swivel gun.

12*th.*—Left Longparish for London.

13*th.*—Proceeded to Norwich.

14*th.*—Arrived, for a short visit, with my old friend Robert Rising, Esq., of Horsey.

15*th.*—Out all day in pursuit of 3 eagles, but never could get them to pitch or fly where I had a chance. In the evening killed at a shot 2 tufted ducks, the only 2 birds I had seen in the marsh since my arrival, and which I got by lying in ambush at dusk, while Rogers drove them to me with his gunning punt.

16*th.*—Out before daylight for the eagles, but only saw them pass over half a mile high.

17*th.*—Went to Yarmouth.

18*th.*—Returned this evening, and went to Mr. Huntingdon's at Somerton Hall.

21*st.*—Despatched Rogers to inspect the celebrated salt marshes at Blakeney and Salthouse, about 46 miles from hence.

22*nd.*—Rogers was back this day by twelve o'clock, with extraordinary expedition, and brought word that this place, like all others on the public coast, was so infested with gunners, that there was no inducement to try it, and consequently I had the great satisfaction to prove that, in my own place at Keyhaven, I was as well off as in any other gunning port I could yet discover.

23*rd.*—Left Mr. Huntingdon's for Yarmouth, from whence I had hoped to take a trip through Holland to Brussels; but as no conveyance was likely to offer for some time, I took my place by the next morning's coach for London.

While at Mr. Huntingdon's we had various sport—coursing, fishing, &c.—but, except killing one day 1 hare and 1 rabbit, I made no attempt at shooting.

24th.—Left the 'Bear' (an excellent cheap inn), Yarmouth, at five this morning by the 'Star,' an admirable coach, and reached Mrs. Nelson's 'Bull' inn, Aldgate, at nine, 124 miles within sixteen hours, including ample stoppages for breakfast, dinner, and tea.

27th.—Left London, after having exerted myself about my new invention, and ordered some repairs to my guns, and arrived again at Longparish House.

28th.—My finger, which had precluded my practising music for six months, being now so far better that I can leave off the dressing, I this day was enabled to play a little.

Game &c. killed in the season up to March 1st, 1821, as below given (the two first days, and many more, lost by my absence in London, and all October cut up with my regiment at Winchester, and afterwards laid up with my hand in a sling, and during all the hard weather):

103 partridges (only 9 since September), 7 hares, 3 rabbits, 2 pheasants, and 69 snipes. Wild-fowl shooting: 5. Wild ducks: 6 curre, 2 tufted, 2 of a curious large morillon species, 1 teal, 6 wigeon, 26 brent geese. Total, 232 head.

Had my finger been well in the frost I should have had grand sport on the coast, and my only satisfaction was that of beating all the other gunners put together.

April 4th.—Embarked on board the 'Lady Cockburn, Captain Blackmore (the best packet, and the most respectable captain I ever met with), and, after being twelve hours on board, we were landed at ten o'clock at night in a French shore boat, and all but capsized coming over the bar, owing to the dreadful awkwardness and incessant chattering of the detestable French (*soi-disant*) sailors, who, through greediness, had loaded their rotten boat like a coal barge, with passengers stowed like a freight of hogs. We could get no refreshment ready till midnight, and consequently, save a small sandwich, had fasted seventeen hours.

5th.—Proceeded for Brussels, and left Calais at eleven o'clock in the day per diligence, by which everyone but a fool would travel in France for comfort,[1] expedition, and economy; and, after stopping half an hour halfway at Gravelines, reached Dunquerque at five. My fasting so long the previous day, and this day being served with some French messes at the latter place, I was ill all night.

6th.—At four o'clock I was hastened into the diligence to proceed. We stopped while I looked at, and the other passengers ate, a breakfast at Mount Cassel, where, being too sick to eat, I had the more time to admire the beauties which the view from this most beautiful mountain presents, and where you see about seven different provinces in a complete panorama, at the head of which stands the château of Marshal Kellerman. We arrived at Lille before one o'clock, having gone 19 leagues within nine hours, which, for France,[2] is flying. In short, the diligence for this particular division of the journey is the best I ever travelled in, and the reason of this is because it takes the letters from all places south of Dunquerque to Lille, and is tied to time. I had the whole evening to inspect the tremendous fortifications and pleasure grounds of this place, and with the advantage of a most gentlemanly Flemish *compagnon du voyage*, who explained to me everything which the place presented. At Lille

[1] If I hereafter note miseries, I still repeat the word 'comfort' because the provocation, imposition, insolence, and delay that I have always met with in French posting are such that the miseries of a diligence when compared to them are enormous. I believe most people will agree with me, except those who make a merit of necessity and pretend to admire everything in France, because they are obliged to admire it in order to avoid their debts and perhaps escape a gaol in England.

[2] From Paris to Rouen, in Normandy, however, I have met with light diligences that go almost as fast as our coaches, but these have occasionally accidents which are never put in the papers like ours.

our accommodations were cheap, and so they ought to be, for they were very bad, and the inn was very properly called the Hotel of Portugal, as its filth was strictly in unison with the country of which it bears the name.

7th.—Was bundled out, bag and baggage, at four this morning, and after tramping down Lille like a gang of gipsies, we waited in the rain till various conversations—of course about nothing—were ended by the conductor and the postillion. We got this machine, like a granary on old wheels though most excellent inside, under way at a quarter past four, and at seven reached the Flemish frontiers. Here my heart was in my mouth, as I had three pair of my patent piano hand-moulds to smuggle, and the very look of the *douaniers* was enough to set an amateur smuggler into an ague, and I, ill to boot, looked as if I had been buried for a week and dug up again; however, I did them, and all ended well. We breakfasted at Tournay at eight o'clock, and at half-past eleven we were halted for an hour to dine at the 'Swan' inn at Ath. Never was I more annoyed at having so ill-timed a division of meals. I, of course, could not eat, and of all the dinners I ever yet saw put on a table, here, to my fancy, was the very best; and the price, with a pint of excellent wine and beer enough to swim in, was but half a crown a head. For want of appetite there I was obliged to beg a quarter of an hour 4 leagues farther, at Enghien, where we had some stinking water, that onions had been boiled in, by way of broth, and a piece of cold veal which was nearer black than white; these we bolted with pepper to disguise the taste of them, and washed them down with beer like soap suds, and, by way of a wadding on the same, had some barbarous brandy. On leaving Enghien we passed a fine deer park belonging to the Duc d'Arenburg, and had a very gentlemanly French companion to explain the same, who being, like myself, shooting mad and music mad, suited me to a hair. In short, we, as usual, had a combination of pleasure and misery, and reached Brussels by a quarter past eight this evening, where we entered the celebrated Hôtel de Belle Vue, and under apprehension that the figures in the bill might soon resemble a swarm of hornets, decided that we would get into lodgings as soon as we could.

8*th*.—On getting up to look out of our excellent suite of rooms, I found myself transplanted from a pigstye to a paradise. I compare my situation to the rising of Lazarus. Our view of the beautiful square at the back, and the delightful park, palace &c. to our front, make this place agreeable in the extreme, and far superior to any town I have been in abroad, and I may almost say in England, for a cheerful appearance.

9*th*.—Got a quarter in the most splendid part of Brussels, not for gaiety, but for the sake of the air, within two doors of the Royal Palace, and looking directly into the best part of the park. For this I pay 200 francs a month, exclusive of crockery &c., which in this place is usually hired. I this day entered my new abode, hired a piano, &c.

10*th*.—Got delightfully settled in our new abode, and had my first lesson in music with Mr. Jerome Bertini, after having lost above six months' practice, owing to the accident to my finger.

11*th*.—Went shopping, saw the Brussels lace made, &c., and was much delighted with the excellence and cheapness of everything in this charming town. The shops are the best on the Continent, and you may look into them while walking on a kind of pavement without the risk of being run over as in Paris.

15*th*.—Went with Radcliffe, in his barouche and four, to inspect the ever memorable field of Waterloo. After reaching the village of this name, which is about ten miles from Brussels, we proceeded in the carriage towards the farm of Gomont, falsely called 'Hugomont' in the despatches, which is about 4 miles beyond Waterloo; and, at a small hamlet, halfway or thereabouts between the two places, we called on the celebrated peasant Jean Baptise de Coster, who was so notorious for having been the personal guide of Buonaparte during the whole of the battle. As I was coachman at the time, De Coster was seated for some time with me on the box of the barouche; and here, of course, I entered as eagerly into conversation concerning the ex-Emperor &c. as the incessant plague of having four blood horses to drive on a bad road full of Flemish coal carts would admit of. At Gomont we left our carriage and spent the morning in seeing and collecting all we could, under the able explanation of this celebrated pilot. Our carriage came for us in the afternoon at the farm of La Haye Sainte, where we were hospitably received by a worthy farmer during a heavy shower, after which we returned to Brussels in time for a late dinner.

23rd.—Being Easter Monday, we this evening drove, in one of the hackney coaches which in Brussels are most magnificent, and 109 in number, to the Allée Verte, which is a delightful drive between two double avenues of trees, and by the side of a broad canal, extending for above a mile, and at about half a mile from the lower town. This may be considered the Hyde Park of Brussels, and Easter Monday being a very grand day there, we met the Royal Family in three carriages and six, and it is really a pleasure to see how happy and affable they appear to be. The very countenances of the King and Queen bespeak the excellent qualities for which they deserve to be upheld as a pattern to other crowned heads. Weather so sultry as to be quite oppressive, and so hot that the water in our room was as warm as we usually drink tea.

25th.—Started for a tour through Holland. Mrs. Hawker and I left Brussels at about eight o'clock this morning by the 'malle-poste,' a machine drawn by three horses abreast, and on grasshopper springs; but it having the roof covered with boards instead of leather, the noise of it is such as to distract the head most unmercifully, particularly as every part of the road to Amsterdam is on pavement. The civility of Mr. Lefebre, the postmaster in chief, was excessive; he offered us coffee, and showed us his very handsome house &c. while the horses were putting to. When we got to Anvers, or, in the Dutch language, Antwerp, 8 leagues, Mrs. Hawker was so overcome with the heat and the shaking, that she felt so far faint as to have been running a risk of illness if she had proceeded, and luckily, Mr. Lefebre's nephew being there, I was enabled to send her back to Brussels under his care, by means of posting. I, of course, wished to attend her home myself, but she would insist on my proceeding. Our misery at this horrid hole Antwerp may be easily conceived when I state that Mrs. Hawker was ushered into a dirty long room, where fifty fellows were smoking, and could get nothing warm, except some pot liquor and chervil, which the people, or rather the pigs, here eat by way of soup; and then, again, the unpacking of the luggage under the shade of a door porch, while the conductor of the mail was every instant urging me to make haste under pain of his being obliged to leave me behind. After having gone 18 leagues from Antwerp, we entered the kingdom of Holland by a little landmark on the Belgian side of a toll turnpike gate. We arrived next at a beautifully fortified town, called Breda. We were then driven by a coachman instead of a postillion, and were no onger tormented with the monkey-like absurdity of whip cracking peculiar to France and Belgium, but had the way cleared by a bugle horn, which, of course, was more effective and by no means annoying to our ears. About eleven at night we reached a miserable pothouse, where we unloaded the mail, preparative to crossing the Waal, which here is joined by the river Meuse and becomes unusually large, and from about a quarter past eleven till a quarter past twelve we were on board a large boat making the passage, during which it was novel to see the quantities of Dutch fishermen casting their nets by the light of the half moon and lanthorns. We landed at a very outlandish-looking place, called Gorcum, where, it being necessary to look very sharp after our baggage, we were, owing to the want of better light, in some confusion.

Having no servant, I had to scramble up the quay with all my things at my back, and though laden like a jackass, not a soul offered to assist me or any other passenger; and, as not a word but of Dutch was spoken, I could not, at the moment, request any help. After being detained about an hour in a large melancholy room, where pipes were offered us, and where we got some excellent hollands, we proceeded in a different kind of voiture, like an English Jarvey, on most cruel grasshopper springs, and with our new conductor, who had passed the river Waal with us, but who spoke nothing but Dutch. In short, all was pantomime for me after landing in this new world, and the only interpretation I could get was from two of my fellow-passengers who spoke French, but so very so-so, and who were by no means obliging with what little they did know of that language. They both smoked, of course, all the journey. This mail, I should observe, shook so dreadfully that I was literally bruised all over, and the noise of it was in my ears for two days after leaving it.[1] The horses, however, were good, fine, spanking animals, sixteen hands high, and although we had only a pair, we went at the rate of seven miles an hour. The roads in Holland are most admirably good, being paved with hard white brickwork, and as level as a billiard table. At break of day we reached Vianen, where we were ferried over the Rhine, mail coach, horses, and all, on huge masses of floating timber, very different from what is commonly known as a ferry boat.[2] At daylight we got to Utrecht, and here the extraordinary change in the style of houses and country appeared as if we had awoke from a dream; and all the way from this place to within a short

[1] By such a shaking a gummy fellow would have been laid up for six weeks; but the foreigners invariably take a warm bath after it.

[2] In the course of the journey we passed in like manner all the large dykes, which were too broad for the drawbridges.

distance of Amsterdam was lined with gentlemen's country seats, than which nothing could be more novel to an Englishman, or more beautiful to an admirer of nature and art. Here every ditch was literally boiling and bubbling with the motion of the finest fish, and, for twenty miles, the fields and marshes were swarming with green plover and other marsh birds.

26th.—About nine o'clock in the morning we arrived in the most extraordinary-looking town of Amsterdam, where the mail took me and my baggage from the post office to the Doelen Inn, the best hotel in the place, kept by a Mr. Cottu, a Frenchman. The moment you enter Amsterdam your respiration is literally suppressed by the suffocating and putrid smell arising from the large, black, stagnant ditches which run through every street in the town, with trees on their banks. The town of Amsterdam is built on piles in the midst of a contagious morass, and is so unhealthy that, out of a population of 200,000, the deaths average 9,000 a year. Not wishing to have my carcase left here, I lost no time in seeing the curiosities of the place, and, instead of going to bed, hired a lacquey, who spoke good French, to whom I paid 2 florins a day, and a curricle, for which I paid 2 florins an hour, as the hackney coaches are, in the greater part, built like sledges and go without wheels. First I saw the King's palace, a magnificent building, though situated in the horrid town. The most striking object here was the large ball room, which is 160 feet long, 100 feet wide, and about 80 feet high, and which they told me was the 'largest *salle* in Europe.' This may, or may not, be the case, but certainly I never saw anything equal to it.

Next I saw the Felix Meritus, an institution to promote all the arts, which here are very laudably encouraged, and where there is a concert room considered the best in the world, I suppose for sound, as it was nothing extraordinary in size or splendour.

I then inspected the Nieuwe Kerk, where the cover or

rather canopy over the pulpit is the most magnificent piece of carving that can possibly be imagined ; and then the old church, where there is some very fine glass painting, done in the year 1555.

The Exchange was my next object, and a very curious one ; it is spacious and good in the extreme, built on arches over the bog and water, and of course well thronged, as there are no less than 30,000 Jews in Amsterdam. Would that I could have heard them in their synagogue, which a gentleman told me was scarcely to be distinguished from 10,000 cats, dogs and ducks in full concert. We then drove to the Pont Amoureux, the ramparts, the Plantage and other places of pleasure in this extraordinary place ; and by the way I omitted to name the only spot in which I could find any comfort, or even breathe, and that was the top of the Palace, from whence I had, without exception, the most novel and the most beautiful panoramic view that I ever beheld.

After having seen everything that was worth seeing, and taken my dinner as I would a pinch of snuff, to save time, I got home quite exhausted about dusk, and just as I had got into a sweet sleep, I was obliged to get up to receive Mr. Fodor, the Clementi of Holland, about my hand-moulds for the piano. He was so delighted with them that his approbation was worth the journey to me ; and Mr. Steup, the celebrated music seller, was to have seen them also, but was prevented, though he took a copy of my book on music, with a view, no doubt, of translating it into the Dutch language. So much for Amsterdam, which, miserable as existence in this town is, I would not have missed seeing for 100 guineas.

27th.—Up at daybreak, and having taken plenty of Madeira the previous night, and fortified myself with Huxham's tincture of bark this morning, I took the first packet for North Holland. We had a short passage across an arm of the sea, and were then towed by a horse and landed at the little village of Buiksloot. The first thing when you arrive in Holland, you are offered a pipe gratis, but they make you pay pretty dear[1] for what, from necessity, you are obliged to drink with it: here, however, I played the old soldier, being armed with a fine ham given me by my friend Radcliffe at Brussels (and without which, by the way, I should have starved when at Gorcum), and a cold chicken. I instantly hired a curricle, for which the fixed price is ten florins, and proceeded for Broek in this still more extraordinary part of the world. The people here are the most cleanly known. (So neat was the inn at Broek that, on cutting my pencil, I, to avoid giving offence, carried the shavings out of doors to prevent dropping them about.) I proceeded in a curious-looking curricle, drawn by fine large high-spirited Gelderland horses, along a dangerously elevated bank by the side of dykes, and was requested not to put up my umbrella, which I wanted to shade me from the intense heat, being informed that I was 'liable to a penalty,' I suppose through danger of frightening the horses of the other vehicles. I inspected the noted village of Broek. Here the carriage is left at an inn, as this place is only accessible on foot. The village is built round the banks of a beautiful little lake, and the streets are cleaner than any English kitchen. The outsides of the houses are most of them ornamented with carving and gilding, and in short are as clean as the inside of an English drawing room. No one dare enter the inside of these houses. The inhabitants are a very rich and independent people, insomuch that I was informed, though I believe it to be a lie, that the Emperor of Austria was made to take off his boots before they would allow him to enter a cottage at Broek. The houses are most charming; never could the hackneyed phrase of 'earthly paradise' be better applied than to this heavenly little place. To name all I could describe

[1] Holland is by regulation the dearest country I ever was in next to England, but the Dutch do not impose on you so much as the French and Belgian innkeepers and tradesmen.

would take a quarto volume ; but, among other remarkable things I noticed, the houses have one of their two doors which is never opened except for a marriage or a funeral. Instead of sparrows, the village is swarming with starlings, which, as the houses are very low, might be killed with a whip from every tree, every chimney, and every kind of perch that they can crowd upon. The storks also are equally tame, and build within a few yards of you on the low trees and chimneys. These birds are the arms of the Hague ; and this is the reason that there is a heavy penalty for killing them or taking their eggs. Among the innumerable neat cuttings of box and other evergreens, here is a whole menagerie of birds and beasts with ships &c. ; in short, I may go on for ever about Broek, but have no time : suffice it to say, that to see it is even worth a voyage of sea sickness for two days. The place is not the least like anything European, but more like China. We then drove back to Buiksloot for the other drive—to Saardam. Here the wall on which we drove was made delightful by a refreshing breeze from the Het (or T'ye) on the left, and on our right was an object not a little interesting to Peter Hawker, the *chasseur Anglais*—a marsh swarming with birds of every description : ducks, teal, curre, shovellers, spoonbills, snipes, storks, great snipes, plovers &c. within shot of the road and bidding defiance to me as I waved my hat at them. How my fingers itched for my Joe Manton, much more for my duck gun. At Saardam we could drive about, as the town was all bricked like the floor of an English kitchen, Here I entered the cottage inhabited by the great Czar Peter of Russia while he worked in disguise as a ship carpenter, and I also sat in his arm-chair.

At a quarter past one we reached L'huys, and crossed the narrow part of the salt water in a boat. Thus, by bribing the driver to go fast, and eating in the carriage, I was enabled to make this usual tour in North Holland, and with strict observation, in an unusually short space of time. Here, by the way, as well as in the other parts of Holland, the waggons are curiously driven; there are so few hills, and those so trifling that they have neither pole nor shafts to the carriages, but the driver, if descending, puts one foot to the horses' hind quarters, in order to keep back the vehicle.

At half-past one I got back to Amsterdam, and at two started in a curricle for Haarlem to hear and play on the wonderful organ. By bribing the driver, I went the three and a half Belgic leagues in a little more than an hour; and hastened to the house of the organist, Mr. Schumann, who luckily was at home, but who never plays under the regulated price of twelve florins. He first played me the Hallelujah Chorus, which had a tremendous effect; next, an imitation of the human voice, which was wonderful; and last, an extempore storm, in which I defy the strictest observer to distinguish the thunder from that of nature, and in which the rain, and the storm birds singing before the tempest, with the solemn echo of the church, had an effect on the feelings which surpassed any sermon that even Mr. Pitman, Mr. Penfold, or Dr. Andrews could have preached. I then ascended the loft, and inspected the gigantic instrument, which the sexton told me has 5,300 pipes; played on it, in my miserable way, for some time; took the organist to the church porch, delighted him much with a sight of my hand-moulds for the piano, gave him a prospectus of them, shook hands with him and galloped off to a little Dutch house to save the Hague diligence. Here I was somewhat adrift, as the dictionary which my friend the Baron de Tuyll, Chamberlain to the King, had lent me, could not conveniently be got at in this hurried moment. I said 'Tea,' put my finger in my mouth, and showed the old woman of the house some eggs: she brought two raw. I turned all into the bowl together, bread, &c., swallowed my mess like a pig, held out a dollar for her to take payment, and jumped into the Hague diligence at half-past five. This machine (were it not that the Dutchmen all smoke inside) would have beat any conveyance in Europe for the combination of safety, comfort and expedition; it is like a parlour on wheels, though not very heavy considering, and carries nine people; the three centre seats are fine leather arm-chairs, and there are two large windows on each side, four spanking Gelderland horses, capital coachman, English harness; pace eight miles and a half an hour, roads all smooth brickwork; fare, five florins and fourteen francs. Coachman allowed no fee for himself, but paid by his proprietor (a good regulation). Reached the Hague, 30 miles, by nine o'clock, and quartered at the 'Maréchal de Turenne,' kept by Mr. Handel, a very civil man, whose waiters were most pleasant, civil fellows, and spoke French fluently, as well as himself. Here I was again *chez moi*; took a pill to set me at ease, and went to bed.

28th.—Intense heat; hard walking and pills being rather derogatory to the safety of my health in a strange land, and with not a soul who cared for anything belonging to Peter Hawker but his money, I sported a phaeton and a *valet de place*, and having cleaned and sweetened myself a little, I drove off quite a dandy to see the lions in and round this beautiful, lively and clean town. We proceeded for two miles (on a fine brick road) through a heavenly wood and double avenue of trees to Scheveningen, where the open sea and sands burst upon your view, after clearing the village, where the fishing boats were innumerable, and the Dutchmen all in a bustle landing their fish for the market, this (Saturday) being the grand day. The fish is drawn to the Hague, in small carts, by either two or three large dogs, and in many of these droll machines a boy sits up and drives like a coachman.

On the shore I met with a very intelligent Dutch fisherman named Maarten Vanzon, who had been in our navy for many years, and who spoke English perfectly well. This was the first time I had heard my own language since I left Brussels; and on no occasion could I have better had recourse to it, as I was anxious to know about the wild-fowl shooting on the Dutch coast; it proves to be as I always suspected, that when the marshes are frozen the birds nearly all leave Holland, because the coast rarely affords mud for them to feed on, and consequently they all repair to England in quest of food, save and except those birds which may be kept in the private decoys.

The shooting in Holland is, in a word, then, magnificent in the extreme during the open weather, when your life is in constant danger of disease, and good for nothing in a hard frost, when the climate may be encountered with safety. At Scheveningen the fishing boys are a great plague, asking for halfpence; and when I gave a few to some of them, they had a battle royal in the style of Crib and Belcher, the pugilists, the sight of which was well worth what I had given.

After leaving this place, we drove to 'The House in the Wood,' the nominal residence of the King, who, by the way, when in Holland, generally goes off to the Grandes-Eaux, a place in Gelderland, I suppose to have good health. At the House in the Wood I was much gratified by the Salle d'Orange, an octagon room in which there were some magnificent Vandycks, Rubens's, &c.; but my pencil memorandums of the subjects having dropped from the carriage, I must say (like a blockhead) that 'the pictures were very fine,' without giving an artist-like description of them. There was a most elegant Chinese room, with a vulgar, citizen-looking glass chandelier, and a most inferior half-Chinese room with the handsomest china chandelier I ever saw. Were I chamberlain, I would advise the good King to change them. I recollect being very much struck with a composition of Rubens, on the subject of the assassination of William; and also his picture of coppersmiths at work. The triumph of the Prince of Orange, too (by Jordaens) is a most colossal picture, as it covers a whole panel of this splendid *salle*. We then went back to the Hague and saw the King's cabinet, where I was ten times better pleased than in the Louvre at Paris, because all the pictures are good. What a feast for an artist! A man must be a brute who could not enjoy this exhibition. Here is a cattle painting by Paul Potter, that cost 100,000 florins, and is the best of its kind in the world; and the inside of Delft Church in two views by Hoeckgeest, that have an effect which beggars all the architectural pictures I ever set eyes on.

Next, the Palace. Here is all the comfort of old England instead of the splendid misery of France. The Dutch are proud to copy us in comfort, and therefore must become the next greatest nation to us. The French are above it, and will therefore stick in the mud all their lives through their cursed pride. Here we see English grates, carpets, and everything proper for a cold winter's day, and the rooms may be entitled to a word of which there very properly is no French translation—'comfortable.' The ballroom is chaste and grand, the family portraits good; and although a trifle, yet every man of feeling must admire the nursery, where the good Queen has taken such pains to place little objects for the amusement of the little Princess Mary Anne, who sleeps close to her bedroom.

Next, the bells at the Hague. I mounted the tower of St. James and remained half stunned though much delighted while they played; examined the barrel and machinery of wires by which they moved; gave the tiger a florin, and after viewing from on high Delft, Rotterdam, and all the other places round this fine green country, descended and proceeded to the fish market. Here four live storks are kept, as the arms of the town; and the stand of dog carts, and the stable or mews of harnessed dogs, are drolly interesting. Hastened home: exhibited, by appointment, my patent piano hand-moulds to Madame Van den Bergh, the female Clementi of the place. Left my sporting work, for the benefit of the Dutch, with Mr. Vandef; swallowed my dinner, and flew to the theatre. Here they play French and Dutch alternately; and, luckily for me, French to-night, so that I could judge better of the acting. Here was a comedy of which I forget the name, and have not time to look for the bill; but, in a word, their comic acting is better than ours, though inferior to that of Paris; and, on the other hand, in serious strains they are superior to the French and inferior to the English. Theatre small, tolerably neat; two good pillars on each side of the stage; house badly lit up with eight pairs of poor oil lamps, suspended in a circle from a plain white ceiling. Three tiers of seats; pit very respectable, and when the act scene dropped, the whole of the people from thence adjourned to walk the streets and groves of trees, having each received a card to return, with merely the word 'sortie' printed on it. Orchestra pretty good and strong. People very well-behaved during the performance, no whistling or blackguard cries from the gallery like England, but all quiet and attentive like Paris. People extremely civil in directing one home at night, and, in short, very well disposed towards an Englishman without any flattery or humbug.

29th.—Sunday. Went to the Dutch church. Their ceremony, Protestant, is different from ours, as to the mere form. They have no bishops, so much the better, but are governed by a sort of commission appointed by the King. After the First Lesson was read, we had a most powerful crash of ill-tuned voices, with a very *very* fine organ; immediately after which about 300 people adjourned and sat down to a table, precisely like the one where the Eton boys sup at Surley Hall on June 4. Here were all the way down the table plates full of white bread, and in this form the Dutch, it appears, receive their sacrament, while the clergyman, who, by the way, has more energy than most of our sticks of parsons, prays for them. The doors being closed for this ceremony, I had a difficulty to make my escape, and the situation I was in would on any less solemn occasion have been a good subject for mirth.

30*th*.—After discharging my bill, which for Holland was very reasonable, at this comfortable inn, the 'Maréchal du Turenne,' I entered the mail curricle cart, a branch from the Amsterdam mail, at eight o'clock this evening, and after going through Delft, halting for some time at Rotterdam, and passing across the rivers Yssel and Leck, reached Gorcum, 14 leagues, at five o'clock on the morning of the 30th, and here it is that the Hague mail and passengers are resigned to that of Amsterdam.

N.B.—In driving out of the Hague we went at the rate of near 14 miles an hour, with two fine spanking Gelderland horses, which never once broke out of a trot, and although we went to Delft at the average rate of 10 miles an hour, yet we were three-quarters of an hour before we reached this place, which, the courier of the mail informed me, was 'a league and a half only,' not quite halfway to Rotterdam, which they call 4 leagues; consequently I am convinced that the leagues in this country, where they call them '3 miles English,' must be very much underrated, particularly as I have been all my life in the habit of making pretty accurate judgments with regard to time in travelling.

We again, after waiting an hour to sort the letters &c., passed the great river Waal in a kind of small craft without a deck, and had an extraordinarily rapid passage of ten minutes. The Waal, I should observe, is passed with the baggage, mail bags and passengers, as follows: in a dead calm, by a large rowboat; in wind, by a kind of vessel; when half frozen, by a boat and people to beat away the ice; and when thoroughly frozen, so as to bear well, by a boat with skates to the keel, and in full sail on ice instead of water, provided there is wind enough to drive it over the ice. We landed at the little public-house on the opposite bank called 'Het Veerhuis,' where we embarked last Wednesday in the night, and here there was a great confusion owing to the bustle of landing an immense train of caravans, carriages, and horses, belonging to the celebrated rope dancer, Madame Sachi, who was proceeding for Amsterdam, and whose mother interpreted to get some breakfast for the Spanish Consul (my fellow-passenger) and myself. My return from this tour was just in time, as last night the fine weather changed to rain and wind, which continued for the greater part of this day. The mail, by the bye, goes without even letting out the passengers, over every river and dyke except the Waal, which, having a conflux of the Rhine and other rivers, would sometimes be too dangerous. Madame Sachi's stupendous caravan, however, was this day shipped on it, horses and all, in a huge ferry boat.

Having entered our Belgian mail coach, we got under way in this part of Holland, and I was most fortunate in my companion, a consul and a marshal in the Spanish army. We fought over our battles in the Peninsula; and he being also so great an amateur musician as to have composed several operas, was not a little agreeable to me as a companion; and from his mania for the pianoforte I was induced to open the box, and explained to him my hand-moulds, with which he was the most elated of anyone to whom I had shown them. This most agreeable man and I were *tête-à-tête* to Antwerp, where we exchanged cards, shook hands, and took leave. His card was—

Le Chev^er^ de Béramendi,
Intendant des Armées d'Espagne;
Consul-Général de S.M.C.
Au Royaume des Pays-Bas.

Having regaled myself with the remains of my cold ham and a chicken, with other refreshment, in the coach, which I advise everyone to do on this road, and partaken of some good things with my Spanish friend, I was, luckily, enabled to enjoy the time allowed for dinner (a miserable dinner) in Antwerp; took a hasty inspection of the cathedral, where there is some extremely fine carving, ancient architecture, &c., and, above all, two remarkably fine Rubens' pictures of our Saviour on the cross; on the left the elevation to, and on the right the descent from, the cross; and there is likewise an excellent Morillo of St. Francis. The statues of St. Paul and St. Peter give a fine effect to the sortie from the aisle of this church.

Just in time for the mail, which I had all to myself to Brussels, where we arrived at the general post office at half-past eight, and by nine I was in my house, where I found Mrs. Hawker pretty well, and was not a little delighted at what I had seen, and at having got so safely and rapidly over.[1] My expenses, in all, were about 18 napoleons.

Distance		Leagues
From Brussels to Amsterdam		44
Amsterdam, by Haarlem, to the Hague		9
From the Hague to Gorcum	14	39
And Gorcum to Brussels	25	
Tour in North Holland, exclusive of water passages		8
		100

In all, at least 400 English miles, and saw all in six days.

May 7th.—Having a leisure evening, I went to inspect the ancient cathedral of St. Gudule. It was not my intention to waste my time in compiling memorandums of a city so well known as Brussels, which, from its infinite superiority over every town on the Continent, and over some towns in England, for cleanliness, beauty, and I may also add the word unknown on the Continent, comfort, is too well acquainted with by all British travellers to require description.

The cathedral of St. Gudule, however, cannot be passed over with impunity. The Gothic architecture of this superb building is fine in the extreme. The old carving of the pulpit by Henry Verbruggen, of Antwerp, is, perhaps, of the kind, the finest in the world; it represents Adam and Eve driven

[1] Being thus safely lodged in my own house again, I, in order to counteract all risk of disease, fever, or bile that may be brought on by fatigue, took the doctor's curse, or, in other words, a dose of calomel, and went to bed, by which means I never was better in my life than the third day after my return.

out of Paradise, and Death appearing to them. The globe of the earth forms the body of the pulpit, and over the canopy is the Virgin and the infant Jesus bruising with the cross the head of a huge serpent, which curls round the tree that supports the pulpit, and raises its erected head to the canopy. The carvings of Christ, the Virgin, and the Twelve Apostles, are fine specimens of statuary, and the old painted glass is no less worthy of observation. Here are sixteen chapels, accessible from different parts of the aisle. In short, the architecture, sculpture, and carving, both in wood and iron, of this cathedral, are well worth a long journey, to any lover of art or antiquity.

9th.—This was the birthday of the little princess, and we had a grand parade of the 6th Hussars, a very prettily appointed Dutch regiment, and the first regiment of infantry. The trumpets of the former and the band of the latter were so admirably fine, that this parade was to me quite a musical as well as a martial treat. The cavalry were very steady while they were inspected, and their horses were well drilled in trotting past; but, unfortunately, the officer of the right division, being perhaps a better man for battle than for show, destroyed the whole order of the column by trotting too fast, and putting the rear in a gallop. The appointments of this regiment were extremely good, and so were the horses. I disliked the manner of carrying their swords, which, instead of sloping with the hand advanced, they bore nearly erect with the elbow squared. The infantry were not so steady under arms as the cavalry, one fellow scratching his ear, another putting his cap right, &c. They marched past much quicker than we do, and their ordinary time was nearly equal to our quick march; and I was at a loss to guess how the officers could salute in time with the foot. No one, however, but the commanding officer, who was mounted, saluted the general. The pioneers had saws as well as axes, and, on the whole, had a look fierce enough to frighten away everything but an Englishman. I could not resist the foregoing trivial remarks, having been myself so long a dragoon, and now a jolly militiaman. In the evening I went to the Grand Theatre, or Opera House. The *salle* is, on the whole, good, but, like all others abroad, badly lit up, and the audience dressed more fit for the diligence than the boxes. As, however, only fools think about dress, I merely remark this because it detracts from the good effect which is produced by the more graceful appearance of a London audience. We had first a vile opera called 'Le Tresor Supposé,' and then Voltaire's tragedy of 'Mahomet,' in which Talma, whom I had before seen in Paris, performed. The plot of this tragedy is, to my mind, so horrid, and the ending so unsatisfactory,[1] that I could scarcely help reflecting that it was written by one who is probably gone to the devil himself; and in Talma's acting, however fascinating to Frenchmen, I could observe nothing particular, except that at the end of almost every sentence he concluded with a sort of twang not much unlike the bellowing of an old ram, and shook both his hands in the air like a man struck with the palsy.[2] There was, however, one scene really well acted, and the first in my life played by Frenchmen that ever made me shed a tear; but here it so happened that Talma had nothing to do.[3] The Prince and Princess of Orange were near to the

[1] Since making this remark, I have to apologise to Voltaire, having ascertained that he had, in this tragedy, a particular view in making vice triumphant; namely, the Pope had prohibited his works, and, out of spite, he wrote the tragedy of 'Mahomet,' as an indirect attack upon his Holiness, and thus he left Mahomet in full possession of all his empire, after the most outrageous acts of villany.

[2] In making this remark I reflect more on the French taste than Talma's acting, as I am informed that he is obliged to sacrifice his own talent to comply with their ideas of tragedy, for which the generality of the French have about as much natural disposition as they have for religion: none at all. Had Talma proper judges, or rather men of feeling, to play to, we might be led to hope he would perform very differently.

[3] The scene to which I allude was the one between Seide, played by Bouchez, a Brussels man that I had never before heard of, and Palmire, by Madame Petipa. The former was really good through the whole piece, but his acting in this scene, just before he is compelled to murder his father, really does credit to his talent.

Ambassador's box, where Baron Tuyll's party and we sat; the audience, on the entrance of each of these personages, rose, and gave a short round of applause.

13*th.*—Hired an excellent coach (for 6½ francs), and went with Mrs. Hawker to pay a visit, and pass the forenoon with the Countess of Bentinc (the governess to the Princess Mary Ann) at the heavenly palace of Laeken, which is about 4 miles from the suburbs of Brussels. Lady Antoinette (her daughter) was so kind as to show us the beauties of this charming place, among which we were most attracted by the magnificent hall and dome. The views from the hill on which Laeken stands are charming, as you look down on the most delightful pleasure grounds, with a lake and a yacht on it, and have the city of Brussels and other picturesque objects in the background. The orangery here is particularly fine, and has in its collection several trees that (Lady Bentinc told me) have been there since the time of Ferdinand and Isabella, which must be 200 years ago. When in Paris, however, or rather at Versailles, I saw some orange trees which, I think, were 300 years old.

14*th.*—Previously to this day, I had taken a place in the mail to accompany Baron Tuyll to Namur, with a view of proceeding from thence to Liège in a curricle. We were to stop at his château on the banks of the Meuse (between these two places, which is the most beautiful part of Belgium), and then to go and see the famous Mr. Berleur's manufactory of cheap guns &c. at Liège. After having done this I should have gone on to Aix-la-Chapelle, to pass my hand-moulds and publications into the Prussian frontier before returning to England. I was so unwell all this morning, however, that I felt but little disposed for a journey on bad roads of 230 miles, which this (going and returning) would have been. I nevertheless rallied as well as I could, and at two got into the mail; but the shaking of the wooden roof made my head so bad, that when we got to Waterloo, I found it would have been madness to proceed, and luckily there was at the inn there a butter merchant for whom a very fair cabriolet was waiting at the door. He readily agreed to give me a seat back, but would accept of nothing till I insisted on his letting me treat him to a bottle of hock (which was here very good for 3 francs), and I of course had the consideration to remain patiently in durance vile till he and his friend had finished it, while I sipped at a glass and pretended to drink also. He drove me home to my own door, and nothing could exceed his good nature and civility. I was, however, an hour and a half remaining on the staircase of my hotel, as Mrs. Hawker, who (from illness) had gone out to take an airing, had taken with her the keys of the rooms, as is always customary on the Continent.

15*th.*—Having last night taken a little magnesia and gone to bed quietly, I was this day very well; whereas if I had proceeded I might have been dragged in this constant wet weather just far enough to be accommodated with a sick bed, where I had no servant, and where, being in Prussia, I might scarcely have made myself understood.

18*th.*—Having now most satisfactorily settled my business abroad (with a view to circulating my patent, publications &c. at Brussels, Paris, Berlin, Vienna, Madrid, &c.), I have no longer any business on the Continent, and as Mrs. Hawker has never been well while at Brussels, I, of course, could not think of staying here for pleasure. I have therefore this day packed up everything preparative to quitting to-morrow.

19*th.*—Hired a pretty good chariot, and at eight o'clock this morning started post from Brussels for Ghent, which is 7 postes (about 39 long English miles), and where we arrived (by means of paying the postillions well) at two o'clock. We put up at a magnificent house called Hôtel de la Poste. We had three horses; the postillion rode on the near wheeler and drove the others, and we went very fast. Here we could get on by means of paying well, but the few times that I posted in France I found that nothing could put the brutal baboons out of their jog-trot. If you have four people in the carriage you pay for one horse more than is actually taken, whether you have three or four. We paid 6 francs a post, and 3 francs (double the regulation) to the drivers, and the barriers or toll gates averaged one franc per post. In short, to bring the matter to a calculation that may be easily recollected, I should say that every ten miles (to do the business handsomely and comfortably) cost a trifle within a napoleon.

Having refreshed ourselves while in the carriage with cold tongue, chicken and Madeira, we lost no time in seeing the chief objects in this fine town, which is the capital of Flanders. The first thing to which we directed our attention was a collection of some of the finest original pictures in Europe, a great part of which has been considerably more than a century in the possession of the proprietor, who, as well as his forefathers, has always been one of the greatest amateurs of the age. The enjoyment of the treat which this admirable cabinet affords can only be obtained by favour, as the collection is all the private property of this gentleman, whose name is Schamp. The servant, however, on having it explained to him that I was a British officer, made no hesitation in letting me and Mrs. Hawker in, and as soon as he saw that I just knew enough of pictures to be fond of looking at them, he withdrew, and was joined by his master, who was most kind in his attention and who seemed delighted with our admiration. Instead of an hour we required at least a day; suffice it therefore to say that he has about eighteen very fine Rubens' pictures, one of them in imitation of Teniers, which being quite different from his usual style is deemed a valuable relic. He has also a landscape by Rembrandt, which is another novelty rarely, I believe, to be met with. He has the best Teniers, and one of the best Ruysdaels I ever saw. Here is, in my humble opinion, the finest painting of fruit that can possibly be conceived, which he told me was done by Heem (Jean David). To speak of the Vandycks, the Murillos, the Rembrandts &c. would absorb my whole evening; suffice it therefore to say that Mr. Schamp had in his collection some of the best pictures of almost every master I have ever heard of, and of many that were never before named to me. Of course we here saw the Flemish school to great advantage, and though I have no pretensions to judgment, yet I was highly delighted.

We next explored the celebrated cathedral of St. Bavon. The first grand object is the pulpit, which I have observed, with scarcely any exception, are, in the churches throughout the Netherlands and Holland, magnificent in the extreme, both for excellence of design and superior carving. This one, done by Laurens Delvaux, in 1745, is a combination of wood and the finest marble, exquisitely carved, and represents an aged man, to whom an angel, trampling on the globe of the earth, opens the book of life. At the head of the church, or chief altar, we have a splendid carving of St. Bavon, and the choir on each side of the aisle is formed of pure marble with such matchless carvings on the tombs of seventeen bishops, which have been interred, that I am only surprised at not having heard them more publicly spoken of. Among the finest, I was particularly struck with that of the third bishop of Ghent, in alabaster; and the seventh bishop with a mosaic portrait over the tomb. The choir of this cathedral is surrounded with numerous chapels, which, of course, have each a fine altar, and old paintings, among which is one very fine by Honthorst, done in 1733; and another, which the Flemish sexton told me was 'the very first picture that ever was painted in oils,' and that it was above 400 years old. The correctness of this as to dates and truth I leave to others to discover, as I merely write at the moment from what local information I can collect. The huge massive brass doors of the chapels are quite a novelty, no less for their stupendous weight than the pains it must have cost to carve them. The two gigantic candlesticks, sent from Charles the First of England, are moulded in enormous masses of bronze, and I should guess about eight feet high. I omitted, among the paintings, to name one of the Paschal Lamb, by Van Eyck, done in the year 1415, which painting is in the Venetian school and still retains its brilliant colour; and also the Resurrection of Lazarus, by Van Veen, the master of Rubens. The church of St. Michael, too, has some paintings worthy of a short observation, and, of course, a beautiful pulpit.

We then saw the botanic garden, the fine public library, and the ancient building which is used as the Hôtel de Ville. We strolled afterwards about the town with our guide, who spoke very good English, and had been in Spain in the same action with myself and in our service. He showed us a piece of lumber called a cannon, left ages ago by the Spaniards, which was about two feet in calibre, and would have required a small tea table for a wadding. We then listened to some very fine bells at the town belfry, which is a tower adjoining the prison, that is remarkable as having been the place of confinement for starvation of the old man who was kept alive by being suckled by his own daughter, and who was consequently pardoned. I observed all the dogs were muzzled in the town, and on inquiry I learnt that such is the dread of mad dogs in Flemish towns, that the police have orders to destroy every dog which they see loose without a muzzle. For the purpose they are provided with balls of poison, and there they lie about in every direction, as much for the sake of getting the dogs' skins, as for any other reason. The streets of Ghent are cleaner and superior to the old town of Brussels; but just after seeing the new and upper town of Brussels, one views almost every place abroad with discontent.

20th.—At half-past eight this morning we started for

Bruges, in one of the celebrated Ghent barges, which in the Dutch and Flemish languages is called a *treckschuyt*, and which may be considered almost as a floating cook's shop. During the whole passage nothing but eating and drinking was the order of the day. We paid 5½ francs each for ourselves, 3½ francs each for our servants, and 1½ franc for our baggage, and had a most sumptuous dinner into the bargain. At a little before one o'clock we sat down to some of the best-dressed dishes that I ever saw put on a table: two sorts of fish, meat, poultry, made dishes, &c. We had two regular courses, besides a third, which included the dessert. After witnessing the superior performance of the cook in a Ghent barge, I was not so much surprised to hear that gourmands often make this excursion expressly to satisfy their gluttonous appetites, and that one idle man whose chief resource was, like many other foreigners, that of chattering and stuffing himself, actually lived in the Ghent barge for six of the summer months, by way of a cheap residence, where he could gratify the fancies of his little mind and great appetite.

At a quarter before three o'clock we stepped on shore at the quay in Bruges, which from Ghent is 8 leagues by water, and 9 by the paved coach road. After walking through the streets, which were very clean though very dull, and taking a hasty peep into a fine church, we went on board a barge, which goes to Ostend, and to which all our things were wheeled in a barrow for the regulated price of 15 pence. The captain had collected about a hundred passengers, whose chatter resembled a pack of hounds in full cry, and to this he added an obbligato accompaniment of a large hand bell, with which he summoned them on board. We started at four, and by half-past six got on shore at Ostend, having been towed by four horses, with the aid of a sail, four leagues, in two hours and a half. Ostend from Bruges by the pavé or coach road is 6 leagues. On stepping ashore at Ostend, nearly all the commissioners who were sent to beat up recruits for the innkeepers were Englishmen, which made the place appear to us like the landing on a British shore; and when we got to the Hôtel d'Angleterre, kept by a Mr. Nicholson, there was not a foreign article or a foreign person to be seen about the premises. It was literally an England in Belgium. I spent the evening in viewing the very fine fortifications, the harbour, and the beautiful sands which distinguish the shore at this place, and then retired, much in want of rest, to a good honest English four-post bed.

21st.—Having now got safe to Ostend, we had to make our choice of two inconveniences: either that of a long passage to England, or to have another filthy French journey of about 60 miles to Calais in order to shorten and have less hazard in our passage. With a lady there would be no hesitation in favour of the latter, particularly as we have no reason to expect that any packet will sail before the day after to-morrow (Wednesdays and Saturdays being the only days), were it not for the following unpleasant circumstance, viz. all those travellers who enter France from Belgium are so tormented at the French frontier custom house, by Dunquerque, that the conduct of these *douaniers* is the talk of everyone. They have literally taken the handkerchiefs from gentlemen's necks, and are so greedy to get possession of everything which they can make an excuse to seize, that they may rather be considered as a banditti than officers of a lawful king; and, according to report, they are insolent in the extreme. Having at present excellent quarters, with beautiful weather and a fair wind from Ostend, we therefore decided that we would, at all events, wait here a day or two longer. After taking a comfortable English breakfast, Mrs. Hawker and I went out for the whole morning with an English commissioner, who explained to us every trifle in the town. The fortifications, the barracks, the sluices, the new works &c. are worth a morning's inspection, and the breeze from the sea is so delightful after the marshy air of Belgium that its salubrious effect on us was like magic. Having in case of accidents provided myself with a letter from Mr. Messel, the banker, of Brussels, to his correspondent, Mr. Herrewyn, of Ostend, I called on this gentleman, who, among other acts of the greatest politeness, took me up to his observatory, from whence I had a fine view of the sea and town. Ostend has so delightful a sea breeze, and the streets are so free from the offensive smells with which you are annoyed in most foreign towns, that were I to be exiled through disgrace, debt, poverty or extravagance, I should certainly choose this as my head quarters, notwithstanding there is here some trouble in getting supplied with good fresh water.

22nd.—Had I not been detained this day I should have lost a sight of what I think the best worth looking at of anything in Ostend, and which never was named to me—it is the Fort Napoléon, a wooden lighthouse at the mouth of the harbour, to which you have access by an immensely long range of planks, and where the depth of water (which is from 14 to 20 feet) is ascertained in the night by a kind of sunk pendulum that rings a little bell, and from this an old man, who is appointed to the station, makes by different lights his various signals to the captains of vessels who may wish to enter.

With the hope of being able to start by the packet of tomorrow, I this day discharged my bill at Mr. Nicholson's hotel; and it is but justice to observe that for comfort, accommodation, civility and cheapness, I never in my life was in such an admirable inn. We had everything in abundance of the very best kind, and our expenses were literally cheaper than if we had bought the articles in the market. Every traveller is bound in justice to proclaim Mr. Nicholson and the 'Rose' inn or Hôtel d'Angleterre of Ostend.

23rd.—Embarked this morning at five o'clock on board the 'Prince of Waterloo' packet with Captain Page, a very honest, obliging man. We got under way at a quarter past five, and at half-past twelve dropped anchor alongside the quay at Ramsgate, having sailed from harbour to harbour, considerably above 60 miles, in about seven hours. We might have eaten an eight o'clock dinner in London had it not been for the custom-house officers, who at this port, although civil, are more troublesome and more strict than at any place I ever entered. We had a gale of wind with showers and squalls for the last two-thirds of our passage. The passengers on landing at Ramsgate are summoned to the custom house to be personally searched; and but for a few masterly manœuvres I should have lost all my little bagatelles. It is only by a miracle that I contrived to save anything I had; never did I meet such a set of devils to outwit as the custom-house officers of Ramsgate. I believe I was the only one but what had something taken away from his or her effects. But reverting to the officers of Ostend, they are altogether as lenient, and particularly in leaving the country; for here, instead of giving, as is usual, a search (though of course less rigid than on landing), they gave no search at all, but merely delivered a permit for the embarkation of our baggage, by which we had not even to unstrap a single portmanteau. After passing two hours at the office of these infernal Ramsgate sharks, with my wits as much on the stretch as if I had been pleading at the bar, I got into a small inn (for the convenience of the morning coach) called the Royal Oak, where I had good accommodation, with most excellent fish, a very reasonable bill, and much more civility than if I had gone, as a mere dirty traveller, to one of those kinds of hornet's nests where you are fleeced with powdered waiters and wax candles, such as Wright's Hotel at Dover &c., and where you pay 50 per cent. extra.

24th.—Left Ramsgate at seven this morning, and at four arrived at Hatchett's Hotel, where we were driven up to the Dover Street door by a coachman who was not only civil but who had more gentlemanly manners than half the people

I have met at the Court of St. James's. I suspect this man had seen better days.

26th.—On this day (by the way, it snowed and was as cold as in January) I returned by the Salisbury coach to Longparish, where I, thank God, found all my family well. During all our travels we never lost or broke a single article, because we had everything numbered and classed for its place, which plan I should always recommend, and particularly to young travellers.

The foregoing memorandums were hastily scribbled at such hurried moments, and in such awkward places, that to put them into language sufficiently good for a common letter would require a revision of the whole ; but as I am now very busy on concerns of more importance, and as they were compiled merely to amuse a few of my particular friends, who would rather seek for my information than my faults, I shall not waste my time on any corrections. If, therefore, this elegant piece of syntax should fall into the hands of a word-catcher, I can only say that I will correct literary errors as fast as he may find them, conditionally that he gives me a bottle of wine for each ; and if he meets with any such mistake subsequent to my revision, I will, as a punishment for my ignorance, give him a dozen of wine, and if a dandy a new pair of stays. By saying this, far be it from me to presume where I have not the slightest pretensions, but merely act on the defensive against some of those half-educated machines who are so fond of saying, 'This fellow cannot write English,' and who seek for the leaves on the tree rather than the effect of the landscape ; in short, people who look at their words as a lady would examine a piece of Brussels lace before they either write or speak, and who, if probed, are generally found to possess about as much genius as a donkey.

June 1st.—As of late years I have not fished regularly, but merely taken my rod as a recreation, when friends were at Longparish, or when I wanted trout, I have discontinued keeping any account of my own performances; but the number of fish brought in to our house during this month has been exactly 212 brace, of which nine-tenths, of course, were given, or sent, to our friends.

July 4th.—Went to London, relative to my hand-moulds; transfer of some stock to the French funds; to see about fresh boring and breeching my swivel gun; to try about getting a patent for the cure of smoky chimneys; and to hear the celebrated pianoforte player Moscheles, &c.

8th.—Having executed all business to my satisfaction, and had the delightful treat of hearing Moscheles, I this day returned to Longparish House.

August 6th.—Went to London concerning a purchase in the French funds, my patent &c., and to inspect the new breeching and boring of my single stanchion gun, of which I saw the means of improving. The plague that I had to superintend this latter work, Mr. Joseph Manton being unfit for business from an accident, was more troublesome than a suit in Chancery. After journeys to Fullerd's, in Clerkenwell, constant attendance at a forge during the hottest time I ever felt in London, we got the gun so far forward that I was promised it by Saturday morning, and took my place per coach for home. Delays, however, occurred; and I, determined to carry my point, as it is my rule, waited at Manton's till near twelve at night on the Friday; when the huge furnace that was required to harden the stupendous breeching, set Joe's chimney on fire, and we had a grand uproar with a row, engines, &c.: nevertheless, I carried my point; for we got the fire out, finished the gun, and I brought it off in triumph, per Salisbury coach, on Saturday, the 11th inst., when I arrived with it at Longparish House.

Weight of gun since reboring: Barrel and breech, 58 lb.; stock, lock &c. 20 lb.; swivel, 5 lb. Total, 83 lb.

CHAPTER XIV

1821

September 1st.—The corn being so much in the way this season, I had made every attempt to postpone the shooting, but to no effect; and no sooner was it daylight than old Payne and his son, two vagabonds under the toleration of Mr. Widmore, were popping away before my house. I, therefore, turned savage and sallied forth to follow the birds, and I did wonders considering the dreadfully bad behaviour of the young dogs I had to shoot with. I bagged 38 partridges, and shot and lost in the barley, while the dogs were running off wild, 8 partridges, and also 2 snipes, which these dogs mauled to pieces in the reeds, but would not bring to me. Making in all, knocked down, 23 brace of birds and 2 snipes.

3rd.—30 partridges and 1 wood pigeon, with only missing one long shot, as I was, this day, not tormented with wild young dogs.

17th.—Had an extraordinary day, under all circumstances. I went out at ten and was home by two. In consequence of domestic misfortune I was so unwell as to be forced to take bitters for the nervous state I was in. I had young dogs that behaved most infamously, and literally obliged me to race, in order to save the few shots they would let me get. The day was windy, and the birds wild; notwithstanding all, I bagged 20 partridges, besides 3 shot dead and lost, without missing a single time, with killing 4 double shots, and making good some very long snap shots. I made one singular shot with the rapidity of lightning, viz. 5 birds rose at about 40 yards; I cut down and bagged 4 (just as they were in line together) at a shot with the first barrel, and knocked down the fifth bird in most handsome style with the second barrel, making in all 23 birds in 20 shots.

Game killed in September 1821: 152 partridges, 1 hare, 5 snipes. Total, 158 head.

October 1st.—Lord and Lady Poulett left me, after our passing together two most agreeable days and musical evenings. Not a pheasant on my estate, so no more covert shooting, unless I choose to go for it to the many friends who have invited me, but whose invitations I am neither in health nor spirits to accept.

3rd.—Went to Sir Thomas Baring's at Stratton Park. Killed, in about five hours, 12 partridges, 12 hares, and 1 pheasant, the only one I shot at, besides 4 birds winged and lost. This was merely my own share of the day's bag, though it happened to be the best share.

4th.—Returned to Longparish.

6th.—Joined the North Hants Regiment, which this day assembled at Winchester Barracks for twenty-one days' training.

The Lieutenant-Colonel having resigned, I was strongly recommended by Lord Rodney for the command, but the Duke of Wellington, although he admitted I had the 'best military claims in the county,' would not allow me the promotion in the event of being able to find a man of higher rank; and, therefore, I have been in suspense ever since the middle of August, for the mere hazard of this eligible step, which always before was quite certain to be mine as soon as the Colonel recommended. What with this and family misfortunes, I could only support myself for duty and the mess by constant stimuli, and the state I have been in would have even gained me the pity of my greatest enemy.

26th.—The regiment was broken up again, and the flattering manner in which my brother officers, without one dissenting voice, expressed a wish (and even wanted to memorial) for my promotion, was most grateful to my feelings.

27th.—Returned to Longparish, after a farewell dinner the previous day.

November 2nd.—Went to Winchester, to wait in durance vile while the Duke of Wellington was passing the final sentence about my promotion, which, luckily, his Grace decided in my favour; and I then, with my mind greatly relieved on this subject, proceeded to Lord Rodney's, at Alresford, where I took my dinner and a bed.

7th.—Went again to Lord Rodney's, for the express purpose of showing his bailiff and keepers the proper plans for getting the wild fowl on his most admirably fine pond (after the plan of a decoy hut, as I had seen in France).

Waited at the pond from five this evening till seven the next morning; but the bailiff having persisted, contrary to my advice, in choosing a very ill-judged position for the decoy hut, we never got a shot all night; whereas if he had complied with my suggestions, we should have had most excellent sport.

8th.—Killed 2 teal and 1 snipe, and at night waited about six hours more in a new hut. Owing to the rough weather, perhaps, the fowl would not leave the water meadows, and only one duck came to the pond, and this immediately pitched before the spot I had now chosen, and was killed by the bailiff, who relieved me in the duty of sentry there, by which he was convinced of the goodness of my plan, as well as my choice of the place.

9th.—Walked in the water meadows from half-past nine till five, till my feet (with the water boots) were literally raw. I killed 2 mallards, 2 wild ducks, 4 teal, 2 jack snipes, and 1 snipe, with coots, moorhens, &c., in short, returned with a bag *omnium gatherum*, besides having lost several excellent chances hrough downright bad luck. Just before dusk I finished with storming the armies of starlings that roost every night in the reeds on Alresford Pond. The first shot I fired nearly half a pound of small shot with a shoulder duck gun into about an acre square of these birds, and how many I killed I know not; but I can swear to having shot 105 at a shot, because we picked up 96, and counted 9 lying on the pond; and these, I expect, were not near the half of what must have fallen to the gun. We kept up the attack till above a bushel and a half were bagged, and how many more may be found by daylight will remain to be proved.

10*th.*—Having put Lord Rodney's people in the proper method for everything concerning the management of his pond and decoy hut, I this morning, after having passed my time most agreeably, returned to Longparish House.

14*th.*—Having previously sent forward all my canoes, punts, baggage &c. I this day left Longparish for Keyhaven Cottage, where I was met by my gunner, James Reade, from the Isle of Purbeck.

15*th.*—A very good show of wigeon, considering the mild wet weather. The tremendous hurricane and rain would only admit of my going afloat for a few hours this evening.

19*th.*—16 wigeon. I got a shot at about 50, but the night was so dark, and the tide falling so fast, that I got none but what we killed quite dead. This is the first time I have fired at birds with the stanchion since it was fresh bored and breeched by Joe Manton.

21*st.*—Went to Poole to superintend the building of my large boat, and take out the licence for her under the name of the 'Wellington.'

22*nd.*—Arrived back again at Keyhaven this evening.

23*rd.*—1 brent goose, and another, that fell on the tide, lost. The first geese seen off Keyhaven this year. I bore down on them in a gale of wind, and fired the stanchion at about 150 yards, flying. Owing to the bad weather, this is the first shot I have fired since killing the 16 wigeon on the 19th.

24th and 25th.—A constant series of wet, windy days, and every bird driven away to the leeward part of the coast.

26th.—I this day received from the Duke of Wellington my Lieutenant-Colonel's commission, which was dated the 15th instant.

27th to 30th.—Incessant hurricanes from the westward, and not a bird left on this part of the coast, as nothing can live to windward.

December 5th.—Availed myself of the still dreadful weather to superintend the finishing of my boat, the 'Wellington,' and receive my licence for her from the London custom house; and accordingly this day went to Poole.

6th.—Had great plague with my gun and boat, in consequence of the workmen having deviated from my plans. I was obliged to remain all this day, all the 7th, and all the 8th at the hotel in Poole, to be at the elbows of the boat builders. I had everything pulled to pieces and changed to my own plan, and then, as I expected, it answered admirably. The uproar of about 100 men and boys dragging the boat to the water, and the christening of her, was a laughable scene. I returned to Keyhaven (in my punt on wheels) with post horses, by moonlight, on the night of the 8th.

8th.—On returning from Poole at night I heard of a few fowl, and, instead of going to bed or sitting down to rest, I drove my canoe to the shore, took her off the carriage, launched her in the rain, and got (just before midnight) 3 wigeon.

N.B.—This chance at a few birds is the first that Keyhaven has afforded to anyone since my shot on the 19th ultimo.

11th.—After a succession of 22 days' terrible weather, we had this day the pleasure to have one fine morning, and got 2 brent geese and 4 wigeon.

21st.—After eight days more of the most dreadful weather

that ever wind and torrents of rain could produce, I being almost sick from confinement to the house, drove, for a change of air, to pass a couple of days with Mr. Bertie Mathew at Lyndhurst, and returned on the evening of the 23rd, when the whole county was inundated; people in many parts dying like rotten sheep; doctors flying in all directions; and, in short, no enjoyment for any creature but doctors, undertakers, and other human reptiles that fatten on the misfortunes of others. Thank God, however, except a slight sickness through the whole house from which scarcely anyone has escaped, we have been, on the whole, as yet, extremely fortunate.

28th.—The weather, which has, day after day and week after week, been most hideously abominable, this day came to such a tremendous hurricane that the whole valley could be compared to nothing but the very rage of battle. Keyhaven is no longer a village, but a sea. The tide is so tremendous that the breakers literally rage and foam against the houses, while the incessant rain is pouring in torrents, and the whole population here are driven to their attics; no communication from house to house except by boats, which can scarcely live in the sea that washes our doors; and the breakers which are bursting at us, as if threatening to swallow our very houses, present a scene most awfully grand. But the distress of the poor people is more calculated to excite our feelings than the inconvenience to ourselves. Thank God we are somewhat less inundated than our neighbours, having as yet saved all our boats and property. We have our punts floating at our door in the street ready to rescue our family in case of danger. What a scene! Shutters, doors, and pails afloat; birds killed while diving and washed up by the tide; and, in short, the best representation I have yet seen of a second deluge. My dear children, instead of being alarmed or ill, were amused with the scramble; and I by way of aping Nero (who fiddled while Rome was burning) sat at my old humstrum, and boggled through a given number of Bach's fugues.

29th.—Before this evening the waters had entirely abated, and we found that we had the good fortune not to have sustained the slightest loss or damage in the deluge, though some of our neighbours have suffered severely. No prospect yet of weather in which we can even attempt to shoot.

30th and 31st.—Most deplorable wind and rain from the westward. Never, never can we see a prospect of even tolerable weather. The oldest inhabitants, and the greatest judges here, consider this everlasting wet wind as a phenomenon that baffles all their judgment. Let us hope, not only for our sport, but for the farmers and the poor, and reasons of more consequence, that 1822 will give us a more cheerful prospect of weather.

1822

January 9th.—Having taken calomel, and suffered severely all yesterday, I was this day considerably better; and we have now the pleasure to see fine weather.

10th.—Got pretty well. Fine weather, but more like May than January. At last had the pleasure of discharging a gun again, and killed 1 brent goose.

11th and 12th.—As hot as May-day, and not a bird to be seen or heard either day or night.

February 8th.—It being now twenty-eight days since I have heard, seen, or even heard of a wigeon, I this day had my guns cleaned up, and discharged my account with Reade.

Game &c. killed up to 11th of February, 1822: 164 partridges (shot but one day since September), 13 hares, 8 snipes, 1 pheasant, 4 wild ducks, 6 teal, 44 wigeon, 9 brent geese. Total, 249 head.

The worst wild-fowl year ever remembered by the oldest man on our coast. The most unpleasant season I ever shot in, and the most unhappy period of my life and affairs in general that ever I experienced.

March 5th.—Returned to Longparish from Keyhaven.

May 9th.—Unwell as I was, I mustered resolution to go to London to attend Cramer's concert, where I heard such an exquisite duet as may rarely be given during a man's life, between J. B. Cramer and Moscheles, on two pianofortes.

June 2nd.—Removed to Longparish, of course with considerable pain from my late illness. Met Lord and Lady Poulett, and their little son, Viscount Hinton, on my arrival. I was all the 2nd, 3rd, and 4th in torture day and night with the gout, and on the latter day, while I had Colonel Hay and other friends, besides Lord and Lady Poulett, with me.

August 19th.—2 teal and 1 wild duck, also another wild duck that the dog let go from his mouth, that I never recovered.

Teal here, in summer, are very rare. I marked them down while fishing; there were 3 in number, and I bagged 2 at a shot, flying, although a long way off, and with a very small gun. The ducks I killed in front of the house. Four pitched down, and by means of going on my stomach, all the way to them, I got so near that if they had sat one instant longer, I must have stopped all four of them, notwithstanding I had no ambush whatever but the mere ground that I crawled on.

26th.—Started about five this morning, with my own horses, and from Andover took four post horses, in order to have the whole day's inspection of the hitherto inaccessible mansion of Mr. Beckford at Fonthill, which is now open to the public by guinea tickets, under the plea of an intended sale by auction. The uproar which the admission to this Abbey has made all over the country led me to expect more than, perhaps, any place in existence could have afforded, and consequently I was rather disappointed in finding that the *tout ensemble* was by no means superior to some other places that I had seen. To enter into particulars would be needless, when I have Rutter's flowery description, and also a specific catalogue of every article; but I shall make a few remarks. The western entrance to the Abbey, by the Gothic doors, the baronial hall, and the library, with every costly cabinet that unlimited expense and incessant research could produce, surpassed (as a *coup d'œil*) for neatness, elegance, and classical arrangement, all that I had ever seen. Nothing could be more tastefully displayed than the various cabinets of the most ancient china, which were no less in variety than the costly gems and exquisite workmanship with which the other innumerable ornaments were composed.

I found the view from the tower to be one of the finest and most extensive panoramic views that I could conceive, and the Gothic architecture of the building is exquisitely magnificent, but here must end all that need be especially remarked in approbation of Fonthill, and on the whole I should say that its chief ornaments were more calculated to adorn the boudoir, or dressing-room, of a princess than to give imposing grandeur to the mansion of a wealthy Englishman. The paintings were very fine, but the collection did not appear to me to be so 'far beyond comparison' as was reported by the Gullivers and Baron Munchausens for which the town of Andover is so celebrated. The most striking ones to me were, the 'Entombment of a Cardinal,' by Van Eyck, and 'Christ in the Garden,' by A. Mantegna; the latter, particularly, is very justly styled in the catalogue 'a very surprising and valuable early specimen.'

The grounds are most extensive, insomuch that the guide informed me there was one walk of sixteen miles. Rutter, however, calls it the nine-mile walk, and I should rather trust to his authority. But nothing can be more monotonous than the objects which are here in view: one endless tract of neatly mown grass walks, or rides, all thickly wooded and without a single cascade, fountain, grotto, figure, or obelisk, and with no other view of water than a long lake which is almost obscured, instead of being heightened in beauty, by the sequestered valley in which it lies.

The gardens, and, in short, the whole domain, I presume, remain unfinished, when I see the contrast between them and the Abbey itself, which was well worth the drive, although the distance altogether, including about ten miles that we drove and walked in the grounds, was about ninety miles. I got home to Longparish House by nine o'clock at night, having travelled most furiously and made about seven hours' very diligent inspection of the place.

CHAPTER XV

1822

September.—Having been for a long time so unwell with a nervous complaint, that I have had neither strength nor spirits to enjoy anything, I have made no provision for shooting, having only two moderate dogs. Never did I look forward to sport with so much indifference, and were it not for the pleasure of supplying my friends with a little game, I would gladly have laid aside my gun.

1st.—This being Sunday, shooting began next day.

2nd.—Never do I remember the first day of shooting so very unfavourable for filling the bag. No turnips, no good clover ; the stubbles as much beaten down and as thin as in November. A strong wind all day with drizzling rain at intervals. The very worst scenting day I ever was out in, and the birds quite as wild as in December. Annoyed by greedy shooters in every direction, who made the birds even wilder than they otherwise would have been, by disturbing every covey on the feed, blazing after them at random, and scouring the whole country from daybreak, so that I, weak and unwell as I was, had enough to do to bag even 24 partridges, which is far more than were killed by the other parties.

3rd.—18 partridges by incessant perseverance, while so unwell that I could scarcely hold my gun. Had I been able to shoot as usual, I should have done about as well as yesterday.

5th.—The country had been so driven by shooters, and the

wind was so high, that scarcely a bird was to be got at; after fagging all day and till I almost dropped down with weakness, I at last got one shot and killed 1 partridge, and then being too unwell to continue shooting I came home.

7th.—Having pretty well cleared the country of unqualified pothunters, I got this day a quiet beat, and bagged 16 partridges and 1 snipe, without missing a single shot, and making several very long shots.

11th.—It being folly to attempt shooting in such a time of hurricanes, and the ground as dry as sand, I this day went fishing, and had some good sport in a very short time; my largest trout was a very little under 2 lb. weight.

17th.—I, seeing the impossibility of sport, did not go out, but Captain Capel and Mr. Richards, with good dogs, and both old sportsmen and steady shots, started, and, after beating our very best country, never got but one random shot, and they literally came home with an empty bag on a fine sunshiny day.

18th.—The difficulty of killing birds put me on my metal, and my friends, defying me to get even 3 or 4 brace, made me desperate. I therefore quacked myself up with tincture of bark, sal volatile, and spirits of lavender, to give me artificial strength for a grand field day, and, aided by markers of cavalry and infantry, I attacked the birds in right earnest (and when I do this I have never yet failed), and in spite of an execrably bad scent, and a gale of wind from the east, I bagged 15 partridges (and another shot dead and lost) and 1 hare without missing a shot. Though I shook like an old man of seventy, I never shot more brilliantly. I of course suffered no other gun to interfere with me, and therefore went alone, so that I could follow up the game at speed when the markers gave the signal, and do as I please, whereas if I have friends, I always lose two-thirds of my shooting by wishing to accommodate them with the cream of the sport.

21st.—Being sadly in want of game, and seeing everyone

beat by the birds, I quacked myself up again with sal volatile, bark, and lavender, and, aided by the same good markers, I bagged 12 partridges, 2 snipes, and 1 jack snipe, without missing a shot.

In the last two days I shot with my beautiful new detonating gun, and I have killed with it 28 partridges, 3 snipes, and 1 hare, without missing a shot.

26th.—Was prevented going out or doing anything till this day through illness in the house, and being also unwell myself. I went out merely to try for a brace of birds for the doctor, who had been a repeated attendant, and in an hour and three-quarters brought home 6 partridges, 3 snipes, and 2 jack snipes.

Game &c. killed up to the end of September 1822: 108 partridges, 3 hares, 1 rabbit, 11 snipes, 2 wild ducks, 2 teal. Total, 127 head.

October.—The pheasants here are annihilated; consequently I made no attempt at October shooting.

23rd.—Having heard that 3 pheasants had by the high winds been blown on my estate, I assembled a levy *en masse*, headed by the ratcatcher and some field-marshal poachers, as if to attack a tiger, and before night I had all three in the larder, after their giving me and my banditti a chase that was far superior to an average fox hunt.

28th.—At night took some decoy birds and waited at the river for some hours, and though a beautiful moonlight and a white frost, I never saw or heard but one duck, which the call birds brought round several times, but too high to shoot at. Our duck shooting (like our pheasant shooting) is nearly annihilated, owing to the breaking up for water meadows of Lord Portsmouth's bogs, called the Parkses.

November 15th.—A grand bustle through the house in consequence of a man having run in with information of a woodcock. I marched against him, followed by a rabble, and in a few minutes flushed him and bagged him.

25th.—Having previously sent on my baggage &c. I this day left Longparish for Keyhaven, but more with the view of changing the air for my health than any prospect of sport, as the westerly winds are, as usual at this season, annihilating all chance of getting either fishing, fowling, or sailing.

December 2nd.—After all shooting had been precluded by several weeks' continual westerly winds and rain, we had this day the pleasure to see better weather, and took a sail in the 'Wellington' with the stanchion gun and large mould shot, and got 1 brent goose, I believe the first killed this season by anyone in this country. Went afloat at night, and towards morning bagged 2 wigeon, 5 being all we saw, and the first that I had seen or heard of since my arrival; I killed them under the moon with the stanchion gun, so we have now made a little beginning.

3rd.—Out again the whole night and never saw a bird, and the same complaint all along our coast.

6th.—Every day west winds, and no fowl. I had this day the mortification to have blown off and then sunk in the creek the most beautiful detonating lock, that I was so proud of contriving, and such a long time getting Manton to make. I used every kind of drag to no purpose, and the last hope will be the next spring tide.

12th.—Having now an easterly wind, I, with my crew, sailed in my large boat the 'Wellington' at five o'clock in the morning, and beat all the way up to the mouth of the Beaulieu river, having twice stood out to the Isle of Wight in a heavy sea before we could fetch our point; we then sailed down, and saw an immense flock of geese, but no wigeon.

On our return about three in the afternoon we renewed by every possible means and invention our search for the gun lock, accompanied by a man named Thomas Mallard, who said he dreamt last night that the lock was found about a yard from the post, and in a line for the 'Duke's Head' public-house, where he eagerly kept probing with a long eel spear, to no purpose for some time; and, as the tide fell a little lower, we shovelled under the water as well as we could, till all hope of finding it was at an end. Mallard then, still inspired with a kind of presentiment by his dream, went to his old spot again, although we felt confident the lock was far above that place, and, most extraordinary, he suddenly struck something hard; down he ducked and up he brought the lock, to my great satisfaction and still greater astonishment.

18th.—The weather has been variable till this day, when it is again north-east but without cold or frost; we have since the 2nd got 5 wigeon, 5 curlews, 2 teal, and 3 godwits, which, little as it is for our hard labour, is the best, by far, that has been done here. In the evening, killed 2 godwits, and at night tried the new system of shoving the swivel gun and punt over the mud, and firing by guess. We had but a poor chance, the birds were so thin and scattered, but we got 1 wigeon, and, by the spattering on the mud, suppose I must have stopped some more.

22nd.—Up to this day we have got but 5 more wigeon. The weather is now frosty, and plenty of birds are, at last, to be seen; but, as we expect, about three gunners for every flock of birds. The excellent shots that we have had spoiled by vagabonds, who kill nothing themselves, is really provoking.

28th.—To this day, 3 wigeon, 2 brent geese and 1 mallard. A fair show of birds; but at no one hour of the day or night can we have time to paddle to a flock before some infernal Christmas popgun is discharged, and the wigeon are sprung by the flash on the shore. This night, we were within half a minute of firing into about 200 wigeon, close to us, when a rascal discharged some popgun on the shore, and sprang them.

Up to the 31st.—9 wigeon and 1 brent goose.

1823

January 1st.—Launched a little punt on my own plan, to carry nothing but the swivel gun, in order to shove it along on the mud, and fire with a string to the trigger. While chiselling down the bow to fit the gun, a golden plover pitched on the mud, and, after shoving a little towards him, I fired the gun, and killed him at exactly 100 yards; got, with my hand gun, also a mallard, after a race, as usual, against a gang of shore shooters.

2nd.—5 brent geese at one shot; at night fired with my little canoe by guess on the mud, heard several birds flutter, but it being quite dark, and I having no dog, got none of them at the time.

3rd.—Killed, at about 200 yards, 4 brent geese and 2 wigeon, besides a towered bird that fell at sea.

N.B.—The scoundrels, on the shore, make a practice of discharging some powder and then claiming the dead birds that float in to them from my shots, while I am getting the outside ones.

6th.—4 brent geese.

7th.—1 brent goose.

8th.—4 brent geese.

N.B.—Was coming home from Lymington, in almost a calm, with my children, on board the large yawl the 'Wellington,' saw 16 geese, and, to my astonishment, they let us get within about 180 yards of them, while shoving with the oars, and a boatful of people. As soon as I saw them stretch their necks to fly, I drew the trigger of the swivel gun, and, to my no less astonishment, down came 4 of them, although they were so thin that I had scarcely the breadth of more than 4 to shoot at.

9th.—6 geese[1] and 3 wigeon, after, as usual, a proper

[1] As brent geese are almost the only ones here, I shall, in future, put down merely the word 'geese.'

scramble against other boats, which we outmanœuvred most gloriously.

10*th.*—Killed, at a shot, with the stanchion gun, at about 150 yards, 2 pintails and 3 wigeon, all dead; also a mallard of a singular plumage, which I believe to be a Dutch fowl.

11*th.*—Had 3 beautiful shots spoiled by the other gunners, and got only 1 wigeon.

13*th.*—11 geese, killed 6 at the first shot, and 3 ducks, and lost, of course, several more that were picked up by the shore sharks, who lounge about with guns for that purpose.

14*th.*—7 geese and 1 wigeon.

15*th.*—7 wigeon, 2 mallards and 1 duck. Killed one of the mallards and the duck at the same shot with the wigeon, and while paddling up to the fowl, two small birds pitched on the barrel of my swivel gun. So severe was the frost and snow that they were, I suppose, benumbed in crossing the Channel.

16*th.*—14 wigeon and 18 geese, the latter in 3 shots, 8 the best shot. Gunners out of number afloat and ashore, and only one bird killed among them except mine.

17*th.*—My sport yesterday made the people so shooting mad that a flock of birds had hardly time to pitch before they were popped at by some boat or other, and among them all but one goose was killed. I therefore let them have their frolic out, till the afternoon; and when the water no longer served, I made Reade shove the canoe over the mud, and by our being dressed in white nightcaps and shirts, we suited the snow so well that we, in a short time, came in with 10 more geese.[1]

18*th.*—11 geese, which, in proportion to the very few I saw,

[1] N.B.—Killed this week: 57 geese, 25 wigeon, 4 ducks and mallards, and 2 curre ducks, making about 88 head, about ten times as much as has been killed by all the Keyhaven harbour shooters put together.

was the best day's work I have made. Out all night again, and my clothes stiff with frost, and when just going to bang into a flock of wigeon, a jealous villain on shore fired in the air purposely to spoil my shot.

20*th.*—We had only time to get 1 duck and 2 geese, as I was all day in Lymington, getting my lock mended, the cock of it being broken.

21*st.*—4 wigeon and 5 geese.

22*nd.*—5 wigeon and 5 geese at the same shot.

23*rd.*—8 geese, 1 wigeon, 2 mallards, 2 ducks, and 1 pin-tail. (The latter I killed at the same shot with the ducks.)

24*th.*—It blew such a tremendous hurricane all day that no boat could have lived, and froze so hard that in one night the whole harbour was like Greenland, and several wild swans passed by. I found a duck frozen to death, and they could not exist anywhere but in little ditches and other well-sheltered places. Reade scrambled over the ice in my little gunning punt, and had the great luck to succeed in shooting a wild swan that flew over him, and we got also 7 geese, 3 mallards, 1 duck, and 2 wigeon.

25*th.*—Everything frozen up, and I could not get out for the snow. Reade contrived to scramble across the ice in my little punt, and, by getting himself in a most miserable condition, brought in 2 geese, 3 wigeon, and 1 duck.

27*th.*—A sudden and general thaw, with a strong wind and an incessant pour of heavy rain. Nothing could be more novel or beautiful than the appearance of the harbour, which was one solid region of ice, with pyramids formed by the drifted snow, and frozen like glass; and on the thaw setting in the whole harbour appeared like a huge floating island as it was carried off by the fall of a high spring tide; and to see this huge movable body in motion with 14 wild swans sitting upon it, as it receded, and looking as if formed by nature for the only inhabitants of such a wild region, gave one more the idea of a voyage in the arctic circle than anything belonging to the shore of a habitable country. Under an idea that every vagabond would eagerly seize the first day's shooting after the thaw, I, to be well to windward of the butterfly shooters, weathered the torrent of rain all day, and, by capital locks and good management, contrived to keep my gun dry for the five shots which I got. The geese were scattered in every direction, so that I could not bag more than 5 at a shot, and so drenching wet was the day that after the first half-hour not a dry stitch could be found to wipe out the pan of my gun, except the tail of my shirt, and while paddling to birds I had three inches of water under my stomach. I fairly brought home 17 geese. I took one very long shot at 8 swans, heard the shot strike them, and afterwards saw one leave the company and drop on the sea, where I dare not venture (about two miles to leeward), consequently had not the good fortune to bring one home. Wet all the evening, a west wind, and as mild as May.

28th.—My swan that I shot yesterday having died and been picked up, there remained 7 of these magnificent birds, and they were seen off Keyhaven sitting among what little ice was left, about nine o'clock in the morning, and every corner of the creeks or on shore contained a gunner anxiously hoping that they might possibly swim or fly near enough for a random shot. Having to contend with all this impediment, and the wildest birds in existence to cope with, I had recourse to a manœuvre which struck me as the only chance. I dressed myself and Reade in a clean white shirt, white neckcloth, and clean white nightcap, and in my white punt went all the way round to windward through a pretty heavy sea; and after getting to where the hill called 'Mount' became a background to the view, in which we appeared, we, dressed thus in milk white with a very white punt, drifted among the floating pieces of white ice till we got within about 180 yards of these monstrous fowls, when I let drive at their necks and knocked down and brought home 2 wild swans or

Invented & Sketched by P. Hawker

Engd. on Steel by H. Adlard.

Commencement of a Cripple-Chase, after firing 2 lbs. of Shot into a Skein of Brent Geese, & Two Wild Swans.

London: Published by Longman & Co.

hoopers. I had to finish one of them with an old musket, or he might probably have escaped; and I wounded a third severely,[1] as three were fairly laid in the water, to the discharge of my swivel gun. As this attack was in full view of the village, I had several people anxiously looking on, and among them my children and all the house with their hearts in their mouths, and in a gale of wind and rain, eagerly watching our proceedings.

Towards the afternoon I was not a little surprised to see 16 more swans. They were, however, very far off, and near to a dangerous sea, and therefore, determined of course to run no risk, I dare only venture to within 220 yards of them; I consequently fired at this distance, and fairly laid 5 of them down on the water, till the others had flown above a gunshot; and notwithstanding this they all recovered, and, I suppose, joined the company.

The 2 that I killed were of equal weight (18 lb. each), one milk-white, the other of a dusky colour; the latter the largest; got also this day 10 geese and 5 wigeon.

The birds here being so incessantly popped at, I am always obliged to use large mould shot (called 'SSG') by day. Of this my gun carries 1 lb. with an equal measure of treble strong, coarse-grained powder, made on purpose, as a common gun or common shot afloat here would rarely if ever hit a bird so as to kill him.

As usual, gunners afloat all day out of number, and nothing done; and, I dare to say, not a little jealous of our invariable success.

29th.—A tremendous gale of wind all the morning, and the whole country armed with popping vagrants, who kept every flock of birds in constant jeopardy with their contemptible noise, and the whistling of slugs, which they kept discharging at everything they saw. The reptiles spoiled me

[1] One was afterwards picked up in the direction he went, so I may safely say I killed three swans at a shot.

another magnificent shot at the remaining swans, one of which, in spite of all, came over my head, and my hand gun, that I was then obliged to use, missed fire. I got but one poor shot, and killed 2 geese, and afterwards a dun-curre duck from a flock of these birds, at which I before refused an excellent shot, supposing from their white noses that they were coots, and, having the sun on them, I could not see clearly till too late ; at night 4 wigeon.

30*th.*—In Lymington about my new punt ; out in the evening ; got 3 geese, the finest I ever saw, and almost white in the breast, the only shot I got, and that a random one flying instead of a magnificent one sitting, owing to a stupid ass trying to out-row me with a huge black boat. About twelve at night got a beautiful shot at about 100 wigeon on the water, but, owing to the experiment of a night sight that was rather too thick, I shot infamously bad, and my whole charge went among the first of the birds, and in the water below them ; so that, instead of 20 or 30, I only stopped 8.

31*st.*—A wet day, and as no jackanapes could get his gun off in the rain it was my only chance ; I therefore sallied out for one huge swan that had been the target of the coast, and had become so wild that he could scarcely be looked at : on my way out I fired a long shot and got 4 geese ; soon after, as I expected, we saw this huge bird, floating about in a rough sea, and in a pour of rain ; I had two punts to manœuvre on one side of him, while Reade and I drifted down on the other ; he sprung at about four hundred yards, came luckily across my punt at about 75 yards, and down I fetched him, like a cock pheasant, with the swivel gun. His fall was more like the parachute of an air balloon than a bird ; he was shot quite dead ; he weighed 21 lb., and measured 7 feet 8 inches from wing to wing, being the largest, by far, of any I had killed ; therefore my misfortune of last night was balanced by getting another wild swan.

February 1st.—An incessant pour of rain from morning till night; and I therefore was at Lymington nearly all day, superintending my new punt. A few geese pitched off near the quay in the evening, but rose an immense long shot. I fired at random, killed 1 goose, and came in again, or I should have been drenched to the skin.

3rd.—It scarcely ceased raining for one half-hour ever since the morning of the 31st ultimo. I went out in a pour of rain, fired one long shot, got 3 geese, and then went, for the day, to Lymington about my punt, and to get some little repairs to my gun.

5th.—Took a sail, but there were no geese near the Channel's edge. Was out at night, but it was so dark that I could not see my gun or the birds; I fired to the sound of some wigeon feeding, but made a wrong guess and missed.

6th.—A tremendous gale of wind, with snow, sleet, and rain; and not being able to exist afloat, I chose this as a favourable opportunity to be again in Lymington, and direct the workmen as to the completing of my new punt.

7th.—Wind and rain nearly all day. Killed 2 geese. Owing to the wet, mild weather, the geese were nearly as wild as hoopers.

10th.—Incessant gales of wind and rain. Though I weathered it all, I got but one shot and bagged 4 geese.

11th.—After having been out all night, and done nothing with the wigeon, owing to the wet, dark weather, I was out again all to-day, but never could get a chance to fire a gun. Except the tremendous flood last year I never saw more sea in the harbour, insomuch that we were occasionally obliged to go ashore and empty out our punt, which was repeatedly half filled; it never ceased raining the whole day. We should have had a few tolerable shots at geese had they not been spoiled by the detestable shore lubbers, who were, as usual, in armies, and who, of course, never killed, or even wounded, one bird among them all.

12*th*.—4 geese, by means of sailing in the 'Wellington,' and firing a pound of balls as they crossed.

I had this day a providential escape from being shot by Joe Wearns, the sailor. He had his gun on board, not having time to take it home, before he came to help 'man' my boat, and in putting on an old stocking that he had for a lock cover, he let the gun go off. The whole contents went within a few inches of my right side, and, as God's mercy further prevailed, instead of blowing a hole through the boat and sending us all to the bottom, the charge was half lodged in the stem post, and the other half stopped by the anchor, which happened to be down in the bottom of the boat. No one has ever been more careful of what persons and what guns they suffer to come on board than myself; and this shows what may happen from the slightest neglect of such a necessary caution, though, as it most mercifully happened, not one farthing's worth of mischief was done to either ourselves or the boat.

13*th*.—Sailed to Lymington to bring home my new punt, called the 'Fox,' and, on my way, fired off the swivel gun at 9 birds rapidly crossing, at about 120 yards, and knocked down 1.

The punt, built by a man of great celebrity, Mr. Thomas Inman, appears to be the neatest and best I ever had. It is somewhat singular that I was yesterday within two inches of being shot by Wearns, and this day within half an inch of having my right eye knocked out by Reade, with an oar; but most fortunately the blow just passed the ball of my eye, and took the upper lid, which, of course, is as black as if I had been fighting. It was a miracle for Reade, as he is the most active, the most careful, and the handiest man I ever saw in a boat, without any single exception.

15*th*.—Went out for the first time in my new-planned punt, the 'Fox,' and nothing could answer better than she, as yet, proves to do in every respect. I may say she is the first punt I ever yet saw that was really free from defect. I contrived to get 2 geese, which, with any boat that I before had, would, to-day, have been impossible.

19th.—Detained from going afloat all the morning by having to stand over the blacksmith while I showed him how to alter the swivel, which he had made wrong, though with a pattern before his eyes. In the evening I got a goose, and the musket missed fire at another that I had wounded so as to get close to. This gun, with a detonating apparatus by old Egg, served me this so many times, that I took off the apparatus and threw it into the sea, in order never to be made to swear any more. Out (as I almost always am) at night for several hours, and though I crawled in my mud punt for more than a mile, I could find but a few straggling wigeon, not worth notice.

20th.—Fine weather, like spring; but the late westerly hurricanes have nearly finished the prospect of sport. Out all day and saw but a few geese, flying in the air, at a distance. Out all night and never found a wigeon.

21st.—A westerly hurricane with a pour of rain all day. A few geese were off in the harbour; weathered it to them, and then dropped down towards them; but, though almost out of sight, could not get within 300 yards. Killed nothing. At night the weather was beautiful. Out, of course, as usual; but not a living bird was to be heard, even in, or out of, the harbour.

22nd.—Wet by day and fine by night. Out both; not a goose to be approached within bullet shot, nor a wigeon to be seen or heard. All the sport here appears to be completely over for this season.

Reade went, this day, to Poole, to see if there were any birds there worth my going for.

24th.—Reade having returned with a fair account of the birds at Poole, I this evening sent on my punt for a few finishing days at my old quarters at Southhaven, as all sport at Keyhaven is now decidedly at an end.

25th.—Got to Poole and then over to Southhaven, after a most abominable journey both by sea and land, the rain falling in torrents, and the wind blowing a perfect hurricane. On arrival at the little hovel called Southhaven Inn, the place was destitute of everything, owing to a dispute with the former landlord, who would not give up the licence to the new one, who had just arrived, but consequently would not unpack his things. There were two rooms, the one solid blue with smoke, and the other with the masons putting up a chimney. This might have done quite well enough, as we meant to be twenty hours out of the twenty-four afloat; but as luck would have it, the wind and rain made us prisoners all the afternoon, all night, and part of the next day. At last matters were settled, and the old landlord walked off, and the other, with his family, began to make things look less miserable, and no people could be more civil, more reasonable, or more anxious to oblige. An immense number of geese in Poole harbour, as well as burrough ducks, curre, &c.; but the very wind which we had to weather had fairly cleared the harbour of wigeon, so that we were out all three nights without hearing a bird. Could get nothing but a few day shots, and consequently killed but 7 geese and 1 curre duck, added to some coots &c. that I shot, for mere pastime, with my shoulder gun.

March 1st.—Having done some business which I had at Poole, I then drove back again to Keyhaven.

The enormous mob of gunners that crowded round to exclaim at my shooting apparatus on the quay at Poole, I could compare to nothing but a Westminster election; and, previously to leaving the town, I rowed over to Ham to see the field marshal of the eastern gunners, who had come there, to the terror of all the Poole men. His name is Sam Singer; I was delighted with him, and we were two hours eagerly conversing with each other; the pleasure of this interview well repaid me for going to Poole, and reminded me of Wellington and Blucher meeting after the battle of Waterloo; and what made the matter pleasanter still, I have killed more geese than he has.

4th.—Quitted the coast for the season, and returned with my family to Longparish House.

Game and wild fowl up to March 1823:

Popgun work inland—132 partridges, 1 quail, 6 hares, 3 rabbits, 4 pheasants, 43 snipes. Total, 189.

Grand gunning work—18 ducks and mallards, 5 curre ducks, 5 teal, 3 pintails, 97 wigeon, 180 brent geese, 4 wild swans or hoopers. Total, 312. Land sport, bagged, 189; sea sport, 312. Grand total, 501; regular wild fowl, exclusive of coots, curlews, godwits, plover, ox-birds, and various other shore birds.

N.B.—The winter was most beautifully severe, but the wind, tides, and moon, particularly unfavourable in their times for serving us. The magnificent shots that I had spoiled by the shore-popping rabble, I can scarcely reflect on with common patience, and the wigeon shooting at Keyhaven was more disturbed and injured by the beggarly army of flight poppers than on any other part of our, or, I may safely say, any other, coast.

6th.—Longparish. Walked quietly out for the chance of a few snipes, and killed 8 snipes, 10 jack snipes, and 1 teal, without missing a single shot. Killed 2 jacks, a double shot; and at another time put up 3 snipes together; bagged two from the first barrel, and the third from the second; had I been prepared with two guns, and gone out in earnest, I should, perhaps, have rivalled all my other days' sniping at Longparish. I shot like a fiend, but the dogs behaved cruelly bad, or I should have made up a dozen couple.

8th.—Some snow and a little frost, consequently no snipe shooting. I got, however, 2 snipes, 2 jack snipes, and 1 woodcock (that had defied everyone here), after a hard chase of nearly two hours, and I finished by making a double shot, off my horse, with snipe shot, at 2 magpies.

11th.—Went to spend a few days with Lord Rodney at

his delightful place near Alresford, and took over my punt and swivel gun and other apparatus for shooting.

12*th.*—Up several hours before daylight, with the hope that some few birds might yet be left on his famous pond; got a shot at a small flock, and picked up 3 tufted ducks, 2 golden-eyes, and 2 dunbirds, at a shot. Then walked in the meadows after breakfast, and killed 10 snipes, 1 duck, 1 mallard, and 1 teal, besides several coots.

13*th.*—A grand battue at the coots, with about twenty guns; 125 were bagged, my share of which was 43; by means of having my punt I killed also 2 wild ducks and 1 mallard at daylight. Had also some fishing with a casting net and trimmers.

15*th.*—Returned home to Longparish.

N.B.—The sensation which my shooting punts and guns made in the town of Alresford was not a little diverting; and the publican, at whose house it stood, never sold more beer than on this occasion; and my man, who acted as the showman, got more pots than his head could well stand, for the trouble of explaining to the multitude the manner of using my large gun and other apparatus.

29*th.*—2 hares, and 1 woodcock (that weighed 1 lb.). I had given up shooting for the season, but was told of this cock, and after a *grande chasse*, with all the rabble I could collect, I found and bagged him, a very long shot.

Appendix since March 6th: 2 hares, 2 woodcocks, 47 snipes, 8 ducks and mallards, 5 tufted ducks, 2 golden-eyes, 2 dunbirds, 2 teal, making 70 head, besides a quantity of coots, 43 of which I killed one morning to my own share at Lord Rodney's, where 125 were killed, making in all 571 head this season, or, including coots &c., about 700 head.

April 19*th.*—Went to London for the Levee, and a multiplicity of other business.

21*st.*—Was presented by my Colonel and Lord Rodney

on my promotion as Lieutenant-Colonel of the North Hants Regiment.

May 7th.—Went to Hamble from Southampton, sailed to inspect Mr. Delme's duck marsh at Tichfield haven (Hill Head), and returned.

28th.—Went to Cowes from Southampton and back in the 'Medina' steam packet, and nothing could be more delightful. We went full ten miles an hour, and so free from any kind of motion that, being on board, with the noise of the engine, was precisely like being in a mill.

June 28th.—Longparish. For these several years past I have never cared about fishing further than to supply my friends, and then lay aside my rod whenever I made up my basket; but finding that it now becomes a kind of trumpery theme for reputation to kill so many fish, in order to chatter about the performance, I availed myself of about five hours' fine weather this day and honestly bagged 46 killable trout, besides a great many thrown in; my first 35 were all particularly fine fish, the largest 1¾ lb., which is the very best size our river is now likely to produce. I suppose some of the cockneys would have posted to York for such a day.

July 2nd.—Mr. and Mrs. Griesbach came to us, and left on the 21st. During the stay, I had some good sport trolling, particularly one day when I caught 5 fish, about 1 lb. each, in six throws, the largest about 2¼ lb. Mr. Griesbach, as a maiden trout fisher, killed 4 brace one day, and my little son Peter, without anyone to attend or show him the way, killed his 12 good trout, with a worm, in a few hours. I made a ridiculously good double shot this evening at a bat and a stag beetle.

CHAPTER XVI

1823

September 1st.—41 partridges and 1 quail, which, considering the nervous state of myself from recent illness, the want of good dogs and the annoyance of standing corn, is one of the best days I ever made. I made 8 double shots and missed nothing.

3rd.—30 partridges, and 6 more shot and lost. The only beat I had was where there were four other parties, and although so weak I could hardly walk, I am quite sure that I bagged twice as much as all of them put together.

6th.—20 partridges and 1 hare, having made 8 double shots; 4 brace out of which were at pairs of old birds, such has, this year, been the havoc among the nests, on our best side of the country, owing to the early mowing of the clover.

20th.—14 partridges and 1 snipe. Scent bad and birds extremely wild, everyone complaining that not even a brace could be got. I killed all my birds by means of walking the ground with both barrels cocked, and blazing, as quick as lightning, just as the birds topped the stubble.

23rd.—While everyone was complaining that not a bird could be got, I went out for scarcely more than two hours previously to going to Andover, and brought home 10 partridges, with missing only one long second-barrel shot. This shows what manœuvring will do.

29th.—A beautiful day, and the birds lay very fairly for the time of year and for our light country. I bagged 16 partridges and 1 jack snipe, and missed nothing.

Game &c. killed up to September 30th, 1823: 206 partridges, 2 hares, 1 quail, 2 snipes, 4 wild ducks. Except killing 4 brace to try a duck gun, I took but twelve days' shooting; which, as I was in indifferent health, badly off for dogs, and had such a multiplicity of business that interfered with my shooting, I consider most admirable sport; and I have no doubt more than was killed by all those put together who were here at it every day. I shot with a detonating gun which never missed fire but once, and made a great many double shots almost every day I went out; the most in one day was eight.

October 1st.—Out the whole morning in one incessant pour of heavy rain with a continual hurricane, and only discharged my gun three times, and all very long shots. I bagged 2 hares, and shot and lost the only pheasant I sprung; he was a fine old cock, and fell in the most handsome manner. A pheasant in my beat is a very rare bird to meet with, we having had none for years. My detonator went as well, in spite of all the rain, as if it had been used on a sunshiny day.

4th.—Slaved all day to no purpose trying to find a pheasant, and came home with nothing but 1 partridge and 1 jack snipe, all I shot at.

15th.—Got one long shot and at last bagged an old cock pheasant, which is now become quite a *rara avis* in this place.

23rd.—Left Longparish at two this morning; got into the Isle of Purbeck about two in the afternoon. Brought Reade over to Poole to have the bone of his bad finger (poisoned by a fish) cut off by the surgeon, and took away my new bitch, brought from Newfoundland. Slept at Poole.

24th.—Got to Keyhaven, and proceeded to Lymington to inspect two new punts building for me by Inman.

27th.—Sent my boat cart to Southampton, and had over the famous east countryman Elijah Buckle, with his celebrated gun and punt, to try experiments, &c.

28th.—Had a grand trial of stanchion guns before a mob of spectators, and found my gun as good as (if not superior to) Buckle's.

November 3rd.—Returned to Keyhaven to renew my experiments and preparations.

N.B.—Scarcely any birds on the coast. I killed only a wigeon. Among the few birds that I shot to try my gun, I got 2 knots and 1 turnstone. Buckle got a little shot one wet day and picked up 4 wigeon, which with mine were the only fowl killed on our coast while we were there.

15th.—Longparish. Had a *grande chasse*, to scour the whole country, wood, fields, and river; and so destitute of sport did we find all our beat, that I bagged only 3 rabbits, 2 snipes, and 1 jack snipe, which were all I fired at.

16th.—Received from France 15 decoy ducks of a wild species trained for *la chasse à la hutte.*

18th.—Having this day completed the hut &c. after the style I learnt in France, we tried our birds; they behaved magnificently and brought down the only two ducks that flew close to me; but my young dog spoiled the shot before I could catch the wild birds clear of the others.

20th.—2 jack snipes and 1 partridge, all I shot at.

First tried all my beat for snipes, then the uplands for game; and passed the night in my new hut for ducks; but no sport whatever to be got. This place seems at present to be completely barren of all game whatever.

December 4th.—I launched the new punt which I ordered to be painted and 'got ready' for sea, and named her the 'Owl,' being a white night bird and the emblem of sagacity or wisdom, on the helmet of Minerva.

15th.—Having sent on my new punt, the 'Owl,' to be

kept on the coast, I this day drove down to Keyhaven, to see if there were any birds.

16*th*.—Scarcely anything to be seen this morning. I got 1 brent goose and 2 grey plover, and was much pleased in every respect with the new punt.

17*th*.—Reade got 3 wigeon a little before daybreak, when it came on an incessant pour of rain, and a tremendous gale of wind, which lasted all day and all night.

18*th*.—Got 1 brent goose; and afterwards (owing to the impossibility of managing my gun in so short and so rough a sea) I overshot a trip of geese, that, had not the lop of the sea canted my gun, I have no doubt I should have stopped half a score of.

19*th*.—Out all day and never saw but 5 geese; got nothing but 2 coots, a long random shot; out all night and never heard nor saw a single wigeon.

20*th*.—A most tremendous day again. Weathered, for a few hours, expressly to try the new punt in a sea. She answered beautifully; but as for a shot, we did not get a chance.

23*rd*.—Having nothing but incessant wind and rain, I this day drove over to Longparish, with a view of passing Christmas, and with the hope that the weather might change in the meantime.

30*th*.—1 partridge, which I wanted and had some difficulty to get.

1824

January 6*th*.—Returned to Keyhaven for the pleasure of a little seaside recreation, but, for want of hard weather, with no prospect of good shooting.

7*th*.—Up by daylight; out sailing and exploring till five in the afternoon, having been nearly to Cowes, saw nothing but a few very wild geese, and getting a shot was to-day out of the question. Out for the night directly I had refreshed myself, and never heard but 1 wigeon, notwithstanding the wind had changed to the east. I impute the destruction of Keyhaven to those rascally launchers shoving their punts over the mud every night before the birds have had any feeding.

8th.—At it all day and night: not a bird to be seen. Wind in its old filthy quarter again, south-west.

11th.—As there is no shooting whatever here, I took a drive to Poole in order to see Sam Singer's new 141-lb. gun and punt; and in the afternoon drove to Uddens House, to see my old friend Jack Ponton, but he was in town, so I drove back and supped at Poole.

12th.—Drove back to Keyhaven. A little frost, but as yet white and therefore uncertain.

13th to 16th.—Not a wigeon to be seen in harbour, either by day or night, though both Reade and I never ceased to persevere. In spite of fair frosty weather and a full moon, not one gunner have we even heard fire a shot, so completely is this place clear of birds; my whole week's sport, and at it every day and all the nights, was 2 grey plover.

17th.—Reade went home, and on the 18th returned bringing me word that the unprecedented bad sport with wild fowl was, if possible, worse at Poole than at this place.

18th to 23rd.—Not a wigeon to be seen or heard.

24th.—Gave up, and left Keyhaven.

N.B.—All the gunners are reduced to beggary by this phenomenon of a scarcity.

26th.—Longparish. The whole country here I find has been in arms after three Egyptian geese, which I suppose must have deserted from some gentleman's pond, or they never would have stood the immense number of shots that a rabble of bunglers have been popping at them; one, by better luck than skill, was stopped by the sixth round of Will Blake, my man, and I have sent it to be stuffed. I rode out all the morning;

but the other two geese, no wonder, have not been seen since. This evening my man Charles arrived with the two grand potentates of all the gunners, Reade and Elijah Buckle, with whom I am trying various experiments and still further improvements in my punts.

27th.—Was instructed by Buckle in the knack of firing the large gun from the shoulder, instead of from a swivel, by which a punt of one-third the usual weight is equally safe. I had, of course, but a small charge, though I was astonished to find how much less was the recoil than I expected. Powder is tremendous for the first inch or two of recoil; but afterwards it is much less powerful than I could have supposed, if received by anything the least elastic.

30*th.*—Reade and Buckle left me, after we had worked hard every day at the punts and learned Buckle's system.

February 9*th.*—Having received 10 more decoy ducks and mallards from France, I tried them this evening, and the only 2 birds that came near my hut they brought well in shot.

11*th.*—Went to Lord Rodney's to instruct his man in the use of some French ducks, that I took him, &c. Even here the scarcity of wild fowl has been such that not a bird had been brought to table. I continued, however, to get a few by means of getting up some hours before daylight, letting myself out of the house and getting over the park pales to the pond, where I had the luck to kill all I shot at.

March 1*st.*—Left Longparish to look at a manor in Norfolk and inspect the lakes and coast.

3*rd.*—Arrived at Yarmouth and received the greatest civility and hospitality from C. Girdlestone, Esq., who, being an excellent sportsman, proved to be a capital pilot and guide for every information.

5*th.*—Went to Horsey to stay a few days at my old quarters with Mr. Rising, where I had a good day's fishing, and in the course of one of my walks killed 2 teal and 1 snipe.

9*th.*—Left Horsey for Yarmouth early in the morning,

and made a thorough inspection of the Breyden flats, which appeared in every respect to be the finest gunning ground I ever saw. Having taken Buckle, the admiral of the swivel gunners, by way of a servant, I had also an able engineer to judge of the place. In short I found the impediment to shooting on the waters so little, and all the gunning ground so good, that I proved it quite unnecessary to be troubled with the care and expense of a manor, and left Yarmouth fully satisfied with my pleasant excursion and the many little things I had seen and discovered.

N.B.—The gunners on this coast, although equipped with huge guns, were about thirty years behindhand in their art ; but so near is Yarmouth to Holland, that the people here have the maiden shots at the fowl before they become wild, as they always are before they reach our coast. Left by the 'Dart' coach at five in the evening, and slept at Norwich.

10*th.*—Left Norwich at a quarter past six, and at a quarter past seven reached London by the 'Times' coach. Had a capital *déjeuner à la fourchette* at Bury St. Edmunds for two shillings each passenger. And the same coachman drives the whole 114 miles every day in the week, not even Sunday does he rest; and one of the coachmen, the famous Mr. Thoroughgood, has in addition to this to walk about thirty miles a week.

11*th.*—From morning till night with gunmakers, book publishers and other people on various business, and got through about thirty long commissions and a few calls.

12*th.*—Returned to Longparish, and found all well.

Game &c. killed in the season :

Popgun work—216 partridges, 7 hares, 1 quail, 3 rabbits, 2 pheasants, 46 snipes.

Duck gun work—2 geese, 8 ducks and mallards, 1 wigeon 3 curres, 4 teal. In all but 293 head.

N.B.—The vilest wild-fowl season in the annals of history, a summer instead of a winter, and half the gunners starving, and on the parish books for relief. Universally bad all over England, and even the decoy men in distress for subsistence.

April 1st.—Got up early, did business at—below Kensington, Hanover Square, Pall Mall, Thames Street, Ely Place, Clerkenwell, Soho Square, Long Acre, Marlborough and Poland Streets, Princes Street, Dover Street, St. James's Street, Fleet Street, Regent Street, called on three friends, found everybody at home, did several commissions to boot, and at six o'clock on the morning of the 2nd left town, and got home to Longparish about half-past twelve o'clock.

28th.—Killed 20 brace of trout, besides small ones thrown in, in three hours and three-quarters.

N.B.—I name this merely as good sport; though I have long left off keeping accounts, because I have killed so much in my life, that I now only take fish when wanted, and not for amusement.

May 12th.—Went to town about my works, my large double gun, and various other matters of business. Had, one evening, an interview with Rossini, the god of Italian music; found him a very pleasant man, and was afterwards much gratified by going to his concert, to which nothing but knowing him could have got me admittance at so short a notice, not being a subscriber. Saw the boat that performed 118 miles in fifteen hours and three-quarters. She is of one-quarter inch oak plank, forty feet long, very sharp forward, tolerable bearings, and apparently crank.

28th.—Went to town in order to bring out the third edition of 'Instructions to Young Sportsmen.' In a few days after, lodged at Mr. Currie's, 20 Regent Street, the best billet I ever had in my life.

June 20th.—Superintended the rebuilding of the middle part of Longparish House.

July 12th.—London. Saw the remains of our unrivalled and immortal bard, Lord Byron, removed into the hearse, and moved off in procession for interment.

August 3rd.—Brought out the third edition of my 'Instructions to Young Sportsmen,' after two months' incessant labour and anxiety with artists, printers, &c. I, of course, sent copies to his Majesty, and other great persons, as well as to some particular friends, and the artists who were engaged for the work.

31*st.*—After quite as much trouble with getting forward my large double gun as I had in bringing out my book, I left town this day, and arrived at Longparish House, which I found still in such a miserable mess, with brick and mortar, that I directly wished myself away again.

CHAPTER XVII

1824

September 1st.—Partridges all in the high standing corn Weather so intensely hot and dry that scarcely a dog would hunt, not a breath of scent, and the birds wild and running all day, and, as far as I could judge, a bad breed of birds. In short, the worst 1st of September I ever was out in at Longparish, for, though I shot as well as ever I have done, yet I could only bag 20 partridges and 1 rabbit.

2nd.—So intensely hot that every person is complaining. Went out between four and five this evening, and even then was almost broiled.

7th.—I got 11 partridges. Missed a bird in shot, which is the first time I have done so this season. I, however, killed him with the second barrel, so I lost nothing by my bungling.

14th.—Out for four hours, and literally never discharged my gun, except at a quail, which I killed. Finding shooting out of the question to-day, I took half an hour's trolling, and got 4 brace of very large trout.

16th.—27 partridges, and, what is somewhat singular, I lost 7 more than I shot. This is an extraordinary contrast with the day before yesterday, when I beat the same ground, with very little in addition, and never got a shot at a partridge. It shows the extreme difference between a good and a bad scenting day. Although this is by far the greatest day I have had this bad season, yet it was by no means a satisfactory one. First, I lost 7 birds that I shot in covert, &c.; second, I had six fair shots spoiled by my horses and men being in the way; and third, I missed three birds within shot, which has been always a rare thing for me to do, and was as sad a catastrophe as losing my purse or my watch; and fourthly, I burnt my fingers by once firing in haste with my hand near the gas-hole of the detonator.

22nd.—8 partridges and 1 hare, and 4 more birds lost. Never did I lose so many birds as I have done since I used detonating guns; as they have always with me proved to hit the birds so weak at long distances, that they get a field or two off and tower before they fall, instead of coming down handsome as they usually did when I used a flint lock.

Game killed in September 1824: 146 partridges, 4 hares, 1 rabbit, 1 landrail, 1 quail, 2 snipes. Total, 155 head.

N.B.—A universal complaint everywhere that this has been the worst and scarcest season ever known, insomuch that I have beat everyone here, and even done wonders by getting the little game above entered.

October 4th.—Decidedly proved that the flint gun shot superior, both for strength and closeness, to the detonator. But, on taking the flint into the field, I killed only 1 partridge and 1 landrail, having from lately used a detonator fired behind four other shots at birds that I ought to have killed. This is a caution to those who have shot well with a flint to 'leave well enough alone.'

9th.—10 partridges, 2 jack snipes, and 1 hare. Was unwell, and nervous as a cat, or I should have killed a leash more birds; as it was, I lost a brace more that towered. Two curious occurrences to-day: killed 2 birds at a shot, and stepped over a hare sitting, when running to pick them up, and then killed hare. Sprung an old cock bird out of Hunter's pigstye in the village when riding home; went in search of him again; found him in the plantation before the windows, and bagged him a very long shot, which happened to be the longest distance of any shot I ever recollect making with a detonator.

16th.—1 pheasant. The first I have seen or heard of since the season commenced. I was walking up our wood without a gun; sprung the bird, and then raced home; raised a hue and cry, and after a little search found the pheasant again and put him in the bag.

November 4th.—London. Seriously ill. I crawled from seeing Sir Everard Home to the chemist with the greatest difficulty, and, while almost fainting in the shop, the first salutation I had was that Chambers, my banker, had just failed for 260,000*l.*, and with all my money, 931*l.*, in his hands. I was ordered to go home and be put to bed, but this affair obliged me to get driven to the City to be satisfied as to the safety of my funded property; but, after all, I was too late, and Friday being a holiday, I had to wait, with Christian patience, till Saturday.

5th.—Lay on my back with violent pain and inflammation the whole day. I dare swallow nothing but tea and gruel, and lost the means of getting fomented by my servant not having arrived, agreeably to a letter despatched. This is like a second edition of my suffering in Spain and Portugal, with an attack on my finances as well as my health.

15th.—Ill ever since, and ill still. More miseries. Pinnock (the man who has my patent) smashed, and to avoid bankruptcy, resigned, all in confusion, to trustees.

19th to 21st.—Worse again. Intermitting fever, gums all in boils, teeth loose; in the essence of misery. To-day received information that my house at Keyhaven was inundated by another tremendous flood; the chimney fallen through the roof by the late tremendous gale; the house and everything round completely inundated and seriously damaged.

December 9th.—After being bored to death with the consummate ignorance, impertinence, and obstinacy of old Egg, who pretended to undertake my large double gun, and, after all, threw the whole burthen of directions on my shoulders, and then wanted to take all the credit himself, I was this day well enough to drive to below Vauxhall Bridge, where we tried the gun; and, in short, the two barrels together (on my plan) answered even better than I expected, whereas if Egg had done it his way, the whole concern would have been spoiled.

14*th*.—Returned to Longparish House, under the idea that change of air would expedite my recovery.

16*th*.—Buckle arrived, and we began building a punt.

22*nd*.—What with the wet weather, abominable damp mortar, and the sad state the house is now left in from the alterations, almost everyone in the house has taken a cold. I had a severe relapse yesterday and to-day, and my eyes were so bad also that I could hardly see across the room.

24*th to* 28*th*.—A pretty Christmas. Myself much worse, a close prisoner, and till now, and now with great difficulty, I could not see to write. Scarce touched a morsel for three whole days, and as weak as a rat. The cook so bad with the rheumatism she could not spit the meat or do anything without help, and in great pain. The kitchen-maid bled, and laid up in the drawing room among the lumber of the mutilated centre of the house, which is deposited there. Poor Charles, my right-hand man and useful attendant in all my illness, was the worst of us all; alarmingly ill, with two doctors, and hourly apprehensions of typhus fever. Hornsby touched sharply with ophthalmia, and bad in his stomach. Kitt the carpenter so poorly he can hardly go on with his work. The plasterer gone off, and laid up with his eyes in a dangerous state, owing to an accident with the lime. Long, the gunmaker, laid up in his bed at Andover and unable to come to me, and the man he sent in his stead very poorly. With the exception of Long, this is all a house illness; though such has been the wet weather that it must be admitted there never was so much general illness here before. This is a glorious salvo for the architect, who will probably swear that his damp walls, wet mortar, and thorough draughts have nothing to do with our invalided family.

29*th*.—Reade came up to see and trim the new punt &c.

30*th*.—I was so far better as to be just able to crawl out and see the punt afloat. All our household a little mended, and Charles this night pronounced by the doctors as likely to live.

1825

January 14*th*.—Buckle, who came to me to assist in punt building, went out after a large flock of teal that dropped in our moors; 15 came by him all in a cluster, and he knocked down 6 at a shot, which, on my property here, is the best shot I ever remember being made. I continued not well enough to go out.

25*th and* 26*th*.—Myself still on the sick list, though constantly employed in building my punt in the new drawing room.

February 16*th*.—Had a grand trial of my new double stanchion gun, assisted by Buckle (the king of the stanchion gunners), and nothing could be more satisfactory than all my inventions proved, insomuch that I may venture to pronounce this gun the champion of England. We were from morning till night firing, and half the night writing down the calculations and experiments.

17*th*.—Had not killed a bird since October 16th, owing to long illness. This day discharged a duck gun at a jack snipe and bagged him.

28*th*.—Although still an invalid, I went to stay a few days with Lord Rodney, to try my new gun and punt on his lake at Alresford; though what few fowl had been there this year had nearly all disappeared.

March 6*th*.—Longparish. Laid my boat up inshore, covered her over with reeds, got the snipes driven to where they always were seen to pitch, raked the reeds with the big gun at random, and bagged 12 snipes at one shot, all dead. I waited half an hour for the flock to come down again, which they were in the act of doing, when my dog swam across to me and drove them off.

Game &c. killed to March 5th, 1825: 160 partridges, 6 hares, 1 pheasant, 1 rabbit, 2 landrails, 1 quail, 38 snipes, 4 wild ducks, 1 tufted drake, 9 teal. Total, 224 head, exclusive, of course, of coots, &c.

N.B.—Lost all the shooting in October, November, December, January, and February, owing to illness brought on entirely by vexation and trouble. Luckily for me, however, the season was the worst ever known both for game and fowl.

17*th.*—London. Suffered much from illness, and was dreadfully inconvenienced by having got into a house in London without a warm corner in it. Had much vexation again with that old rascal Egg; and, after much trouble with my solicitor, and Joe Manton for a mediator, got off for 200*l.* for my gun, and it will take 20*l.* more to replace the bad work therein. Old Egg made an indirect appeal for 300*l.* for the gun, and 25*l.* for his time; and then mitigated this into a demand for immediate payment of 200*l.* for the gun, 10*l.* for his time, and 4*l.* 11*s.* for a loading rod and a deal box. After giving me immense trouble, he proposed to toss up for the 4*l.* 11*s.*, and it was pretty evident he knew how to throw tails; so I cried 'Tails,' caught him in his own trap, got his receipt in full of all demands, witnessed by Joe Manton, and on a 10*s.* stamp, and at a great sacrifice washed my hands of one of the most aggravating and ungrateful fellows that ever disgraced the name of a tradesman.

April 11*th.*—After being four weeks in the very essence of misery with being stewed in hot water, physicked, leeched, and butchered, I, this day, went with Macilwain to consult the most extraordinary old bear that ever appeared in a civilised country, the celebrated Dr. Abernethy.

12th.—Consulted, on my case, with Sir Henry Halford, the prince and the Lord Chesterfield of all the medical practitioners.

25th.—After having undergone two more infernal operations, that did me more harm than good, I this day withdrew myself from the attendance of Macilwain, and went again to Sir Everard Home, having been now just six weeks under severe treatment to no purpose. Lord send me a speedy delivery from illness and doctors. Here have I been a sufferer more or less, without any one permanent step to amendment, since the 1st of November.

June 23rd.—Saw Graham ascend in his balloon, after first having a long conversation with him. Favourable weather, and the sight most beautiful.

30th.—After being very busy, in order to leave the fourth edition of 'Instructions to Young Sportsmen' in the press, I this day returned to Longparish.

July 19th.—4 snipes, and should have killed 4 more had I not taken up an old flint gun, which put me out, after the detonators.

N.B.—The hottest weather known since the memory of the oldest man here, was this day, and several days previous to it. It was for this novelty that I went after these snipes that I had heard of.

August 10th.—Launched my fourth edition of the 'Instructions to Sportsmen.'

12th.—London. Met Tom Moore, the poet, and some other scientific men at Longmans' dinner.

13th.—Saw the living skeleton in Pall Mall.

23rd.—Left London for Longparish.

24th.—Proceeded to Mr. Ponton's at Uddens House, Dorset, for what little black-game shooting England affords.

Particulars of the greatest day's west country poult shooting on record:

25th.—9 heath poults or black game, having discharged

my gun but nine times; and, on one occasion, as Ponton was a long way behind me, we all felt confident that 2 birds fell to one barrel of my gun; if so, I bagged 5 brace; but at all events 4½, which is, in this country, a miracle, being far more than was ever done before, insomuch that 2 brace of black game in a day is here considered most brilliant sport. I made two doublets and five single shots, some very long ones. Ponton also shot as well as possible, and, as almost a matter of course with him, never missed. He killed 3 brace, exclusive of the doubtful bird before named. In short, our day was 8 brace of strong, full-grown black game, the greatest sport here on record, the talk of all the country, and an article for the public papers. This was my maiden day at English black-game shooting, and a most glorious one it was. We found but 11 brace the whole day, and this was considered a wonderful show of these birds, except in winter, when they all flock together, and can never be shot by fair means. In a word, this was, taking it 'for all in all,' the most satisfactory day's sport I ever had in my life.

28th.—Sunday. Went to morning church at Ham Preston, and to afternoon service at Stape Hill Convent, where, by a lucky accident, I got a good view of all the nuns. This is a poor though wild and romantic little place, established by Lord Arundel, on the heath just outside of Ponton's Park.

30th.—Left Uddens Park, and in the evening arrived again at Longparish House.

CHAPTER XVIII

1825

September 1st.—I never knew the scent so bad, or the birds so wild, on the 1st, as on this day; notwithstanding which I bagged, with only my two old bitches, neither of which are extraordinary, 42 partridges, besides 6 more shot dead and lost, 2 hares, 2 quails, all I saw, 1 landrail and 1 wood pigeon.

2nd.—Rested, as I always do after the first day, for many just reasons.

3rd.—31 partridges, 1 hare, and 1 snipe, entirely through having shot most brilliantly, as the birds were so extremely wild that many sportsmen could not even get a brace.

5th.[1]—40 partridges, making, exclusive of a wood pigeon not game, 120 head of game in three days; or, putting it on the average, 20 brace a day for three successive days. Though the ground is, notwithstanding the heavy rain in August, so dry, and the birds so wild, that everyone complains of getting but little sport, yet by means of able manœuvring, rapid attacks, and rapid shooting, I have been doing wonders, considering the country I shot in.

7th.—21 partridges, 1 landrail, and 1 wood pigeon, which, considering how very windy it was, and how very wild the

[1] This is the first day in my life that I could in our wild lawless country have what I call my 'butcher's halloo,' after the first day. This means the three cheers that I and my army give whenever the number of twenty brace in one day is made up.

birds were, is quite equal to the preceding day's sport. I made seven doublets, and missed nothing in reach. Indeed, I have not missed a fair shot this season.

10*th.*—An incessant hurricane all day. After my bagging 8 partridges, besides 2 more killed and lost, and 2 snipes, there came on such a thick, drizzling rain, that I gave up shooting, galloped home, and sallied forth with my rod, and had a most wonderful day's fishing. Colonel Halton and I, including what we threw in, caught 40 brace of trout. I remember at one time killing 5 good fish in seven throws of the rod.

12*th.*—A wet, drizzling morning; went with a casting net to get bait; then attended Mr. Painter to give him a few finishing lessons in fishing, at which he had excellent sport. Caught two very large trout myself, and several smaller ones; and, in short, was occupied till about twelve, when the rain blew off. I then went home, took a snack, and gave the birds another and a farewell attack for the present. I bagged 24 partridges, 2 hares, 1 landrail, and 1 snipe, by dint of good generalship, with my army of markers, and shooting with a rapidity and accuracy that after my long illness I despaired of ever recovering. Long, the gunmaker, was among the spectators; and much pleased he was, as he had bored one of the guns on which I played such a glorious concerto. Here ends my shooting for this trip to the country. A most glorious beginning, with a splendid finale.

Grand sport. I here give a list of game &c. killed up to September 12th.

Out altogether but five whole mornings and two half mornings. Some unprecedented sport trout fishing; and 9 heath poults (all in one day and in nine shots), to which add 166 partridges, 7 hares, 2 wood pigeons, 3 landrails, 2 quails, 8 snipes; besides 10 more partridges shot dead and lost, which would bring the list to 207; reckoning fairly, however, as to what I bagged, the total is 197 head.

13*th.*—Drove over to Lord Rodney's to see him relative to our regiment meeting, to play at soldiers and swallow sloe juice on the 28th of this month.

26*th.*—Having received orders for twenty-eight days' training of the North Hants Regiment, I this day left town and arrived at Longparish, in order to prepare for playing at soldiers and swallowing sloe juice.

27*th.*—Went out to get some birds for the Duke of Clarence, despairing of success as no one had been able to do anything. I persevered, however, and killed 16 partridges; and the next day, the 28th, I joined the regiment at Winchester.

October 1*st.*—Too busy soldiering to think of pheasant shooting, though I had some very tempting invitations with promises of extraordinary sport.

12*th.*—Having got a few days' emancipation from sloe juice and pipe clay, I this morning mounted the rostrum of the 'Telegraph,' and arrived, on some business, in the far more agreeable town of London.

15*th.*—Returned per mail (*alias* the paper cart) to our Bacchanalian servitude in Winchester.

25*th.*—Our training, thanks to my stars, is this day at an end; and so should I have been also, had I been obliged to weather another such a month. What with sitting till midnight over sloe juice, occasional suppers &c. (kept up till morning), plays, balls, grand singing, dinners, &c., in short, one incessant round of company, I was almost worn out, as this to me is the very devil. The little duty which I had to do was the only mental recreation which this sink of dissipation would afford. This evening we all went over to Alresford House, where Lord Rodney gave a grand dinner, and beds to the whole regiment; and we sat up till two at music.

26*th.*—Tried some experiments on the lake (accompanied by Reade, who came to me on purpose) for the amusement of the officers and a large concourse of spectators assembled from all parts, and astonished my lookers-on by some excellent shots at coots, the only fowl then on the pond. Previously to this, by the bye, I turned out at five in the morning—after being up till near three—in order to storm an enormous army of starlings, into which I blew off the great double gun with 30 ounces of small shot, just before sunrise. What I killed it is impossible to say, but, from the appearance of the huge hole blown through the phalanx of birds, my spectators guessed at least 500, though I could get but a mere share of those which fell, as nearly all of them dropped in the reeds and on quagmires. What I bagged at the time, however, was 243 starlings at one shot.[1] The feathers which the wind blew towards and over us, after the shot, I could compare to nothing but a heavy fall of black snow.

28th.—The first quiet day I have passed for some weeks. The transition was like the stopping of a noisy mill.

December 13th.—Returned to Longparish.

17th.—After passing the morning at Andover, I this day, though suffering with a severe headache, went out at a quarter past two, and was home again before four o'clock with 5 snipes, 5 jack snipes, and 1 teal, which I killed without missing a bird.

19th.—1 snipe and 2 jack snipes, and was then driven home by rain, which was no loss, as, by what little I could see, I had nearly cleared off all the snipes here on Saturday.

1826

January 2nd.—Sent Reade and Charles to remove my new gunning flotilla, for a trial on the sea, to Keyhaven.

[1] P.S.—*December 27th.* My man Charles came home from a mission to Alresford, and brought back word that, since I was there, the reeds were cut, and the workmen found between 200 and 300 more starlings. If so I was right in guessing that I killed 500 at a shot, and they say that all this army of starlings evacuated their garrison the day after I besieged them.

3rd.—They and I arrived safe at Keyhaven.

4th.—Employed all day in getting our apparatus in order.

5th.—Though it blew a tremendous gale, from east by south, my sailors and I were anxious to try our new punt, the 'Lion' to-day, it being Thursday, which we superstitiously fancy a lucky day. We began working up to windward, at daylight, in order to drop down on what few geese were arrived. But it so happened that the first birds we fell in with were about 60 wigeon. My punt was so invisible, that we got well in shot of them; but, being loaded only with mould shot, and having to fire through a tremendous surf, which took the charge from the object, I got but one old cock wigeon, though we had the satisfaction to find that everything answered remarkably well. All sport at an end by ten o'clock A.M., as the water had then left the mud; and nothing could live outside, as it poured with hail, sleet, snow, and rain, and blew ready to tear the very trees up.

6th.—A gale of wind all night and all day, with a tremendous pour of rain; fired one shot, a long one, and got but 1 wigeon; and was then, as yesterday, imprisoned by the weather from ten in the morning till night.

9th.—A frost and fine weather. Reade went out to reconnoitre the creeks in my old Poole punt, and merely took my old forty-shilling shoulder gun a few hours before daylight. He happened to fall in with a newly migrated bunch of fowl, all in a heap, and got close to them, and at one shot with this gun killed and got 5 ducks and mallards, 12 wigeon, 2 pintails, and 1 grey plover.

10th.—Calm weather, scarcely a bird in harbour; did fairly, for the little chance there was. Got 1 pintail, 1 scaup drake, 1 wigeon, and 3 grey plover.

12th.—A butterfly day; every jackass afloat with a blunderbuss or a swivel gun; all the fowl driven out to sea, and there enjoying a dead calm. I killed 4 coots, and then came in, and went to bed after dinner. Turned out again at midnight, and on the morning of the 13th, about half-past two, got 13 wigeon, by starlight. Every one quite dead.

14*th.*—Out from after midnight till seven this morning. Foggy weather, and wigeon, as they always are then, too restless to be done anything with. Out from two till night; not a bird in harbour, and I killed nothing all day, except a jack snipe, that I discharged my musket at. I this day heard that, notwithstanding the very cold weather and hard frost, there was scarcely a bird to be seen in Lymington market, or even to be got from any of the gunners, so unaccountably scarce have they as yet been. Not a goose to be seen or heard of; a bird that this coast has generally afforded in all weathers. Sent Reade to crawl in the mud sledge about eight, I being afraid, after my late illness, to crawl on the mud this season. He got 4 wigeon, but found the birds very 'ticklish.'

16*th.*—Out at four; few birds, and no tide to get at them: got but 1 wigeon and 2 coots. I then went to Longparish, and providentially arrived just before a dreadful fire took place in the village; by which means I had the pleasure of being somewhat useful to the poor sufferers, by starting a subscription &c. on the morning of the 17th, just before the engines had subdued the flames. Three houses, Morrant's, Mersham's, and Siney's, were burnt to the ground, and not a vestige of property was saved.

18*th.*—Alresford (Lord Rodney's). 9 dunbirds, 7 tufted ducks, 1 golden-eye, 1 morillon, 1 teal, 4 snipes, 8 jack snipes, and several coots, that got shot with the other birds. I missed only one shot, and that at a snipe, far out of reach. My best shot, with the duck gun, was 9 mixed fowl. But the whole country was, and is now for ever likely to be, ruined by the preserve of Mr. Alexander Baring, of the Grange Park, who feeds and monopolises, merely to ornament his water, and tickle his fancy, half the fowl in Hampshire. I drove there, expressly to see his collection, and I am confident

I saw not less than 8,000 fowl on the water before his house.

21st.—A mild, foggy day, and no chance for sport. Took a cruise all the way down Channel, as far as off Newtown in the Isle of Wight, in the gunning punt, and though out from five in the morning till two in the afternoon, never got a shot.

Out again at night from seven till eleven; heard a few wigeon, but the tide was not high enough to get at them.

23rd.—No chance by day, and the only one we had, at night, spoiled by some rascally shore popper.

24th.—Out by day and night again. Very foggy, and consequently no chance with the wigeon.

25th.—4 wigeon. Out all day and all night, with but very poor chances.

26th.—Out all day and all night; no chance till about one in the morning.

27th.—Got 9 wigeon; only found one little trip of about 16, and caught them under the moon. Some more were picked up, so I guess I did vastly well with them. In the evening was unlucky, at the only shot at geese I have had this year. I got within 150 yards of about 300, and owing to a trifling derangement of my swivel gun, I shot a yard under them. Again, after midnight, I was unlucky. I had been lying for three hours alongside a fine trip of wigeon; at last I got close in to them, and when in the very act of raising my gun to blow a double lane through them, at about two in the morning, an infernal custom-house boat opened the point, and put them up.

30th.—11 wigeon and 1 brent goose. Nothing but a few small trips were in at night. About three I shot at 6, and stopped them all. A gale of wind and rain in the afternoon, but I hurried back from Lymington, where I went on some law business, and saved my tide for the geese. I knocked down 3, but I was forced to come home, owing to the heavy sea. This was the only shot I got after working hard till dusk.

31*st.*—Took our tide at half-past two this morning; out till daylight; tremendous rough weather, and not above 20 wigeon in harbour, and we came in with a wet gun without having fired a shot. Took the evening tide, but never found a bird. Westerly gales and all appearance of what little sport there is being nearly at an end for the season.

February 1*st.*—Out three hours before daylight; no wigeon in harbour; got a wild duck and a godwit while sailing in to breakfast. It then set in a warm wet day; out from two in the afternoon till seven; no birds on the tide, and a fog at night.

2*nd.*—Out before five this morning, being determined to persevere; no chance for a shot, and there was too much wind and hazy weather to attempt anything in the evening; consequently, the lot of every gunner was a blank day.

4*th.*—Arrived in London.

Nothing particular occurred in town, except the bankruptcy of Joe Manton and the sale of his effects.

13*th.*—Keyhaven. We were prepared to turn out at half-past one this morning, but it came on hazy and wet, with a westerly wind; so all chance was at an end, though when I left London only the day before yesterday we had a fine east wind with a pretty hard frost. Thus we were, as usual, made 'gaol birds' of again. In the afternoon we took a sail and landed on the shingles of the Needles, where all the dunlins and curlews go at high water, and defy the gunners. I popped away at the dunlins, and knocked down a couple of dozen, and also shot a cormorant, or, to use the slang term, 'lowered a parson,' but we should have buried a cask, and tied a cat to a peg, to have done well. Then we might have had good sport. We went out, four hands on board, or this expedition might have been dangerous, as we had quite as much sea 'as we knew what to do with.' On our return, about six in the evening, Buckle had arrived to pass the evening here, and try some experiments with me to-morrow.

15*th.*—Wind and rain morning, noon, and night, and not a bird to be seen or heard. Keyhaven more like a cell in Newgate than a place for recreation, during such cruel weather as we have hitherto had to undergo.

16*th.*—Wind and rain all night till daylight this morning, when at last it was tolerably dry overhead, though a strong westerly wind. We were this day very anxious to try the new elevation of the gun, as we had evidently been shooting under before. The only shot I got was at dunbirds, into which I fired both barrels, and a most satisfactory little shot I made. I picked up 58, nearly all dead, which was two-thirds of what I had to shoot through. Thus far, everything appears to answer extremely well. No fowl about to-day; out again about sunset; wind very fresh, but no water over the mud.

N.B.—The discovery of this improved elevation for the gun has tenfold repaid me for running down here again. Had it not been for this, I should have repented my journey, as the wild fowl have now almost all disappeared, and I dare say may have already migrated to their breeding country.

17*th.*—Wind from the westward ready to blow the house about our ears, and a deluge of rain; not a bird to be seen or heard, and the whole country apparently cleared off by this unfavourable wind. Not the most distant prospect of having anything more to shoot at.

Reade ran out in the rain and 'lowered a parson' (shot a cormorant). This bird made some fun for us. He had thirty shot through his skin; three flat fish and an eel were taken out of him, and three shot through the flat fish, also through undigested stuff like meat. So that Reade had shot fish, flesh, and fowl flying; and in spite of this blow the nine-lived glutton led us a chase for twenty minutes before he got sick enough to be caught, although shot at, within 40 yards. by a shoulder duck gun. He was disposed of as follows: the skin to make a dandy collar for a coat; the feathers to make me drawing pens ; and his carcase begged by my boatman Williams, who engaged two friends to partake of him for a delicate Sunday's dinner. Employed all hands the whole of this afternoon in packing up and putting away our coasting paraphernalia, preparative to leaving Keyhaven to-morrow.

18*th.*—Left Keyhaven.

Fowl killed to February 22nd, 1826: 46 snipes, 2 geese only (scarcity this year unprecedented), 7 ducks, 64 wigeon, 2 teal, 3 pintails, 19 dunbirds, 4 grey plover, 2 godwits. Total, 149 head of fowl.

My new shooting outfit in every single item proved to answer inimitably, so that all we wanted was a more plentiful season, as this one at Keyhaven proved to be the worst ever known. All I could boast of, therefore, was having killed more than all the other people put together.

March 18*th.*—London. I was till now an invalid, but being this day a little better, I went (wrapped up) in the evening to Covent Garden Theatre in order to hear my favourite overture of 'Der Freischütz' conducted by the immortal composer himself, Carl Maria Von Weber. Nothing could be more sublimely beautiful, and the applause that was drawn forth by the appearanee of this great composer was no less flattering than just.

19*th.*—Sunday. The best sermon (for explanation of the Scripture, analogy, metaphor, language, logic, and energetic delivery) that I have ever yet heard, was this day preached at St. Mary's, Bryanstone Square, by the rector, the Rev. Mr. Dibdin, on the subject of St. Paul's shipwreck.

May 2nd.—Left town, meaning to pass the night at Virginia Water provided I could be admitted to see the King's Park, the boundary of which is close to a little inn called the 'Wheatsheaf' at that place. On my arrival I was informed that no one could be admitted after two o'clock ; and that even before was a particular favour. I went to Mr. Turner, the head ranger, and on making known to him who I was, he very politely sent a keeper with me, who showed me all the King's fishing boats, aviaries, Greenland canoe, and, in short, everything that could possibly be inspected except the interior of the King's cottage, which no one is allowed to see; and after walking several miles on the borders of the lake, surrounded with some of the finest forest scenery I ever beheld, and twice crossing it in one of his Majesty's punts, I returned, highly delighted and quite tired, to the inn.

Mr. Turner was a scientific wild-fowl shooter, which, of course, formed an immediate kind of masonry between us; and I have perhaps in part to attribute to this his very great civility.

17*th.*—Took a run in the 'Eclipse' steam packet to Margate.

18*th.*—Saw and went to church at Margate. Took a row out and bathed, went to Broadstairs &c. and saw all worth seeing; and, on the 19th, left by the 'Dart' steam packet at eight in the morning, and landed on the Tower stairs at half-past two, making the passage of about 84 miles besides offing &c. in six hours and a half. Nothing can surpass, in every respect, the perfection of these packets. Every accommodation, good living, reasonable charges, music on board, and, in short, every inducement to make it pleasant.

20*th.*—I remained in London to bring out the fifth edition of my sporting book; the third having been sold in ten, and the fourth in nine, months.

July 10*th.*—Longparish. Left for Keyhaven to see a few days' work done to my boats, to arrange about my new purchase of Coombs's little place, &c., but was detained some hours at Winchester, in consequence of a sad accident with my fine favourite brown horse. On going, very slowly, down the hill about three-quarters of a mile from that vile town, he fell with such violence as to pull me out of the gig; and, most unfortunately, a large flint took his knee directly across the sinew and divided it like the pinion of a fowl. In spite of all the farrier's hopes and consolations, I made up my mind to the loss of this valuable horse, that I could have had 130 guineas for, and proceeded, as well as I could, with the chestnut horse, to Keyhaven.

18*th*.—After having several annoyances with this chestnut horse, rearing up like a goat and then lying down like a pig, &c., I this evening drove as far as Southampton on my way back to Longparish.

19*th*.—Returned to Longparish, and, on my way through Winchester, found my horse, as I expected, in a dreadful state; but the farrier, Mr. Dixon, a clever man, still wished me to try him another week. But on the 21st a note was brought me over from Winchester, saying it would be charity to kill the poor beast. Thus was there an end of the finest gig horse that I ever was master of.

August 1*st*.—London. Word brought to me that my other horse, the chestnut, had been thrown down and broke his knees. The accidents are now out of number, everywhere, owing to the roads having been without rain for so many weeks. I had also a letter with the particulars of the death of one of the oldest and best friends I had in the world, poor Jack Ponton, my old brother sportsman, and one of the best shots; and, what is far better, one of the best men that ever lived. Thus have been cut off, in the prime of life, our two greatest shots in the district, if not in the kingdom; poor Wardell last summer, and poor Ponton this summer.

CHAPTER XIX

1826

September 1*st.*—Friday. In London, being as yet too unwell to venture away for shooting.

2*nd.*—Finding myself, however, rather better, I went quietly out of town by the ten o'clock coach this day, and got to Longparish for a six o'clock dinner. The report as to birds was favourable, except that they were so extremely wild that not even the best shots had done anything worthy of mention. As for me, I never voted shooting so great a bore as just at this moment; and, were it not for my wish to supply a few friends and the farmers, which I could not trust to the bunglers here to do, I would gladly have left my guns in their cases, and gone somewhere for a healthy excursion and change of scene.

4*th.*—My first day. The weather mended considerably; but the country was so extremely barren as scarcely to afford a vestige of covert for the birds. The stubbles were all trod down by sheep and 'leasers,' and, owing to the previous dry weather, there were no turnips large enough to shelter the game. The birds were plentiful, but much wilder than ever I knew them in September; insomuch that scarcely one covey in ten would allow even the dogs to come within gunshot. I, however, by means of mustering a good army of markers, and harassing the birds by repeated charges of cavalry, so completely tired them down at last, that I performed this day the most that ever was done by me or anyone in the annals of Longparish sporting. I bagged 56 partridges and (for our country in one day, a miracle) 7 hares in nine hours: never lost a bird the whole day. Owing to the extreme wildness of the birds, I was, of course, obliged to fire many random shots; but notwithstanding I was so weak from having been unwell, I may safely say I did not lose a bird by bad shooting the whole day, as the only two fair shots I missed were at single birds, both of which I secured with my second barrel. Taking everything into consideration, this is the greatest day I ever had in my life.

5th.—Had a general day's rest for men, horses, and dogs, and everything except the birds, which were, of course, a little popped at by other parties. The bad weather came on again this afternoon.

6th.—A hurricane of wind and a deluge of rain. *N'importe.* I have had sport enough to last me a week.

14th.—A wild windy day, and the stubbles as bare as the meadow. I could only get 15 partridges, 1 hare, and 1 snipe; though, in spite of being very unwell, I shot famously. Such is the state of the country now that a good bag would require more exertion than I am equal to at this moment.

16th.—15 partridges.

As the strong, dry, easterly wind appears to be now set in, and good sport at an end for the present, I worked hard (though I shot well) to get the above 15 birds, which will just complete my promises to friends, and make up an even 50 brace in the one grand day and three quiet mornings' shooting. On completing the 100 partridges I left the field, truly happy to get rid of the trouble of such unpleasant shooting.

Game killed in September 1826: 122 partridges, 8 hares, 2 snipes. Total, 132 head.

What with being unwell myself, and absent in London, I was only out 5 days. My first day was on the 4th, when I bagged 63 head, and, I believe, beat all England. This was posted, as a miracle, in all the papers, because the birds were never known to be so wild; considering all things, I shot famously.

October 9th.—Another of my best and oldest friends dead, Mr. Bertie Mathew, whose funeral I attend to-day, unfit as I am for anything, from my serious illness, much less for a melancholy undertaking like the present.

November 1st.—London. Having got well enough to limp about, I this day went down to Fullerd's, at Clerkenwell, in order to fire my old swivel gun, which I had altered to my new spring plan, and it gave me great satisfaction.

14*th.*—Longparish. Up to the eyes in experiments and preparations. Captain Ward—my new pupil, whom I set up with a man, a gun, and all my wrinkles—arrived this day, preparative to a grand trial of our two unrivalled gigantic guns.

23*rd.*—Busy jobbing, and did not pull a trigger till to-day, when I just walked out and got 1 miserable snipe, Reade being gone to Purbeck for his family, and I am now waiting for him.

25*th.*—Reade, with his wife and two children, took up their quarters (which I lent them for six months) in my cottage at Keyhaven that I lately purchased of Mr. Beck, after some delay in my being able to remove the previous tenant. This chiefly detained me here, as there is not a bird on the coast.

December 2nd.—Keyhaven. Detained by bad weather and illness—said by Doctors Badger and Nyke to be gout, and by Sir E. Home not to be gout—till this day, when I started for Longparish. After being dragged about Southampton to do my commissions in a 'donkey fly,' I proceeded on my journey home. I took a shot out of the gig and killed 2 partridges belonging to some squire or other just to try how the new musket would reach them, and how old Lazarus (my grey horse) would stand fire. Both the gun and the horse pleased me much better than I should have done the squire had he seen the shot. While last in Southampton a rogue charged me 3*s.* 6*d.* for a 'fly' for about twenty minutes. I swore I would never give 3*s.* 6*d.* for a fly again, so I got the donkey one at 1*s.* 6*d.* the hour. But *che sarà sarà,* the vehicle was so small that I thrust my elbow through the glass, for which I had to pay 2*s.*; so, after all, it was to be that I must pay 3*s.* 6*d.*

1827

January 5*th.*—Being much better and we having now had several days' frost and snow, I this day started for Keyhaven. Just after I left the yard at Longparish I was called off after a particularly large woodcock, which, after several hours' search and a hard fag, I contrived to pocket the first shot. A great victory over the usual bad luck of Friday, and a magnificent bird to begin the new year with.

6*th.*—Arrived at Keyhaven this night, and (strange that it should almost always happen so) brought a change of wind to the filthy south-west, and a wet evening. Not a bird has been killed yet, and scarcely any birds have been seen here, though the weather was, till this day, so favourable for sport.

8*th to* 10*th.*—Wind, rain, and every other kind of miserable weather that, as if by magic, I always contrive to conjure up on my arrival at Keyhaven. Reade, after working four whole nights, got 2 wigeon, which are perhaps, at this moment, the only 2 in our district. Thank God, however, I am better, so I pocket the affront of having nothing to shoot at, so long as I derive benefit from the sea air.

19*th.*—This evening the weather set in fine with a beautiful easterly wind; but, till now, we have had nothing but wind and rain from the miserable west; and, except killing a cormorant, I have never pulled a trigger, though I persevered regularly throughout every night and always came home with an empty bag.

22*nd.*—At last we have the blessing to enjoy severe

weather: frost, snow, and a tremendous gale from the eastward all day; we could hardly live in it, but of course persevered. I got two shots: first bagged 10, and second 6 wigeon; we came in as wet as shags with 16 wigeon.

23rd.—29 wigeon, 1 teal, 1 dunbird, 11 godwits, 1 plover, and 1 knot, making 44 head, besides 4 dozen of dunlins and many wigeon of mine that other people got. My best shot was just before daylight. I picked up 15 wigeon and 1 teal on the spot; and, had not the left barrel of my gun missed fire, I should have doubled this shot. The only time both barrels went was at 12 wigeon on the edge of the creek by daylight; I killed them every one, and bagged 10 of them. No one else in and around Keyhaven has yet done anything, so I have every reason to be content.

24th.—Wind dropped westerly after a beastly white frost; birds suddenly disappeared again.

I had been up since three this morning for a grand daybreak shot, which I was within two minutes of firing when all was ruined by a jackass with a blunderbuss in a washing tub.

25th.—6 wigeon; the right barrel missed fire, or should, of course, have doubled the number.

This night the brutal west wind shifted, and things look better again.

28th.—Sunday. An abominable westerly wind again and cold miserably stormy weather, as bad for birds as for oneself.

29th.—Out in the morning, and had no chance for a shot. Out in the evening, and it was too dark for flight. Reade out till ten at night; and it was too dark and thick to do anything with what few birds were in harbour.

30th.—Beastly rotten cut-throat weather, enough to suffocate you all day, and at night as thick as mustard. Several wigeon still remain; but we must have starlight, or moon, before we can attempt getting another shot. We could shoot without seeing, but then the wigeon will never keep together in thick nights.

February 1st.—Finding that the vagabond mud launchers made a point of working over the mud every night, before the tide flowed, I this day purchased of Lieutenant Harnett, R.N., the prettiest mud punt and mud gun in all this country. So now Reade and I can cope with the mud-crawling reptiles 'at all tacks.'

Wet weather all this afternoon, and then a wet night. Reade went out after midnight to try Harnett's new set-out; he got 2 wigeon towards the morning, at which he made such a shot as to be, beyond anything, pleased with the bargain I had made for the mud gun and punt.

2nd.—Was not out to-day, and merely fired a shot with the musket, with which I killed an old cock wigeon from the quay. The wind changed this evening to north-east, and things look better again.

3rd.—The wind got well away from the old miserable quarter, west, and stood north-east with clear frosty air. Reade came in with 3 wigeon about three this morning. A gale of wind all day, and consequently no living outside; and, being the 'dead of the nip,' we had no water inside harbour; we had therefore no chance even to see birds this day. About midnight Reade got 3 more wigeon with the new launching punt, which, at this time of tide, is the only possible means of getting a bird.

5th.—Out the whole day sailing at sea (the only thing we could do), and brought home but 1 wigeon.

7th.—Reade came in this morning with 12 wigeon (by launching, which is the only remedy for this detestable, ever-dry harbour).

7th.—Harbour dry, and a tremendous sea outside; I got but one little shot all day, when I killed 2 coots. No flight at night, nothing but mud work. I launched about for two hours with the new mud punt after a few straggling birds, and came in at nine without shooting. Reade went off again before midnight, and came in at daybreak with delightful success; he brought in 21 wigeon, 18 of which he killed at one shot.

What a country! that an old rattle-trap mud punt should be the only way of going after fowl, and that all the other guns and punts would, nineteen days out of twenty, be comparatively mere lumber.

8*th.*—Tantalised again with a fine easterly wind, a dry harbour and a hurricane outside—and, notwithstanding the wind, there was no evening flight. Reade went off for the night about six o'clock in the only effective craft—the mud punt—intending to crawl in the slush through the whole of the blessed night.

9*th.*—Reade had got but 2 wigeon the whole of the past night. It was so cold the birds would not sit on the mud. A tremendous gale all day; the harbour as dry as a ploughed field, and no boat could live outside. Every floating gunner a prisoner; and I, for exercise, took a walk and killed a roost of small birds, the only game on the manors of this desert. Reade went off mud crawling at night, but never heard a single fowl; I went to flight, saw nothing but a wild duck and a coot, both of which I knocked down and brought home.

10*th.*—Dry harbour and a gale outside; made an attempt to get out, but was forced to put back; and on coming home (within a quarter of a mile from the quay) I was very near doing wonders, though (as the devil would have it) I did nothing through unfortunately having small shot in my gun. Reade paddled me up to within 130 yards of a huge sea eagle. I let fly, beat him down, and then up he got, and went away out of sight. I had scarcely done watching for him when five hoopers came directly towards me, and then hove up at about 120 yards; I let fly the other barrel, but, for want of being loaded with mould shot, I lost both my grand prizes.

12*th.*—Reade, who had wallowed in the mud since midnight (directly Sunday was over), came in this morning with 11 wigeon, which he got at one shot about two o'clock from my new mud sledge. Nothing in harbour to-day, though a pretty fair tide. I was out from nine at night till two; got a shot at about 14 wigeon and bagged 9. Reade went on at half-past two mud launching; he brought in about daylight 2 wigeon, and would have had about 6 more had not his gun flashed in the pan.

13*th.*—No birds about, though cold frosty weather, so I took this day for doing some jobs to my punts. Out all night; a cold, white frost; slack tide in spite of the full moon, and not a bird in harbour, or even outside. Sorry Keyhaven for a gunning place! Reade relieved me soon after two, when the water fell; and, after crawling on the mud till half dead, and till daylight appeared, he never saw, nor even heard, a single fowl.

14*th.*—There being nothing else to do, I turned my wits to a few miserable geese that had, ever since October, been the public target of every shooter, from the launcher to the armed cobbler, and never had one reduced from their company. By way of a valentine, I mixed them up some boluses (like blue grapes) sealed in a sort of shell cartridge. We had the excellent fortune to get within about 300 yards of them, when I let fly and bagged one brent goose, and another fell dead on the breakers, where I dare not follow. This is poor sport, that it should now be working a miracle to get one goose, when, a few years ago, I have knocked down over 100 in a season. *Tempora mutantur.*

15*th.*—Reade came in at daylight this morning, after a whole night's crawl in the mud sledge, with 19 wigeon, which he killed at one shot about five o'clock. Nothing does in this country but mud crawling, as when we have a wind for birds we have no water, and when we have a wind for good tides we have no birds.

After going to Lymington on business I renewed my game with these gun-defying geese; they started up as usual at 300 yards, where my boluses floored 5 of them, with the two barrels, each loaded with 20 ounces. A Yarmouth boat took off 2 before our faces before we could get the punt afloat, after running aground to shoot; all that I bagged of them, therefore, was 3 brent geese. Had we not made haste to get within hails and damns of these chaps, they would have got all our birds; but on our coming up they sheered off, and left us the three which I got. There being no tide for night shooting, I trudged off (among divers journeymen and rag-tag fellows) to the flight. All I saw to fire at was 1 mallard, which I bagged, and this was the only one killed among the whole army of shooters that lined the marsh and the shore.

16*th.*—Reade, having had bad luck with his gun flashing in the pan during the night, came in this morning with only 1 wigeon. No tide for me so I was again a gaol bird for the day, in spite of a frost. O Keyhaven, Keyhaven! not even a wherry could have lived outside, so what was I to do?

17*th.*—Reade came in this morning, after mud creeping all night, with only 1 wigeon. A calm sea at last after a white frost. Went off on tide in the gunning punt; and, after crossing the Channel close into the Isle of Wight, almost to Newtown, we fell in with a trip of wigeon, of which I got 6.

18*th.*—Sunday. Was packed up last night in order to start to-morrow morning for Alresford, when there set in suddenly the most tremendous gale of wind from the east, and the severest frosts that we have had for the last three seasons. I, of course, countermanded the march, to see what would be the issue of such delightful gunning weather.

19*th.*—A gale of wind all day; the harbour half frozen, and all the vagrant gunners racing up and down the shore like Bedlam broke loose. We, with great difficulty, got through the ice and weathered the wind in the creeks, but outside not even a vessel could have lived. I got a beautiful shot at 8 ducks, and the gun flashed; and these birds sat till I primed and flashed again; but, on retreating to rectify the gun, they flew up. I got another (indifferent) shot afterwards, and bagged 2 ducks and 1 mallard, and with the hand gun killed a fine old cock pintail and a golden-eye. Plenty of wigeon, but all where we dare not go.

20th.—2 mallards and 1 duck on the mud at 81 yards (measured) with a shoulder gun (old Fullerd).

21st.—4 wigeon and 1 brent goose; a fine show of birds, but the poppers so innumerable that they could have no rest day or night, and so bad were the chances that, I believe, I was the only gunner who got a bird to-day.

22nd.—Weather rather more calm; wigeon all to the eastward at sea; worked with my shell shot and got 3 brent geese and 1 burrough duck, all at enormous distances; not another soul could get near enough even to tickle one, so unusually wild were the birds.

23rd.—Reade, after the sovereign remedy (for this beastly country) of mud creeping all night, came in with 12 wigeon this morning. The only time that a punt could get water was from eight till twelve. A fine day, and every dandy turned gunner. Not a chance for a fowl, and I believe I was the only one who fired a shot.

24th.—Reade came in, after a blank night at mud crawling, and I was out all day and got but 1 wigeon. A tide at last, so went out at night; a fair show of birds, but as dark as the grave. Fired twice, by the sound: got 6 wigeon the first shot, nothing the next.

25th.—Sunday. A thaw after a white frost; and wigeon triumphing in the air all day, as if they knew it was a day of rest.

26th.—A gale of wind from the west, with thick drizzling weather and all the wigeon disappeared; everything indicating that the sport for the season, at all events on this coast, is nearly at an end.

27th.—Packed up all our traps, preparative to evacuating Keyhaven to-morrow by daylight.

A singular coincidence—the last shot I fired or required to fire I broke the lock of my great gun.

Last season, the last shot I required to fire I broke the swivel. How very kind of the traps never to give way till on the very point of being laid up for the summer! Our smallest great gun is luckily quite right; and this is all I want for a few little shots at Lord Rodney's, as I have an old punt, the 'Fox,' there in waiting.

28th.—Left Keyhaven, and after travelling at the rate of four miles an hour, in one incessant pour of rain, with a heavy load, the old horse and I arrived at Alresford House just in time for a six o'clock dinner, and after just twelve hours drenching.

March 1st.—Alresford. A hurricane of wind all day; and, at last, such a tremendous fall of rain, that I got wet through, and came home, after getting 4 tufted ducks, 3 dunbirds and 1 teal. The birds were so scattered that making a shot was impossible; and I should not have fired once the whole day had it not been to avoid the disgrace of an empty bag.

I was at the taking up of three cwt. of eels, at the weir, this morning.

5th.—Got up at three; climbed over the park paling, and was entrenched by a quarter before four. Got one shot only at 1 duck and 1 mallard, both of which I killed; discharged my gun after at 2 coots and killed them, and here ended my morning's work. So completely is the season over now.

6th.—Left Lord Rodney's for Longparish, and precious gales of wind and pelting storm I had to encounter for the last two hours of my drive, with a very heavy load, and the roads like a quagmire.

Game and wild fowl &c. killed in the season up to March 5th, 1827:

Game—122 partridges (all in four days except 1 brace), 8 hares, 1 pheasant, 1 woodcock (all I saw), 3 rabbits, 8 snipes (all I shot at). Game, 143 head.

Fowl—8 geese (the most killed by anyone on our coast), 209 wigeon, 12 ducks and mallards, 1 burrough duck, 11 curres, 1 pintail, 3 teal. Fowl, 245 head.

Sea-waders—5 curlews, 4 coots, 16 godwits, 9 plover, 146 ox-birds (in three shots), 2 olives. Waders, 182.

Grand total, 143 game; 245 wild fowl; 182 waders; 570. Best shot 17 wigeon, 2 teal, and 1 duck.

April 12th.—London. Had a grand day from six in the morning till twelve, with Joe Manton and his myrmidons firing with, and regulating the new elevated sights of, my huge double swivel gun, which we wheeled down to Bayswater, to the astonishment of the gaping multitude and idle followers.

17th.—Was from nine this morning till five in the evening with John Hussey, Joe Manton's celebrated borer, putting a fresh inside to this gun, down at Fullerd's den in Clerkenwell. It was shameful to see what a miserable inside the gun had before we rebored her, and then she looked and shot beautifully. My men Charles and John drew home the gun all along the New Road up to Manton's, lest it might come to harm by being left, as the tiger who took it there on Saturday evening was run foul of by a Paddington stage, on the strength of which he showed fight, and the gun was left at the mercy of a London mob while Smut and Jehu (who descended from his rostrum for a round) put themselves in battle array, and would have fought a battle worthy of the 'Morning Post' record and Marylebone Office cognisance, but for the interference of the stockbroking passengers, who feared, perhaps, that their 'blunt' might be in jeopardy during the fracas.

May 2nd.—Gave the great double gun a final trial at Bayswater, attended by some of Joe's best men. Found her wonderfully improved, and therefore satisfactorily ended all the trouble I have had with this job.

June 16th to 18th.—London. I continued very ill in bed, and could take no sustenance. As if we had not trouble enough, the chimney very kindly took fire, and we barely escaped the usual levy of engines, by a chimney sweeper, a hero in his way, wetting himself to the skin, and then going up through the fire, by which he succeeded in putting it out.

29th.—Longparish. We dragged the river to get baskets of fish for the Duke of Clarence and others; but, although we caught about 50 brace of trout, not one fish among them was more than $\frac{3}{4}$ lb., so very small do the fish run this season.

July 11th.—Left Longparish for Cowes. No smoke ships after three, so forced to boat it; got becalmed, broke an oar; should have been starved but for some bread and cheese and sour beer, at Calshot pothouse, and never reached Cowes till midnight.

12th.—Went to Southampton, to superintend some boat jobs that were doing for me. Slept at the 'Sun' inn on the quay, where the noise was such that all I ever heard before was pianissimo compared to it; thirty fellows screeching drunk, and singing till daybreak, in one room; an argument on politics in another, and a gaggle of more than average chattering women in another; people to and fro all night, and the waiters running about like mad dogs; but, *per contra*, I had a good bed, and, what was a miracle in Southampton, no fleas.

13th.—Went to Keyhaven, a transition to pure sea air, and quietness to boot.

16th.—Cowes. A grand tour round the island by the 'Medina' steam packet. Captain Knight, the master, was to have gone first to the eastward, and then, after seeing all that I had not seen, my boat would have met me in the evening off Keyhaven; instead of which the captain went the wrong way first, to oblige some company, and consequently I had to go all round to Cowes again, and then work my way back to Keyhaven in the evening. The packet made the round in a little better than seven hours. The day was delightful, and the scenery most interesting, though none so good as that at the Needles. At half-past seven, I started in a hack gig for Yarmouth (twelve miles), which I did by nine, and then took a boat and was rowed the six miles across to Keyhaven, where I landed at a quarter past ten, supped, and went to roost.

24th.—Cowes. Went to see that beautiful place, Norris Castle, and after passing a pleasant day with a party, was highly amused at the grand evening parade here, by a very tasteful singer and performer on the guitar, who appeared, in every word and action, to be a highly finished gentleman, and who, report says, is an officer in the Guards who is thus collecting money for a great bet. He seemed, when aside, to be hand in glove with all the first circle, and had been, the previous evening, dancing with the nobility and gentry at the yacht club house.

26th.—Made a third attempt to go to the Needle rocks, and, for the third time, was disappointed owing to the weather, as it blew so fresh we were obliged to put back, and, for the third time, our provisions were cooked in vain. Ever since I arrived here the rocks have been the object of my first cruise, and not one day have we yet had that would do. Towards noon the weather became boisterous, and threatened a regular miserable, wet-blowing evening ; so my musical friend Langstaff and I resolved to be a match for St. Swithin ; and, as every horse and wheel was in requisition for Southampton races, and we could not find a boat, we hired old Sadler's lobster cart, the value of which, horse and all, was about 4*l.*, and toddled into Lymington to the high diversion of ourselves and petrifaction of all the staring dandies, and repaired to old Klitz, the Clementi of the place. There Langstaff joined in a trio while I went foraging, and it then came on a determined wet night, for which we were well armed ; as we brought off a fiddle, a tuning hammer, and all the music we could borrow, and sat in with a good fire, for a thorough batch of such noise that neither the wind nor the rain was thought of.

31*st.*—This morning, between six and seven o'clock, I started for the grand regatta at Cowes; and, what was much more grand to me, to survey some duck shooting ground after the show was over. We were to have gone in the 'Cornwallis,' but, as we found her aground, we proceeded in Reade's boat. On our arrival, the place was all in an uproar, similar to the Derby at Epsom, with the addition of a military band, and an endless display of colours. Nothing could be more dull than the yacht race itself, as there was such a want of wind, and the vessels were so completely covered with canvas, that they appeared more like an enormous display of linen hung out to dry, than any objects that were contending for speed. At four o'clock I left Cowes, and joined Captain Ward on board his yacht the 'Guerilla.' We proceeded to Portsmouth, where, for want of wind, we did not arrive till nine, when we dropped anchor nearly alongside my old friend the 'Victory,' the immortal Nelson's ship, in which I once went a voyage, and slept on the very couch where this hero breathed his last. We went ashore at Portsmouth, as Ward had business there, and the place was 'out of the frying pan into the fire,' for what with jollifications for the Lord High Admiral and other naval men, here was, if possible, more noise than at Cowes. We did not get back on board till twelve, when we 'turned in,' and prepared for weighing anchor at daylight. This we did next morning.

August 1*st.*—Through want of wind and water we could not enter Langston harbour, the place to be surveyed for possible future fowling, till the afternoon, being made prisoners for a very long morning; we therefore amused ourselves with some bad line fishing, and then eating what we caught, added to some more fish that we got with a 'silver hook.' We dropped anchor in Langston harbour about three, when Singer, Ward's gunner, and I lowered a punt in which we kept surveying the harbour till near ten at night. Though shooting was not my object, Singer would ship Ward's beautiful stanchion; and had it not missed fire, owing to a little sea that we shipped, I should have made a grand shot of curlew jacks.

N.B.—Langston harbour is, without exception, the finest gunning place I ever saw, but, if possible, more infested with gunners than Keyhaven.

2nd.—Got under way, long before we were up, in order to be sure of getting to Cowes before nine, when the third day's regatta was to commence. As vessels were desired not to cross the course, we waited in the rear till the eight yachts, which started for the prize, were under way, and had got half a mile ahead. We then bore away and fairly passed seven of them, having the advantage also of even the 'Julia,' which was far ahead, insomuch that I think the 'Guerilla,' if well manned and in proper order, would have beat them all, and got the prize.

This regatta was beautiful, as there was a pretty breeze, which made the effect of it quite different from the other. We arrived at Keyhaven about half-past twelve.

6th.—After twenty-four days passing before there was one sufficiently calm to venture to the rocks, we this day had beautiful weather, and made a very pleasant excursion there. Though the scene was nothing new to me, yet I could always enjoy the beautiful scenery and the terrific grandeur of the cliffs. It was at least two months too late for the rock birds; all that I shot at was a willock, the only rock bird I saw, and a green cormorant, and these I bagged, besides landing and shooting at 3 rabbits, all of which I killed at one shot and sacked. No Leicestershire fox hunt, on record, could surpass the chase that we had with the shag, *alias* cormorant, *alias* 'parson.' After flooring his reverence from a little rock, and leaving him 'keel uppermost,' the invulnerable devil rallied, and led us a chase of between three and four hours and among other places to which he led us was into a subterraneous cave among the rocks, where the boat bumped about, and the cavern echoed so as to put us in mind of the incantation scene in 'Freischütz,' and the old cormorant of the devil Zamiel; but, after unkennelling the 'gentleman' and going twice to sea again after him, we shut up his daylights, and brought home our bird in triumph as a present for my man Williams, whose teeth vowed vengeance against him for his ensuing Sunday's 'blow-out.' I this day tried my old plan of the bell, string and flag, for moving the rock birds off the cliffs, which, had there been a thousand, would have started them every one, as not a gull or cormorant would sit a moment after this novel attack was made, but came pouring down on the sea, and were even accompanied by young nest birds that were so badgered by the sight and sound of this as to take their maiden flutter down on the occasion. We concluded our day's pastime by collecting specimens from the beautiful vari-coloured chalk rock in Alum Bay.

8th and 9th.—Was employed trying my large gun, regulating the elevations &c. Since being fresh bored, I found the gun wonderfully improved, both for strength and closeness, and as an example I must memorandum the best shot. Reade fired both barrels together, at half a sheet of brown paper 1 foot 10 inches by 1 foot 1 inch, and into this, at 90 yards, he put 52 No. 2 shot. The single shots were about in proportion, and all well driven for strength in the board. I killed seabirds just for a little trial at living objects, and no birds could have died in better style.

10*th.*—Was all day in expectation of Captain Ward to try our two unrivalled guns, as great improvements had been made to both of them since the last trial that we made. He arrived, in his yacht, off the quay after a miserable passage, and slept at my cottage here.

11*th.*—The trial being completed to our infinite satisfaction, as possessing the *ne plus ultra* of guns, Captain Ward dined with me early in order to sail for Southampton to-night. I accompanied him on board the 'Guerilla;' and after taking a bottle of wine with him there, and seeing him under way in a gale of wind, I went home in Reade's boat, and owing to losing a hat overboard, and getting into a vile mess to recover it, we had a most cruel passage home. Wet to the skin, and twice forced to get overboard up to our middle.

13*th.*—This afternoon about five o'clock I was witness to a melancholy accident, on the very spot where we were in such a bad predicament the night before last. Four men started in the highest glee to sail out of Keyhaven harbour and back, each in a separate boat and without oars on board, which was their foolish agreement, and one of them, Thomas Salter, a man unused to boats, 'capsized,' in 'gibing,' and suddenly disappeared, boat and all, to the horror of all the spectators. It was an hour before he was dragged up, a corpse, and above two hours before the boat was discovered and dragged up from above six fathoms of water. Mr. Davison got his horse, while I wrote the note for the coroner, and we sent my man Bagshore off for him about eight o'clock this evening to Ringwood.

14*th.*—If one could indulge in drollery on a melancholy occasion, we had some reason to do so. Bagshore, or rather Mr. Davison's horse and great-coat, with which he was equipped, was taken for a gentleman on his arrival at the inn in Ringwood, and after being hailed with the usual salutation of bell ringing, ostler calling &c. was shown up in style to a room, charged eighteenpence for his tea, and billeted for the night in the best manner the inn could afford, with scrapes and bows on his departure. And my 'gentleman' having a little *esprit de corps* about him, lugged out his 'blunt' for 'all hands,' under hope that Mr. Davison would indemnify him, which he kindly did.

Mr. Baldwin, the coroner, punctually and politely attended my summons by twelve this day, and after hearing from me all the particulars, he went through the form of a jury close to our windows here, where the body was brought, and of course gave 'accidental death.'

21*st*.—Fired a barrel of the great gun at 3 'jack' herons at about 120 yards, and winged them all three, to the super-exquisite gratification of the coroner, who with his mongrel dog played an able first fiddle in the 'cripple chase.' These imperial grenadier-looking birds 'showed' such fight against the dogs, that we, being without mud pattens, were nearly an hour before we got them all. They kept retreating over the mud, and occasionally disputed ground with the dogs, in a manner that was quite *à la militaire.*

CHAPTER XX

1827

September 1st.—The greatest day on record here. 102 partridges and 1 hare, besides 3 brace more birds shot and lost.

N.B.—A cold, dry, strong, easterly wind, with no scent; but I took care to have a fine army of cavalry and infantry, and made ample allowance for the wildness of the birds by the rapidity of our charges. I had no dogs but poor old Duchess and Sappho, both, like myself, among the 'has-beens.' I started at nine, had the first 'butcher's halloo,' or three cheers for 20 brace, at two. A second 'butcher's halloo' twenty minutes before six, and I then worked like a slave for the glory of making up 50 brace off my own gun, which I not only did, but, on turning out the game, it proved that I had miscounted, and had gone 1 brace over the desired number. I believe, under all circumstances, and at all events in our district, this nearly doubles any day on record in the annals of its sporting history.

2nd.—Sunday. Nothing so fortunate as this, because it keeps all the raw fools off, and allows the birds a little time to forget what has passed.

3rd.—50 partridges and 2 hares; the greatest second day in my annals. A still stronger easterly wind. The ground like rocks of stone, and the dust flying like Irish snuff. Birds walking about like poultry, and so wild that even in woods and rushes they would not stay to be fired at, but kept running off like hares; and, in short, nothing could be done with them till they were dispersed by cavalry and infantry, the labour of doing which made the day's work more like a hot and severe action than a day's sport and pleasure. Every man, dog, and horse was so exhausted as to be quite knocked up.

4th.—Busy ticketing off a houseful of game. Drove to Andover, and heard that no one round had done a fourth what I had. My whole army much exhausted, and a general resting day. A few shooters popping about, but nothing done. There rarely ever is after a grand field day, as the birds have not recovered their nerves to settle quietly.

5th.—Another general resting day; men, horses, dogs, and birds still unfit for war. A few poppers over all the ground as usual, but *n'importe.*

6th.—At them again. Another brilliant and unprecedented day. 56 partridges and 3 hares.

N.B.—A cold, dry, easterly wind, with a scorching sun again; never found a bird for the first hour, but at last discovered that the main army of the partridges had entrenched themselves in a piece of thick clover, on the estate of Sir Henry Wilson, of not more than three acres. His friend and steward, Captain Clark, very kindly gave me leave to enter this garrison of game, and directed me to give them no quarter; so in this one little field I bagged 10 brace of birds and 1 hare without missing a shot. Indeed, this was the only sport like easy September shooting that I have seen this season. The birds then returned to and dispersed on my own shooting ground, which was well planted with markers, and here we did gloriously. But had it not been for this lucky circumstance, I doubt whether we should have made a good day's sport; and I am quite sure we should have been puzzled to make up 200 head of game in three days, which everyone was anxious I should do. As it was, however, I made up 214 head of game in three days' shooting, viz. 1st, 102 partridges and 1 hare; 3rd, 50 partridges and 2 hares; 6th, 56 partridges and 3 hares. Total, 208 partridges and 6 hares, making 214 head besides lost birds.

I every day returned home with my cavalry and infantry in proper form of procession, instead of allowing them to straggle in like a vanquished army or disorderly banditti, which attracted no small admiration and laughter among the friends who were with me.

Having now done what I believe never was done here before, and what possibly may never be done here again, and supplied all the farmers and my friends with game, I shall here terminate the war against the partridges; and, at all events, leave them to others till I want game again, and can have proper scenting weather to kill a few birds in a quiet way.

15*th.*—Mr. Childe the artist arrived at Longparish, and Mr. Joseph Manton, preparative to a painting being made of our *partie de chasse.*

17*th.*—Assembled my myrmidons for one more grand field day, in order to have some of their likenesses. Mr. Childe attended as a strict observer, and Mr. Joseph Manton shot with me. Our united bag was 48 partridges and 1 hare, and we returned some time before the day was over, in order that Mr. Childe might complete by good daylight the necessary sketches of the group. My share of the bag was 28 partridges, but had I shot entirely by myself, and been able to waive the usual ceremony of shooting in company, and galloped up to all my birds, as heretofore, I am confident I should have killed 30 brace of birds. I therefore calculate that by taking out another sportsman the larder fell 6 brace short; because to follow birds up, as I ought in this wild country, I must do that which in company would be unsportsmanlike and ungentlemanlike to whoever was my companion; and Joe Manton, not being one of the quickest movers, either on horseback or on foot, doubly retarded several of the necessary attacks.

18*th.*—Stayed at home with Mr. Childe to arrange for the

FIRST OF SEPTEMBER, &c.

Sketched by J. Childe, Engraved by H. Adlard. & Published by Longman & C°.

disposition of the picture &c. while a friend and Joe Manton went off shooting. Nothing in 'Hudibras' or 'Quixote' could be more ludicrously crisp than the result of their day. They were to beat us all by going in a quiet way, and meant to astonish us by showing what could be done by one dog and a little poaching on our neighbours. But (yes, but), as the kitchenmaid (and the devil) would have it, the aforesaid dog unhappily fell foul of a tub of buttermilk just before starting, with which he so preposterously blew out his paunch, that he was pointing all day, not at birds, but to open both his ports in order to be relieved of the cargo he had taken in; and before he was sufficiently in trim to do anything but make his deposits from one port and cast up his accounts from the other, it was time to come home for dinner, and the finale was a deluge of rain. So much for buttermilk. Joe Manton suspected I had played this trick as a punishment for his challenge; but I was as innocent of the hoax as they were of the murder of game, they having got but 7 birds all day.

19*th.*—50 partridges and 4 hares, besides lost and divided birds, to my own gun and exclusive share, in 6 hours' shooting with Mr. Henry Fellowes, who is one of the quickest, coolest, and best sportsmen I ever entered a field with. He had a rascally gun that quite spoiled his shooting, though I could see he was a good shot. Had it not been for this, I dare say we should have killed 100 birds in the six hours, notwithstanding we had a very wild, windy day, and a pelting storm just in our best shooting, which spoiled the ground for at least an hour after it had ceased. We had only one gun each.

Joe Manton, Mr. Childe, and L—— hung on our leeward flank, and got 11 brace and 1 hare.

20*th.*—Joe Manton left us for town, highly delighted and astonished with what he had seen.

25*th.*—A tremendous gale of wind all day, with occasional

showers. The birds so wild that everyone laughed at me for going out; and I so ill that I could compare myself to nothing better than the buttermilk dog that accompanied Joseph Manton on the 18th, a memorable day. However, I worked 10 brace of birds; I said I would have them, and I did have them; and all within less than four hours; having bagged, besides 4 towered and lost birds, 20 partridges and 1 snipe. And all done by dint of rapid snap shooting.

27th.—While my man Charles was gone to Southampton, with despatches for Buckle, relative to building me another new punt, I pottered out on a pony in order to get a few more birds in a quiet way; but I was forced to quack myself up, for the sortie, with Huxham's bark and sal volatile. I started at half-past twelve, and came in at half-past four with 24 partridges, 3 snipes, and the only landrail I have seen or heard of this year, and all without once missing a shot; though, in spite of beautiful weather, the birds were so wild that half those I fired at were snap shots. I made five double shots and three cannons in the course of the day, and under all circumstances I consider this the best day's sport I have had this season.

29th.—Having enjoyed some of the best September shooting that I ever heard of, and wanting no more birds just now, I this day left Longparish for London.

Game killed in September 1827: In seven times going out, viz. four whole days' shooting, 258 partridges and 10 hares. One scrambling, ill-managed day, with Joe Manton, 28 partridges, and two little quiet sorties of four hours each, and without markers, 44 partridges, 4 snipes, and 1 landrail; making in all, 330 partridges, 10 hares, 4 snipes, 1 landrail. Total, 345 head, besides about 12 brace shot dead and lost. This is the best sport I ever had, or that ever was known here in the memory of the oldest man living. Though far from being in good health, I never shot better. A good breed of birds, but they were particularly wild every day this season.

October 10*th*.—Arrived at my healthiest of homes, Keyhaven.

13*th*.—A few wigeon appeared; went out to reconnoitre, but got no chance.

17*th*.—Got my maiden shot of the season, from which I picked up 2 brent geese, 2 pintails, and 1 wigeon; and these were all the birds I had to fire at, except 1 other goose, that went off severely hit, and dropped off at sea. These 3 are the first geese that have been heard of this season, and very early it is for them.

I then came home and went game shooting. At the close of the day, however, I made up a brace of partridges. We then had quite an event with an old hare, an animal that is thought as much of at Keyhaven as an elephant. I let fly at her a scrambling shot, a long way off, and through the potatoes; down she came, and the dog had a hold of her. Off she set again: Bagshore, Mr. Davison, myself, and a whole banditti had a chase after her for nearly half an hour, till, at last, we gave her up. Soon after she was chased by an old woman, who caught her by the legs, and who let her go in a fright when she began to squeal, for fear that she (the said old woman) should be scratched. Then we heard that this wonderful hare had run into some one's house, and Lord knows how many stories. In short, she was cut all to pieces, and is, no doubt, dead; and she was the first living creature that I had pulled a trigger at, without bagging, since my arrival in this place. After this curious affair I went home, shipped water boots, shifted my shot, and went out for snipes. All I fired at was 1 snipe and 1 jack snipe, both of which I bagged, except discharging my gun at, and killing, a swallow, just to say that I had shot wild geese and a swallow in the same day. Here ended my three heterogeneous sallies in shooting this day; and, at night, my waggon, with my workman,

Buckle, and all the traps for finishing the new light punt arrived, and this is now my chief business at Keyhaven, as the weather is still too mild for sport with wild fowl. What with the hard fag in the day, the uproar of unloading a large freight of traps and goods, and quartering off the myrmidons attendant on them, I had this day quite as much work as would have served any moderate man's exercise for a fortnight.

20th.—While my men were jobbing, I went out for four hours in order to get a partridge, if possible. The scarcity of game was quite ridiculous. I saw but 6 birds, and these a snap shot. My first barrel missed fire, but with my second barrel I got 1 partridge, and just saved my charter of never having a blank day.

24th.—Busy jobbing. About 20 wigeon dropped in off Pennington Lake. Reade and I went off to them in the 'Lion.' I let fly both barrels of the swivel gun, and stopped 12 of them at about 110 yards, with which I had every reason to be satisfied.

25th.—A gale of wind and rain all the morning. In the evening it abated, and we tried the new punt, in an unfinished state, just to 'trim her on all tacks,' and nothing could answer more beautifully than she did. While busy at the punt, a very fine fat knot pitched on the mud, and I ran in for my musket, and got him. This was the only shot I fired to-day.

31st.—New punt finished and painted to-day. I went out for about four hours, and never saw but a leash of partridges the whole time; and when I put my leg on one hedge, these birds were flying over the other, at the opposite end of the field. I just saved my charter of never having a blank day by accidentally springing one snipe and bagging him. The only shot I fired.

November 1st.—Sailed all the way to Pitt's Deep, in the 'Lion' punt, and had such a fine side wind that we made the passage there and back at the rate of seven miles an hour

We had thus an opportunity of surveying about twenty miles of coast, and in this we saw but one flock of birds, and these off at sea. I was much amused with an interview with old Harnet (the emperor of the Hampshire gunners), whom I had not seen before, since I was a Johnny Raw at the science (about eleven years ago), and he was in ecstasy with my set-out and new inventions. I got no shots, except firing one for the edification of the said Harnet at a mark, which not a little astonished him.

2nd.—The new punt having been finished last night, Stephen Keil left us this day, and such a workman, I believe, never used a tool. Among other house jobs, this morning he made a capital bootjack in fourteen minutes.

4th.—Sunday. Had a pleasant sail to Yarmouth, where I went to church. Nothing extraordinary occurred, except that the parson forgot to read the Gospel.

7th.—Named the new punt the 'Dart,' and gave the myrmidons a five-shilling wet on the occasion at Reade's new pothouse the 'Gun,' where not only my beer, but lots more of the brewer's, was quaffed on the occasion; and not one of the Lord High Admiral's launches could have been launched off with more determined energy.

8th.—Made my first sortie with the 'Dart,' in order to try her at sea 'on all tacks.' Nothing could answer more beautifully.

11th.—Sunday. Went, as usual, to church at Milford, where on this occasion our parson forgot to read the Gospel.

13th.—Left Keyhaven for the 'Dolphin' inn (the flash hotel of Southampton), and the only place there where I ever tasted of real comfort. I was busy the whole evening settling little bills for the 'Dart' punt, which came to 32*l.* 2*s.* 6*d.* And so admirably superior has all turned out, that, had it cost twice the money, it would have been well worth it.

21st.—Keyhaven. An easterly wind again. Took a cruise in the 'Lion' in hopes the geese would be blown over with this wind; but the only fowl I saw or shot at were 2 teal and 1 tufted duck, all of which I killed with one of my new cartridges, in the left barrel of the 'champion' gun. While stretching my legs ashore, I trod up a snipe, and floored him with the cripple stopper and duck shot.

22nd.—Started for a regular day's cruise, to survey the whole coast, at daylight, in the 'Lion' punt, with a north-east wind. Worked up beyond Leap till we were about fifteen miles from Keyhaven, and except a few geese on their travels in the air, we never saw one single head of wild fowl, though the frost (a rascally white one that always brings rain) was so sharp that we were half starved with cold. We anticipated a delightful passage back, but no sooner had we completed our trip to the east, than the vile white frost changed the weathercock to the west, and we had consequently the wind in our teeth both ways.

24th.—Cold wind from the north, with a little frost. I got 5 wigeon out of 10 which I shot at, and of which I did not expect to get one in the tremendous sea that they fell in. I fired the great gun into the only company we saw (about 25), and brought down 4 with the first barrel, and 6 with the second, after they flew up from the breakers.

30th.—Having now completed all my little finishing jobs to my satisfaction, and established ready for the winter the best 'turn-out' of gunning punts and guns in the known world, I this day left Keyhaven, and arrived at Longparish House.

December 1st.—Being sadly in want of a little game, I weathered a day's hurricane, with pelting storms every half-hour, and got an old cock pheasant (the only one I have set eyes on this year), 3 partridges, 1 jack snipe, and 1 rabbit, which, with 1 moorhen and 2 birds shot and lost, was all I fired at.

3rd.—Fagged all day, and brought home but 5 partridges, 1 rabbit, and 1 pheasant.

4th.—I tried to catch a few fish, to show Mr. Davison what our sport would be if it was the season, and, in little more than an hour, I caught 6 brace of fair-conditioned trout.

5th.—11 rabbits, 5 hares, 2 snipes, and 5 pheasants, to my share of a shoot at Hurstbourne Park, in killing which I never missed one shot, except at a hare that popped behind a stump which took off my whole charge. I killed 4 of the rabbits without seeing them, by firing at random, just ahead of them, as they ran across in the covert.

6th.—Pottered over my old beat, round home, and bagged 2 pheasants (all I saw) and 7 partridges, besides 2 more partridges that towered and were lost. This I did by banging away at all distances, as the birds were extremely wild.

8th.—7 partridges, by means of blazing away at all distances, for the lottery of taking heads and wings, as the birds were so wild that fair shooting, even in turnips, was totally out of the question.

27th.—2 partridges, 2 snipes, and 1 jack snipe. Thus have I been slaving for two days to make up one small basket of game for a friend. I never in my life saw the birds so wild, or the country and weather in such a deplorably dull state; the very look of the fields is enough to give a sportsman the horrors.

Incessant wet weather up to and on the 31st, so that there has not been the least chance for any more shooting in 1827.

1828

January 1st.—A deluge of rain from the north-east, which we hope and trust will clear the weather, and bring us over a few fowl.

2nd.—A fine black frost, with a N.E. wind, and, before I had been two hours on the road for Keyhaven, the fickle cock must needs ''bout ship,' and get S.W. with an eternal bellows of wind, and spouting of rain the whole afternoon and night. Such was the damage done on many parts of the road, that it was quite a matter of doubt whether all communication was cut off or not. However, after getting sick with some stuff yclept 'mock turtle' at an inn, but more like leather and glue, I reached Keyhaven late at night, and luckily found that the place had escaped very well from the floods. Not a fowl had been seen for many weeks, except a few very wild geese. This I fully anticipated, and therefore, had I not had some arrangements to make, should not have gone down till the weather was better settled.

We just loaded the great gun and put all 'in trim,' in case anything should appear.

4th.—A few very wild geese were seen off below Pennington, and no sooner had we started in chase of them, about three miles to leeward, than there came on the most tremendous weather I ever was out in: a hurricane that almost tore up the very mud, hailstones that peppered us like a volley of musketry, and as heavy a fall of rain as I ever saw, with an *ad libitum* accompaniment of thunder and lightning. Reade was drenched to the skin, in spite of all his 'dread-nought' garments, and the punt had a complete freight of rain water on board. But notwithstanding all this, and although the storm lasted more or less for four hours, yet my 'sou'-wester' dress so defied the elements that I came home as dry all over as if I had been sitting the whole time with dandies in a drawing room.

5th to 7th.—Incessant bad weather.

8th.—The weathercock flew backwards into the east, with a gale of wind, and rain, all the morning. This being a better quarter for birds, we weathered it, to explore; and as it blew so hard that we could not row the punt on end, we towed her along the banks all the way to off Lymington. We then flew down the wind most beautifully all the way home, though saw nothing but one flock of geese, which a lubberly fellow had spoiled our chance at. Being anxious to try a new cartridge of my own invention, I took a shot with it at 2 grey plover, which were sitting, with 3 dunlins, on some piles, and got the whole 5 of them, so that I hope my cartridge will answer.

10*th.*—Frost and snow. Things looking up. I got 10 wigeon about five this morning, and Reade 1 wigeon only in the night. It snowed all the afternoon, so that we did not go out for the evening tide.

Frost and snow the previous night, and Reade got 6 wigeon. But about twelve to-day there came on a rapid thaw with a transition from the coldest to warm weather, and towards the afternoon there came on the old detestable and everlasting west wind, which, as if by magic, blew off every flock of fowl that had assembled on our coast. I had no chance to-day for a shot with the large gun.

12*th.*—Nasty, foggy, rotten, undertaker's weather. No fowl. Shot at the dunlins, picked up 43. I stopped about 60. Got 2 coots, at about 160 yards off, and coming home I knocked down a large speckled diver. So much for the gunning here now. A deluge of rain all the evening and night, with an atmosphere hot and sickly.

13*th.*—Sunday. We had such a tremendous hurricane soon after midnight, that our beds were shaken under us, with an attack of thunder and lightning that may be compared to the heat of a severe battle. About two hours before daylight we were hastily called up with the alarm of an immediate inundation. The sea broke over the beach and came raging up to our very doors, so that we were in the greatest alarm for the safety of our property. Though we have experienced floods before, we never were so suddenly and unexpectedly visited with one as on this day. Providentially, however, all ended well, and I contrived with extreme exertion, at the risk of being washed away, to secure all my valuable punts, and with scarcely any damage, though two of them were swept away, but just recovered in time on the lee shore to save their being beat to pieces. The damage that must have been done at sea is horrible to reflect on, and it appears worthy of remark that this sudden and awful visitation should have occurred on Sunday, the 13th, when the first two verses of the evening Psalms for that day are so appropriate to the occasion. Before night the waters had abated, the weather became tolerably calm, and perfect safety was again restored.

14*th.*—A dead calm, with a fog, and the water as smooth as a looking-glass. Went with a large punt off under the Isle of Wight, got a shot at a few ducks, and to my surprise stopped 4 of them; but not wishing to run the risk of losing the tide back, I came away well pleased with 1 duck and 1 mallard. In the evening the wind got to the eastward and blew a gentle breeze with thick rain.

15*th.*—Wind more southerly; the bellows and water engines on again—everlasting puff and slush; lovely weather for doctors and undertakers, but the essence of nuisance to all other people.

16*th.*—The wind backed and blew strong from the east, which occasioned the arrival of several large flocks of wigeon; but they were very wild and too much scattered to afford a good shot by day. I banged off at long distances, and got 4, 3, and 2, making in all 9 wigeon bagged.

The wind then flew to the southward, with more rain. Reade got me 4 more wigeon; and I went out at night, but was driven home again by a pour of southerly rain. The springs so high that we were forced to launch a punt in the larder, as a ferry boat for grub, coals, &c. A lovely time! Nothing but howling of wet gales of wind battering against the windows, of eternal everlasting rain, and the barking coughs of men, women and children. Everything seems to promise a second edition of Noah and his cruise in the ark.

17*th.*—A gale of wind and slush again. I weathered it out, as there were several birds off. I got only 2 wigeon, though had a fine chance at about 300 geese, but the big gun was so full of water it would not go off.

18*th.*—Left Keyhaven merely to go to Longparish for a

day, and therefore had but one shirt, and the mere clothes on my back. Owing to the floods and rain I was obliged to sleep at Winchester, and I went over to Longparish on the 19th. No sooner had I arrived there than a most distressing letter, on a most nefarious business, called me on to London, where, in a dress scarcely fit to be seen, I arrived on the 20th and proceeded that night and all the 21st to business; and I may say that in those two days I saw more roguery than I had before met with in all the rest of my life.

21st.—Returned to Longparish, wishing to be in the country just now, though I had left my man Charles and all my gunning things at Keyhaven. The country was so inundated that getting sport of any kind was out of the question. Never were the floods, in the memory of man, equal to those here now. Having H.R.H. the Duke of Clarence's commands to get some game for the Duchess (a forlorn hope I feared), I slaved all one day and got 6 partridges and 2 pheasants.

Game &c. killed to February 1828: Popgun work—375 partridges, 15 hares, 12 rabbits, 12 pheasants, 1 landrail, 22 snipes, total 437; swivel-gun work—3 ducks and mallards, 44 wigeon, 2 pintails, 2 teal, 2 geese, 1 black duck, 1 tufted duck, total 55.[1]

N.B.—Owing to the worst season ever known, and being much interrupted with business, my wild-fowl shooting for this year has been almost annihilated.

February 19th.—London. I had received some days ago a very brilliant account from Reade of the birds at Keyhaven. Matters being a little right now, and having received yesterday a second despatch from Reade, I resolved on making an appendix to the campaign by going down *solus*, and roughing it for a few days.

[1] P.S.—Since closing this list, I had to go down to Keyhaven for a week, and from the 20th to the 23rd of February I bagged 36 wigeon and 2 brent geese. This brings my fowl to 93 head and my grand total to 530 head of game.

Keyhaven. I was ready to go afloat at ten this evening, but it came on a rascally fresh wind from the westward, which embargoed the novelty of my breakfasting in London, and killing wigeon above 100 miles off within fourteen hours, which I was almost sure of doing, as there had been a prime chance every night.

20th.—Tide served about two in the afternoon; plenty of birds, but the harbour ruined by dandies chasing and firing at them with ball. About four a gale of wind and a pour of rain drove the dandies home, and we then fell in with a trip of wigeon; but not till all was wet and only one barrel to fire, and this, unluckily, loaded with large mould shot. I blew it off, and picked up 14 wigeon and 1 brent goose. A gale of south-west wind and rain for the remainder of the evening and night.

21st.—7 wigeon and 1 brent goose: bad weather again.

22nd.—8 wigeon, and the day finished with wind and rain.

23rd.—Foggy weather, which never does to get at birds afloat. Out from four till ten, and at night, when I got a little straggling shot across the haze, and picked up 5 wigeon.

25th.—An incessant gale with constant thick rain from the west. The very weather to extinguish the wild-fowl season. We weathered it morning, noon, and night under our new water covers, but neither saw nor heard a single bird the whole time.

27th.—Arrived in Park Street.

28th.—Saw in London in the Regent's Park 15 wild wigeon and 5 tufted ducks.[1]

June 4th.—Drove down to see my son Peter at Eton, and a pour of rain having embargoed me till two 'clock, and the requisition of every animal and vehicle for Ascot races having monopolised all better conveyance, I had to work my way down with an old horse and chaise, in order to be in time for

[1] The French decoy ducks that I presented have, no doubt, called them in there, on their nightly passage.

the grand Etonian gala of 'the boats.' A party of us rowed up to Surley Hall in the procession with a prime four-oar, and I never saw the spectacle more brilliant or more to advantage. The King sent the boys plenty of his royal wine in return for their taking up the little Prince George of Cumberland, and most royally drunk some of them got with it. What with the gaiety of the scene, among the merry little fellows on the one hand, and the reflection of my younger and happier days on the other, I hardly know whether the being elated or affected was more predominant on my feelings.

On the 5th I spent the whole morning in shaking hands with old friends &c., and first among them my esteemed old tutor, Dr. Goodall, now Provost of the College; and after having partaken of the kind hospitality of my old schoolfellow, and Peter's 'Dominie,' Captain Dobson, I returned to dinner in London.

22nd.—Longparish. Fished (to amuse Mr. W. Griesbach) in a bright sun, dead calm and north wind (with a fly), and killed 4 brace of trout. This is equal to 30 brace in a good time and in a good month for fly fishing.

July 29th.—Left Keyhaven at half-past four, drove to Southampton; boarded the 'George the Fourth' steam packet at eight; and at a quarter before eleven landed on the quay at Havre de Grâce. Passage 112 miles.

30th.—It was a matter as if of life and death for me to get off this morning at nine by the 'steamer' to Rouen; it being the only conveyance till the next day, except a vile night coach or vile French posting. They all defied me to get my passport in time for the steamer, as the 'consul was never at his office till eleven, and lived out of town,' and a Madame Moncey (who seemed to lead all Havre by the nose, having an official situation in the custom house) was quite indignant at my not taking her word to this effect (as all the other passengers without passports had done) and paying her the same homage that others did. I ran all the way to the country seat of the consul, whom I caught just going to breakfast; and he, luckily, having a blank form by him, favoured me with a passport; so I floored the omnipotent Madame Moncey, and got under way for Rouen. Though the road to Rouen is but fifty-five miles, yet the passage is seventy-five miles, owing to the innumerable windings of the Seine. This is perhaps one of the most lovely passages in France.

I landed soon after eight at Rouen, where, after securing the only vacancy in the morning diligence, I inspected the magnificent cathedral of this place, built by the English in the reign of Henry IV., and then passed a short bad night in a sorry nest, seven storeys high, at the Hôtel de Lyon But, as I am now an old foreign traveller, it would be needless to recapitulate the mixtures of novelties and miseries with which I have, over and over again, filled the pages of my former journals. I have, therefore, but little to remark on this excursion.

31*st.*—Left Rouen by the diligence at six this morning, and arrived in Paris by nine at night, by way of Louviers, where we breakfasted at ten; Mantes, where we dined at half-past two; and St.-Germain, which is about 4 leagues from the metropolis. The short way is 32 leagues; but I preferred this route, as being the most beautiful journey on the banks of the Seine, and because I had been the other way before. A French post league being 2½ miles English, the journey to-day was just 90 miles. I have nothing to remark on this road, since I was in France before, except that the diligences are cleaner and go better: you have no conductors or postillions to pay, and the latter have doused their butter-churn boots for life guards' jack boots; have left off powder, and amputated their colossal pigtails. I this night took up my old quarters at the Hôtel Montmorency, Rue St.-Marc, No. 12.

August 1*st.*—Called on my old friend Mr. Kalkbrenner, No. 33 Rue Chantereine, and then passed my time in the

Louvre till it was the hour for dinner, after which I went to the French opera.[1]

2nd.—Engaged in various little matters, and, in the evening, called on another god of the piano, my other friend, Mr. Jerome Bertini (who is now the Clementi of Paris), at No. 8 Rue Montaigne du Roule. He was out teaching, though half-past eight at night; but madame, his wife, the great harp player, was *chez elle*, and not a little surprised to see me. I must surely astonish both my old masters by this popping suddenly upon them, who scarcely knew whether I was dead or alive.

3rd.—Bertini came up to me this morning before breakfast, and I never saw a fellow more alive at seeing another than he was at seeing me. We breakfasted together, and he then adjourned to Pleyel's to play me some of his new music. The remainder of the day we spent at Versailles, but were prevented from enjoying it, owing to the wet and stormy weather.

4th.—About various business till the middle of this day, and then passed the remainder of it in the Jardin des Plantes, where there were innumerable additions made since I was last in Paris, the giraffe and many other curious animals, as well as a great increase in every other branch of natural history.

5th.—Spent a part of the morning in the Luxembourg; some of the pictures here were the best, for effect, I had seen for a long time; and one in particular by the president or chief of the Academy at Rome. Went in the evening to the 'Favart' or Italian opera. Meyerbeer's 'Crociato in Egitto' was the piece, and, as usual, the orchestra at this house was most delightful; but I hardly knew whether to condemn or approve of the introduction of Turkish cymbals in this orchestra. They seem to be the order of the night, now, in the Paris

[1] *La Muette de Portici*, in four acts, with the dancing included. A very spirited opera; but the music rather in the noisy school. A tremendous orchestra, with the addition of double drums and Turkish cymbals.

bands. The best singer, to my taste, was Madame Pisaroni. A Monsieur Donzelli also showed great talent, and I preferred him to our London tenors.

10th.—Since the 6th I have been to the Louvre, the Luxembourg, the Tuileries, Versailles &c. but made no memorandums, as nothing particular was there beyond what I took down in my former visit to Paris. This evening I went to the Tivoli, which is very different from what it was a few years ago. The ground on which this once grand fête was held is sold, and the place now substituted is farther off, and not nearly so well adapted to the purpose. The old Tivoli was as far superior as the new one is inferior to our Vauxhall. No Russian mountains, no balloons of fire now, and, in short, a poor, miserable place, but little better than a country fair, except having one fine temple for gormandising, and a capital band for the quadrilles. But this is a matter of course: leave a Frenchman alone for eating and dancing.

12th.—Mr. Kalkbrenner gave me a seat in his box this morning, to hear the pianoforte pupils of the Conservatoire play for the prizes before a full audience in the theatre of that establishment, which is called the Ecole de Musique. The performance began at nine o'clock, and the great Cherubini sat in state as the harmonic judge, surrounded by a kind of jury of other mighty dons. The first batch of pupils were seven girls, who each played the same piece, and then read an MS. at sight. The piece was Kalkbrenner's, and the MS. was Cherubini's. Monsieur Adam, the old man who for many years has been pianoforte master to the Conservatoire, and who was Kalkbrenner's master, sat by the side of the pupils. It became tedious and monotonous to hear the same thing played over so many times, and, as a matter of etiquette, all applause was withheld. At last the first act of this exhibition came to a close by a vase being handed round among the judges, and their placing therein little things similar to our balls in 'blackballing' at clubhouses, when three of the young ladies were called on, and severally addressed as best, second best, and so on for the prizes; and on Cherubini finishing his short oration to them from the grand box, there was a great burst of applause. The next part of the exhibition was to be young men playing a concerto of Kalkbrenner's; sat out three of them, but when I heard there were to be five or six more, I could weather it no longer, so took the liberty to 'bolt.' Went to see the new building La Bourse on the Exchange, a superb and commodious edifice lately completed in Rue Vivienne. The imitations of sculpture here are so well 'brought out' in the painting, that I could hardly persuade myself but what they were real statues.

15*th*.—Went (by admission ticket) to the church of Notre-Dame to see the King and all the royal family celebrate the day of the Virgin Mary, one of the greatest festivals in France. The town was in confusion the whole morning, with the rattling of carriages, ringing of bells, and bustling about of the civil and military; and about two o'clock the cathedral doors were opened, and those who had tickets were admitted, and, no doubt, also many without them in the general confusion. From two till near three we sat in the cathedral and saw all the different processions arrive: the counts, the peers, the mayor, the priests, the masters of ceremony, &c., and punctually at three the grand procession began to enter: the priests, the bishops, the marshals, the Duke and Duchess of Angoulême, and then the King, walking under a large canopy superbly ornamented. I never saw a monarch with whose countenance I was better pleased, he looked the picture of affability and good disposition; and so well does he carry his age, that I thought he looked quite as young as, if not younger than, his son the Duke of Angoulême. I had seen him before, in old Louis's time, when he was Count d'Artois, and he does not appear a day older, though when I saw him last must have been about nine years ago. The ceremony performed in the cathedral was what they call vespers; an immoderate bellowing of the basest of base voices, with the blowing away of two serpents, and all the noise that hands and feet could bring forth from a huge rough-toned organ; and, by way of a finish, the silver Virgin Mary was started from the altar, and carried halfway over the town with all the procession from Charles X. down to half the rabble of Paris, among such a noise and stink as a man may go his life and never hear or smell again. We thought the noise in the church pretty well, but it was a mere whisper to that out of it, particularly the bells, which would have almost drowned that of a cannonade. In short, this evangelical spree was kept up till about five, when the King arrived at the Tuileries in his state carriage; and his other carriage (with eight horses) was ready to take him back to St.-Cloud as soon as he had rid himself of the trappings for the levee of the silver Virgin. Although I am too great a 'heretic' (as the Spaniards would call me) to enter into the spirit of the Catholic religion, yet no one could say but the show was extremely well worth seeing. In the evening I looked into the French Theatre; but, as it was too hot to sit out a play, I merely went into the second gallery. But there was nothing particular to observe since I was there before.

17*th.*—Having now done what business I had here, and prepared to start for England again, I shall just memorandum down a few short remarks as to the changes that have taken place since I was last in Paris.

Travelling: Road and travelling much the same. The *messagerie*, or diligences, altered to huge treble-bodied machines, and painted yellow instead of green. No conductor or postillions to pay, but a moderate charge made in lieu of it. Inns as dirty and uncomfortable as ever, charges dearer, and winės not so good. Posting and the *malle poste* in every respect the same.

Paris: Every article dearer than it was, but now the

French have a fixed price, so that you have not to bargain like a Jew to avoid being cheated, as you were once obliged to do, in even the best shops. The cooking is much the same —most exquisite for those who like made dishes, and prefer messes of butter, sugar, and Lord knows what to plain, wholesome food. Our English sauces—cayenne &c.—may now be had, if called for, at most of the *restaurateurs'*. The wines are decidedly not so good as in former times, and you have still the same difficulty in getting a good-sized glass to drink out of at your dinner. There are, however, some English people who have set up soda and ginger-beer shops, so that, by going to them, you have now the means of quenching that insufferable thirst which is produced by the greasy, sugary, salt, and acid mixtures, that the French dishes abound with, not to say a word of the tricks that are now played as to meat, wines, and spirits.

Amusements: French opera rather improved. Italian opera rather fallen off: their band, which I thought the best I ever heard, is now no more than equal to that of our opera. Dancing, if anything, in rather less force. Tivoli miserably bad. Boulevards as gay as ever. Tortoni's still the best ice shop, and Very's (in the Palais Royal) now become the best *restaurateur's* in Paris. Formerly I thought it about the third best.

State of things: Great improvement in the paintings of the rising French artists, particularly in the school of David. Military nearly the same—*gendarmes*, as usual, a pattern to the whole world for their orderly and respectable behaviour. Cuirassiers not so well mounted as formerly, cavalry rather fallen off than improved in appearance. Even the King's stud are but moderate-looking animals. People here all appear to be in the height of affluence, you rarely see a shabby-looking person; and, in short, the people of Paris appear to spend a great deal more money on their dressing, eating, drinking, and amusements than do those in London.

From all appearances, therefore, we may conclude that France is in a very flourishing state.

18*th.*—Left Paris at six this evening by the diligence, to go the other, the short, road to Rouen. There being an opposition on this road at night, we travelled a very fair pace, and were as quick in all our changes as the Southampton coaches. We rumbled along all night in this stupendous machine, like a movable hayrick driving a herd of bullocks before it, and two other diligences at our heels, and we never got more than a few seconds' stoppage all the way from Paris to Rouen. Our conductor was an infernal hog, and quite brutish to several female passengers who wanted to alight a moment, which he would hardly allow. Refreshment out of the question, except what I had the sense to pocket, and grope out in the dark to eat. Between four and five in the morning we descended into the valley where stands the town of Flueris; and the four diligences descending the mountain under the opening of daylight on a fine morning, the 19th, had a novel and beautiful effect. The diligence weighed 11,100 lb., the freight with twenty inside passengers and luggage, 5,500 lb., making in all, 16,600 lb. We had seldom less than seven horses, three at wheel, and four abreast leaders, all driven by one postillion; and in the mountainous parts we had nine horses, on which occasion an extra boy in a blue frock and white cotton nightcap drove the two leaders. The first refreshment we got was 1½*d.* of milk on reascending after passing the town of Flueris. An old cribbage-faced woman, surrounded by beggars, waylays the coach at this ascent with her cups and pitcher. Nothing worthy of remark occurred till we approached the town of Rouen from the tremendous hill of St. Catherine, the view from which is so charming that people often make a point of staying a day in Rouen on purpose to go and look from thence over the town and the Seine, if it so happens that their journey does not bring them by way of this heavenly landscape. The hill is tremendous, and the coaches while descending by the winding road have a novel and beautiful effect. I should not omit to mention that two Frenchmen had such a quarrel about their seats in the night, as to come to the scratch and collar, and almost to a fight; and, before daylight, they were as thick as two pickpockets. We got to Rouen by seven, having performed the journey, 32 post leagues, 80 English miles, within thirteen hours, which for France is very fair going. Nearly the whole way is paved, and the diligence nearly as rough as a butcher's cart, so the shaking may be easier imagined than described; and, as if we had not noise enough with an everlasting volley of rumble and chatter, the horses had all bells. But, after all, the convoy of these four machines had a very lively and somewhat pleasing effect. Trunks just looked into at Rouen, merely to see we had no liquors, which pay a small barrier duty. After a good, though dear, breakfast at the Hôtel de Lyon, Madame du Roy, I proceeded by a branch diligence, just like the other, and for which you are booked at Paris, for Dieppe. Here we had a very civil gentlemanlike conductor, who was himself chief proprietor of the coach, and it is to him that I am indebted for the precise state of the weight &c. before mentioned. We left Rouen at nine, and got into Dieppe a quarter before four. The distance is 14 leagues, 35 English miles. Nothing particular occurred on the remainder of the journey, except our having to walk through the fine oak wood of Malawney while the diligence performed the winding ascent of the road, which was so tremendous a drag that the moment you have reached the summit of the hill, nine fresh horses are put to, and the others taken away ready to drop. English horses would have jibbed with such a freight.

N.B.—I could get no place but the *rotonde* (behind), which happens to be cheapest. The middle is called *l'intérieur*, and the front *le coupé*, much the best place, but generally bought up a week beforehand. The rookery place 'aloft' is called *l'impérial*, and a most imperial tumble a gentleman would get out of it if any accident happened. These hasty remarks are all I have time to make, as I must now proceed to see and do various jobs at Dieppe.

P.S.—I forgot to note that poor old Delarne is dead, and his widow keeps on the house where I am now put up. Dined at the table d'hôte; and, in the evening, went down to see the superb baths and public rooms that have been erected since I was here some years ago. I never saw a place so improved. I always liked Dieppe as well as any place in France, because it is almost the only French town that does not stink abominably. Finished the day with a refreshing walk on the shore, and then a warm salt bath to rectify all the shakes and dust of the twenty-two hours' rough journey.

20th.—Went a little way out of the town to investigate the particulars of the *pension Anglais* (English school), kept by Messrs. Williams and Sparke, at a sort of country seat called 'Gaudecote,' and was more pleased with this than any other establishment that I had seen in France. The remainder of the day was spent in running about and seeing the few 'lions' of the place, which I found so very pleasant that my detention in it became a day's pleasure, instead of a day's quarantine. Had an excellent dinner at Madame Delarne's table d'hôte, and among many other good things, we had capital roast beef, and good Bordeaux claret at fifteenpence English the bottle. Price of the table d'hôte, two francs and a half for dinner, cider, dessert, and in short, everything but wine. Got my heavy things on board the packet preparative to starting early to-morrow morning for England.

I never was asked for my passport through the whole of my journeys.

21st.—Got under way by the 'Eclipse' steam packet, Captain Cheesman, at half-past six this morning, and landed on the chain pier, or new quay, at Brighton at half-past five in the evening, making a tolerable passage of eleven hours. For the first three hours all was as smooth as a duck pond, and a capital breakfast was set out on deck; but, towards the latter part of the passage, the wind freshened in our teeth, and the berths and basins were more in requisition than the eatables or drinkables. Passage from step to step on quays, 80 miles, fare 2*l.* The very devil's own work at custom house. No fault of Mr. Lewis, who is the chief and a very gentlemanly man, but the neglect of there not being built a custom house nearer to the quay. The whole contents of the packet were transferred to three carts and drawn off all through the town to a distant and bad situation, where the crowd was immense. Many people despaired of even getting their night things; but I brushed about instead of going to eat, and literally got the whole of my baggage cleared off and in the barrow before any soul was clear, though forty names were down before I came. There is a right and a wrong way of doing things.

I never saw any place so much improved as Brighton has been since I was here last.

30*th.*—Left London by the 'Times' (Southampton) coach at a quarter before eleven, for Longparish, and got home about six o'clock.

CHAPTER XXI

1828

September 1st.—Longparish. Strong wind all day from the east; ground as dry as Lundyfoot's snuff, but a moderate breed of birds, and my two dogs on their last legs. I therefore performed a miracle by bagging: 60 partridges (besides 6 more lost), 4 hares, and 1 quail. My son Peter killed 3 brace, his first essay. We never in our lives had such a fagging day and such hard slavery to keep up our charter. Our army were literally worked off their feed, to the joy of my commissariat; but they drank their extra hog-tub full of stiff swizzle, which cost me more than the half of the sheep that they left.

2nd.—I gave a general day's rest, as every sensible shooter ought to do; but, as other Johnny Raws were worrying the poor birds, I gave Peter leave to go with a borrowed dog; and he bagged 3½ brace more, besides 4 brace killed by his follower.

3rd.—By slaving like a negro from ten till five, I contrived to satchel 48 partridges (besides 3 brace lost), and 3 brace more that Peter killed, as I took him out and gave him several shots. Weather so dry that the only plan was to walk all day with both barrels cocked, and snap down the birds as they rose wild from the stubbles. Cruel hard labour, and no sport for the poor dogs.

4th and 5th.—Dogs all footsore, so I rested these days; but Peter, who was red-hot for sport, went out with only the house dog, which was of more harm than good to him, but he contrived to bag his 2 brace on the 4th, and his 2½ brace on the 5th.

6th.—Was anxious to finish with 20 brace, and never had such a hard run to make up the number. The dogs were so done that even the falling of a bird would not move them from my heels, and I stood at 19½ brace for the last hour before nightfall. I had no alternative but marching up and down at a rapid pace, without dogs, and treading the stubbles till I was ready to drop, but determined to die game. I fought to the last; but, through over-anxiety and fatigue, I missed two fair shots; but, at last, just at the farewell of daylight a covey rose from the feed. I 'up gun,' and down came a bird as dead as a hammer, a long shot; so I bagged the 20 brace, gave three cheers (a butcher's halloo), and came home in triumph with 40 partridges on a pole.

7th.—Having decided on taking Peter to Dieppe, in order to place him at school, I therefore started this morning for London.

8th.—Doing business all the morning as fast as a 'cab' could drive me about. Then started by the 'Age' coach, and got to Brighton about half-past eight. 'Ship' inn a perfect hornets' nest; a grand ball in the town; a packet just in. No beds to be got except out of the house. All the good grub eaten up; much delay in getting bad. Not grogged and cribbed till twelve; beds procured in dirty lodging houses. 'Warmunt' in great force, more scratching than sleeping.

9th.—A drowned man brought ashore. Sea looking rough and blue. Peter and I proceeded to France. Got under way by 'Talbot' steamer, Captain Norwood, at a quarter past ten, and had our legs under the cloth of Mother Delarne's table d'hôte, in Dieppe, about eleven at night, after a fair passage of eleven hours and a half. Ran foul of a French vessel coming in; no harm done.

Though I never was asked for my passport the other

day when in France, yet I was this time troubled beyond anything by the police, so people should never depend on them. They have, it appears, fresh officers on duty (in order to relieve each other) every month; and it entirely depends on them whether you go free, or are molested about your passport every step you take. Custom-house people, as usual, lenient and very civil; and, by a very little *ruse*, I escaped all duties for Peter's things. All, of course, in the usual confusion on landing at night; and I was not in bed till twelve.

10*th.*—Up and dressed by six. Settled all Peter's affairs in about two hours. Got all his baggage cleared. Rigged him with a few traps, blew him out at Delarne's, got my passport with great difficulty, and with the loss of half my breakfast, and all just in time to a minute to board the steamer while she was getting under way for England by eleven o'clock My reason for hurrying back was to avoid the tremendous weather which I suspected was working; and to prove my judgment, I have since my arrival at home seen the account of the 'dreadful passage' that was encountered by the next packet. Out all night in great danger; forced to put in to Newhaven, and I don't know what all.

The fairest possible wind and a pretty time at starting, but before we had been an hour at sea, there came on a complete deluge of rain and, towards the afternoon, a tremendous squall with thunder and lightning. Forced to douse all sail and ease the engine. But after striking the ground three times, we got alongside the chain pier off Brighton about half-past eight and were landed soon after nine. I weathered it well; ate boiled beef below while others were 'cascading;' wrote letters, lent a hand in the squall, &c. Having but little baggage, I was allowed to be cleared off on board, so I ran up to the town, secured a place, then swallowed a cup of tea, and set off by the ten o'clock night coach for town, not having courage to face any more of the live stock in the Brighton blankets. Had the inside of the coach all to myself, the best possible company at night, wrapped myself up in a cloak, and though I am a vile sleeper, and particularly in a coach, I on this one occasion played such a good bassoon that I never heard till on our arrival in town, about half-past four, that we were all but killed in the night. Coachee fell asleep, got partly foul of a van, horses ran up a bank, a wheeler and a leader floored and left sprawling, and coach all but over, and we under the van, and I perhaps to have been cracked like a kernel (Colonel) in a shell; a bad pun, but a true state of the case. But, thank God, all ended well, and I was over the stones and in bed in London before six o'clock in the morning on Thursday, the 11th.

13*th.*—Left London by the 'North Devon' coach, and arrived about half-past ten at night again at Longparish House.

15*th.*—Longparish. Went out to try and get a few more birds for my friends; but the game had been cruelly driven about in my absence, and the easterly wind had this very day returned, and blew strong; and, to mend the matter, I was ill; but, notwithstanding all, I did wonders for the third week, by getting 32 partridges.

N.B.—Heard of a jack snipe having been seen to-day.

17*th.*—Went out quietly without markers, and bagged 21 partridges and this snipe.

Killed altogether, in only five mornings' shooting: 201 partridges, 4 hares, 1 quail, 1 snipe. Total, 207 head.

N.B.—A bad breeding season; more old birds than young ones.

20*th.*—20 partridges. Dry easterly wind, birds as wild as hawks, no scent; and my two old bitches had scarcely a leg to stand on, though I had given them two days' rest.

22*nd.*—As this day commences the fourth week in September, the birds, in our very wild open country, had, of course, got quite wary. Bagged 18 partridges and 1 hare.

Made one rather extraordinary shot; 3 birds crossed

each other, at the regular interval of about 10 yards apart; and, when all three got in a line, I 'up gun' and floored the whole trio with one barrel. They were all killed quite dead, picked up instantly, and all three proved to be full-grown birds.

29th.—Had the variety of shooting, hunting, and fishing all within five hours. It blew a hurricane all the morning. I first bagged 10 partridges. Then had a spree with the harriers, which I fell in with while shooting; and, by way of a wind up, I got my rod and killed 6 brace of very fine trout for dinner, &c.

Game killed in September 1828: 264 partridges, 5 hares, 1 quail, 1 snipe. Total, 271 head.

N.B.—Out but ten times.

October 2nd.—A particularly fine day; and, as I might as well try for an elephant as a pheasant, I availed myself of this time to try our wild partridges on the hills. I was at first out of luck: broke the cock of my gun, broke my horse's bridle, tore my shooting jacket, and, what was more annoying to me than all, missed four shots; however, the luck soon turned, and I ended the day with shooting brilliantly and bagging 20 partridges.

3rd.—A strong southerly wind; and, it being a good fishing day, I took my fly rod out for about an hour before dinner, and killed 3 brace of fine trout; and, among them, one which weighed 1½ lb. He was as red as a salmon, and as full of curd as a new-laid egg; so I crimped him and made a most delicious dinner on him.

9th.—A tolerably fine day; and I had the extraordinary luck to bring home 20 partridges and a magnificent old cock pheasant, for which there was a hue and cry in search of me, just as I was coming home to dinner. They had marked him down in our moors; Duchess soon pinned him, and I had a most beautiful easy open shot at him. I think, under all circumstances, considering that I had only one pony and one man out, a new gun stock to try—with which I never shot more brilliantly in all my life—I never had a better day in all my annals of sporting.

22nd.—Put myself on the rostrum of a Newbury coach, at Winchester, and took a run down to Keyhaven, in order to overhaul my craft, make some experiments &c. preparative to the winter.

23rd.—Went out to explore a little, boat leaked, came home and caulked her; heard that the curlews had taken a strong haunt on my artificial island, where two beautiful shots had been missed at them by the 'Sams' here. Saw but 2 curlews there, and floored them both, with a blow off of my right barrel, when coming in from my reconnoitre. Not a wild fowl to be seen.

24th and 25th.—Up to my eyes in wind, rain, dirt, gunpowder, and experiments with my patent cartridges again. Too busy to look after birds; fired but at one living target, and that was a cormorant, which I killed dead, at above 100 yards. After coming home from my day's experiments, settling some business, bills, &c., I worked my way up, on the outside of the mails; and, with my nose half nipped off, by that vilest of all vile weathers, a rotten pinching white frost, I got home to Longparish House about a quarter before one on the morning of the 26th, or (as a Frenchman would more properly say) 'after midnight.'

27th.—Heard of 3 pheasants that had beat the other shooters. I nabbed them all in about an hour.

31st.—A nasty raw cutthroat gloomy day; birds walking about like fowls; came home without having had a shot. Shipped my boots and went to the river, to save my charter of never having a blank day. Got the first jack snipe I have seen this year, and one whole snipe (at 75 yards); all I saw, and all I shot at.

November 5th.—A tremendous fire on the hill immediately in front of our house. It broke out about eight in the evening, and proved to be 5 large ricks, belonging to poor Farmer Ray; and, as there had been no lightning, and this was on a desolate hill away from the village, it was too evident that this was the revengeful work of some damnable incendiary. The hill was in an uproar all night, and the effect was awfully grand.

10*th.*—A cold raw day. Walked out and had the good luck to get 1 snipe, 2 jack snipes, 1 teal, 1 mallard, 2 rabbits, and 1 woodcock (the first one I have seen or heard of in this country since goodness knows when). I made a most brilliant snap shot at him the first moment I caught sight of him.

12*th.*—Having had a fine easterly wind for nearly three weeks, I put myself on the rostrum of the old 'Oxford' coach, and ran down to Keyhaven, where I arrived about nine this evening. Found, to my astonishment, that there had been scarcely any wigeon; and, a few hours after midnight, there came rain and a westerly wind. It seems like magic how this almost always occurs to me the very day I arrive.

13*th.*—Out all day in very unpleasant weather, and never saw the least chance for sport. The wild fowl had all left.

14*th.*—A tremendous gale from the southward all night and all day, with heavy rain. About 20 fowl were seen 'off.' The 'Lion' punt weathered it most gloriously; and I had the great luck, in spite of the heavy sea, to stop 5.

27*th.*—Walked out for an hour, and just saved my charter of never having a blank day, by bagging 1 miserable jack snipe. Such is the shooting here just now.

December 20*th.*—Went out to try a new gun stock; discharged my gun ten rounds, and brought home 5 snipes, 3 jack snipes, and 2 partridges, which were all I saw.

N.B.—The 3 jacks were killed with some *éclat.* The first got up as I was carrying the bitch over some water; I dropped the bitch into a cold bath, cocked, 'up gun,' and down jack, all as quick as a conjurer; the other 2 jacks were killed right and left, a double shot.

Total killed up to Christmas 1828: 388 partridges, 7 hares, 1 quail, 2 rabbits, 8 pheasants, 1 woodcock (the only one I have seen these two years), 56 snipes. Total, 463 head. Wild fowl: 2 mallards, 5 wigeon, 3 teal. Total, 10 head. Grand total, 473 head.

1829

January 1st.—Keyhaven. Weather a little finer. Put off (by way of a little start on New Year's Day) at three this afternoon; got 4 curlews. Never saw or heard any other birds

2nd.—I explored all day, but, from what I saw and from what I heard, there does not appear to have been a single trip of fowl on the coast, except a few very wild geese, that old Harnett flashed in the pan at and drove out of the country just before I came to where they were.

5th.—New moon and a northerly wind. Things looking much better. No birds arrived yet, but I walked out with the musket to try a new dog, which appears to do well, and saw 1 teal and 1 wigeon, both of which I bagged, and which the dog brought to me in prime style.

6th.—10 brent geese. No wigeon come yet, and this was the only shot I had all day.

7th.—A northerly wind, but no wigeon come yet.

8th.—A fine north-east wind, though no frost, and scarcely any wigeon to be seen; and what few there were had mixed with the geese, and were wilder than ever I knew them.

9th.—Out all day, and never got a chance. Not a wigeon to be seen, and the very few geese that were about were so wild that it was quite impossible to do anything with them.

10th.—Got a long shot at a small company, and brought in, close to Keyhaven, 3 brent geese, after having been three miles beyond Lymington without a chance of a shot. I took them in by sailing to them, as the few that are here are now so well up to a paddling punt as invariably to rise at 400 yards.

12*th.*—A furious easterly wind; no showing our noses outside the harbour, and, being 'the dead of the nip,' no water in it; so we were prisoners for the day, except Reade, who crawled about on the mud; but it blew so strong he could not even work his launching punt to what few birds he saw.

13*th.*—The gale continued. Reade out mud crawling from morning till night, and he got 8 wigeon. I walked out with the musket, and got a wild duck, a very long shot (with snipe shot), and then went half the day in chase of a beautiful old gander barnacle, a rare bird here, and I had the luck to bring him home, at the expense of being in a miserable mess, by following him 'through thick and thin.'

14*th.*—Out from five in the morning till five in the evening, and never got but one very long shot, with which I had the unexpected luck to bring in 3 brent geese. The rascally blackguard 'mud launchers' have totally ruined this country, and they now rarely ever kill anything themselves.

17*th.*—Magnificent weather; fowl pouring in by thousands; cruel bad luck. Flashed in the pan at about 1,000 wigeon; again at as many geese, and, after drawing and squibbing, flashed again at a splendid hooper close to me. To complete my sorrows I found my lock broken, and had to leave all my sport and go off with my gun to Lymington. I got but two shots off; with one I bagged 8 wigeon in the breakers, and with the other 2 geese at a very long distance. Reade got also 7 wigeon. Reade was out till Sunday morning came, and got but 3 more wigeon, owing to as bad a run of luck as I had.

19*th.*—Reade, who had been wallowing about in his mud sledge from the break of the Sabbath till daylight, and got three shots, came in with 17 wigeon, and we found 5 more dead wigeon after breakfast.

Out from nine at night till one; had a glorious chance spoiled by a wretched tailor of a fellow spitting off his popgun, but, the tide being slack, I had no other chance for a shot.

Plenty of birds, and a fine time for wallowing on the mud again in the mud sledge, for which only this essence-of-mud-country in general serves.

20th.—A foggy, white frost; Reade came in with 10 wigeon, after crawling in the slush all night. I went out 'on tide,' having got my gun well repaired, and brought in 14 wigeon, 1 pintail, and 1 tufted duck.

N.B.—I fired at 3 tufted ducks, and stopped them all; but, seeing a large flock of wigeon pitched near, I dare not finish off the 2 cripples with the musket, but proceeded with the second barrel of the great gun to attack the wigeon, as there were three other boats advancing on them; what I fired at them was a patent cartridge, and I bagged 22, besides towered and crippled birds; but the tide was such that, if I had attempted to get any more, I should have been carried out to sea. As it was we were off to the shingles, and had to remain there an hour before we could 'stem the tide' to get back.

21st.—The 'Lion' punt brought them to action at last. All I got on the spot, however, was 32 wigeon, 2 mallards, and 1 coot, at one shot; but including what others brought me, I killed 53 wigeon, 2 mallards, and 1 coot, at one shot. The greatest work that has ever been done here.

To make this brilliant shot the more extraordinary, I should name that it was done about half-past twelve o'clock in the day. The gunners to windward had driven all the birds down to Keyhaven, and they congregated, about 1,000 strong, just off Shorehead in the shallow water, and by having a favourable time, I just slipped into them before the other gunners could come up.

I went out again after taking some refreshment, and was all but getting nearly as good a chance again; but a four-oar boat happened to spring the fowl when I was within a few minutes of doing the business. Coming home I got 6 grey plover with one barrel, and lost 3 more, and made a capital flying shot at a wild duck with the other, and I knocked down a tippet grebe eighty yards off with the musket; so I began well, emptied all my barrels well, and, in short, made a most satisfactory day in every respect.

In the afternoon I had only just come in to refresh myself, and wipe the gun. Off again at ten, out all night, and the severest night I ever remembered. My cap froze on my head, and it blew a gale of wind; but I had so much to do that I perspired the whole time, except at intervals when my hands were so frost-bitten that it was with the utmost difficulty I could grope out the traps to load, and particularly to prime the gun. The man who followed me to retrieve my dead birds fell overboard, and was obliged to go home in order to avoid being frozen to death; and I thus lost at least a third of my birds, which fell into the hands of the leeward shore hunters, who lurk about after gunners, as vultures follow an army, at all hours of the day and night, when there is a hard frost and a chance of good plunder. The labour of working for the fowl was an odd mixture of ecstasy and slavery. I brought home, shot on the spot and caught on the ice at daybreak by self and helpers, 69 wigeon and 1 duck, making in all 101 wigeon and 4 ducks and mallards, besides the 6 plover and the old coot, in eighteen hours, as I was out from past twelve in the day till six the next morning. The gun missed fire twice, and I missed one fine shot owing to the spray of the sea freezing on the punt, and forming a mass of ice that threw the barrels above their bearings. My best shot in the night, or rather at two in the morning, was 30 wigeon with one barrel. The left barrel snapped, as the lock had broken again, but on getting home to the candle I luckily found it was not so far gone but that I could make shift with it on being a little rectified.

Had not this misfortune occurred and my follower remained with me, I really believe I should at least have doubled what I did.

22nd.—After sleeping a few hours I was off again. It 'blew great guns,' and froze the oars as we rowed; had cruel hard labour to row to windward, as the ice prevented our towing the boat up along shore. Saw seven splendid hoopers!—gave up everything for them. Lay alongside for the tide to flow for hours. Not water enough at last! so Reade had to steal overboard and shove the punt with his chest while I crept 'abaft' to 'give her life forward.' The sun came out, and my cap was too white and glared, so, while lying as close as I could, I rubbed it with water and gunpowder, as I had seen the old captain of the hoopers look 'ticklish,' which I suspect was at my cap. For want of more tide, we could only get within about 130 yards of these swans; but, having shifted my common shot to some glorious pills for them, I tried my luck. First barrel missed fire by the lock cover catching the cock; but, as it blew a gale, the birds never heard this, so I cocked again, and held up the cover with the little finger, while I pushed off the trigger with my thumb, and instantaneously banged in the detonating barrel as these huge monsters began to flap and sprawl, and gave them such a broadside as they little expected. As 2 of them were far detached I had only 5 to shoot at, and I had the satisfaction to bring home in triumph 3 of these wild swans, and kill a 4th, not got, that I saw tower and fall, where I should soon have been as dead as he was had I been rash enough to follow him off in such a sea as that on which he dropped. I never made so splendid a shot in my life, and Reade's agility in 'shipping sail' and 'cutting off' one of my birds that was only winged from going seawards, was one of the most finished manœuvres I ever saw. We just got up in time to blow out his brains with the cripple stopper before he reached some breakers that would have swallowed us. We had a miserable time in getting these swans, but were amply repaid for our wetting and labour.

Our next game was a flock of mixed birds. We dropped to leeward and loaded, and bore down on them as quick as we could to save the tide, to a part where there happened to be water enough. Terribly plagued with our huge shipmates on board, and my follower, as usual, skulking behind, and thinking more of his dinner than the sport, instead of being up and ready to relieve us of this encumbrance. These last birds were scattered, and I had to fire across their line; but I got 5 ducks and mallards, 5 wigeon, 3 curlews, and 1 brent goose at the shot.

N.B.—While in full chase under sail to force the punt over the flooded mud the gale carried away her mast, and we had both to get overboard and strain ourselves like slaves by working inch by inch for about 300 yards to shore her into a creek, or we should have had to leave her on the mud and hail our other boat to retreat in. During our dilemma the dirty pirates to leeward carried off I know not how many of my other dead birds, that had floated to the lee shore while we were chasing the cripples to prevent their going to sea; and our follower, who had orders to be near us, did not reach his post in time. The ruffians here have literally lived well on my lost birds, insomuch that, before the frost set in, I could command any loafer for a shilling, and now I can get no one to go with me unless dearly paid, as they can do so much better by stealing my dead birds, and selling them to the neighbours round at a trifle below the market price. They all carry an old musket if they can, and just pop off a half charge (perhaps with only powder) to justify the possession of your bird by swearing that they fairly shot it. This roguery I have watched no small number of times by the help of my spy-glass, which, of course, I always take afloat to save useless rowing after fowl.

23*rd.*—It blew such a tremendous gale of wind that it was by sheer slavery a man could row on end, and the shore was still so frozen that we could not approach it to tow the punt to windward. Reade, however, by working like a horse, got us up to near Pennington, from whence we dropped down on the fowl, and they were literally so cold as to be flying up and pitching again every moment, which, by their thus seeing into the punt, spoiled all chances for a heavy shot. But I got in all 28 wigeon, 1 duck, and 1 curlew in the only 2 shots I fired. The first shot I stopped 42 (I always stand up and count what lies on the water the moment I have fired), and the second, a very long one, 17. So tremendous was the weather and sea that I was obliged for safety's sake to allow about 20 dead birds to be carried to sea before my face, and all within 70 yards of the boat.

24th.—A very hard frost, but the wind more moderate. The birds were frozen out of harbour, and not even in at night. I went outside for the day, but found them wild and much scattered, as the moderate weather had drawn forth the gentlemen gunners, who generally perform the part of excellent 'gallibaggers,' a term used by the clods for anything to frighten away birds. All, therefore, I could do to-day was to bring home 18 wigeon, 2 brent geese, 2 curlews. My best shot was 14 wigeon bagged. Thus ended the best week's wild-fowl shooting I had ever enjoyed, or ever heard of.

It is worthy of being summed up together, being as follows:

Monday.—22 wigeon	22
Tuesday.—24 wigeon, 1 curre, 1 pintail . . .	26
Wednesday (night included).—101 wigeon, 4 ducks, 6 plover, 1 coot	112
Thursday.—5 wigeon, 1 curre, 5 ducks, 1 goose, 3 hoopers, 3 curlews	18
Friday.—28 wigeon, 1 duck, 1 curlew . . .	30
Saturday.—18 wigeon, 2 geese, 2 curlews, 1 plover	23

Making in all: 198 wigeon, 2 curres, 10 ducks, 1 pintail, 3 geese, 3 hoopers, 6 curlews, 7 plover, 1 coot; which is, 217 wild fowl and 14 waders.

Grand total, 231 head.

26th.—A sudden change of weather had taken place in the night, and by daylight this morning we had a decided thaw, with warm wind and rain. Was routed out of bed and all the house thrown in confusion by an alarm about 3 wild swans having dropped off in view of our windows. I shuffled on my clothes, bolted my breakfast, and did all else as quickly as possible; and, after some little manœuvring, I got at the swans, and made the most superlatively double shot that mortal man could wish for. The old cock sat up in majestic state on the mud, where, by going up a creek, I could just get the gun to bear on him. The other two birds were in a hollow, where the shot would hardly have touched them. I fired the first barrel at the old captain, and killed him as dead as a stone; and instantly knocked down one of the others quite dead, as he flew up, with the second barrel. The first bird was 115 yards, the second 120; I paced the distance on the mud. Thus I had the glory to sack 2 more wild swans, and killed 6 (including the one I lost the other day) out of the 7 that had appeared at Keyhaven.

Afterwards, like a resurrection, 7 more swans appeared, and I had done their business within a few yards' punting, when a diabolical wretch spit off a popgun at some tomtit or lark on the shore, and drove them all to sea. Towards the afternoon I had all but got the seventh swan of my old company; he rose, out of shot, but crossed the punt, and both barrels missed fire. The detonator had got damp from the rough sea, and the flint lock had caught in the gun cover. I then went after smaller fowl; but the whole country was so full of poppers ashore and afloat that I had better been in bed. I got but one shot, with which I bagged 7 wigeon.

27th.—11 geese, 13 wigeon, and 3 scaup ducks. First shot 9 geese, second shot 2 geese and 13 wigeon, third shot was at 4 scaup ducks, all of which I stopped.

The birds happened to be in harbour, and I had this day two following boats, so I never lost but one bird that I know of; a very pretty little day, and excellent shooting.

28th.—Tide for night shooting at last, for which we have to thank the very wind that drives the birds away—south-west. Out from two till six in the morning; got a shot, and bagged 13 wigeon, all dead, and lost several of our cripples, owing to our follower rowing off after some sea weeds which he took for dead birds, and the wigeon he ought to have had escaping in the meantime. In bed from seven till nine, out again from half-past nine till eight in the evening. Country ruined by floating poppers; so we gave up and pottered about the harbour. Saw 2 scoter ducks, birds I never met with before, except stuffed in museums; blew off a cartridge and floored them both; and had a chase of more than an hour before we could get near enough to finish, with a detonating musket, one of them which was winged, though I had three boats with me. I then shot and killed 3 scaup ducks out of 4, then got another little shot at 3 more scaup ducks and a golden-eye. Floored them all; lost 1 scaup duck, that beat us by diving, and bagged 2 scaup ducks and 1 golden-eye duck. Blew the gun off at a few curlews coming home, and killed 1 curlew at 200 yards. Nothing of a bag, but exquisite shooting, capital fun, with the chases these diving ducks led us, and a very pleasant day's diversion.

N.B.—I was all but killing the last remaining swan of my original company; but a raw amateur spoiled my shot when I was within one minute of getting into him, up an excellent creek, which I had reached unobserved by the bird, and up which I was working with the almost certainty of getting close on board him.

29th.—Up at three and out till half-past eight. A fog came on, and then, of course, shooting afloat was annihilated, as birds will at such a time never let you come near them. A cold rime fell that was more disagreeable than anything I ever felt before; and this is the first time I ever felt really chilled in gunning. On getting home I made a good breakfast, put my feet in hot water, and turned into a warm bed, by which I was quite comfortable in a few hours, instead, perhaps, of taking a serious cold. All people should do this.

Out at two in the afternoon, and it came on most tremendous rain from the south-east all the evening. I had just time to pop at 3 wigeon, and I killed them all dead, and make a long shot at 1 brent goose, which I knocked out of the company, with small shot, at about 150 yards. There were plenty of birds, but my man having neglected to bring my south-wester defiance jacket, and I, thinking with Falstaff that

> The better part of valour is discretion,

turned tail, and came home for the evening about five o'clock wet through.

30*th.*—No tide and a very slack time to-day, so I went into Lymington to get the hammer of my flint lock hardened, as I had lost several shots through the steel missing fire. On my return home, Reade, who had been out all the morning, congratulated me on escaping a blank day, which he had had, owing to innumerable shooters driving the birds out to sea. I went afloat in the evening and got 3 brent geese, besides shooting 2 more that fell on tide, and which our fellows never got for want of proper exertion; and this shot, a preposterously long one, was the only chance I got. There being no water, I sent Reade mud launching at dusk, and he came in at half-past nine with 26 wigeon, killed at one shot.

31*st.*—Reade came in this morning, after being out again since midnight, with 25 more wigeon, making in all, killed by his mud launching in my little punt the 'Mudlark,' 51 wigeon in a night; and, by finding 6 of his cripples this morning, he made the first great shot up to 32 wigeon at one shot, launching, which is the greatest work he ever did or had ever heard of. A north-easter, but very little frost. This just favoured the operation of mud crawling.

February 2nd.—Reade stuck to the mud every night, and got in all 40 more wigeon.

3*rd.*—Reade came in with 13 more wigeon, after his usual

night's crawl, there being no water for me or anyone to go afloat.[1]

To-day I went out at eleven round the 'outside,' and at four brought in 12 brent geese, which under all circumstances I thought capital sport.

Some water to-night. Went afloat about nine. Nasty white frost and fog—birds all scattered and ticklish. Could get none together. At about eleven found a few birds before gun. Floored the whole trip without ever seeing them.

Reade and I just made up to-day a score of wigeon and a dozen of geese. Too thick for Reade on the mud at ebb tide, so no launching to-night.

4th.—Prepared to go off outside the beach, but wind and rain came on, and prevented us. So had but two chances the whole day; the first a most beautiful one at geese, which was spoiled when we had all but done their business by some miserable preventive men spitting off a popgun at a cripple.

5th.—Wet weather, but a strong northerly wind. Got 6 brent geese; 2 with the first barrel, and 4 with the second. Fired another shot, but too far off. Birds cruelly disturbed by boats out of number.

6th.—11 brent geese; 8 with the first barrel, and 3 with the second. The only chance I got the whole day, and, I believe, the only birds that were killed by anyone, though all the gunners were working round me in every direction.

7th.—Reade had been out all night, and never got a bird, owing to the thick, hazy weather, and I was out all to-day, and never got a shot. Towards evening the wind became more northerly, but no water for me to-night, till near twelve, which would encroach on the Sunday. So Reade was mud crawling till just before twelve, and got 4 wigeon.

9th.—A mild pleasant day, birds outside, between the

[1] N.B.—Reade, by crawling on the mud while there was no water for a floating punt, brought in 104 wigeon in four nights; and his best shot, a most miraculous one for 12 oz., was 37 wigeon, picked up at one discharge of his gun.

beach and the Needles; tried them, but there was too much 'lop.' Worked the rest of the day inside, at straggling 'trips,' and brought home 8 brent geese and 4 wigeon.

Reade got but 2 wigeon all night, launching, and it came on too thick before the water served for me. This is the sixth time I have had the kitchen fire kept in till morning, and been baulked by hazy weather from getting out.

10*th.*—Out the whole day, and got but 2 dun divers (out of 3 that I shot at, and stopped them all) and 1 brent goose.

11*th.*—Reade had been out the whole night, and could do nothing, owing to the thick hazy weather.

Nothing inside all day; tried the outside, off Milford, having towed above a mile from Hurst Castle; but the sea was so rough that the birds and punt were jumping about, and nothing could be got together worth firing at, and we were too happy to retreat from this unpleasant berth, and determined not to venture again unless the sea should be like a mirror.

12*th.*—A nasty rotten day, with small rain, and a fog as thick as possible; the vilest of vile weather for night, and but little better for day shooting. Neither Reade nor I could attempt anything, but we rowed down to Hurst and back, just at the close of the evening, and blew off the gun at the dunlins (for a pudding); we picked up only 28, but had the company been clear of a ridge of mud that took the shot, I am confident we should have got 100 at least, as I had taken the precaution to whip in a dose of small shot for these little gentlemen.

13*th.*—Dead tides, thick nights and no chance for gunners morning, noon, or night. Out all day, and never fired a shot. I got two golden-eyes.[1]

[1] N.B.—The golden-eye is here provincially called 'gingler' or 'ginging-curre,' from the noise of its wings. Bewick speaks of the 'morillon;' and Leadbeater, our great London ornithologist, laughs at him, and says that what he calls the morillon is only the golden-eye, which never is in high feather till at a certain age, and even then not till the spring of the year. So one or the other must be wrong.

14*th.*—Reade had been out all night, crawling on the mud, and I the whole day, and never saw the chance to get a fowl.

16*th.*—Reade, who had been crawling on the mud ever since the clock was past Sunday, got a little shot about five this morning, after lying on the mud in a heavy rain for two hours, in hopes of being able to see his birds, which he kept lying in shot of; but hearing a rival scavenger on the move at the same game, he let fly by guess and brought in 6 wigeon. I went out from eight till ten, in hopes of water, but there was no tide to speak of. I got a scaup duck, at which I made a brilliant flying shot with the musket, and this is the only living fowl we saw all the time we were afloat. Mild wet weather, and birds beginning to leave the country very fast. Prepared to go out at half-past eight in the evening, when it was time for high water; and after beginning to undress for bed, at a quarter past nine, I looked out, and saw the tide had made three-quarters of an hour after its time, so I shuffled on my things again and got afloat. I brought in 5 wigeon out of a little scattered trip, which was all I had to shoot at.

17*th.*—Reade crawled all night and till seven in the morning, and brought in but 2 wigeon. A good tide to-day, but a dead calm, and as warm as in May. I went out from nine till two, and brought in 6 brent geese. I used as a last resource the 'L.G.' boluses in Eley's cartridge, and I am confident the first 3 birds were killed at near a quarter of a mile. I blew off at about 2,000, and took about ten yards' elevation. It was complete artillery business.

A good night tide at last; out from nine till half-past twelve. Brought in 15 wigeon; birds scattered like fieldfares, so that I got but few at a time. A change of weather, a white hoar, and then an easterly gale, all within a few hours to-night.

18*th.*—Reade out after my cripples before daylight, but the shore lubbers (who keep dogs on purpose, and partly live by other folk's birds) had been before him. A tremendous gale from the eastward all day, and a sky as thick as mustard. We were up about half-past seven, and with difficulty worked about four miles to windward, to drop down on the geese; but the hazy weather, as it always does, made the birds extremely wild, and we were all but coming home without a shot. At last, however, I fired across a trip flying, and I knocked down 3 at an incredible distance with the left-hand barrel and Eley's cartridge.

Turned into bed all hands at five, hoping for a spree from nine till two, as there is now good water, but it blew great guns, and after being up from eight till eleven we were forced to return to our berths. The gale moderated, and the wind got south, about four in the morning.

19th.—Reade, after a long crawl, came in with 5 wigeon. I was out from nine till two in the afternoon, but got only 1 brent goose, as the birds had been so tormented by other people that no boat could get within 500 yards of them. Turned into bed from six till nine, then out till past two in the morning; never heard a bird till one, when at the very critical moment for a shot, there came on suddenly a most abominable fog, the vilest of all the vile weathers to ruin a shot, and particularly at night. I popped, a long way off, at a few stragglers and got 3 wigeon. I then heard more, and lay in wait for them till two, when the water went off, not choosing to injure the harbour by advancing any more on birds while a fog was on. No man who values his own sport ever should, when the season is so far gone.

20th.—Extraordinary weather; a thick fog with a sun and a strong breeze of wind. The fog was our only enemy. The geese were heard off 'Stivers.' We tried them, though with despair, after losing three-quarters of the tide through waiting for the fog to clear; and luckily for the geese to-day, the fog suddenly blew off, as unluckily for the wigeon last night it suddenly came on. We consequently got a very long shot instead of no shot at all, and brought in 4 brent geese after a most glorious and hard cripple chase. I never saw such fine fat birds in my life as those we had the luck to get. So difficult is it now to get at a goose, that people will not believe you have killed one till you produce him. Turned into bed all hands at six this evening, in order to get a snooze to windward, in case the night should clear up at high water. Up at a quarter before ten, and out till four in the morning. Fine at first, but wind and rain at last. Wigeon nearly all gone; got but one poor little shot at about 7 stragglers (all that we found), and brought in but 3 wigeon, with which I was well content, as I wanted just that number to make up the last basket for H.R.H. the Duke of Clarence.

21st.—A gale of wind from the southward all day with a tremendous high tide. Plenty of geese off, but the wind blew the punt about so that we could do nothing, and drove them all to leeward. This will be a lesson to me for the future never to meddle with geese in very rough times till just at the ground ebb, when they are feeding and quietly settled for a good target.

23rd.—A strong wind from the eastward; out from twelve till five; got a long shot, flying, with one barrel, and bagged 4 brent geese after the other gunners had been driving the flock all the morning without being able to get a shot. This shows the superiority of my punt &c.

24th.—Got my fifth brent goose that I had shot yesterday, and afterwards was off the whole day, and never saw one single bird in harbour, or even all the way to three miles above Lymington, though we had a strong easterly wind. This I impute to the mischief done by two notorious monsters, from Itchen Ferry, who infest the coast, and fire ball at everything they see, and rarely ever kill a bird. They have punts like washing tubs, heavy guns like blunderbusses, and are all boots and breeches, and look like banditti. They act as scarecrows or 'gallibaggers' by lying on the mud at low water, and driving about under sail at high water; and would have long ago been starved but for fishing in summer, and getting other people's cripples in the winter.

25th.—Having packed up my 'alls' to leave Keyhaven for the season, I went off in the rain from three till seven this evening, in order to give the birds (if any) a farewell salute. I discharged one round and got 1 brent goose, and with the other 1 curlew; at such immense distances that I will now give the other gunners leave to get a shot if they can, for I have well scared the last remnant of the feathered tribes here.

I began with the curlews and finished with the curlews this prosperous season.

26th.—Left Keyhaven.

Most brilliant and glorious season; proof how my plans repay me.

Greatest shots.

1st: 16 geese.

2nd: 30 wigeon with one barrel.

3rd: 53 wigeon, 2 mallards, and the coot, with the two barrels fired together.

4th: 4 hoopers out of 5 with the two barrels.

5th: A double shot at 2 hoopers, and killed both dead; the one with the flint barrel, sitting, and the other with the detonator, flying (the first at 115, the second at 120 yards).

Best sport: 101 wigeon, 4 ducks, 4 mallards, 6 plover and 1 coot, in eighteen hours.

Wild fowl &c. killed up to February 25 (inclusive), 1829:

Swans	5
Barnacle	1
Brent geese	96
Ducks and mallards	17
Pintail	1
Wigeon	433
Teal	4
Curres	15
Scoters	2
Dun divers	2
Plover	10
Curlews	14
Coot	1
Olive	1
Total (574 wild fowl and 28 waders)	602

All killed just in eight weeks to a day. Add game killed at Longparish before Christmas (388 of which were partridges, and 56 of which were snipes), 463 head; and grand total makes 1,065 head.

28th.—Longparish. Busy all day putting my traps away for the season; but hearing that a few snipes here had tempted divers vagrants to salute the premises with popping, I went off a little before three in the afternoon, and by a six o'clock dinner contrived to pretty well clear the country. I found altogether 11 snipes, and I did for 9 of them, the other 2 got up too far; but as 2 of my birds fell in a withy bed and were lost, I have only to score 3 snipes and 4 jack snipes, added to 3 moorhens and 1 other, which increases my grand total to 1,076 head.

March 2nd.—A very severe black frost, and a strong north-easter the whole day; and I had to weather it outside the coach to London, where I arrived this evening at half-past six, and, thank God, found all well. I never was colder in my life; and, on seeing such glorious gunning weather, I sorely regretted being fried out of Keyhaven by the warm summer-like weather which we had had latterly at that place.

18th.—Longparish. Walked out with my gun (for the few hours I could leave my workmen) and got 4 snipes and 2 jack snipes; all I saw, and the only six shots I fired.

19th.—Incessant jobbing every day at my new invention for the invisible approach to land birds, till the 24th. In one interval of leisure I took the first chance of the season for fly fishing, and killed 20 brace of trout in about two hours, or rather less, and, notwithstanding an easterly wind and occasional sun, the fish rose beautifully, and many of them proved in excellent season, though some mornings the water was hard frozen.

25th.—Tried my invention, to see which the emperor

Buckle, grand 'admiral' of the 'gunners,' had come over from Southampton ; and it answered most exquisitely.

26th.—Having succeeded most beautifully in everything, and left the workmen to 'finish off,' I this day returned to London.

April 21st.—After having been more or less unwell ever since I came to town, and several days confined to my bed and the sofa, I this day completed several repairs and improvements to the locks and breechings of my large gun, and got all safe away from the hornet's nest which Joe Manton's manufactory was in while he was in gaol, and this billet beset by 'Philistines.' His men worked under and for me, and had to keep an incessant eye lest anything should happen on the premises. No other workmen in London could have done such a job well to my fancy.

28th.—Longparish. I caught 24 brace of trout in a few hours, though the cold weather still continued.

June 8th.—London. The best Philharmonic ever known, and a duet between Sontag and Malibran considered the best piece of singing ever heard in this country.

July 7th.—Longparish. Took two hours' fishing this evening, and killed 25 large trout.

9th.—Made a droll trial of a new-stocked duck gun, which was well done by my carpenter Keil. I knocked down, in seven shots, 6 bats and 1 moth. A duck at dusk flight may therefore know what to expect.

10th.—Fished and killed 20 very large trout indeed, and I then left off, not wanting any more fish to-day.

END OF THE FIRST VOLUME

COLONEL PETER HAWKER'S

DIARY

VOL. II.

L^T COL: P. HAWKER.

From a Bust by Wm Behnes, Esq. Engraved by H. Robinson.

THE DIARY

OF

COLONEL PETER HAWKER

AUTHOR OF 'INSTRUCTIONS TO YOUNG SPORTSMEN'

1802—1853

WITH AN INTRODUCTION

BY SIR RALPH PAYNE-GALLWEY, BART.

IN TWO VOLUMES—VOL. II.

WITH ILLUSTRATIONS

LONDON
LONGMANS, GREEN, AND CO.
AND NEW YORK : 15 EAST 16th STREET
1893

LIST OF PLATES

IN

THE SECOND VOLUME

THE DIARY
OF
COLONEL PETER HAWKER

CHAPTER XXII

1829

September 1st.—Longparish. The most deplorable first day on record. I very unwell. A wet morning with a north-east gale, that prevented our throwing off till near twelve o'clock. Only one borrowed dog to shoot with, not one breath of scent, birds most lamentably scarce, and as wild as at Christmas, and a variety of particular bad luck to boot, owing to one of my gun locks being out of order. Disappointed of all my good markers, owing to the harvest not being near over, and so nervous I could not have hit a cow but for the aid of bark and sal volatile. I contrived, by working till I was half dead, to knock down 16 brace of birds, but, having lost 5 brace out of the number in the corn, for want of a retriever, or, at all events, a better scent, I was obliged to come sneaking home with only 22 partridges, 3 hares, and 1 quail. So much for the 1st of September, 1829.

3rd.—Renewed my pursuit of the most miserably woeful shooting, and did wonders, considering all. I actually brought home 24 partridges, 20 of which were old ones, as grey as badgers, and two squeakers, which I killed to encourage a puppy.

Everyone is disgusted with the unprecedented bad shooting of this September, and many have already thrown aside their guns.

5*th.*—A westerly wind and a wet day. Went out a little before two in the afternoon; and, with a drizzling rain the whole time I was out, came in, before six, with 20 partridges; but, to cancel all, I missed four fair shots. This is what I rarely did in a whole month's shooting, but the present state of my digestive organs is such that I must compound for want of nerve.

7*th.*—Was out the whole day, and beat over the whole estate. I never worked harder in my life to make up a bag; but the birds were so very scarce and so very wild, that I literally never got but one really fair shot the whole time I was out; but, by blazing away at everything, and shooting as well as I could wish to shoot, I contrived to bring home 14 partridges. I shot with one of my old guns, and was far from being in prime nerve; and therefore I now impute my four vile misses on the 5th to the stock of a new gun, which I had on trial, and which, consequently, I mean to return.

Specimen of a sorry first week: 80 partridges, the average of which was about seven old ones to one young one, 7 hares, with 1 quail and 1 landrail, making but 89 head in the four days I was out. The worst week on record; and I had only a borrowed dog to shoot to, and had been so harassed by bother and business as to be quite unwell.

This looks very poor after the September of 1827, when I bagged, besides what I lost, 102 partridges and 1 hare the first day.

14*th.*—The first tolerably fine day we have had since I returned here. Went out, with my musket, and joined Captain Symonds over Mrs. Whitby's manor, round Newlands, the most beautifully wild country I ever saw, but a most severely stiff one to get about in. The most impregnable fences I ever met with, and blind ditches, six feet deep, to half the fields on the manor. We had fair sport, considering that this is not a professed partridge country. My share of the bag was 4 partridges, 1 hare, 1 rabbit, 1 landrail, 1 wood pigeon, and 1 turtle dove (all I shot at).

29th.—Got 1 hare and 2 partridges, which I wanted, and for which I have to thank Eley's cartridges, as the birds were so wild they would hardly let you enter the field with them.

Game bagged in September 1829: 105 partridges, 10 hares, 2 rabbits, 1 landrail, 1 quail. Total, 119 head.

The worst season in the memory of the oldest man; so, being in bad health and without dogs, I gave it up, as did many other sportsmen.

October 1st.—Shot in a part of Wherwell Wood. My share of the killed was 3 pheasants, 2 hares and 1 partridge, all the shots I got, and most of them long ones. As we spared hens, the whole bag, among four of us, as Lords Charles and George Paulett were with us and made up eight barrels, was 8 cock pheasants, 5 hares, 1 partridge and 1 rabbit.

6th.—Keyhaven. Toddled out without a dog of any kind to see if I could have the luck to get a snipe with my old musket, and had the extraordinary luck to drop in with such a flight as I never saw here before, and knocked down 6 couple, with one miss-fire. As it was, I made the best day on record for Keyhaven; but if I had had a proper double gun and a decent dog, I should have performed what, in this place, would have been considered a miracle.

14th.—Keyhaven. Left here by way of pleasant conveyance in a yacht. Wind changed, carried away mizen-boom. Heaviest sea known for a long time off Calshot. Gentlemen all sick and wet through with a happy mixture of rain and breakers, and a foul gale in our teeth. Lost the coach, and had to gig it home to Longparish. Horse fell down, and rolled over twice, broke a trace, and consequently the man and I had to walk a great part of the way in the rain and dirt. Relayed with a horse at Winchester that Weyhill Fair had 'taken all the shine out of,' so could only toddle along by sheer flagellation, and was almost perished by a northerly hurricane, and one of the coldest nights that ever nipped a nose.

19th.—Having seen all the gear &c. packed on the boat carriage, I this afternoon returned to Keyhaven. We had a narrow escape from accident with the Lymington coach. A high-couraged young horse, that 'Wiltshire' had to break in, took fright at a barrow going down hill. He kicked over the bar and dragged the coach to a ditch, into which we were all but overturned.

20th.—Keyhaven. Just stepped out with the musket, to see if there were any more snipes come. Found 5, 4 of which I shot at and killed. This evening, about four o'clock, the convoy arrived safe, with all my newly done-up apparatus, punt, great gun, &c.

22nd.—Walked the marsh again. Found nothing but my old friend the jack snipe which escaped being shot at the day before yesterday, but to-day I bagged him. I never saw a living creature in all my wet walk. In the middle of the day we had wind and rain, but about an hour before night it came on fine, so I launched the punt and rowed 'up along' ashore with the great gun; but there were no fowl.

26th.—A fine day, but no fowl to be seen. Tried a few shots at marks, and found the gun wonderfully improved since newly done up; but had to alter one of the new touchholes, which, merely from being too small, missed fire twice out of three times. This shows how necessary it is always to try a gun well before you go into real action with it. All the flesh and feathers I could see, by way of living targets, were 'old Francis' (a heron) and 'the parson' (a cormorant), both of which I killed, quite dead, at a good hundred yards.

29*th*.—Afloat all the morning, with a fine north-east wind, but never saw a chance. Fell in with Buckle, who had not yet had a shot.

November 2nd.—Went afloat again, to see if there were any fowl come, but the coast has, as yet, a very sorry appearance.

7*th*.—Having put all my 'gear' in most superlative order, and left everything ready for my recall, on the arrival of the fowl I this day left Keyhaven for Longparish.

9*th*.—Longparish. 3 partridges, got by mere random firing, while out with Ford, Lord Portsmouth's keeper, to try my puppies that he had to break. He is a capital shot, and, after coming home, he laid his gun cocked on the ground, threw up two penny pieces himself and then took up the gun, and hit one with each barrel before they fell. He could never meet with anyone who did the same, but there was some art in throwing up the money. As I have never yet been beaten, I was anxious to do the same, and I did it.

16*th*.—Had another day with Mr. Coles and the Lords Paulett, and though we scoured the whole of the best coverts with a regular battery of five double guns, not one fair chance occurred for killing a pheasant, and, indeed, the only shot was one that I blew off at, about eighty yards from me, and he fell wounded in the high wood. Such is the deplorable state of the shooting this year.

December.—While detained in London on particular business, I had the mortification to see a fine easterly wind, and wild fowl hawked at every corner of the streets. At last I received a pressing summons from Read, at Keyhaven, on the 6th, entreating me to come off the next day, the 10th, but I could not possibly leave town till the next day.

11*th*.—I mounted the 'Telegraph' at eight, and was in Keyhaven Cottage (just one hundred miles) within the twelve hours. But most wonderful and remarkably unfortunate, I had no sooner got about halfway on my journey down, than my implacable enemy the weathercock flew into the west, and it began a hurricane and rain just as I entered the gig which took me from the coach at Lymington. The gun and punt were all ready to take me afloat at nine the same night; but the weather ruined everything, and, instead of breakfasting in town, and perhaps getting a fine satchel of birds before supping at Keyhaven, I was obliged to turn into bed, and from the wetting I got, so unwell that I was indebted to some little management for not being laid up here in the very essence of misery.

12*th.*—Keyhaven. Went out for a few hours, while the tide was over the harbour, having to weather a gale in which we could scarcely 'row on end;' and had the mortification to see armies of birds travelling over the harbour on their route out of the country, solely in consequence of the brutal, abominable, ruinous, and detestable westerly wind.

14*th.*—Out from a quarter past twelve, directly the Sunday was passed, till three this morning, while the tide served well, and with a beautiful bright moon, but never saw or heard one single trip of wigeon the whole time. About nine this morning we had the blessed satisfaction to see that the weathercock had gone to the right about, and brought us back the easterly wind. We then had the pleasure to see some flocks of birds off on the tide; but it was too rough to do anything out at sea. We cruised round the harbour from one till five; all I fired at was (one barrel) at 4 curlews, all of which came into the larder. This shot, although at mere rubbish, was a satisfactory beginning.

15*th.*—Nipping white frost and fog; out from one till near four; a fine moon. Birds scattered about like fieldfares, and very 'ticklish;' got 2 wigeon out of the only 3 I could get together. Lay down till eight; off all day; but the fog and wind with it made a miserable time. Saw some wigeon on tide, and lowered 2. So came home, and 'blew myself out,' and got to bed soon after dark.

16*th.*—Read out all night, and got but 2 wigeon, the

birds were so scattered. I was out from three till near six; but the tide was out, or I should have had a fine shot. Out again from nine till three in the afternoon; bagged 4 brent geese, the first that I have heard of being killed this season. I shot them out of a small company at an immense distance, with my left-hand barrel; and this was the only shot I fired all day. But one of the mud crawlers spoiled me a superb shot at wigeon.

17*th.*—The 'dead of the nip,' and no more water this moon. Out all day and never got a shot. We tried to work the birds at sea between Hurst and the Needles; but although the punt worked as well there as a boat could have done, yet the motion was such that the birds could see into her every time the waves lifted; so we resolved to abandon this place for the future.

18*th.*—A tremendous gale with sleet and rain from the eastward; no water inside, and no living outside. Read crawled about on the mud with the 'Mudlark' punt, and brought in 5 wigeon.

19*th.*—Fine clear weather, with a north wind, but no chance for a shot, as the 'nip tides' are now on for a week, and therefore there will be no water over the harbour; and what birds there are remain out at sea till night, and then come in to the dry oozes, where nothing but mud crawling can get at them.

20*th.*—Sunday. Breakfasted at half-past three, and worked my way up, so as to get in the box of the 'Telegraph' at Southampton, and arrive at Winchester in good time to breakfast and to go to the cathedral, where the service was beautifully performed; and, after church was over, I got a hack gig and drove to Longparish.

N.B.—The very day that I left Keyhaven, there set in a heavy fall of snow, and a most beautiful frost.

22*nd.*—Took my artillery up to Lord Portsmouth's for a shot at the ducks on the park water; but there was such a heavy fall of snow that we thought it prudent to raise the siege and leave them quiet.

23rd.—Renewed the siege at Lord Portsmouth's; took but one shot, not wishing to disturb the fowl too much; but the birds were so scattered that I could only get 11, viz. 7 ducks and mallards, 2 dunbirds, 1 tufted duck, and 1 coot; some more were stopped, but they made their escape to the rushes, &c. Went up the river in the evening, and, though it was one of the severest nights that ever was weathered for wind, frost and snow, yet I never got but one chance, and then the gun missed fire. I never saw this country so ruined for sport in my life.

25th.—London. Sad accounts from many parts of Hampshire and other counties. I had this day, too, to witness horrors of another description. Having to cross the street, we just escaped the track of a coach and horses run away without a driver, and before our very faces were eight people knocked down and severely wounded, and among them two ladies weltering in blood and carried off on shutters, one with a broken thigh and apparently quite dead. The equipage came in tremendous contact with the window of Mr. Hale, the hatter, Oxford Street, corner of Regent Street, and I never heard such a horrid crash or beheld such an alarming sight. To name the people frightened and slightly hurt would be endless. The further progress of damage was prevented by the gallant behaviour of a policeman, who in seizing and holding the horses got such blows as to be taken off severely wounded.

The result of the horrid accident was that the two Misses Delisle [1] were so severely injured that one only came to her senses to-day, and the other was to have her broken thigh set for the second time by Brodie this afternoon. A French

[1] Their poor mother has been confined on the sofa for seven weeks, and the first she heard of the accident was a double knock, and her two daughters brought in on shutters apparently dead.

gentleman was dangerously wounded; six more taken to the hospital; the policeman had three of his ribs broken, and his chest beat in; and the coachman from whom the horses escaped was thrown from the box and much hurt. Add to this list many people who were knocked down and slightly bruised. Left for Longparish.

27th.—Left Longparish this afternoon, and contrived to get to Keyhaven by nine o'clock, notwithstanding the severe frost and snow.

28th.—Up at four in the morning, and afloat till five in the evening. A dead calm, and the frost so hard that our beer froze up in the bottles. Hot enough, however, what with thick clothing, rowing, &c. Gunners in every direction. Saw 17 hoopers, 1 eagle, and lots of fowl; but they were eternally chased, and I could not meet one man who had got a bird but myself. Had spoiled for me a splendid shot at 7 swans, and another prime chance at burrough ducks; and brought home 7 wigeon and 1 pintail.

29th.—A determined 'black snap,' water jugs in bedrooms all frozen. Harbour all ice, and birds all off at sea; thick snowy nights, and no time for wigeon. Out from dawn till afternoon, got three shots only. I was the only gunner who had a bird in his punt this day.

30th.—Keyhaven. The hoopers dropped into Keyhaven harbour, and I was all but 'doing them.' The water was low, and we had to go up a winding creek that showed us broadside too much. I could therefore only get within about 160 yards before they hooped and flew. I let drive both barrels into them; but no lucky shot happened to take their vitals, and therefore I only peppered their feathers.

31st.—All day in chase of the swans.

1830

January 1st.—3 brent geese and 1 old cock sheldrake, one of the finest and cleanest specimens that any museum could have shown, and therefore I sent him to the prince of ornithology, Mr. Leadbeater, to stuff for me.

2nd.—Still a severe frost, with a north-east wind. Read had been out all night, and never found a wigeon, though hundreds were travelling over, very high. I was out from dawn till dusk, and saw nothing (except what I got) but one flock of geese, at a distance, and 17 hoopers, travelling over, but they never offered to drop. So I got all I fired at, viz. 1 brent goose, 2 scaup ducks, and 1 golden-eye. All the other gunners had a blank day. Read mud-launched till Sunday came in, and got but 4 wigeon.

4th.—Knocked down 1 golden-eye with the musket, the only trigger I pulled all day. We were up, and at breakfast by five, to take the day-dawn chance, but it snowed and rained all day till the afternoon, when we turned out and saw nothing but 2 hoopers, that I lay in shot of, for two hours, and could get no water to bring the gun to bear on them. Not a fowl in all Lymington market, no chance for anyone, for want of water to clear the mud.

6th.—Read came in after a night's mud launching, with 13 wigeon, 1 pintail, and my wild swan, that I floored yesterday, which he rowed down and caught near where I shot him. I went out, with the moon; got 5 wigeon about eleven, but could do no more for want of water.

8th.—A return of northerly wind and frost. No tides again in consequence, though this is but one day before full moon. Read came in at daylight from mud crawling with 7 wigeon, and I got 6 brent geese about noon.

9th.—Shot but one barrel all day, and brought in 9 brent geese; 5 more were picked up by a sailing boat, and carried off in view of me. Out at night, a fine time; but the moment the water whitened the mud, off to sea flew every wigeon in harbour.

11th.—A severely cold gale all day from the north, with some frost. Discharged my gun but once all day. Picked up

10 brent geese. No wigeon about. Read, who had been mud crawling all the previous night from twelve o'clock, when Sunday was over, came in with only 1 wigeon and 1 goose.

12*th.*—Read had a blank night on the mud, and I a blank day in the harbour ; a gale from the north enough to cut a man's nose off, no water inside, and no 'living' outside. Too cold for wigeon, but plenty of geese and some swans, defying all gunners.

13*th.*—Read came in from his nocturnal crawling bout with 5 geese and 2 wigeon. I went out in the afternoon. I got but one little shot, and picked up 7 brent geese.

14*th.*—A severe 'black snap' with snow. Read had a blank night, the wigeon frozen off to a milder climate. Out all day, bagged 10 brent geese.

15*th.*—Made a long flying shot with the musket at a lough diver, or female smew,[1] a bird that I had long wanted for my collection. Then got a shot at 3 brent geese, and 'floored' them all. It snowed most heavily, and coming home I saw about 11 of such birds as I never saw before. I put the first barrel into them, when much scattered, and hit down one. I then up with the second barrel, as they clubbed, and cut down 3 more. But one out of the 4 fell where I lost him. I followed the remainder all day, and could get no further chance but a blow off with 'Eley's cartridge' at about 300 yards, and down I fetched another. So I bagged 4 in all. They proved to be 4 white-fronted geese.[2] The most beautiful fowl that ever I saw brought home for a cabinet.

16*th.*—After being all the morning in Lymington, tormented with old Charles the gunmaker, I had just time to swallow my dinner, and bustle off after about 50 more of these extraordinary outlandish geese. I put both barrels into them, and picked up 12 white-fronted geese.

[1] The first I ever saw, or heard of, on our coast.

[2] Or laughing geese from Hudson's Bay. The *Anas albifrons* of Linnæus ; and the *l'oye rieuse* of Buffon.

17th.—Sunday. Very severe weather, harbour frozen, and nothing to be seen in our walk with a glass after church.

18th.—14 brent geese, 3 sheldrakes, and 2 curlews; 3 geese the 1st shot, 3 sheldrakes the 2nd shot, and 9 geese and 2 curlews the 3rd shot.

19th.—Out before daylight, and near two hours cutting our way through the ice. A tremendous sea, and little to be done; blew off at 7 swans, so far that the shot was spent. Out till night; no other chance.

20th.—The most tremendous day I ever saw. Sleet, rain, deep snow, thaw, and then hard frost again, with a gale of wind from the north-east that one could hardly stand against, for fear of being blown off one's legs; every kind of outdoor work suspended, and everyone driven home to his house. Of course no shooting even on shore, much less afloat.

21st.—A calm frosty morning. Out an hour before dawn, but had to slave through ice till long after sunrise; got but two shots all day. Second shot got 2 wild swans. The two I got were fine birds, but the one that escaped was the old captain of the 6 I shot at, and the finest bird I ever saw. We were so blocked up in ice that we compounded for twelve hours' starvation, neither being able to get back nor forward, but by sheer slavery we battered our way home (about a mile) to Keyhaven. In the evening we were driven home from our second sortie by a south-west wind, with sleet and rain.

22nd.—The gale abated so much that we were enabled to get afloat very early this morning. The first game we viewed were 2 wild swans, which, having plenty of water, we set into with ease, and I cut down the old white one with the first barrel, and the young brown one with the second barrel as dead as September partridges. The next shot was at 9 of the outlandish geese, but I only got 2 of these white-fronted geese. The 3rd shot I got 3 brent geese at one shot with my musket. I never made such a shot with a popgun in all my life. I had a cartridge of 'Eley's patent,' containing but $1\frac{3}{4}$ oz.

of No. 2 shot, and there were five geese in a line; the one dead was eighty-five paces, and the two winged fell short at about a hundred paces. I never could have believed this had I not seen it, and done it myself. The 4th shot was at about 220 yards with the swivel gun, at an old single swan. I knocked him down like a cock pheasant (flying), of course with a barrel of the great gun; and, after exulting in my prize, the old scoundrel recovered, hobbled over the beach to sea, and bid us defiance. He will, of course, be a prize for some one.

23rd.—The frost returned with a 'north-easter,' and a heavy fall of snow, and fog. Out for a few hours, but could not get a chance to shoot anything.

25th.—White frost, and of course a butterfly day after. Everyone that could muster a punt was driving about, and the consequence was no one could get a good shot. I brought home 3 brent geese, which were 3 more than I expected.

27th.—Read could get no chance with his nightly mud creeping. On my return from Lymington about twelve, he had just put off and got an old swan; and I renewed the attack, and made two such shots as I never saw in my life; and the three birds all proved to be 3 old gander hoopers, one of which was five feet two long, and full eight feet from wing to wing. I had no other chance, but such birds as these were enough to content one for a week's sport. In bed by eight, out again from eleven till three; fine when we started, but came on as black as a hedge before the tide flowed.

28th.—Out from eight in the morning till a four o'clock dinner, and never discharged a gun. So many gentlemen poppers were flying about the harbour that not a bird could pitch, and the geese were absolutely banished from the place.

29th.—Captain Ward took a shot with a barrel of my gun; and bagged 3 of the white-fronted laughing geese out of 7 that dropped in off the quay, and I afterwards fired a barrel, a very long shot, and got 1 laughing goose.

30*th.*—Read came in with 1 wigeon, after a hard night's mud crawling, and I was out all the afternoon, and found the coast as free from fowl as at midsummer. Read crawled till twelve, and bagged 4 wigeon.

February 1*st.*—Out from dawn till dusk, and brought in but 2 scaup ducks, though it froze so hard we had to beat through ice for above a quarter of a mile before we could get under way. Dead tides; and the geese so wild that 500 yards was the very nearest we could get to them. Never on record was the sport so bad in a frost.

2*nd.*—The coldest day within the memory of any man in Keyhaven. A gale from the north-east that no boat could 'row on end' in, and such a severely nipping frost that whatever was dipped in water became petrified in a few seconds. I walked out with the musket and sprung a mallard, and my hand was so benumbed that I absolutely lost the shot, from not having power in my thumb to cock the gun. Read went off by day crawling, and he and his punt came home looking like a set-out of glass, and himself half frozen: he got only 1 dun diver and 1 wigeon out of 5 that he stopped and could not follow. Never, never did I witness such a bitterly severe day.

3*rd.*—The tightest snap on record. All Keyhaven harbour petrified in one night to one solid body of ice. Wind enough to bite a man's nose off. Out at dawn: four hours cutting our way through a mile of ice, and obliged to leave gunboat and all at Pennington, or be made prisoners at home till the weather changes. Fought through it like Britons, and floored 30 wigeon and 1 goose in the 3 shots we had. Pumps, pots de chambre, basins, beer, and every liquid but spirit turned into a solid body of ice.

4*th.*—Up at five. Tramped over the marshes to Pennington, where I had left the punt, laden like donkeys with traps and rations for the day; but the wind came on so violent that we were obliged to fight back through a heavy sea, and 'knock off' for the day before we pulled a trigger.

5th.—7 burrough ducks and 3 scaup ducks. A fine day, and birds so driven about that no good shot was to be had, insomuch that my best shot was at 4 burrough ducks, all of which I killed. Dreadfully hard labour to tramp to Pennington, and thrash for an hour through blocks of ice before we could get out or come in again.

6th.—Got but one shot all day, and bagged 7 brent geese and 5 wigeon.

7th.—Sunday. A complete break up of this unparalleled frost, with a whole day's wind and rain from the westward.

8th.—Keyhaven was itself again. No longer Iceland or Greenland, and we had the comfort of getting our craft home and ending our miserable tramps over Pennington marshes and ditches, to get afloat, and then to cut our way through ice. Such was the wind and rain that by this day it had cleared the whole harbour.

A good tide at night. Out from ten till two. Came on a fog with wind and rain, which scattered the birds. Fired one shot at random, and got but 2 wigeon.

9th.—Discharged but one barrel all day, and that with Eley's cartridge, which went like a ball (at about 250 yards) through 1 brent goose. A fine moonlight night; but the wigeon were all scattered like blackbirds and thrushes, insomuch that I, who was out from half-past ten till two, got but 2 wigeon, and Read, who mud-launched from three till seven, got but 1 wigeon. Birds all in threes and twos, nothing to shoot at.

10th.—Got but one long shot all day, and just saved my blank by getting 1 brent goose. Out from 11 till 3: made one pretty little shot soon after midnight, having killed nearly all the company; got 16 wigeon and 1 curlew.

11th.—White frost, followed, as usual, by a butterfly day. Every dandy afloat, and of course no one could get a shot, so came home to do some jobs and get some rest. Out from eleven till four. A fine shot spoiled for me by a wretched mud launcher, blew off at random in self-defence and got 2 wigeon.

12th.—Birds attacked again by all descriptions of gunners. Nothing killed by any.

13th.—Read shot 2 wigeon after a whole night's mud launching, and I 2 brent geese after a whole day afloat.

15th.—Out from five in the morning till seven in the evening, and never got but two shots. The first I knocked down 2 brent geese (at near 300 yards), and the other was at 3 scaup ducks, all of which I brought home.

16th.—Out all day, and just saved a blank by making a good shot at 6 geese. A fine day, and the whole coast literally besieged with boats and punts, and, as far as I could learn, no one got so much as a bird.

17th.—Read had three successive blank nights crawling on the mud.

18th.—Our punt leaked with the unmerciful usage of this unprecedented winter, so that we were busy to-day overhauling and caulking. We dropped out for an hour or two in the afternoon, and blew off one barrel at the geese as they flew past. Killed two of them in handsome style. They were taken up before our faces by a yacht in a sea that we could not weather, and, to justify this, some fellow blew off a bullet from a popgun, which was much nearer killing us than any of the geese.

19th.—Read got in the night 7 wigeon mud crawling, and I made one very long shot at the geese. I fired but one barrel, expecting nothing, when down came 6 brent geese, and I had the luck to get every bird of them.

20th.—Read had a blank night's crawl. I got 5 brent geese and 1 wigeon out on tide by blowing away large shot at long distances. Afloat from eight till twelve: fine starlight and hard white frost: never heard but a few stray single wigeon: and not a gun was fired the whole time we were out. Symptoms of the sport being nearly over.

22nd.—20 brent geese; 12 one shot, and 8 the other. No

JAMES READ, WITH HIS NEW LAUNCHING-PUNT, [illegible]

Drawn by C. Varley. Engraved by H. Adlard.

London: Longman, Brown, Green & Longmans, 1844.

dandies or gunners out to-day. This shows what we can do when all is quiet.

23rd.—A very thick fog, and of course nothing to be done afloat. Out for a few hours, but the geese would not sit a minute together.

24th.—Ash Wednesday. A combination of such weather as one could hardly think possible to exist, viz. a strong breeze of wind and drizzling rain, with a fog so thick that nothing could be discerned more than 200 yards distant. The very worst weather of all for shooting afloat.

25th.—A very heavy fog again, but it cleared away about noon. We then went out, and came in with 10 brent geese; but they were so wild I had to fire 3 shots to get this number.

26th.—A happy mixture of wind, rain, and thick fog all day. A few geese came close to Keyhaven; put off to them, but in this weather, of course, could do nothing.

March 1st.—Made a successful finish of a bad season. Saw nothing all day but a small company of geese: got, in all, 7 brent geese. Coming home about six, I closed the evening and the season by killing a single old gander as dead as a hammer at 152 paces. Never was a season closed by a more splendid shot.

2nd.—Left Keyhaven this morning, and arrived at Longparish this afternoon.

4th.—Tried my 'invisible approach' (for the first time) at the few fowl that were left at Lord Portsmouth's. I got up to them with ease, and floored the whole of the lot I shot at, viz. 6 wigeon, 2 teal, 1 duck, and 1 mallard. A successful close of the wild-fowl season.

Game killed in the season: 122 partridges, 14 hares, 1 landrail, 1 quail, 3 pheasants, 3 rabbits, 38 snipes. Total, 182 head.

N.B.—The worst list for many years, owing to the unprecedented scarcity of all game.

Wild fowl killed in the season: 11 ducks and mallards, 149 wigeon, 2 teal, 21 scaup ducks, 2 dunbirds, 3 golden-eyes, 2 pintails, 1 tufted duck, 1 scoter, 12 burrough ducks, 154 brent geese, 20 white-fronted geese, 9 hoopers, 29 plovers. Total, 416 head.

Grand total of game and fowl, 598—a sorry season, compared with the last.

April 3rd.—It was so cold to-day that cartloads of ice were brought in.

8th.—It was so hot by day as to be quite overpowering; and so warm at night that one could scarcely bear any clothes, beyond the sheet, over one in bed. This specimen of our climate is worthy of record.

22nd.—Routed up at two in the morning, with some rascally thieves that were caught dragging our river, and before thirteen hours had elapsed I had all their business executed, and the two miscreants in full march for Winchester.

June 28th.—London. The printing and completing of my book made it necessary for me to remain in town. Went down to see my good patron, the *ci-devant* Duke of Clarence, proclaimed King by Joe Hawker, the Richmond Herald, the latter in a dress like the knave of spades and on a piebald horse; and in my life I never was in such a long-continued and frightful mob.

July.—Busy all this month, preparing a sixth edition of my work on Guns and Shooting.[1]

August 17th.—Ended all my book labours, and this day launched the sixth edition of my sporting work, dedicated by permission to his Majesty William the Fourth, our most excellent King.

[1] 'Instructions to Young Sportsmen.'

CHAPTER XXIII

1830

September 1*st.*—Longparish. Wonderful success, all things considered, and with such a scarcity of birds as even surpassed that of last year. I went out with two wild borrowed dogs, at half-past nine, came home to dinner at half-past one, and then went out again. I bagged altogether 34 partridges, and mostly all fine full-grown young birds. On the whole, I think this one of the luckiest days on my list. No one else did anything worth speaking of, and the scarcity of game was a general complaint.

2*nd.*—Despatched for his Majesty the finest 16 young birds I ever saw together. Having cleared the larder for presents, I was obliged to take a few hours' shooting this evening, and in these few hours I had the luck to get 10 partridges.

6*th.*—My new puppies came home, and I bought also a nice little setter. Went out to try them in a tremendously rough day, and with showers that wet us to the skin, and, in spite of all, I got 20 partridges and 1 quail. I never missed, and made five brilliant double shots. This, considering the weather and the scarcity, is one of the best days on my record.

11*th.*—A wonderful day, considering the scarcity. I bagged 22 partridges and 2 quails. What I killed this day were mostly all old birds, and I did something extraordinary, which was, to kill three times successively a pair of old birds with one barrel, by contriving to catch them like a billiard cannon as they crossed each other.

13*th.*—Was out from ten till six, over the Bullington and Furgo country, and literally never saw but 26 birds the whole day ; and thought myself well off to get what I did, 7 partridges and 1 quail.

16*th.*—Lord Poulett came, and we went to a roaring jollification at Sir John Pollen's.

17*th.*—Went to get some bait, and caught 365 minnows at one throw, and 406 the other.

18*th.*—Rode out with Lord Poulett, in a quiet way, till near four, and never got but one shot. Then galloped off by myself in right earnest, and in half an hour killed 8 birds and 1 heron. This shows the difference between the twaddle and the vigorous in shooting.

Game killed in September 1830: 154 partridges, 7 quails, 1 landrail, 5 hares. Total, 167 head.

Most admirable sport considering that the scarcity has even far exceeded that of last year, and I had not one good dog. I have beat everyone, and exceeded last year by one-third.

October 1*st.*—A wonderfully lucky Friday, and the greatest day I have made on my own little inclosures for many years. I bagged 4 pheasants (all I saw, and all superb large cocks) and 6 hares, besides a 7th caught by the dogs, and all without missing a shot, though several of them were at very long distances.

4*th.*—Went out for a few hours after breakfast, previously to going over to Mr. Fleming's, to meet Moscheles, and hear some delightful pianoforte playing, in order to try a new gun stock, botched up in the country, and rectified per Lancaster. Never set sight on a pheasant, but bagged all I levelled at, viz. 3 partridges, 2 hares, and 2 rabbits.

6*th.*—A curious circumstance occurred. Charles Castleman (who accompanies me shooting) put up an old hare in some thick rushes, into which he jumped upon her, broke her hind leg, and instantly seized her. This is the first time in my life that ever I heard of a man catching an old hare after she was up, and without snares.

18*th.*—Out all day to try hedgerows for hares, fields for birds, and river for snipes, and in the whole blessed day never set eyes on but two living creatures in the way of game, 1 partridge and 1 hare, both of which I pocketed, as the taking out of a game bag now would be ridiculous. Never was this country so fairly cleared as at present. What with the unprecedented scarcity, the rivalry of shooters, and the march of intellect in poaching, the game is all but extirpated.

November 9th.—London. The grand procession of the King and ministers going in state to the Lord Mayor's dinner was this day to have taken place, and we had excellent seats. But, in consequence of an alarming letter to the Duke of Wellington, the procession and all the unprecedented pageant was put an end to, 8,000 troops assembled round the metropolis, and everyone intimidated with the threatening horrors of revolution. And what did it all prove to be? A gang of discontented pickpockets worked up for a row by shoeblack Hunt and printer's devil Carlisle, who, after inflaming them, of course sneaked off to their beds of safety, and the affair ended in all these mighty revolutionists getting a confounded good thrashing from about 500 police, by whom those who were not active enough to escape got 'had up' and well trounced by the magistrates.

14*th.*—Longparish. Much more serious cause for alarm than the rows of the 9th. A house on fire so close to our back premises that we were on the very point of collecting what we most valued for removal. The house was burning to the ground, and most awful was the sight when I was roused from my bed about six. But providentially, and thanks to the vigilance and exertions of the police, the fire was extinguished before it caught the haylofts at the back of our house, or Lord knows what might have been the consequence.

20*th.*—Alarming riots in Hampshire, conflagration of many

of our near neighbours' property, and 300 men surrounding the farmers at Longparish.

22nd.—Longparish quiet again, in consequence of the farmers having all agreed to an increased allowance to the poor.

23rd.—Dreadful accounts from Andover, Winchester, and many other parts of Hampshire and the adjoining counties.

December 1st.—Most horrid accounts from various counties, but things looking better in Hampshire owing to the energy of the magistrates and the Duke of Wellington's rapid movements for the county arrangements.

4th.—Longparish. A half-year of public and private events such as I never had to experience before, and may never have to experience again. Death of George IV. Accession of King William. Revolution in France. Resignation of the Wellington Ministry. Riots and incendiaries all over England. Warlike preparations all over the Continent, and revolution in Belgium. A house burned down within a few yards of my town residence, and a narrow escape with my two daughters from a lamentable crush of persons, by a coach run away with on the pavement at the corner of Regent Street. In short, so many events, both public and private, that it would require more time than I can devote to a memorandum book to recollect and enumerate them all.

6th.—All the rioters dispersed, and the country perfectly quiet.

30th.—Keyhaven. Tremendous wind from south-east, only good for mud launching. Read brought in at daylight 9 wigeon and 1 goose; and in the evening 6 wigeon and 1 pintail. I got only 3 wigeon and 1 scaup duck. Westerly wind, hurricane, and rain all night.

31st.—Weathered it from eleven till three, and got 6 wigeon, 1 mallard, and 5 coots. Towards evening the gale abated, and the wind got more in to the northward. Read mud-launched from dusk till eleven, and then went afloat with me from eleven till two, but the late westerly gale had swept off all the birds to the eastward of our country.

1831

January 1*st*.—Read launched from three till seven this morning, but never found a bird. I went afloat from eleven till three in the day, and got 2 wigeon, 4 dunbirds, 1 teal, 1 laughing goose (the first seen this year), and 3 coots.

N.B.—I began the new year with a pretty little shot. I fired, under sail, a barrel at 5 dunbirds and 1 teal, and turned up all quite dead. A dunbird at Keyhaven is a *rara avis*.

4*th*.—Out, by moonlight, from two till near six; never found a bird; and Read, who launched both before and after I was out, found nothing. This is in some degree to be accounted for by two red-hot gunners having come to lodge under our noses, and being eternally mud launching. Out from two in the afternoon till dark, and never had the chance for a shot.

5*th*.—Read came in this morning, after a night's mud crawling, with 3 wigeon; and I was out all day, and all but coming home empty, when I got a long shot at a very large company and bagged 10 wigeon. A fine easterly wind set in this afternoon.

6*th*.—Read was out all night and got nothing, and I out all to-day and never pulled a trigger.

7*th*.—Read had another blank night owing to divers bad luck. I was out all day (though so poorly I could hardly sit up in the boat), and got 2 mallards and 4 golden-eyes (7 of which I fired at and stopped 6 at about 120 yards).

8*th*.—Read another blank night mud launching, and I another blank day on the water. We went off at daylight in such a cruel white frost that we had to cut our way to Hurst through one continued channel of ice, which had all frozen in one night, and to get through which took us between two and three hours; and because the frost was a blackguard white one, not a bird was to be seen.

10*th.*—The white frost was of course too suddenly severe to last; and yesterday was a warm damp day with south-west wind; but to-day the weather flew into the north-east, with rain and a strong breeze. Neither Read nor I had the chance to get a shot, but the amendment of weather now gives us better hopes.

11*th.*—Read a blank night and morning mud crawling. A tremendous north-easter, and no water, so I could not get afloat to-day. Stepped into the marshlands with the popgun, and got 1 wild duck and 2 snipes.

12*th.*—Read, after a night's mud crawling, brought in 8 wigeon, but not a chance for me all to-day.

13*th.*—Read a blank night, and I just saved a blank day by getting 1 brent goose. The most execrable season on record, and all the gunners nearly starved for a livelihood, though the weather has not been so bad for gunning as in many far more abundant seasons than this.

14th.—Read a blank night's mud crawling, and I a blank day afloat; a fine easterly wind too.

15*th.*—Read another blank night, and I just saved a blank day by knocking down 1 brent goose with a mould-shot cartridge at about 300 yards. Never, never was there such a miserable season for all kinds of shooting.

18*th.*—Not a chance to be got. The vagabond mud crawlers have totally annihilated our once fine country.

28*th.*—Out at night from nine till half-past one, and never heard or saw a bird, though a cold, frosty night, with a full moon and excellent tides.

Read has had some fair luck mud launching, having killed in the week 36 wigeon.

29*th.*—Out all day and all night and never found a wigeon; got nothing but one golden-eye; then Read crawled till twelve and got 5 wigeon.

31st.—Read brought in 3 wigeon after a crawling bout from two till five this morning. I was afloat all day, and never pulled a trigger. A precious pretty gunning season!

February 1st.—A tremendous gale of wind all day; harbour a complete sea; towards evening, at the ground ebb, I dropped off, and made a shot into some 100 geese.

2nd.—A tremendous hurricane, with an overwhelming fall of snow, and with the wind south-west. An extraordinary influx of fieldfares, not less than 20,000 dispersed round Keyhaven and Westhover, and so tame that you might have kept firing from morning till night, though I found it impossible to get more than 5 at a shot. After killing as many as I wanted, without even moving from the hedge I took shelter under, I weathered the storm and got 4 golden plover, besides one I wounded out of a flock, and which I followed for miles through this unmerciful weather. Went afloat in the evening and got 3 brent geese, and had not my first barrel (which had large shot) missed fire I should have had a fine bag. It was quite laughable, when the storm ceased this afternoon, to see and hear the levy *en masse* of tag-rag popgunners blazing away at the fieldfares. The whole country for a mile round was in one incessant state of siege.[1]

4th.—An absolute hurricane. Walked out all day with my gun, and was almost blown off my legs. Never set eyes on one living creature to shoot at.

5th.—As it blew too fresh to go afloat, I sallied forth to near Lymington, where I had heard of 3 cocks having been seen by the hare hunters last week, and after a long search I had the good luck to bag them all.

7th.—A heavy westerly wind. Afloat from six till ten this

[1] The next day, when the snow had changed to rain, all this enormous army of fieldfares had completely left the country. It was somewhat singular that, although these fieldfares were tamer than sparrows, yet they were fat as butter, and I never ate any more delicious birds in my life. I had about four dozen in all, and might have had a sack full if I had made a business of it. This is an occurrence that may happen once in a century.

morning; saw nothing but about 10 stray geese in a heavy sea. Read mud crawling eternally all nights, as usual, and not a chance to get a bird. Patience exhausted, and a precipitate 'bolt' decided on, so began to pack up this afternoon.

14*th*.—Longparish. Dreadful conflagration on our premises. Roused from my bed at half-past three this morning with the horrible sight of our premises on fire, as had been previously threatened by an incendiary letter. I had intended to start for London at six, which this catastrophe, of course, prevented; and most providential was it that I had not gone, for, had it not been for my incessant exertions with about six hundred people and plans of arrangement for the engines, heaven only knows what would have been the end of this. I was engaged stimulating and keeping in line to the river, after all our pumps were exhausted, several hundred people (and many most unwilling ones) [1] from half-past five in the morning till the afternoon; and then working and running about till ready to drop till near four, when the fire was got down. Among the buildings consumed were broiled to ashes the whole of our poultry, the barn and all the corn in it, and the largest and finest oat rick in the country. The coachhouse and stables were on fire, but saved by timely exertion. I was in one incessant bustle till near twelve at night, when I went to bed quite exhausted, and had no sooner fallen asleep than I was unnecessarily alarmed by another cry of 'The fire again!' which, on my getting up, proved to be another fire at a distance, which, owing to the extreme darkness of the night, appeared at first like a conflagration of our further premises.

15*th*.—In one incessant bother with business and lookers-

[1] N.B.—The two principal inventions of mine, which, I may safely say, saved 800*l*. worth of property, as the other ricks &c. ran parallel within 8 feet of the property consumed, was the drawing from the fire to the river, about 280 yards, a mob of people that would not leave the exhibition, which they came to stare at, by means of placing one cartload of beer at the river, as a counter attraction, and another batch of beer in the centre; and then combining the two engines so as for one to play into the other; and by thus prolonging the alignment only was it possible that I could continue to supply water to save my remaining property.

on concerning the destroyed premises. My night's rest spoiled again by an alarm of the watch, who had heard thieves whistle about the remaining ricks.

16*th.*—Harassed all day with the arrangement for, and trial of, a woman before the magistrates, on suspicion of writing the incendiary letter. She was committed to gaol for trial at the assizes. Up till twelve arranging the watch, &c. Nothing can exceed the state of apprehension everyone is in at this crisis.

17*th.*—Busy again all day concerning the late events, and everyone in the village in a perpetual state of jeopardy. Fellows heard about last night, though not on our premises.

22*nd.*—Have been now a clear week in perpetual jeopardy, and on constant watch with a gun in my hands for either incendiaries or thieves who have been heard about in several places.

Game &c. killed up to February 11th, 1831: Game—173 partridges, 7 quails, 1 landrail, 17 hares, 5 rabbits, 10 pheasants, 2 woodcocks, 23 snipes. Total, 238. Wild fowl—11 ducks and mallards, 3 teal, 103 wigeon, 12 curres, 9 geese, 2 pintails, 1 scoter, 4 golden plover. Total, 145. Grand total, 383 head.

One of the worst game seasons on record. The worst wild-fowl season on record, and the most lamentable season on record for private as well as public affairs.

Concatenation of events in the past season: Alarming state of the country, with tremendous riots and incendiarisms. An alarming fire after midnight within a few yards of us, when at our house in Upper Gloucester Place. Witnessed the horrible accident in Oxford Street. L—— seized with a paralytic stroke. My house in Boston Street broken open and near being sacked by robbers. Awful conflagration of my premises at Longparish through a diabolical incendiary. The worst shooting season in the memory of the oldest man living. The whole Continent in a state of fermentation, and nothing but confusion and discord at home. These are merely a few of the memorandums that I can immediately recollect. So much for the times up to the March quarter, which let us hope to God will commence their improvement.

April 19th.—A sharp frost and a north-easterly gale, which I had to face on the box all the way to London this day; and I am sure I owe my escape from ague to a hot bath, rhubarb, and soda, by which I cheated the doctor out of at least 10*l.* by finding myself all right the next morning.

May 12th.—Longparish. Was earnestly solicited to attack an unprecedented breed of perchers in the Bullington rookery; but as business prevented my getting off till near one in the day, and I lost two hours more in having to return to Longparish for a relay of three more guns and a larger freight of ammunition, I had in all but about 5½ hours' actual shooting, in which time I got and distributed to the poor the enormous number of 216 young rooks, and at least 100 more were picked up by outskirters and other parties.

13th.—After being at Andover all this morning, I slipped on my shooting jacket about six in the evening, and before dark got 6 dozen and 5 more rooks in the little rookery at Longparish. Although I hate such tame sport, yet the novelty of killing so many, and the pleasure of gratifying the poor clods with a 'blow out,' induced me to sacrifice my head and shoulders for once in a way. I think I shall have the bang of guns and caw of rooks in my ears for a week to come.

14th.—A north-easterly gale of wind with thick ice, and much damage done to all vegetation. A hard winter on the 14th of May.

26th.—I caught such a cold that this is the first day I have been about since I came up. I had an eye somewhat injured by the detonating gas from my gun, and my cold flew to it, and so inflamed it that I was advised to apply leeches, and these so swelled my face that I was laid up quite blind for several days and obliged to keep my bed, and in short a very great sufferer. Now, thank God, I begin to recover my sight again, and the first use I made of it was to go to London to see Lancaster and suggest an appendage to the cocks of all my guns, in order to prevent, in future, the escape of detonating gas.

June 20th.—London. Having lodged the money for my son's commission and done divers business, I heard with ecstasy the wonderful Paganini.

30*th.*—Keyhaven. Took a sail to the Needle rocks this afternoon, and brought home 30 willocks, which is the best sport of any one gun here this season. The birds had been driven all day by four other parties and were very wild, and the boy that I sent aloft to drive them out of the cliffs turned frightened, and would not go near enough to throw over the bell and string. I had therefore every disadvantage, or should have got perhaps treble the number I did.

August 1st.—Started for town at six this morning, but the grand uproar of the King opening London Bridge suspended all business.

9*th.*—Peter was gazetted.

13*th.*—Mary and Sophy arrived in town, to resume their studies at school.

16*th.*—Peter arrived, bag and baggage, from Dieppe about seven o'clock this evening.

24*th.*—Peter was presented this day to the King at the Levee (by me).

25*th.*—Peter left town for Longparish, and I attended Lord Hill's Levee to return thanks for his commission.

31*st.*—After having been very unwell with the influenza, that has, more or less, affected everyone this season, I this day went down to Longparish for a few days' change of air, but in poor trim for what little shooting there is.

CHAPTER XXIV

1831

September 1*st.*—An incessant pour of rain from daylight till dark, which put a stop to all shooting, and which I had reason to exult at, as I was so unwell all night that a day's hard fagging might have laid me up with a fever.

2*nd.*—A stormy day, with thunder and lightning and tremendous showers. Went out at eleven with Peter, and my bag was ten brace of birds, which, though the worst first day on record, was vastly well for the little we found, as wild as the birds were. So little as I got, I did as well as it was possible for anyone to have done.

3*rd.*—14 partridges, all I shot at. Birds scarce and extremely wild.

4*th.*—Sunday. Was at Hurstbourne Park and Andover, where, as far as I could learn, all the other sportsmen were far more unsuccessful than ourselves, so the complaint of scarcity appears general in this country.

Mr. Fellowes informed me that the sport has been so bad that instead of sending off baskets of game, as usual, he was sending off letters to his friends, to say that none was likely to be got this season, beyond the immediate consumption of the house, and that an excellent sportsman had been sent out the whole day, and only get seven shots on Lord Portsmouth's best property.

6*th.*—Wet again. Shot after twelve o'clock, and bagged 14 partridges, having missed nothing, either far or near.

During my stay at Longparish, I have killed just 21 brace of birds without once missing a shot.

N.B.—On the evening of the 6th, the day before my return to town, a man of our village just come home from Winchester gaol, confessed to me that he had in the spring destroyed above a hundred partridges' nests, and another man had feasted on above 200 partridges' eggs, besides destroying others, and all this they confessed was done to spite the lord of the manor, who is universally disliked. Thus all our shooting is to be annihilated for the sake of spiting one individual.

7th.—Returned to London, heartily glad to get away from such dull sport, and to prepare for our campaign with the militia at Winchester. All London in an uproar, preparing for the coronation to-morrow. An incessant rattle of carriages all night.

8th.—Up at five, in order to get to the United Service Club before any dangerous crowd was likely to be assembled. Doors opened at eight, and the procession passed about a quarter before eleven, and returned again at a few minutes past four. I never saw so many people together in my life, nor did I ever before witness so grand a cortège. The state carriage surpassed description for its happy combination of profuse splendour and chaste good taste. I never before saw a profusion of excessive finery without some approach to what is tawdry. But here everything was good taste in the extreme. What with the time occupied in seeing the lions, durance vile, and working home through mobs, we could not get home till past six, and then, after a late dinner, we had a few shillings' worth of Jarvey to see the illuminations.

9th.—Busy all the morning with parchments and other troublesome concerns. I have not had a day's leisure, or a comfortable night's rest, for these three weeks.

October 11th.—Winchester. My regiment completed their twenty-eight days' training. The performance of our regiment was the astonishment of everyone, and particularly the military, as, with a very few exceptions, the men were all from the ploughtail, and our officers entire beginners, except nine, who were all, more or less, on the sick list, so that I was so incessantly occupied that I had scarcely time to get even sustenance. This, however, arose chiefly from the lamentable waste of time at mess, as is the custom in all trainings, and what with jollifications, invitations, balls, plays, shoals of visitors, drunkards, guttlers, and idlers, we were in one eternal scene of confusion and interruption. The town was for the twenty-eight days in a bustle like a field of battle. The Duke of Wellington had finally settled to review us and the 90th Regiment, and to dine with us, but the 90th received a sudden and mysterious route for Scotland, and the Duke was prevented from leaving London. So that the climax of our hard labour was a finishing field day to astonish the natives. I had the command for the last week, while Lord Rodney was absent on the Reform Bill, and was literally obliged to go through it with a plaster on my chest and suffering from severe cold.

12th.—London. The whole town running wild about the rejection of the Reform Bill. Many noblemen assaulted, and nothing thought of but politics.

November 7th.—Received a most polite note from the Chancellor of the Exchequer, Lord Althorp, in approbation of my publication and suggestions for improvement in the Game Laws.

8th.—Received a letter from my son Peter to inform me of his arrival with his regiment, the 74th, at Templemore, in Ireland, on the 1st.

December 8th.—Went out the only dry hour in the day, with a cold and sore throat, to try for a snipe for a sick friend; got 3 jack snipes, all I sprung, saw, or heard of.

9th.—More frightful fires again, lighting the atmosphere before our windows; one last night again at Sir Henry Wilson's large farm; another two nights before at Bourne, and another at Abbot's Ann. How truly shocking is this renewal of the hellish system of last year! The night of the 12th was the most terrific I ever remember here; a hurricane, a deluge of rain, and tremendous thunder and lightning nearly all night.

14*th*.—I crawled out for the first time since my illness, and with a black dose to work off in the field, bagged 2 pheasants, 1 jack snipe, and 1 hare, all I saw.

1832

January 2nd.—Keyhaven. 5 wigeon, 1 dunbird, 1 golden-eye, and 1 coot. Out from daybreak till dark, and began the new year well, by firing a long shot at 2 wigeon and bagging them both, and finished the first day of it well by shooting at a dunbird and a golden-eye flying with the big gun, and bagging both of them at one shot. A fine easterly breeze, and a fair show of fowl off at sea.

3*rd*.—At it again all day, after a candlelight breakfast; got 7 wigeon and 2 coots, besides some cripples lost. Had extremely bad luck in getting our shots spoiled by continual poppers and sail boats.

4*th*.—South-west wind again; out all day; got but one little shot; picked up 3 plover and 24 dunlins, nearly all the company.

5*th*.—4 wigeon and 1 brent goose.

6*th*.—8 wigeon, 3 brent geese, and 1 pintail. Killed two of the geese with one shot, and all the rest with the other.

7*th*.—Read made one little shot at last, after crawling on the mud every night since I came here, and brought in 6 wigeon. I was out fourteen hours and killed but 2 ducks; lost a splendid chance at a large flock of wigeon close to me, owing to both my cartridges 'balling,' and besides this I got in the worst mess I ever was in by shipping a hollow sea.

9*th*.—A wet day and a westerly wind; weathered it afloat in the afternoon, and just saved my blank by knocking down a single wigeon with the popgun.

10*th.*—Wet all the forenoon. Went into Lymington, and heard universal complaints about there not being a wild fowl to be bought. Went afloat all the evening, and again just saved my blank by getting 1 golden-eye. Strong westerly wind and thick rain; a woeful time for sending all the birds out of this country.

11*th.*—More rotten weather; a regular emetic of rain, with a brutal west wind; gaol birds all day, with damp, smoke, and all other nastiness. Read crawled on the mud, and got 4 wigeon in the previous night, but we could not attempt to go out to-day.

12*th.*—It having held up a little in the night, Read had his nocturnal crawl, and came in this morning with 4 wigeon.

13*th.*—Read had some luck in crawling at last; he came in this morning with 19 wigeon, 15 of which he got at one shot. I was afloat all day, but never saw a chance.

14*th.*—Read had a whole night's crawl for nothing. Out myself from morning till night, and got but 1 wigeon.

16*th.*—Read brought in, by crawling from one till six this morning, 6 wigeon. We were then out from daybreak till five, and got but 1 wigeon and 1 goose, all we shot at. A fog, and consequently nothing to be done. Read crawling all night as usual, but got nothing.

17*th.*—5 geese; the only shot I got, though afloat all day. Out from eight till two in the night, but the harbour was, as is usual at full moon, cleared of fowl by the shore poppers before the tide made over the mud.

18*th.*—Had a good shot at last. After Parson Harrison's gunner (old Head) had been fumbling after the geese for about three hours, without being able to get within a quarter of a mile of them, and had given them up in despair, I caught them just at the ground ebb, and blew both barrels into them with mould shot, and although at an immense distance (Read thought near 200 yards) I knocked down, short on the spot,

28.[1] I was left in a state of jeopardy on the mud after this shot; my dog being nearly drowned was of no use to me, and I actually lost some dead birds that I had in my hand, and I should have lost more had I not taken off my neck-cloth to tie them together with. Read had much trouble to save the punt from being left aground, and several pirates availed themselves of our distress to take away birds, except Sam Singer, who kindly assisted us. The best shot this that I have ever known to be made in our Lymington district.

30*th*.—Read was out from two till daylight, and never got a chance to shoot; and I was out from daylight till three in the afternoon, and never pulled a trigger. A dead tide and no birds.

31*st*.—A precise repetition of what we did yesterday.

February 1*st*.—New moon, a high tide, and a southerly wind. Read had another blank night, but I, by firing long shots, saved my blank to-day by getting 2 geese and 2 curlews.

2*nd*.—Read had another blank night. Not a wigeon in the country; the rain and squalls have banished the wigeon from the coast. I was out all day and was coming home empty, when I got 2 golden-eyes.

3*rd*.—Afloat all day, and got but one shot at a few straggling geese (all I saw), and just saved my blank with 1 brent goose. Not a bird to be heard of in all the markets; a westerly wind, and the season dying away to a dull finale.

6*th*.—Busy all day putting away the shooting gear &c. preparative to quitting Keyhaven.

9*th*.—Longparish. Took my 'invisible approach' up to Lord Portsmouth's to try and get a couple of tufted ducks

[1] Making 40 wild geese at one shot, as was afterwards proved by 12 more being picked up.

N.B.—I saved the dog from drowning by tying up 12 geese with my neckerchief to make an island for him; and to prevent its floating off, I stuck the pole into the mud. My patten string broke, and I was in a miserable predicament, though in the midst of a glorious massacre.

for Mr. Fellowes. Bagged 5 tufted ducks and 2 dunbirds, besides losing 2 more tufted ducks and another dunbird.

N.B.—I first shot at 10 fowl and stopped 7. The other 3 then pitched, and I wheeled up to them and bagged them all. These were all the birds there, except a few wild ducks that flew off before I began operations.

13*th.*—A cold easterly wind, and weather that would be worth a guinea an hour at Keyhaven. Was there ever anything so truly provoking?

15*th.*—Alresford. Up at five, though not in bed till one, with the hope of a little finishing shot here. The only fowl on the lake were 6 tufted ducks, which swam in good shot of my ambush, and I was only waiting to let them swim altogether (which they were just about to do) when 2 great swans flew in and drove them off; so I finished with a blank morning, and took my leave of Alresford pond. My system here was enough to wear me to death, having a large party in the house to play the amiable with till after midnight, and then to steal out of the mansion and walk a mile in the dark every morning, as the fowl seldom remained on the pond when the people began to pass for their daily work, particularly as there were then occasional flight poppers near the high road. No lord chancellor was more in need of a little quiet repose than I am. Left Alresford this day at twelve o'clock by the 'Age' coach, and arrived (by the new route viâ Guildford &c.) in London about half-past six, where I found all well.

N.B.—The very night I arrived in London there set in the most beautiful hard frost, with a continuance of the north-east wind. Nothing can exceed my bad luck in weather. It always happens that I am never to be at Keyhaven in the only weather that suits that place.

Game &c. killed up to February 15th: 56 partridges, 1 hare, 1 rabbit, 2 pheasants, 13 snipes. Total, 73 head game. 95 wigeon, 38 geese, 5 curres, 3 dunbirds, 10 tufted ducks, 1 pintail, 7 ducks, 3 teal. Total, 162 head wild fowl. Grand total, 235 head only.

N.B.—Owing to the almost annihilation of game, I never had so little shooting at Longparish for many years.

23rd.—Got a letter from Read, by which I heard that, notwithstanding the beautiful frost we have had almost ever since my departure from Keyhaven, there has been no fowl worth naming at that place. This was very satisfactory to me, who had so regretted having left the coast at the only time the weather had suited all this winter.

March.—Busy all this month about remanufacturing and again bringing out my 'patent hand-moulds' for the piano.

29th.—Went to the funeral of Clementi at Westminster Abbey.

May 1st.—The trouble, vexation, and business that I have had pressed on me all at once, through the whole of the past month, would have driven many people crazy. What with people breaking in my debt, tenants not paying, my landlord absconding, trouble and sickness in my various establishments, incessant bother with all the workmen about my patent, which is now out, books to correct for press, frequently twelve miles a day to go besides, &c., I have often gone without a dinner, and been so exhausted and worried as scarcely to close my eyes the whole night.

June 20th.—Left Keyhaven at half-past four, and arrived in London at half-past four in the afternoon, and then had to proceed with much troublesome business relative to the delay of solicitor about lease, &c., and to prepare for removing into another town house.

24th.—Sunday. Driven about all yesterday like a mad dog, with beginning to move house, and the negotiation all in confusion owing to the delay of the gentleman's lawyer. Tormented with troublesome concerns about Longparish, where I ought to be, and unpleasant accounts from Keyhaven, where I ought to be also. In pain morning, noon and night with my wound, which I had not felt for sixteen years before, and on the eve of moving all my furniture to-morrow, and summoned to sit on a horrible special jury that very day. When am I to have no more than man's average lot of botheration?

25*th*.—Got up in cruel pain, and in the midst of house moving (which had been going on ever since five o'clock), and had to be down at Westminster Hall by nine; kept there in constant pain till near seven in the evening, and I was so ill that during a part of two other trials I was obliged to go out and lie on the floor. On my arrival home I threw myself on the only sofa then left in the house; and, by way of refreshment (as I of course had to starve the whole time), I received a perplexing letter about the Longparish concerns, a melancholy letter from Keyhaven, and a bothering communication with a gun about some new-fangled patent, a letter from Mr. Roberts about the insurance and other things of the new house; one from Coutts about the sale of stock, and by which I had not given the order precisely as it should have been. Shepherd wanting me for the examination and discharge of some bills he had paid on the old house, and various orders relative to discharging all rates, taxes &c. of the new one. Wanted for many other trifles; and, in short, worried to death, I sat down to a morsel that I had no stomach to eat, and then, after having many little items to do, I followed the furniture and my family to No. 2 Dorset Place, where I went to bed, and what with pain and bother, scarcely closed my eyes the whole night; and at half-past seven on the 26th had to get up and be off again for Westminster Hall, where I was luckily soon dismissed, and paid a guinea as foreman of the special jury. I then took the said guinea to Brodie, who prescribed for me and sent me off to doctor myself.

N.B.—I was summoned on Saturday night; and the next day being Sunday, and Brodie not to be seen, I could get no certificate to escape the jury, and therefore had the option of getting saddled with an incompetent doctor for the sake of his certificate, or being liable to 100*l.* penalty for non-attendance.

July 3rd.—Having had bother enough to drive a fellow crazy, with an obbligato accompaniment of pain and illness, I this day left London for Longparish, preparative to my entering a second series of trouble, bother, and business about my property in the country.

4th.—Caught an immense freight of trout by means of hauling at about eleven at night, when these fish are so stupid that they lie for the net to take them up, and without even requiring a stop net as by day. This is the way that night poachers can so easily clear a river if free from weeds.

5th.—Keyhaven. No sooner had I arrived at Keyhaven than the wind and rain set in. I told everyone it would, and they laughed at my superstition, as there never was a more apparent set in for the finest weather ; but I never yet have failed to the best of my recollection in bringing on rain when I came to Keyhaven.

12th.—Incessant westerly winds till this day, consequently all coasting pleasures were embargoed, and the only pastime for exercise was with a casting net in the marshes, where I occasionally had plenty of fun with such rubbish as shoals of roach, small eels, little flat fish, &c. But to-day we had a regular butterfly morning, and took another sail to the rocks. The birds were not so plentiful as on my last cruise, but I succeeded admirably in getting them under way from the 600 feet precipice by means of my old invention of sending aloft a strong-headed fellow to lower a bell and flag with 100 yards of pot line. Nothing, however, was attempted till we had been out nearly six hours imprisoned, or rather drifting off to sea, in a dead calm, during which time I had a great treat in boarding a 'Torbayman,' to whose freight of fish Billingsgate was a mere stall. Towards evening there came on a pretty breeze, when I soon killed 5 couple of willocks; no sooner had we got into the marrow of the sport, than there appeared such an awful approach of weather that we were obliged to make all sail for home. But before we had even fetched back to the Needles, there opened on us a complete battery of thunder and lightning, and such a gale of wind as made the very timbers shake; and all the way from there to Keyhaven this running fire, more or less, continued, with such a pouring torrent of rain as not a sailor on board had ever before witnessed. But we providentially got safe into port (all, of course, drenched to the skin) about seven in the evening, when, at the moment of our landing, I could compare the thunder and lightning to nothing but a field of battle, and the thunderbolts to cannon balls flying about our heads.

29th.—London. People dying in every direction with this dreadful cholera, and many of them close to my own town residence.

30th.—Left London for Longparish, to see about the building of Bullington, and also about the building of a new punt, for which Buckle is now here. Wet weather, and the corn not in; but a fair account as to the breed of birds. Disease here as everywhere else. Poor Peter, the blacksmith close by, was last night enjoying his pipe in company, and at six this morning was found a corpse in his bed.

31st.—I was obliged to go over to Tom Langstaff to get something to put false life in me, or could not attempt to go shooting the next day.

CHAPTER XXV

1832

September 1st.—42 partridges and 3 hares.

A wonderful day considering I was hemmed in on all sides by contending parties, and so weak and ill that I could take nothing but an egg with a little brandy and milk to support me. I, however, shot most capitally, and never had better reason to be pleased; and the masterly manner in which I outmanœuvred the green-livered lawyer and his gang, who made every attempt to ruin my beat, was even better sport than the shooting itself, and worthy, I trust, of any cavalry and infantry general.

3rd.—Had too many things to attend to of more consequence than the shooting; but found time to bag 19 partridges, 1 hare, 4 quails, and 1 landrail.

5th.—46 partridges and 1 hare; one of the best days on record, when we consider how the lawyer has injured the country. My 56 brace in former times, when with a large army and free from all nuisances, was nothing in comparison to this. I never missed, except three long random shots.

6th.—Cavalry, infantry, and dogs all done up. A fresh army called on to harass the enemy. Goodchilde and another bloody shot arrived at ten with fresh dogs; and I sent them into the inclosures to have a day's sharp-shooting, we having pretty well scoured the hills.

N.B.—They bagged 15 brace and 1 hare, having worked from morning till night.

8th.—Out the whole day; and though I slaved like a horse and missed nothing, I could only bag 16 partridges and

1 hare, which was the greater part of what I found. This shows the effect of that blockheaded, green-livered lawyer going to war about the game, and never allowing it a day's rest. The consequence is that what is not shot must be banished from within his boundary.

Game killed the first week, or rather in the first 4 days' shooting: 123 partridges, 6 hares, 4 quails, 1 landrail. Total, 134 head.

Excellent sport considering the innumerable disadvantages.

10th.—20 fine full-grown young partridges, after gloriously outflanking the lawyer, and slaving all day till I was quite exhausted. This bag is miraculous considering the annihilated state of the only beat I could take.

21st.—Out all day and never saw but two small coveys of birds, and those very wild. Bagged 3 partridges and 1 hare, which was all I fired at. This shows how soon our shooting is at an end in this country, until the winter sets in, and the shooting parties and foxhounds drive out a little more game from the preserves and coppices.

October 1st.—Wet weather at last. Started with a chosen banditti to try if my estate would afford 1 pheasant. Out from seven in the morning, and wet to the skin, till a five o'clock dinner. All the pheasants I set eyes on the whole day were 3 splendid cocks and 1 fine young hen. I knocked down every one of them, and all long brilliant shots, but lost one for want of poor old Rover, whom Joe had the mishap to shoot in the hind leg when firing at a rabbit, and whom we sent home on the pony to be fomented and nursed. My bag was 3 pheasants, 2 rabbits, and 1 jack snipe, the latter a proof that emigrants are moving; and these, with the cock pheasant shot and lost, were all I fired at, and indeed all I saw; so that our 1st of October was a very satisfactory day.

2nd.—Went up to London to procure some things for the new punt, and to get some repairs done to the locks and breechings of my great gun; also to pay some bills, and see about my sporting book, which is already out of print again.

18th.—Returned with all my traps to Longparish, and was nearly losing my life by a frightful accident in Whitchurch. On my way home I drove to a shop for Monk (my old Peninsular servant) to run in and get a few Whitchurch biscuits; and while he was gone in I was about to turn the chaise round, when the wheel caught in something near the step and broke it, on which the horse plunged forward and overturned the chaise with such violence that I was thrown out and stunned; and there I lay entangled with a gun and a dog in a chain between my legs, while the horse was kicking everything to pieces, except the dog and me, who were repeatedly grazed by his very heels. I succeeded, however, in saving myself, with some severe bruises, and the gun with some little damage; but was so benumbed with the shock, that it was some time before I could tell whether my bones were broken or not. Monk came out of the shop, and was just in time to save further mischief, at the risk of his own life; and I had for some time been lying where no one dare come to help me. However, I, thank God, had a most providential escape, and arrived at Longparish with the wreck about seven o'clock at night. I fomented and physicked, and passed a miserable night; but in the morning I sent for Dr. Perry to cup me in the back, where I was hurt, and was then so far better as to be able to get across the room with the help of two sticks. I omitted to say that in this accident I was rendered helpless by having to hold a gun, as well as whip and reins, and a dog in a chain between my legs. Moreover, the reins broke in the very plunge that the horse made.

19th.—In bed and on the sofa all day, and occasionally in much pain. It is somewhat curious, too, that I should have received a blow precisely on the spot where I was shot in Spain.

21st.—Able to go without sticks. This evening Read

arrived, to arrange the final trimming and sailing of the new punt.

23rd.—Continuing to improve, and, indeed, pretty comfortable, except the soreness of the old wound that was torn. Hobbled down to the river, crawled into the punt, and tried her trim, &c. Sent Monk on horseback to Southampton for more copper work, as Read is crazy to get off to Keyhaven this splendid easterly wind.

24th.—All hands on from daybreak till about half-past four in the afternoon, when we started the punt on the boat carriage for Bullington, in order to avoid the danger of that vile road in the dark; and I arranged that Read and two helpers should leave this, with a fresh horse, after midnight, and then take on the punt with good turnpike roads in order to save his tide to-morrow morning, in sailing her from Southampton. We were so hard run to get her off that I had to take a 'trap' or two from the 'Lion' and varnish her after she was on the carriage, so as for her to be drying and travelling at the same time, the weather being so favourable that there was neither dust nor dirt.

25th.—The expedition started, with the punt on the carriage, at two o'clock this morning; that is *après minuit*, as the French more properly call it.

I was again hopping about all day among the workmen, getting some *ne plus ultra* 'wrinkles' done for the great gun, covers, &c., and also hard on about repairing the wreck of the chaise, and taking the opportunity of greatly improving the way in which the body was fixed on the carriage.

Read got under way from Southampton quay by half-past ten, and sailed off for Keyhaven with a beautiful breeze and tide in his favour. The weather was delightful, and nothing could have been better managed. The crowd, as usual, was no common one, on the arrival in a strange port of one of my punts.

29th.—Received a despatch from Read to announce the safe arrival of himself and the new punt at Keyhaven.

30th.—Returned to town, in order to prepare about 150 pages of my seventh edition, the sixth being out, and the booksellers crying out for copy to begin reprinting, as many orders could not be executed till another edition was ready. Good luck and great honour, but a miserably inconvenient time for me.

November 9th.—Having done enough to leave the printers employed for a few weeks, and having corrected the two first proofs, I this day left London for Longparish, with a view of collecting all my traps together for the coast, that being their proper station, and I never had such a pinching cold journey before.

10th.—South-east rain from morning till night, and a regular doctor's and undertaker's day.

13th.—Followed my shooting outfit to Keyhaven; arrived there about eight this evening, and found that everything had got down safely and comfortably. No prospect of sport; indeed, I knew this before I came, but my grand object was to try all the tackle, having (except the gun, newly done up) an entire new set-out, on a somewhat different, and, I hope, improved plan.

N.B.—The greatest number of wild fowl yet killed by any gunner all this season that I have heard of was three wigeon. Quite marvellous, when in former years I have known hundreds killed in October.

The tide did not serve till nearly four this afternoon, when the rain ceased, and the wind continued to blow most furiously. This was the very time to try the new punt, and we were just ready by the time the tide was. She answered splendidly at all tacks, and we had the great good luck to see a little trip of wigeon. I blew off both barrels together, and knocked down 7 at an immense distance, which was most unexpected, and a very lucky start for the first shot of the season and the first of the new set-out. My new invention of a landing, or rather cripple, net, decidedly saved me two of the birds I got.

15*th.*—Our good luck attended us, though the coast was all but destitute, as the only three living creatures we saw were 3 brent geese, all 3 of which I brought home to Keyhaven Cottage. They had been heard of, and seen for weeks, and tried by many, but without success. I followed them for nearly the whole time we were out, and at last got them near a creek, where I turned up 2 with the first barrel, and the other with the second.

17*th.*—Out from an hour before daylight till twelve, and never saw one single fowl.

19*th.*—As there was nothing worth going afloat for, I amused myself with a little in Mr. Pryce's mudlands with old Rover and the popgun, and in a few hours cleared off all that was there, viz. 9 coots, 7 moorhens, 1 snipe, and 1 jack snipe, without missing a single shot, and sent to Mr. Pryce, to make him a substantial pie for his vassals.

20*th.*—Paltry as our sport has been, I have got more birds than all the gunners on the coast for the whole season have done, put together; and never fired a blank shot. Having had a most satisfactory trial of all my new set-out, I this day put my things by till there shall be better weather and better sport, for London, where I was much wanted, for a week or two at least, to see to my seventh edition, now at press.

22*nd.*—London. A beautiful north-east wind, now that I have left Keyhaven. This is always the case, but my book could not go on without me, and therefore I was obliged to come up, if only for a week.

December 6th.—I this day, thank God, got to the end of preparing for a seventh edition between 500 and 600 pages of my sporting book, having, for the last several days, worked about fourteen hours out of the twenty-four.

11*th.*—Having worked in right good earnest all yesterday and to-day, as chairman of Mr. Portman's Christchurch division committee, and hunted up the various electors for the poll, I, among my numerous brother constituents, had the pleasure to see him hailed this evening at the illuminated 'Yorkshire Stingo,' tea garden public-house, by a triumphant majority of 997, above even Sir William Horne, the other deservedly popular candidate, for whom I had also voted.

12th.—Attended Mr. Portman and Sir Samuel Hawker (his nominator), to the hustings, where we had a royal noise, but no serious disorder, and where Mr. Portman and Sir William Horne were this day most ably and eloquently proclaimed by Sir Peter Laurie, the Lord Mayor (though here in the more humble capacity of returning officer), as duly elected for the borough of Marylebone. As this is the leading borough of England, let us hope that it will be an example to all others ; first for its good order and peaceable conduct throughout the whole of the polling, and though last, not least, for its good sense in neither being humbugged by the ranting 'Rads' on one hand nor the Joe-Surface-hypocrite 'Conservatives' on the other.

26th.—Went down to Keyhaven, but not with the least idea of gunning, as there had not been a single fowl killed since I left the coast. A scarcity to this degree is a phenomenon, even let the weather be what it will.

Not a bird even seen by anyone up to the very last day of this year ; a circumstance that, even in the mild weather, no one can account for.

1833

January 1st.—1 tufted duck was seen in the marsh. I took my double gun, and got him, and also 2 snipes, all I fired at, and this made a very lucky, though a very small, beginning of the new year.

Found in the garden the nest of a 'long-tailed Dick,' with 3 eggs.

Received the first copy of my seventh edition of 'Instructions to Young Sportsmen' this day from Longman & Co.

7th.—Longparish. The wind having continued north-east ever since I came away to spend some days here, and I having received a despatch from Keyhaven to say some birds were come, I this day mounted the Oxford coach and returned to Keyhaven.

8th.—Keyhaven. Got afloat again at last. Fired a long shot with one barrel, and got 4 wigeon, which was as good luck as could possibly be expected. No one had yet done so well. Out from ten at night till two A.M. Heard a 'fair show' of wigeon, but all left as the tide 'creamed' the mud. Read on from two till six, and never heard a bird, the effects of the unmerciful way in which this harbour has been treated.

9th.—Got 1 brent goose. No other chance all day. Tried the beach flight at night, but no one there got a shot, though the number of people coming home was like a congregation from a church or chapel. A fine easterly wind, and yet no sport for anyone; indeed, my goose was the only bird shot all day.

10th.—Read, after mud launching all night, went with me all the way to Hampstead Ledge, where we landed in the Isle of Wight. We then came full sail, in such a sea as no other punt would have lived in, across to Pitt's Deep, four miles below Lymington, and then home. We saw but very little, though got 6 wigeon and 1 merganser.

11th.—2 wigeon. A deplorable show of birds considering the easterly wind; but the harbour has been ruined. Only 2 birds in all the Lymington poulterers' shops to-day, when I was there on divers commissions.

14th.—Out from five in the morning till half-past five in the evening and never got a shot, though a strong easterly wind. This proves the ruin of our coast.

15th.—Out some hours before daybreak; got 4 wigeon (all I shot at). Boarded Buckle, who came in his craft to lie here, but had done nothing, and complained that the gunners everywhere were starving, though we have had, and now have, as fine an easterly wind as ever blew.

17th.—Out all night. Shooters out of number, and not one shot for anyone, and yet a fine wind.

Game &c. killed in the season to February 28th : 149 partridges, 7 hares, 4 quails, 1 landrail, 3 rabbits, 3 pheasants, 5 snipes. Total, 172 head. Wild fowl : 4 ducks and mallards, 19 wigeon, 4 geese, 1 merganser. Total, 28 head. Grand total, 200 head.

April 10th.—Longparish. Engaged with a party of fishing gentlemen who unexpectedly popped in on me. Three of us killed 50 brace of trout in a little more than four hours.

14th.—Very poorly ; half London indisposed with the influenza, and literally not one sound inmate in the whole of my establishment.

16th.—Had the honour of a private audience with his Majesty, to thank him for the high compliment of my being permitted to dedicate to him my work on 'Guns and Shooting,' and to present him with an elegantly bound copy of the seventh edition, of which his Majesty expressed his approbation, and received me with his usual kindness and condescension.

May 3rd.—Longparish. We had a capital morning's trout fishing. General Sir S. Hawker got 11 brace. I got 16 brace in about three hours.

18th.—We have now had the weather so intensely hot for this last week that the water is everywhere tepid, and we cannot bear even the sheet alone to cover us in bed. Never in my life did I feel the heat so oppressive ; perhaps from the sudden transition after the winter that we had late in spring.

August.—In an excursion this month to that paradise, Alum Bay, where I took a gun to get a few dozen of those delicious birds the wheatears, I knocked down a curious owl that Groves, on whose ground we were shooting, had been long trying to get ; so I made him a present of it in return for his civility. On my getting home and referring to the unrivalled engravings of Bewick, it appears to be either a short-eared specimen of the horn owl or the short-eared owl, which he describes as rare and valuable. At all events I gave away what I may never again, perhaps, shoot for my own collection.

CHAPTER XXVI

1833

September 2nd.—Longparish. The wind rather abated, but the birds were as wild as hawks; and I never in my life saw a worse show of game on the first day. We, however, did wonders considering all circumstances, as our bag was 30 partridges and 1 hare; no doubt by far the best day's work that has been done in this country. The green-livered lawyer with his myrmidons, as usual, drove the whole country before us, but found himself, as he always has been, well beat, and heartily laughed at.

7th.—17 partridges.

N.B.—Splendid shooting and a wonderful bag considering that the birds were wilder and more scarce than they generally are in December. A gale of dry easterly wind the whole week, and the ground as dry as Lundyfoot snuff. Not a wheat stubble in the whole country that afforded more lay than an average barley stubble and not a turnip large enough to hide a squeaker.

9th.—21 partridges; five double shots, and not a blank shot fired.

Game killed the first week, or rather in the first four days' shooting: 97 partridges, 3 hares. Total, 100 head.

Strong north-east wind all the week. Only one dog. Birds driven off the feed every morning by the green-livered lawyer's gang on purpose to spoil my sport. But, in spite of all, I never shot so well in my life, having literally missed but one fair shot in the whole campaign, and beat all the other fellows to atoms, though they had the whole country and fresh hands and dogs every day.

October 7th.—Went out with Joe and ratcatcher Siney on a forlorn hope, to get a little game for friends, and had, to our utter astonishment, a miraculous day, viz. 10 partridges, 2 hares, 2 rabbits, 1 snipe, and 1 old cock pheasant; the latter we drove out of covert into the village and chased for two hours, and at last bagged, after a harder run and more noise than we could have had with any average fox hunt.

11th.—Left Keyhaven at half-past eight this morning, and arrived at Longparish House at a quarter-past four P.M., making about forty-five miles in seven hours, with the little grey mare and gig, without a whip; and she wanted to run away with me the last stage. It poured with rain, and my umbrella broke all to pieces, so I had a luxurious drive of it. I fed at a pothouse in Redbridge, the 'Ship,' and had a delicious lunch and exquisite ale for a shilling, in a room with a Broadwood piano, and the best works of Clementi, Cramer, and Herz, which were the practice of the landlady's daughters. Here we have a specimen of the 'march of intellect' in the highest degree.

12th.—Got up at half-past six, took my fresh horse to Basingstoke in an hour and a half (fifteen miles), and mounted the box of the Odiham coach. Arrived in Dorset Place about a quarter before three, and, thank God, found Mary considerably better. Had two droll catastrophes on the road: first, an old woman, while gone in for a drink at an inn, had her barrow of vegetables capsized and gorged by a drove of bullocks; and second, young Thurnwood, who drove for Goodchilde, ran foul of a stone cart, which fell backwards, and hung the horse up by the neck till we had driven almost out of sight, when we just saw him come tumbling down like a cock pheasant.

30th.—Had a whole day's rifle shooting at Chalk Farm with Long, the crack rifle shot, and discovered that my rifle shooting was quite equal to my other shooting; we never missed the target the whole day; made a great many bulls'-eyes, and the four last shots I fired (without a rest) at 150 yards, and put into the space of an apple two shots out of the four.

December 2nd.—Received a letter from Read to say the fowl were come in great plenty at Keyhaven.

4th.—Ran down to Keyhaven; but I had scarcely reached Staines when a westerly hurricane and rain attacked me the whole way, and on the 5th it blew great guns all day, with repeated squalls of rain. Every fowl was swept off the face of the coast, and, after having done what business I had, I was the whole day immured in a kind of imprisonment that Newgate would have been preferable to.

31st.—Longparish. From the day of my return up to this very night, we have scarcely had any intermission from the most determined hurricanes and constant wet days I ever remember. Let us hope that all the troubles of the past year will evaporate in this sweeping tempest.

1834

January 1st.—Longparish House. So much trouble and business that I have only taken five days' shooting up to this New Year's Day, and it's over with the sport now unless the winter fowl come. Incessant rain, and country most desolate up to the last night of the old year. 107 partridges, 5 hares, 2 rabbits, 1 pheasant, and 1 snipe, is the list up to 1834; of course a very poor one compared to former seasons, though quite satisfactory, because I did wonders for the few chances that I had, and I never shot better in my life.

7th.—Walked out with Mr. Griesbach in the forlorn hope of finding a snipe or two, but saw nothing, though I saved my blank by shooting 3 trout at a shot, and one of them was in good condition. The east end of the village all in excitement about 2 wild geese being over in the fields, and how Fiddler Blake and Miller Dance (who missed them, a fair shot) had driven them away. I rode off at once with the pony and a telescope, and after a very long reconnoitre I spied one of these geese about a quarter of a mile off in an open field. After much manœuvring and crawling (to the very earth) like a toad for two gunshots and more, I got so near as to give him such a sickener with the first barrel that I made him 'haul his wind,' and fall a dead shot to the second. In my whole life I never was more proud of my shooting generalship than in bringing home this said grey goose.

N.B.—On seeing Leadbeater in town, who has my goose to stuff, he told me that it was a very curious and a very valuable species that he never saw before; and that this bird has completely 'floored' him in his ornithological knowledge, which we all know to be about the best in Europe.

28th.—Received a most deplorable account of the incessant rain and hurricanes at Keyhaven, and of the total banishment for these last six weeks of every fowl from the coast. Read congratulated me also on the narrow escape of my two splendid punts, the 'Dart' and the 'Petrel,' by their providentially not having been put into the boathouse, which was blown down, and consequently everything within it annihilated. Two of my worn-out punts were in the ruins, but this was of no consequence.

29th.—The first fine day that we have had for several weeks.

As a relief from being constantly confined to the house, I went out occasionally during the last week in a drizzling breeze, and exercised myself with fly fishing. The trout rose well, and we always got enough, that were in fair condition, to make a good fry for dinner. Had we made a determined chase of it, we should, no doubt, have done enough, for the month of January, to make a chatter for half the clubs in London. Left for Windsor.

31*st.*—Saw the Castle. Paid a visit to dear old Eton College.

March 13*th.*—Poor Leech departed for 'another and a better world' at about four o'clock this morning.

N.B.—I am not over-superstitious, but it was a singular occurrence that about half-past one, shortly before Leech died, the bells in our town house rang so as to alarm all the neighbours and the police, and not a soul was about, though our people got up to see; and the previous night Longparish House was literally assailed and attacked at the windows by a screech owl—a bird I had not heard of or seen there for many years.[1]

20*th.*—The greatest trial of all—the following my poor dear friend to the grave. When the hearse drove up to bear away his last remains from the house where he was for fifty years cherished in the bosoms of my family, I had to undergo what may be easier imagined than described.

Nothing could be more satisfactory than the result of all our business, and the excellent arrangements throughout the funeral of my dear departed friend.

N.B.—Within about these last twenty months I have taken the same white cambric handkerchief to four funerals of those who were dear to me.

April 4*th.*—Keyhaven. A day's peace and quietness. My first for many many months.

7*th.*—Availed myself of a most beautiful day to take a sail round the Needles and to Alum Bay; and not having fired a gun the whole winter, I took my little 'cripple stopper' and popped off a roost of wheatears, &c. The very

[1] Since my writing this, my daughter Mary received a note from her mother in London, in which she added a P.S. to observe that towards four o'clock on the morning of the 13th she was awoke by a most tremendous rattling of her shutters, without anyone or any wind occasioning it; and that she was dreadfully frightened, and observed that 'some one was going to die!' she knowing nothing of what had occurred here. These mysteries are facts, to be accounted for as we please.

first day's healthy pleasure I have enjoyed the whole season, and no small relief to my eternally worried mind.

May 1st.—London. Busy with Spottiswoode's printers, *vice* my poor old friend Davison deceased, about the fourth edition of my little book on music.

28th.—Keyhaven. Having done all I had to do, I treated myself to a day's pleasure, as every poor chimney sweeper has a holiday in May, and a royal day I had of it, having made the best day's rock-bird shooting in the annals of Keyhaven. I brought home 42 willocks, 3 puffins, and 1 razor-bill; and I never missed a shot except one, when the shrouds of the boat were in the way of the gun. My day is quite an event here.

July 15th.—Being anxious to see about my son Peter, who has been very ill in Ireland, I took my place for Holyhead by the 'Wonder' coach, and got a lift down to St. Albans.

16th.—Went on by the 'Wonder' coach to Shrewsbury, where I arrived about ten at night. The very best coach I ever travelled by. It does the 154 miles within 15 hours, including breakfast, lunch, and a hasty though well-managed dinner at Birmingham. Fare only 1*l.*

17th.—Proceeded at seven by the branch 'Wonder.' Had the very best breakfast I ever ate at Llangollen (30 miles), with, of course, a Welsh harper to accompany it. Had the box seat with the coachman's full explanation through all the splendid scenery of North Wales, which country, for about 85 miles that we travelled in it, has such roads, in the hands of Government, as may defy all Europe. They are for the most part cut through solid rocks, and are flanked by stone walls the whole way to Holyhead. The gates are all of one tasteful fancy pattern, and the milestones as neat as monuments. The vale of Llangollen, the descent from the mountains into the valley, the terrific 'Swallow' waterfall, the fine view of the majestic Snowdon within four miles of the road at Capel Curig, and, above all, the 'eighth wonder of the world,' the Menai Bridge, were sights any one of which were worth the whole journey. The counties we went through were Denbigh, Merioneth, Caernarvon, and Anglesea. The weather was delightful, and I had the luck to fall in with my old friend Mr. Vaughan, the celebrated singer, who travelled with us all the way to Capel Curig, where he was met by another old friend of mine, Mr. Gaven, who took him and his daughter off to his country seat, and wanted me to go too. The dinner at the 'Penryn Arms,' Bangor, was worthy of a duke—salmon taken from just before the windows, exquisite Welsh mutton, and everything first-rate.

We got to Holyhead, 106 miles, about half-past eight. In one minute after we entered the inn all the fine weather suddenly changed as if by magic. There set in a drenching pour of rain with the heaviest thunder and lightning I ever yet beheld. Instead of these memorandums I should write an octavo volume, even to name all the beauties I had seen; but when we have most to do and to see, is just when we have the least time to write.

Embarked at ten this night on board the 'Escape' packet and went off in a tremendous night of thunder, lightning, wind, and rain, and had a heavy sea, particularly on the Irish side of the Channel. I was stowed in the only vacant berth, near the steam boiler and furnace; and should have been sweated to death or suffocated had I remained there the whole passage. So I crawled out and lay on the cabin floor, surrounded by seasick passengers, and bombarded by the brisk fire of chairs, boxes, and other 'traps,' that were all in confusion from the neglect, to everything and everyone, of the beastly steward, who took all the money the moment we got on board, with a regular charge of half-a-crown for himself, and then left us all adrift.

18*th*.—Landed at Kingstown about half-past six in the morning, in a constant pour of rain, and amidst a scrambling mob, whose noise I could compare to nothing but some hundred irritated curs at a badger bait. Was whisked to Dublin, nine miles, in the 'Royal Mail,' by a red-hot coachee, who was all but giving us a royal somerset by furiously charging round three sharp corners.

Got into Macken's Hotel, Dawson Street, and found that Peter had got better, and bolted off to join his regiment at Belfast. So there was another journey for me. Had I known this, I'd have seen 'dear Ireland' at the 'divvel' before I'd have ever set my foot on her 'elegant' shore.

A regular downright thorough wet day from morn till night. Saw what I could of Dublin, by means of jaunting cars and umbrella. Took a copy of my book on music to my old friend and master, Logier, and was petrified with the performance in his unrivalled academy. Booked the box seat, the inside being full, for the Belfast morning mail of tomorrow.

19th.—Heavy rain continued. One incessant gale and water-spout in our faces all the way to Newry, 50 Irish miles, where an inside became vacant, and I took it, though not before I was wet to the skin, and where I ate sparingly of the worst dinner that could be imagined. But little to remark on this miserable journey through a miserable country, except the deplorable state of the ragged and lousy peasantry, and the wretched stye-cabins which they and their pigs and poultry inhabit.

On the side of the agreeable I have to note that superb trout and salmon, just out of the river, were offered round the coach at about twopence per pound. Dundalk is a beautiful and a very sporting-looking place, with a fine coast for wild fowl and grand mountains for grouse.

The coachman, guard, and mail were nearly as good as in England; but the horsekeepers and all other attendants ragged and barefooted. Distance 80 Irish (that is 103 English) miles.

On my arrival at Belfast (which, by the way, is worth all the rest of the country put together), I was met by Peter, who, although he had been nearly dying, was so recovered as to have resumed his duty, and been out in the rain all night with his regiment in getting down a tremendous fire. My cares about him were therefore at an end, thank God, and I had only to spend a day or two to enjoy the company of him and his brother officers before I went home.

The rain kept on, and continued pouring away all night. I escaped cold by rubbing myself all over with whisky, and having a warm bed and hot tea.

20th.—Went up to the barracks, and spent the whole day with the officers, and never got back to my hotel till between one and two in the morning, as we sat seven hours at the mess. In the afternoon I marched to church with the regiment, this day being Sunday, and then took a drive to see the country. Much delighted with the 74th's excellent kind fellows; capital mess, splendid band, and in every respect a regiment that I felt proud to have placed my son in.

21st.—Went to the parade with the Colonel; made a minute inspection through the ranks of the regiment, and no corps could be in more beautiful order and discipline. Attended the practice of the band for two hours, and they played me a symphony of Mozart and another of Haydn in the first style. The drums, bugles, and bagpipes were also capitally drilled by Signor Mazocchi, the bandmaster. Peter being on duty, I took another drive with Mr. Davies. We went to Carrickfergus, and inspected the celebrated old castle, where the 74th have a detachment, and from the bomb-proof summit of which we could see all over the opposite coast of Scotland with the naked eye. The distance there and back is just twenty-two English miles. My enjoyment of all this beautiful scenery was much damped by the severe pain I was in with a bad foot, and my consequently being so lame I could but with difficulty limp on a stick. I was obliged to hire a car to go to and from my hotel to the mess, and another to get back at night. Had a sober party and an early 'bolt,' which was well suited to my unpleasant situation.

22nd.—Discharged my little bill at the Commercial Hotel, which, by the way, proved one of the very best houses I ever ate or slept in, and after breakfasting there with Peter, who came down to see me off, I embarked on board the 'Corsair,' trading steamer, and got under way for Liverpool about half-past eleven o'clock.

I write this at sea.

Delightful heavenly weather, sea like a mirror, with just air enough to fill our two long-sails. About 20 miles from Belfast we passed the Copeland Islands on our left, and ran close alongside the picturesque little harbour of Donaghadee, the passage from which is 20 miles across to Portpatrick, in Scotland, the land of which was quite visible to the naked eye. About eight in the evening we ran close alongside the Isle of Man, where our captain fired two rounds of cannon to delight us with the grand echo through the continuation of majestically bold rocks that surround this beautiful and picturesque island.[1] No sooner had daylight disappeared than there rose directly ahead of us a most beautiful moon, within a day or two of the full, and our passage was more like a gondola party or a Venetian water serenade than a commercial steamer for Liverpool. The captain, Mr. Gowan, was a most obliging and pleasant man. We had excellent attendance, splendid cabin, boarded all the way, and bill only 6*s.*, which, added to half a crown for the steward and 1*l.* 1*s.* passage, cleared me for 1*l.* 9*s.* 6*d.* except giving a shilling to a most obliging cabin boy, who made me up a prime bed on a large horsehair sofa, where I lay as well as in a hotel, and had my regular dress, shave &c. in the morning.

[1] I made a sketch with a pen while flying by at twelve miles an hour, and at all events it is more like the Isle of Man than St. Paul's Church is.

23rd.—Dropped anchor in the beautiful harbour of Liverpool at half-past seven this morning, making a delightful passage of nineteen hours. Landed in a boat at 6*d.* each, and was then driven in a thing (an old coach put across two wheels) to the Royal Hotel. Breakfasted, and had above an hour to see the town, in a car, being too lame to walk. Much delighted with Royal Exchange and public room. Thought Nelson's monument the *chef-d'œuvre* of all English productions. It literally made me cry, there was so much feeling in the composition. Admired St. Luke's Church and the cemetery, where was Huskisson's monument, though, as yet, poor and unfinished. Thought much more of Liverpool than of Dublin, there was not that poverty-struck, beggarly look about it.

Went per omnibus to railroad about ten. Started five minutes after, and flew to Manchester (32 miles) in an hour and five minutes, deducting two minutes' stoppage halfway for greasing, and setting down passengers for Newton and its neighbourhood.

Terrific travelling, as I was, by my own choice, allowed to leave my seat and be perched on the summit of the mail carriage, where I had to lower my head on entering the subterraneous causeway. Fortunately I had a pair of spectacles, and by 'shipping' them I had such an awful view of the whole concern as no other place could have afforded. But had I not been provided with these my eyes never could have borne the intense current of air and the occasional volley of black dust that flew from the engine. The guard of the mail has a place on purpose with his back to the train, and well sheltered by his letter box. I am delighted at having sat where I did, now, thank God, it is all safe over, but they'll not catch me there again; it was more awful to me than anything I have weathered at sea.

Lost the only feeding hour I had, hopping about in search of my first music master, Cudmore, who had moved and was not to be found ; so I left a book I had for him to the mercy of the porter of the inn.

Proceeded for Birmingham at a quarter-past twelve by a coach called the 'Railway,' in order to avoid having to stay in the putrid air of this most filthy town till the night travelling began. This coach went by way of Stockport, Congleton, Macclesfield, and Stafford, where we stopped at the 'Swan' inn, Mr. Meeson (his name ought to be recorded), and where we had the worst dinner, the worst attendance, and the least civility of any place in my memory. Passed all the country where the potteries are; this made a variety, as we had here another kind of smoke and stink. Arrived in Birmingham soon after ten at night. No coach on to town, so booked for the first in the morning, and went to get a few hours' rest at the 'Castle,' where I sat, till my bed was ready, with a pleasant intelligent bagsman, over 'cold-without-sugar' and a cigar. Fair inn, tidy bed, no bugs, reasonable charges.

24th.—Left Birmingham by the 'Tally-ho' coach at seven this morning, and arrived at the coach office in Islington at half-past six in the evening (108 miles).

CHAPTER XXVII

1834

September 1st.—Deplorable prospect for a field day. A heavy pour of rain till near eleven, when it held up for about two hours with a strong gale of wind, and then it poured away again till half-past four. Country all day as wet as a river; and birds, of course, continually on the run. Only one dog, poor old Bess; but by sheer slavery, luck, and good shooting, got 18 partridges, wholly through splitting one immense covey over two large fields. I gave up my bitch (the only other dog I had) to Joe, to work the inclosures, and he got 5 brace and 1 hare, so that our day was 14 brace. We had our usual spree of outflanking and racing round the green-livered lawyer, who had a whole platoon of cock-a-doodle shooters as usual, and did all he could to spoil our sport.

2nd.—Splendid sport, considering the birds were as wild as hawks, and the dogs were so tired that we were obliged to tread the ground ourselves. I bagged 27 partridges and 4 hares, and Joe 7 brace and 2 hares, making in all 41 birds and 6 hares.

3rd.—Wind as usual, with more wet weather again. Got but 11 partridges and 1 hare, though we shot most brilliantly. Lawyer's party not out, so we conclude dead beat; and all of us, with our animals, properly knocked up.

4th.—Lawyer rallied and out again in full force, so I raced out instead of resting. Did capitally; I bagged 14 partridges and 1 hare without firing one blank shot, though I had some very long ones.

N.B.—I this day shot with Lancaster's new 'patent primers' for the first time, which he had put to my favourite and celebrated old flint gun of Joe Manton's, and a better tool was never handled by sportsman.

5th.—Rested, and physicked the lawyer by sending out a friend to shoot (a dead shot), who got 8 brace.

20th.—3 snipes, 1 duck, and 5 partridges. So oppressively hot that I fainted away in the snipe bog and missed 3 shots, two of them close under my feet. I never suffered so in my life, nor ever before was so overcome by the heat.

30th.—Feeling better I went out on the pony to try for a few birds, and got 7 partridges, but I soon became so faint that I shot miserably, or should have killed 3 or 4 brace besides these, as we found more birds than I had seen before any day since the first week.

Game killed in September: 105 partridges, 6 hares, 11 snipes, 1 duck. Total, 123 head.

October 1st.—Breakfast prepared at seven, old Siney and his curs in attendance, and the usual preparation for the 1st of October; but the result was that not a single pheasant could be found on the estate. We, of course, never expected above 2 or 3, but a sheer blank day is what we never before witnessed. I was so ill that I gave Joe the command of the first sortie, and all that came in then was a huge polecat, caught by terrier 'Trip.' I then put myself at the head of the banditti, and we worked till night. The bag was 3 partridges and 1 hare.

What with a bad night's rest from illness and the fatigue of this day, I was completely done up. So much for the 1st of October, 1834.

2nd.—Better, though still weak. Rode out and got 3 partridges that I wanted, though the birds were very wild, notwithstanding the weather was as hot as in the dog days.

3rd.—Drove down to a retired stream below Bransbury, and had some good pastime with my casting net. In less than an hour I caught 17 dozen and 7 immensely large gudgeon, besides a quantity of dace and some fine trout.

4th.—Took a few hours' shooting in Wherwell Wood, and my share of the bag (the best of the party) was 1 partridge and the only 4 pheasants I fired at.

6th.—Got kidnapped into a most deplorable shooting excursion in the miserable deserts of Wiltshire with Mr. Montague Gore, and instead of loading a cart, as I was led to expect, I never discharged my gun but ten times; I got 6 partridges and 1 hare. Fired two divided shots (both of which were bagged) with another gentleman, and hit a bird, a long shot, that towered, but was not bagged. I went off at eight in the morning, and never got home till near ten at night, and the poor mare had, I think, above fifty miles of it in the gig before her day's work was completed; and I may bless myself that I was not lost on the downs, and consigned to a bivouac for the night in getting home again. Of all the horrible counties I ever saw, I think the Wiltshire downs have a decided claim to pre-eminence.

17th.—London. Went to see the ruins of the Houses of Lords and Commons, burnt down last night and still burning.

30th.—London. Up to now constantly on about my troublesome property, but received this day a flaming despatch from Read about the quantity of fowl arrived at Keyhaven; so I decided on starting without loss of time, if it was only for change of air and peace to cure my cough, though I told everyone I should bring a westerly wind, as I always have done.

31st.—Started per 'Telegraph' at eight, and arrived at Keyhaven about a quarter before eight this evening, and I *did* bring a westerly wind.

November 1st.—After bustling about to get all my traps in order from daybreak till past nine, as I had not been in the new punt since the early part of the winter before last, I went afloat nearly all day; and, as a matter of course, the change of wind had cleared the coast. The only 2 birds we fell in with were a single brent goose that I killed handsomely with a barrel of the long-laid-aside stanchion gun, and a large grey plover that I made a very long shot at with the cripple stopper, after crawling on my knees for about 300 yards. So, sorry as the bag was, I at all events began capitally with the little I saw for the first day of my season.

3rd.—Availed myself of a calm day to explore the whole coast. Started in the 'Petrel' punt at eight, and landed on the quay at Cowes (15 miles) in about two hours and a half. My set-out raised a complete mob among the Royal Yacht population of this place. After taking refreshment and passing about an hour in the town, we rowed the punt down tide along the whole coast, and all we saw was one large flock of wigeon, high in the air and travelling back to the eastward. This proves how soon the wrong weather puts an end to the chance of getting fowl.

4th.—Made another survey, but to no purpose; never saw a single bird of any kind, so finished the afternoon with paying all my little bills that were due here, and getting rid of all the business I had preparative to mounting the coach to-morrow morning.

5th.—A precious comfortable trip up to Longparish from Keyhaven to-day. Was told to meet the 'Pilot' coach at Everton at a quarter past eight. Walked there by soon after eight, but had been misinformed as to time, as the coach was gone, so had to tramp in 'double quick' for Lymington till within half a mile of the town, where I gave a warren boy a shilling to put me up with his rabbits and try to catch the coach. Horse no goer, so we failed altogether. Took a pony and gig and got to Hythe, twelve miles, in an hour and five minutes. Crossed the ferry, nearly three miles, in a quarter of an hour. A gale of wind, and should have been capsized and drowned by a squall had I not seized and let go the sheet.[1] Ran all up Southampton streets and got to the office a quarter of an hour before the coach came in. Wonderful quick work. Got to Winchester soon after twelve to see lawyer Bird, but he was not at home. Mounted a two-horse slow coach at two, from which out got Bird, and after a hasty interview with him in the thorough draught of a gateway, I went on by this *adagio* conveyance. A tremendous hurricane and heavy driving rain all the way to my farm at Furgo, the nearest point to which I was set down. The farmer out, so left my wet trunk for a countryman to bring on to Longparish. Umbrella broke and useless in the gale. Paddled it over the wet fields, with a gale and waterspout all the way, that I could scarcely make head against, to Longparish, where I arrived, wholly unexpected, and as 'wet as a shag,' a little before five, and was put naked into a warm bed till my clothes could be got at and dried, and some sustenance provided. I shall not in a hurry fail to 'remember the fifth of November.'

6th.—Went to try for a cock that I fancied I saw, but found nothing. Then worked down by the river, where I got a cold bath. On riding over Redmoor dyke 'bridge' old Bob, my horse, shied aside, and down we both came from a bridge of some height into about three feet of water, I under and old Bob on me, and I could not get above water till my breath was nearly gone. We were both completely out of sight for some seconds, as the markers informed me. But I stood true vermin and tried the islands afterwards for snipe, while Siney galloped home to get fresh clothes ready. Saw but one jack snipe, bagged him, and dined on him in commemoration of the event; and had an evening's employ to clean up my watch, and every other article that was kept under water with the old 'horse' and 'his rider.'

[1] While the sailor was engrossed in a long yarn about the wonderful exploits of 'Colonel Hawker, the great gunner,' little aware that he could have quoted Nathan and said, 'Thou art the man.'

20th.—Keyhaven. A tremendous gale of wind from the north-east all night and all day, and all night again. No boat could row on end. Dead tides, and some geese off, on the mud, near the breakers.

22nd.—Gale and rain continued. Sick of being a prisoner. Fought our way out in the punt, and waited from daylight till near twelve on board a salt lighter, then dropped down on the fowl: got 1 brent goose and 8 wigeon. My pattens came untied on the mud, and I came home in miserable mess, that took us four hours to clean up and rectify.

24th.—A cutting north-easter. Up at four, but it 'blew great guns,' and all we could do was to work through 'Stivers' creek, and 'make fast' the punt to windward, so as to be able to drop down outside without having to face a wave. No birds at all; so went home, overland, and returned to our craft at midday. Beat the marshes for snipes in the meantime, but no sport. Sadly slack crisis; no water inside from dead tides, and no facing the wind outside, and all the birds slipped off, Lord knows where, though weather most beautiful for fowl. Home to Longparish to-day.

27th.—Having left my punts &c. all ready for my immediate return, I drove off on my way back to Keyhaven, a the most ominous of all bad weather, a severe white frost gave me warning that I had but a few more days to embrace. Indeed the change seemed, at one time, so near at hand, that I had all but turned off my gig, and proceeded up the Winchester road to London. However, my destiny was to proceed; and not wishing to bother the old mare with another forced march, I left her and Monk to 'take it easy' at Redbridge, and mounted the 'Pilot' branch coach with Jemmy Judd, who set me down at Everton, from whence I toddled with my pack at my back to Keyhaven, and saved five shillings' worth of fly. I arrived before I was expected; and Read, who was knocked out of his bed, where he had gone to bottle himself up for a mud launch, told me there had been a splendid show of birds the very two days I was away, and gave me brilliant hopes for the morrow; but, alas! Old Nick's wind came on in the night, and the pinching 'sniveller' was changed to a tempest. We, however, got under way on the 28th, as the tide was well over the harbour, and had a cruise down to below Lymington, in which we saw nothing except Buckle and two of his brother gunners anchored in the very bull's-eye of our beat. In short I never pulled a trigger, except blowing off a barrel and killing 10 shore birds, that were settled on a new-invented raft of mine, the very first tide after Read had moored it. If we could only have weather and water, how this raft would do the plover!

December 1st.—Keyhaven. Cruel weather. Tired of being a prisoner. Drove to Christchurch, and while the mare was feeding, inspected the beautiful church there, which, from its deviation from correct order, affords, perhaps, more interesting variety than any cathedral I know. In short, it is well worth seeing. I then drove on to my old rendezvous, Poole, where I was amused with seeing all the brother gunners of my infancy, who were delighted to see 'the Captain' again, as they called me, and did some commissions in salt fish, and attempts about getting a real St. John's dog &c., and, in short, anything to kill the monotony of a west-wind embargo, and with some hopes of changing the weathercock. Returned late to Keyhaven.

3rd.—A butterfly May day. Out all the morning, and saw nothing but a small flock of geese, which were so well fed, and so wild, that they would not sit for ten minutes at a time in any one place. Was informed that all the birds, by thousands, had got into Sowley Pond, where keepers were on watch, day and night, to preserve them for the 'pleasure' of Lord Montague looking at them.

4th.—Having given up the gunning for a 'bad job' till the weather changes, I went into Lymington to do some business, and then drove on to look at Lord Montague's 'thousands' of birds on Sowley Pond, of course with a popgun and cartridges, but the 'thousands' turned out to be one small company of wigeon, about 7 straggling ducks, and nearly 1,000 coots. The wild fowl were out of shot; so I discharged a barrel for the public good, and drove them off to sea, and then drove myself home.

5th.—Read, who was out all night mud crawling, got 6 wigeon, having shot, some time after midnight, at a company which, from place and number, I can almost swear were the birds I had started out of my lord's nursery at Sowley Pond.

8th.—Longparish. Availed myself of a few hours' leisure from business this afternoon to try for a snipe, and had excellent luck. I bagged the only 8 snipes I saw, and 1 woodcock that had long outwitted everyone here, and at which I made a most brilliant shot, after some masterly manœuvring, and a sharp chase of nearly an hour.

10th.—Returned to London. No schoolboy was more happy to escape from birch, Latin, and mutton, than I was to return to Dorset Place.

17th.—By way of a climax to my worry of mind with lawyers, I was this day sentenced to an awful operation by surgeons. I called on my friend Sir Benjamin Brodie, the head of the profession, who examined me, and said, if I wished to live, I must suffer this, and be ready for him about half-past two on the third day. All this day, after eleven, all the 18th, and till about twenty minutes to three on the 19th, was I kept in a state that may be easier imagined than described. At last the awful rap at the door announced the arrival of the carriage with Sir Benjamin and his assistant. The operation lasted about thirteen minutes. No pen can describe the agony I suffered, though I was highly complimented on bearing it as I did.

For about fourteen hours I lay in such excruciating pain that all opiates were unavailable, and I kept getting worse and worse, till, at last, I was quite resigned to lose my life.

23rd.—Sir Benjamin, who had attended me every day, came a little before seven this evening, when he thought me so far safe as to postpone his next visit till the day after to-morrow.

Game &c. killed up till the end of December 1834: 118 partridges, 8 hares, 4 pheasants, 25 snipes, 1 duck, 2 brent geese, 10 wigeon, 7 teal. Total, 175 head.

1835

January.—London. Here begins the new year, and God send I may have a pleasanter one than the last, which brought me throughout a series of afflictions and difficulties.

1st.—Just downstairs, after having been confined to my bed and room for above a fortnight.

12th.—On taking up my paper this morning I was much hurt, and could scarcely eat my breakfast, at reading the death of another old and highly esteemed friend and brother 'gunner,' Captain Ward, whom I had met in excellent health, and just going to prepare his yacht and punt for fowling, but three days before I came up to town.

April 16th.—Black frost and snow.

17th.—Good Friday. Black 'north-easter' with a stiff breeze, and with frost and snow. Absolute winter.

18th.—The few days' severe weather ceased, and it became spring again. What a climate is ours! Went down to Stoke Newington House to see Mr. Wood relative to his relieving me of Longparish House for a twelvemonth. Mr. Wood was here on a visit to the rich heiress, Miss Crawshay, who, house and all, is to become the property of the curate. Lucky dog! Leave a parson alone for getting the best of everything.

20th.—From morning till night in a bustle, owing to all things coming in a clash, as is invariably the case, and raced about like a hard-driven bullock in a mob. Booked Mr. Wood's and my places for Wednesday to go to inspect

Longparish. No sooner up than down, but *n'importe* in a good cause.

22nd.—Went down with Mr. Wood, and made every preparation for delivering to him Longparish House.

23rd.—While I was fishing (I got 25 trout), the carpenter and my men were employed relative to examinations, inventories, &c.; and on Mr. Wood, after a more minute inspection, doubting whether I had a sufficient supply of articles to suit his style of living, and finding the place not in such good order as Mrs. Wood would require, he declined proceeding any further in the affair unless I could make an immediate outlay that would at once swallow up the whole year's rent.

24th.—Thus have I had all this trouble and a journey for nothing. So much for house and land property. If you want to kill a chap humanely, shoot him at once; but if you want to worry his life out with successive years' plague without profit, give him land, in the present times, and some unoccupied houses.

May 7th.—London. The best performed opera I ever saw. We were taken to the box of Grisi, whose acting surpassed even Pasta. The opera was 'Otello,' and her Desdemona was perfect. Rubini, Tamburini, Lablache, and Ivanhof were never greater than this night; nor did I ever hear the orchestra go to such true perfection. I seldom notice town spectacles, but this was one in a thousand.

14th.—The most intensely crowded Drawing Room I ever was at, and a deluge of north-east rain from morning till night. The fight of carriages in Grafton Street was awful, and my 'Jarvey' cracked like a lobster. I expected a wreck every moment, and blessed myself that I had no females in charge. All the servants half drowned, and I could get no escape without the drenching of all my finery, till at last I bribed a chairman to work me to a Jarvey stand, where he shipped me from his sedan to a coach, a precious wet one too, insomuch that I dare not sit down in it, but crouched and held on all the way home. So much for being a courtier this wet day.

June 16th.—Longparish. Netted the river for the King. Killed 63 brace of trout in two drags, besides as many thrown in, and about a bushel of large dace.

July 15th.—London. After being all the morning at the concert of Benedict, which was by far the best of the season, I this day adjourned from the Opera House to the Freemasons' Tavern, where was given the grand farewell dinner to John Cramer. Much as I abominate a public feast, or rather public fast, I must admit this to have been a real intellectual treat. On the whole, nothing could be better conducted, nor could any man living have had a more cordial reception than my old and talented friend John Baptiste Cramer.

27th.—Left London and arrived at Longparish. Found the country completely burnt up by the long-continued easterly winds and overbearing heat; and, in short, not a degree cooler than London, where the heat has long been such that it was impossible to get a night's rest, at least for me, without lying on a mattress without any covering whatever.

28th.—Busy all day regulating the cellar and other things, and cleaning and varnishing all the pictures in the house. In the evening we had a tremendous storm, with thunder and lightning, and such a deluge of rain that half the rooms in the house were wetted through the ceiling.

August 7th.—Fly-fished for several hours in a good wind, and got but one fair brace of trout. Never in my whole life did I see the fish so sulky in good angling weather. They were all at the bottom running for minnows. Tried the river for fowl; got 1 duck and 1 snipe, the only two shots I had. This was Friday, and I thought I could defy the spell by the goodness of my gun and shooting; but Friday would be Friday. I fell down in the river, filled my gun, got a ducking, and consequently a miss-fire at a most beautiful shot. And then 2 more ducks passed me while I was 'done out of' my gun.

18*th.*—Started for a few days' inspection of Jersey and Guernsey, having never seen either of these islands. I got a berth in the custom-house boat, and dropped down the Lymington river just as it grew dark, and had not the officers fired three pistols for the captain to 'heave to,' the packet would not have stopped for me, and I should have had to go back, like a fool, in the middle of the night. As it was, however, all was well; I got safe on board the 'Liverpool,' and had one of the finest passages imaginable in the very best steamer I ever set foot in. We left the Channel about nine.

19*th.*—Brought up close alongside Guernsey about seven in the morning. Here we waited an hour, and, as the weather was so delightful, I determined on embracing a good passage to go on and see Jersey first. We got under way at eight, and dropped anchor off Jersey (thirty miles more) at eleven; but, owing to the multiplicity of passengers in both this packet and an inferior one called the 'Ariadne,' added to the negligent scarcity of boats, we were imprisoned under a broiling sun, and peppered with the blacks from the evaporating steam for the greater part of an hour, and in a state of exhaustion and starvation for want of a good breakfast. The chief beauty to remark on our passage was a view of rocks called the Caskets, which we opened about half-past four, and of which I took a hasty flying sketch, such as it is. But as to attempting to sketch, or even describe, the *coup d'œil* of St. Peter's, the only town in Guernsey, it would be too long a job. Suffice it to say that it presents such an endless detail of bold rocks, and innumerable houses of all sorts and colours, that nothing short of a hard laboured panorama would give a proper idea of it. An intelligent gentleman who had long resided there told me that in the island of Guernsey there were no reptiles of any kind, though they were common in Jersey as in England.

On our left going to Jersey we had a fine view of the island of Sark, and, in short, went along a coast of the boldest, and, of course, the most dangerous rocks I ever saw. On landing at Jersey I went to the 'Albion' hotel, a passable tavern for such a place as St. Helier's, the capital and great seaport of this island. The passage, the seamen said, was 140 miles; 110 from off Lymington to Guernsey, and thirty more from quay to quay afterwards. Fare, in best cabin, only 11*s.* 6*d.* including a shilling for the steward.

20th.—Having yesterday seen the town of St. Helier's, I got up this morning, and with a one-horse car made a minute survey of the country round, with which I was not a little delighted. First I went to Grouville, where the chief subject for a sketch was the church; we then went to the village of Gourey, and ascended to the celebrated old castle called 'Mount Orgueil,' in which Charles II. was secreted, and from which he made his escape to France by a passage through the solid rock, on which this splendid ruin stands, and by the excavation of which it is chiefly formed. The view of and from this castle is magnificent. We then proceeded to a delightful little rendezvous for pleasure called 'Prince's Tower,' which commands a panorama of the whole island, and which is fitted up and laid out around with more taste and neatness than any public refreshment place I ever met with. There is a winding gravel path by which you ascend to the tower, and then a most commodious winding staircase which leads to little octagon eating-rooms in every storey, from which you have windows to see over the island in all directions. We then drove back to St. Helier's in the evening, and ascended the ramparts of the fortified rock, where you have a view equally fine in its way. Here is a memorandum of the views; now for a short summary of observations.

People civil and obliging. Things about half the price of England. No taxes, no duties, and a free port for all commerce. First-rate fruit, as cheap as dirt. Capital market.

Town much like a French one, but far cleaner. Religion chiefly Protestant, the service performed in French, both languages fluently spoken in every shop, though with an accent peculiar to the natives. Town and country swarming with apples. Farmers all in a very small way, but for the most part freeholders. Plenty of employ for the people, and I never saw or heard of a beggar in the place. Only one other town besides the capital, and the only public conveyance on the island is from 'town,' as they of course call St. Helier's, to this place, St. Austin. You have a fine 'currency' profit on either English gold or Bank of England notes, being allowed 21*s.* 8*d.* for every pound, and 13*d.* for every shilling. This, and the total release from every duty of either excise or customs, is what makes Jersey, and I believe Guernsey too, so much cheaper than France and other foreign places.

21*st.*—Made a further reconnoitre of everything in and about the town. Found the prices of everything a mere nothing; for instance, best French brandy 1*s.* 4*d.* a bottle, that is 1*s.* 3*d.* English; tea, 3*s.* per lb.; snuff, 1*s.* per lb.; India silk handkerchiefs, 4*s.* each, and less if taken by the piece, and, in short, almost every article in the same proportion. While inspecting the fish market (which, although not in great repute, abounded with coarse fish, such as conger eels, and was fairly supplied with good fish of most kinds) I met the old Adjutant of the 14th Dragoons, Ben Shotten, who had settled in Jersey, and told me he could live for within one-third here of what it cost him in England. In the afternoon I took a small boat with one man, and rowed over to Elizabeth Castle, where I spent some time, and saw the armoury, King Charles's boots, &c.; and we then rowed to the hermitage close by, where, after such a climbing of rocks as I never before had to encounter, I mounted up to the old cave of St. Helier, the ancient hermit, after whom the capital was named, and got home just in time to escape a most terrific thunder storm, in consequence of which I gave up an expedition that I had in view, of going in a hired oyster smack to survey the Choissée Islands, a place with about twelve inhabitants, and swarming with birds of all kinds, and about twenty-seven miles south of Jersey. The storm threw such a darkness over the whole country and town, that we were obliged to light a candle before I could see to pen down these memorandums. This evening the whole town was in a royal uproar with a grand dinner, given by the officers of the Jersey militia to the General, Sir Colin Campbell, in honour of his Majesty's birthday, at the 'Sun' inn, which was close adjoining my quarters. Cannons, drums, trumpets, guns, two hundred jolly boys getting uproariously drunk, with incessant hurrahing and singing, bands of music, fireworks, rabbles of boys by hundreds screaming ready to split the rocks, and, in short, such a spree as could not be surpassed if Old Nick's dominions were broken loose.

22nd.—As I wished to land on and go over the island of Guernsey on my way home, I had no other alternative of doing so than embarking about half-past eleven last night on board the 'Ivanhoe' Weymouth and Guernsey post-office packet, and there waiting in durance vile till three this morning in a beastly craft only fit to convey Irish pigs across the Severn, till there was water to float her out of harbour. At this hour we got under way, and were above four hours doing the passage, which the 'Liverpool' would have done in three. As in all post-office packets, the accommodation was vile; the ladies were so little separated from the gentlemen as made it quite indecent, and, as there was no female attendant on board, nor indeed any but a superannuated old steward, the gentlemen who had their ladies there were obliged to go in to assist them where others were. We had a rough passage, with some heavy rain, a rolling vessel, and an almost general mess of sickness. We 'fetched' Guernsey soon after seven, and there I put up at the 'Crown' inn on the north pier. As soon as I had refreshed myself with an indifferent breakfast, I went to the celebrated market, in order to see it early, and therefore in full perfection. Nothing could be more abundant, but things were not so cheap as in Jersey, the people much more inclined to cheat, and the currency money allowed here is only $\frac{1}{2}$*d.* in the 1*s.* The fruit market was superb, the fish market immense, but for the greater part consisting of colossal shell fish. In the poultry market turkeys were 6*s.* a couple, and young pigs 16*s.* a couple. What delighted me the most was to see the English gentlemen, like sensible fellows, choosing and buying their own things, instead of trusting to and having to be encumbered with a set of beastly lazy, idle, discontented servants, overfed and underworked, and, in short, live lumber. Here I met the half-pay officers and other refugees from English plunder and humbug, with their market basket in one hand and a lobster in the other, the wife with the fruit, and the child with the flowers, and so on. What I call the height of independence and domestic happiness. The streets here are more like the French, and not so pleasant as those of Jersey. About twelve o'clock I took a car with a most intelligent and loquacious driver, and started for a tour round the whole island about twenty-four miles, and there was no house, person, or thing but what this fellow was perfectly acquainted with, and volunteered the history of. We first mounted the immense hill of streets that leads to the fashionable part of the town, passing by the house of Lord Saumarez, the college, the hospital, and all the fine houses of the rich merchants, to Fort George. From thence we went half a mile and back out of our way to the famous tower erected to the late General Sir John Doyle for making the roads, and this I ascended by a winding staircase in total darkness, to enjoy perhaps the finest view that all this part of the world can afford—on the one half circle the whole island of Guernsey, and on the other the islands of Jersey, Sark, Herm, Jethou, and Alderney, with the coast of France in the background. Country afterwards not very picturesque, more for a farmer than a painter. Rich land, small proprietors of about from six to ten acres each. Country all divided in small crofts, with either stone walls or banks, all fortified with strong furze. Wheat put up in stacks of about two to the acre. A great deal of mangel wurzel, parsnips, beetroot, and brocoli in fields. Ploughing done twenty inches deep for this, and sometimes 14 beasts required to one plough, either French horses or bullocks, or both. No cows but those of Alderney admitted, and these were larger than what we call Alderney cows in England, and the very finest I ever saw, some giving, the guide told me, forty quarts a day. Passed village of 'Forest,' and near there drank wines a penny a glass and paid a penny for a stiff brandy grog for dinner. Continued round by the villages of St. Martin, and St. Peter's in the Wood, having afterwards on our left a fine view of the 'Rock in Bay,' Richmond barracks (now sold for the land) and the island of Leo. There are ten parishes in the island, with one church and either two or three dissenting chapels to each. French language for Divine service and everything is used throughout the country part of the island, though both languages universal to all ranks of people in town. Put in at the 'Royal Oak' at St. Saviour's, a noted, indeed the only, house for eating and pleasure parties out of the capital. Here we refreshed and rested ourselves and horse, and saw an enormous ox, and some very large and well-shaped pigs. We then put to the horse and started on our other round for the capital, St. Peter's Port, through the village of King's Mill, where at the house of a Mr. Moulin there were the very largest sized oranges growing against the wall, adjoining the parlour window, and there were in most places very fine myrtles, and aloes nearly as large as in Portugal. Near this place there is erected a manufactory for distilling brandy from potatoes. After then we passed the village of Vale, and re-entered the town on the north side without having to descend the huge hill we had mounted, and drove by the seaside and esplanade home again to my quarters, where, by the way, the windows of both my bedroom and sitting room looked off from a rock directly into the sea, and over the most superb view of the town, Cornet Castle, and the distant islands, that could be imagined. I took a kind of tea-supper, and went to bed as tired as a dog between nine and ten, having had no rest the previous night. My reason for thus making such a toil of a pleasure was to secure the 'Liverpool' for Monday, and the intervening day being Sunday, when it is not much the custom to travel about here. But after all, I found the 'Liverpool' had been suddenly bought up for a voyage to Spain or Portugal,[1] and there would be no packet for England till Tuesday.

23rd.—After a good night's rest, of which I was sadly in want, I got up to pen down these memorandums, which I was too tired to do, as usual, at night, and went to St. Peter's Church, which is so precisely the same, both in the building and the service, with our chapels in London, as to need no description. The canopy of the pulpit was formed like an immense oyster shell, and sloping from behind the preacher, which had a novel effect, and perhaps assisted in throwing out his voice. The Sabbath is kept here even more strictly than in England. Not an article of any kind to be bought, and there is no fish market on Monday because the fishing on Sunday is prohibited.

24th.—Had intended to cross over to inspect the island of Sark; but a heavy sea, through which I might not have been able to get back, prevented my going this 9 miles passage. So I devoted the day to exploring everything in and about the town, and, amongst other things, I was much pleased with the college and the hospital. The former is a splendid building, and beautifully regulated. The latter has many well-contrived advantages for doing, by mechanical means, all that is necessary in the baking, cooking, washing, and other labours of an establishment of about 300 patients.

25th.—Having now seen all I wanted to see, or rather all that my limited time and the contrary winds would allow me

[1] Sold, as I since heard, for 11,160*l.* to run from Falmouth to Lisbon.

to see, I this morning put up my things, previous to another sortie in the town, an early dinner, and a start by the afternoon packet for England; and never did I feel more regret at leaving a strange place where I was unknown, than I do at leaving the two islands I have visited. I came to them out of mere curiosity, and for the benefit to my health of a sea voyage to where it would cost me the least, and where I expected to find a place only fit for poverty-struck refugees. But, to my agreeable surprise, I found everything so far before either France or England that I should have no objection to take my leave of both, and end my days in either of these well-regulated, independent, and happy islands.

26th.—I remained packed up for the steamer, but the wind was so strong and contrary that she never came in all yesterday, being wind-bound at St. Malo. Here I am, therefore, and cannot go far out of the way lest she should be in and out again. Saw a fine haul of fish close to the town, and the moment the fish were caught and collected in one great heap, a horse, with two large panniers, was brought down to take them as quickly as possible to the market, where alone fish is here to be sold. About six this evening the 'Beresford,' the long-detained Southampton packet, appeared, and a little before eight she arrived off the harbour, and everyone said we must hasten on board, as she would not stop many minutes. Off went I and the other passengers; but instead of her bringing up to take us in, she ran 'right into the docks,' owing to some damage, as they said, done to her in the bad passage, from which she could not proceed till early to-morrow morning; so I had to pay porters and boatmen for nothing and return to my hotel, which I was not sorry for, as I prefer a day passage to one in such a night as this.

27th.—The packet was to leave at five this morning, and I gave orders to be called a quarter before four. Woke up, looked at watch, wanted only ten minutes to five, and not a soul up. Flew from my bed to the street, and luckily a little shift of wind had penned the tide, so that the dock could not float out the packet till six, or my passage must have been lost. As it was we got under way at half-past six, and came into the Channel off Hurst at half-past five in the evening, after making a rapid passage, in spite of having a breeze directly against us for the greater part of the way. We had for the first three hours a rough, and afterwards a very pleasant, passage. At one time, near Alderney, we steamed seventeen miles in the hour. On arriving off Yarmouth, I sadly feared I should not get a boat to see our signal, and indeed none did; but most fortunately a boy in a Freshwater boat cut across to us just in time, and gave me a passage to Lymington; otherwise I should have been dragged all the way to Southampton, and kept by the custom house till perhaps past the Lymington coach time of the next morning. But as it luckily was, I landed unobserved, walked over the marsh to Keyhaven, and had all my things brought safe to me, with my own cart, early next morning. Thus ended my amusing, cheap, and satisfactory excursion, and, I thank God, found the children well, and that they had been well amused with our good neighbours during my absence from Keyhaven.

CHAPTER XXVIII

1835

September 1st.—A good show of birds, but scarcely a point to be got the whole day. County as bare as a seashore, and we were forced to walk up (wild as hawks) all we killed; not even the dispersed birds would stay a moment where they pitched, unless in hedges. Joe and I shot together, and both performed splendidly, indeed never better. We bagged 22 brace and 1 hare between us.

2nd.—In a bustle all the morning packing off birds and notes; my usual occupation the second day. Walked out after dinner to get a brace of birds I wanted. Fagged hard to get seven long shots; bagged 5 partridges and lost another. The green-livered venomous reptile of a lawyer and his myrmidons were on, of course, from morning till night as usual, but have no chance against us, though they have the whole manor, and we are confined to our own fields.

3rd.—20 partridges. We have, as usual, beat all the country hollow; but the shooting is sheer slavery. The ground like hot cinders, the heat like India, and getting a point out of the question. All must be done by walking the barren lands with both barrels cocked, and popping at all distances the moment the birds top the stubble. We all came home so exhausted as scarcely to be able to move.

5th.—Slaved all day and got but 6 partridges A perfect farce to go out, everyone giving it up as unprofitable slavery.

7th.—14 partridges, and Joe 13. We gave up the bitch

and our marker to Goodchilde and his friend, who worked from morning till night and bagged 23 between them. We saw nothing of the lawyer to-day, though we gave him a royal benefit between our three parties, killing just 50 birds.

9th.—A very stormy day, and birds wilder than ever. I got 15 partridges. N.B.—I owe my bag to-day to two extraordinary shots. I began with firing at 5 birds, and bagging 4 of them with one barrel; and finished my evening with springing 4 birds on an oat stubble, and blowing all 4 of them down at one shot; 3 fell short, and the old cock flew and towered and was also bagged. These extraordinary shots occurred, I conceive, owing to the tremendous gale of wind, and my having taken out my miraculous 'Old Joe,' a gun which I can pitch with more rapidity than any other I have, and am, therefore, frequently able to catch the birds before they have time to divide. Add to which this gun cuts out all my others for throwing a regular circle of shot.

11th.—I was out from one till six, and of all the years I ever was a sportsman I never saw such a bad day's shooting; it was a real Friday. The birds got up regularly at about 100 yards, and there was such a tempest the whole afternoon that I could hardly keep my hat on my head.

14th.—I fagged from ten till seven, and never got but 7 shots. We had a fine 'spree,' as the lawyer was between both our beats, and I worked round him as a cooper would round a barrel, while he got little or nothing.

18th.—A prisoner with physic; a wet day, and the lawyer hard on at shooting, but I flew out and flanked him, and got 2 birds and wet to the skin.

25th—A fine butterfly day at last; I got 10 partridges. Splendid sport. The green-livered son of a —— the lawyer drove my preserve, but I flanked him and beat him handsomely.

29th.—A capital day for fishing. I killed 12 of the largest trout I have seen this year within the hour; and, had

I not been engaged, and therefore obliged to go, I might have done something extraordinary.

Game &c. killed up to Sept. 30.—238 partridges, 12 hares, 2 rabbits, 1 quail, 6 ducks, 18 snipes. Total, 277 head.

October 1st.—Up to breakfast at six, and out the whole of a stormy day, till near six in the evening, and a fourth of the time standing under shelter of trees, to avoid being wet through. Had an army of myrmidons and curs to scour every inch of wood or hedge that I could sport on; and, in the whole day, only set eyes on 3 pheasants, all of which I killed in brilliant style, just as they were flying out of bounds, and bagged instantly the first time of springing them. Under all circumstances I never had a more satisfactory little day's sport.

2nd.[1]—The first time for some years, I was this day jackass enough to be kidnapped into a downright country visit; and what follows is a specimen of this 'pleasure.' I was to have previously gone over to shoot 'a splendid bag of game,' but luckily a wet morning prevented my joining the sportsmen, who, although good shots, I believe, got but 7 head between four of them. Now to the set-out. The girls and I, in order to meet my old musical friend, the well-known Signor Sola, accepted a kind and friendly invitation at Quarley House, a pretty seat in a desert seven miles beyond Andover, with an obbligato accompaniment of bad roads. The girls, women-like, were all agog for the 'spree' as soon as the rain had stopped, and the treacherous sun began to show his phiz; but when it was too late to retreat, the pitiless storms, as I predicted, began to pepper away on us and our uncovered vehicles. We made a short halt in Andover in order to pick up the life and soul of all sport, Tom Langstaff, who had borrowed the brewer's pony phaeton, and 'prime' grey prad. Whether the 'sturdy beast' had had too much grains or not enough, it matters but little; as all required for

[1] A bad attempt at the much-about-nothing style of Walter Scott's novels.

my journal is to say that he was considerably slower than a good tidy donkey; and in spite of whipping, whistling, chirruping, and charming him with all the hands and mouth that I could muster, his pace was no more than five miles an hour. We arrived at Quarley about four, and, according to the feeling and roaring of my 'chitterlings,' I guess it must have been near eight o'clock before we sat down to a grand dinner, which had waited long for the return of the chasseurs and their light bag of game. Nothing could be more kind or hospitable than the friendly treatment of our host and hostess; indeed we were so regaled as to be unfit for music in any other way than for merriment; and, had we not 'fought shy,' should have 'all been drunk together.' After a batch of rattling play, jolly singing, buffoonery, waltzing, quadrilling, and joke cracking, we proposed ringing for our vehicles, and were thought quite unsociable for 'cutting our sticks' so early as a quarter past one o'clock. Up drove our carriages, escorted by a party of men with flambeaux, which was headed by the Squire himself, and he ran with us very fast till we got through a new cut to the turnpike road. I should observe that the shipping and starting of the cargo was worthy of a picture by Hogarth, what with the music, changing of clothes, fiddle, guitar, and all such like; while my mouth was alternately occupied in blowing a mail horn and puffing a cigar, and my two hands in full occupation to put life into the brewer's 'prad.' To do him justice, however, we did coax him into a much better pace; and this I impute partly to his being 'homeward bound' and partly to a 'jolly blow-out' of the Squire's corn and beans, which of course took the shine out of all his former grain diet—perhaps unavoidable mixture of cocculus indicus and other brewer's fare. Well, we got to Andover, bid good night to Tom Langstaff and his Cremona, and I then got behind my own horse, 'Old Samson,' and rattled along at the rate of twelve miles an hour, till there came on a dense fog that it was not only extremely difficult, but even dangerous, to proceed in; and our laughter was soon changed to horror by seeing the whole horizon in a blaze of awful fire, and this in the direct line of my own property, which, thank God, it proved not to be. We reached Longparish House soon after three o'clock, and smelt of smoke as strong as if we had been attending the engines; though, from the intervening hill, we could not till next day ascertain where was the conflagration. We got to bed exactly at four, and were all quite sick and unwell the next day. So much for country visiting.

3rd.—On being called about half-past eight this morning, I was shocked to learn that there had been no less than three fires since midnight on the property of my friend Lord Portsmouth—two at Hurstbourne, within less than a quarter of a mile of where we turned off, and one at Tufton, about a mile farther, in which three horses were destroyed, and the carter had the narrowest possible escape of being burnt to death. The Andover engine, it appears, came directly after us, as it did not arrive till about three o'clock. Went, in a pouring wet afternoon, to view the remains of the fires, and the awful sight of four beautiful horses that lay broiled to death, and found that all four of the carters were so burnt that they escaped absolutely naked, though providentially with not very serious injury done to themselves, except the loss of all they had. Called at Hurstbourne House to offer any assistance in my power to my friend Mr. Fellowes, and was detained a little time stopping a row and bloody fight in Hurstbourne.

In the evening Signor Sola and Tom Langstaff arrived to dinner for a 'spree' and a glut of music, which we had in perfection till twelve o'clock.

5th.—Out all day, and, in spite of good weather and good shooting, could only get 4 partridges and 2 jack snipes, the only two I saw. The birds are now so wild that it is an absolute waste of time to slave after them.

6th.—Went to Southampton.

7th.—Got into the morning packet for Ryde, and in taking a glass of soda at Cowes, where I landed for about a quarter of an hour, the cork, which the chemist cut the string of, flew into the ball of my right eye, which at first I thought was blinded for ever, and the sensation was like a pickaxe striking through my head. I was blind in this eye all day, and in great pain, but I proceeded to Ryde, which place I never saw before and had now only one eye to see with, and was quite delighted with this most beautiful of all watering places.

November 3rd.—London. I went into our United Service Club to get some soup about four o'clock, and Sir F. Egerton came in and said he had just marked down a woodcock in the little shrubs of the park, close to the club house; and, had it not been so late, General Mundy would have gone to the ranger and got leave for me to go and kill the woodcock for the King. What a novelty this would have been!

6th.—An easterly wind and a good report from Read. Took the box of the 'Eclipse.'

7th.—Left London at eleven and got to Keyhaven at eleven. Of course I changed the weathercock. The wind had been all the week north-east, and I turned the cock to south-west and rain before I reached Winchester. There had been birds, and Read had had some sport.

10th.—A fine gale of wind from the eastward. Had the punt up to Pennington, but as yet seeing no birds off at sea we would not go off in the wash on an uncertainty, so brought her back dry and comfortable. I shot a green scarfe shag with the cripple stopper, and had fine sport with him and my terrier; but lest the dog should swim his very heart out, I settled this crippled parson with my second barrel.

11th.—The gale abated and we had a fine day, in which I was at sea from nine till past six, and never found a bird on tide. We walked ashore to Sowley Pond, where we saw a few dunbirds, &c. Never discharged a gun, except a shot with which I got a heron, coming home.

12th.—Read crawled on the mud since midnight, and came home this morning with 7 wigeon. Though a strong north-easter, there was not a bird off to-day.

14th.—Had a precious day's excursion; not for sport, but business. Having received a note from Joe yesterday to say that my waggon would be in Southampton early this morning for a load of coals, and would bring there an old punt that I wanted and a new pianoforte that I had bought, I drove into Lymington, and then mounted the box of Judd's coach to Southampton because I particularly wanted to see my faithful old carter, John Reeves, who had irretrievably hooked himself into the service of the lawyer—that marplot of everyone and everything in the parish. Well, having done my business with John and some other commissions, the next thing was how to get the punt and piano to Keyhaven. I hired a little coaster for 15*s.* and away I went with my cargo about one o'clock, with every prospect of reaching Keyhaven about four or half-past; but, alas! the uncertainty of wind and water. In order to save the tide I was obliged to 'dine with Duke Humphrey,' and content myself with a few buns and a bottle of porter, that I dare not wait to touch till we had got clear of the harbour. Before we had gone far we were suddenly becalmed, and, in short, the result was we dare not attempt to land at Keyhaven, as we never got to off Hurst till near seven, and then in total darkness. We there dropped anchor nearly half a mile from the beach, and had the delightful option of either starving on board all night, or taking to the old punt, which was not caulked and therefore leaked like a basket, with the vessel's two huge oars by way of paddles. Preferring liberty on any terms, we trusted to Providence that we should gain the shore before the punt could fill, and off went I with the captain and his mate like three unfortunates escaping from a wreck. We reached the beach, ran up for help, and the only boat we could get was a little thing just fit for two men to row in. We went off to the vessel, got out the piano, and off we came with such a freight of us that I really expected every moment we should sink. However, we fetched Keyhaven, with an awful roll of the piano and the two heavy fellows who rowed me ashore. So much for anyone but a slave being condemned to make a trip in a coaster.

15*th.*—Sunday. Nothing occurred to-day, except we heard of the captain and his mate having 'held on' and 'lushed it' ashore all night, leaving the boy on board to satisfy his appetite with sleep, in a cold easterly wind. The boy volunteered to see the coast. Query, will he volunteer again?

16*th.*—Afloat all day; went about twenty-four miles, and never found a bird, though a beautiful northerly wind. Heard from the Itchen Ferry men, who came down to drag for oysters, that they had not seen a bird all the way from the Southampton river to off Lymington, and that the whole of the gunners at Southampton, who regularly come to our West Channel, had only brought in one bird among them during the whole of last week. The coast is ruined till there comes frost enough to bite one's nose off, and snow to bleach up all inland vegetation.

17*th.*—A westerly wind. Went out in the punt, without the great gun, merely to try a rifle, and could not even get a gull to shoot at. Had no other arms on board but the popgun, loaded with small shot for the chance of dunlins, and set close up to 3 wild ducks, which I peppered with this feeble concern, and all 3 of which I must have killed dead had I had the great gun on board. How ridiculous, and yet provoking, that the only shot all the week occurred when I had no proper gun to shoot with. But it always is so.

December 9th.—Having been worried out of sleep and appetite, I resolved on a few days' sea air before I returned to town ; so sent Monk, my coachman, on to Southampton last evening to have the mare and gig fresh and clean. Made for the eleven o'clock coach at Bullington, and, after wasting half an hour, found that both coaches had ceased running, and my only chance was to catch the one o'clock coach at Winchester, which I could do only by driving our slow sulky pony and butcher's cart about eight miles in the hour, and this I did, with five minutes to spare, by the persuasive argument of a blackthorn stick that I cut, as the only tool that would tell on the pony's buffalo hide. On my reaching Southampton, Monk, instead of being quite ready as ordered, had wandered away with a pot companion, and kept me waiting an hour all but three minutes; so, out of all patience, I was just driving off alone, leaving word for him to follow at his own expense per coach, as a salutary lesson for him, when he just met me turning the corner, with his face like that of a red lion, and his eyes blinking like an owl in the sun. I got to Keyhaven about seven, instead of four, as I ought to have done.

N.B.—I always change the weathercock when I go to the coast. I came off (not thinking about shooting this time) in a westerly wind, and before morning we had a north-easter and a hard black frost.

10*th*.—In the afternoon I shipped the great gun in the punt and took a cruise. It blew a heavy gale, so that I could not go far out, but I saw off at sea about a dozen geese, and a fine trip of wigeon, such as I had not seen before this season.

14*th*.—A calm day with a south-east wind ; took a rush-light breakfast, and started at daylight for a long cruise up to the mouth of the Beaulieu river. Bagged 8 wigeon : the first lot of birds I saw was 4, which I got close to, and bagged all of them with one barrel ; the second, a large company that were very wild, and into which I pulled both barrels, flying, and got 4 more ; if I had had large shot, proper for

150 yards, I think I should have knocked down 20. We did not get home till half-past six.

16*th.*—Went into Lymington with my punt having a few jobs to get done there, but never set eyes on a bird, though we had good weather. Fell in with a fleet of professional gunners, who had done nothing for this fortnight. Last night a stormy petrel flew against Hurst lighthouse, and was taken alive; I bought him for a shilling, and had him booked per coach to Leadbeater to stuff for my collection.

17*th.*—'Knocked off' for the present, and cleaned up and put away all the gear preparative to returning to town.

N.B.—Read was mud crawling every night, and during the whole time I was here brought in but 2 wigeon. We have to thank the mud crawlers for the ruin of our coast.

20*th.*—London. Sunday. Sadly disappointed. Had made up my mind to go and hear again my favourite preacher Dr. Dibdin, the Paganini of the parsons, who had through debts and difficulties been a long time absent, but my cold was so bad I dare not go to church, and was obliged to sit prisoner, with a poultice to my neck, and aching bones, all owing to yesterday's horrible woman, who would have a thorough draught in the coach in the coldest weather that had been felt for years. To-day we have frost and snow in right earnest; the very weather for geese, and even hoopers.

21*st.*—Splendid weather, and I much worse. The swelling in my neck quite insupportable, though I supposed it to be a mere boil. Went to Brodie, who pronounced it to be a carbuncle, and said it was the wisest thing I ever did to come to him just in time, or I might have lost my life, as Colonel Broughton did, by not having it opened in time. Sir Benjamin performed the operation immediately, and a pretty severe one it was, and then sent me home to be laid up for a day or two, with poultices &c., and with every hope of my getting well in the course of a week.

N.B.—How singular! Last year I was operated on upon

December 19, and laid up all Christmas, and this year on December 21 again for a totally different case. And both times during the only good wild-fowl frosts that we have had for some years.

27th.—Sunday. After church and some visits, I went to the Regent's Park to see the immense mob that were admitted for skating; and if all the cattle in Smithfield had enjoyed a month's run there, they could not have done more damage to the grass &c. than was caused by this free admission. The trees that had been white with powder-frost for eight days were now beginning to thaw, and the wind was getting to the west, which I told all the philosophers it would of course do when I was near getting to Keyhaven.

28th.—Left London per Southampton 'Telegraph' at a quarter past eight this morning, and drove up to the door at Keyhaven Cottage at a quarter past eight this evening, making the journey, as usual, in just twelve hours, and just 100 miles. A westerly wind.

N.B.—During the past week the sport has been excellent, though merely with ducks, mallards, and wigeon, as scarcely any geese or other more northerly birds had appeared, which was the best possible proof that the very severe weather would not last. And when the west wind set in, the country was, as usual, clear of all wild fowl.

31st.—A south-east wind. Went afloat, and saw nothing but a mallard.

1836

January.—I write this at Keyhaven, where I came just too late for the good weather, having been detained in town by illness.

2nd.—A fall of snow, and a sudden change of wind in the night, has brought down a fine show of birds, though they are wild and scattered, and consequently I could not kill many at a shot. But by working from morning till night, we brought in 12 wigeon, 4 mallards, 4 teal, 5 godwits, and 1 knot plover. I refused a shot at 5 pintails within forty yards, while setting up to about 150 wigeon, that I must have done wonders with had not 3 wretched curlews sprung from a creek and frightened them to sea.

3rd.—Sunday. The wind shifted back to the miserable west again. Read, our 'mud worm,' indulged in his hobby of 'launching' till after midnight, though brought in but 1 wigeon.

4th.—A tremendous gale from the west all night. Read got 3 wigeon before daylight, and we went off, on a forlorn hope, as far as we dare go, and I brought in 3 ducks and 3 mallards, which were 6 birds more than I expected. Out at night from ten till past one; but though a full moon and west wind, we had not tide enough to get near what few birds remained for the high water. Read never went to bed, but crawled on the mud till morning, and came in with 10 wigeon. We then went off for the whole day again, the 5th, but never saw a chance for sport, though out till dark. Miserably dull day for everything, except a rich jaw between mud crawler Read and Buckle, who met afloat after a previous quarrel.

6th.—Out from soon after eight till dark. A splendid calm for the open sea, so went about ten miles up, and landed near Gurnet Bay, in the most desolate part of the Isle of Wight; and, if I had had a dog, might have poached some game while two hours waiting for the ebb, which did nothing for us, as the swarms of birds that were here yesterday had shifted to Christchurch Bay; and, in short, we had a blank day, and brought home everything we took out, except the victuals.

7th.—A south wind, with heavy drizzling rain. Went up Channel to take a rope to Buckle, and lunched with him, in his floating den, on fried sprats. Put off from his craft and got 1 brent goose; a very long shot, and the only one I have had a shot at this year, as the geese appear to have forsaken our coast altogether. Coming home in a heavy rain, I had the great good luck to bag 6 pintails at a shot with the one barrel of the swivel gun, and in my life I never had so long a chase as I this day had with one of these birds. There were about 13 in the company, and I think I should have floored them all if the wet weather had not induced me to neglect loading the other barrel. Turned into bed from eight till ten. Off from eleven till four in the morning, but the birds all left the harbour directly there was water over the ground (their old trick, unless they are 'young comers,' or the weather is hard). So I proved that night shooting now is time and rest lost, except for a mud crawler like Read.

8th.—A wet day. Out in the evening, though saw nothing except a good show of wigeon at flight time, all of which flew too high, and appeared to be bound far to the eastward. Read crawled all night, and came in at daylight with 3 wigeon.

9th.—Another wet day. Went 'well breeched' for the evening flight, but the birds all went over in some fresh place, instead of where we saw them last night.

10th.—Sunday. A splendid hurricane from the east, and a right glorious fall of snow the whole day.

11th.—Out several hours before daylight, and Read like a madman with his confidence of an immense day; and, after all, there was not a bird to go after. The swarms of fowl that appeared (lost in the snow) yesterday had all gone out to Christchurch Bay, and, in short, we gave it up, and came home, in a dense fog, about twelve. I then proceeded to look at Sowley Pond, which had been black with fowl in the snow storm. Had a precious wet drive home, with the weather-cock south-west and a heavy gale. And thus ended the beautiful hard frost and snow that had raised our hopes of grand sport.

12th.—Out at daybreak, and again all the evening. Got but 4 wigeon, and did wonderfully well in killing even them.

14th.—A terrific westerly gale, and a blank day.

15th.—A most ferocious gale of wind from the west the whole night. We thought our house would come down; it literally shook our beds. About eight this morning the gale was beat down by heavy rain; it then moderated, and we went off, unluckily, just ten minutes too late for water, to one of the finest shots I should have ever had. We got nothing, and came in about twelve.

16th.—A sharp white frost, with a northerly wind and fine day. Out from daybreak till evening, and never got a chance for a fowl. Read, who was out all night, got 2 wigeon.

17th.—Sunday. A pinching white frost with a butterfly day.

18th.—A westerly gale and a blank day.

19th.—A sudden change from west to east. A few birds down, and with them a host of blundering blockheads from Itchen Ferry, who drove them to sea. Never fired a shot.

20th.—A south wind. Out all day, and found only 6, and got 3, brent geese, in the very middle of all the Southampton gunners. I should have got the other 3 with the other barrel had it not been that one of these fellows attempted to paddle up to them where they had pitched near their shot companions.

21st.—A south-west heavy gale, and a blank day. Boarded Buckle in the afternoon, and even he had not got a bird the whole week.

23rd.—A precious excursion. Up at five to pack and breakfast. Walked to Everton in a gale of wind and drizzling rain to mount Judd's coach at eight. Misinformed as to time, and was ten minutes too late; so had to tramp three long miles more (with a part of my things at my back, and Tommy Chissel carrying my trunk) in wind and rain to Lymington. Coach, of course, gone; no other conveyance till evening, so obliged to hire a fly, as soon as I had ascertained there were no letters for me at the post office. Just as I was preparing to start, with the fly at the door, the Keyhaven postman ran up to me with a basket, which I opened in great haste, and alongside a goose which came in it was a letter from Peter, to say he had received an extension of his leave, and was therefore ready to join me at Keyhaven. Well, I stood at the flyman's door for some minutes, hesitating whether to drive back to Keyhaven or on for Longparish; and, as I had some business there, decided on the latter in order to get rid of it. Went a good pace in order to be in Southampton by twelve to save Dalton's coach to Winchester, where my gig was to be in readiness. Got in a quarter before twelve, and floored again. No more Dalton, his coach had just stopped for the winter, and no conveyance till night except a hired one. So had to work on in a hack gig to Winchester, where I found Monk and the mare. After having walked the first five miles on a turnpike road, an inch deep in slush, and gone the other thirty miles with damp feet, and a shirt ringing wet with perspiration at the price of a shilling a mile, besides the drivers and gates, and in a day that no humane man would have turned out his dog in, I got to Longparish about half-past four.

24*th*.—Sunday. Shivering like a dog in a wet sack from the miserable damp and cold I had to undergo yesterday.

30*th*.—Met Colonel Sheddon of Lymington, who was delighted yet panic-struck to see me, as his son, in a letter received the previous day, had informed him of my being drowned off Lymington on Monday night, when I was at Longparish, playing duets with Bill Griesbach.

February 7th.—Keyhaven. Mild as April, and all the birds singing. This (being Sunday too) was no day for shooting, and the accounts of the gunning were miserable, as Read and his opponent Buckle by incessantly opposing each other had nearly banished the wild fowl, without getting anything worth their labour.

8*th*.—Took a cruise in the punt, to try my rifle, though

never got a chance, and get some sea air, but would not disgrace myself by putting the great gun together for nothing, so took 'old Fullerd' for the fun of popping at a passing 'parson' or bagging a few dunlins for a pudding. What should I see, however, but 9 geese, which happened to pitch on the mud 108 yards from where we had water. Up we went on a forlorn hope, and off I fired the gun, with the bare possibility of stopping one by some lucky shot, when, to my utter astonishment, down came 4 of them. One, however, recovered, after we had all but got him, and joined the company, but the other 3 geese we brought home. About two o'clock it set in a wet day, and coming home, we fell in with the other six, a splendid shot for a stanchion, but (for want of water only) a little too far for 'old Fullerd.' I tried them, but it was no go.

9th.—Out again for the day, and had reason to repent the want of the swivel gun. We got within a hundred yards of about 60 geese, and they all drew up in one solid cluster, with their necks stretched up like a bundle of asparagus. But just as I rose up to discharge the shoulder gun, they all sprung and dispersed into the wind. I fired after them and beat down 4, but it was so rough that after nearly filling the punt with the breakers in the shallow water, I bagged but 3 brent geese. We therefore decided on shipping the great gun to-morrow, though I suppose when we are 'well breeched' there will be no more chances for great sport.

10th.—Put off with the great gun in the afternoon, and saw about 70 geese off Pennington Spit, but there came on such a gale and heavy sea that we were too happy to give them up, and make our escape home, through Stivers Creek.

12th.—The large company of geese were in view with a glass from our window, off Pennington Spit. Off we went in a strong breeze, and down we dropped on them, but on approaching the flock we got into such a heavy hollow sea that we had more to mind the breakers than the birds. I blew off at them at about 250 yards, and knocked down 1, but we were obliged to raise the siege and pull into shelter, with about a hogshead of water on board, and make a vow that we would abandon the cruise for these birds till we had either 'water over the ground,' or a more moderate time for 'the outside.' Any punt but mine would have been filled and washed on 'the edge,' with a comfortable sousing of gear and all hands.

13*th*.—The first fine moderate morning since I came, and, as the devil would have it, that stupid scarecrow, Dan'l Paine of Itchen had arrived last night at the Hurst pothouse, to disturb our harbour at daybreak, which he did so effectually by popping at ox-birds that, before the water was up for a stanchion, not a living creature remained. We were therefore 'done out of' everything. I, however, saved my blank by bringing in 1 duck and 1 golden-eye, the only two shots I had, except killing 1 superb spotted diver with the popgun. In the evening I went to a late dinner, with Mr. and Mrs. West, at Arwood's Lodge, a stretch of friendship that very few are favoured with by me, and as a matter of course I paid rather dearly for my pleasure. I did not leave till about twelve o'clock, when I had to drive home, about three miles, in the gig, and it was so dark that, for the greater part of the way, I was obliged to walk in front, and literally feel the way lest we should be lost or capsized among the innumerable ditches and pitch-dark turnings on this ram's-horn road, and to make it all the more agreeable we had no lamps, and there came on a cold thick drizzling rain which we had to weather with that virtue, patience, all the way to Keyhaven at the pace of a 'black job.' I of course caught cold. Here is another specimen of the delights of dining out in winter in the country, a thing I generally avoid as I would a mad dog.

15*th*.—Fine weather, and off all day, but nothing to be seen.

16*th*.—Not a chance to be seen.

17*th and* 18*th*.—Such a ferocious north-easter that not a boat could row on end, and I booked for London on the

19th. Here again we have the very essence of my turning the weathercock.

19th.—Arrived in town by the 'Eclipse,' almost perished with cold, and in the finest gunning weather we have had this year—a black frost, and a gale from the north-east. And by way of a pleasant home to leave for in the very fine weather I had been praying to have, I was assailed with a concatenation of annoyances in private and other matters that made my situation like that of a toad under a harrow, or a cat among a pack of dogs.

20th.—On the tramp, and at work with head and heels all day.

21st.—Called on the park keeper relative to presenting to the commissioners a beautiful goose that I had spared from the first shot I made at Keyhaven, and kept in my garden the whole time I was last there, and brought up with me, as we could no longer stand the damage he did to the cabbage plants. He lived on the grass, but was for ever marching about, and his feet were the ruin of everything.

22nd.—Turned the goose off on the ice in the Regent's Park this morning. Accounts in town of the awful devastation on the northerly coasts occasioned by the late unprecedented hurricanes, and among them the wreck of a kind and worthy man, named Paxton, whom I had just got a situation for at Scarborough, and who was on his passage from Lymington, where I had just taken leave of him. The crew, however, were saved, and let me hope, at least, some of the property too, though this I could not learn at Lloyd's, but the secretary promised to send me word when known.

29th.—Had the satisfaction to learn, from Lloyd's Norfolk agent, that Paxton and his property were saved from the wreck. So busy that I was obliged to go about all day with blue pills in me. Busy in the afternoon about Joe Manton's tombstone, for which I was solicited to write the inscription.[1]

[1] To the memory of Joseph Manton, who died, universally regretted, on the

In the evening I went to the new theatre of our unrivalled vocalist Braham, which I consider as decidedly the most chaste and neatest I ever saw at home or abroad.

March 2nd.—Mounted the box of the 'Telegraph,' and ran down to Keyhaven. I merely did this to recover myself after the worry I had in town; but, hearing there were still some geese about, and my punt not being yet taken from her moorings, I had my gun put together.

3rd.—A south-wester, and very wet all the morning. Went out for a few hours in the afternoon, but could expect nothing, as the coast was lined with an army of periwinkle pickers, who were preparing for a vessel, that was to sail for London to-night, fifteen tons of winkles; and may they get a quick passage out of our country, say I.

4th.—Out all day and went a long distance, but never saw anything, though heard that a great many geese had been seen last week, and that 3 had been killed by that bungler, Dan'l Paine, of Itchen. In the evening there set in another heavy gale from the south-west.

8th.—A fine northerly breeze, so we sailed in the punt all the way to off Leap. But the late gales had swept every fowl off the coast, and we came home just before dark with a blank day, though after a most delightful and healthy sail.

N.B.—My great gun was loaded last Thursday morning, and though it remained afloat till this afternoon (Tuesday) in such seas, rains, and hurricanes as we seldom see, yet on discharging the barrels, both went off as well and as smart as a clean gun the 1st of September.

9th.—Went on a miserable though satisfactory expedition. Having sent on an old punt to Christchurch, I started very

29th day of June, 1835, aged 69. This humble tablet is placed here by his afflicted family, merely to mark where are deposited his mortal remains. But one everlasting monument to his unrivalled genius is already established in every quarter of the globe by his celebrity as the greatest artist in firearms that ever the world produced; as the founder and the father of the modern gun trade; and as a most scientific inventor in other departments, not only for the benefit of his friends and the sporting world, but for the good of his King and country.

early this morning in the gig with Read, to row all over and inspect the harbour, from the Haven House at Mudeford up to the town of Christchurch. We started in a humbugging white frost, which appeared all very well for our purpose, as a dead calm suited it best; but no sooner had we got to within about three miles of Mudeford than there set in the most beastly gale of wind, with heavy rain, that the clouds could vomit up, and this continued for the whole day without one moment's intermission. Determined not to be bullied by the weather, after driving ten miles of heavy road, we got into the punt, with two shoulder guns, and went all over the harbour, till we landed in the town of Christchurch, where I had some fun at hearing of my own fame from the barber bird-stuffer and others who knew me not, but from whence we could not return against the torrent of water that the wind had brewed up. So we left the punt, and tramped by land, in water boots, two miles, with all our gear at our backs, and then drove home to Keyhaven in one eternal torrent of rain and raging blast of wind. But we were repaid for our misery by finding the harbour such as to be well worth trying on a future season, or even driving over to with a shoulder gun any fine day.

10*th.*—A strong westerly wind and rain nearly all day again. Busy taking the great punt and gun into store, and cleaning up and putting away all the gear thereunto belonging; as every fowl has now left our coast, and we have only to 'knock off' for the season.

Game &c. killed in the season up to March 15th, 1836 (a general failure all over the coast, and every gunner in disgust; the geese appear to be banished altogether): 130 partridges, 1 hare, 3 rabbits, 3 pheasants, 21 snipes. Total, 158 head. 20 ducks, 54 wigeon, 6 pintails, 6 teal, 2 golden-eyes, 8 geese, 13 plover. Total, 109. Game, 158; fowl, 109. Grand total, only 267.

24*th.*—London. Went down to Kidbrooke to see Mr.

J——, but as he was from home, I gained nothing for my lost morning but a trial of the new Deptford railroad, by which I returned, and which I found far inferior to that between Liverpool and Manchester, because the road was rather on the curve and the wheels were too high, from which circumstances the motion was not so easy as that on the other railroad, and our pace was much slower, as we were eight and a half minutes doing a little more than two miles, while on the other railroad we went about double the pace, and with half the motion.

April 25th.—To London from Southampton by the 'Eclipse' coach. We had for a travelling companion the celebrated Lord Stuart de Rothsay, who generally works up and down outside this coach in the garb of an old skipper, and either in the name of his valet or with no name at all. Though I remembered him at Eton, and had once dined with him when an ambassador, I also preserved my *incog.* lest I should have annoyed him by a recognition.

29th.—Winter. Frost and snow. Alone from morning till night, and I have not passed so pleasant a day for these fifteen years; what with writing, reading, and strapping hard at my long-lost music, I could have stayed up till daylight next morning. 'A man ought never to be so little alone as when he is alone.' I this day received a letter from Mr. Black, the great publisher in Edinburgh, offering me twenty guineas a sheet to write for the 'Encyclopædia Britannica,' but my engagements with Messrs. Longman & Co. and the extreme pressure of private business obliged me to decline this handsome offer and high honour.

May 13th.—Went to Longparish to see and decide how to proceed with the new lake that I have begun, and also to get some more of my rents in.

14th.—Longparish. A cold white frost this morning. Tried a fresh-bored duck gun ('Old Egg'), and found that it shot one-third closer, and with double the strength, since Lancaster rebored the calibre to my order. Having done this, and all the business I could do for the present, I indulged in an afternoon's 'spree' with Mr. W. Griesbach. We dragged four baskets of trout out of Mole's Hole; shot as many rooks as we could tell what to do with, and ended the evening with a 'flare up' at the bats, and then a batch of duet playing.

15th.—Ran down to Keyhaven to see my stone walk complete, which proved to surpass anything I ever saw, and to be the admiration of the whole country. This is one of the many things I was thought a madman for attempting, and afterwards worshipped for having done. What short-sighted asses most people are!

21st.—Drove to Christchurch to see Charles Tucker about doing up my old punt I had left there, and then drank tea and spent the evening at Mudeford, in order to see the salmon fishing, but was here disappointed, as not a fish was caught while I was there, though several had been taken within these three days, and some 20-lb. fish. Old Joy of Christchurch had, however, a royal catch of mullet, of which I took a few. He caught 14 cwt. in one evening. I finished my day with a drive along the beautiful shore of Mudeford, and an inspection of an old steam packet that is hauled up on an eminence and let into the cliff, by way of a fancy summer house for Lord Stuart de Rothsay, who employs a caretaker and showman to take care of the concern.

28th.—Returned to London, half starved with the cold winterly weather, and much gratified with meeting the beautiful procession of King's birthday mails, as well as with Williams's dexterous driving of our coach through the crowd occasioned by these and the equipages returning from the Drawing Room.

29th.—Influenza everywhere, owing to burning sun and chilling north-easters. Vegetation all but annihilated. Came home from bank in steam omnibus in half the time of the others. Nothing could go better.

June 30th.—London. Up to the end of this month I had scarcely a moment to enjoy a meal; what with bother, business &c. I was seldom in bed till one, and awake again writing down memorandum at daylight. The heat was so intense that at night one could not even bear a sheet as a cover. *Quantus equis, quantus adest viris sudor.* Horace, hem!

July 1st.—We went this evening to the benefit of the tenth muse, or goddess of the stage, Malibran, and so intense was the heat in the boxes that my very skin was stained from the dye of my blue coat. So no more benefits for me this season.

5th.—The weather has become so intensely hot and oppressive that it is even difficult to breathe. Talk of winter, it's all nonsense; this is the weather to make a man a cripple.

6th.—I hopping all over the town in pain that made me holloa out. All our places booked for leaving town. What with pain, packing, bill-paying, and bustle, the confusion was awful. Every servant so occupied there was no one to help the cripples, and the doctor not to be found, and most probably again in a sponging house.

7th.—So bad that I was obliged to ring up Charles to dress me in time to be stuck on the box of the 'Telegraph;' in short, a regular second edition of the old journey from Talavera to Lisbon, when I spent a week among the mountains with a bullet in my carcase. Got helped into a jolting fly on my arrival at Lymington, and crawled out of it at Keyhaven about eight this evening.

8th.—Having scarcely been able to lie otherwise than on my back all night, I was so stiff to-day as to be a complete cripple, the rheumatism having, as I before forgot to mention, set into the very part where I was wounded.

18th.—The worst Overton Fair for many years; and I was

obliged to think myself very lucky to sell eight score of lambs at 16*s.* 6*d.* instead of 1*l.* 6*s.*

August 1*st.*—Mounted the 'Red Rover' for a few days' visit to Lord Rodney at Alresford. A house full of company, and all the luxuries that could possibly be thought of.

3*rd.*—Left the dinner table about ten for a couple of hours' eel fishing, to be shown the way they fish at Naples. It is to have a row of lamps in front of a broad punt, by which you see the eels when they cannot see you, and then kill them with a spear. The night was too rough, and hardly dark enough; so that the bailiff despaired of my seeing enough to learn the plan; but, in spite of all, I did manage to kill 1 fine eel, and had a stroke at 2 or 3 more, which I could not see sufficiently to kill. Lord Rodney tells me he has killed 30 or 40 sometimes in a few hours' cruise. Nothing can be more novel or beautiful than this pastime; and it was so clean and dry that I need not have unshipped my dandy dinner dress.

4*th.*—Left Alresford, after having as usual received the greatest kindness and hospitality, and drove home by an improved road through Lord Ashburton's park. We came home on 13 miles of beautiful road instead of having to travel 21 miles of hilly turnpike with two gates to pay, and a heavy drag through the whole town of Winchester.

5*th.*—Busy all day with farmers, lawyers, horse dealers, clods, workmen, and other bores.

7*th.*—Sunday. Sailed to Yarmouth, and heard a parson who could preach, the Rev. George Burrard.

19*th.*—Keyhaven. Lord Chief Justice Tindall walked down from Newlands expressly for the purpose of seeing my punts, guns, and gear, which he entered into the spirit of with observations worthy of a judge; and went away evidently much pleased with my divers originalities.

20*th.*—After a series of fine days, of which we profited by seeing everything in the neighbourhood, both by sea and land, we had this day a westerly wind and rain. In the evening it cleared up, and we saw a splendid frigate put back owing to bad weather, and anchor off Yarmouth. Off we went to see her. It proved to be the 'Madagascar,' 46 guns, whose captain, Sir John Peyton, knew both Mrs. Hawker and myself, and whose hospitality was unbounded. The band played while we took tea, and the middies waltzed and quadrilled. We then adjourned to a splendid cabin aft with a capital Broadwood piano; in short, we had a regular merry soirée on board, and did not leave till past nine, when the marine drums struck up their watch-setting. We had a contrary wind back, and through breaking an oar and other reverses did not get home till near midnight.

22nd.—Went in the yacht of Colonel Sheddon and Mr. Hare to a grand regatta at Cowes. The King's prize was won easy by Mr. Lyons's yacht, the 'Breeze.'

31st.—Proceeded by the midday coach for Longparish; and, on the coach setting me down, I had the mortification to find that, while I was waylaid by two loungers in Winchester, a green sub. of some padnagging regiment had walked off with my portmanteau instead of his own; so I was obliged to send the only man I had for everything, in consequence of the harvest, off to Winchester with a cart and the very horse I wanted for to-morrow; and luckily he got back with my trunk a few minutes before ten at night. But the green man had the worst of it, as all his shooting things were gone off to Reading.

CHAPTER XXIX

1836

September 1*st*.—A dry gale of wind all day, and not one breath of scent. Birds ran away from almost every point, and were as wild as hawks. Nothing could have been done, but for the thin barley, in which we severely punished them in the afternoon; and though at one o'clock I had only got 6 birds, our day wound up with just 42 partridges.

N.B.—My last 3 birds I shot so late that I could not see the gun, so that I never was so hard run to get a 'butchers' halloo,' or three cheers for 20 brace. One thing I did that was worthy of my youngest days; I charged a covey against a high wind till they dropped exhausted, when I sprung from my horse, à la Ducrow, without stopping, and bagged one with the first, and two with the second barrel, leaving the horse to proceed *solus* at full speed, till Mr. Griesbach charged after him on the grey and caught him. Under all circumstances we consider this as one of our most miraculous days on record.

2*nd*.—Friday. A wet day, a glorious godsend against the blockheads who can't resist driving the birds the second day. Fine in the evening, when the green-livered son of a —— the lawyer turned out 'full drive,' so I flew out, flanked him, and bagged 8 brace.

3*rd*.—Another splendid day. I bagged 30 partridges besides 4 lost; and Joe Hawker, who was with me, and this day shot beautifully, got 27. Our combined bag was 60 head.

We worked round the lawyer's grand party as coopers would work round a barrel.

N.B.—On finding I had 29 birds, I slaved hard to make up a round number (that sounds fuller in the mouth), but without success, and had given it up as it grew dark ; when, on leaving the very last field, a covey sprung from the feed, and I shot one through the head, which fell and was bagged at about 80 yards. To-morrow being Sunday, I was up till past midnight—game distributing, note writing &c. though tired as a dog, and had not dined till near ten.

4th.—Sunday. Heard all their bulletins, and found I had 'beat' all the country 'hollow.'

5th.—A wet morning, and a gale of wind all day. Went out quietly at twelve, and came home to a late dinner with 13 partridges and 2 hares, besides having lost 4 birds in the barley, and never fired but one blank shot the whole day. I shot capitally.

N.B.—The birds are now so wild that we may take our leave of all further chance for great bags ; and, having now supplied all my requisitions, I shall either give up shooting or merely ride out to get a few birds when wanted.

7th.—Got 20 partridges, and never fired but one blank shot.

Game bagged the first week (I was out but three whole days and one half day): 103 partridges, 2 hares, 1 snipe. Total, 106 head, which, with 80 birds, besides 2 hares, 2 snipes, and 1 rabbit, got by Joe, who shot every day, makes the combined lot 191 head—exclusive of an unusual proportion shot and lost in standing corn for want of scent as well as of a retriever.

10th.—A splendid little 'spree' with the lawyer. While I was detained with people on business till half-past twelve, he bombarded all the best beat that is now left for me to shoot on, and had planted his marker under my firs to watch the birds that he had made up his mind to shoot in my tenant's corn ; when, at about two o'clock, I made a rapid charge of cavalry, by which I completely cut him out, and at five came home with 20 partridges (besides 2 lost), 1 hare, and 1 quail, the only one I have seen or heard of this year ; all of which he had driven from his own ground, and most of which I killed before his marker's face, and without missing a shot, which was extraordinary, because I was so unwell that I was scarcely able to fag. This is one of the prettiest little bits of shooting I ever made in all my sporting career.

12th.—In one constant row like a house on fire from the moment I got up till three in the afternoon, when I rode over to Bullington to announce to the keeper the surrender of Mr. Gore's lease and do other business at that place. I took a gun in my hand, but it appeared useless, as all the country was cleared, and it blew a bleak blast from the north. All I shot at therefore and got was 1 hare, so I rode home to prepare for blowing out some neighbours with a haunch of venison ; and, just at the last hour, who should I see but my old friend the lawyer, so I made a rapid charge to leeward of him, and picked up 9 partridges, besides 1 lost.

21st.—Keyhaven. Went across to Mr. Guy's 'mudlands,' and got 3 snipes and 3 jack snipes. I never saw so many jack snipes in so small a space before ; about a dozen kept getting up under my feet one after the other. But I was so unwell that I missed several shots, and was obliged to go home instead of following up the sport. If I had been well, and had had two double guns and one good dog, I really think that, by working all day, I might have got 15 or 20 couple ; a phenomenon for Keyhaven, where 3 couple in a day is thought brilliant sport.

22nd.—Tried the bog again ; but, as is always the case, the great flight of snipes had taken their departure.

28th.—I read to-day with tears of the death of the unrivalled Malibran ; and I also lost my beautiful Newfoundland dog, of the distemper.

October 1st.—A most ferocious gale with a deluge of rain. But no disappointment to me, as my spies of last evening had looked round the feed near every wood or hedgerow I have, and not a single pheasant was to be seen or heard of.

7th.—Went down to Chatham and found my son Peter, thank God, in excellent health. Had a pour of rain all night and all day, and felt sadly damaged by cold and being harassed. I dined with him and slept at a kind of canteen hotel, where the noise was awful, all the windows rattling with the wind and rain; a church clock so close that it vibrated my very bed, and at daylight the bugle boys of 'the Rifles' came to learn their lesson under my window.

8th.—'Turned out' at seven, breakfasted at eight, took a hasty inspection of the dockyard till near ten. Then mounted the coach, when the rain set in again, and got worked up to Blackheath; sent on my trunk to town and ran down the dirty fields for an hour's heavy business at Kidbrooke. Then ran down to Deptford and just caught the coach; worked my way through the borough just in time to send off Peter's money before Coutts' had closed (to-morrow being Sunday, and Peter to march for embarkation before post on Monday), and then flew up to Dorset Place just in time to answer an important letter by the last moment of the post. A list of commissions ready for me as long as a carpenter's bill, but too exhausted to do more than a few of them this wet night.

9th.—Sunday. Quite unwell and without appetite; but no rest for me, even on the Sabbath day, for the moment I had got out of church I was obliged to cab it, omnibus it and run it the whole morning, to do calls on business with people that I could only catch, or find time for, on a Sunday.

10th.—On incessantly from seven in the morning till ten at night, and only a quarter of an hour to each meal. Did more in a day than all my servants would in a week. Peter countermanded, and another officer allowed per Adjutant-

General to take his place, so he will return to the depot at Perth. What a godsend that I did not give 300*l.* for his exchange, as he wished!

11*th.*—London. One hour's pleasure while here—Moscheles played me his new pieces when I called to see him.

17*th.*—Longparish. Hunted like a wild boar from eight in the morning till a six o'clock dinner. I was literally bombarded with a rushing of people on business all in a heap. Surveyor about my plans for letting the farms. The doctor about my health. Buckle, just arrived from the coast, about punts and guns. Keele about divers jobs. Dance to settle his rent, and argue for divers more things wanted. The parson, on a mission from the hospital, and his brother, to see my 'lions.' Lieutenant Criswick on a visit (who had not met me for years). J—— on divers jobs. M—— about several items. L—— about some bills. Mr. Earle, the lawyer, with all his memorandums of agreements for tenants, business about the pond, and divers letters to write for the post. Worst of all, 2 pheasants in the wood, and obliged to send Joe to kill them, which he happily did, I not having one minute in the whole day, and even losing my music with Langstaff, who was all adrift without me. This they call amusement. Lord deliver me from the delights of a country clod squire. On again after dinner with persecution and botheration, and in short was not in bed till one o'clock in the morning, and obliged to wind up with a pill, though booked for more business to-morrow.

Memorandum of game &c. killed this season: 135 partridges, 1 quail, 4 hares, 10 snipes. Total, 150. Coast birds, 10 godwits, 3 knot plover. Total, 13. Grand total, 163 head.

N.B.—Had no time for shooting.

18*th.*—Prisoner from illness and slave with business. A partridge pitched in our lawn, and I walked down in my great coat, and made a brilliant shot at him.

19*th.*—A couple of wigeon pitched by my pond before I

was up, and I sent Buckle with my right barrel, that was left loaded yesterday, to blow them over, which he easily did and brought them in. All day I was baited again, with people of six different trades. 1 cock pheasant was heard of, and I went and bagged him after a 3 hours' chase, for which loss of time I had to lose all the comfort of my dinner. *Mais n'importe*, as I've no appetite.

20th.—Busy all day completing my new-invented paddles for the punt, which worked beautifully, though I have my doubts as to whether the birds will stand them better than sculling.

27th.—I got to Keyhaven to-day about eight, and found a delightful relief from business, and a fine change of air, though, as I never yet failed to do, I turned the weathercock from a lovely north-east to a dirty westerly gale. Heard that there had been a good show of wigeon and geese last week, so put the 'Petrel' punt afloat, and cleaned up all, in hopes of fair weather to try for a shot. On all the afternoon, and got everything for gunning put together and in order for the season.

29th.—A tremendous gale of wind all day from the north with a little sleet and snow. The very weather we are glad to see, though dare not venture out in, and so now let us hope to have not only leisure but weather for birds.

31st.—Out on tide all day and never got a shot; as an Itchen blackguard, yclept Dan'l Paine, had employed himself all yesterday to drive away every flock of birds that had collected here, and he kept banging about all the Sabbath day for 1 goose and 1 plover. I'll 'serve him out' for it with a threat of the penalty if he thus annoys us again.

November 8th.—Longparish. Got a half-holiday to-day; and started with my unrivalled 'Paganini' gun and old rat-catcher Siney to try our wood about two o'clock, but our day ended in a 'chapter of accidents,' owing to the first head of game started—a gigantic wild cat that ran to earth in a badger hole. To begin, I had a tremendous fall and broke the splendid and beautifully fitting stock of Paganini, which was worse than any injury to myself short of a broken bone. We then had a battle of dogs, in which old Hillery's sheep dog was all but killed; we then heard the screams of old Hillery's boy, who was all but killed by his ferocious old father for joining us; and the day ended with a three hours' digging for the cat, which was at last got at, and fought its way through the whole pack of dogs and mounted a tree. Charles Castleman then ran home for Siney's old musket, and blew the infernal old 'warmunt' out of the tree and brought her home in triumph. She weighed above 12 lb.

10*th*.—On from morning till night, with about a dozen active fellows well primed with beer, weathering some heavy showers, at planting round my pond; and it was like magic, the rapid change we made in the appearance of the place. I had to gallop backward and forward to the men cutting stakes and pulling trees in our wood; and while the men were at dinner, the only hour I could spare, I rode to the bog and found 4 snipes, 3 of which I got.

29*th*.—Keyhaven. The most savage hurricane I ever beheld. Went in water boots to view the terrific sea, which ran as high as a church; and such was the hurricane that the noise of the waves was completely silenced by the wind. The sea had made a breach in the beach, and we prepared 'all hands' to remove property for a flood, as in 1802; but, providentially, the wind shifted so far in as to prevent any further apprehension of serious consequences.

December 6th.—Longparish. I had the luck to find that I had sustained no very serious damage by the late unprecedented hurricane, that has laid so many places in ruins, and caused the loss of so many lives in both town and country as well as all over the coast. It was quite awful to see the damage on each side of the road all the way from Lymington to some miles beyond Southampton.

21st.—Up before daylight, and opened the flood hatches of my new pond by ten o'clock for the first time; and the effect of the pond when flooded, with the little waterfalls, amply repaid all my long trouble by answering to a focus in every respect, and even surpassing my expectations in its splendid appearance.

22nd.—On all day in Southampton. Went over in the new floating bridge to Itchen, and spent a delightful evening at the pianoforte with the Apollo of the place, Mr. William Griesbach.

24th.—Busy with solicitor and banker at Andover. Finished the new punt and finished the pond and all the inclosure; and this evening (that of my birthday) paid off every bill, and discharged all the workmen employed for this pond and inclosure, so that to-morrow, Christmas Day, I can look at this greatest improvement that has ever been made on the estate, and fairly call it my own property, as well as my own invention.

25th.—Sunday and also Christmas Day. Splendid frost and heavy snow. Crazy to be off to the coast.

26th.—The severest frost and heaviest fall of driving snow that I have seen for several years. Monk went off in advance for Keyhaven at two this morning, and, as all this day has turned out, with a drive that could only be surpassed by a Russian campaign. Everything, and even the pond, frozen over; so we finished our 8 months and 3 days' hard labour just in time, as the severe weather set in Christmas Day, the very day after the work was completed and the men paid off.

This afternoon the snow was in all the by-roads level with the hedges, and consequently in many places eight feet deep. No coaches passed, and all travelling stopped. A gale of wind from the north-east, and many degrees colder than I ever felt it in all the course of my life. Absolutely petrifying. My following Monk for Keyhaven to-day was impossible; and I have no guess how far he got before the overwhelming snow hurricane came on, though he started with hard roads and fair hard weather.

27th.—The only coach that passed to-day was the mail from London, which had to work over a bridge near here by the help of shovels. My boat lashed on the boat carriage, and I 'all hot' to be at Keyhaven; but no prospect of getting out of prison. Snow eight feet deep on the turnpike.

28th.—Imitated the only man I condescend to imitate—Buonaparte. A second Moscow business, though without the failure. The turnpike from near Sutton to Winchester being, for six or eight miles, up to the tops of the hedges filled with snow averaging seven feet deep, I started a direct steeplechase for Winchester by crossing the turnpike at the only passable place, and then taking my boat on the carriage across the fields like a foxhunt, avoiding the turnpike as death and destruction, though keeping it in view as a beacon of direction. I had twelve men altogether, and every hedge we came to, we had to cut through a block of snow about six or eight feet high; then cut the hedge through and assist the carriage over it with all hands, and then drive away over about half a mile of clear arable country, where we could proceed above four miles an hour. My man Charles and I took it by turns to gallop forward on a rough-shod fast horse, and, with one pioneer behind, to probe and ascertain the next safe breach to be made, while the rest of the troop were cutting the previous one. Nothing had passed. Everyone defied me, and swore I was mad. Had we failed, the Lord help us; as I doubt if we could have been quite sure of completing our retreat, when within two miles of Winchester, before dark. At last we came to the grand difficulty, an impassable dyke and a wood, when I, who was in advance as pioneer and surveyor, was hailed by a gentleman shooting; so I advanced towards him, and he directed us all one field to the right, where we had only to cut through for about ten yards in five feet of snow, and then enter the turnpike road at about a mile and a quarter from Winchester, where there had been a levy *en masse* to clear the snow in order to rescue Parson Dallas, who had been blocked there in his carriage, and could only be saved by this great undertaking. We then entered the town of Winchester in glorious triumph, to the utter astonishment of everyone who heard of us; and after giving my old horse the good cheer he deserved, as well as all the men (a man should always take care of his horse first), I drove comfortably on to Southampton, where I left him for the night to follow with the boat carriage, and proceeded by the 'Tally-ho' coach to Keyhaven, where I arrived safe, after all my unparalleled difficulties, about ten o'clock at night Thanks to God for my safety, and for having done what has perhaps never been done before, at all events among the Hampshire hogs.

N.B.—I had only time to swallow two buns and a glass of beer, as the only half-hour I had in Southampton was to run about, on commissions, in water boots, in which, by the way, I had travelled all the way from Longparish, and nothing like them to keep one from cold.

29*th.*—Longparish. Castleman brought in the boat carriage and horse about one o'clock, after being detained so long at the custom house (for the licence) that I was afraid some accident had happened to prevent the perfect success of the expedition. I could not get afloat till near three, when it was very rough. The new punt answered beautifully, though I only used her as a following boat, because I took the grand set-out of all, the 'Petrel.' I got one little shot only, and brought in 4 wigeon and 1 scaup duck; for we had just time only to make a beginning and get back before it was 'pitch dark.'

30*th.*—Very severe weather. Plenty of birds off at sea, but too rough to attempt getting there. Fired but one very long shot, and got 2 wigeon.

31*st.*—Weather so severe that the mud was frozen, in consequence of the tides (being just now at the 'dead of the neap') not flowing over it, and the birds were all at sea feeding on the floating weeds. Too much sea to shoot in the Channel, so that there was this day no sport for a punt; and last night not a chance for Read with his 'launching.' I went out about one o'clock, and all I saw was 14 geese, at which I made a capital shot while bobbing on the waves. I pulled off one barrel at them (with mould shot) and knocked down 8. A pretty little shot to finish the old year, and, please God, to lead to success in the new one.

1837

January 2nd.—Began the new year very well. Read mud-launched from two till dawn and brought in 11 wigeon; and I went outside of Hurst, and brought in 17 wigeon.

3*rd.*—No fowl to-day. Read had no chance with his nightly mud crawl, and a little shift of wind had driven the birds westward. My gun missed fire at the geese. But I came home early in order to despatch baskets of fowl for his Majesty and others.

4*th.*—A mild, calm day. Off at sea from morning till the afternoon, and then in the creeks with my new punt, which answers beautifully. Brought home 19 wigeon and 4 geese; 15 the first shot, 4 the second shot; and the geese with the shoulder gun from a creek, where I had to launch and then crawl for an hour. I never had such a filthy, laborious job, and never in my life made so long a shot with a shoulder gun. There were five punts and boats innumerable off in the mirror calm, but not a bird did any of them get, except, I believe, 'nabbing' a few of my cripples.

5*th.*—A south wind. Too rough to go off in Channel for wigeon, and no chance for geese to-day, so all I got was 6 birds.

6*th.*—A westerly gale and heavy rain, with high tides.

Dropped down to off Lymington, and had a shot with one barrel of the swivel gun only; picked up 9 wigeon, and let some more go, rather than risk my life by facing the breakers. I never made a better shot in my life, considering I had scarcely more than two dozen birds to shoot at.

7th.—9 geese and 1 wigeon in two shots, as it blew so hard I was obliged to abandon half my dead birds, rather than run a risk of being swamped by following them to sea. A strong westerly wind with fine tides, and a good show of geese, though extremely wild. Read has 'launched' every night, and never got a bird.

9th.—Gave up my whole tide for shooting to the pursuit of a splendid eagle that appeared off Hurst. I had all but got him, when a lubber rushed out with a musket and scared him away. He, however, returned in a few hours, and gave me a second chance by sitting on Hurst beach within range of my great gun while afloat, but the baker drove by and put him up, when he flew several miles westward. I therefore came home, much disappointed, and left word with the boys to hoist me a signal if he appeared, as I found he had been seen three days in succession within a few hundred yards of the same place.

10th.—Tremendous wind and rain all night and all day. Nothing more heard about the eagle. Busy till two rectifying gear and cleaning up. Lots of geese off, but no getting at them in the rain, which always makes them restless. Put off for an hour or two, and got 2 wigeon.

11th.—Gale turned to dead calm and nipping white frost with north wind. Every fellow turned gunner, and no chance to be got from the birds being so disturbed. Just saved my blank by bagging an extraordinary fine old cock wigeon with the 'cripple stopper,' and had another distant view of the eagle, hovering off the Isle of Wight; and, no doubt, driven from his old haunt here by the rabble of poppers afloat at Hurst.

12th.—Out long before daylight, but not so much as a little pop shot to be seen, though hundreds of birds were travelling over, cannon-shot high. In about eleven, when a most savage south-wester set in, and peppered away its deluge of heavy rain.

13th.—Gale of wind and rain all night, and nearly all this day.

14th.—Sudden change from west to a cold north gale. No water inside. Too much sea off. Fired but one shot, and that with the shoulder gun at about 100 yards, and just saved my blank by bagging 1 goose.

15th.—The eagle came again on the beach, as if he knew it was Sunday.

16th.—Out from daylight till dark, and just saved my blank with 1 mallard; not a wigeon to be seen. Read mud-crawled all night, and never heard a bird.

18th.—2 geese; the only shot I got, and that at above 200 yards, besides 2 more that got away. Not a wigeon or other fowl to be seen. But Read at last, about midnight, got a shot on the mud, and bagged 9 wigeon.

21st.—Longparish. Never was there so much illness as now. Twenty-six people lying dead at Southampton of the influenza.

22nd.—Sunday. Confined to my bed from last evening till this afternoon with this influenza.

23rd.—Half the village and three-fourths of my men thrown out of work by this infernal disorder.

24th.—Well enough to get out, though very weak from the influenza. I got on the pony and rode to the common, where I found 7 snipes, and never left one to tell the story. No bad work for a fellow scarcely able to crawl.

25th and 26th.—Still poorly. Incessant cold, then raw, rotten rain, and almost everybody more or less unwell.

27th to 30th.—Continued rotten weather, and this influenza everywhere, though I got better.

31st.—I started for the coach, and this evening arrived at

Keyhaven, hoping to get into a healthy change of air. But, on my arrival on the coast, I found that since I left the sickness had been even worse than inland, and the deaths far more numerous. Read, his family, all the tradesmen, preventive men, coasters, in short, everyone has been or is now suffering from the universal influenza.

February 4th.—The summer weather changed to a stiff easterly wind; so I put the great gun in the 'Petrel,' and tried another cruise. Fell in with 12 geese, and gave them both barrels while tossing on a heavy sea; knocked down 2 with the first, and 4 with the second barrel. We then emptied several gallons out of the punt, got dry mats &c. and sallied off again, when we saw above 100 more geese; but such was the sea that we dare not attempt to shoot any more this afternoon.

6th.—Having sprained my trigger finger while showing some things to Sir W. Symonds yesterday, I turned out today with some inconvenience, and it was still too rough for sport; but I continued to bring home again 4 geese.

7th.—Afloat, but did not get a shot; the geese kept shifting every ten minutes from one place to another, and then went off ten miles to the eastward.

8th.—Out again, and killed an enormous large diver with the shoulder gun; but the setting in of a south wind, with a determined wet day, drove us home; and Read finished this pleasant trip with first getting wet through and changing, and then going down to moor the punt off, and falling overboard and having to change again.

9th.—Off all day, and never saw the shadow of a chance; the only flock of geese that the unfavourable change of wind had left would not let us get within a quarter of a mile of them. Read has mud-crawled for a fortnight and never heard a wigeon; and Buckle, who has been about here for some weeks, is totally sickened with blank days. In short, it appears now to be 'all up' with coast gunning.

10th.—A ferocious dirty south-wester all day and all night. Rain spattering the windows like the drums of a padnagging regiment, and the wind howling like a pack of hungry wolves. No moving on land, much less on water.

28th.—Went up to London to settle a load of accounts and business that had accumulated in my long absence from town, and to show my injured finger to Sir B. Brodie.

March 2nd and 3rd.—Busy from morning till night; scarcely time to eat a meal, as I worked doubly hard in order to get over the misery of being in town in a fine north-east wind with a lame finger.

4th.—London swarming with wild fowl; wigeon as low as 1*s.* a couple in the streets.

13th to 15th.—Keyhaven. An incessant gale and the most piercing cold north-east wind. In short, winter in spring, which I long ago predicted. This weather about three months ago would have been worth a guinea a puff, but now it is an absolute nuisance, as it precludes the possibility of going on the water (for healthy air and the only flock of geese that remain), and is too late even to stop, much less to bring, other wild fowl.

16th.—Rough, but more moderate than it was, so went afloat, and, as the devil would have it, all the Billingsgate periwinklers were out this day, and thronged the shore for nine miles, so good-bye to the 150 geese, and adieu to shooting for this season.

20th.—Bitter winter, frost, snow, and a black north-east gale of wind, but all of no more use than a kneebuckle to a Highlander. Too late. Birds gone long ago, so we have our noses bit off for nothing.

22nd.—Game &c. killed in the season: 136 partridges (never shot at a partridge after September, except 1 that pitched in the lawn and I bagged), 1 quail, 5 hares, 5 rabbits, 1 pheasant, 24 snipes. Total, 172. 5 ducks and mallards, 1 burrough duck, 1 scaup duck, 81 wigeon, 33 geese, 15 godwits, 3 plover. Total, 139. Grand total, 311 head.

N.B.—As poor a season as ever was known, except one good week just after the snow. The coast is ruined, and we have no game shooting after September.

23rd.—Longparish. The incessant snow ceased about three this afternoon, when I was at last able to get out of the house. I therefore waded off in water boots, and took my gun for the chance of a snipe. I saw at least 40 all in a flock like plover, but at such a time one never can get within a hundred yards of them.

April 11th.—Keyhaven. Loaded my heaviest shoulder gun, and tried to get to the eastward, but was soon driven back by strong wind and heavy snow. Fell in with a small detachment of the geese, which let us get well in shot, but they were so scattered on the waves that I could only shoot 1, and that I dare not follow, so I came in, and spent the evening in revising the drama that I brought here for that purpose.

May 18th.—London. Flying about like a dog in a fair to stir up divers people, lest all things should not be in in time for the girls, and after a general action with plumassiers, dressmakers, barber, tailor, jobman, and Lord knows what besides, I shuffled on my finery and drove off 'as big as bull beef' with the girls for the Drawing Room, where they were presented by Lady Rodney to the King, and to the Princess Augusta, who presided for the Queen, as she was invalided at Windsor. We got over the operation without accidents or fainting fits, and arrived back at Dorset Place soon after four, when I shifted my things, and posted off to a filthy den in search of a journeyman who is making my new-invented tambourine; his residence was in a dirty court very far in Westminster, but he having just 'shot the moon,' I had to follow him to a cockloft in St. Giles's, which made a happy variety just after the Court of St. James's.

29th.—As the King and Queen were both too ill to attend

to-day, the Princess Augusta did all the duty at Court; and of all the mobs I ever was in, I never met a more uncomfortable place than the Drawing Room was to-day. I thought it never would be over, and so badly were the carriages regulated, that the ladies were obliged to walk out among the mob like girls at a fair, and I only got home just in time to bolt my dinner and shuffle on a coat and waistcoat for the Philharmonic concert.

30*th.*—A most glorious treble concerto of Bach at the concert of Moscheles, who played it with Thalberg and Benedict.

31*st.*—Dined with Moscheles to meet Thalberg, Madame Schroeder, Devrient, Galtz, Moeser, and others, who gave me an evening of absolute enchantment.

June 1*st.*—Out from nine to-night till near five in the morning, at the grand carnival in the opera house for the benefit of the Spitalfields weavers. It was the grandest ball and the greatest assemblage of fine folks that I ever saw. The Court was nothing to it. But I went to support the concern, as I have property in Spitalfields, and to please the girls, who were charmed with the spectacle, otherwise I should have made a more agreeable use of my time and money.

13*th.*—After being busy every day, and much engaged with taking my daughters about to enjoy the splendid musical talent that now swarms in town, and after being up nearly all night through having to go to the last most glorious Philharmonic, where Thalberg almost drove me crazy with delight, I this day got on the box of the 'Light Salisbury' and went down to Longparish.

21*st.*—Keyhaven. Received a 'Morning Herald' announcing the death of our beloved sovereign and my kindest benefactor, King William the Fourth, whom it pleased the Almighty to take to 'another and a better world' between two and three o'clock yesterday morning. Although this sad event was what we had reason to dread every day, yet I felt it so much as to be unable to do anything.

23rd.—Availed myself of the first fine day to sail to Alum Bay and ascend the heights in order to see young Coleraine descend the cliffs for young birds, &c. The way he does it is this. He has two very long ropes each about an inch in diameter. The one he fastens to an iron bar, which is driven into the ground, a few yards from the awful precipice, and the other he ties round his body. He then descends, clinging with his hands and feet to that rope which is fastened to the bar, in order to lighten the weight on the other rope that is made fast round his middle, and held by his partner, with a lad in reserve, in case of wanting further assistance. When he has taken anything, he stows it between his shirt and his breast, and gives a jerk to the rope that is held by the man as a signal to be hauled up again. The only danger that I could see, and which alone deterred me from trying the experiment, was the risk of getting injured by stones and pieces of chalk that might fall before the usual caution of 'Look out!' could be heard through the roar of the sea and the noise of the parent birds. This I would obviate by a kind of cap that I could invent. I would not have missed this sight for 5*l.*, though for want of wind we did not get home till eleven at night.

In the afternoon I sailed off to the back of the Isle of Wight, in order to have a view from below of Coleraine, who appeared by appointment at four o'clock, and descended the cliffs, where I was close under with a large telescope, so I saw him take 4 more gulls (that we brought home) as well as if I had been on the rope with him.

28th.—Went up to London per 'Salisbury,' and on my arrival was informed that General Sir S. Hawker had been sent for express by our good King, and arrived from Boulogne in time to pass two days with him previously to his dissolution; and that his Majesty desired to be affectionately remembered to me, my son, and my daughters.

July 8th.—A most dismal day in town, with every shop and almost every house shut up for the funeral of his late beloved Majesty, which took place in Windsor at eight o'clock this night. I should have been one of the procession, had not Lord Munster been deprived of all influence in the arrangements. I might have gone with a ticket as a mere looker-on, but this, of course, I declined; as a funeral, and particularly the one of a sincere friend, is the last thing I should wish to undergo as a mere exhibition. From nine till eleven this night it was truly afflicting to hear the minute guns and bells all over the metropolis announcing the departure to their last resting place of our dear King's mortal remains.

9th.—Sunday. I was taken so sick and unwell all night, that I expected to be laid up to-day; but fortunately I got relief, and was well enough to go and hear a most beautiful sermon by Dr. Dibdin on the death of our lamented monarch, the whole of which, as well as the service, was a severe trial to the feelings of anyone, much more of those who had long enjoyed the kind friendship of his late Majesty.

13th.—Put the prads in the britchska at twelve, and arrived with them at Keyhaven at half-past nine at night, as fresh as larks.

N.B.—Everyone gloried in my driving to the coast, as the country was half ruined by long easterly winds and dry hot weather; and it never yet failed to turn the cock and bring rain. I did turn the cock, and brought about an hour's light rain.

24th.—Into Andover, but business out of the question till the afternoon, on account of the election; which, although there was no contest, turned out to be one of the most amusing uproars I ever wasted my time at, thanks to Mr. Marsh, who spoke admirably and showed consummate ability, by the ready wit that he shot off at the blackguards whenever they dared to interrupt him.

31st.—Hard on in the City from breakfast till six, and then out again till near bedtime. One of my jobs was to choose some port and sherry in the docks, where the port-wine cellar alone is nine acres and a half of ground.

August 10th.—All in a bustle, preparing for 'the family' and their awful freight of baggage, which (except enough for a regiment) was coming on per Jones's 'Fly' waggon first, and then by the Odiham coach this morning from London. Willum Watts, our clod carter, left at daylight with rat-catcher Siney, as a baggage guard, to drag home the trunks &c. Monk left at eight, with old Samson and my cart, to 'bring into port' the maids and the lighter 'traps;' and I left at eleven with the prads and britchska, to drive home 'the ladies' from Basingstoke. All had a good passage but myself, who had a narrow escape of getting my neck broken. My horse 'Tom Brown' shied at a road waggon, and then 'took the rust,' which I fetched out of him instanter. He then plunged and broke the splinter bar. Here I was done; and left *solus* on the road, without a prospect of anything passing. At last I made the trace fast to the stump of the bar, cut off the strings of my flannel drawers to prevent it slipping, and thus toddled into Whitchurch, where I lashed on a piece of timber, proceeded to Basingstoke, and brought my cargo home in triumph. The whole army were safely lodged in quarters before dusk, and, thank God, without any further accident.

19th.—Ran down to Keyhaven to recruit myself with rest and sea air for the shooting fag of September.

N.B.—I just kept my charter, as we had heavy rain for the last six miles into Southampton, and a strong westerly wind at Keyhaven.

21st.—Rain set in in the evening, and we had wind and rain all night; so the farmers, who prayed that I might go to Keyhaven to bring rain, for the turnips and all that was burnt up, were quite right, and I successful in their petition.

28th.—Though I had been out sailing in the Channel every day, yet it was too rough to weather the back of the island till this day, when at last I had good weather to try the rock birds again. But on reaching the cliffs we found that every bird had left the country, and after a long day's beautiful sail I returned without pulling a single trigger. This is unusually early for all the birds to be gone.

CHAPTER XXX

1837

September 1st.—Longparish. A cold, stormy day; no lay for the birds, which were as wild as hawks, and of which there proved but a sorry breed. But in all my life I never shot better nor saw my dogs behave better; in short, the performance was perfection, though the supply was poor. I bagged 24 partridges and 2 hares without one miss, and I made seven brilliant double shots.

The dogs caught besides 2 birds and 1 leveret; and Joe, who had the advantage of the inclosed country to himself, bagged 26 partridges, so that our spread on the table was, in all, 52 birds and 3 hares. One of our very worst first days for number, but one of our very best for good shooting.

2nd.—Wonderful work again; a stormy day with showers, but to-morrow being Sunday I took the field, contrary to my custom, the second day, though did not begin till one o'clock in the afternoon, and was home to dinner soon after six I bagged 20 partridges and 1 landrail; I never fired a shot without bagging, and made five glorious doublets of the greatest difficulty. Having once 'made a cannon' at 2 birds crossing, and consequently got 3 with my two barrels, I bagged 21 head of game in 20 shots.

Joe shot like an angel also; he discharged ten rounds and pocketed his 10 birds in brilliant style. What care we for all Europe?

4th.—Wonderful work again considering the lamentable

scarcity of birds. I bagged 20 partridges and 1 snipe. But I this day missed one shot, the first miss I have made this season, and up to which I had bagged 65 head, including fourteen double shots without one miss. I was very lucky in 'making cannons'[1] to-day, as I got 2 at a shot three times, and 3 at a shot once. This is the most consummate beauty and difficulty of the art, and always more than covers the misses of any good shot.

6th.—Miraculous shooting again, warmer weather, and bagged about the half of what I saw. I was out from ten till five, and came in with 22 partridges and 1 hare, without missing even a long shot or losing a bird. I made five doublets, and, by means of three 'cannons,' got my 23 head in twenty shots, and many very long shots among them.

9th.—Better, and meant to shoot, but there came on a hurricane of wind with showers every two hours; so, not wishing to look little with an empty bag, I shipped my sou'-wester and went fishing, and had a most glorious bit of sport. The 3 first fish I landed weighed 6½ lb., and I came home with 11 brace, besides throwing in about 9 brace more that were rather too small to kill when I had such an abundance of first-rate ones. I was about four hours at it, and left the water while they were taking like bulldogs, because I thought it a shame to kill more than I knew what to do with.

11th.—A tremendous stormy day. I attacked the trout again, and brought home 12 splendid fish, besides throwing in nearly as many more. I was scarcely three hours at the river.

12th.—Too busy to go out till two in the afternoon, and a stormy day; but I wanted a bird or two for the house, and I could only get 3 partridges by means of very long shots. I killed a cuckoo that flew past me like an arrow, and

[1] Catching 2 birds as they cross, and then firing so quick as not to allow them to open again.

I took him for a hawk, as I never saw a cuckoo so late before. I killed also a little wheatear, which here is a *rara avis*.

13*th*.—Called down to the lower common this afternoon with a report that 2 or 3 dozen of snipes had been there yesterday, though only found 6, and those very wild. I then took the rod and caught another splendid dish of trout. I, however, kept but 4 brace, as I wanted no more, and my best fish was $2\frac{1}{4}$ lb. good weight.

15*th*.—6 partridges, with another wheatear, and had a providential escape from being killed and mutilated. My horse fell at full gallop and pitched head over heels, and nothing but my crawling off with the rapidity of a weasel saved me from being pounded to a mummy by the revolving croup of the horse.

16*th*.—An exquisite musical treat. Thalberg at Winchester, with Mori, Albertazzi, and others. Busy in assisting about the concert, but unfortunately could not get either Mori or Thalberg to come home with me, as the one was obliged to post all night for Birmingham, and the other was obliged to proceed to London the moment he had finished his most exquisitely splendid performance. It seemed like a romance to have such gods among the Hampshire hogs.

Game killed in September: 103 partridges, 4 hares, 1 landrail, 1 rabbit, 3 snipes. I never shot better, and never shot so little. I killed 91 head of game with only one miss, and made seventeen double shots out of eighteen. What with incessant business and the scarcity of game I have had no season at all. Total, 112 head.

October 2nd.—I never saw a pheasant, though I beat all our prime places with a good squad of men and dogs, and all I got was 1 rabbit and 2 partridges, as I was so unwell I was obliged to leave the chase and come home to lie down.

4*th*.—Got on the coach and ran down to Keyhaven to get my punts there put in order for the winter.

7*th*.—We paddled out at dawn and at dusk, but saw no

fowl, though there had been some in the late east wind. Now we have it west with rain, keeping up my charter.

21st.—Having put all things in order, I went afloat the whole day, but never saw a fowl. The day was so hot I could scarcely bear my shooting jacket, much less a gunning dress.

24th.—A hurricane from the west all last night. Calm this morning. Out at daylight; got only 1 pintail and 1 curlew.

25th.—Out at daylight, but driven home by heavy rain and high wind.

26th.—Went all the way to Pitt's Deep, and found the coast destitute of everything, and never discharged my gun. Buckle and I came home in despair, and gave it up till better winds blow.

November 8th.—London. I attended the Horse Guards' Levee to-day to lay before the Commander-in-Chief my claims for an honour, and was most kindly received by Lord Fitzroy Somerset.

9th.—Had a capital place at the United Service Club, and a comfortable stare at her Majesty and all her procession on their way to the City banquet.

14th.—Longparish. Received this day the kindliest memorials in my behalf from Lord Combermere, our general of cavalry, and my friend Sir John Elley, who was Adjutant-General, which I this day forwarded copies of for General Hawker, my former Lieutenant-Colonel, to lay before the Commander-in-Chief.

16th.—Went to Southampton, and saw the remains of the awful conflagration, where twenty-one persons were burnt to death.

18th.—Keyhaven. A bitter cold white frost, but a north-east wind, and a looking-glass calm. Up by candlelight, and got all my great set-out afloat. Went all the way to Cowes before I saw a bird. About to land for some lunch, when we saw about 40 ducks a mile off. Sculled for them half seas over, when we saw the most sudden change of weather that we had ever seen or heard of; so gave up Cowes and the ducks, and made for the shore near Eaglehurst, and got on the safe side just before there set in a strong wind with rain from the west; and, in short, we had to work ourselves all the way to Keyhaven, about eighteen miles, close to the shore, against the wind, because the Channel became so rough that we dare not take the tide back as intended. We got back some hours after dark, and in all our lives we never had such a severe blank day. Not a shot, and 'wet as shags.' Had I lunched at Cowes, I must have slept and spent the Sunday there. This is a lesson never to trust to a frost again when there is any white in it.

28th.—I this day got a letter from General Hawker, inclosing one from Lord Hill, to express his regret that it was against rule to give me the Order of the Bath, because I had left the army. Most glorious letter to 'show off' with, but no order to be got as yet.

December 5th.—Longparish. Very cold easterly wind. Having half a day to spare, I scoured the whole country both for game and snipes, and all I saw was 1 hare and 1 rabbit. This shows how completely the shooting here is now annihilated.

7th.—Extraordinary weather. Wind east, with snow and sleet, though without frost, and yet so chilling that I literally could not play on the piano, the keys were so cold, and it was so dark as to require candles at half-past three. Every labourer was complaining that even his work would not keep him warm; and as for me, I have been petrified ever since I was bit by the white frost on Saturday, and should like to have returned this day to the more genial climate of the coast.

9th.—Went to Keyhaven, and the change was like magic; the report of the gunning, however, was miserable. Read had been on day and night mud crawling in his small punt, with cold winds, and even snow, and had not got a bird.

11*th.*—Lovely weather, and out all day, but not a bird in the country except a few geese, that would not stay three minutes in a place from having been so persecuted by the bullets of the lubbers from Itchen Ferry. Read out all night with a splendid full moon, and never saw a fowl.

12*th.*—Out from daybreak till a late dinner; and the only shot I got was at 2 golden-eyes, both of which came home to the larder.

13*th.*—Out from dawn till night, and never saw a chance. Read crawling on the mud all night, with a beautiful full moon, and never saw a single wigeon. The scarcity is unaccountable.

14*th.*—Persevered, but nothing done; and there came on a south-west wind. Read crawled all night and found nothing. I was off all day, and soon after daylight had a tolerable shot at about 20 geese; and, for the first time these four seasons, my great gun missed fire. Really, such gunning is enough to tire the patience of Job.

15*th.*—Nothing for Read all night, and no shot to-day, though the rough weather gave me a view of about 100 geese in the wash.

16*th.*—Read another blank night. I dropped down with the wash, and took a snap shot at the geese, and knocked down 9, and had the luck at last to bring home some geese, thanks to my new cartridge, as nothing else would have reached them.

21*st.*—Moderate, with a north-easter; but not a bird in the country. Busy, on the mud, about a contract for cutting a lake through Stivers, and direct from our harbour to the West Channel.

22*nd.*—Read crawled all night in his mud punt, and never saw a chance. We then turned to and cleaned up all the gear, preparative to my returning to Longparish for

Christmas. Never, never did we see such a blank time for fowl as this.

31*st.*—Longparish. Sunday. I have been so employed with business, friends, and music, from breakfast till after midnight every day this week, that I was quite indifferent to the week's rainy and unpleasant weather that we have had, and if we, please God, enjoy the new year as we have done the last week of the old one, we shall have no reason to complain.

1838

January 1*st.*—In spite of wind and wet weather, we had a glorious New Year's Day, by sending the tilted cart for Tom Langstaff and his fiddle, and playing from one in the day to one in the night, except at our meals, where, with Signor Sola's merry face and jokes, we were not a moment free from glee and harmony.

2*nd.*—As at Sola's earnest entreaty we had a dish of trout for New Year's Day (which, to my astonishment, were in fair season), I this day took about half an hour's fishing, and killed as many as we could eat for dinner, and some of them were as red as salmon. This shows the mildness of the winter.

4*th.*—Obliged to be up two hours before daylight, and in Winchester before nine o'clock this morning, on two vexatious actions, by Parson Cockerton and Bill Wickham, against Charles Heath, my tenant, in both of which we came off triumphant, thanks entirely to the splendid talent of Mr. Smike, our leading counsel, whom we primed at every point with strong facts to bother our opponents, who looked as if they had been over-dosed with emetics and jalap. By this sudden call to court I lost all my morning's music with Langstaff, who came over again, and I only got home just in time to dress for my dinner party. Up till two in the morning, with music, singing, fun, and dancing, so that my incessant excitement continued for twenty-one hours.

5*th.*—Badgered away from a batch of Beethoven to go

after a cursed cock pheasant that I never found, but I saved my blank with a rabbit, which was all I saw in four hours.

6th.—Signor Sola left us for London, after delighting us for a fortnight with his good performance and useful assistance in music till after midnight every evening.

8th.—A glorious black frost and north-easter. In Keyhaven soon after eight; no time to eat, and could only get through my jobs by running in 'double quick' instead of walking.

9th.—Keyhaven. Lovely weather. Pumps and water jugs frozen, and a furious easterly gale. Read was out yesterday, and his gun missed fire three times; and once he was so eager to pull off his worsted glove to shoot, that he seized it with his mouth, and literally pulled out one of his teeth, which fell into the punt.

To-day the birds were not in such swarms as yesterday. I fired my two barrels in a heavy sea, and stopped 2 mallards, 1 duck, 2 pintails, 5 wigeon, 2 teal, 2 plover, and 5 dunlins. We came home wet and frozen, and yet perspiring with bustle and excitement.

10th.—Intense frost and snow, but wind more moderate. Lots of shooters out; but nothing done, and thousands of birds frightened off to sea. I got only 2 wigeon, 1 duck, and 2 godwits.

11th.—Made a capital shot, having, from one barrel only, picked up, from one shot, 21 curlews. We had a chase on the frozen mud for two hours. These birds were so heavy, and the frozen mud in such a state, that we were obliged to go back to the punt for a rope to drag them along. My second barrel missed fire, by the cock catching the gun cloth, or I might have doubled the shot. Got also an enormous eider duck. Intensely hard weather, but wigeon so driven by boats that they were not allowed time to give us a chance.

12th.—I got 4 golden-eyes and 1 wigeon. Only out from dawn till midday, having business. To bed at six, out at eleven, stopped by snow. Read crawled from two till four, but heard nothing.

13*th*.—Intense frost; up and at breakfast by seven. Gale of wind from east, so could not get out till three in the afternoon, when I could pass through Stivers and drop down from Pennington to the Camber. Had one scrambling shot in a rough sea, and, to my surprise, bagged 6 wigeon.

14*th*.—Sunday. Read had been out till twelve last night crawling, but not a bird could live on the frozen mud; so now all must be day work. Never did a treadmill man hail the Sabbath as a day of rest more gladly than I did this day, for, what with incessant gunning, furbishing, and being my own servant here, no galley slave ever worked harder than I have done this week, though I am, thank God, all the better for it.

15*th*.—Capital day work: 1 duck, 1 goose, 38 wigeon, 32 plover, and 2 godwits. The first shot I got 18 wigeon and 1 goose; the second, 17 plover and 2 godwits; the third, 18 wigeon. The others were little pop shots. So exhausted when I came home at night, that I was obliged to swallow two glasses of sherry before I could stand to clean up my gear, in order to turn out again by midnight, should the weather permit.

16*th*.—Entreated by Read to go out from midnight till four this morning, but I told him it was too cold for birds at night, and I was right, as I had all but a blank; the birds in were a mere nothing, and all scattered. Up again at seven to prepare, and started as soon after as I could eat a breakfast. Out till dark, but little to be done, as the report of my sport, of which there were plenty of witnesses and exaggerators, had called every boat in requisition; and the order of the day was dandy bullet shooters, who, of course, got nothing, but they drove every flock to sea, and the Channel was literally barren. I, however, got one shot at a flock of geese above 200 yards, and, to my surprise, knocked down 6 geese.

17th and 18th.—Ashore all day in consequence of a part of my detonating lock having so worn away that I had three miss-fires on the 16th. Mr. Clayton, the gunmaker from Lymington, and I were on, by candlelight, on the 17th and best part of the 18th, forging and filing in our kitchen, and I hope with success. I had also a severe press of business on other matters, and was raced about the house all day. I sent Read off, and he brought me in 5 wigeon and 1 goose.

19th.—A day's work equivalent to the treadmill as to exercise and diet. From seven till eleven working with pick-axe and shovel to get to the water with the great gun and punt, and then cutting away the ice for half a mile to get out of harbour. Afloat all day; both our meat and our beer so frozen we could not eat the one or get a single suck at the other. Landed at Hurst just as night set in, and walked in the dark three miles home in water boots and with heavy lots at our backs, two miles of which was on shingles, that were the only things not frozen; and consequently as heavy as in open weather. The gun did well after the repairs, as far as we tried it, which was two shots; our bag was 7 geese and 6 wigeon.

20th.—Up hours before daylight, and tramped round the beach to Hurst. Made a glorious shot: 42 wigeon and 9 geese at one shot, and had not my primer missed fire, should have had about 30 geese at another shot. The boats helping themselves to my fleet of cripples off at sea with popguns, put an end to shooting for the rest of the day; or I might have got 100 birds, and must have hired a cart to bring them home.

21st.—Sunday, but, what with baskets, letters, church &c. I could hardly call it a day of rest. Indeed, I was up at daybreak, in order neither to neglect my commissions nor to miss going to church.

22nd.—Up at five and tramped again to Hurst by daylight. A general thaw and weather turned mild with a strong south wind. Birds, as is usual on the break up, congregated in immense flocks; but so harassed by sail boats that I could only get three flying shots, with which I sacked 15 geese, all at above 200 yards with heavy mould shot. At three in the afternoon we sailed home to our own quay at Keyhaven, and were 'hard on' cleaning up all the transported gear till eight in the evening.

23*rd.*—Off at daylight; much embarrassed with floating pans of ice, but got extricated by shipping sail. Fired a shot about eight o'clock, and cut down 22 geese and 1 wigeon; but such a heavy sea that I lost several both of the dead geese and wigeon. A cold easterly wind again.

24*th.*—A candlelight breakfast as usual, but such a tremendous hurricane from the east, that nothing could move to windward; and the ice that came to leeward blocked us up for the day, while 16 wild swans sat and bade me defiance before my very windows. On like a slave, with five hands cutting away the ice, while the wild fowl were flying round me every minute; but having greater objects in view than popping down single birds as they flew over the quay, I stuck to my work of ice cutting, cartridge making &c. Several other little trips of swans were flying about, and so tame that two were killed by the common shore poppers with their miserable muskets.

25*th.*—Gale continued, swans blown to leeward, and 24 more travelled over from Poole. Much trouble to get to windward. Dropped down on a host of fowl; both barrels missed fire; they pitched again and both barrels missed again. Made for shore and drew the charge. Found that Read had put wadding first and powder after; sorry blunder. Off again; refused a fine shot because 5 swans were to leeward; got close to them while all in one solid cluster; must have killed all dead, but flint flashed in pan; up they flew, all abroad; caught two as they crossed, with other barrel, and only No. 1 shot; cut both down short in high style, but one, the old cock, managed to reach the beach and go off to sea; so, instead of clearing the harbour of the only 5 swans in it to-day, I had the mortification to come in with only 1 wild swan;[1] after rectifying the flint barrel again, I blew it off at a long distance, and got 1 goose, 2 ducks, 2 wigeon, 1 golden-eye, and 1 burrough duck; a curious mixture at one shot.

26th.—Strong wind, but not so furious but we could row against it. Brought in 3 wild swans; 1st shot at five close to us, but in so heavy a 'lop' that the splash took off the shot; 2nd shot at 7, got 2, both splendid old birds, and another fell dead, off at sea; the latter was a very long shot, as the birds were old and wary. We were on with three boats for two hours before we caught the old captain of the swans, as he took to the breakers and made for Yarmouth. No other shot to-day,[2] as we gave up all fowl for the glorious sport of killing the hoopers.

27th.—Most glorious sport; 49 geese and 2 such splendid wild swans that 1 weighed 20 lb. all but 3 oz. Another old swan fell dead at sea. I had only four shots; the first, a single swan a long way off; the second at 10 swans, an immense distance, when I killed 2 with the 1 lost at sea; the third, shot 20 geese and sacked all; the fourth, shot 29 geese and sacked every bird. I had three punts to cut off every cripple from reaching the Channel.[3] Never was there a more satisfactory day to finish a week.

28th.—Sunday. Severe work writing, basket packing, bill paying, church, &c. A general thaw with strong south wind and heavy rain this evening.

29th.—Very high tide all the forenoon, and the harbour besieged like a field of battle with bullet spitters in boats, and

[1] Two more wild swans picked up on beach since this entry.

[2] Our bag to-day was gigantic: 3 swans, and an enormous conger eel as thick as my thigh.

[3] The cripples were so thick that I sailed into 4 and blew down 2 with the first barrel, and another 2 with the second, of my 'cripple stopper.'

absolute legions of snobs on every point of the shore, one incessant fire the whole day, and not a single bird knocked down. Having had several narrow escapes of bullets while attempting to approach the geese, I went quietly home and gave up all further attempts till the ragamuffins had had their 'whack' of popping off blank shots, and at four in the afternoon I took the 'ground ebb' and landed 23 geese, 15 one shot and 8 the other. Weather mild the whole day, and wigeon all at sea. No more wild swans seen or heard of.

30*th.*—A dense fog, so did not go afloat, but took a stroll alongshore with Captain Vassal and some young gentlemen. A fine wild swan flew over our heads within shot, and pitched close to Highlea Point. The gents watched him till I came off with the punt, and, after setting near a mile to him, while he kept swimming away, we at last got up and I shot him as dead as mutton, and gave him to the captain. We then heard some geese and paddled off to them, and fired off one barrel only (as I could not see to shoot the other for fog). I knocked down 16 geese and sacked 'every man John' of them. I then ran into my house for a lunch; but when I came back to the punt there were no more fowl about, but I blew off a barrel at some mixed shore birds that sat on the mud thrown up by Dowden's work at my leak, and the filth that I had to wallow in to catch them. Considering the distance of the three shots and the disadvantage of the fog, I consider this the most satisfactory day of the campaign.

31*st.*—25 geese. Afloat from ten till three, and about two o'clock we got about 2,000 geese in a place where we could not fail to get a shot, when a rascally shore snob popped up his black shoulders and popped them all off. In my whole life I never saw so fair a chance to kill 100 geese at a shot, as we had a perfect ambush, and the birds were all standing in a phalanx. As it was, I blew after them and got 4. I then came home, as the harbour swarmed with bullet poppers afloat and snobs ashore, and when they were got rid of I went out for two hours just before dark, got one shot, and picked up 21 geese, making in all the above 25 fowl to-day.

February 1st.—19 geese; had but two shots all day, as the harbour was besieged with poppers afloat and ashore. One of these two shots, I got 12 so near home that the shot rattled on the slating of my house. I sent Read to crawl at night, and he got in all 14 wigeon.

2nd.—Sail boats off all day, looking for cripples, so I stayed in till half-past three in the afternoon, but there set in a north wind that cut the tides, and enabled all the geese except a few to go to the high mud, five miles off. I fell in with a fair lot about sunset; but just as I was within a minute of shooting, up jumped the geese, and 'bang' went the gun of Buckle, who cut down 5. I should have had about 15. I then steered for home, resigned to a blank evening, when I saw a few birds under the little moon. I got close to them and fired, but not one rose, and when we rowed in there lay dead 12 geese, so I annihilated the whole company of them, and this on the very edge of my own new-cut leak. So after all I came home again in triumph.

3rd.—20 geese the first shot, 3 geese (a long random flying shot) the second shot, and 34 geese the third shot.[1] The latter splendid shot was made under a curious circumstance. I had given up shooting for the day to open my new leak through the mud, just finished, to pay for it, and to lush the Keyhavenites with four gallons of swill; and while we were waiting for water to go through the leak, about four in the afternoon, the grand company of geese took the mud, when I put off to them, and shot flying as the tide was too late to shoot sitting, and sacked the above lot in presence of all the procession. It was consequently moonlight before we entered the leak, and I should have had a second cut at the geese under the moon had not a shore snob popped off his piece.

[1] Making 57 geese brought in to-day (in three shots), besides many of my dead birds that were bagged by the boats and shore sharks.

We then, with flags flying, and all the guns in Keyhaven firing, and three hearty cheers, opened the passage, and 'all hands' adjourned to the pothouse to wind up Saturday and drink 'luck to Colonel Hawker's leak.'

4th.—Sunday. The sharp frost continued. Busy sending off a corn sack stuffed with geese for my North Hants tenants, lots of baskets, letters, &c. What with church and all, I had enough to do between early rising and a candlelight gentleman's dinner on a fat goose.

5th.—Intense weather. Off at daybreak. First shot 6 enormous milk-white old wild swans, with the flint barrel, the detonator having missed fire,[1] or I should have had 12 more. Second shot very long, 2 wild swans; third shot, 10 geese, with the detonator, the flint having missed fire. These were the only three shots I had, as I was so taken up with the swans that I literally went through 2,000 wigeon in musket shot, and in getting the last of the above 6 swans I never in all my sport was in such danger, as I went over my knees, and saved myself from sinking by making a handle of my shoulder gun by laying it crossways on the mud. I was over my knees and my pattens buried every step, and so exhausted that I made for the shore and lay down on the ground before I could recover to proceed home. I then washed out my gun, and swallowed some porter, and got taken back to my punt in the custom-house boat.

6th.—What with dead tides at dawn, and dusk and floating bullet poppers all day, there was little to be seen except 400 yards in on mud; all the shots I had were two. I got another splendid old wild swan (besides hitting 2 more down that the snobs finished), and with the other shot I bagged 6 geese at an immense distance, as they crossed me on my way home at night.

[1] Another white one picked up dead on the beach, and a brown one knocked down with an oar (by some boatmen) half a mile off, making 8 at one shot of one barrel, though only six fairly sacked. We had a cart to bring the 6 up (and also the other 2 shot), as they all averaged 20 lb., making about 160 lb. besides the 10 geese, which brought the sack to just about 200 lb. cargo.

7th.—A general thaw with tremendous south wind all last night and all to-day and heavy rain. Went a little way down the harbour in the afternoon, and just saved my blank by popping down with the great gun 7 geese as a small flock rapidly crossed me to go out for the night.

8th.—Tremendous westerly gale all day, with a heavy pour of rain. Kept ready from morning till sunset, but no birds in and no living out of harbour. Read crawled at night, but got only 2 wigeon and 1 burrough duck.

9th.—A wet hurricane all day, so went off to pay visits and bills, but at four P.M. the storms abated, so we weathered it till dusk. I got one shot in a rough sea a long way off, and knocked down and bagged 13 wigeon.

10th.—Extraordinary change of weather. Up before daylight, and all was deep in snow, with a hurricane from the north-east. Ready all day, but snow and wind too much to weather. Went off in the evening, but thought it prudent to return, though discharged one barrel, a very long shot, and got 4 beautiful burrough ducks, making just 600 different birds fairly bagged up to this (Saturday) night [1] since I came here on January 8, just a month ago! and of which list 459 are ducks and geese.

11th.—Read, who would crawl in his pig trough last night, got but 1 wigeon.

12th.—A hard white frost; out at half-past six; got one shot and bagged 12 geese. Came in to lunch at one, and went out again, but the whole coast was so swarming with sunshine poppers that I gave it up, and went to assist Dowden in putting the booms to my new leak, which is now complete.

13th.—Out at daybreak; coast so bombarded I could only bag 3 geese. Went out again at three P.M.; 'Sams' all tired; got a fine shot, and bagged 8 geese and 16 wigeon. Read crawled at night, and in two shots got 14 wigeon.

14th.—Intensely cold gale of wind from the east-south-

[1] Fowl 459, waders 141. Total, 600.

east. Prisoners till three in the afternoon ; got one long shot, and killed 8 wigeon. The main army of geese never came in to-day.

15*th*.—A ferocious hurricane from the east-south-east all day, so that nothing could 'live' afloat, and one could hardly stand on one's legs ashore, and most intensely cold to boot. I therefore amused myself with jobbing, writing, music &c. and took my dinner at three. About half-past four I was just stepping out to Read's house, when 4 splendid old swans passed over from the sea and pitched inland ; I flew to arms, and was off like a greyhound, but already about thirty shore snobs were in full chase. They, however, all being 'green,' raced in competition to windward, and I, who was last, ran to leeward, knowing the birds would smell the snobs and come over me. Up they got, out of all reach of their pursuers ; down I lay on my back ; over they came, and down I brought the old captain of the four swans as flat as a flounder and dead as a hammer, and this saved my blank for to-day with my 19th wild swan. It was impossible to do better, as the 4 birds were all apart, and away flew the 3 others to sea. I never did anything in all my shooting that pleased me better than this.

16*th*.—A tremendous hurricane from the south-east all night and all day, with snow, rain, hail, and sleet. Shooting, even on land, out of the question.

17*th*.—Most extraordinary weather. A gale of wind, with severe frost all night ; at six o'clock in the morning everything was frozen ; at seven the cock flew to the west and it poured with warm rain, and before ten it was as mild as in May ; and about the middle of the day the sun shone, and it was so hot we were obliged to 'douse' a part of our gunning cloths. At 4 P.M. we had a cold, wet evening, and before dark it was dry and mild. We were out from ten till six, but the birds were all at sea, and we brought nothing home except a crested grebe, killed with the popgun, the fifth that I have got this season, though I never saw one in this country before. I fired one long shot at a swan two miles at sea, and hit him very hard, and marked him drop on the mud, and afterwards saw three men hunting him down, and then killing him. I should have had one good shot of geese, but an ass blew a bullet at them just before we had arrived in shot. Read crawled till midnight, and got 4 wigeon. A white frost.

19*th.*—Up at three, hoping to catch the wigeon in harbour, but it came on so dark and so windy from east-south-east that we would not start till daybreak. Dead tides, and scarcely any birds, so got but 2 geese all day.

20*th.*—Out at daylight, but all the birds were gone about twelve miles to the eastward. The coast was destitute.

Memorandum of fowl killed to end of February 1838:

1837, old year.—In mild weather: Waders—3 curlews, 8 plover, 25 dunlins. Wild fowl—3 wigeon, 1 pintail, 3 golden-eyes, 6 geese. Total, 49.

1838, new year, from January 9 to end of February.—In (and after) severe weather: Waders—31 curlews, 48 plover, 5 godwits, 1 redshank, 64 dunlins. Fowl—217 wigeon, 2 pintails, 5 wild ducks, 2 teal, 6 burrough teal, 1 eider duck, 1 tufted duck, 5 golden-eye ducks, 4 dunbirds, 298 geese, 19 swans. Grand total for winter campaign at Keyhaven, 758, of which 573 are ducks and geese.

Best shots: 28 curlews—42 wigeon and 9 geese—20 geese—28 geese—23 geese—34 geese—8 swans (1 barrel).

N.B.—In 18 of the days shooting 262 geese and 18 swans.

March 12*th.*—A fine sunny day; off from about eight till three. Not a bird of any kind to be seen or heard of, except about two dozen very wild geese, at which I took a long shot, hoping to get a couple to make up my 300 in the new year, and to my surprise down came 6 geese, to add to the above list; thus I closed a splendid season with a capital little shot,

RETURN TO KEYHAVEN, AFTER A DAYS GUNNING, IN THE WINTER OF 1838.

Drawn by C. Varley.

Engraved by H. Adlard.

London: Longman, Brown, Green & Longmans.

and retired from the coast without leaving as much as a plover to look after.

19th to 21st.—London. On like a slave from early in the morning till late at night, with lawyers, booksellers, bankers, creditors, debtors, artists, tenants, gunmakers, workmen, &c.

22nd.—Returned to Longparish ; most heartily glad to get out of town, and came inside the coach, being still so unwell with a settled cold, that such a brutal day as this outside might have been the death of me. Nothing but cold, petrifying, sour storms, most wet and furious, from the north-west.

23rd.—Bitter winter. Heavy snow, and piercing cold winds ; and all of no avail, as 'gunning' is over, and all foreign fowl have left our part of the country.

April 19th.—London. Piercing cold, with snow almost every day, which I was obliged to bustle about in, preparing the eighth edition of my sporting book.

30th.—Out on a stick for the first time after being confined to my bed for ten days.

May 8th.—Keyhaven. Read, Buckle and myself, all cripples. Most singular, all the three great gunners cripples, and plenty of whimbrels about and quite tame.

10th.—Up to the eyes in model working and book revising. Heavenly weather and sea looking like a paradise, though a brisk north-easter. What a climate is that of England ! Yesterday insufferably hot ; this evening frost, and obliged to light a fire.

23rd.—London. My illness and my business just admitted of my going this day, for the first time, to her Majesty's Levee, which was immensely full. I was presented by General Lord Combermere, as my Colonel, Lord Rodney was unwell in the country.

31st.—Every day occupied with divers artists, bringing out my book ; and much bothered, as I had to destroy some sketches done all wrong while I was away, and to insist on having my old able friend Cornelius Varley again. Splendid theatrical, musical, and operatic treats this month; though too busy or ill to accept half the tickets offered me.

June 21st.—The last Drawing Room of the season; so of course an awful crowd and a vapour bath. Had to wait above three hours for carriage, therefore could not get home till ten minutes before seven. Found a ticket waiting for me for Grisi's box at the opera. Galloped off in a cab to ask Lady Rodney in Pall Mall how we were to go. Answer: 'No more Court costumes now.' So had to strip, and bolt my dinner, and got there by half-past eight; but a row in the house had luckily kept back the performance half an hour. Fullest house I ever saw. Home exactly at two; so had a day's real town life—what they call 'pleasure.'

22nd.—Hunted like a wild boar from the time I got up till eleven at night, and then obliged to work for the press till a quarter before three in the morning.

25th.—Had a dinner party at home, and afterwards a music party, and everyone present voted it the merriest they had passed for years. We did not break up till past two; and I had then to work for the printers till half-past four, as they wanted the sheets per eight o'clock post.

28th.—The Coronation. Up at five in order to get down to the club by seven, after which time the streets would be scarcely passable for ladies. So numerous were the applications for seats at our United Service Club, that there had above a week ago been a kind of raffle for good seats, bad seats, or no seats at all. I had the luck to win the very best for my girls, and of all the pageants that it was possible to behold, this was the most magnificently splendid. We had a sumptuous banquet at the club, and did not get home till near seven, and were in sad confusion owing to a man not bringing the lamps we required for the illumination; but I made shift without them, and then sallied off till near one to view all the grand illuminations, fireworks, &c., which surpassed anything I ever saw before; and, in short, it was nearly daylight before we got to bed, so that my bustle and excitement this glorious day continued little short of twenty-four hours.

29th.—Took the girls to the large Coronation Fair in Hyde Park, which is to be kept up three days; but found it more of a place to amuse the lower orders than to attract the fashionables, though the drives round the outside of it were thronged with carriages, and the bustle of the West End made the streets quite a misery to get through with ladies.

July 4th.—Westminster Abbey being open to the public gratis, and even without tickets, I went this day, the last of the two days it was open, to see it; and a most awful crowd I had to encounter, though the sight was gorgeous in the extreme.

12th.—Persecuted with printers, and other bothering book fellows, in the City all day; and then on from half-past three in the afternoon till three o'clock after midnight compiling and copying fair a list of contents, plates, and various other matter for my book, and other business concerning it. Who would be an author, if it was always to be like this? Formerly I had good help in all the dry mechanical labour; but with the printer's gang of careless jackasses I may as well ask for help from Bedlam.

14th.—Saturday night. Sent in the last proof sheet. Of all the happy deliveries I ever had to offer up my thanks for, this is one of the most emancipating. In short, what with printers and engravers, and the bustle of this crazy season in town, I have been in one absolute state of effervescence for three months.

23rd.—Worked my way to Longparish in order to dine with Mr. Fellowes, who wished me to meet Lord Brougham and Sir Richard Sutton, the celebrated great shot and sportsman.

August 15th.—Longparish. A reconciliation took place between me and my old enemy, the lawyer, through the friendly intervention of Mr. Fellowes, so that all scrambles and skirmishes in the field of sport will be happily at an end; and they never would have occurred at all but for the mischief-making lies of gamekeepers, who have since left the lawyer's service, and to whom he had unfortunately given credit, without giving me a chance for explanation. Hence arose all the war. And now for peace when I have hardly health and spirits to enjoy it.

27th.—Keyhaven. A grand day with the Yacht Club; dining at Hurst Castle, I went under sail with the girls in the 'Petrel' punt, which excited more curiosity than any bark upon the Channel, as people could see nothing but ourselves, the sail, and flags, there being just breeze enough to make the punt invisible at a moderate distance.

CHAPTER XXXI

1838

September 1*st*.—Too unwell to begin shooting till near twelve o'clock, and never did I see a worse first day, birds as wild as hawks, small in size, and so much heavy corn standing that the shooting ought to have been put off for at least a fortnight. I, however, shot capitally in spite of all, and bagged 25 partridges, besides 3 more lost, and never missed a bird, except two long random shots, and I made five brilliant double shots. Dogs behaved as well as they could do, considering a vile scent and birds on the run all day.

3*rd*.—Rather better, and out all day; and though I shot most gloriously I only brought home 11 partridges and 1 hare. I lost 3 birds, and Charles, who was with me and shot capitally, added 4 brace more birds to the bag. We met Mr. Fellowes's party just going home, and all they got in the whole day was 4 old birds and 4 very young ones, and they pronounced this to be the vilest shooting season on record. So, miserable as my bag has been, I have far surpassed all my competitors.

N.B.—Though I beat my whole estate I did not see so many birds as, in former times, I've bagged in a day.

8*th*.—A cold north wind, and the very few birds to be found as wild as at Christmas. I got seven shots, and only one fair one among them, and bagged 6 partridges. What a vile first week, and yet I believe no one has beat me.

10*th*.—As Monday, after the rest on Sunday, is generally

the best day in the week, I went mounted over the open country all the morning, but all I could bag was 7 partridges. So wild were the birds that I fired seven blank shots, and yet I feel confident that I shot straight every time I fired. The season is so bad that going after game this year is a toil instead of a pleasure.

14th.—Left for Keyhaven to join the girls, who had returned there from their visits in that neighbourhood, and attended the benefit of our friend Miss Chambers at the Southampton Theatre this evening. Never was a town so crowded, four public meetings and a morning concert besides. I could not get a seat in the coffee room of the inn, as even this was filled with men, women, and children, it being the day, both out and in, for packets.

28th.—Went from Lymington per steamer to Portsmouth to find out the monument to my great-grandfather, and see my friend Captain Symonds, now a patient in Haslar Hospital. Found a rich ancient tablet in the garrison chapel, which I ordered to be repaired at my own expense, and surprised the clerk not a little when I made myself known and showed the crest on my seal as corresponding with that on the monument.[1]

Game bagged in September: only 52 partridges and 1 hare, though I never shot better. Out but five times, and found the birds so scarce that I gave it up and returned to the coast. The same complaint all over our country, insomuch that I killed the most of anyone the first day.

[1] Richly carved in marble with arms and crest over, and inscribed as follows:

'Near this
place lyeth the body of the
Honble Colonel
Peter Hawker,
Late Lt Governor of
Portsmouth,
Who departed this life
the 5th of Jan^y^,
1732, in the 60th year
of his age.'

October 1st.—Keyhaven. Took a hard day's fag with Mr. West over his wild rough country at Arnwood, accompanied by Major Keppel. My share (the best) was 6 partridges, 2 cock pheasants, and 3 hares.

4th.—A strong north-easter, and some wigeon come: so I launched the 'Petrel' and the great gun, so as to get out for a few hours in the afternoon, and I should have had a good shot if I could have been ready about an hour sooner. I did get in shot of about 50 wigeon, but the tide sunk so low I could not bear the gun on the birds.

8th.—The wigeon have kept about here ever since the 4th, but were always on a 'lop of the sea.' I was out from six till three P.M., when just as I sat down to dinner the wigeon appeared. I left my dinner and put off, and got close in to them, where I lay for near half an hour, but they were all scattered abroad. But when I saw them in the act of 'jumping,' I caught 3 together and took another with the second barrel, and brought in these 4 wigeon. There were other gunners about, or I would rather have left them till I could have caught them properly placed for a shot, and perhaps cut up two-thirds of the company.

21st.—Longparish. On my way to call at Lord Portsmouth's after church to-day, I witnessed the scene where the frightful accident occurred yesterday with the Salisbury coach at Hurstbourne.

25th.—Longparish. Up for a candlelight breakfast. Went for the first time on the new railway: did 38 miles in an hour and thirty-one minutes: in town soon after twelve.

30th.—London. Off to Bank; sold some consols about half-past eleven, but had to wait till one while papers for New York stock were preparing. Being for this time a prisoner, I wished to amuse myself with an inspection of all the Bank; so went to my friend Timothy Curtis, the Governor-in-Chief, who was delighted to see me, and said I never could have hit on a better time, as the Prince Louis Napoleon, Buonaparte's talented nephew, was expected every moment to see all the machinery of the Bank, by appointment. Waited till one, but no prince; so went and completed all my American transaction just in time to save an outward-bound ship with the papers. Back again to Curtis; prince and all his staff come, and on my being introduced, he was quite delighted, as he said he had long wished to know the author of his favourite study on the *chasse*; nothing could be more flattering or agreeable. Saw all the bullion, machinery, bank-note making, steam engines &c. Had bags holding 1,000 sovereigns each in my hand (they weighed 21 lb. each bag), and then had 3,000,000*l.* in my hand in 1,000*l.* bank notes. Had a splendid luncheon with Curtis, his ladies, and the prince and staff, and then flew to Coutts's to execute my power of attorney at four. The prince walked out with me to his carriage, with all the staff following behind; and the street was so mobbed to see this new 'lion,' *vice* old Soult, that we could scarcely proceed any pace. His highness then entered a splendid carriage, and I flew off in a cab, not having time to crawl along in an omnibus. Indeed, such has been the pressure of my business that I never could have got through it in the time I've been in town, had I not cabbed it on most occasions. Now, thank God, I've done all in a most satisfactory manner, and booked my place for leaving town to-morrow morning. Up to the eyes in accounts from half-past six this evening till twelve at night.

31st.—Returned to Longparish by Salisbury coach, and viâ railway. On arrival found notices for a lawsuit, and a requisition for my coming to see my jobs done at Keyhaven. Never at rest.

November 5th.—Up before daylight; off early to Winchester; long consultation with solicitor about lawsuits; on to Southampton; down to Northam about Ward's punt, &c.; busy with Buckle and gunmaker Burnett, and heaps of commissions. On per 'Pilot' coach, and at Keyhaven Cottage about half-past eight in the evening, the tranquillity of which peaceable place, after the incessant bustle I have been in ever since I left it, was a relief that was like a heaven on earth. No birds.

15*th*.—Keyhaven. There being no birds on the coast, though an easterly wind, I never took up a gun till to-day, when I went up to Arnwood to try for a cock with my friend Mr. West, who with his keepers and a cry of spaniels beat all his best country, but the only cock we saw the whole day flew into my very face, a close open shot, just after I had discharged both barrels, and I never could find him again, though I beat for hours.

23*rd*.—Longparish. I had, thank God, the satisfaction to hear that my son Peter was just getting under way with a fair wind, and in a capital transport (the 'Elizabeth') with a very pleasant party, and he wrote in good spirits. May God protect him wherever he goes.

26*th*.—Deadly cold, with an easterly wind and a fall of snow. I had such a bad cold that I could not get warm in bed or up, and got warm by a strange recipe. I was busy at accounts, and was suddenly called off after a woodcock; away I went in the snow, got wet through, and at the same time perspired with heat from the tremendous long chase I had with 2 woodcocks, which kept all my banditti on the run for nearly three hours, as they were so very wild, but I bagged them both at last.

29*th*.—Ferocious weather still on day and night. No stirring out without a tattered umbrella and a drenching to the skin. Every chimney choking with smoke, and every tree in danger with the gale. We pray to God that Peter may, ere this, have either reached a different atmosphere or put into some foreign port.

December 1*st*.—On to Keyhaven, and long before I reached Southampton all the wind and rain returned. Got to the Cottage about nine, all the coaches being late owing to the bad roads. On my arrival found that everyone had been having fine sport during the easterly wind, but the awful south gale last week had not only put an end to the shooting, but caused a serious flood, insomuch that all my things were of necessity moved to the upper floor, and the villagers, and even their pigs, were obliged to be sheltered in the bedrooms. Luckily, however, I sustained no damage worth naming.

8th.—A fine day at last, so I completed my chief business at Keyhaven for this cruise, which was to place all the booms in another new leak that I had cut by contract (at my own expense) through 'Stivers' mud for nearly half a mile, in order to get to 'Pennington Leak' without going round by Hurst. The job was completed for 8*l.*, which I paid old Dowden the navigator the moment I landed, and ordered two gallons of 'heavy wet' for the men to drink success to my 'new cut.' Mrs. Whitby was kind enough to present me with the booms, fresh cut, from her own plantations.

9th.—Sunday. Most awful accounts of the disasters in the late terrific hurricane, and among them the narrow escape of the 'Barossa' transport, the one that followed the 'Elizabeth' a few days after she had sailed with Peter. My anxiety about him, therefore, must be intense, till I, please God, hear some tidings of the latter ship, in which he sailed.

20th.—Returned to Longparish.

N.B.—Such was the scarcity of wild fowl on the coast, that while at Keyhaven for nineteen days I saw five gunners 'on' day and night, and in the whole time they only got 3 wigeon among them all. I therefore withheld launching my grand set-out for two reasons; the one that I would not waste my time and the wear and tear of gear for nothing, the other that I would not have it said that the poor gunners were half starved because my great gun had driven away all the fowl. I therefore devoted my time to the completion of my new leaks through the mud, and other preparations for a better prospect of good sport.

30*th.*—Received a letter announcing the death of General Sir Samuel Hawker, which took place in town on the 27th, and which melancholy event will restrain our gaieties and put us in mourning.

1839

January 5*th.*—As a specimen of what the shooting here now is, I must record that Mr. Sola, who was eager to have a day's sport, was obliged to amuse himself with the killing of sparrows and other small birds, as he could not get even a blackbird, much less a head of game.

9*th.*—Frost. Off for Keyhaven.

10*th.*—Scarcely any birds yet. All the better, as it will take me a few days to recover my strength, after being confined so long to the house.

N.B.—Not above three couple of birds killed here during my twenty days' absence at Longparish.

11*th.*—Frost ended in a set in of dirty 'sou'-wester,' with a constant batch of wind and rain.

19*th.*—Another tremendous gale and pour of rain all day, after the usual forerunner, a most petrifying white frost; weather that of course puts a stop to gunning, and the chance of birds. Read has persevered mud crawling night after night, and never saw the least chance for a shot. My gear continues still in store.

22*nd.*—A fine day at last, north wind, clear sky, and a little black frost.

31*st.*—From the 22nd up to this day we have had the most unpleasant weather, and the coast has been so destitute of birds that the poor gunners cannot earn even a few shillings a week. Nothing but white frosts, followed by westerly hurricanes. This morning, however, there set in a severe black frost, with a strong northerly gale and snow, so I got my small punt, and a light single stanchion gun, in order, not thinking it worth while to launch the grand set-out unless some good flocks of birds made their appearance.

February 1st.—A black frost, with wind north-north-west; but not a bird in the country, except a few geese that Read tried and could not get within a quarter of a mile of. He was out all last night with a bright moon, and never saw or heard a single fowl.

2nd.—Read crawled all night, and not a bird was to be seen or heard, either by night or day, on the whole coast. I availed myself of a fine sunshiny dead calm to try two shots at a mark with a new cartridge in my light stanchion, and the result was such that we had only to regret the want of a living target, on which to repeat our experiments. But the coast is done, totally done, for this season.

3rd.—Sunday. A warm bird-singing day.

4th.—A rotten wet day.

5th.—A May morning, ending in an afternoon and all night wet and windy sou'-wester.

6th.—Rotten heavy weather, but more calm.

7th.—Rotten wind and rain all day. Had a general furbish of all my 'traps' preparative to 'bolting' the day after to-morrow, as I could weather it no longer and had plenty of business in hand.

8th.—Savage wind and rain from the south-west. Called on all the good neighbours, and ordered my fly to take me off for to-morrow morning's coach.

9th.—Arrived at Longparish.

13th.—Went up to London.

21st.—After an incessant round of business with lawyers, bankers, executors, brokers, book publishers, binders, musicians, artists, gunmakers, and other tradesmen, attendance at the Horse Guards' Levee and the Queen's Levee &c., I this day returned (doing the thirty-eight miles railway in an hour and twenty minutes) per 'light Salisbury' coach to Longparish.

22nd.—A letter from Peter, who, thank God, had weathered all the awful hurricanes and landed safe in Barbadoes on December 20, after a passage of only four weeks and four days.

Lamentable list. The worst season in the memory of man. Game &c. killed up to November 26 only, as I never got a shot after, there being no game worth going out for, and the awful and destructive hurricanes, which began towards the end of this month, having driven home all the wild fowl from the coast:

Wild fowl: 1 teal, 5 wigeon (young birds in October). Total, 6. Waders in September: 2 godwits, 2 plover, 1 curlew. Total, 5.

N.B.—Seeing the failure of all the gunners, I never launched my punt this season.[1]

Game: 58 partridges, 6 hares, 7 pheasants, 8 rabbits, 1 woodcock, 4 snipes. Total, 84 head. Grand (or rather paltry) total, 95 head only.

March 4th.—Left Longparish for Keyhaven, not for shooting, as there is none this year, but for change of air, for this influenza that I and almost every one have suffered with. When in Winchester on my way through to-day I found that the assize court was crowded to excess, and would be all this day taken up with the case of Sir John Milbank stabbing the Southampton attorney, Mr. Pocock.

5th.—Found myself quite another man already from the change of air, and there came on a dry easterly wind.

9th.—Frost and snow, with a strong north wind; in short the weather of a proper, hard, healthy winter, though too late in the season to do any good. I went out to see if this set-in of fine hard weather had brought any fowl, and if so I should have launched at least my small swivel gun next day. But nothing was to be seen, except about 100 geese that would not let you get within a quarter of a mile of them. So much

[1] N.B.—Scarcity universal, and London supplied from Holland.

for fine weather setting in 'a day after the fair,' though it was sadly wanted for the health of the people, as I found that half this neighbourhood was laid up with the influenza. The effect of the hard winter and sea air acted like magic in curing me, and did me more good than all the medicines and warm baths I had taken.

7th.—Rowed out again, accompanied by Read, Payne, and Guy, in hopes of their driving the geese over my head by surrounding them on the mud; and I perhaps might have got one, but Buckle set into them with his stanchion gun, fired a blank shot, and away they all went. On my return home to dinner I had the mortification to receive a letter from my solicitor stating that the jury, for want of a better judge, had been humbugged into a wrong view of my legal case, and Charles, as well as my tenant, Farmer Diddams, was ordered three months' imprisonment. A most rascally, ignorant, and unheard-of piece of injustice. So much for the villanous laws of this country.

9th.—Fine hard winter still, but nothing afloat. Followed a flock of golden plover over a stiff country for four hours; but, at last, could only catch them so dispersed that I had the option of one or none as the last chance, so let fly and brought in 1 golden plover.

11th.—Out all day again in search of the plover; but the wind having shifted from north to east, they were not to be found. Intensely cold weather, and half the neighbourhood under the doctors with influenza. Fired some shots at small birds, all I could get to shoot at, with a self-priming copper-cap musket, that Westley Richards sent me as a present to try before he submitted it to Government. But although ingenious, I fear it will be too complex and not waterproof enough for the service.

18th.—Left Keyhaven in a piercing north-east wind and snow (though we literally had summer only three days ago) for Winchester, where I was all the forenoon employed in seeing my man Charles in gaol, relative to steps against the perjured blackguards who got him in there. Arrived at Longparish almost frozen at six in the evening, and had the satisfaction to receive another letter from Peter saying he was quite well, and had just weathered a severe earthquake.

31*st.*—Longparish. Very unwell ever since I came, from the general and horrible complaint called 'influenza.'

April 1*st.*—Winter. A bitter cold easterly wind with snow and rain. 7 wild geese were seen flying over to-day.

2*nd.*—Though the piercing cold continued, I this day saw 3 swallows flying up and down the river. A curious circumstance—grey geese and swallows in the country at the same time.

18*th.*—London. On returning from a call on Sir Benjamin Brodie, I ran foul of the grand wedding of Lord Douro, and got a capital post to view all the great dons, and the great ladies with their grace, lace, and giblets.

May 9*th.*—Cold as at Christmas again, whereas three days ago we were broiled with heat.

10*th.*—Intensely cold, with a north-east gale. People driven to great coats and furs again.

12*th.*—Sunday. Bitter cold. It was just thirty years ago from this day that our affair of the Douro took place.

14*th.*—Yesterday it was as hot as in July; to-day it was as cold as in winter, with occasional sleet and snow.

15*th.*—Epsom races, and actually snow at the 'Derby.'

23*rd.*—Ran down to Longparish. Tried trolling for a couple of hours this evening with Lord Saltoun's brass 'kill-devil,' the only artificial bait that I ever found to take in our river. It answered well; and though a vile evening for fishing, I killed 5 brace of large trout, besides what I threw in.

24*th.*—In my life, I never saw the vegetation so cut up as by the late winter, that we had about a week ago; when there were three days' snow, with ice half an inch thick. The oldest person never saw the like before.

25*th*.—Frost at night, cutting north-easter all day with a bright sun. Lovely weather for wild swans and geese; but the very devil for vegetation. Proceeded to Keyhaven to order some jobbing, repairs, painting &c., and on passing through the New Forest observed the greatest part of the trees appeared as if they had been set fire to, owing to the foliage being killed by the late severe weather.

28*th*.—Off from morning till night between Hordle and Christchurch with my large net, that I've had for three years, and never before wetted. We did pretty well, having brought home just 20 brace of fish, viz. 14 bass (largest 7 lb.), 3 mullets (best 2 lb.), 12 flounders, 4 small turbots, 1 sole, 6 very large gore fish.

29*th*.—A few hauls with net on our own shore; but the weeds were so thick, and my cadgers so drunk from the profits of yesterday, that we did but little and gave it up. We got only 5 bass (one 9½ lb.), 1 flounder, 1 gore fish, and 1 monster called a cuttlefish, which I never saw before (common as the shell is for pounce). We cut him open and threw him into the sea, and he made half an acre of water black with his ink; which, after he was thrown away, my cadgers told me was very valuable.

June 1*st*.—Took a day's sail to that delightful place, Alum Bay, and then round the Isle of Wight cliffs. Had my gun with me, but there was so little wind under and off the heights, that it was impossible to sail in quick enough to shoot the rock birds. Several parties were out on purpose, and I could not see that they got a single bird. I did contrive to bring home a few.

5*th*.—Longparish. Rose betimes and bustled along to Hartley Row for fear of being too late for the railway from there for town, but found it went at one instead of twelve, so had to kill an hour. This gave me an opportunity of walking about half a mile to see the arches that have lately fallen in, and one of which I had gone over one journey in the 'Hampshire Hunt' coach. The engineer, it appears, perseveres in establishing tunnels through stuff like brown sugar, instead of cutting a ravine and building a suspension, or, if no good ground to hold it, a common bridge. A stupid fellow.

20th.—I was taken so ill, that I despaired of being able to go to Hampton Court to-day to attend a picnic given by my old regiment, the 14th Light Dragoons. I, however, got the doctor to quack me up for a makeshift, and we started. We got down to Hampton Court just time enough for me to inspect the Palace &c. before dinner, and I was not a little gratified by the kind reception I met from my old regiment, though there was not one officer and very few of the men that had been in when I was with the 14th.[1]

July 6th.—Keyhaven. Took a refreshing sail to the back of the island, and on passing the Needles I observed a large boat at anchor with five men in it, two of whom were constantly winding away in a manner similar to drawing water from a deep well. I gave the order to 'lower sail,' and go up to this boat, which proved to be one on a diving speculation, and the diving man, who was some fathoms under water and had already been there an hour and three-quarters, was to come up again at the end of two hours, so I of course waited the other quarter of an hour to see the diver and hear what he had done. The winding apparatus that I saw incessantly at work was very finely manufactured, and made for the purpose of inflating air into the diving machine, or rather waterproof diving dress, of the man who was working under the sea. At last the diver came up rather exhausted, and as soon as he recovered his weakness he drew out from his large bag pockets several articles that were of no value except for a

[1] Brown, the bandmaster, Heatley, the trumpet major (a piccolo boy in the band in my time), and Fitzhenry, an old mungo and pupil of mine on the tambourine, soon proclaimed me as the officer whose squadron won the trophy of the 'Douro' (which they were wearing), and the respect shown to me by 'all hands' was such as I could not but feel; and particularly the honour of my health being given (with a statement of the circumstance) the first toast (after that of 'the ladies') when the dinner cloth was removed.

mere curiosity; the best prizes having already been taken up, as the vessel which went down there close to the Needles was the 'Pomone' frigate, wrecked thirty years ago. The 'hands' of the boat then said, 'Sir, please to remember the diver,' so I gave them a shilling and said, 'I shall still longer remember him if he gives me a bit of the copper, or anything worth a farthing, as a trophy of what I have seen,' on which the diver gave me a little thing as portable as he could find.

11th to 13th.—Immured in the town of Winchester with all my witnesses during the infernal uproar and row of the Assizes. Mr. Smith had to fly like a bird on the railroad repeatedly up and down from London. On one occasion he left at one in the night, and was back and at breakfast in Winchester by twelve in the day (eleven hours) with deeds and documents collected. Mr. Earle opened my case, and was answered by a terrific jaw from Mr. Butt, who, in order to preclude the fulminating reply of Mr. Earle, declined calling any of his witnesses, and consequently left all their lies and romances uncontradicted. As God's mercy would have it, I had insisted on a special jury (all thorough gentlemen, who were above the influence of a counsel's humbug), and they gave a verdict in my favour. The expense of course must be serious; but what am I to do if people will rob me and won't listen to proposals of fair arbitration?

20th.—London. Battle of Waterloo from morning till midnight preparative to our leaving town early on Monday morning, the 21st being Sunday. A severe day, too, on Sunday. Had to get up very early to read prayers and do business besides, as the only chance I had to get a pair of horses (which I was quite at a loss for want of) was at eleven (church time) this day, when I bought a pair of greys. While the horses were being shown off to me, the Wesleyan Methodists were in full cry in a chapel over the mews. Tried the horses in a spare omnibus (the only vehicle to be borrowed), then trotted and galloped each over town and country, then tried each separate in a gig, and in short bought them, and gave orders for their leaving town next day. I then flew off to Moscheles (the only day he could do business), and had a long and most satisfactory discussion with him on a trial of my 'hand-moulds,' after waiting till he had played three fugues and a concerto of Mendelssohn for his Sunday's practice. Then made a string of indispensable visits, that I could not catch a moment to do before. Read the evening prayers. Baited with bills, packing, and 'good-bye-ers' till twelve at night, and went to bed as tired as an old dog after the 1st of September.

22nd.—Flew by the rail to Basingstoke in two hours. We then posted home to Longparish House.

This evening at dusk a curious bird, that all the clods have been after for weeks, flew over me. I ran in and had to put a gun together, as all my things were dismantled. I shot the bird. It was quite white with a few yellow marks, and appeared more like a white canary than anything else. Perhaps a bird strayed from a cage; but I'll send it to Leadbeater, and 'time will show' what it is.

25th.—Had over Tom Langstaff with his fiddle, and enjoyed the first day's leisure and pleasure that incessant worry would allow me for several weeks past.

August 3rd.—Keyhaven. Fine weather at last; so I was enabled to take a delightful sail. Put into Hurst in order to inspect and bring away a specimen of the new paving composition, for the manufactory of which 'Crusoe's' beach cottage is let to a London man. This material is made from a stuff called 'bitumen,' like lava, which, from being pliant and somewhat sticky, is rendered as hard as iron by the process of boiling it with a certain composition; and it may then be ornamented with beach pebbles ground up so as to look like granite. The man employed in it showed me several specimens laid out in squares, stars &c. as ornamental paving for halls and such like.

20th.—An eventful day for exertion, grandeur, novelty, &c. At half-past one, being disappointed of my donkey chaise, I had to amble at a jackass trot to catch the coach before it passed Everton. I proceeded to the excellent little inn of Mrs. Osbaldeston at Redbridge, to dress in my best, and join the splendid gala of Captain Colt at Rownam's house. I then drove on in my carriage, and arrived about half-past five, just as the innumerable host of fashionables were sat down to a banquet similar to that of a lord mayor. The wines flew at an awful pace, and the speeches after dinner were like a meeting in parliament, and I had the honour of being kindly victimised on the occasion by our hospitable host as the leader of the shooting world. We then had a concert till near eleven, fireworks equal to Vauxhall till twelve under the able directions of Captain Rich, dancing till two, then a gorgeous sitting supper, and a finale with dancing till half-past three, when the carriage came again from Redbridge and took us worn out to our beds at the inn. Vercellini, who had no refuge to fly to but a night's lodging under a hedge, as every sofa in the house as well as every inn in the neighbourhood was crammed with visitors, lay on the inn sofa for the night, and we almost burst with laughter at the account of the concatenation of troubles he was in through arriving before us at the inn without his 'cue,' and being taken for a madman or wandering impostor.

21st.—This morning Vercellini was as lively as a lark, and singing his roulades in the garden. We then turned to at music till breakfast, and sang a grand duet of Donizetti. To relate all the fun and catastrophes that occurred during this expedition would fill a novel for Colburn, but my head is too distracted to write more than a sorry memorandum.

CHAPTER XXXII

1839

September 1*st.*—Longparish. Sunday. Shooting, such as it now is at Longparish, postponed, owing to the corn not being cut, and a good job too, as it's a disgrace to the laws to begin so early.

2*nd.*—After tremendous gales and showers for three days we had this day a regular set in of rain as well as wind, so while the tyros were getting their wet jackets and almost empty bags I went to do all my commissions.

3*rd.*—More wet weather, and the wind raging enough to blow one's teeth down one's throat. A sorry time for those who would not postpone their shooting.

5*th.*—Went to inspect Mr. Weld's champion yacht, the 'Alarm.'

10*th.*—Took the field about eleven o'clock to-day, and of all the sorry first days I ever had at Longparish this was the worst. It's all over with our partridge shooting. Had I brought home every head of game I saw, my number would not have amounted to what was a few years ago an average bag. Though I never shot better than to-day, I only got 13 partridges and 1 hare. I missed but one shot, and that was in attempting to secure a quail with my second barrel, at which my first had missed fire. The other shooters, as far as I could learn, had even worse sport than I had, though the weather, for the first time this month, was tolerably fine. Good-bye to good sport on the Longparish estate, till our surrounding neighbours have less mercy on the vermin and poachers, and more mercy on the game.

11*th.*—Rested myself and dogs, *and dined with the lawyer* at seven. He had been all over his best preserve, with Lords George and William Poulett, and their three pair of barrels got but 7 brace among them, so it proved that I had done no worse than my neighbours.

18*th.*—A windy day with a few showers. Took out my gun to try if it were possible to get a few birds for the house, and, to the astonishment of all, I brought home 18 prime partridges, and I lost another in the high turnips. I only fired my gun twenty-one times, and the only two blank shots were out of reach. In short, I never shot better, and considering the season is the worst on record, I never had a more astonishing day. I only started at twelve, and was home a quarter before five. But I was lucky in dispersing birds in the wind.

20*th.*—A treat worth all the game shooting in the world. Thalberg at Winchester for his farewell performance. Drove the girls over, and a delightful treat we had, as he was far more extraordinary than when we last heard him in town ; his miraculous combination of working in four parts with intense feeling and electrifying execution decidedly proves him to be the greatest pianist that ever sat before the public.

Ran down for a change of air to Keyhaven.

N.B.—No sooner had I reached Southampton than the wet weather set in again.

26*th.*—As some trips of wigeon had been seen, I availed myself of this the first fine day, though a strong westerly wind, to launch my light punt, the 'Dart,' with the single stanchion gun, and took a long cruise beyond Pilewell, where I fell in with 9 wigeon ; but the coastguard were at exercise and drove them away. Coming home 5 more travelled past, but did not stop. I saw a rare bird in the marsh, a phalarope, and got him with the cripple stopper.

Game killed in September (shooting so bad that I went

out but four times, and then only for half a day): 40 partridges, 1 hare, 1 landrail. Total, only 42 head.

Our shooting has been all but annihilated by the taking of eggs, the severe weather in May, the destruction of hedges and turf banks for firing, and the mowing of the wheat.

October 1st.—As we have not had any pheasants, except by chance a stray one, at Longparish for several years, the 1st of October is no longer an eventful day for me.

16th.—London. Saw that splendid invention, the daguerreotype.

18th.—Returned to Longparish after knocking off what some twaddlers would take three weeks to do in three clear days.

Universal complaints about the scarcity of game with all the gunmakers, powder men &c. in London.

19th.—Longparish. After being baited with business till near one, I turned out for a bit of pleasure with as fine a brigade of men and dogs as ever took the field, and did wonders, considering the scarcity. We found five pheasants, all in the country I believe, and every bird of them came home to the larder.

November 21st.—This is the grand day for the meeting on Chambers's (my bankers) bankruptcy; but as I had sent a power of attorney with my vote against that scorpion, old M——, and the other diabolical assignees, I had no occasion to go up on purpose, though should have much enjoyed the baiting of these scamps had my lawsuit called me to town about the same time. So I started in a pour of rain to Keyhaven, not a little delighted to get there.

25th to 27th.—Bad weather, which was rather *à propos*, as I have been three days a prisoner with illness.

28th.—Better, but sick and weak still. Buckle came ashore to see me, after having earned only 4*s.* 6*d.* the whole month. I took a little walk with him for some air; we saw a cock wigeon in the 'mudlands,' so Buckle hauled his punt over the bank, and I got the bird with the popgun just before there set in a wet afternoon.

December 6th.—All the wild fowl in the whole of the large town of Southampton to-day was one stinking 'curre' duck. Not even a decoy-caught wild duck in the town or market. What can be worse than these beastly white frosts; or, in other words, petrified, poisonous fogs? Not a bird at Keyhaven.

7th.—A cold damp southerly wind. Too much sea to go out.

8th.—Sunday. A strong easterly wind, but damp and deadly cold instead of bracing, and so dark I could not see to read in church, nor, by the way, hear either, for the constant coughs and sneezes of the congregation.

9th.—A cold damp east wind. Took the punt to bring home some things for the house from Lymington, but brought back again the charge that had been put into my single stanchion gun on last Saturday fortnight. Not even a chance for a shot.

10th.—Bitter cold, and damp east wind. No fowl; a sure sign that this east wind is only a humbug, and 'bound' for a south-wester and rain. Blew off my gun, which went like lightning, though loaded 18 days.

16th.—A fine day at last. Afloat at daybreak, but never saw a fowl, and came home with nothing but an old crow that I knocked over with the popgun. A pinching white frost at night.

17th.—The white frost broke into a damp southerly gale. Not a bird to be seen.

N.B.—I this day saw, by mere accident, the following article, under the head of different regiments, in the 'Naval and Military Gazette' of the 14th inst.:

'74th. Lieutenant Hawker is about to return from the West Indies on sick leave. He is son to Colonel Hawker, whose "Hints to Sportsmen" have gained a just celebrity.'

I at once wrote to my agent in town to go and learn particulars, as I had not heard from Peter, though I wrote every foreign post day, and yet received no letter since one on September 24, when he was in good health, and had been having grand sport with the tobago plover and other birds.

21st.—A fine day at last, though a heavy south-wester. Had a general furbish of all the gear and stores, and put them away, preparative to going inland for Christmas, after the most barren year for sport in the memory of the oldest person living.

25th—Longparish. Went (Christmas Day) to our church, where Mr. Greene read a prayer for fair weather. The church is beautifully ornamented and altered; a fine painted window over the altar, and some fine specimens of carving from the Continent, all of which is presented by our worthy vicar, Mr. Greene.

26th.—The pinching white frost that bit our noses all last night, turned this morning into another most determined wet day. Accounts from Peter to November 5, when he was, thank God, 'quite well.' So the news in the paper was all false.

27th.—Wet again, but outwitted the weather by having a jolly good day with Tom Langstaff and his fiddle.

28th and 29th.—Sunday. Petrifying white frosts.

30th.—Ditto, and so deadly cold that one could get no warmth in bed, up, in doors or out of doors. Everyone complaining of chills. This night, soon after ten, began Mr. Fellowes's grand ball at Hurstbourne Park, when I dressed up and went, though so unwell I could hardly stand, and shivering with cold 'like a dog in a wet sack.' Never was anything more handsomely done, and the sitting supper for all (above one hundred of the *élite* of the county) was quite the best I ever saw. We went in a bitter cold white frost, and came away, about three, in a pour of rain.

1840

January 9th.—Keyhaven. Everyone complaining of chills, and nearly all the gunners ill from the late poisonous weather. Not a bird yet come to the coast.

13*th.*—Longparish. Unprecedented weather, and, what I never saw before, eight white frosts running, with wind south-south-east. So deadly cold that everyone complained of not being able to get warm, even with exercise; and not so much as a fieldfare or a few larks, much less a head of game, to be seen or heard of. The dullness of the country now is absolutely lamentable so far as concerns outdoor amusement.

18*th.*—Bitter white frost. Started, bag and baggage, with the whole family, in the Whitchurch chariot and my carriage at half-past eight this morning for Basingstoke. The roads were so vile that we were nearly three hours doing the 15 miles. We had nineteen heavy packages, besides innumerable little things, and all was shipped with the regularity of clockwork by means of my patent plan of not only numbering, as most wise people do, but by tying a piece of scarlet binding to distinguish every article that belonged to my party. What a contrast between the awful freight of a batch of females, and a gent with his one portmanteau!

22*nd.*—London. Rain and a hurricane all day; tiles and chimney pots flying about like Waterloo. Few men have had a sharper day's work than I to-day, viz. after paying bills and doing several commissions in the City, I was with Parkinson having a tooth drawn at eleven. Then a long business with Chambers, my former banker, in the Fleet Prison; ditto at the 'Times' office; then down to the Court of Exchequer in Westminster Hall, where I had a consultation with counsel about my lawsuit, expected on every day. Then an interview with several officers at our club about getting Long the appointment of furbisher at the Tower; then with Mr. Hatch, the secretary of the Army and Navy Club, about Peter's concerns. Then with Jones about a clever six-barrel pistol; with Eley about cartridges, and with Lancaster and Long about guns. Then up to H——, near Tottenham Court Road. Then down to Mr. Gunther's at Camden Town on the business of a new piano for Keyhaven, and on transferring to him my 'hand-mould' business. Then a long visit at Moscheles' about musical lessons and divers musical novelties. Then to settle a bill and give some orders in Park Road, and home just in time to save the post with some letters on business to the country. Swallowed my dinner about six, and afterwards had a stiff pianoforte lesson from Bertini, who by mere chance dropped in and invited me to a good 'strap. Went to bed at eleven, as tired as a dog after the 1st of September.

24th.—Ferocious weather and another deluge of rain all day. At Westminster again to-day, but trial not to come on, and to-morrow the judges will be all occupied on the point (of our humbugging laws) which relates to the notorious Frost.

25th.—No lawsuit till about Tuesday, as the Court of Exchequer is occupied to-day with the case of the notorious Frost, and will not resume equity cases till next week.

29th.—The rain ceased. Judges decided against Frost. I was directed to be in the Exchequer Court this day at two, and when I arrived my trial was over; so unexpectedly did it come on that Wickham's leading counsel (Butt) and his solicitor and my solicitor were all too late, but both my counsel, Earle and Smirke, were there, as was also Mr. Smith, my solicitor's clerk, who gave us a full report. Judgment was deferred till the judges had conferred together, and Mr. Butt got leave to have a new trial in case their verdict did not suit him. Judges Park and Alderson took my part, but I am fearful as to Judges Gurney and Coleridge. We were much amused at the blustering Mr. Butt arriving too late to spit out his jaw. Here ends my business in London for the present.

31*st.*—Went down, viâ railway and Salisbury coach, to Longparish, where I cut through all my bills, inspections of work done &c. with railway speed, and with only a few hours' sleep, in order to get out of the place before the damp of it should make me unwell again.

Lamentable list of game up to February 1, 1840: 42 partridges, 1 landrail, 3 hares, 3 rabbits, 4 pheasants (all I saw), 8 snipes (all in one day). Total, 61 head only.

The fact was that the game season was so bad I gave up shooting, and resigned to Charles Heath, my keeper, the hard labour of getting about 5 head a week for the table. I never shot better; but there was nothing to shoot owing to the destroyed breed, and then the floods and hurricanes.

February 3*rd.*—Keyhaven. In a bustle since this early morning putting things to rights, unpacking the new piano &c. when about 30 geese dropped inside below Pennington. We left one bustle for another, dried some powder, launched the 'Dart,' the light single-gun punt &c. in hopes of catching the geese before the ground ebb; but, after all, we were about a quarter of an hour too late, and they left us for the eastward.

4*th.*—Weather more awful than ever; a tremendous hurricane and an awful flood. It came on last night at twelve. My punt the 'Dart' was torn from her moorings and washed inland, but saved by the coastguard. To-day at high water (eleven o'clock), the sea swallowed up the whole quay, and I galloped off for help from Milford; but at one the waters happily abated sufficiently to induce us to withhold the removal of further articles from the ground floor, and we now remain all anxiety about the tide of this night, with a raging hurricane and a pour of rain, though, thank God, a few more points from the awful south. After remaining on guard, 'all hands,' till past twelve at night, when it was as dark as it possibly could be, we retired to bed in safety, as the change of wind had providentially arrested all further danger.

5*th.*—In the morning all was as well as if nothing had happened, save a few shillingsworth of damage to gear &c. A strong north-wester all day. Had I not been here, I should most likely have had one of my splendid punts knocked to pieces, as I had her carried into the yard in spite of Read and others, who advised me to let her swing near the quay, where, soon after I rescued her, there was a fall of water like Niagara, and she must have caught the current and been dashed down a fall of about eight feet.

10*th.*—Terrific weather all night and to-day; but as the tides are luckily now at the neap, we are pretty safe from flood.

N.B.—The Queen's wedding day; but I lost nothing by not being in town, as J. Hawker, *alias* Clarenceux King of Arms, told me he could get no admissions to the ceremony for me or anyone. So all I can do is to drink 'to the royal pair' among myself and myrmidons.

11*th.*—A letter from Peter dated December 20, when he had got quite well, thank God, and had been enjoying some splendid shooting and fishing, and had got a large alligator while on a visit at the seat of a Tobago planter or squire. Weather so much better this afternoon that I put my light punt afloat again and went off again, but had not gone far when the weather set in with all its fury, and continued all night.

17*th.*—A fine day at last, with a light air from the eastward, and no sun, the very best of times for gunning. I therefore got up by candlelight, and once more enjoyed the sea breeze in my light punt, but came home about one, after having gone many miles and seen nothing. Went off again about two, when it was quite calm, and rowed off in Channel, where I made a capital shot at 6 black velvet ducks. I floored the whole of them at about 120 yards The only dead one floated out past Hurst, where I dare not follow him.

18*th.*—A fine heavy gale from the east, though we fear too late to bring us any sport.

19*th.*—Gale from east. About 60 geese off; the most seen this year. Weathered a heavy sea, and was dropping smoothly down 'cock sure' of a good shot, when 10 more flew over and drove them all miles to leeward. The 10 flew past us in a heavy sea. I 'up gun' and down with 5 of them, and made my retreat with the first geese shot here this year. Came in at two and drove to Noah's marsh, where there have been some snipes, but found nothing but 1 jack snipe and 3 water rails, all of which I cleared off. In the evening 'Buckle' anchored a mile to windward of us, so that our further sport with these few geese will be done for either by his banishing them from the ground, or by his lying directly where he must have the first shot.

20*th.*—A prime north-easter, with a healthy black frost, and a few blossoms of snow, but, alas! two months too late to be of much service. Out from daylight till afternoon, and saw only a few geese far off at sea.

21*st.*—Out, but too rough to 'live' outside, and nothing on coast but a few geese, though as severe a winter's day as could be wished for.

22*nd.*—Hard black frost and furious east gale all last night and all to-day. Went off about four in the afternoon, and weathered some stiff breakers to a small trip of about 15 birds, and cut down 10 of them, a splendid shot for its extreme difficulty.

24*th.*—Intense frost and severe east gale all yesterday and all to-day, though nothing on our coast except one fine set of geese that remain where no boat could live.

25*th.*—Moderate. Out at daylight and saw the geese, but the gale sprung up again and I dare not follow them. Found the remainder of the 15 birds in the same place I fired on Saturday; there were 5 left, and I bagged 'every man John of them,' viz. 5 wigeon, and thus had the glory of annihilating the whole company.

26th.—Bitter cold gale and frost. Up at daybreak, having had the punt previously sent on to Pennington, so that I could walk to her after the tide was too late to float her inside. The plan answered so well that I fairly outwitted the grand army of geese, that had increased to about 300. The birds were all feeding under the lee of the mud at the edge of a most awful sea, and we popped on them from a place of perfect safety; but having only No. 1 shot in the gun they were about eighty yards too far, the consequence was I only knocked down 5. Had I been loaded with mould shot I think I must have bagged 20, as I caught the company all in a line, but at two hundred yards my shot was too light.

N.B.—Not another fowl to be seen. So much for good weather when it comes too late for fowl to migrate.

March 2nd.—The severe frost and north-easterly gale of wind never ceased all yesterday and all to-day, but not a bird has it brought on the whole spy-glass view of our coast. It's too late now for hard weather to do any good, and the gunning may be pronounced a blank for this season. I betook myself to the fields for exercise, and walked at least ten miles in search of golden plover, though never saw but 16; and some starlings and fieldfares spoiled my chance while I was crawling, by driving them up with their flutter and chatter. If I had been all day in the treadmill I could not have had a harder day's fag than I had to-day, and all for nothing.

4th.—Ash Wednesday. The most intensely cold north-east gale that ever blew into mouth and ears, and the coast looking as if uninhabited by man, and destitute of all living creatures except a few hungry gulls. My only reason for not 'cutting my stick' is the chance that either a calm would give me one fair trial at the geese, or a fall of snow might drive a few wild ducks from the private ponds.

6th.—Moderate. Went afloat outside and bagged 2 geese at about two hundred yards out of a little company of 14. As the geese were 'up to' the white punts I made my punt drab colour, with a wet of inland soil, as salt mud would stain the paint, and put on a drab gunning dress. This, by the way, should always be done in bright sun or moon, though at all other times white is the only colour.

7th.—A light breeze. Up with the larks, and cruised about twelve miles up Channel. Saw nothing the whole day but one small trip of geese that rose a quarter of a mile off, and thus convinced myself that all further attempts for this season would be only a waste of time, so came home by two o'clock, put my punt in store, and 'struck' for the season.

Sorry list of the past vile season: 30 wigeon, 2 mallards, 5 geese (most killed by anyone), 4 black ducks, 11 plover, 4 godwits, 7 curlews. Total, only 63 head. Add 11 snipes and 53 game, and my grand total is only 127 head, though I believe I've done the best of anyone. What a miserable display, though I never shot better or worked harder in all my life.

10th.—Left Keyhaven for Longparish, and on the 11th I arrived safe in Dorset Place, London. The train did the forty-eight miles five minutes under the two hours—the quickest passage I have had.

N.B.—No winter birds at Longparish, and complaints of scarcity even in the London market; so that the splendid weather (which still continues) has been of no service whatever from its having come too late.

17th.—London. At Chalk Farm (where I met all the leading gunmakers) to see a trial of cartridges invented by T. T. Berney, Esq., of Morton Hall, near Norwich, who had previously called to request my attendance. The cartridge consists of a spiral spring, which is filled with the shot and calcined cinders, and strongly wadded with about an inch of moss next the powder. The performance nearly doubled anything I had before seen, and these projectiles must be capital for open or for coast shooting; but, as the spiral spring is a deadly missile wherever it hits, they must never be used for common sporting. Mr. Berney promises experiments with a swivel gun in about six weeks, and was kind enough to show me his plan for firing his stanchion at plover by means of an elliptic spring attached to the saddle of a mule, he having one trained for this purpose. I never met with a more ingenious or intelligent gentleman than this thoroughbred old sportsman, Mr. Berney. I could, however, scarcely enjoy my view of his experiments as I was so unwell, and the weather was most piercing.

21*st.*—Not a wild fowl in London, except cartloads of rotten birds packed in boxes of ice from Norway.

23*rd.*—Took a copy of my sporting book to leave at Buckingham Palace (agreeably to his Royal Highness's permission) for Prince Albert, and then returned a visit with which I was honoured by Prince Napoleon Louis Bonaparte. After my attendance on these personages I went into our club, where I had the misfortune to receive a letter from Peter, dated on his birthday, January 19, announcing his alarming illness with yellow fever, which was, and I fear still must be, raging in Tobago. Out of six seized he was the only one alive ; but, thanks to God, he gave me every hope that he has got out of danger, and when, please God, well enough to be removed, that he would use all interest to get home on sick leave, in which I fervently pray that he may succeed.

April 4th.—Being detained here by the postponement of Wednesday's Levee till Monday, the 6th, I had luckily not left town, when I had this morning the satisfaction to receive a letter from Peter dated 'Off the Lizard' (Cornwall) on board the 'Louisa Baillie,' West Indiaman, bound for London, announcing his safe arrival in sight of English land, and his amendment in health, after having been given over for death, by the yellow fever.

N 2

7th.—I was all day till six, cutting about and racing round the West India Docks; and then waiting on the pier in a pour of cold rain, with cutting north wind, to see if any of the ships coming in was the one in which Peter is, but no tidings as yet.

8th.—A postman's knock about twelve. Made sure it was a note from doctor about Peter, when 'Lo! who obeyed the knocker's rattling peal' but Peter himself! He had left the ship beating off Margate Roads, and very wisely flew up to town by the Margate steamer. His getting aboard this ship was a mere chance that decidedly saved his life; he could not have lived till the packet sailed, and the 'Louisa Baillie,' a first-rate West Indian of near 500 tons from Demerara, happened to put in at Barbadoes, and took him off the moment he got his leave. Thanks to God, all my fears are now at an end; and Peter is looking as well as ever.

May 11th.—London. One of the finest Philharmonics on record, at which we had the literally magic performance of the wonder of the world, Liszt, the Paganini of the pianoforte, whom I had previously heard on the 8th, when he made his *début* at Parry's concert; and whom I knew when a boy in England fifteen years ago. To describe his energy, effect, and execution, baffles all the public writers. In short, no one can compete with him in wildfire and electric effect, and his graces are of the highest order. So let us place him and Thalberg as the Gog and Magog of the piano, like two super-exquisite paintings; Thalberg as the sunshine, and Liszt as the storm, surpassing all other artists.

12th.—We made up a dinner party for Peter and friends, and on an appropriate day, which never occurred to me till the day came, for it was the anniversary of the 'Douro,' where my squadron gained the trophy for the 14th Light Dragoons in 1809.

June 4th.—Being apprised by Mr. Earle last night that judgment would be given to-day in my lawsuit, I went this morning again to the Court of Exchequer, where I had the great satisfaction to hear the judgment on every point given 'for' (me) 'the defendant.' Mr. Butt, however, after badgering the judges for near an hour, at last got a rule granted to have some legal points argued again at Michaelmas term. As my enemy in the country made so sure of swamping me, I only regret I could not send him a pigeon with despatches to give him an appetite for his dinner.

12th.—After leaving my name among the innumerable calls of congratulation at Buckingham Palace, I went to inspect the supposed two bullet marks on the wall near where the would-be assassin, Edward Oxford, fired two pistols at her Majesty and Prince Albert on the evening of the 10th. From what I could learn the villain was only about three paces off when he fired; and the bullet marks, if such they were, measured thirteen paces apart, and were evidently well directed, except rather behind. Her Majesty was driven at a quick trot; and by the blessing of Divine Providence, the scoundrel omitted to make the proper allowance for a cross shot.

20th.—Ran down to superintend the completion of, and pay for, some work at Keyhaven, where I arrived about seven in the evening, after having encountered a regular uproar, and seen a fine sight, during the three hours I had to wait for the coach in Southampton. It was a grand public breakfast to the Duke of Sussex, on the completion of the railroad; and what with guns, bells, bands, mobs, and processions, the city of London was comparatively quiet to the town of Southampton on this gala day. The Duke with the Duchess of Inverness, his wife, were close behind our train, with a separate engine; so that we were in the very thick of the great reception.

21st.—Sunday. Keyhaven. Thanksgiving for the Queen's providential escape, but no sermon on that subject. The singers, however, were determined to outdo the parson, and brayed out the four verses of 'God save the Queen,' to which the clerk appended an 'Amen' at the very top of his voice. All this was just previous to the last prayer after the sermon.

July 7th.—London. My lawsuit ended at last with a glorious victory on all four issues; the parties having declined the further litigation of a 'writ of error' before all the other judges, and agreed, as awarded, to pay all costs.

27th.—Battle of Waterloo, or family in uproar, preparative to our all leaving London to-morrow; a van of advanced baggage started, and the .onfusion and noise of tongues and door bell terrific. I raced on commissions till four, and then at all my intricate half-year's accounts in the midst of all the row.

29th.—I arrived in the charming air and quietude of Keyhaven Cottage.

August 4th.—Keyhaven. Anniversary of my purchasing a troop in the 14th Light Dragoons in 1804, when only 17 years 7 months and 11 days old. This to-day is just 36 years ago; as I am now these odd months and days over 53. *Tempus fugit.*

5th.—I was surprised to hear that a few months ago Lieutenant Harnet died; the man who, by his invention of mud 'launching,' has for some years ruined our coast, on the glory of which I made for him an epitaph.

PETER HAWKER'S EPITAPH ON LIEUTENANT HARNET.

Dedicated to the writer's esteemed friend, the Hon. William Hare.

1

Good reader, here Lieutenant Harnet lies,
Who ruin dealt to all the Hampshire coast,
By 'launching punt,' a plan he did devise
(Of which some imitating quacks now boast).

2

The ooze that once for authors formed a theme,
On which our Gilpin and our Daniel wrote,
No more has geese, or swans, or ducks 'in team,'
No sport we've now for shoreman, punt, or boat!

Inv^d. & Sketched by P. Hawker. Eng^d. on Steel by H. Adlard.

MUD-LAUNCHERS, on the oozes, off LYMINGTON, shoving their PUNTS up to WIGEON.

London, Published by Longman & C°. 1844.

3

Lieutenant Harnet crawled upon his knees,
  And shoved this punt before him in the night,
Till all his kinsmen thus the birds did tease,
  And drove the fowl for miles at ev'ry flight.

4

Let's hope Lieutenant Harnet's gone aloft,
  For good he was, and all must wish him well ;
Though had he gone below, and ta'en his craft,
  I wot the devil he'd driven out of hell.

6th.—Insufferably hot. Nightingales in my garden within reach of a whip from the windows of the Cottage.

24th.—By way of a tonic I this day sailed to Alum Bay, ascended the heights, shot 20 wheatears for a delicious roast, brought home some nice little hen lobsters and prawns, blew myself out like a pointer, and found myself quite another man.

31st.—Left Keyhaven for Longparish after some baths, and sailing almost every day, by which I found myself much better than when I left. Three hours in Southampton, and went all over the colossal steamer, the 'Oriental,' previous to her starting to-morrow for Malta and Alexandria.

CHAPTER XXXIII

1840

September 1*st.*—Longparish House. Having only arrived here last night, and much to do, we could not throw off till near twelve to-day, when we had a broiling sun with a strong north-east gale, and the ground as dry as Lundyfoot snuff. But I did wonders considering this and the degenerated state of our once fine country, and the extreme wildness of the birds, having bagged, in little more than half a day, 24 partridges, besides 4 more shot and lost. Our combined bag was as follows:

Partridges bagged: myself 24, Peter 8, Charles 8 and 2 hares. Total, 40 birds and 2 hares.

3*rd.*—Bothered and hindered again till near twelve, when I went out with one old dog, and bagged 24 partridges without one miss. I gave up the 'Furgo' country, and all the markers, except Siney, to Peter and his friend Captain O'Grady, or I might have made a grand day. But they bagged only 8 birds between them.

6*th.*—Sunday. Heard all the shooting bulletins of my neighbours, by which I ascertained that, with my one dog, I had beat everyone in our country.

8*th.*—Plastered up my swelled face, and worked like a slave for the larder, but the birds were become so very wild I could only bring home 12 partridges. Mr. Fellowes shot over Tufton on Saturday, and his bag was one squeaker. What a pass our country is come to now the farmers mow the wheat, and destroy all the turf hedges for fuel!

9th.—Face no better, so laid myself up. This afternoon Buckle arrived from Southampton to enter my service, and to assist me in building a land-and-water punt, that I had some time ago invented.

15th.—Cold windy weather. Tied up my face and went out for about four hours in the afternoon, and brought in 8 partridges and 1 hare, making three doublets and three single shots, and missing nothing. No bad work for a cripple in the hands of the doctor.

16th.—Dragged the pond for 2 jack that had got through the grating when less than gudgeon in size. The one weighed $5\frac{1}{2}$ lb., the other $4\frac{3}{4}$ lb., and we caught also 12 small jack. We pulled out several brace of tench and perch; one of each we kept and weighed. The perch was 2 lb., the tench $1\frac{3}{4}$ lb. They were put in when about the size of sprats, in 1837. We took also, and let go, several trout from 3 to 4 lb. each, which were put in when about $\frac{1}{2}$ lb. in 1837.

26th.—Buckle left me for Southampton to prepare for a winter at Keyhaven, I having engaged him in my service.

29th.—For the first time for several days I've left the house and premises, being unwell, and busy with the punt. I went and killed 4 large trout that were wanted for dinner, the best of which was nearly 2 lb. This must end angling, as the fish, I see, are beginning to spawn.

N.B.—Never shot after September, except killing October 1st 2 pheasants and 4 rabbits, and December 2nd 3 jack snipes. Our game shooting was annihilated, so I laid aside my gun.

Game killed in September: 80 partridges and 1 hare. Total, 81 head.

October 1st.—Mustered an army, and scoured the whole of my liberty for the chance of a stray pheasant, and bagged 2 pheasants and 4 rabbits. We found but 3 pheasants the whole day, though we had fine calm weather and a good scent. The third pheasant was a grand old cock that rose out of bounds, a very long shot; but I hit him so hard that he most likely dropped dead, though we hunted for two hours and never could find him. Except this bird I bagged all I shot at.

5*th.*—Keyhaven. Still very unwell; at Batramsley, to see Captain Vere Ward on the subject of selling his gun, punt and gear. Coast literally swarming with birds, and even the clods killing wigeon with muskets. Buckle arrived this evening, and, on his passage here, this day killed and brought me for the larder 29 wigeon and 1 pintail in 2 shots. House in confusion at night, to get all in order for a daybreak start to-morrow. Most untoward arrival of fowl, as I came to take Mr. Price's cottage for Buckle and on other business, and; not with the least idea that there was a fowl on the coast, much less the greatest October flight ever known.

6*th.*—Off at daylight, shot at about 40 wigeon across the line, got 5 wigeon and 2 teal. A better shot than I had right to expect. Got no other chance, as I had to come home with my punt leaking like a basket, from having had not a moment of daylight to overhaul her for this sudden turn-out. Weak as a rat, and no appetite. In the evening the easterly wind ceased, and the cock went to south-west: so I suppose I shall find that I have arrived just in time to be too late. Had I been here and in proper order to get afloat a week ago, I must have killed at least 200 or 300 birds, judging from the bags that have been got by the most contemptible bunglers.

8*th.*—Went off from six till six with the punt less leaky than before, but to no purpose, as the fowl were all gone, except a small trip off at sea.

11*th.*—Sunday. Green peas with a goose at dinner, my apple trees in blossom, and woodcocks in the country.

24*th and* 25*th.*—Longparish. A prisoner still. The latter day I got a letter from Mr. Berney to put me off from a grand pheasant shooting week at Morton Hall, Norfolk, in consequence of his fall from a ladder.

November 13*th.*—Keyhaven. An awful hurricane, and the most alarming flood that ever was known here. About twelve o'clock I had just begun a letter to Peter, when I was obliged to throw down my pen and fly in water boots for help to save my property; had I not providentially been here, all my valuable guns, punts, and gear might have been ruined. The sea banks burst, and the water was soon a foot deep in all the lower rooms of the houses, and such was the torrent against the doors that, had they burst open, as we every moment dreaded, our house must have been swamped. Retreat was impossible, as no one could either wade or row against the violence of the current that swallowed up the road. About four the water suddenly abated, and we then opened the doors, and let it pour from the rooms as from a mill hatch, and we were then enabled to climb over hedges to lay in a night's provision from Milford. We were all on guard the whole night, and, as God's mercy had it, the wind flew from the south to the north-west, or heaven knows what must have become of us. This providential wind saved the whole village, by cutting the tide to only a moderate height, and at daylight in the morning all was well, except an awful breach in the bank, that will cause us to dread more than ever a south hurricane.

14*th.*—Half the boats in the harbour blown out over the banks into the marsh fields. Coots, rabbits, and fish lying dead among the general wreck of gear, gates, pales, and other property. Many floods as I have seen here, this one has been of all others the most awful and alarming. But, thanks to God and strong assistance just called in time, I saved the whole of my furniture and valuable gunning property.

15*th.*—Sunday. Called up at three this morning with a cry of 'The water! the water! for God's sake get up, sir!' This awful breach in the bank had let in even an average tide in such an alarming way that the water was again nearly up to my house, all owing to the sleepy indolence of a Mr. McLean, who neglected to stop the breach while a mere trifle. I went to him at his window, and with some difficulty persuaded him to send to a carpenter to make a temporary check by piles, gates &c. till the navigators could come on Monday. The carpenter, all asleep, could find nothing, and came down at his leisure, and condemned my idea. At a quarter past ten the break in the bank might have been stopped in an hour, but Mr. McLean was gone off to church and Sunday gossip, and I could get no authority. I offered a mob of clods a shilling apiece to turn in and stop the breach, but they would not hear of it unless they had 5*s.* each, so there it ended. In the afternoon the master navigator came and said I had advised admirably, but then it was too late, so we now remain at the mercy of Providence, with every prospect of alarming weather till to-morrow.

16th.—After our being on watch all night, there came on a serious influx of water before daylight, but at half-past six this morning it fell back without entering the house. Frightful gales all day, and nearly south. The navigators came at one, but could do nothing, from Mr. McLean having provided no marl or faggots, and it blew too fresh for a temporary stoppage with gates and such like. All operations at a standstill, and Mr. McLean riding out at his ease. No prospect of proceeding. So I took the postman's letter cart, flew up to Mrs. Whitby, who acted (like Buonaparte) in one minute. She instantly ordered all her men with teams to strike from their work, and to begin digging and drawing down six loads of marl preparative to to-morrow, and by four o'clock two loads had arrived, previously to which she came down herself followed by her bailiff.

17th.—A southerly wind having blown last night, we were in great alarm for the tide at a quarter before seven this morning, but a shift of wind about two checked the flood, and by nine o'clock the water had abated sufficiently to go on with ten men, besides Payne and myself, hard at repairing the awful breach. It poured with rain during the whole of the job, but, by dint of cheering on the workmen with good words and 'lush,' I had the place that had given way in the bank stopped up by two o'clock in such a manner as to put an end to all danger even in a gale of wind. The men had not left the place one hour before there set in a strong gale from the southward, that might have done us most serious damage. Had I not been exerting myself like a fellow fighting for his country the whole time, through the whole of this undertaking, Lord knows how the affair would have ended. But now our danger is over, and we may go to bed and sleep in peace.

18*th.*—Alas! little did I think yesterday afternoon, when penning the foregoing day's journal, that we were in one hour after to be visited with a more terrific hurricane than that of the 13th. But the navigators had not left us more than three hours in a pour of rain than there set in another hurricane, the most awful ever known here, and another flood over all the banks, and with still more awful appearance, as it kept increasing and washing against the houses from six till half-past nine, which was more than two hours after the second high water, and with the night as dark as the grave, and had not this breach been repaired just in time, the whole of the bank must have gone, and the village become a complete wreck. We were in absolute horror till near one in the morning, when there suddenly and most providentially came on a dead calm, and then a north wind that stopped the awful accession of the morning tide, which otherwise would have been over the banks again hours before daylight. After this the weather flew round again to the southward, and so threatened the place that we all turned out with the navigators in one incessant pour of rain the whole day to repair other parts of the banks that had been washed away by this second flood.

Two floods in one year, much less in one week, were never before experienced here, and, what is most extraordinary both of these came within the period of the neap tides. In the afternoon the rain continued to pour on us in torrents; but for the safety of life and property no one would strike work, till at last there set in an easterly gale that completely checked the sea for this evening's tide, and hope and joy then beamed on every countenance 'in spite of wind and weather.' To prove the suddenness of the floods I should name that poor Captain Symonds, who is ill in bed, had the tide all over his rooms, four feet deep, before he could save his furniture from saturating, and a duck, while roasting on his spit, was suddenly emerged into its former element. So furious was the sea last night, that it came over the beach, and the spray flew up to the top of the lighthouse. A general wreck last night of chimneys, windows &c. all over the neighbouring villages. This beats all we have ever yet had to weather.

19th.—A splendid easterly wind, and all comfortable, except having to clean up the messes that have been made by the late overwhelming floods and hurricanes. Received the thanks of the whole village for being their preserver, and went to Lymington to recruit my exhausted larder and cellar.

N.B.—I omitted to mention, when noting down this flood, that such was the certainty of our total wreck, had the morning tide (before daylight) not been checked by the change of wind about one o'clock on the 18th (just after midnight), that I had made up my mind to row all the punts out of the yard, which was under water, and lower the guns and the inmates of the Cottage out of the upstairs windows as soon as the 'ground ebb' should moderate the current, and then seek refuge inland with our lives saved and my valuable guns and gear rescued, leaving the Cottage and furniture to the mercy of the waves; for had the banks gone, as I made sure they would, one thousand men could not have made a new foundation quick enough to save the village before the return of the tide would have washed away their labour, even had the tide fallen low enough for them to work, which by all good judges was considered as very improbable.

22nd.—Sunday. A fine dry day, with a north wind and easy tides. What a contrast was to-day from last Sunday, when we were all in constant fear! The country papers of to-day gave a full account of the late flood and hurricane, and, I was flattered to see, did full justice to my exertions in saving the village.

25th.—All the London papers that come down here have, I see, an account of our flood &c. taken from the three county ones; all different reports, but still true, in substance, and I received congratulations on all sides.

29th.—Longparish. Another petrified fog, enough to paralyse a Newfoundland dog. Received this day the resignation of Buckle, to my great delight, as on trial he proved to be only live lumber, and his punt proved so unfit to weather a sea with two persons, that had I gone on the season with him I might have endangered my life.

December 7th.—Left Longparish, and went, for a change of air from the pestilential vapours of that low water-meadow country, to Keyhaven. During the thirteen days I was at Longparish I never was fairly warm the whole time, though we had fires in almost every room, and a stove in the gallery; and such was the illness in the village, that my family were busy every day in ordering little articles of sustenance for the poor sufferers.

10th.—Keyhaven. Out all day in a heavy sea, and the only chance I got was at the ground ebb, when I blew off, coming home, at 4 godwits. Read, who came to my employ, got this morning 2 wigeon.

N.B.—Got a hare for my larder, which was an animal of novelty. Mr. Sleet, the master of Squire Legh's yacht, saw something at sea which he supposed was a dog or a fox. He lowered his boat and chased it, and it swam so fast he could hardly row fast enough to catch it; and on coming to close quarters, he said it dived like a water rat; and, in short, he killed it with his oar, and it proved to be a fine fat hare, and he brought it to me for my dinner.

11*th.*—A splendid east gale all night and all day, but too furious to row against. Wild fowl of all sorts to be seen off in the foaming waves. This is as it should be, and a change that we have long wished for.

14*th.*—North-east gale and sharp frost. Up at six. Read put off on mud, and got 12 wigeon. I discharged but two rounds all day, and bagged 16 wigeon and 1 duck. I saw 15 dead ones floating in the heavy breakers before my face, which were got by other people. I should have had two more still better shots, where I could have got all of my birds, but a dirty scoundrel, named Dan'l Paine, of Southampton, the public nuisance of the Hampshire coast, came in his rough weather boat, and blew off his slugs and blunderbuss, and drove the fowl from the shore head, getting only a couple, that he disturbed the whole harbour in chasing.

15*th.*—Out from daylight till dusk, but the weather being moderate, though not calm, the whole Channel was in arms with blank-day poppers in boats, and consequently all I got was 3 wigeon, 1 pintail, 7 godwits, and 1 grey plover. Read got no chance last night, as the mud was frozen, and a heavy fall of snow all the evening.

16*th.*—Afloat at daybreak and off in Channel before the 'tormentors' had arrived; had one shot and bagged 20 wigeon, after which the water was full of boats all day. Harbour frozen, and a heavy fall of snow all the evening.

17*th.*—Under way again at break of day. Intense frost and heavy fall of snow, with a gale of wind; and after weathering it till it was useless to remain out any longer, I returned home without firing.

18*th.*—Up at daylight. Intense frost and heavy snow, with a gale of wind, so could not get afloat. Read crawled about all day in his mud-launching punt, and came in in a miserable mess with only 4 wigeon. I advised him not to go out, but nothing could keep him in.

19th.—Cutting weather again. Up at five, and off before daybreak. Got 4 wigeon that flew up at dawn before I could shoot sitting, 6 geese out of a small company at a long distance, and 1 dunbird. I never had more satisfactory sport, though the chances were small and my numbers few; because I did wonders in the face of old Buckle, who moored himself in my way to oppose me, and enlisted a chap of our village to help drive the harbour.

21st.—Intensely cutting gale of wind. Up and out as usual by candlelight; weathered some ugly seas, and then worked along the Channel's edge. Brought home 17 wigeon, 1 teal, and 1 mallard; best shot 12 wigeon and the teal. I fired in all three shots, and never used the popgun, having no opportunity. One shot was at 2 mallards and 1 duck. The gun flashed, and so good is my lock cover that the birds never jumped; so I pricked and primed, drew again, and knocked all three of them down.

22nd.—The coldest north-east gale I ever had to weather. No living outside in the Channel, and inside the harbour all frozen. We tried a few birds in the 'wash' just inside the breakers; but being to windward of them we had no chance to shoot, so I came home about two in the afternoon and just saved my blank by making one immensely long shot at 4 ducks, that I cut out of a company of 10.

23rd.—Hard frost, but wind more moderate; birds at sea, where it was too rough to shoot; and scarcely anything to be seen in harbour. I made a shot of 2 geese and cut down 5 burrough ducks out of 7—a very long shot on the mud. These are the only two triggers I pulled all day, not having once used the popgun; and in the evening we cleaned up all the gear preparative to my going inland to eat my Christmas dinner with my family.

24th.—Kept up late last night by the chimney of the

kitchen taking fire, which I extinguished by a wet flannel on the 9-foot ramrod of my long gun after much alarm.

29th.—Up at daylight, and by two in the afternoon got the great 'Petrel' punt and large double gun put together and in complete order, as Read's account of the increase of geese justified this trouble, though I find that all the birds killed in my absence at Longparish by all the gunners together did not exceed about 10 couple, and these only wigeon. We put afloat for only an hour and a half just before the day was over, and bagged 5 geese.

30th.—Off at daybreak. A looking-glass calm with bitter cold white frost. All the birds off for miles at sea, and Channel mobbed with float poppers. Drew but one trigger and picked up 10 geese out of a small company, and 2 more were sacked by Yarmouth water sharks. Came in early, and as clean as if I had been taking an airing in a close carriage.

31st.—The white frost of course turned to wind and rain, and the hard weather broke up. Everyone expected a grand day's sport, as is generally the case; but, to the utter surprise of all, the birds remained all day for miles at sea, and not a fowl ever came inside the Western Channel.

1841

January 1st.—Off an hour before daylight; but not a fowl in Channel or harbour.

2nd.—Wind north-west by north; a splendid breeze to sail the punt all 'up along,' both out and back. Went all the way up to Need's-oar Point, about 12 miles, and saw nothing the whole cruise of the Western Channel except one very wild company of geese on the tide a mile from land, and a few ox-birds on the shore.

4th.—After a west gale, and then a white frost followed by rain and snow, the wind set in north-east again. I got one very long shot and bagged 4 geese; and had not a sudden current 'slewed' my punt round when within ten yards of firing at about 300 geese, I should have made the greatest shot of my life. In the afternoon we had some light snow, and the birds were all on dry mud five miles to windward; and a bird frightener from Southampton brought up in Pennington, so we despair of the grand chance that was looked for to-morrow at the ground ebb.

5th.—Got but 3 geese and 1 scaup duck, as the whole coast was so infested with shooters that birds could scarcely pitch. No wigeon to be seen.

6th.—The bird frightener in Pennington, 'Buckle' in Oxey, 'Joe Parker' in Lymington leak, all the Yarmouth float poppers cruising up and down, and, in short, not a peaceable place for a bird to pitch. They all tried the geese, but 'no go.' At last about 10 birds pitched down just between the crafts of Buckle and the bird frightener, who were both on board. I put off from under Pennington walls and cut down 5 of them before their faces—the only birds killed by anyone the whole day; and though a trifling shot I had a great victory over the other gunners and the floating snobs.

7th.—Read, who had been crawling night after night in the mud punt and never getting a shot, at last came in this morning with some birds, viz. 9 wigeon, 1 mallard, and 1 pintail. We then went off for the day with the frost so intense that our beer froze in the bottle; and I did well, considering how the birds were persecuted by surrounding shooters. I fired three rounds, though with only one barrel, as there were no flocks worth a second pull. 1st shot, 36 plover; 2nd, 7 wigeon; 3rd, 8 wigeon; all in the view of my many competitors.

8th.—Up at daylight; and an hour cutting through the ice before we could row. None of the shooters had any birds except myself. I beat them all put together, though had but three poor chances, all long shots, and at miserably small companies of no more than the size of a covey of partridges.

1st shot, 5 wigeon; 2nd, 6 wigeon; 3rd, 2 wigeon, 2 ducks, and 1 mallard. Read had a blank night mud crawling.

9th.—Read came in with 16 wigeon that he got at one shot on the mud in the night. I pulled but one trigger all day, and came home with 3 ducks, 2 mallards, and 2 wigeon. The time at sea to-day was miserable, and even dangerous; so that we could follow nothing. A violent gale from the south, and all the ice for miles drifting to leeward in pans of half an acre large and four inches thick. On entering Keyhaven harbour, it was blocked by drifted ice, and that beat back by the river sluices; so that our only alternative to get home was to ship full sail, and cut our way through; which we providentially succeeded in, or must have been beat back to leeward, and at our wits' end to have escaped being carried to sea and swamped. In all my gunning campaigns I never encountered anything more formidable than this. It was tantamount to being in a field of battle. But my splendid 'Petrel' punt did her duty; and we got her hauled on the quay and well lashed, in case of a seriously high tide to-night.

10*th.*—Sunday. The gale of last night luckily abated in time to save danger to my punts, the three best on earth, and turned to a bitter white frost, after heavy snow. A pour of south-west rain all the time we were in church; and at night another white frost, enough to kill a Newfoundland dog.

12*th.*—Our harbour was in one pan of ice, half a foot thick, and our boats in danger every night. People defied the removal of the ice, because it could not be broken. I had it cut across with pickaxe and spade. Then I put a grappling iron into it, and pick hole; and, having sunk the buoys by poking them under the ice, so as to prevent their holding the ice, I, by means of a long towing line and powerful lever, got the whole field of ice under way; and off it went like one large island at the first ebb of high water; making our harbour as clear as in the month of May, and enabling everyone to resume his boat moorings in safety. This is the second service I have lately rendered to our little village. This job retarded my shooting so long that the Southampton bird frighteners had cleared the coast before I got off, and the only trigger I pulled was at 3 mergansers; I shot them all, and the splendid old cock merganser I sent off immediately to Leadbeater to stuff for my collection.

13*th.*—Torrents of rain, hail, and snow, with a gale of wind from the south-east, which worked round to the north-east, and was so cold as to scarcely melt a particle of the ice, but rendered every path and road like a piece of glass. I had put off in the morning early; but before I could get half a mile up Channel, was driven back by the furious weather. This is the first time I've got into my punt without bringing home something. In short, I've not before had a blank day, nor have I fired one blank shot with either stanchion or 'cripple stopper.'

14*th.*—Strong north-easter. Off at daylight, and came home in the middle of the day 'as wet as a shag,' it having come on to pour in torrents of cold rain. I got one shot and brought home 17 wigeon. Read has persisted in mud crawling every night, though he gets nothing.

15*th.*—A fine day and all the birds off at sea, except a small company that I caught on tide just under the Isle of Wight. I pulled one trigger and came home with 8 wigeon. Went ashore at Hurst, to clean up all my gear on the beach, after the saturating of last night's incessant rain on everything while moored, and then heard all about the flock of geese that had flown against the lighthouses on Wednesday night. Carpenter of the 'night light' got 5, and Page of the 'low light' got 4; and at one time the whole company of geese were sprawling about in the yards; but it was so dark that the lighthouse men could not see to knock down or catch more of them.

19*th.*—Though the wind got into the north, and I was off

at eight and out nearly all day, I never saw a chance to fire off even the popgun. In the evening, the Southampton bird frightener resumed his anchorage in the heart of our best 'feeding ground;' so I rigged up Charley Page, of Hurst, with powder and shot, in order to make this interloper's station too hot to be desirable; because, while this lubber is stuck up there, not a bird can pitch on the best place for killing either wigeon or geese.

20th.—A hard frost, and the cold more pinching than any day we have yet had. Out at daylight, but no chance while the bird frightener infests our coast. Charley 'served him out' with a popgun, as he was fumbling at the only few geese to be seen.

21st.—Intense frost, but too white and too pinching to be genuine; as, in one night, it froze the whole harbour half an inch thick, and we had a job to row out of it at daylight. The bird frightener kept the coast clear; and in return I hired a footman to follow him, so that he could not shoot; and Charley Page performed his part in this office, as well as in jaw, most admirably.

22nd.—The white poisonous petrifying frost of course turned to a south-wester and rain. I again cleared the harbour of ice with ease, by having yesterday sunk the buoys of all the moorings under it; and then made Peter Fifield cut it across, so as to be free to float out at the first ebb. Off at eight o'clock, but no chance of a shot of any kind. I had, however, some novelty and some fun. The one was seeing a battle between two ravens and a huge eagle, who dropped his grey plover that he held in the fight, and on which bird I dined; and I should have shot the eagle had not a second fight with some gulls made him rise again and fly up to the Isle of Wight cliffs. The other was a savage row between Charley Page and the bird frightener, who at last, with a mouthful of bitter curses, got his vessel under way and sailed off for Southampton. Joy go with him.

23rd.—Tremendous wind and rain from the south-west all night, and in the morning a strong northerly breeze. Saw the eagle again on wing, and sailed after him for miles, till we saw him pitched with five crows flapping over him, but he would not remain long enough in one place for us to 'settle his hash.' No sooner was the bird frightener blown out of harbour than a few geese returned to their station, though not more than about 18. I used them kindly by leaving them in peace till the ground ebb, when they began to taste the feed, on which I fired one shot and blew over 9 of them.

26th.—Up at daylight, but there came on wind and rain; so I worked for several hours to put all our stores, ammunition &c. in proper order, of which it was much in need, and about twelve the weather cleared up enough for us to get afloat. But the only bird I saw the whole day was a single laughing goose, which I killed dead as a stone at 125 long strides of Read on the mud, and I am sure every step he took was far more than a fair yard.

27th.—Not a bird to be seen off or in harbour.

28th.—A white frost. Never saw a wild fowl the whole day.

29th.—Availed myself of a fine day and a dead calm to make a long cruise all the way up Channel to opposite Cowes, and never set eyes on a fowl the whole trip, except a small flock of about 30 geese. I tried a new mould-shot cartridge at about 300 yards, and down came 2 of them; so I came home with 2 geese, and well pleased with this extraordinary shot. The whole coast is ruined by the Southampton fellows both for shooting and fishing, and these cadgers do so little that they are almost ruined by starving one another in opposition for everything. The once retired wilderness off Need's-oar is now swarming with vessels for gunning, eel picking, and periwinkling.

February 1st.—Extraordinary change of weather. Yesterday as hot as in June, with fog and small rain. To-day such a cutting north-easter that the water froze on the oars all the time we were out. I got one shot at a small company, and picked up 7 geese and 3 teal; the latter I never knew anything about till I bagged them, as the 3 were among the geese, and all came in for my charge. Got caught in a sudden gale off Pennington, and Read most dexterously let the punt drop down sideways, putting her bow to the heavy breakers, till we 'fetched' the safety of my leak; and, after shipping about twenty-five gallons of sea, we got out of the scrape most gloriously, though we resolved not to risk such a chance again.

2nd.—Intense frost and some trouble to extricate punts from moorings. No water inside, as tides were so dead and the mud frozen. Off from daylight till four, and obliged to walk Hurst Beach till birds dropped in outside; but, as the shooters had driven them all to the eastward, I got but one chance and brought in 4 wigeon and 1 pintail.

3rd.—The hardest frost I ever weathered. Harbour a sheet of ice and a cutting gale from the north-east, which knocked up such a feather-white sea outside that, after pacing Hurst Beach for five hours waiting to go afloat, we were obliged to retreat. I, however, saved my blank by knocking down with the popgun 1 wigeon, and also 1 brown goose,[1] an immensely long flying shot, with which I first tipped his pinion; and I put him alive in our garden in hopes he would survive for the Longparish pond.

4th.—Most bitter weather. Cut the punt out of the ice and secured her on the quay, and brought the gun up to the house. No one could row a boat, as the oars formed in clubs of ice, and the boats were like bodies of glass. All communication cut off from the sea, which ran mountains high with the furious easterly gale. In short, the whole place was a region of ice, without a living creature to be seen on it; and gunning, of course, at an end till the weather became

[1] Like the laughing goose, but with no bars on the breast. Leadbeater thinks it a variety of the laughing goose.

less severe. No one in the place had ever before experienced such cutting weather.

5*th*.—Weather for whales and white bears only. Water jugs in bedrooms so frozen that they were all one solid block of ice. Read would go out in the afternoon launching on the ice, and he came in half frozen and wet to the skin with 4 wigeon. He changed his clothes and would go off again. A furious east hurricane set in at nightfall, and we all feared Read was lost, and his wife was in sad alarm. I ran all the way to Highlea Dock, and the gale was ready to cut my nose off, and there I saw his punt turned up, and happily found that he was all right, and had missed me on his way home by having got into his house just before I started.

6*th*.—Annihilating weather. A most vicious petrifying tempest all night and all day, and all night again. Everything frozen, and a wind that one could hardly walk against.

8*th*.—Wind less violent, but frost harder than ever. Rain fell and froze as it lodged. Harbour in cliffs of ice. Read launched his mud punt over ice, and got 10 wigeon and 2 mallards. Yarmouth mail, frozen out of Hurst and Lymington, came over beach on foot. Thousands of birds off outside of the frozen region, which, as yet, nothing but a launching punt can be got over, and that with great difficulty.

9*th*.—Bitter weather, and everything like glass. Walked over beach to Hurst to see if there was any creek open to moor a punt, in case I put in there. The Camber was open, but the land passage (for punt carriage) in such a state that I could not attempt it, so I decided on waiting till I could get some passage by water. Plenty of birds and floating shooters out of number, though scarcely a bird killed, except Read bringing home 2 geese and 3 wigeon.

10*th*.—Found an open place off Highlea, and cut our way through the ice to it. Then got off for a few hours (while water served to get back again) and brought in 10 geese. The only shot I got.

11*th.*—A sudden thaw with south wind and rain. Went from our anchorage (to which we walked over the mud) to Hurst for a windward berth; but through fears of the drifting ice retreated to Keyhaven and anchored under the wall, as the quay was worse blocked up than before. Went off to some straggling wigeon about four o'clock, and just saved our water back again. Cut down 10 with the first barrel and 3 with the second.

12*th.*—Rain all night, and a fog all day. Went out with a compass on board and made two capital little shots; saw 7 geese, and floored the whole company; then saw 4, and floored them all. The ice was nearly all gone to-day, so we got a berth on our own quay again.

13*th.*—All in order for an early start this morning, but there came on a southerly gale of wind, with a pour of rain, that never abated the whole day. I, however, saved my blank with a good shot of starlings out of the drawing-room window.

15*th.*—Constant south gale and heavy rain all last night; off at daylight, and, after fighting through a heavy sea, got one chance and bagged 8 geese, after which it blew so hard and poured so heavy that I was obliged to go home and remain a prisoner.

16*th.*—Out at daybreak. Blew off both barrels, and picked up 15 geese. Afterwards was all but shooting into about 1,400 geese when a brute from Yarmouth popped off his rusty musket under sail, and sent the birds off for miles. Otherwise I was certain of making the greatest shot ever known. I really think I should have bagged 100 birds. About ten o'clock all was over for the day, as the mud was like a fair with periwinkle pickers and eel spearers. The only 2 swans I've seen this year would have pitched but for the crowd of people about. But they bore up and flew to sea for Poole.

17*th.*—Out at daylight, and in rain all the time; but the

geese never came to-day, and by eleven o'clock the whole coast was so mobbed with periwinkle men to freight the crafts for Billingsgate that not a bird would come to the mud.

18th.—Out at daylight again with my new-invented loader, which answered admirably. A breeze, with a fog. All I saw was 21 geese. Caught 7 in a lump and bagged them all, and on the others rising 3 were together, and I got all of them with a No. 3 shot cartridge, and thus brought home 10 geese out of nothing to expect. All were killed dead except 2, and both of those I floored with one barrel of the popgun. Thus have I done well in a fog, the very weather that I and every other gunner had hitherto discarded. At one the periwinklers and the beastly Yarmouth sailing boat, the 'Carrion Crow,' as I call her, drove both myself and all further chance away.

19th.—Started at daylight again, and went, with compass, in a fog, all the way to Pilewell Leak. Fell in with a company near Lymington, and picked up 8 geese. Then sailed into about a dozen curres, a good shot with the other barrel, and at the instant I drew they jumped up, and by this accident every bird escaped. This is the first blank shot I've fired the whole campaign.

20th.—Up hours before daylight, but such a gale came on we could not get outside. We had a rough day, and torrents of rain, and had only the recompense of 1 goose and 1 burrough duck.

22nd.—An intense white frost all last night, and such a dense fog the whole of this day that nothing could be attempted. Read got 5 wigeon after midnight, and we all turned out at six this morning, and after waiting till one in hopes of the fog abating enough for us to venture out, I gave it up and metamorphosed myself into a gentleman, and did some commissions in Lymington.

23rd.—Fog-bound till afternoon, and then the periwinklers

were all over the shore, so that, having no chance, we made our first blank day. Our morning, however, was turned to good account by making the punts tight after some leaks caused by fighting under heavy sail against the pans of ice in the late frosts.

24th.—The fog turned to a dark north-easter. Off early and cruised all day; picked up 13 geese at one capital shot, out of the only company I saw the whole day.

25th.—Up with the larks again. Saw one company of geese, as wild as wild could be; followed them all the way to Pitt's Deep, about seven miles, but the punt jumped so much on the sea with the strong north-easter that they would not stand the show and noise; at last they crossed me, flying rapidly, and down I dropped 5 with one barrel.

26th.—Out from daylight in a squally north-wester; brought home 11 geese in two shots, though never saw more than about two dozen the whole day; 5 more geese fell dead where it was too rough to venture, and another, winged, stole away on the mud, so that what I knocked down in all was 17.

N.B.—My shooting this trip has surpassed all I ever did, saw, or heard of; from December 29 to February 26, both days inclusive, I never had but one blank day, and then only out for a few hours after a day's jobbing; and, except firing at some curres that jumped at the instant I pulled, and trying an experimental cartridge at about 350 yards, I never fired one blank shot the whole cruise, though out every day that I could 'live' for eight weeks and four days. The show of birds this season has not been more than the tenth of what we had in 1837–1838, though the miseries of weather were tenfold greater, and the wear and tear of ourselves and gear the severest on record.

Wild fowl I have killed at Keyhaven up to the end of February 1841:

Ducks and mallards	19
Teal	14
Scaup ducks	2
Dunbird	1
Wigeon	185
Pintails	4
Burrough ducks	6
Brent geese	145
Curious brown brent geese	2
Merganser	1
Plover	23
Godwits, waders, &c.	13
Olive	1
Shore birds	179
Total	595 head

Nearly all killed with my large 200-lb. 'champion double duck gun' and with only firing two blank shots. Such a performance, I believe, is unprecedented in the annals of gunning. We had the most intensely severe winter on record; and yet not a tenth of the wild fowl that we had in 1837–1838. Not a single wild swan ever came to our part of the coast, and the only 2 I saw the whole winter were a pair flying over on their travels. Leadbeater never had so few fowl to preserve any winter as this; notwithstanding it was the hardest winter I remember, for the few weeks at a time that each frost lasted.

March.—London. I left my great 'Petrel' punt at her moorings in Keyhaven harbour, meaning to run down again for the chance of a few more geese (which birds rarely leave till April) before I took my gear into store, and 'knocked off' for the season.

8*th.*—With Eley, 'Uncle' Bishop, and all the crack gun fellows on logic and new experiments.

9*th.*—Keyhaven. On my arrival I heard that a good show of geese were still in the Channel; so I decided on making a few days' more cruise before I 'knocked off,' because geese are never so good as in March and April if you can get them.

11*th.*—North-east wind and cold again. Up at six and cruised all the way to 'Park Rails,' and never saw but 4 birds (geese) the whole day's trip. The 'winklers, it appears, have banished all the geese which otherwise would have abounded here in March, as they always used to do whenever the winter had been hard enough to bring them to our coast.

12*th.*—Took a cruise, but the birds appear to have left the coast altogether.

15*th.*—Summer come back again; and butterflies on wing.

16*th.*—Bade adieu to gunning for the season.

June 9*th.*—London. Went over the awful ruins of Astley's Amphitheatre, which was burned down yesterday morning. Having known Ducrow (through once offering to him a melodrama), I gained admittance immediately on sending in my card, and a more lamentable sight I never beheld.

19*th.*—Went down to Woolwich to see the launch of the 'Trafalgar,' about which there was more fuss and difficulty than in any other public exhibition. Sir William Symonds had kindly given a written order for myself and family; and this order was backed, in writing, by Sir John Barrow, Secretary of the Admiralty; but, after all, no one could pass the police without a ticket for each person; and these tickets could only be issued by Captain Hornby (Superintendent of the Dockyard), to whom I sent in my card and my order; and who, being too busy to see anyone, sent out a written memorandum that my name should be put down for tickets, which he could not promise. I then, after much difficulty, got on board the 'Trafalgar' under the shed. She was so low 'between decks' that I could nowhere stand upright; and her build was, in my opinion, nothing equal to the modern ships of my friend Sir William Symonds.

20*th.*—Received three tickets from Captain Hornby, which was an agreeable surprise, as I feared he had only given me some hope, to avoid the trouble that might arise from a direct negative. So far, however, from backing out of serving me, he kindly sent the tickets for the very best station.

21st.—Got down to the Dockyard soon after ten, by which means I had the choice of seats; and so well were I and the girls situated that we were close to the Queen when she named the ship. Of all the sights I ever beheld I never witnessed any so grand and splendid as the launch of the 'Trafalgar.' I had the offer of being on board while she was launched; but this I declined, because, for the sake of novelty, I must have been precluded from being able to see the christening. She was launched at half-past two; and nothing on earth could be better or more comfortably arranged than the whole of the superb sight and the accommodation. But the crowd afterwards was awful; and had I not put up the carriage nearly a mile off, I could not have been home till midnight.

July 5th.—Keyhaven. Up early and prepared for a sail to the cliffs, but became out of humour for sport by hearing of the horrible death of my factotum poor Eley, the cartridge man, with whom I was in perpetual communication, and who was the most punctual, respectable, and intelligent of all the sporting tradesmen under my patronage. He was blown to atoms by fulminating powder at his factory in Bond Street, where I was in the habit of repeatedly going to give him hints and advice; and often have I advised him not to extend his practice to the dangerous trade of making percussion caps. His loss will be irreparable to the sporting world; and no one will feel it more than myself.

8th.—London. Directly I set foot in town I went, with 'Uncle' Bishop,[1] to the factory of poor Eley, where I was astonished to see that scarcely any damage had been done beyond the appalling accident that blew him to atoms. His

[1] The famous manager of 'Westley Richards'.'

own son was within two yards of him, and people were working in the factory, at the time the explosion took place; but so little was the expansion that, although he blew up 2 lb. of fulminating mercury, not even a paper was burnt; and the walls were no more disfigured than if cold water had been thrown over them. In short, a few panes of glass being broken was all that could be seen in the way of damage. The usual quantity of fulminating mercury that people venture to mix at a time is from $\frac{1}{4}$ to $\frac{1}{2}$ an ounce; and how so clever a man as Eley could have run the risk of mixing such a quantity was the surprise of everyone.

24*th*.—After an indescribable concatenation of worry and vexation in London, and after having waited four days till a succession of gales from the south had abated (with my passport signed and our things packed up), I this morning soon after two o'clock entered the Boulogne packet at London Bridge Wharf on our long-talked-of trip to pass a week or two in France. The 'Magnet' packet, for which I had secured berths, was so full that men and women were all huddled together like dead bodies in a cholera hospital; and a drizzling rain with a pitch-dark morning put an end to the superior comforts of remaining on deck. At three o'clock precisely we got under way; and such was the mess of sickness and suffocation that we were obliged to sit under umbrellas on deck for the whole of the passage after we had passed Gravesend. The stewardess was drunk, the steward a stupid fellow, and all the men on board, except the mate, a sorry 'ship's company.' The packet itself was good, a capital sea boat, and with fair wind, two lug sails, and steam, did the 140 miles in 10 hours to a minute, though two hours were absorbed by bustle and bother at the custom house before all was clear, as the *douaniers* now are become much more strict and tedious than they were in my many former trips to France. On landing we put up at a nice little hotel, recommended me by an old friend, Mr. Moscheles, called the 'Ship Hotel' in

Rue de l'Ecu, in which we had the luck to get the best apartments I ever had at any French inn. Nothing, out of England, could be more comfortable than they were. We dined at the table d'hôte with about twenty-one persons, and, to our surprise, all were either English, German, or Americans; not a Frenchman was there at the table. Being too tired to perform a long slow journey on the morrow, we decided on resting the Sunday in Boulogne, and booked for Lafitte's diligence on Monday for Paris.

25th.—Sunday. Went to the English church at eleven. Service performed by two fairly good parsons, and music nicely got up by the amateur English of the place, who are at the chief expense of this exclusive place of worship; and to which therefore there is a charge of 1 franc entrance to non-subscribers, and a very just one it is. After church we visited the celebrated library and museum of Boulogne; and the latter is, I think, without exception, the best I ever saw in my life for its extensive display of ornithology. It contains, in addition to all that museums usually offer, some good paintings and the finest statuary; but its greatest curiosity is an Egyptian mummy of some great personage, that is in such perfectly good condition that the hair and even the teeth are as perfect as when in life; and the printed inscription near it states its age to be 1511 years before Christ. We then made the best of our time to see the Catholic church, the cemetery, and the town in general, not omitting the magnificent harbour entrance, extensive sands, &c. And I have no hesitation in saying that, as far as I have yet travelled, I pronounce Boulogne to be the most desirable place in France.

26th.—We entered the *rotonde*—the only place to be got—of Lafitte's diligence at nine this morning, and arrived in Paris at six the next morning (the 27th)—140 miles in 21 hours. We had no fault to find with the pace that was travelled at, considering the hideous machine and the poor palfreys that were flogged before it, and the stoppages for changing were even too quick to be pleasant, but in other respects everything was most miserable. We had a beastly dinner at three at Abbeville, my old quarters, and could get nothing all the way from there to Paris but a bit of sour bread and a glass of vinegar wine, and the conductor locked us up and would never attend to us the whole night without my first lustily bawling out signals of distress. We were shook till our bones ached, and literally crammed with dust; never was there a more miserable 100 miles travelled than that through the famine land of Picardy, from Abbeville to Paris. On arrival, half dead, we had to be overhauled by the excise, which took nearly an hour, and we then got into Meurice's flash hotel, where there are now 150 English, and which is more like a barrack than an inn for comfort. We lay down, too tired for sleep; and, after cleaning up, took the morning to get rid of our first commissions and see the Louvre. All that was new to me here were the naval models, and an imitation of the original horses that I had before seen on the triumphal arch that leads to the Tuileries at the time when the Emperor was first banished to Elba; the eagle is renewed on everyone and everything, and a most elegant lady, the Duchess of Orleans, was surveying the pictures with us like any ordinary person. We at length mounted our six very high storeys to a seven o'clock dinner, and went to bed as tired as dogs.

28th.—Took a coach and saw Père-Lachaise, where the best monuments I had not seen were those of a Russian countess, Elizabeth Demidoff, Marshals Suchet and St. Cyr. No tomb as yet for 'Ney,' but the palisades and the flowers within them tacitly pointed out his remains. Next saw the fortifications (which were proceeding rapidly with 100,000 workmen) beyond the suburb called Belleville. Next the Invalides, where the greatest sight to me was the splendid tomb of the late Emperor Napoleon, with all the trophies of his glories around him, and his hat and sword at the foot of the marble coffin which covered those wherein were embalmed his mortal remains. All was within an iron railing, and shrouded in a darkness that was illumined only by the splendid lamp which was suspended above the coffin; and the regularity with which each person was admitted to pass was, like everything of the kind in Paris, admirably well arranged. We inspected the Place Vendôme, Place de la Concorde, Champs-Elysées, &c., all of which, with many other things, I had seen and noted down many years ago. The only new sights here were of a kind of obelisk, in the Place de la Concorde, presented to Louis Philippe by the Pacha of Egypt, and the enormous cannons taken at Algiers. Dined at Café Riche; then went to the opera of 'Le Serment,' in which Dorus Gras was splendid; and saw the ballet of 'Le Diable Amoureux,' which was the only ballet I ever enjoyed in my life. It was in three acts, and on a plot that made it not only interesting, but most exciting, and nothing could be more magnificent. Took ice and coffee at Tortoni's, and came home even more tired than yesterday.

29th.—The great annual fête to-day. Commenced with seeing the grandest fair imaginable in the Champs-Elysées, where, among other innumerable shows, spectacles, and little sights, we took about an hour in the newly built 'Cirque National'—the Astley's of Paris—which is, without exception, the most splendid amphitheatre that can be imagined. A Madame Cinizelli was the most distinguished equestrian of the day. This is one of the best evening spectacles, and was opened to-day only on account of the glorious fête of July. At seven we went to the front of the Tuileries, where all the bands of the garrison played in one grand concert before the good King and Queen, of whom we had a capital view when they came and stood on the balcony. The moment this was over, we adjourned to the illuminations, after which the best that ever were in London were no more than a few rushlights, and soon after nine there commenced a series of fireworks that no pen or tongue could describe. The one for the finish was called a 'bouquet,' which threw the whole atmosphere into one gorgeous blaze with a fiery garland of flowers some hundred yards in circumference, and so well imitated in fire that the foliage was like a fine colossal painting. The fête having kept us worked hard from breakfast till bedtime, we could see no other 'lions' to-day.

30th.—On hard again at seeing the 'lions'—those for to-day were: the Eglise Madeleine, a church long ago begun and now nearly finished; the small chapel built by Louis XVIII. to commemorate his murdered brother, Louis XVI., of whom and of his wife are fine monuments or statues with the 'last will and testament' of each inscribed beneath; the magnificent triumphal arch on entering the Champs-Elysées, begun by the Emperor and finished by Louis Philippe; the Chamber of Deputies; the Chamber of Peers, with the Luxembourg, and the boudoir of Mary de Medicis; the churches of St. Sulpice and of Notre-Dame. During our many hours' drive about the town, I was struck with the wonderful changes that have taken place since I was here nearly twelve years ago, and for all these the French have to thank Louis Philippe, who has not only been indefatigable in completing all the works unfinished by the Emperor, but has wisely condescended to imitate the English by cleaning and paving the streets, and getting rid of all stinks and nuisances, for which Paris was formerly the most offensive place, next to Lisbon, that I ever had to encounter.

31st.—Visited the Bourse, the Jardin des Plantes, the Gobelins, the Panthéon, the Artillerie (or ancient armoury), and several other smaller sights. In the evening we went to the Théâtre Français, which, although the most fashionable place next to the opera, is, to my taste, the least amusing of any spectacle in Paris. I found the house much improved and far cleaner than our own theatres.

August 1st.—Sunday. Henri Bertini came from Versailles to see me about my patent hand-moulds, which I brought over with the improvements made since I had them in Paris some eighteen years ago, and I appointed Tuesday for him to meet me about them. At three we went to the English Ambassador's church, where my old tutor, Mr. Lefevre, was the reading parson. It was forty years since I saw him, and our meeting was quite an event. In the evening walked in the Champs-Elysées, which was a sort of fair, but no dancing, as formerly.

2nd.—Up early and off by railroad to St.-Cloud; but could not enter the palace because the King was there.[1] Caught a *fiacre* to take us on to Sèvres, where the chief specimens of porcelain are exquisite and are actually framed copies from the finest painters; and for which they ask from 30,000 to 40,000 francs apiece. The china in general is now but little superior to our very best, and nearly double the price. Our next 'lion' was the sight of all sights—Versailles, which took us the remainder of a long day, and worked us off our legs. After the gardens, we went over the whole of this most enormous and gorgeous palace, where there were all the victories of Buonaparte, restored to the walls by Louis Philippe; and these were, of course, all new (and not a little interesting) to me. This present King had expended an immense sum of money in putting the palace at Versailles in the highest order; and never since the days of Louis XIV. (who built it, and who was the only king that often frequented it) was this place in such a splendid state. We refreshed at a good *restaurateur*, Hôtel de France, and came home in the evening by another railroad. There are two to Versailles: one works round a half-circle on the right, and the other on the left of Paris; so that by going with one and returning with the other, you go round a circle outside the intended fortifications, and are so elevated that you survey Paris and the environs to great advantage nearly the whole way.

[1] Since the infernal attempts on his life, the attendants deceive the people as to his movements. It was given out that he would be at Fontainebleau to-day.

3rd.—Met Henri Bertini at the piano factory of Erard, Rue du Mail, No. 13, and presented him with a complete set of hand-moulds, book &c. to make what public use he pleased of. I then went with the girls to show them the royal library, and attended them shopping; and we ended the day with a 'lush' at Very's and a view of all the gaieties of the Palais Royal.

4th.—Made every preparation for leaving Paris to-morrow, on our return home, having got through all the best sights; and being heartily tired of the expense, noise, confusion and humbug of this place of splendid misery. I made a second sortie, and got permission to see the *salle* &c. of the Opéra Comique. Went over the whole of this new theatre, which is beautiful. The alternate boxes of the best class are fitted up with a private room. The theatre is very rich, chiefly in white and gold, and with some effective and fine statuary. The saloon is rich, and in great taste; and the floor of it is of various wood to imitate mosaic. To my taste the prettiest theatre in Paris, and well worth seeing. Dined at our hotel,[1] and concluded by going to the Théâtre des Variétés.

5th.—Left Paris at a quarter past seven this evening for Havre (all the day coaches being full for some days), and arrived in Rouen at a quarter past seven in the morning.

6th.—Havre. Such is the posting opposition in France now, that the changing of the horses is more rapid than in

[1] Specimen of charges here, which are a mere trifle more than at other hotels.

	fr.	cents
Tea or coffee	2	0
One small chop or cutlet	1	10
A bottle of claret	7	0
Best Burgundy from 7 fr. to	10	0
Ordinaire (hogwash)	2	0
Picardon (the least acid and by far the best for its price)	4	0
Port	9	0
Sherry	8	0

Sixty-five servants, seven head men cooks.

N.B.—Judge what a scene of uproar for the whole twenty-four hours. A State inquisition—a Bedlam—I don't know what to call it.

England; and the diligence from Paris to Rouen (with a butcher and a savoury Dutch peasant for inside 'shipmates' in the *rotonde*, which here holds eight instead of four, and which was the only place to be got—I have not a laugh in me now, or should write the account in true colours) actually travelled about 2 miles with the off-leader's bridle off, and the head-stall and winkers dragging on the road and between the horses' feet, because the coachman would not stop, for fear of being passed; and racing is very properly forbidden. From Paris to Rouen we had the *coupé* and went the lower road; and having a bright full moon till the weather changed after daylight, we saw the rich country of Normandy nearly as well as if we had gone by a day coach. Our arrival at Havre was even worse than at Rouen, though luckily the weather cleared off again. The town was so full, owing to the cheap fares of contending packets, that we literally had to walk all over the place for an hour before we could get a hole to put our heads in; and, at last, we got into an inn with everything dirty, and sheets so wet that we dare not even lie down with our clothes on. This retreat from Paris beats all.

N.B.—I'm so bothered, and have such confused moments to seize a bad pen and ink, that I can scarcely write common sense; but still I must book, lest I forget. No alternative remained for us but lying on the sofa all night, or embarking in a packet that was to sail at ten, and with rough squally weather; so I engaged to go off with Captain Forder, of the 'Monarch.' After paying 16 francs for a filthy chop and three little soles at this execrable hotel, we bundled off, bag and baggage, just before dark, and got on board the packet; and had I not taken the double precaution to get my passport revised in Havre (which in Paris they told me was not required) the gendarmes would have taken me out of the vessel, and forbid my proceeding to England, having come on board expressly for that purpose. Well, at ten we got under way ; and no sooner had we cleared the harbour than a strong wind with repeated squalls of heavy rain beset us for the whole night ; and so contrary was this wind the whole way, that the captain was obliged to force the engines in a manner that was quite awful, in order to perform the voyage in any decent time ; and to compete (as far as prudence would admit) with a dangerous narrow opposition packet, a Frenchman called the 'Hamburgh.'

7th.—We landed on Southampton pier at one, making a passage of just fifteen hours, and a more unpleasant one I never weathered, except that the packet was a first-rate sea boat, and the cleanest I ever sailed in, with the greatest attention and civility from everyone, from Captain Forder down to the lowest hand on board. After the usual bother and anxiety at the custom house, which I got clear of with great success, we proceeded by the four o'clock train to Winchester. Lord Adolphus Fitzclarence and another great yacht gentleman rode in the carriage with us, and we laughed at our change of company from the butcher and the Dutchman of yesterday. We luckily got a hack chariot that had just taken a family to the station, which saved some time, and we arrived at Longparish House a few minutes before six, making our journey from Paris to Longparish within the forty-seven hours. As if all our campaign was not enough, even here we had to meet with trouble. The whole of the servants and baggage that ought to have been here to receive us, and administer that comfort we so much stood in need of, had never arrived. They put off their start to this very day, and so slightly warned the rail police of their intended stoppage at Andover station that the whole of their heavy baggage was carried on to Southampton, and they had to remain at the station all day till an express got there for an up train to bring it back, and even then some articles were missing. This never happened with me, and I warrant would not have been the case had I been there. They all arrived about a quarter of an hour after us, and a precious mess of confusion it was for people who had been fifty hours in boots and without a change of clothes. Now all is over I am delighted that we took the trip, as the sights we saw and the miseries we had to encounter will be something to think of as long as we live.

CHAPTER XXXIV

1841

September 1*st*.—Lord Glentworth and I went out, from the middle of the day till a late dinner, and so few birds were to be seen, and those few so wild that I got only 6 partridges, and Lord Glentworth 1, and 1 hare. I expected vile sport, but not quite so execrable as this. The farmers, it appears, in addition to mowing all the wheat stubbles, and destroying for fuel all the turf banks, where birds could breed free from rain and the scythe, have been using a solution of 1 lb. of blue vitriol in a gallon of hot water to fortify each sack of sowing wheat from becoming smutty, and most people think that many birds have been poisoned by feeding on this corn. Our whole combined bag was only 7 birds and 1 hare. What a miserable first day! What a contrast with my bagging 52 brace, besides 6 birds lost, and 1 hare off my own gun, and with missing but two shots in the whole performance! If it's to be like this, I must either cadger for shooting at other people's houses, or send in my resignation as a field sportsman.

6*th*.—On approaching the house, after not firing one shot all day, I reflected that I never remembered a blank day before; so I turned round instead of going in, and tramped up to the inclosed country, where I worked till dark, and came in with 7 partridges.

8*th*.—Lame with my foot again. Poured some eau de Cologne over my stocking, and went off on the old mare with my gun, expecting to break down. But I so 'mended on it' by the friction of walking the turnips that I got on well till a six o'clock dinner, and had a capital day considering the vile season. I bagged 14 partridges, and missed but one long shot. This is the only day of this season worthy of record, and for my good luck I have to thank Mr. Henniker Wilson's party, who drove a few birds over from Barton Manor, though got but very few shots themselves. On the whole, however, my day was splendid for this lamentable season.

11*th.*—A sad, unlucky day. I got but 2 partridges, and missed a fair shot, a thing I have not done for many seasons, and on my coming home soon after three, in disgust at having found only 8 birds all the time I was out, I fell in with Charles, my keeper, who was weeping for his unrivalled dog that he had accidentally shot dead. I have been a sportsman for more than forty years, and never yet had such an untoward season at home or abroad.

22*nd.*—Wanting a brace of birds, I started about half-past twelve, hardly expecting to get them, and had the miraculous good luck to disperse a splendid covey that was driven to our home field by the Hurstbourne Park shooters, and to come home in triumph with 16 partridges. I killed all I saw, thanks to Eley's cartridges, with which I made such a succession of long shots as I never saw before in one day.

November 1*st.*—Keyhaven. Up at five so as to skim the coast before the Southampton lubbers. Cruised all the way to Pitt's Deep, and never saw but 9 wigeon, which a vessel put up, though a fine lot were seen by captains of vessels during the north-easter. Saw 18 geese off at sea, but had no chance to fire a gun, except at three dun divers on my way home, and I killed them all.

2*nd.*—Sport so bad that I took the gig and 'knocked off' some visits round Becton and Bashley, a savage country like the wilds of Ireland, and a cruel hard drive for my horse.

3*rd.*—Tried it on again, but the coast was almost barren.

Got 2 wigeon, all I saw, and 1 brent goose at above 200 yards out of the only 12 I saw. Not another fowl did I set eyes on in a very long cruise.

4th.—Read crawled on the mud (his filthy hobby) last night, but heard not a bird.

5th.—Out all day. Coast destitute of all wild fowl.

9th.—Up at four, and took a long cruise to explore the coast. Not a bird in the whole Western Channel, except the one small company of geese that have been so popped at by bullets that even 'on the ground ebb' they would not let me come within 400 yards of them. In short, I gave up gunning as hopeless till a change of wind.

18th.—London. I went to hear Adelaide Kemble in 'Norma,' and I think her quite the best English singer we have.

20th.—After having cut through business and commissions with railway speed in four days that many snails would have taken some weeks to do, I left town for Longparish. Had the Bishop of Winchester for a companion. The trip up, I had Commissioner Elliot, just landed from China.

December 2nd.—London. Busy about my new musket for Government, and saw Colonel Peel (Sir Robert's brother) at Ordnance Office. In sad suspense all night about the safety of my property at Keyhaven, lest the bank should burst as it did last year, when I saved the whole village by timely exertions.

3rd.—A letter from Keyhaven to say the floods had abated without entering my house, and that all my property was safe. Hard on again about my new musket, on which I had received a most flattering communication from Colonel Peel as to the Master-General's attention to my suggestions, and his intention of conferring with Lord Hill on the subject. Raced to death with divers business, and in the midst of it served with a summons for a special jury. Flew to Smith to buy me off if possible. But after a long dance to find the Philistine, his attempt failed, as he had been bribed so often that he was afraid of being 'blown' and ousted.

4th.—At musket again. Incessant rain morning, noon, and night.

5th.—Sunday. Had so many visits to pay after church that my cab hire came to *7s. 6d.*

6th.—Eternal rain all day. At Ordnance Office again about a conference with Westley Richards.

7th.—Served on jury. Only an hour at Westminster Hall. Got my guinea, and bolted like a scalded cock, lest I should be hooked for a second election, as several of our jury were, and on a case that stood fair for a week's work. Completed all my business and got my musket finished by bedtime.

15th.—Keyhaven. A lot of geese off yesterday, so was prepared for launching the light single-gun punt to-day; but there set in another south-west gale with pouring rain, so all I could do was to send a man about in the wet to try my new military musket, which seemed to defy everything.

17th.—A moderate day at last. Got 3 geese out of a small company at above 200 yards, and 2 curlews out of 3 that I fired at, a very long shot.

18th.—A pinching white frost with a north-east wind, cold enough to cut a feather. Got 2 geese, and gun flashed in pan at a company of 60. No sooner had we landed and cleaned all up than there set in the heaviest fall of snow I ever saw, which continued till about two in the morning, and then began to melt so fast as to fall from the house in such large pieces that I was woke up, and thought the chimneys were blown down and the slates breaking.

20th.—Intense frost and cutting north-easter all day, and yet I got no chance except just saving my blank with 1 wigeon. Read has crawled every night in his mud punt, and always came home with an empty bag. Poor show as yet.

21st.—Though a hard frost there were no birds, except

the few very wild geese that have been here since October. Buckle appeared for the first time this season, but has killed nothing.

1842

January 8th.—Breakfasted by candlelight, and got the champion gun and gear all in order for launching while it was daylight. No birds killed yet, but many said to be come and lying far off at sea owing to the moderate weather and the many gunners in our Channel.

10*th.*—Breakfasted by candlelight and launched at daylight. Brought home 2 tufted ducks, 3 golden-eyes, 5 ducks and mallards, and 1 wigeon. Splendid shooting and nothing missed, though a poor show of birds to shoot at.

N.B.—I have not been warm since a cold I took, Saturday three weeks, in spite of sudorifics, sulphur baths, &c., so I dreaded the risk of beginning the campaign to-day. But, instead of it making me worse, I got into a glorious perspiration from fatigue and excitement, and feel 50 per cent. better.

11*th.*—3 geese, the only chance I got, as a shift of wind to the south with a stiff breeze had filled the Channel with sailing bullet poppers, and the coast was cleared of all the birds, which went far off to sea. Old Buckle had arrived with an empty bag, and as savage as a bear.

12*th.*—3 geese again, the only chance I had all day.

13*th.*—A tremendous gale from the south-east from morning till night, with torrents of rain, hail, sleet, and heavy snow. Not even a dog could show his nose out of doors.

14*th.*—An extraordinary reverse of weather, a dead calm, with a day like summer. Not a bird to be seen, except 2 geese, both of which I bagged with the only shot I fired.

15*th.*—Took a long cruise over the whole Western Channel, and went as far as Need's-oar Point, off Leap, and then I went off Cowes, Hampstead, and Newtown, and (except a few ducks that rose before a steamer) never set eyes on a single company of fowl. Not even in summer did I ever go so far without a shot at something. Our log must have been fifty miles, as we were sailing in the punt near twelve hours.

23rd.—Sunday. Read all the week has crawled every night and all night on the mud, and never got a single bird. Not a fowl has been killed by anyone for days.

24th.—Read crawled all night in his mud punt, and he had the luck to get two shots just before daylight, and brought in 10 wigeon and 4 pintails. As soon as the water served I went off, but found no chance, and we were too happy to escape from a heavy sea and retreat by Pennington Leak.

25th.—A strong north-wester. Off from nine till one, but never saw a chance even for the popgun ; so, rather than have quite a blank day, I took off my gunning frock and walked ashore over a little bog in Mr. Pryce's 'mudlands,' thinking I might get perhaps one snipe. I had the good luck to obtain eight shots, 1 bird fell off in a field, and I killed dead and pocketed the other 7. This evening the coast was all alive with cannon and fireworks for the christening of the Prince of Wales.

26th.—A nipping white frost till near daylight this morning, when Read came in after his night's crawl without having heard a bird, and just in time to escape a violent change of weather. I made a most brilliant shot at a merlin hawk that flew over me as swift as an arrow, and though at least fifty yards, I cut him down as dead as a stone with snipe shot.

27th.—Read came home blank this morning, after a long mud crawl, on the winds abating. He fell in with old Buckle in the night, who had done nothing all the season, though eternally at it, and following the birds in his vessel with two punts on board.

29th.—Never set eyes on a bird all day, except 9 geese that I blew off at without success with mould shot at 300 yards.

31st.—Up directly after midnight, started about one, and

came in about seven in the morning. Was unlucky, or should have had plenty of wigeon. I had a miss-fire at one lot, and was just a quarter of an hour too late on the tide to bear the gun on a company of about 70. Came in with only 1. Lay down for an hour, and started about nine for the geese. Out all day; the only shot I got was at 9, out of which I got 3 geese.

February 1st.—Prepared to go out again at one this morning, but it blew so hard one could not hear. After the tide was gone, Read mud-crawled and heard nothing. At nine we cruised as far off as Pilewell, and owing to changes of wind went from Keyhaven and back without using our oars at all. This is a very extraordinary occurrence. We found the whole army of periwinkle men on the mud for miles, so of course came home till the afternoon tide would wash away this rag fair rabble. All the wigeon on the coast were this day together on the sea off Hurst beach. I made out about 430 as near as I could count with a glass, which proves what lies have been told about the 'many thousands' that were every day off at sea.

2nd.—Up at two and out till daylight. Heard a few birds and lay under them for a shot without moving till I heard Lymington clock strike four and then five, but it came on too dark to fire at a small trip by sound, so I let them go, and moved down to Mount leak. Nothing there but a few single birds. On landing I had reason to rejoice at a blank, as Read, whom I trusted to load the gun, had forgotten to put the shot in, and had left the ramrod in one of the barrels for that purpose, so had I fallen in with a shot I should have come home *sine* wigeon and *sine* ramrod. So much for operations in very dark weather.

22nd.—Went to see the 'Kent' steamer, which was wrecked under the cliffs of Becton last Saturday morning before daylight. The master, Captain Lakeman, ran her aground about five in the morning, in a heavy fog, for want of using his lead-line to try the depth of water, having steered north instead of east.

23rd.—Got afloat. We saw about 300 geese, and had not the sea been so rough as to toss us about too much, we should have made a shot.

24th.—Afloat again, and got caught again in torrents of rain. Geese off again, but no doing anything in such weather, they would not rest a minute.

26th.—Bad weather again; that horrid brute Dan'l Paine has driven away all the geese with his blunderbuss and bullets, so that only about a score are left, and they went off in Channel under Yarmouth. I went after them, and bagged 3 geese as they flew off the waves, and 2 more came down that I dare not follow. The bad weather then returned, and we were too happy to fetch land in safety.

27th.—A terrific hurricane in the night and all this morning. My 'Petrel' punt, with the great double champion gun in her, rode out the gale at her moorings in gallant style.

28th.—Went afloat about ten and got as far as Oxey leak, where there were about 80 geese, but we saw bad weather coming and got home just in time.

Sorry list of the past barren season: Game total, 83. Wild fowl—5 ducks and mallards, 22 wigeon, 4 pintails, 3 golden-eyes, 2 tufted ducks, 20 brent geese. Total, 56. Other coast birds—1 merganser, 3 dun divers, 4 curlews, 7 plover, 48 shore birds. Total, 63. Grand total, only 202 head.

N.B.—I never shot better at game or wild fowl; but such was the scarcity of both that I regret having taking out a licence for the one, or knocked about my best punts and gear for the other, during this nasty, hoar-frosty, blustering, rotten winter.

March 8th.—Out early again, and at last had a chance to try the geese; but they rose more than a quarter of a mile off, so we voted it useless to cruise any more, and returned home, and thus wound up the most execrable season on record.

9th.—Another hurricane. Heavy rain nearly all day, with heavy squalls of wind. At about eight this evening the wind increased to the most furious hurricane I ever saw; but most providentially it came when the tide had ceased to flow outside, or Lord knows what might have been the consequence. This truly awful gale continued all the time the tide was ebbing; but, as God's mercy had it, a squall of rain 'hove' the wind into the west before the flood began to make. Such was the fury of this tempest that no one could walk against it; and we were so shook in our beds that sleep was out of the question. Boats out of number driven from their moorings, and two of Read's boats were blown about on the quay like a man's hat, and considerably damaged. How truly lucky I was to get all my valuable punts and gear safely housed yesterday!

12th.—Returned to Longparish; and in Southampton heard the report confirmed that Dan'l Paine, our mad and drunken frightener of wild fowl, was no doubt lost more than a week ago, as his boat, gear, and hat were picked up at Hillhead, and he had not been heard of since. He was recorded in the South Hants paper as a person patronised by me; but I never spoke to him in my life. Though he did more mischief to our coast than all the other gunners put together, and no good to himself, yet I sincerely regret the poor fellow's untimely end, and the only wonder is that he was not drowned long ago.

17th.—London. Busy in the City. Tortured with a toothache. Whipped in to the dentist, who ridded me of a tooth like a three-legged stool, which he hung fire at drawing. But I would have it out, and a blessed delivery too!

April 4th.—Went down to Keyhaven. Took the train at Winchester, as on Saturday, the day before yesterday, the long tunnel halfway between Andover station and Winchester, called 'Waller's Ash,' had fallen in and killed five workmen, besides wounding four more severely, and others slightly. By working all Sunday, however, the directors had got the line open again this day. When in Southampton I ascertained that the body of poor Dan'l Paine had been found in a place called 'Park Hole,' a few miles above Lymington Creek, and that he was taken home and buried rather more than a week ago.

5th.—Weather colder than in winter, with a cutting north-easter and frost; and some geese and even a few wigeon were still about; but having housed all my gear I took no trouble to go after them. A grand 'lion' to be seen. A whale about one hundred feet long was washed ashore in Totland Bay, nearly opposite Hurst. Boats, steamers, and all craft in requisition to see it.

6th.—Another lovely day for the whale; boats from all parts, and the Lymington steamer with a band of music. Went a second time, with General and Lady Elizabeth Thackery (who kindly invited me to take a passage in their boat), and took a sketch of the wonderful monster; and I cut out and brought home a few of the curious combings that are attached to his upper jaws, and which are the whalebones so general in use.

7th.—Company from all parts, this being considered as the last day of the whale, which, report said, was to be cut up for oil this afternoon and to-morrow.

8th.—The whale was sold for 24*l.* to a man in the island, who, instead of cutting it up on the spot, decided on towing it away with a steamer for exhibition, and then dissection. To-day the whale was high and dry, owing to the low fall of spring tides, and those who went had a famous view of him on the bare sands.

9th.—The steamer and all boats were prepared for a visit to the whale, and away I went with Read, but no whale. The purchaser had towed him off at daylight this morning, and all parties came home disappointed, particularly myself, as I had prepared for making a finished drawing of him on a large scale, to supersede the little hasty sketch that I took the other day.

30*th.*—London. Down to Woolwich about another committee which the Master-General had ordered on my new patent army musket, and for which I am waiting in town. Went over the Arsenal, the largest guns in which carry a hollow shot of 96 lb. and weigh 4¼ tons.

May 4*th.*—Down to Woolwich, and before the Select Committee with my musket, models &c. Having heard from everyone that this Committee made a point of rejecting everything that did not emanate from themselves and furbishers, I read to and left with them my protest against their own musket, now in use, and left a copy of what I said with Colonel Peel for the Master-General. The Committee never give applicants an answer as to their opinion, but concoct a letter after the party is gone, and send it in to the Board of Ordnance for the Master-General. So thus rests the musket job, on which I have taken so much pains, and all for nothing but a wish to do good to the service.

7*th.*—Longparish. Took the only three hours' recreation I've had for many weeks; killed 8 brace of tidy fish, besides lots thrown in. Received advice this evening that Peter was gazetted captain in the 'Gazette' of last night, May 6th.

12*th.*—Keyhaven. Took a sail to the cliffs at the back of the island. Put my little popgun in the boat for the chance of a shot, but saw scarcely anything; and there came on such a heavy sea and such a strong southerly wind that we sailed home against the tide, after being off a few hours. I got 3 willocks and 2 terns, all I fired at, in five of the most difficult flying shots out of a jumping boat, in which we got a pretty good wetting.

16*th.*—Took a sail in Read's boat in the Channel; and, to my surprise, saw the whole shore lined with godwits, all working to the eastward.

17*th.*—This afternoon we went off with an old leaky punt

of mine, and one single shoulder gun, and in a few hours I brought home 21 godwits, some red in their summer plumage, and some grey in their winter plumage. The two best shots were 6 sitting and 5 flying. Wind, heavy sea, and a vile punt. Had my grand set-out been in commission, I calculate I should have killed 150.

18*th.*—Off again with the same set-out this afternoon; but being fully aware that, as godwits rarely remain two days in the same place, I should find none where I shot yesterday, I went up with the flood tide about seven miles to the eastward, where I fell in with the rearguard of their army, consisting of a few small trips only. I, however, killed 18 godwits and 2 turnstones; my best shot was 9 bagged, added to 2 that escaped, out of not more than two dozen in the company. This afternoon I took No. 4 instead of No. 1 shot, and had I done so yesterday I should have trebled my number.

N.B.—A party, hearing of my sport yesterday, eagerly boated it to where I had been, and never killed a single bird.

27*th.*—Longparish. I went out for about an hour and a half with fly rod, and brought in 24 prime trout. Not being in an enemy's country, I left off when I might have caught, perhaps, as many more.

June 1*st.*—London. Presented Peter to the Queen, at the fullest Levee I have seen for many years, as it was the last of the season, and the first after the diabolical attempt on her Majesty's life last Monday.

7*th.*—An interview with Sir George Murray, the Master-General of the Ordnance, at the request of Colonel Peel. Sir George, on seeing my models, seemed fully to coincide with my views of the musket, and nothing could exceed his kind attention. But still the Select Committee and their armourer will have their own way.

21*st.*—Called at 70 Pall Mall to inquire for my kind friend and patron, Lord Rodney, who a few days ago was sitting with me in Dorset Place, but who had since been very seriously ill. The answer to my inquiries (which, of course, I had made every day) was, 'Sir, Lord Rodney is no more.' Never was I more distressed.

July 2nd.—Returned to Longparish, where on arrival I found the different official letters relative to the pay of the staff, the stores &c. of the North Hants Regiment, for which I now become responsible till a colonel is appointed, *vice* Lord Rodney, deceased.

4th.—At Winchester the whole morning, taking up the regimental stores, pay of staff &c.; and no sooner had I done all the needful, and posted my official to the Secretary at War, than I heard, and found to be correct, that the commission for the colonelcy of the regiment was signed by the Duke, and going for gazette by to-night's post, in favour of Lord Wiltshire, a young man, the son of the Marquis of Winchester. This is the Duke's recompense to me, who gained the trophy of 'Douro' for the 14th Dragoons, was severely wounded under his Grace in the Peninsula, major of 1815 in the North Hants, and lieutenant-colonel of 1821, having served six years major and twenty-one years lieutenant-colonel, and being more than qualified (by landed property, as by law required) for a colonelcy, and within a few months of twenty-seven years a field officer in this regiment.

23rd.—Keyhaven. Sailed to Alum Bay, and had a lovely day on the heights, after a swim off the rocks below. Got some wheatears for dinner in trying my new military musket. A bad show of them this year. All the rock birds gone some weeks ago. Saw Bill Coleraine, who told me he had got but twenty-two dozen eggs the whole season; whereas in former times he used to get his thirty dozen before breakfast in one morning. The worst season known for sport on the heights.

August 4th.—London. Down early this morning with Mr.

Godfrey, the bandmaster of the Coldstream Guards, to hear a practice of my march called the 'Prince of Wales's Quick Step,' which 'went' splendidly, though, of course, only a mere trifle. And this, by the way, is the anniversary of my being made a captain, as I got my troop in the 14th on August 4, 1804, when I was only in the eighteenth year of my age.

CHAPTER XXXV

1842

September 1st.—My daughter was married this morning to Mr. Charles Rhodes. If a man has any feeling in him, nothing, short of death, can more acutely try it than the parting thus from a child so dear to him as my darling Mary has ever been to me. May God be a Father to her wherever she goes, and inspire her husband with that ardent affection which she so justly deserves.

5th.—Took my first day's shooting, and, although far from well, fagged from ten in the morning until dinner. So scarce and wild, however, were the birds, that I came home completely knocked up, with only 5 partridges.

10th.—Better, but still in pain. Went out on the old mare, and had the worst luck on record. It blew a gale of wind, and I crawled about till I found a good show of birds, but old Don ruined my sport by running into every covey, and such vile retrievers were he and the old bitch that at one time I killed 2 birds with the first and 2 more with the second barrel, and lost 3 out of the 4, and I winged a stone curlew in some turnips, and even he got away. All I got was 5 partridges, 1 hare, and 1 landrail. I had three miss-fires, owing to a heavy shower, and all the good shots happened to rise after I had blown off at long ones. Had I been well and in luck, with good dogs and a reserve gun, I do think I should have killed 20 brace.

All I killed in September was 26 partridges, 1 hare, 1 landrail, 4 snipes, and 2 teal: 34 head.

October 5th.—Keyhaven. Took a long cruise, saw very few birds, and those so thin there were not two together, and as wild as in March.

8th.—Took another cruise, but never saw a chance, though the weather continued beautiful. Heard all the birds were gone to Poole, where they remain in peace, owing to the enormous quantity of herrings and other fish now occupying the whole time there of the coast gunners. Their profits in fishing are, I am told, enormous—one night producing more than a whole season's gunning.

December 19th.—Keyhaven. Not a fowl on the coast, and Read coming home every morning from his nightly hobby, mud crawling, without seeing or hearing a bird. I, of course, have not been such a fool as to put my punt afloat this visit to Keyhaven, nor have I even taken a popgun in hand, as there is literally nothing now by sea or land. Flowers blowing and blackbirds whistling.

29th.—Longparish. So mild was the weather that I put my fly rod together, and soon caught a large dish of trout (6 brace). We had all these fish broiled for dinner and breakfast, and they were quite as good as in the early part of the fishing season.

1843

January 16th.—Keyhaven. Not a single wild fowl in all the market of Southampton, and nothing whatever done or even seen in my absence. The news of the place on my arrival about a quarter before eight this evening was all about the damage done, chiefly to houses, by the hurricane of Friday morning, and that a flood was just avoided by the late raising of the banks, which would never have been done had I not constantly bothered about it. Sam Singer was all but drowned in the gale; as it was, his craft was washed aground, his punt and gun were washed ashore, and he had to swim for his life, and then to be laid up ill from cold and exhaustion, from the water he had swallowed in swimming.

18*th.*—Went to Lymington to see and offer assistance to Sam Singer, but found that he had recovered and left the place. On my return home, I boarded a Brighton mackerel boat, a thing I had for years wanted to see, and inspected the whole set-out. The nets, it appears, are a mile and a half long and only 4 fathoms deep, and are therefore worked on the surface of the water, as the mackerel always swim far from the bottom of the sea, which this kind of net never reaches, though when they come near land, as in Portland, then the common seines, which sink with leads, are used from the shore.

21*st.*—Heard of Sam Singer at Hurst. Sailed down and brought him up to spend the day and to 'blow' him 'out.' He told me that his loss in the hurricane was a spy-glass, a 'cripple stopper,' and his great-grandfather's compass, and was most loquacious and amusing about his late trip for duck shooting with two swell gents to Norway. He had done nothing on our coast this winter, and was quite sick of English gunning.

February 2nd.—My other dear daughter was this day married at Christchurch, St. Marylebone, to the Rev. Lewis Playters Hird. I never felt anything more acutely than parting from this dear child, and may God be a Father to her wherever she goes. My family are now all disposed of, and I remain as the mere scaffold on which has for more than twenty years been building, as it were, the edifice of their education.

19*th.*—Keyhaven. Rain! Wonderful how I turn the cock always when I arrive on the coast. Birds almost as scarce as before, in spite of the late intensely severe weather. Only 8 wigeon and 3 geese killed by all the punters put together during my four weeks' absence on business.

20th.—A butterfly day. Went afloat, but got no chance for a shot, though saw a few geese flying a long way off at sea, and a small trip of wigeon with them. I had only launched the small set-out, and went more for my health than with the expectation of having a shot.

27th.—Wild fowl only 32 for season. No shooting for anyone on the coast this year.

March 21st.—London. Took a lesson of Professor Richter in his new discovery for perspective, by which it is said a housemaid may, in one lesson, be taught to draw anything from a spoon to Westminster Abbey or a large landscape as correctly as a member of the Royal Academy.

May 16th.—My cause was tried to-day in that blackguard bear garden, the Sheriffs' Court, in an alley at the back of Holborn; and though the evidence, and the summing up of a counsel who sat as judge, were all as strong as possible on my side, yet the jury, a set of uneducated people, gave a verdict for the rascally plaintiff and his black lawyer. Instead of paying the least attention to the evidence on the summing up, this beggarly lot of jurymen were guided entirely by the nefarious lies that were spouted out after all power of reply was past by the most finished blackguard I ever saw as counsellor, a fellow who, I am told, was a journeyman tailor, who practises only in this court, and is hand-in-glove with all the low jurymen that are procured for it at a few shillings each for the whole list of causes for the day. Never, therefore, let a defendant go to this court if he would resist imposition. We, of course, moved to 'stay the writ' for the High Court of Exchequer, and the judge readily granted this request to us, which he had refused in two other cases. But, as the sum in dispute was under 5*l.*, we query if the Barons will grant us a new trial in their court.

July 10th.—In Hanover Square Rooms at half-past seven. Queen came at half-past eight; close to her all the evening. Her first turn at Philharmonic, and perhaps her last, as, in consequence of that dry mathematician, old Spohr, having the command, we had all noise and no melody.

August 26th.—Longparish. Licensing day, on which came on the grand fight, before the full bench of magistrates, relative to the spirit licence for my property, the 'Bullington Cross' inn. I had got nearly one hundred signatures, in opposition to which the black parson had enlisted all his own coterie, backed by some trumpery fellows whom he had humbugged; and never was there a harder fight. Old C—— held forth with a long speech; lying as fast as a dog would trot, and made out a case on which, to all appearance, we had not a leg to stand on. But when the brute had 'spun his yarn,' it was my time to administer the antidote, which I did in no measured terms; and the fellow looked as if he had been horsewhipped. The court was then cleared for decision, and out we went among the farmers of the market, before whom I told old C—— he was 'a liar;' and off he sneaked like a mongrel cur as he is. The decision was such that I gained the day and got the licence.

CHAPTER XXXVI

1843

September 1*st*.—Longparish. No shooting worth going out for.

5*th*.—Started about half-past eleven. I was five hours without getting a shot.

9*th*.—Slaved all day, and came home with 13 partridges, the most that has been yet done here with one gun; and I now long as much to get rid of my gun as I formerly did to take it up, for such is the sport here in these days, that it is slavery instead of recreation to take the field.

26*th*.—Went to Keyhaven. No joke going by steamer, as the delays at Cowes and Yarmouth, and the roundabout course she takes, keep you nearly double the time occupied by coach, and without anything to eat. I told everyone that the intense heat and long-continued dry weather would turn to rain on my approaching Keyhaven, as I never yet remember losing my charter. All laughed at me, but I was right, and the weather turned so wet and cold that we were obliged to have a fire.

September list for 1843: 50 partridges, 1 landrail, 1 hare, 4 snipes, 2 wigeon, 2 godwits. Making in all only 60 head.

N.B.—A miserable breed of game, and had there been a good one I had no time for pleasure this month; though, sorry as my list is, I did as well as my neighbours who had more time for sport.

November 1*st*.—Taken very ill, and was put into my bed,

which I did not get out of till the afternoon of the 3rd, when, thanks to Dr. Badger's good management, I was rid of the fever, though, having taken only toast and water, I was extremely weak.

4th.—Prince Alexander of the Netherlands, who is over here, sent to me to advise about a rig-out for gunning on the coast of Holland, so I secured him Sam Singer, and wrote about the famous gun that I built for the late Captain Ward; and on the 7th Captain Hudson (of the Guards) was to go off with my written prescription to Southampton, I being too ill to see to anything myself, and being also in the midst of troublesome business with my lawyer. It seems I'm never to have peace; and all this illness, as the doctor observes, is from downright worry and incessant excitement.

19th.—London. Up to this day I've been harassed, ever since I came to town, with the tedious expensive proceedings of an entail and trust, which could only be made strictly legal by lawyer's jargon, and which required a conveyancer. All the other parts of my new will, which I thought it best to make, is 'A B C,' and I did it in a few hours myself (and in a fiftieth part of the gibberish used in the lawyer's infernal rigmarole) by writing grammar, English, and plain sense, instead of technical jargon.

25th.—Got under way for Keyhaven, shut up in the close britschka; and having but one mare to draw this heavy 'trap,' I lashed on a carthorse to tow the whole concern through the rivers, up Withers's cruel hill, and through the slush to Barton, from whence the mare got on at an 'andante' pace to Winchester. At Southampton I secured Captain Ward's lovely gun, at the dirt-cheap price of 50*l.*, for Prince Alexander. Wrote a long letter of advice to his Royal Highness, and arrived at Keyhaven about nine at night.

December 4th.—Keyhaven. Our coast literally destitute of birds for several weeks; and the very few gunners who went out had nothing but blank days and nights.

13*th.*—In pain all day and in terror all night, and could not turn in bed without two people to raise my body, and a third person to ease my head; never in my life did I undergo such continued pain.

14*th to* 16*th.*—Confined to my bedroom, and for the greater part of the time to my bed, in spite of cupping, poultices, fomentations, colchicum and calomel.

21*st to* 23*rd.*—Keyhaven. Damp, rotten weather. Birds singing; flowers blowing; and doctors full of business.

24*th and* Christmas Day.—Weathercock with head where tail ought to be; dark, damp, rotten, cutthroat-looking weather; flowers blowing; bluebottles buzzing; doctors galloping in every direction; a Philharmonic of blackbirds and thrushes; an armistice from guns and shooting; the poor punters driven to oyster dredging, eel picking, day labour, or beggary; not even the pop-off of a Milford snob to be heard in that unrivalled garrison of tit shooters.

1844

January 1*st.*—Keyhaven. After a most furious night of wind and rain from the south-west, the weathercock this morning flew into the north, and occasionally to the east, with squalls of sleet, snow, and rain. This of course leads us to hope the new year will bring better weather.

4*th.*—Seeing no prospect of weather for a shot, and being liable to be called up to Longparish on the new year quarter business, I availed myself of a very high tide to bring my small punt ashore again, and stow her in the boathouse after her having been afloat about five weeks and never taken once from her moorings, as there was literally nothing to go out for to shoot.

15*th.*—On the whole day getting the great gun and 'Petrel' (with all the divers apparatus) afloat, as hundreds of foreign fowl had been seen in the Channel. Had a most satisfactory launch, as she and the cripple-catching punt, though laid up for, I believe, three whole years, were 'as tight as bottles.'

16*th.*—Off at daybreak and out till half-past four. But the fowl were not near so numerous as they had been yesterday. An intense frost; but it turned rather white, which is a bad omen. I got but 4 wigeon and 3 teal. The birds were off in the Channel, where there was too much sea to shoot, and I lost nearly as many as I bagged.

17*th.*—Off all day; but the birds were off under the Isle of Wight, and so scattered in a rough sea that we were obliged to put back and leave them.

23*rd.*—White frost, and then a beautiful day. Up at six and off. Went all the way to Need's-oar Point, having gone over nearly 40 miles of water; and, except a few straggling ducks that rose a quarter of a mile away, I saw nothing. A blank day, never even popped off the cripple stopper. Other gunners off all day, and all had blanks. A precious pretty gunning season!

31*st.*—Received a most kind letter from Prince Alexander of the Netherlands, expressing his delight with the gun I had sent him. His Royal Highness's first shot was 6 teal, his second 12 curlews, and his third 29 teal. A princely beginning. Heavy fall of snow all day; but no frost as yet.

February 2nd.—An intensely cold winter's day, with deep snow and a biting frost all night. Too severe and too sudden to last, I think.

3*rd.*—Keyhaven. One of the coldest days I ever weathered, and so slippery from the frozen snow that I did not reach my Cottage till near nine o'clock; having had scarcely a morsel all day, and being almost petrified with the cold.

4*th.*—Not a bird killed by anyone in my absence in London.

8*th.*—Began to work for my ninth edition, for which Longmans are crying out most lustily; having all but exhausted the eighth. No chance of more birds this season, I believe.

13*th.*—Another most vicious white frost. Dandy weather in the afternoon; went afloat. All I saw was 2 brent geese and 1 duck, and which I put in the larder.

14*th.*—A candlelight breakfast, and afloat by daylight. Made a long cruise, and except seeing some ducks at sea found nothing but 8 geese all day. Got up to them, and should have had 4 or 5, but the gun was loaded by Read in the dark, and the right barrel missed fire for the first time for six years. They all split abroad as they rose, and I picked out one bird, a brent goose, and killed him handsomely with the other barrel. Mr. Childe, the painter, arrived here this evening to do some sketches from nature for my new edition of 'Instructions to Young Sportsmen.'

Mr. Childe busy sketching; and I at his elbow every day hammering into his head the designs I wished for, and after such trouble as I would not go through again for 50*l.* I got rid of him and drove him off to the coach next day.

19*th.*—Was from morning till night 'hard on' with Read, Payne, and old Peter, housing my punts and gear, and putting away all my great guns in store, as it's now all over this season for a chance of getting a shot.

Sorry list of game &c. up to February 19th, 1844 (the worst year ever known in Great Britain, and even Ireland):

Game—50 partridges, 1 landrail, 2 hares, 3 rabbits, 17 snipes. Total, 73.

Wild fowl—1 duck, 7 wigeon, 4 teal, 3 geese. Total, 15. Other birds—14 plover, 4 godwits. Total, 18. Grand total, 33.

Grand and sorry total, 106 head.

Much illness and town business all the season; but had I been well and at leisure, I could have done nothing, as scarcely a gunner has killed even a dozen wild fowl all this cruel season.

March 16*th.*—Longparish. A letter from Sam Singer, who

has come home from Holland with a gold watch and honours, and the Prince's gun, for me to get made into a detonator.

26th.—Went by Great Western Railway, the very best in the world, to Bristol. Went all over the leviathan steamer, the 'Great Britain,' while my dinner was preparing, and slept at a good hotel, the 'Cumberland.'

27th.—Up at daylight. Ascended the heights, and went over all the beauties of Clifton, and was down again about half-past ten before the steamer (the 'Victory,' Captain Parker) could be in, and in about half an hour in she came, and, thank God, with Peter on board. Worked him off by rail at one, and got him safe into Dorset Place at six. He was reduced to a skeleton, though not so helpless as I expected to find him.

May 1st.—London. Working hard at my ninth edition of 'Instructions to Young Sportsmen' up to, and on from, this day.

6th.—On hard, till late this night, every day, and baited with untoward domestic calamities the whole time I was slaving for the press.

7th.—By being up till twelve last night, and up at four this morning, I contrived to get ready a batch of my book business.

8th.—On like fury with Varley the artist, engravers, woodcutters, Longmans, lawyer, banker, gunmakers, agents &c. from the time I got up till night, and bound for ditto and ditto every day.

July 31st.—To Windsor to take the royal copy of the new edition of my book on shooting (that is published to-morrow) to Prince Albert, and also a copy for his private secretary, G. E. Anson, Esq., who was much pleased with the book. The Prince had a swarm of officials, or I should have seen his Royal Highness. Saw his guns.

August 29th.—Married to Helen Susan, widow of my old friend, Captain John Symonds, R.N., at half-past ten, at

Christchurch, Marylebone, and almost driven crazy with the death of one wife and marriage to another coming all at once. More fit to be buried than married.

31*st.*—At half-past seven boarded the 'Dover' steamer. Lovely day, and in Ostend at four. Scramble as usual, and a Jarvey man, who drove me to consul for passport, charged too much, and was taken off to prison, with a roar of laughter from the surrounding mob. No complaint of mine, but the police demanded information as to what I had paid. Put up at 'Ship' hotel.

CHAPTER XXXVII

1844

September 1st.—Left for Brussels at half-past four o'clock by railway, which was admirably well conducted, and reached Brussels at nine.

4th.—Left Brussels at a quarter before seven by railway, and arrived in Cologne (44 leagues) at a quarter before six, where our passports were revised on entering the Prussian frontier. Railroad admirably conducted.

5th.—Saw the principal sights of Cologne. Cathedral by far the best, and here we had the good luck to arrive in time for the last half-hour of a sublimely beautiful mass, in which the organ playing, by a Mr. Weber, was perfection. The treasure and relics in this most magnificent cathedral I've not time to enter into. After a very grand table-d'hôte dinner, which was somewhat ridiculous from the messes introduced, such as boiled lemons &c., we went by railway, as good as the Great Western, to Bonn. This town we were delighted with, having lost not an instant to explore all we could before dark. The two grand 'lions' were the Munster Cathedral, with the bronze statue of St. Hélène, and the birthplace of Beethoven, at No. 934 Rue du Rhin, over which we were shown by an old man who was bred up from a child with this immortal composer, and who was so eager to explain all that was interesting, that we could hardly get away from him.

6th.—Left Bonn with regret. The steamer started a little before eight in the morning, and, after a short stoppage at Coblentz, making 120 miles against the powerful stream of the Rhine, we landed about eight in the evening at Mayence, where we got into a huge hotel called 'L'Hollande.' We had dined on board the steamer at a large table d'hôte, where we had ices and all other luxuries. In this trip, for which we had a lovely day, we had the best possible view of all the celebrated beauties of the Rhine, to describe which would be impossible, even had I time to sit down and write. The passage from Bonn to Mayence gives you all the best part of this enormous river, as to rocky mountains, 'cloud-capped towers,' vineyards, country seats, and a winding course through almost every landscape that can be imagined, and absolutely bewilders you with one beauty crowding on another before you have time to sketch or even think of them.

7th.—Up early, and with a voiture and a commissionnaire surveying what was to be seen in Mayence, which is a large garrison town with about 8,000 troops, a mixture of Austrians and Prussians, then crossed the bridge of boats over the Rhine, and proceeded by railway to Frankfort, 22 English miles. Here we got into an enormous place, called 'L'Hôtel de l'Empereur Romain,' which from our entry to our departure proved to be the worst house I ever was in; dirty, dear, bad attendance, and no civility.

8th.—Sunday. Went to Homburg (about 12 miles), and back at night. Here we had a scene of the greatest gaiety imaginable; and not only that, but disgraceful scenes of gambling on the Sunday. The grand emporium for all this is a magnificent building called the 'Kursaal,' behind which there is a splendid range of walks to the mineral waters, with an excellent orchestra, and every kind of refreshment.

9th.—After a few hours about the town, we took the railway to Wiesbaden (about 30 English miles), not a little delighted to get out of the noisy, dirty, expensive town of Frankfort.

N.B.—Our move to Wiesbaden was the commencement of our return home; and, by my losing no time in our advance, we had just completed the little tour intended, when the dry and hot weather turned to wind and rain, which began this morning, and I should say with thunder; but such was the noise in Frankfort that I doubt if the thunder could be heard in our hotel.

At Wiesbaden, which is quite the pleasantest place we had seen in Germany, we put up at the 'Hôtel de Quatre Saisons,' a splendid house, with the best table d'hôte I had seen. After an early dinner, we hired a carriage and a commissionnaire, and were driven to the top of the mountain to see 'Die Platte,' the Duke of Nassau's grand hunting palace, from which there is a view that can scarcely be surpassed by any country seat in Europe. We had not time to see much of the town itself, which appeared so superior to the others we had been in, that, had I been in good health and with leisure to remain abroad, I would gladly have sojourned at this place for some time.

10*th.*—Went by omnibus (3 miles) to Beberich, on the right bank of the Rhine, and there embarked (about ten) in the Düsseldorf steamer; and about nine at night landed at Cologne in rain and utter darkness, and where we had a miserable scramble for our baggage; and I was all but getting my teeth knocked out by a porter meeting me with a huge box, that just grazed, and cut a little, my lip. Good hotels full; so had to take refuge in one called 'L'Hollande,' which seemed to be unrivalled for dirt, misery, rudeness and inattention, and where I had nearly broken my arm, and got a severe blow on the head, by falling out of a nasty little elevated Prussian bed.

11*th.*—Got off, by an early train, to Liège, which we found to be one of the best and by far the cheapest places we had been in. We went to the Hôtel de l'Europe, where we had a room fit for a prince: a superfluously good dinner and dessert, a breakfast, and a carriage to the railway (the next morning) all for one napoleon. I amused myself with visiting the two chief gunmakers (Monsieur Lessence Ronge and Mr. Vivario Plomdeur), where a 'first-rate' double gun cost but from seven and a half to nine napoleons to those who were bold enough to run the risk of using it. The Palais de Justice, the market square, and the arcade were three objects worthy of notice in this magnificent town, which I had expected to find dirty like Birmingham, and had merely taken refuge in it to divide the long journey of 68 leagues from Cologne to Ostend, which by rail takes at least sixteen hours.

General memorandum.—Railways in Germany, Prussia, and particularly in Belgium, extremely well regulated; and most particularly for the baggage, for which there are check tickets for every article. Hotels enormously large, and living quite as dear as in England. Tables d'hôte usually at one o'clock, with an endless variety of everything calculated to disorder the stomach, and wine little better than hogwash. All the beds so narrow as not to be large enough for one well-fed gent or lady. Attendance generally bad, on account of the enormous number of persons that one hotel will contain; and a general uproar, noise and confusion. People as a rule civil; but, of course, they play into each other's hands to pluck John Bull all they can, the same as in all other frequented parts of the Continent. Travelling miserably slow in all ways, except by railroad.

15*th.*—London. Arrived. Cleared off all German dirt with a good wash, and all foreign diet with a dose of blues. Weak as a rat, and much in need of a day's rest.

23*rd.*—Longparish. Having arrived on the 21st (after a series of such worry and confusion as no pen can describe, and then a tour in Belgium, Prussia, and Germany), I took a gun out of the armoury to-day, in order to see if I had nerve enough left to kill a partridge. This morning I started, in a cold easterly wind, and scoured the whole of my inclosed beat; and came home without a single head of game. I popped away twice, but too far to kill. Not wishing to lose my charter (of never yet having had a blank day), I went off to the hills for the whole afternoon, and slaved all the way to Bullington. I then used Eley's cartridges, as the only chance of getting a bird. I fired six times and got 6 partridges. Though half dead, I never made more extraordinary shots. Here is my first day, and not a very tempting one to make me wish for a second, unless the wind should change, or there should be better 'lay' for the birds.

October 1st.—Keyhaven. The long north-easter changed to a southerly breeze. Went on the water to try if I could recover my impaired health and appetite, and did wonders with what few plover were on our coast. I got three shots, and cleared off nearly all I saw. Never did I make a more lucky little beginning afloat. I brought in 8 grey plover and 8 knot plover.

November 4th.—Longparish. Scoured the whole country with a gang of beaters (as a grand finishing *chasse*); but the only shot I got was at one old cock pheasant, that had defied everyone since the 1st of October, and which I properly outmanœuvred, and killed in prime style.

5th.—Keyhaven. There had been a good show of wigeon, and Read had bagged 16 at one shot; so I bustled till very late at night, and then before daylight, to get my punt and big gun in order, as everything was laid up in store, except the light punt which Read had launched.

6th.—The north-easter flew to the west; and I had, of course, brought some rain as usual. We were off from very early till near three, but never saw a chance; though about 200 wigeon (all in one flock) rose before a steamer, close under Yarmouth.

16th.—A foggy breeze, which about four turned to a drizzling rain. Weathered it from that time till dark, and came in with 12 wigeon. Birds extremely wild, as they always are in foggy weather. Nearest of my two shots about 140 yards.

18th.—Out hours before daylight, but the wigeon were all gone. The only shot I fired was at a little bunch of mixed birds on a raft of weeds; and I literally cleared off the whole company. This day two new Keyhaven gunners made a grand start, to be on day and night, viz. Harry Troth and Harry Rook; and with two very fair turns-out, all on my system, but not to my advantage.

22nd.—Read out mud crawling all last night, and got but 2 wigeon. I out all to-day, and saw not a chance but 1 grey plover that I killed with the cripple stopper.

N.B.—The last week of November was such a failure that, although Read, Troth, and Parker were all on in hot opposition all day and all night without intermission, every bird killed for these last eight days and nights was 1 curlew and 1 wigeon. As for me, I had cleaned up my gear, and brought my gun ashore. It was high time, when all shooters and no birds.

December 4th.—A fine westerly wind. Many flocks of birds came down Channel, but only a very few would alight owing to our two new tyros being planted off all day like scare-crows, which prevented their coming in. I got 5 wigeon by going off in a heavy sea, and might have had a brilliant day if our little shore had been no more disturbed than usual.

5th.—Off from before daylight till evening, and never pulled a trigger. An intensely cold white frost, and nearly all the birds had been driven away by the tyros. I should have had one beautiful shot at a little mixture of teal and wigeon, with 3 pintails, but a rascally boy with a popgun and a yawl rowed them up out of downright spite. These are the delights one must weather in big gunning.

7th.—Intensely cold with a very hard white frost, and yet an easterly gale. Up at five, and got 5 wigeon under the dying moon, and 11 more at daylight, making 16 wigeon.

9th.—Off before daylight, but the tyros had cleared the shore before me. Lots of birds, and, at last, some geese arrived. Went all the way to Pitt's Deep to get away from these disturbers of sport, but found they had made the birds so wild there was scarcely a chance to come in shot. Came home about three, and launched the grand set-out, the 'Petrel,' the big double gun and the following boat.

10*th.*—Off at daylight, and out till five. A bitter cold easterly wind and frost, and so much sea that we had a miserably wet time in getting six miles off to avoid the new tyros. Got but one shot all day with one barrel of the great gun; knocked down 8 brent geese, 2 wigeon, and 1 teal.

11*th.*—Up before daylight, and off to Pitt's Deep; but no good shot to be had. Got only 2 brent geese, with 1 plover and 11 dunlins, and did well to bag them.

12*th.*—Weathered a heavy sea, and bitter cold easterly gale up to Pilewell; beset with shooters in every direction. Made two shots, and brought in 14 wigeon, 1 tufted duck, and 1 brent goose.

13*th.*—A heavy gale all day from the eastward; went up to windward, and made one pretty double shot; 10 geese with the first barrel.

14*th.*—Frost and snow. All the birds driven away by the tyros to the outside of Hurst. Weathered it all day, and got but 2 wigeon; a long shot at a few scattered birds.

15*th.*—Sunday.

16*th.*—A wet day, and the frost all gone, though still an easterly wind. Weathered the rain for a few hours, and made one double shot, a very long one, and knocked down 5 geese with the first barrel and 5 with the second.

17*th.*—Out in the dark. Got at daybreak 4 wigeon; birds by hundreds at break of day, but so driven by all kinds of floating shooters that a good shot was impossible.

18*th.*—Out in the dark again. Harbour driven all night by strange gunners. No one got any birds but I, who brought in 3 wigeon, 1 mallard, and 4 brent geese.

19*th.*—Off at daylight. Cold easterly wind with heavy

rain. Got but one very long shot. Knocked down 2 geese that fell a great way off, and were 'prigged' by sailing boats. Came home after a long dull cruise.

20th.—Up at six, and went up to Lymington mud. Caught the grand army of geese near a creek at last, and was all but firing when off popped an infernal gun to windward. 3 burrough ducks came and pitched on the spot where the geese were, and I cut them all up quite dead. A tremendous east gale came suddenly on, and we had enough to do to reach home and save ourselves.

21st.—A tremendous frosty gale from the east all day. No boat could go off. Read mud-crawled, and got 3 wigeon, and crawled again in the day till he filled his punt, his boots, and his gun with salt water.

23rd.—Off before daylight, but so cruelly driven by rival shooters was our harbour that I never had a chance for a shot all day. Read had mud-crawled since twelve last night, and came in with 3 wigeon.

24th.—Read crawled all night in a bitter cold hazy frost, and came home blank. I went off at daybreak and had one long volley into the geese, with which I brought in 12.

26th.—Read came in after a night's mud crawling with 6 wigeon. I breakfasted as usual by candlelight, and was out all day; but it proved a farce to be off, as there were more than fifty poppers afloat for a Christmas spree, and not a bird could pitch. I heard at least 200 shots, and I am not aware that one single bird was killed.

27th.—Read came in with 4 wigeon, and had not his gun flashed twice he said he should have had 40, as the mud launching was never better than last night. I was out all day, and got but 2 brent geese, a very long flying shot, and the only one I fired.

28th.—Read had a blank night's crawling last night, and I a blank day to-day. The shooting is almost annihilated by green, greedy, unfair, bungling bird drivers.

1845

January 1st.—Up to Pilewell and back, but never saw a chance, as the birds were all driven to the eastward by the sheer bad usage of bungling bird drivers; but I saved my blank with a glorious brace of rare birds—2 barnacles. While my punt was at the quay, and Read mopping her out, and I just going to eat a second breakfast, these two birds came over and wheeled round over some popgunners, that would have scared them off by a useless discharge out of reach, but for my men, who prevented their firing. I ran out, jumped into the punt, and set off to the birds on the mud, just before the quay, and cut them up both quite dead before a multitude of spectators. I never saw or heard of but 3 barnacles so far south as our coast, one that I shot ashore many years ago and these 2 splendid specimens, one of which I shall send to Leadbeater to stuff for my collection. This was a lucky hit with which to begin the new year, and may our good luck continue.

2nd.—A calm, cold day. Went to within a few miles of Cowes, and never had a chance. Drove the grand army of geese down before me to near Keyhaven, but they went on the mud, 400 yards from any creek. I lay alongside them till near dark, when they rose, like a roar of thunder, to go off to roost at sea.

3rd.—Read got 1 brent goose early in the morning, but there was no chance for my gun till the very end of the day, when I went off; and just as I entered my own creek that I made, a large detachment of the grand army came from the east, and 'took the ground' about 150 yards from one of the 'spreaders' that I had cut. I had not put the shot in my gun, and was obliged to crawl out to do it, as we dare not rise. We then poled up the 'spreader,' but the water was too low to allow my gun to bear on the birds. I levelled the gun, and lay ready to fire when the tide rose; but before I had lain many minutes the geese all flew up without having seen us; I blew into them, and down came 20 in handsome style before a multitude of spectators, who were delighted. We never had a more amusing cripple chase, as only 5 birds were dead, owing to the immense distance at which I was obliged to fire; and, consequently, Read and I on the mud, and Payne in my following boat off at sea, were in full chase for nearly an hour in all directions.

4th.—2 brent geese, a long flying shot, and the only chance I got all day. The birds had enough of me last evening, and removed their quarters to Pilewell.

6th.—Up in the dark. Wet weather came on, and not a chance was to be seen. The geese were all to the east, but we dare not run too far to leeward with a stiff south-wester. Heard all the gunners' reports in Lymington, and found that I had killed more birds than all of them put together.

7th.—Up at six, and off the whole day, but never had a shot; so brought my gun and gear ashore for a thorough good furbish, putting the great punt to her moorings in order to be ready if there should again come a chance for some birds.

9th.—Busy all day ashore. Meanwhile the whole army of geese appeared under my windows, but I was not prepared, and the tyros flew out and drove them away.

14th.—As there were lots of geese about yesterday during a heavy south gale, I put my great gun afloat again to-day. I, however, saw but few birds in comparison to those of yesterday, and the only chance I got was 2 brent geese, at an immense distance, for want of water, which prevented my making perhaps the best shot I ever made this season, as the geese were all together, and, what is unusual, indeed very rare, they kept feeding till daylight was gone, instead of going off to sea at sunset. We both got out and pushed the great punt over the mud till we could move her no longer; so that had there been two inches more water we might have got close to these birds, about 200, all in a lump together. No such chance again, I fear.

15th.—Out again, but never fired a shot, or even heard the report of a gun all day. Weather mild, and nothing to be seen but a few geese that would not remain in one place long enough at a time to set up to them in the punt.

16th.—Up at a quarter to six and off till one, but neither fired nor heard a shot. Off again from three till six, and, after waiting on about eighty geese for near two hours, and then getting them in such a good place and so thick together that I must have stopped half the company, an infernal scoundrel ran in at them with a black sailing boat and drove them to sea for the night.

17th to 19th.—Sunday. South-westers and heavy rain. Not out, but kept great gun afloat and loaded for the chance of the geese, which occasionally appear in one grand company.

21st.—White frost and butterfly day; nothing about but one flock of geese that would not rest five minutes in one place. Got 6 shore birds with the popgun, and then blew off the large gun, in order to clean it out a little, and though the flint barrel had been loaded since the 14th and the detonator ever since the 13th, and left the whole time afloat in the most miserable wet gales that it was possible to weather, yet both barrels went as instantaneously as if fresh loaded in a sunny day. I once had this gun afloat for several weeks, and it went equally well.

N.B.—Not a bird had been killed while I was away; but on my arrival I had the delight to hear that Harry Troth, the man who ruined our Keyhaven harbour, was gone off, bag and baggage, into Norfolk to be under keeper of Hazeborough Lighthouse, for which appointment both he and I have to thank my own exertions with the Trinity Board, where I received the most polite attention from Mr. Herbert, the commander and secretary, on whom I waited the moment I got to town this last time. Never was there a better appointment.

It has put a starving family into comfortable independence, and ridded Keyhaven of a redhot young gunner, who did more harm in one week than our harbour had before suffered for nearly a quarter of a century. Troth's punt being a very pretty one, built by Sam Singer's workmen on my plan, I took care to secure her for 2*l.* lest she may again be launched to the ruin of my amusement.

February 8th.—A hard frost and some easterly breezes. Afloat all day, and should have had some geese, but was 'flanked' all the afternoon by some greenhorn dandies, who spoiled me a capital shot in their Quixotic, and of course unsuccessful, attempt at killing a goose.

10*th.*—Saw some geese, but, as they were too far in on the mud, I left them to 'get a good haunt,' as the tyros were no longer in our harbour.

11*th.*—An easterly gale, with hard frost. Brought home 14 wigeon. Geese to the eastward, so had nothing to do with them.

12*th.*—The hardest frost this year, but so much white in it as to make it suspicious as to continuing. Afloat from morning till night; brought in 14 wigeon, and a splendid wild swan, the first heard of this season. I fell in with 4 swans off Pennington Lake. They were all scattered, and about to rise when we got within about 200 yards of them. I took one with the first barrel and 'floored' him, but he recovered and rose. In the second barrel I had swan shot, and cut up my bird handsomely. After bagging him, I took up the spyglass and saw the first bird lying sick on the mud. To make dead sure, I reloaded the great gun, and we paddled up close to him and were just getting the gun to bear when an old fool named Dagville, from Southampton, a notorious coast nuisance, fancied he could 'put salt on his tail,' and drove him from under our noses to where he may never be seen again. Always some lubberly ass about when a fine chance of a shot occurs.

14*th*.—A fine day, with a little frost again. Up before daylight and cruised all the way to Pilewell, but not a bird did I see, as the water was low, and the mud covered with periwinkle men for five miles to supply two vessels just arrived to get supplies for Billingsgate. Came home at twelve, dined at half-past two, and went out again from four till after dark, when the tide was up and the coast clear. Made a lovely shot, the first I got: 10 brent geese, at about 160 yards, out of the only little company I saw.

15*th*.—A sharp frost, and yet the 'winklemen were on the mud all day, so I drove into Lymington to leave a hamper with my last 10 geese, the fattest I ever saw, directed to Mr. Anson, for Prince Albert and her Majesty at Brighton.

17*th*.—Up at half-past four, out till eleven, when the 'winklemen mobbed the mud. Dined at five and went out from seven till ten under the moon; found some wigeon, but no water, so left them quiet for a higher tide.

18*th*.—Off at daylight again, but not a chance, as the tides were so dead that the 'winklemen were on all day.

19*th*.—Another early start, but no birds, though an intensely cold easterly wind.

20*th*.—A bitter cold white frost. Afloat early, and never felt the cold more severely. Not a bird to shoot at. In by twelve, and, after a second breakfast, drove to Barton, where I heard that the wild fowl were swarming under the cliffs, where no boat could venture with safety. Saw about 2,000 wigeon, covering about two miles of water, and consequently so thin that, had their legs been tied to an anchor, no gun could have killed more than two or three at a shot; and the coastguardmen there told me that most of them flew at night to the Christchurch rivers.

21*st*.—A bitter white frost. Not a chance all day. Afloat by moonlight from eight till near one A.M.; wigeon so scattered that we could hardly get two together. Brought in only 4.

23rd.—Sunday.

24th.—Out all day. Brought in 6 pintails, 5 splendid cocks and 1 hen, the first I had shot at this season. I fell in with 10 of them, and cut up 8 in fine style, but one beat us in a heavy sea, and another scrambled across the mud and got 'prigged' by a clod and his dog. A strong north-wester, but the beastly old 'carrion crow,' a boat-sailing bird pirate from Yarmouth, drove the place so unmercifully under sail that we lost all chance for some geese that again appeared. Prepared to go out from ten till two at night, but the wind set into the moon, so I went to bed.

25th.—Read crawled on the mud before daylight, after the moon had cleared itself from the wind, and brought in 5 wigeon. I went out till one, and then out again in the afternoon. Not a bird to be seen, and a wet south-wester after this morning's sharp white frost.

March 1st.—Easterly gale, winter again; about 300 geese off my 'leak,' a splendid place to steal on them. All but getting a fine shot, when that smutty old 'varmint' cadger Dagville, of Southampton, drove them all off with his trumpery set-out.

5th.—Intense frost. Pain in limbs and quite stiff. Shipped lots of poor man's plaster and went afloat; and, instead of getting worse, I found great benefit from the sea air and excitement, and should have had some fair sport had it not been for the Yarmouth blackguards who followed me on purpose to prevent my shooting. (N.B.—Such has been the ruin of our fine channel, by the sailing scoundrels from Yarmouth, the mud crawlers of Keyhaven, and the banditti of shore snobs, that at this moment about 2,000 wigeon remain for miles at sea under the cliffs, and betake themselves at night to all the fresh waters in the country.) The coldest night known for many years. Read, after crawling on the mud all night, brought in 1 wigeon.

6th.—Tremendous north-east gale, and water freezing to

the oars. Afloat early, and got one small double shot at the mouth of Pennington Leak, and then retreated for the safety of our lives.

7th.—Severest weather known for years. Harbour frozen up, and such a sea in the Channel as no punt could face. An absolute Siberia to weather, and yet not the chance of a shot for a recompense. Reade had a blank night and I a blank day, and glad to get home in safety.

8th.—The frost relaxed and the ice became broken, so as to leave the harbour clear at ebb tide. Very few birds, and all of them in the wash of the heavy breakers. Shooting impossible. Thousands of wigeon at sea under shelter of the cliffs, and now we want a south-wester to beat them out of this berth of defiance.

10th.—The bitter north-east wind kept howling away all yesterday and all to-day. Nothing inside the harbour, and an awful sea outside.

12th.—Cold, though moderate, weather; so went afloat all day, and was not in till past eight in the evening; got 2 brent geese at about 300 yards with a mould cartridge, and afterwards 9 wigeon.

13th.—The most bitter day that ever was weathered. Intense frost, with a north-east hurricane that one could hardly stand against. Prisoner for the day, of course. But in the evening tried 'the flight,' knowing the birds must fly low, wild and cunning as these were become after five months' incessant siege. But no! The birds actually fluttered against the tide all the way round Hurst rather than fly in their usual course, because they had not the power to mount up for 500 feet above ground as usual in order to avoid the popshooters. I was busy all the morning writing, and, among other things, sketching some amendments to the game laws, on which a committee has just been appointed in the House of Commons.

14th.—A north-east gale, with the hardest frost known

for years. Water jugs frozen in bedrooms, harbour blocked up &c. &c. Weathered a heavy sea, and bagged 3 brent geese. After I got home, and put the punt to distant moorings from the frozen harbour, I marked down 5 ducks and mallards in the Keyhaven river, and got 2 mallards and 1 duck, an immensely long shot, with my wonderful 'old Fullerd' shoulder gun that had not been used for two seasons.

15*th.*—A Siberian gale the whole day. Small birds starved to death with cold. No living afloat; and, in short, petrified with cold, and all for nothing. Too late to bring foreign birds, and all the stale birds blown farther westward.

16*th.*—Sunday. Heavy snow all day, and intense frost. Redwings and thrushes half starved, and rabbles of boys knocking them down with sticks in a bitter north-east gale.

18*th.*—Read came in with 25 wigeon, in two shots (16 and 9), the best mud-crawling shot for many years. Afloat myself all day, but never saw a chance.

24*th.*—Out all the morning, and again from nine till two under a lovely moon, and with a fine full calm tide, and never heard a bird.

25*th.*—Out from ten till two for the chance of the rough drizzling rain bringing in a few birds. All I got or shot at was 1 brent goose, and I then, finding all shooting was at an end for the season, mustered 'all hands,' and brought up to store all my gear, my great gun, and my punt, and bid adieu to the longest, though by no means the most successful, winter I ever had to weather.

Wild fowl &c. up to Lady Day: Wild fowl—6 ducks and mallards, 206 wigeon, 10 teal, 6 pintails at a shot, 3 tufted ducks, 3 burrough ducks, 94 brent geese, 2 barnacle geese, 1 wild swan. Total, 331.

Waders—37 plover, 14 godwits, 4 curlews, 1 olive, 2 ring dotterel, 196 shore birds. Total, 254.

331 wild fowl, 254 waders. Grand total, 585.

36 game, 585 fowl &c. Grand total, 621 head. A very long and yet not a brilliant season.

April 11th to 14th.—London. Laid up in bed unable to even sit up, and on the 14th (Monday) lost the Philharmonic on the Queen's night.

15th and 16th.—Laid up still, and on the latter day lost going to Charles Kemble's readings.

May 3rd.—Longparish. Better, and availed myself of the first two hours' leisure I had to hobble to the river with my fly rod, and caught 6 brace of large trout, but all so badly in season owing to the winterly spring, that one I threw in again, half starved, and the others proved unworthy of dressing.

12th.—Whit-Monday, and anniversary of our fight at the Douro in 1801.

July 15th.—Keyhaven. Up at six, and off all day and till nine at night in the 'Solent' steamer, first at Portsmouth, and then home round the island, after being all day in the thick of the grand naval review, and near to the royal yacht, in which were her Majesty and Prince Albert, with the King and Queen of the Belgians. The Queen Dowager and Prince George were in other yachts, and never before was there such a magnificent naval sight. The splendid ships reviewed were the 'St. Vincent,' 120 guns; 'Trafalgar,' 120; 'Queen,' 110; 'Rodney,' 92; 'Albion,' 90; 'Canopus,' 84; 'Vanguard,' 80; 'Superb,' 80.

These eight line-of-battle ships formed the experimental squadron under Admiral Sir Hyde Parker, and after the review majestically sailed off for their trial cruise in the Bay of Biscay &c. with a fine, fair, and brisk breeze. The day seemed made on purpose for the occasion, and in my life I never saw such a magnificent sight.

16th.—As busy as busy could be from morning till night.

22nd.—Busy every day up to this day with painters &c., having six punts to repair, and consequently such a prisoner (to keep them up to their work) that I've had no holiday except going to the royal show last Tuesday, and having now got all done that required my presence I booked my place to get away to-morrow. This afternoon the royal yacht, with the Queen and Prince Albert, passed Keyhaven, and possibly the Prince may have recognised the place, the engraving of which he so admired in my book on sporting that I dedicated and presented to his Royal Highness.

23rd.—Left Keyhaven for London per morning coach, and then on by express train. In the next carriage to me were the Duke of Cambridge and Prince George, and we went from Southampton to Vauxhall in ten minutes under the two hours.

CHAPTER XXXVIII

1845

September 1st.—Though taken so ill that I scarcely closed my eyes all last night, yet I contrived to weather the hardest day's campaign that we have had for many years. We were out from ten till eight in a dry north-east gale, and the birds, of course, as 'wild as hawks.' Nearly all snap shooting. Did miracles considering all things. I bagged 27 partridges, and not a small bird among the whole lot. On our return home the whole banditti were so dead beat as to be worked off their never-before-failing appetites.

3rd.—Another severely hard day, and not home till near eight o'clock. Brought in 29 partridges and 2 hares. Charles Heath, who joined us after beating the outskirts, got 11 birds and 1 hare; so that our combined lot of partridges was just 20 brace, on which old Siney petitioned for a 'butcher's halloo,' in which we indulged him, though our shout in good old times was always at every 20 brace from my own gun alone. All hands so dead beat again that we could hardly crawl home from the hills.

6th.—Another hard day, and still a cold easterly gale. Not home till eight. Never shot better. Brought home 19 partridges and 4 hares, and never fired a blank shot the whole day.

8th.—By blazing away at all distances I contrived to bring in 18 partridges and 1 hare.

19th.—Brought home my old master, the great 'lion' of

Europe, the Chevalier Kalkbrenner, and his wonderfully talented son Arthur, who came to pass a day with us.

20th.—Kalkbrenner entreated me to let his son see me shoot; so to oblige them I went out in a gale of wind. But I only got one very long shot, and by accident happened to kill and bag the single partridge that I fired at, and but for this lucky hit I should have had what I never before experienced—a blank day.

Game killed in September 1845 by myself: 134 partridges, 10 hares. Total, 144 head.

A fair breed of birds, but as wild as hawks on and from the first day. I was out but eleven times in all, and seldom for more than half a day. Though weak and unwell, I shot brilliantly, but could not fag as usual.

October 1st.—Up early, and scoured all our inclosed country, finishing with our little wood, before we came home to lunch. Not a pheasant to be seen the whole day. But after a fagging expedition on both sides of the river we came home to a seven o'clock dinner with 2 hares, 1 rabbit, 1 snipe (the only one yet seen), and 3 partridges. Most excellent shooting, and a satisfactory day, except not being able to find one single pheasant. All of us as tired as dogs, and a grand blow-out in the hall for all the beaters and markers by way of climax to the first of October.

6th.—London. While in town I took the opportunity of putting my name in a long list of other names petitioning the Queen for what the 'Duke' refused—some little mark of honour for the Peninsular war of seven years, similar to what was granted at Waterloo for three days. I entered myself thus at the 'United Service Gazette' office: 'Peter Hawker, Lieutenant-Colonel, formerly Senior Captain of the 14th Dragoons, and commander of the squadron that gained for the regiment the motto of "Douro."'

29th.—Keyhaven. Took a sail, with a brisk wind, all over our channel, and every bird that we saw was 7 wigeon, off in the breakers, and these were the very first Read had set eyes on this season, though out repeatedly in his punt. In times of old we had generally killed the best half our winter birds before the end of October, provided there was no hard weather to bring over a second flight.

November 1st.—Left Keyhaven for Longparish. On arrival at Southampton found that not a wild fowl had been killed there, though the wind was north-east. Having a spare half-hour I saw the magnetic telegraph at the rail station; and the gentleman who exhibited this wonderful invention, after he had conferred on all his official messages, asked me if I had any trifling question to ask for experiment. I said I would beg the favour of him to say, 'Are there any wild fowl at Portsmouth now?'

5th.—Longparish. Having heard that a pheasant had been seen on my estate, I sallied out with a levy *en masse* and scoured all the country side, and bagged 2 splendid cock pheasants, all we found. Never saw one hare all day, though the foxhounds drove Wherwell Wood in full cry, and passed us in gallant style.

7th.—Drove, for a day's business, into Andover. Best horse taken so lame that I drove her in jeopardy, and saved her from falling twenty times. When within a mile of home I turned round to bow to Counsellor Missing, and at that very instant down came the mare and broke her knees. Why was all this? Because we took Friday for a day of business, and, moreover, a single magpie foretold our disaster; but thank God it was no worse.

12th.—Took my banditti out all day in search of another cock pheasant that had been seen, but never found him.

15th.—Heard of the old cock again, but could not find him, nor could I get a shot at a single head of game.

1846

January 5*th.*—Bitter white frost again; and in order to shake off the shivers that I've had for a week, I shipped my long water boots and waded up the river. I killed in good style all that I shot at, viz. 3 jack snipes, 2 of them a brilliant double shot to front and rear, with 9 moorhens and 3 divers. I then shifted my boots, and beat all our wood and the rows, and the only head of game I set eyes on was 1 rabbit, which I bagged. The shooting here now is an absolute waste of time, but still I was well pleased to have such a satisfactory beginning for the new year.

13*th.*—Keyhaven. Afloat at daylight. Found that scarcely a fowl had been killed, though the increase of punt shooters was awful. I saw, off at sea, about 80 geese, and about half as many wigeon, and heard that many more were off outside the beach, but that all the army of gunners put together had not made up twenty couple the whole season.

15*th.*—Took a sail all the way up to Pilewell, and about the Western Channel; never saw a wild fowl, or even a plover, the whole day, so of course gave up all thoughts of launching a punt. The other gunners all complained that it was useless to go out.

My punts were all newly done up for gunning, and I never was better prepared for wild fowl; but I found the unprecedented scarcity of birds at Keyhaven to be such that I would not disgrace myself by putting a great gun afloat. A general complaint all over England about the scarcity of wild fowl, cocks, snipes, and all other winter birds.

February 11*th.*—London. The first Levee of the season, which I made a point of attending, as my bad foot prevented me from going last season, and I had not yet made my bow since the great kindness of Prince Albert on the dedication to his Royal Highness of my ninth edition. Coming home I found a lady's jewels in the cab that I hailed, and, of course, took immediate steps for their being restored to her.

June 17th.—London. Went with my old friend General Brotherton to Woolwich to see the wonderful effect of Charles Lancaster's new conical rifle ball, with which he some weeks ago hit a target five times in twenty-four shots at the incredible distance of 1,200 yards.

25th.—Went again to Woolwich to see another trial of Lancaster's conical rifle ball. For the first hour's shooting he had the disadvantage of strong wind and rain; but at last he overcame the want of proper elevation, and the weather moderated, and he then hit the target (nine feet square) six times out of nine successive shots at 1,200 yards.

CHAPTER XXXIX

1846

September 1st.—Longparish. A dry north-easterly breeze all day. Birds extremely wild, not only when together in coveys, but even after they were dispersed. The only good lay in the country was one large piece of high turnips. Here I found about 40 birds, all dispersed about the field; and yet, although my two dogs were over-careful, I never got a shot at one of these birds. However, by sheer slavery, and being out from half-past nine till half-past seven, I did contrive to do miracles by bringing home 20 partridges and 6 hares. Furgo Farm was without any lay at all, and almost destitute of game. I therefore went off to Bullington for the afternoon, or must have come home with only 4 brace and 1 hare. Having no appetite, I became so weak towards the end of the day that I could hardly stand, and consequently missed 2 fair shots. Except this momentary breakdown, I shot splendidly all day; and had there been lay for the birds and scent for the dogs, I should, no doubt, have bagged my 20 brace. We were all completely knocked up; and as for me, I was so dead beat that I scarcely slept the night. So much for the first day of '46.

3rd.—Another severe day with the wild birds in the dry north-easter. Out from ten till seven. Brought in 20 partridges. So dead beat that I could take nothing but some tea when I got home.

5th.—Out for half a day near home (being too weak for the grand beat round Bullington), and bagged 12 partridges, having made some very long shots, and fired but one blank shot, and that a long second-barrel one.

1st week, out two days and two half-days.—63 partridges, 9 hares, 1 rabbit, 1 snipe. Total, 74 head.

The country was never so bare, birds so wild, or scent so bad as this first week of September.

26th.—Took out my rod, and in my life I never saw the trout more kind. In about an hour I caught enough to have filled a large hand basket; but, not wishing to destroy trout at this season, I kept only 4 brace of first-rate large ones. If I had fished all day, and kept all I caught, I might have gone about bragging of my 40 or 50 brace!

N.B.—The barren state of the fields, and the dry easterly wind, made the shooting so bad for the whole month of September that I gave it up, and went to town after the first week. The birds would scarcely allow even the dogs to come within two gunshots of them; and even when dispersed would run all over the country, instead of lying for a shot.

October 1st.—Had the usual muster of all my myrmidons with the forlorn hope of getting 1 pheasant the first day; and left not a yard of my beat untried. After a fag, from seven till a seven o'clock dinner, I had the luck to bring home 2 pheasants; these were all I had a chance at. But we sprung 2 more pheasants that we chased for hours; till at last we got each of them out of covert, where we could have made dead sure of them. Unluckily, however, they were a few yards out of bounds, and there I declined going.

15th.—Started off in search of a rare bird that had been seen yesterday, but when I ran home for a gun he was gone. To-day I fell in with him, and, after following him about the river for near an hour, I crawled up to him, and did his business with Eley's cartridge. The name of the bird is the 'grey phalarope,' and though Bewick says 'it has seldom been met with in the British Isles,' yet I once before killed one near Keyhaven. The bird, as Bewick says, is a native of the Arctic regions, and is somewhat less than a snipe, with feet like a coot and partly webbed ; it swims like a dabchick, and runs like a plover.

16*th.*—Went out to try a water dog, for which purpose I killed 3 coots ; but the dog was 'no go.' The only sporting bird I had a chance at was a little jack snipe that I got ; and coming home, what should I see and kill, but another phalarope !

21*st.*—The country being, just now, destitute of everything but wind, rain, and dirt, I returned to London.

31*st.*—London. Went to see Mr. Charles Lancaster after his miraculous escape in firing the new gun cotton, and the first-rate strong double gun that it blew all to atoms. This extraordinary composition, which everyone is eager about, strikes me as having more expansive than projectile powers ; and therefore more dangerous and less effective than any gunpowder, except for blasting rocks and such-like uses, for which it is the best material in existence.

November 11*th.*—Having been unwell with the influenza, and the long batch of wet and unhealthy weather having changed to a dry north-easter, I this day ran down to Keyhaven for change of air.

12*th.*—Keyhaven. A brisk north-easter with a little black frost. Up at daylight, and not having launched a punt all last season (as there were no birds), it took me a long time to get even the small set-out in order ; and what with caulking and other jobs, the day was gone. I went out from three till dusk. It blew too fresh to venture far, and I had no chance for a shot ; but I saw 24 geese, the first that had yet been heard of.

13*th.*—Had prepared to go off before daylight this morning, but was taken so ill that I was obliged to give it up. Read therefore went instead of me ; but he never saw the geese, nor did he hear any birds in the night, though crawling till past twelve.

14th and 15*th.*—Sunday. Laid up with the influenza, but lost nothing, as Read had been slaving to no purpose, day and night. My punt and loaded (single) stanchion gun remain afloat, and the east gale continues.

16*th.*—I was, thank God, so much better as to be able to go off, for a few hours, afloat; but the wind had hauled out to southward, and there were no wild fowl about; but I blew off my five-days-loaded charge in a glorious manner at smaller game. There were 14 plover pitched on some sea-weed; and I was just in time to get before some other gunners who were after them, but who behaved very civilly—not to spoil my shot (for which I gave them something to drink), and I had the luck to bag every one of the plover.

20*th.*—A furious hurricane all last night, from south by west (the very focus for a flood), and so fearful was I of the sea bursting over the banks about half-past ten (when there was yet an hour to high water), that I kept a fly nearly an hour at the door before I would venture away to Lymington, where I afterwards went. A wreck off our north shore. 'Hands' saved. Cargoes of railway timber rescued by our coastguard, who got a poor little goldfinch, drowned in his cage. A few wigeon swept into our harbour from their constant haunt of the open sea, which they could no longer live in.

21*st.*—Still rough, wet and squally. Out all day, but chiefly at dirty work in the mud; as the furious tempest of yesterday had carried away the bed of seaweed from my plover island, and nothing was left for birds to pitch on; so I lashed the new cargo within an old net made fast to the surrounding stakes of the fence.

23*rd.*—Up early, and by afternoon had completed another island (of reeds nailed with laths down to a large frame, and moored with an old chain and sunk post, so as to be always afloat, at one regular level, for the gun, at all tides—when there would be water over the mud), and my mock birds[1] answered so well that the curlews all came and sat with them for some time.

24*th.*—About five this evening I had a splendid chance for a grand shot, but had a most annoying disappointment. There came on a dead calm, and every curlew, plover and dunlin in the country had concentrated on my island. I put in a cartridge of small shot, and got almost on board them under cover of nightfall, and, to my great surprise (as it had never occurred since we got all the patent cartridges to perfection), the cartridge 'balled' and flew out to sea like a cannon ball, and, except one dunlin that lay dead (Lord knows by what means), I never touched a feather; and away went a cloud of birds, out of which I expected to fill two bushel baskets.

25*th.*—The westerly gales and rain having put an end to all chance of sport on the coast for the present, I had this day a grand furbish, and laid up what little gear I had put in commission.

28*th.*—Longparish. A stiff day to prove my 'pluck.' Went to bed last evening after dinner with a chill that I took in a deadly cold 'sniveller' coming home from Andover; and my sudorific did not warm me till near morning, when I got up at seven and breakfasted, in order to be ready by daylight. I then went off to the river for 3 teal that I did not find. Then off with a cry of dogs and followers in search of 2 cock pheasants that had been seen on my estate, and after our beating the whole country in despair, they at last flew out of 'Tracy's Dell' pit. Though a long and intercepted shot, I

[1] 'New Dodge.' Recipe for making a mock bird that I defy any gunner to distinguish from a living one at the distance of half a gunshot. Take a piece of wheat straw, and double it up to about the size of a curlew or plover. Tie or sew it up tight in some brown silk or stuff of any kind. Tie under it a piece of white linen rag for the silvery breast. Then roll up in a ball some pine tow (oakum has a smell of tar which wild birds may not like), and tie it up in the brown stuff. Run a wooden skewer through this ball, so as to come out like the bill. Sew this head to the body, and run two skewers through the centre of the body for legs.

hit one of them so hard, that after a chase as good as a fox hunt we put him in the bag. We then persevered till we found the other, which I blazed away at through a thick hedgerow, and which we had another long chase to get. Coming home, a hen sprung within a yard of me on the wrong side of a very little hedge. This artful bird gave me the hardest chase of all ; but at last I killed her at about 75 yards with a patent cartridge, just as she was flying out of bounds. We were then all so knocked up as to need refreshment. Afterwards stormed the 'Moors' wood, though found nothing there. I then shipped my long water boots and waded the river for snipes ; but the white frost had made what few there were as wild as curlews. I, however, cut down a miraculously long double shot with two of Eley's cartridges. I pocketed also the only jack snipe I saw ; and then blew off my two barrels, by killing a double shot at 2 moorhens. Here ended a most satisfactory little day.

If this is not a good day's work for a man who is weak and suffering and without appetite, I know not what is.

December 10th.—Received this morning an account of the death of one of the oldest and best of all my friends, Sir Charles Morgan, of Tredegar Park, who died last Saturday, in the eighty-sixth year of his age. Another severe blow for my valued friend, poor Lady Rodney (his daughter), and a sad embargo on all the princely hospitality of the Christmas at Tredegar.

15*th.*—Keyhaven. Up by candlelight, and on from seven till half-past one getting the great gun afloat, and also her tender the 'Feather' punt, both of which had been laid up for two years in store, as there was nothing to put any punt afloat for last year. Read, Payne, Peter Fifield, another and I were all in one furious bustle the whole morning to get through the jobs of caulking, powder drying, cutting through ice, to get afloat &c. We went out for a few hours to see that all was right ; but it was the wrong time of tide to expect a shot, or even to see any fowl, though we heard that there were thousands on the coast.

16th.—Out from daylight till dark in as cold a north wind as could be weathered. Both water and land in one continued siege by bungling shooters afloat and ashore, so that scarcely a place could be found for the fowl to pitch and rest on till one could go into them for a shot. I got but two little shots the whole day, though did handsomely with them; the first was 10 grey plover, the second 4 wigeon.

18th.—A nipping white frost; out all day, and never had the chance of a shot. In the afternoon the sea under the Isle of Wight was like a mirror, and there were several trips of wigeon floating down on the ebb, where I should have got a good lot of birds; but there were no less than seven boat-loads of popgunning blockheads, who destroyed all prospect of firing my gun.

19th.—The white frost (as I told everyone it would do) broke up at the spring tides of the new moon, and we had last night a westerly gale and rain. It blew and rained hard all this morning, and, as is usual on the break up, the wigeon came into the harbour. But the sport was spoiled by a greenhorn stanchion gunner, who frightened all the birds and nearly got drowned into the bargain. Read went off in self-defence, and got 1 duck and 1 wigeon. I, not choosing to run a race with opposition in a pour of rain, remained at home to write a batch of letters, and despatch a basket of fowl for Prince Albert at Windsor Castle. I went out in the afternoon, when the rain abated, but there was not a fowl in the harbour.

21st.—Up before daylight, and off in such a gale of wind and rain that the birds could hardly weather it at sea, and therefore I expected they would come inside at high water. They did so; but in spite of wind and weather the shore snobs kept up such an incessant fire at birds a quarter of a mile off that it was folly to expect a shot. I was all but firing at about

50 ducks and mallards that I got all in a line, when a blockhead cracked off his popgun and put them all up. The coast here is absolutely ruined.

1847

January 1st.—Longparish. Began the new year with a capital shot from my decoy hut at 2 mallards and 1 duck, the latter a most extraordinary bird that I sent to taxidermist Leadbeater, with one of the mallards that had beautiful pink (instead of white) under his wings. I then shot at 2 more ducks and bagged them both. An excellent start for 1847.

11*th.*—After a bath nearly hot enough to scald a pig, and a dose of paregoric and sweet spirits of nitre last night, I was, thank God, so much 'to windward' to-day as to be able to put on my thick wild-fowl coat, and try my two large shoulder-duck guns 'Big Joe' and 'Old Fullerd'—two such guns as I think are unrivalled.

16*th.*—Having heard from old Read that there were again some birds on the coast, I this day started for Keyhaven. Old Read greeted me on my arrival, and said the birds were wild and much scattered; he had seen some geese.

18*th.*—Keyhaven. Up an hour before daylight to put the great gun anointed with neat's-foot oil and all the gear afloat, but could not get under way till near eleven, and the tide obliged us to be in by four. I brought home 11 brent geese and 1 wigeon. I should have had treble the number but for the bunglers afloat and ashore, who spoiled me two fair shots. A good show of birds and the weather most beautiful; an easterly wind, and a frost not too hard.

19*th.*—A dead calm. Under way about eight o'clock, and cruised twelve miles 'up alongshore;' but above Pilewell nothing but gentlemen gunners in all directions, and the weather being too fine the birds were all at sea, and would not venture in harbour, or even in channel. The only chance

I had was at a few stray ducks and wigeon, nearly under the Isle of Wight.

25th.—A tremendous gale all yesterday (Sunday) and all last night, which drove the wigeon from off at sea to the harbour and western channel. I had finished breakfast long before daylight this morning, but a torrent of rain kept me from going afloat till near eight, and then the tide was gone and the birds had got off in Channel. I took one shot and knocked down 15 wigeon.

26th.—Off again at daybreak. Saw a few wigeon, but they were so driven about by bunglers in sailing boats that I had only one passing shot at a few rapidly flying across at about 200 yards. I knocked down 2 in brilliant style, but the winged one beat us in a heavy sea, as the weather this day was very rough. I also punted up to a single goose with Westley Richards's extraordinary shooting musket, and killed him dead at above sixty yards.[1]

27th.—Another daybreak attempt, but the rain and hurricane of last night had blown away nearly all the birds, and I just saved my blank by popping off my pistol to put up some wigeon that were buried in the waves, and I knocked down a few of them at an enormous distance.

28th.—An awful hurricane all last night and till daylight this morning, and there would have been a flood had not Mrs. Whitby by my entreaties raised her banks fifteen inches, as the sea was even now within ten inches of coming over the banks. I landed my large punt, the 'Petrel,' in the road, and from there housed her in the boathouse. While the men were furbishing up the things I took the musket to blow her off, and had the luck to get the very bird I had long tried, even with the great gun, a huge saddle-back gull that was

[1] When I got home I weighed the barrel of this uncommonly good gun; and it proved to be precisely 6 lb.—the exact weight also of the two barrels of my unrivalled cripple stopper (called 'Bloody Burnett'), that none of my sporting doubles can compete with, although they all carry the same charge. This tells in favour of having plenty of metal, and particularly near the breechings.

blown by the raging tempest into the marsh close by; he measured 5 feet 3 inches from tip to tip of wings. I once killed 5 at a shot of these huge monsters when a youth, and a lieutenant in the 14th Dragoons, but had never killed one since that 'olden time.' The south-west gale had driven everything far to leeward, so that for the present all gunning was 'done for,' and I therefore prepared for a start away from Keyhaven for Longparish.

February 9th.—I got to Keyhaven again before six to-day. Read's report on my arrival was meagre as to wigeon, but rich as to geese. *Demain nous verrons.* Never could finer weather come for a gunner. A black north-easter, and all inland a region of snow.

10*th.*—Up by six, and saved high water to get the 'Petrel' afloat, and ship great gun and gear.

Afloat for about two hours, and never got a chance. And no wonder, as the shore snobs to windward were all day long making war on the scattered larks and thrushes, and I heard at least three hundred pops in the course of the morning.

11*th.*—Out the whole day, no chance.

12*th.*—Off at daylight. Such a savage white frost (the forerunner of wind and rain) that we had to beat our way through ice for nearly a quarter of a mile. I got a shot at 2 ducks and lost them both, and at 2 wigeon, and bagged them both, and these were my only chances from morning till night. There were several companies of birds off in channel, but the snobs would not allow them time to pitch, and the geese never remained five minutes in one place.[1]

13*th.*—Not a chance for a wild fowl, though out all day. But the onset (the first thing in the morning) amply compensated for what would have otherwise been a blank day. Having loaded one of my barrels with a 12 oz. (No. 6) cartridge of Eley, in order to be prepared for a large flock of dunlins that were generally seen very early in the morning, I

[1] Read, after mud crawling all night, brought in a wigeon.

made it my business to attend to them, and luckily caught them on a fine stage of floating sea-weeds. I cut a lane through them, and mowed them down as with a scythe, picking up 178 dunlins and plover. My other barrel being loaded with shot for geese, I would not degrade this great shot by discharging it with what would not have done proportional justice.

15*th.*—A gale of wind and heavy rain, which brought the birds into harbour. About half-past ten we weathered it and dropped down on them, and by using two cartridges of 'A A' shot I had the luck to bring in 5 of the best brent geese I've killed this season. We were no less pleased than astonished at the distance at which I killed these birds (about 300 yards). But a fair shot now is next to impossible, as all the birds are become extremely wild.

16*th.*—Off again in wind and rain, and should have had a better chance than yesterday, but the geese had no time to pitch for the shore poppers.

17*th.*—Afloat early as soon as the tide served, and left Read with a signal flag and the great punt to windward, and Payne and his punt with another signal flag to leeward, and waited at home for my letters and paper, instead of off in the punt. But no signal was made to call me, and when I walked overland to the punt about eleven I found that hundreds of geese and wigeon had come down with the high wind to drop in our flooded harbour ; but not a bird of them could pitch, as they had a royal salute from the kill-nothing-poppers ashore, and the sailing about the harbour of the blank-firing 'snobs' afloat. The 'break-up,' therefore, which for a few days (if windy) was always our grand time to make great shots, was so completely 'done for' that I availed myself of the after-flood tide to get everything ashore. Here ends the gunning season, in the whole of which I've fired but one blank shot, and that out of reach.

18*th.*—The harbour swarming with birds, owing to the

constant wind and rain which had cleared it of the 'one-suit-of-clothes snobs,' and old Read had bagged 1 goose with his old rattletrap mud gun.

20th.—Game killed in the season: 87 partridges, 16 hares (all in September and all I shot at), 3 pheasants (all I saw), 40 snipes and jacks, 6 rabbits, 3 wood pigeons; total, 155. Wild fowl: 39 ducks and mallards (36 of them from my new decoy hut), 31 wigeon, 1 pintail, 2 teal, 1 sheldrake, 28 brent geese. Total, 102. Coast-waders: 2 phalaropes, 1 saddle-back, 39 plover, 313 dunlins. Total, 355. 102 wild fowl, 355 waders. Total, 457. 155 game, 457 fowl &c.; grand total, 612 head.

N.B.—No game shooting worth going out for after September, and Keyhaven ruined by 'snobs.' I never shot better, both by land and by sea, so am content.

April 11th.—Peter was married to Miss Fraser, of Stirling, N.B. I was married to Peter's mother on the 19th of March, 1811. God send him good luck, and less trouble than has, up to the present date, been inflicted on his father.

25th.—Went from London to inspect Tonbridge Wells, and never was I more glad than to get away from this pigeon-plucking watering-place, the only way to see which without a royal fleecing would be to bargain a fly man, and run on direct to 'the rocks,' with a basket of grub, then walk back and survey the town, and when tired, rest in the rail carriage till you were hurled back to the London Bridge terminus.

May 13th.—Longparish. Having a demand for fish, I brandished a fly rod. The trout were so sulky, owing to the cold storms, that it took me a long time to catch 10 brace.

15th.—Took out my fly rod and got 6 brace of fine trout, besides lots thrown in, in little more than an hour.

CHAPTER XL

1847

September 1st.—Longparish. A dry and strong gale of wind all day, with heavy showers after four o'clock. Birds constantly on the run and wilder than ever, and scent most miserable. Furgo Farm almost barren of cover as well as of game, so went on for the afternoon to Bullington. Did absolute wonders, considering all circumstances. I came home with 28 partridges and 3 quails, and out of all these 31 very fine full-grown birds there was not one old bird. This is what I never saw or even heard of before. We got home at eight o'clock quite tired, yet delighted with this extraordinary day.

List of game killed in September: 136 partridges, 8 quails, 1 landrail, 5 hares, 12 snipes, 1 teal, 1 spotted gallinule. Total, 164 head.

All my best shooting was over at Bullington, where I could only take a few hours' sport at a time, as I was too weak to go far and fag hard, and was much interrupted by business.

October 1st.—Only 2 pheasants on all my estate—both cocks, and both came home to the larder, after as hard and grand a chase with a village rabble as ever old Smith had, with his crack foxhounds. We had five hours of it, before the two birds came to hand. I got 1 very old cock pheasant, and Charles Heath, who went with me, got the other, a young cock, and also a hare, and these were every head of game we saw.

On my return home before three, I found that my new cloth kite had arrived from town, so, tired as I was, I went off to try the effect of it before the day was over, and it answered so well that in two double shots off near Bullington, I killed 4 partridges. A most satisfactory day, notwithstanding it was Friday.

8th.—The birds would not let us get into the same field with them. Determined to 'serve them out,' I loaded 'Big Joe' with Eley, started at five in the evening in the cart, and was in again by half-past six, with 10 first-rate young partridges. Nothing like a duck gun from a horse and cart on the road to fill a bag, when all popgunning becomes a wild-goose chase.

16th.—Keyhaven. Availed myself of the first leisure day to put my gear and small punt ready, in case this easterly wind should stand, and bring more birds. Some wigeon have been seen, and Read has got a couple. After seeing that my punt was all right and tight, I tried the experiment of the kite, and it towed the punt so well that we think it will manage my large one also. The one we tried was the mere toy that I got the 4 partridges with on the 1st.

November 8th.—London. A letter from Read to say he had just got 32 wigeon at a shot, besides shooting 9 more that he did not get.

10th.—Came Read's second letter, to say not a bird had been seen or heard of since he posted his first letter, so it's lucky I did not go down. This shows the uncertainty of wild-fowl shooting.

December 16th.—Keyhaven. Tried a large new kite on my improved plan, and it flew and answered admirably on shore, as well as in propelling a boat. Coast literally destitute.

28th.—A beautiful black frost. Up by candlelight, and ran down to Keyhaven. On my arrival old Read said there were plenty of wigeon, but they kept far at sea, and he had seen none in bounds, but nevertheless I ordered the grand set-out to be launched early to-morrow.

29th.—Up long before daylight, and got my fleet all in order by ten o'clock; and no sooner were we prepared for action, than round flew the cock to the southward, and away blew the frost. It is quite laughable that whenever I come to Keyhaven, I turn the weathercock the wrong way. We took a cruise up the Channel, but it was so rough that, had we gone far, we could not have got home in safety. Not a chance for a shot.

31*st.*—Old Read crawled on the mud all last night. Got two shots and came in with 6 wigeon. The day being calm I went off early, and cruised till the afternoon, but never set eyes on a single fowl, as the wigeon had gone off to sea, where no punt could safely follow them.

1848

January 1*st.*—Out all day, and never saw a single wild fowl.

3*rd.*—Off at daylight and persevered till the middle of the day, but the only wild fowl I saw was 1 brent goose, which I brought home.

4*th.*—Breakfasted and off again at daylight; but never saw a wild fowl all day.

5*th.*—Heavy wet gale nearly all day, and yet there was not a single wild fowl blown from sea into harbour—an event worthy of record.

22*nd.*—The moment I got out of the fly, on my return to Keyhaven to-day from London, I proceeded to get the gun and all the gear into the punt, so that I may not have either to do work on the Sabbath day or have a candlelight job on Monday morning. The reports on my arrival were flaming ones as to quantity of birds, though few wigeon and not one goose had been killed.

24*th.*—Up and breakfasted by candlelight, and cruised all the way up to Pilewell in a sharp frost and fine easterly wind. Saw but one flock of geese (about 60), which were half a mile in on the broad oozes off Pilewell. The wind increased to a gale, and we had a job to get back. The birds were, as usual, outside the beach and far at sea, so that their abundance afforded us no advantage. Though I had no chance for sport, I was well repaid for my long day. I had been too ill to eat with an appetite for some weeks, and when I came home I devoured my dinner like a greedy pointer.

26th.—A furious easterly gale all day, and a cutting black frost. At half-past two we went afloat for a few fowls that were to be seen, and, after escaping such a heavy sea as I had seldom before weathered, we came in with but 1 wigeon and 1 mallard.

27th.—Most bitter easterly gale, with intense frost. Went off twice, and saw a decent company of mixed fowl (chiefly geese), but dare not face the breakers to shoot.

28th.—The hardest day's frost I ever knew. The harbour a desert of ice, and the snow falling the whole day. We put the 'Petrel' into the run of the sluice hatches after breakfast; and before two o'clock she was penned in with an inch thick of ice, so that we had to batter away before we could drag her ashore. Small birds starved to death, and chased by the boys to catch them. Water jugs frozen in bedrooms; and, in short, so over 'tight' (as gunners call it) that all sport was stopped for want of being able to get afloat; and we were absolute prisoners for the whole day.

29th.—The intense frost relaxed so much this morning that the ice became soft enough to cut through it; and we battered through the frozen region with our punts; and after sheer slavery from seven in the morning till half-past one in the afternoon, we glided into salt water off Hurst, where (the whole time that we were at hard labour) the 'snobs' of Yarmouth and the coastguard poppers of Hurst were blowing off their trumpery shoulder pieces, in sail boats and wretched punts, at a whole army of birds; and out of about 40 rounds, never got so much as a single dunlin. When we arrived the whole coast was clear; but at last a few geese came down and dropped in. We sculled off to them and bagged 9 brent geese. In the afternoon there came on such a sudden thaw (with a shift of wind to the south) that with the help of our sails we cut through the soft ice, and lodged our punts safely at Keyhaven. In my thirty years' campaign I never had a more severe day than this.

31*st.*—Wind flew back to north-east, with snow and sleet. Out early; came in at two with 10 brent geese, and ready to go off again, but a torrent of snow and a gale of wind prevented us.

February 1*st.*—Up soon after five, and afloat at daylight. A sharp white frost, and about nine there came on a light sailing breeze. The consequence was that every jackass was afloat, and we might as well have been in London as in our punts. Came in about three, never having pulled a trigger.

2*nd.*—Off at daybreak. In the afternoon the sailing snobs came on in nine boats, and drove away all the birds, of course killing none, and I had consequently a blank day.

4*th.*—A south-west gale, with thick drizzling rain all day. The very weather to keep off the 'snobs,' so brought in 9 brent geese. I had this day all but made the greatest shot in my life; about 300 geese pitched within eighty yards of Keyhaven leak, which I had safely cleared, and then lay under the mud, with the birds 'end on,' and, when within a minute of shooting, an ass, in a dandy's craft, popped at some rubbishy shore birds and sprung the company of geese.

5*th.*—A continuation of wind and thick foggy rain. Just what I wanted to choke off the snobs and dandies. Brought in 20 brent geese (6 the first shot, and 14 the second shot).

7*th.*—A thick fog, which brought out an army of shore poppers. Got 5 brent geese; and other people afloat got more from my shot than I did, as we could not see our 'cripples' and 'droppers,' and were obliged to take out a compass in each punt, to avoid getting lost.

8*th.*—A butterfly day, and every jackanapes out in a boat. Never had a chance, though out from morning till night; and should have come home empty, but for the recovery of 1 brent goose that I lost yesterday. This evening a large basket of pheasants came to me from H.R.H. Prince Albert.

9th.—A tremendous westerly gale. Kept, of course, to windward, and when the geese came from the eastward we dropped down wind on them, in an absolute sea that the tide made over the mud. My detonator missed fire, or I should have got 20 birds. I fired after them, flying, with the flint barrel, and got 5 brent geese.

10th.—Went off to an army of geese, but a sail boat sent them away miles to the eastward, and we came home for a time. About five the army of geese returned and pitched in a capital place; but a floating snob flew after them and drove them to sea.

11th.—A butterfly day again. Another mishap with the detonator, or I might have had 12 geese. Came home and again overhauled the tormenting lock, and found that the chief fault was want of power in the main spring. Overhauled my bag of extras and found an old spring that was put by as too stiff, but on trial it went very well and blew off six primers in succession; so we sallied forth again, though only just saved our blank with 1 goose; as a 'gent' had moored his yacht at Hurst, and sent his two myrmidons to drive the harbour all day with a huge machine called a 'punt,' and a stanchion gun like a barber's pole. Otherwise, in spite of the summer-like weather, we might have had some shots; as the geese were all day about our harbour by hundreds, and only required proper treatment to be heavily slaughtered.

12th.—The geese had been so persecuted all yesterday that we never saw but one lot of about 60 the whole day, and, after following them from morning till night, I caught them off near the breakers at nearly the dusk of the evening, and brought in 4 geese with one barrel, the detonator again having failed.

15th.—A heavy gale all last night, and a pouring wet day.

Off in rain to an army of geese, but my shot spoiled by two floating clowns.

16*th.*—No geese. All 'far at sea' in a white frost and dead calm. To-day I was obliged to get my great gun ashore and take out the breechings, in order to take them and the left-hand lock into Lymington, where I was the whole day with Clayton putting a new 'beak' to the cock that had worn too short, and had missed fire at the five best shots at geese I've had this season.

17*th.*—Up long before daylight, and got my breechings in again, with plenty of 'hands' to help lift the huge barrels into the vice, as yesterday the ropes slipped, and the weight had all but smashed my trigger finger and broke Read's neck. We escaped but by an inch. Got afloat again by twelve in high order, but neither birds nor tide to give us a chance this day.

18*th.*—Got 8 brent geese; the only shot I fired, as at last the detonator went as well as ever after this repairing of what was worn away by more than twenty years' hard work and rough usage.

19*th.*—3 brent geese; the longest shot I remember ever to have made. The birds were sitting, and such was the distance that I had to level about a yard over them, and consequently they were shot at sitting, but killed flying.

21*st.*—Up hours before daylight, and cruised all the way 'up along' to Pilewell. Not a bird on the coast.

23*rd.*—Yesterday being a wet day, with a gale of wind from morning till night, we could do nothing; but to-day we brought all our guns, gear, punts &c. ashore, and after a thorough good cleaning, with six men to help, I housed them all for the season. Though we have had but a tolerable season with the geese, and the worst on record with all other fowl, yet we have bagged more than all the other punters put together. The country is ruined by the enormous increase of tyro 'snobs' both afloat and ashore. Poole, Weymouth, Southampton, the same, as I hear from all quarters. Why won't Lord John take my advice, and have a *porte d'armes* tax like the French?

Game &c. killed in the season: 173 partridges, 8 quails, 1 landrail, 5 hares, 1 pheasant, 22 snipes: 210 head. Wild fowl: 5 ducks and mallards, 1 scaup drake, 3 teal, 12 wigeon, 76 brent geese: 97 head. Waders &c.: 1 spotted gallinule, 1 green sandpiper, 2 dun divers, 2 golden plovers, 2 olives, 5 curlews: 13 head. 210 game, 110 wild fowl &c. Grand total, 320 head.

March 30th.—London. I've nothing to note down during the past long, wet, and dreary month of March, except that just after I left Keyhaven there were some awfully high tides, and there had been no more shooting for Read or any one since the day I laid up my guns and gear. And, turning to more serious matters, all Europe has been, and still is, in a state of revolution.

April 3rd.—So intensely hot that we were obliged to put out all the fires, and yet I have not seen for the whole year so many wild fowl as were this day in the poulterers' shops and hawked about town. They were, no doubt, caught in the decoys on their way home to Norway &c.

5th.—Longparish. Tried experiments, in the course of which I proved that the coarse coast 'gunning' powder, even in a stout shoulder gun, shot more than one-fourth stronger than the No. 1 sporting powder, though the one cost a shilling and the other *2s. 6d.* a lb. I always thought and argued that this would be the result; and now I've taken the trouble to prove it. Just before dinner I fancied a trout; but it was a dead calm, and a cold north-east wind, with a bright sun; so I turned poacher, and got 3 fine trout with a stick and wire.

8th.—Returned to London. All in commotion with the expected grand 'shindy' on Monday. Artillery and troops moving in all directions, in order to be prepared for the monster meeting of the rabble of Chartists.

10*th*.—The Chartist meeting, instead of a bloody fight with the military, as many timid persons were fearful of, was all over before two o'clock, and, as far as could be learned, no casualties occurred, beyond a few skirmishes with police and crowd, so ample and wisely managed were the preparations of the authorities, both civil and military, the latter under the Duke of Wellington. A very thin Philharmonic this evening, owing to the fear of many ladies to venture out; but a good concert, and a most inspiring effect produced by the appropriate performance of 'God save the Queen' by full chorus and the best orchestra in the world.

11*th*.—London all quiet again.

29*th and* 30*th*.—Intense white frost, and ice thicker than a penny piece.

May 18*th*.—London. To-day I received a letter from Longparish informing me that 'Squire Smith's' diabolical foxes had just destroyed five broods of spring chickens with 3 hens, 2 valuable ducks with their two broods, having in the winter cleared off every one I had (about 35) except these 2, and though last, not least, my 2 favourite brent geese that I had brought quite tame from Keyhaven. A curse light on all clodpoll preservers of foxes.

27*th*.—The fullest birthday Drawing Room that I was ever at since the days of George IV., who made one 'monster meeting' do for a season.

June 14*th*.—Returned to London again, after having passed at Longparish the most miserable ten days I've encountered for a long time. Heavy rain almost all the time I was down; trout so sulky as to show but moderate sport, and so poor as to be only fit for frying or broiling. Nearly all my poultry destroyed by foxes; three meadows of mowed hay lying 'done for' by the rain, and everyone looking as black and as miserable as the weather.

July 3*rd*.—Down to Longparish on further business, and also to clear off my quarterly accounts to midsummer. To-day the 'dog days begin,' and curious ones they are—a deluge of wet weather, and as cold as in winter. Further annoyances here as usual. The cursed foxes, in spite of dogs with long chains posted at every accessible point of the farm-yard, have had a further slaughter of what poultry they had left, and also took nearly 2 dozen of my pond-fed, pinioned wild ducks. The trout so cruelly swept away from the hatch hole below, that not a decent fish remained in the part of the river that I keep in hand. These are the blessings of being proprietor of a 'beautiful place' in the country.

CHAPTER XLI

1848

September 2nd.—Drove over to Bullington. Put the horses up at the 'Cross,' and shot over my manor. Had capital sport, considering the corn and the extreme wildness of the birds. I got 22 partridges.

4th.—I started for my usual beat over Furgo Farm. Here I fagged for nearly four hours, and got but 5 shots. We then ascended Furgo Hill to the part that borders on Tidbury and Bullington; and here we found a fine lot of birds. But it was then past two o'clock, and I was so exhausted with heat, fagging, and fasting, that my nerves were quite gone for shooting; and I was obliged to leave my sport for a little rest and refreshment. I renewed my shooting about four and kept on till seven, and arrived home about eight (dogs and all completely 'done for'), and brought in 22 partridges, 3 hares, and 1 landrail.

Charles Heath flanked us all over the Bullington side, and had capital sport, as he got 23 partridges, making up our combined bag to 49 head, which, since our good old days are no more, was an immense lot for our larder.

5th.—A general day's rest for ourselves and dogs, though a very busy one for me with basket packing, letter writing, &c. I was so 'dead beat' that, had I fresh dogs and fresh ground, I could not have stood another day's shooting.

6th.—Shot on the borders of Furgo and Bullington, and came home with 18 partridges. The most satisfactory day I've yet had, as I made four double shots, and never fired a blank shot the whole day. As the birds were wild this was good shooting.

8th.—Poorly and weak as a chicken. Crawled out a few hours before dinner with my rod, as it was a dark blowing day, and got 3 brace of trout.

9th.—Having quacked myself to windward with a tonic, I never shot more brilliantly even when without grey hairs.

I went over to Bullington in a windy day and brought home 18 partridges, 1 landrail, and 1 hare, without missing a shot, although I had but one close easy shot the whole day.

Game killed by me the first week: 84 partridges, 7 hares, 2 landrails, 1 rabbit. Total, 94 head.

Nearly all killed at Bullington, as the game at Longparish is not worth speaking of.

16th.—Went out between eleven and twelve; so weak I could hardly sit on the pony; but my 'pluck' carried me on to Bullington, and I came in with 12 partridges.

18th.—Busy at accounts till one; got to Bullington about three, and it was near five o'clock before I picked up a bird, as the fields were occupied by shooters in every direction, with a dry north-east wind, in which the birds were all on the run. I shot well, and killed 7 partridges, having slaved hard to make up this number, because it completed the general list to 100 brace of partridges up to the present time.

19th.—An extraordinary coincidence with fish. The weed cutters brought in a carp about 3½ lb., a fish never heard of in our place. A jack was seen in our pond, and we netted him: he weighed full 6 lb.; and I wired a tench above 2 lb.

The very best partridge season we have had since the good olden time, thanks to my little manor at Bullington, as the shooting on my farms at Longparish is nearly 'done for,' and the breed of birds in general has been bad.

Game killed in September 1848: Specification of grand total—226 partridges, 16 hares, 4 rabbits, 2 landrails, 2 snipes. Total, 250.

October 2nd.—This being the first day of pheasant shooting, we kept up our annual 'blow-out' in the hall, with a muster of curs and myrmidons, for the almost forlorn hope of a stray pheasant on the estate, and made our usual early start to scour our woods, and every place in bounds. After some hard fagging for hours, with markers well planted, there at last sprung up an old cock pheasant. The old cock then made for our wood, which obliged us to beat it all over a second time, though to no purpose, till I luckily twigged the old rascal at perch, and of course blew him down, thus bringing to the larder 1 pheasant. A hen bird had been seen yesterday, but we could nowhere find her. We came home to lunch at half-past one, meaning to turn out again and beat the rest of the day for the hen; but there set in such a determined wet afternoon, with a gale of wind, that I dismissed my followers, and gave up all thoughts of being able to go out again. About five in the evening the rain abated, and I went off in hopes of catching the hen at feed, but without success. At one time I dreaded a blank, but got all right by bagging 3 rabbits.

N.B.—The pheasants are now so destroyed by foxes and rail 'navvies' that even Mr. Fellowes saw and got but 1, and Mr. Coles, I hear, 1, when formerly his first day was 7 or 8 brace or more among his party.

7th.—Made a couple of brilliant shots at 2 teal that dropped into our river this morning. I then went out for the day over Furgo and Bullington, and although the weather was so hot as to be quite oppressive, the birds were wilder than ever, insomuch that in spite of heading them they would not lie even in high turnips. All I could get was 3 partridges, all long random (cartridges) shots. I had, however, much diversion in another way by falling in with the Ethiopian Serenaders, whom I had before seen on the stage in London. They were at my public-house, 'Bullington Cross,' *en route* for Bath. They gave me a regular performance, which was a *chef-d'œuvre* of the kind, and then accompanied me a little way for the chance of seeing me shoot; but in this they were disappointed, as the birds would scarcely let us get into the same field with them; so they wished me good morning, and went back to the 'Cross' for refreshment, for which I had of course left a trifle with the landlord, who, it appears, had already been puffing me off to them as one of the 'lions' of the sporting world.

18*th.*—A wet north-east wind every day; and the weather became so intensely cold this afternoon that sleet and snow were falling, and everything seemed to predict a summons for wild fowl at Keyhaven.

23*rd.*—Ran down to Keyhaven, after an absence of fifteen weeks from this day, to settle all my little bills, poor rates, taxes &c. and to overhaul my craft and gear, though with no view of shooting, as even in the late north-easter but few fowl had been seen; and now we have a furious gale from the south-west, insomuch that I should have deferred my visit could I have foreseen the dreadful weather in which I was caught soon after I left my door at Longparish. It 'blew great guns,' and poured 'cats and dogs' till I entered Keyhaven Cottage, and kept on most outrageously the whole night. Old Read met me with a face as long as a double bass, and said he had been almost living on the mud night and day, and had as yet got but 6 birds.

25*th.*—Not a wild fowl could I hear of that has been shot, though some flocks had been seen off in the rough sea above Pilewell, and also in Sowley Pond.

26*th.*—The furious weather so far abated that I was enabled at last to inhale a sea breeze afloat; so I put the popgun boat in the water, and took a survey of the coast with a musket, in case of an odd bird *en passant.* To my surprise I got 1 wigeon out of 4, which were all I saw, and which I could not get together to kill more, though I waited patiently for hours under a pour of rain. I then went on shore and beat all the marshes, but never saw one snipe.

27th.—A gale of wind and driving rain again all day. About 100 wigeon were blown into harbour, but having no punt afloat I told old Read of them. I weathered it along shore to see him shoot; he, however, stopped but 3, 1 of which fell into other hands. I came home so wet that I had to change, and Read was like a 'drowned rat.' The weather is a downright misery; nothing but south-westers and rain.

28th.—Heavy gale, with drenching showers. 'Bolted' back to Longparish, having now done all I had to do, and it being impossible to get afloat or have any enjoyment of Keyhaven till there came some alteration of weather, and the deluge of fresh water had subsided. I don't know when I had a more unpleasant six days to weather. But it is well I went down, as my lock-up stores would have been much injured by the damp, which exceeded all that was remembered here before, except in the awful sea floods, which, if they do come, have always been in November.

31st.—Longparish. A report of a pheasant. Mustered 'all hands,' and beat everywhere all day, but never found him.

November 6th.—Just as I had breakfasted, old Jack the shepherd sent to say he had seen this rascally old cock pheasant I had tried for so often fly towards my wood. So I went quietly up to the covert, and after a long search up he got, and down I fetched him in brilliant style, and as dead as a hammer. Never was there a more satisfactory little day's sport.

7th.—Drove over to Laverstoke House (an old haunt of mine in bygone days, and where my son was born) to see my old friend, Sir Peregrine Maitland, who has taken this mansion for a year. He was born in Longparish House, which his father rented of my father while his command of the 1st Horse Guards obliged him to reside in and near London. Moreover Sir Peregrine was my brother sportsman when he resided with his sister, Mrs. Warren, in Longparish, at Middleton House, and was the very best shot I ever saw in all my life, and the person from whom I acquired a brilliant style of shooting, and of whom I am proud to call myself the pupil. This was about forty-five years ago, when he was captain in the Guards and I a lieutenant of Dragoons, so that we are now (both of us) a little the 'worse for wear' and the effects of Anno Domini.

11th.—Heard that a few more snipes were come. Went out and bagged 3 snipes and 5 jack snipes, all I shot at and all I saw. It was a dark, dull day, and therefore doubly difficult to kill everything in prime style.

14th.—Having received a good report of wigeon on the coast I ran down to Keyhaven.

23rd.—Keyhaven. Put off to a few stray geese that were scattered on the waves (the first seen this year), and knocked down 2.

28th.—During the whole of my sojourn at Keyhaven (where I've been just a fortnight from to-day) not a bird has been killed afloat by any gunner in the place; and, as far as I could learn, no birds have been killed all the way 'up along.'

December 24th.—Longparish. Sunday. Intense frost again, with a cutting east wind. Up very early in order to distribute my Christmas beef to the poor before church time. A satisfactory beginning for the new year of my birth.

25th.—Christmas Day. A total change of weather. The hard frost broke up with a south wind and rain. Read sent me a summons by to-day's post, but I withheld sending him orders till I heard further from him now that the wind was changed.

30th.—Though unwell with a cough and cold I sallied off in my water boots, and came in with 4 snipes and 6 jack snipes; a grand day, and I never shot better. I missed but one shot at the only other jack I found.

1849

January 1st.—So dark a day that we could hardly see without going to the windows. Very damp and cold, with a gentle breeze from the east. Capital weather for wild fowl if it should continue, and thereby lead, as is usual, to a black frost.

2nd.—Intense frost, with a cutting easterly gale. Went off to Keyhaven, where I arrived soon after four (high water), and just in time to launch the large 'Petrel' punt.

3rd.—Got the following punt and all in order, so as to get afloat about two; but it blew so hard that we got a wetting without being able to fire a shot, though there were clouds of wigeon on the breakers. I never felt such intense cold as with this very hard frost and bitter north-easter.

4th.—Read crawled on the mud all last night, and brought in 8 wigeon at five this morning—when he called me up to go out. But then there set in heavy rain.

N.B.—For the very many years that I have frequented Keyhaven it has scarcely ever been my lot to go down there without bringing wet weather. All the natives say, 'The frost is sure to turn to rain and drive away the birds when the Colonel arrives at his Cottage.'

6th.—Up by candlelight again, and out till three, when the tide would no longer serve; but never had a chance, as the geese were too much persecuted to venture near the shore, and the sea was too rough to come near them afloat, as the punt jumped like a rocking horse. Thus have I been out four cruises and never discharged a barrel. In the evening the weather cleared up, and promised to be fine and frosty again. In all my coasting career I never had such a hard and unprofitable four days' gunning.

8th.—Yesterday afternoon there set in a furious wet gale from the south-west (after a bitter white frost the previous night), and this day it poured and blew. I went afloat from nine till dark and got but two little shots; the first at a few geese near 300 yards, and bagged 2 brent geese, and the second at a few mixed shore birds that I cleared off. The stanchion 'gunners' were so numerous that the birds could find no clear place to pitch on, so went off to sea and would not come in again.

9th.—Up at five, and off at daybreak for a long cruise ten miles to the eastward. Here the coast was less infested with gunners, though equally disturbed by poppers in sail boats. The weather was fine, and consequently the birds were nearly all gone off to sea. We saw but one company of geese, and these birds were driven off by blank shots from the sailing boats. I blew off a barrel, and just before I got home had the luck to kill 8 brent geese out of a small and very wild company.

10th.—All in order and breakfasted by daybreak.[1] A furious westerly gale. The very weather for me, as it embargoed the amateurs. I, however, never saw so few birds in harbour as were driven in by this gale. My first chance was at 12 geese, 8 together and 4 detached. Pulled off one barrel at the 8, and 'floored' the whole lot. One was prigged by a pirate in a sailing boat, the other 7 brent geese I brought home. This enabled me (with birds in house) to send off 10 geese and 10 wigeon to Prince Albert. The only other chance I had was at a mixture of geese and wigeon, for which I waited two hours to let the tide 'pinch' in order to get them together, and when within a few minutes of shooting two rascally shore snobs popped off a blank and sprung the company.

11th.—A north-west hurricane all last night. Read crawled again all night on the mud and got 1 wigeon. Finished my breakfast an hour before daylight for the chance of the gale becoming less violent, and thereby enabling us to propel the punt to windward. The gale, however, increased to an absolute tornado, in which no craft could venture on the water, and the very houses and chimneys shook.

12th.—The gale abated after midnight, and Read went mud crawling about three this morning, and came in with 3 wigeon at seven, when I met him on the quay in a dead calm,

[1] When Read brought in 3 wigeon after a midnight mud crawl.

with moonlight and white frost. We then went afloat all day, and I never got but 1 wigeon out of a couple that I shot at in the rolling surf. Not a single company of birds to be seen in either harbour or channel, unless in weather where no craft could 'live.' All the birds frightened off to sea, which is now their constant quarter when it is possible to shoot inside.

13*th.*—Read got in the night by mud crawling again 6 wigeon, and at daylight there came on a stiff westerly gale. I went afloat at daylight and was off all day, and got but one poor long shot in a sea, and bagged 2 wigeon at 200 yards. Shooters innumerable, as is every day the case now. The coast is absolutely 'done for.'

15*th.*—A most unsatisfactory day. 'Done' out of one of the greatest shots that could possibly be made. After my being out the whole morning about 200 geese came in and pitched within a splendid shot of my own leaks, and it being half flood I got up to the head of a 'spreader,' all hid by the mud and there lay close to them, only waiting for the tide to raise the gun so that I could bear on them. About a quarter of an hour would have given me the chance of 50 or 60 geese at a shot, when no less than three other punts came scrambling in; and the result was that I could only get a long random shot after the birds had risen above the mud, and with which I shot 6, and (2 having got away and been bagged by a Yarmouth boatman) but bagged only 4 brent geese. In all my gunning career I never had a more bitter disappointment. I should perhaps have made the greatest shot that ever was heard of, as the birds were all clustered in one close column, through which my two great barrels must have mown them down like a swath of corn.

16*th.*—A dead calm. Read crawled all night, but got no shot. He knocked us up at five to go out in channel, but at seven there came on wind and rain. The geese came up about eleven. Went off in a heavy rain, but the shot of a 'snob' drove the birds away miles to the eastward. They returned again an hour before dusk. No water to get near enough. Tried one barrel, a very long shot, and luckily bagged what I knocked down, viz. 4 brent geese. Just in time, as two other swivel guns were advancing on them. Came in at dark in a miserably wet mess, as it poured and blew most cruelly.

18*th.*—Up by candlelight and afloat all the morning, but no fowl to be seen. Off again about two, when we saw a large flock of geese a long way to leeward. Had to go outside through a heavy sea to get round to them. Got up a creek, and lay under them for two hours. The gale kept other gunners in, so the coast was our own; but still we were destined to interruption; a cursed flock of large gulls attacked the geese and drove them away. On our arrival at the quay we saw nothing of our following boat with Payne, who had remained outside to intercept the cripples, if I had shot. It came on pitch dark with a frightful gale of wind, and no tidings of Payne for some hours. Both Read and I pronounced him to be swamped and drowned, and every preparation was ordered for a search with all hands, when practicable, which could be of no avail till daybreak. After having given him up for lost, in came Payne a little before eight at night, with his gun and all safe, and 1 brent goose in his hand that he had been rash enough to chase to the Fiddler's Race, where not another punt but mine, the 'Feather,' could have lived, and where no one but himself would have had the madness to venture.

31*st.*—Longparish. Availed myself of the first fine day to have one more trial at the game, and from all reports I almost feared a blank. I, however, had the luck to wind up with one of the most satisfactory days on record, considering the extreme wildness of the birds in a cold north-west wind. I did not start till past twelve, and came home at five with 5 partridges, which was all I saw, and, wonderful for the last day of January, 1 quail.

February 2nd.—Fog and drizzle all day. Country dark,

wet, and miserable. All equally flat on the coast just now, as Read writes that no birds whatever have been killed since I left Keyhaven.

10*th.*—Got 1 wild duck and 1 mallard from my decoy hut. No other chance, now, for the use of a gun. Wet, miserable weather, and the country destitute of all kinds of sport except hunting, which I've given up ever since I came to a sensible age.

20*th.*—Keyhaven. Up very early, when everyone remarked it was the first time for thirty years that the Colonel came down without causing rain (the weather had been splendid for ten days). Before the fly came to the door, however, to take me on my way to Longparish, there set in a determined wet day. On my arrival, among other letters there was a returned one from the General Post Office for Sam Singer, to whom I had written, but who has 'shot the moon,' without leaving an address, and who, it appears, had bolted to Holland as dry nurse in gunning to some dandy gents, in consequence of not being able to 'get a crust' on our annihilated coast.

22*nd.*—Game &c. killed in the season myself: 191 partridges, 14 hares, 3 landrails, 2 pheasants (all I saw the whole season), 1 quail, 11 rabbits, 32 snipes. Total, 254 head.

Wild fowl: 5 ducks and mallards, 1 tufted duck, 3 teal, 26 wigeon, 27 brent geese. Total, 62.

254 game, 62 wild fowl, 15 waders. Grand total, 331 head.

A good game season, but one of the worst wild-fowl seasons on record.

Charles Heath: 99 partridges, 2 pheasants, 3 snipes, 2 wild ducks, 20 hares, 12 rabbits. Total, 138.

Siney (with hare licence): 5 hares, 6 rabbits, 10 ducks, 3 teal, 1 wigeon, 3 wood pigeons, 6 snipes (caught in gins). Total, 34.

P. H. 331, Heath 138, Siney 34. In all, 503 head.

28*th.*—London. Sported my Peninsular medal this day at the Queen's Levee.

March 22nd.—Went with Mr. A. Lancaster down to the Redhouse at Battersea to try the effect of my new 'dodge,' and it surpassed all that we could expect; it beat every gun on the ground, and made both the Lancasters stare at the result. My plan was simply to throw away the solid breech for our grandfathers' old plug, and ignite strong cannon powder by a projecting platinum touch hole. The result was never failing fire, extra strength, closer shooting, no recoil, and a defiance to wet weather and bad usage. My plan is for single guns, as in double ones it would bring the locks as far apart as in olden times, and, moreover, it is here not so much wanted, because in double guns we can get a central fire without impeding the sight of the barrels.

April 11th.—Longparish. I devoted this day to experiments with my improved ignition of guns, and the result was magnificent, as the old patent breeching and fine powder were almost doubled by my saucer plug and 'sea gun' (largest cannon) powder. I wound up with a sally up the river and brought in 1 snipe and 1 magpie.

17th.—A heavy fall of snow.

18th.—A hard frost.

19th.—The severest wintry day, and one of the heaviest falls of snow that I have ever seen. Rooks and other birds taken alive, in a state of exhaustion, from being unable to get food or to fly. My prediction at Christmas came to pass. I said that for our spring in winter we should have winter in spring, though I never could have thought quite so late as this.

May 4th.—So intensely hot that we got rid of fires, and sent for ice to cool our beverage.

6th.—Sunday. A bitter cold north-easter, and fires renewed.

7th.—Ditto. I never remember such a change as this even in our changeable climate.

June 13th.—London. Went to the Horse Guards, and got old Monk (my servant in the Peninsula and ever since) his medal with six bars on it, viz. Orthes, Nivelle, Pyrenees, Vittoria, Albuera, Talavera. A glorious trophy for him to wear, when I've treated him to an appropriate uniform.

July 12*th.*—Keyhaven. Having lots of little commissions in Lymington, I sailed in there after breakfast. Old Read got under way to return with me here, but when off 'Jack-in-the-basket' he ran foul of a pile and staved the boat, with a hole large enough for three cats to run through abreast. She was a third full in no time, and we were all but sinking, when I made him shove in two pairs of huge water stockings that I had bought, as well as a spare sail, and we kept baling and sailing with splendid wind and weather, till we, thank God, landed at Keyhaven in safety. At one time I was fully prepared for the loss of the things I was bringing home, and a swim for my life.

August 4*th.*—London. This day, the forty-fifth anniversary of my being gazetted Captain in the 14th Dragoons, I had an interview at the Ordnance Office with Sir Thomas Hastings and Colonel Anson, by desire of Lord Anglesea, relative to my new ignition gun for the army, which I had left with Wilkinson to rectify the rough work of young Lancaster, and it was agreed that I should have a meeting and a trial of my gun with the new Ordnance musket in the ensuing autumn.

28*th.*—Keyhaven. Rain as a matter of course, which I never fail to bring, and there set in a wet evening.

N.B.—All the farmers had prayed that 'the Colonel may not come down till harvest was over.'

CHAPTER XLII

1849

September 1st.—A good breed of birds; but a hot, dry, easterly wind, that made them wilder than I ever saw them on the first day. About half-past two there set in a squall, with two hours' heavy rain, after which the ground continued so wet that birds would not lie at all. Considering all, however, I had excellent sport. I bagged 18 partridges and fired not a single blank shot.

3rd.—Had a long hard day and killed 24 partridges, in doing which my only two blank shots were fired when coming home dead tired towards the close of the evening.

Game killed the first week (though I never shot better or fagged harder than the few days I was out, my bag was far short of that of last season, owing to the want of lay for the birds, and the dry easterly winds that destroyed all scent):

71 partridges, 3 hares. Total, 74 head.

12th.—A pouring wet day. Mr. Longman drove up to the door from Farnborough for a few hours' angling, and, though a beginner in the art, caught the finest lot of fish that I have seen this year. He landed 9 brace, some of them near 2 lb., and caught all his trout with a fly[1] under heavy rain.

13th.—Went out at one o'clock, though so weak I could hardly fag, and in all my life I never saw the birds so wild. In spite of every dodge, I had been out four hours without getting a shot; and about five was coming home resigned to my maiden blank day when up sprung a wild covey, that flew towards me, and I made a most brilliant double shot; and

[1] The 'brown alder' fly.

afterwards cut down a bird that flew up in the road. So after all I did get 3 partridges.

14th.—Mr. Thompson, a good fly fisher, was here all the morning, and took but one trout, though a splendid fish of about 1½ lb. and well fed; while on the other hand, Mr. Longman, a beginner in the art, killed, the day before yesterday, 9 brace. Here is a proof of uncertainty as to the rising of fish, even in good weather.

20th.—A cold north-easterly gale all day. Such weather as would have called me to Keyhaven for early fowl, plover &c. had not the place been in a state of siege, by an army of red-hot green 'gents,' who scare away everything. No weather for partridges. I, however, went off all day; and by outflanking the birds I got 7 partridges and 2 snipes, without missing a shot.

24th.—A regular butterfly day, and I thought the birds would lie. But no; they were, if possible, wilder than ever, and would not let the dogs come near them even in turnips. Though I fagged all day and missed nothing, I came home with only 5 partridges.

This morning I had a letter from Keyhaven to say some wigeon and plover were come, but that the tyro 'gents' and 'snobs' were on so fierce that the place would no doubt be too hot to hold the birds for long. Otherwise I would have gladly left this treadmill partridge shooting and gone off to the healthy sea air, as I used to do.

26th.—Out all day; got two shots, and brought in 2 partridges. A north-east gale, and the birds up the moment you entered the field they were in. No recipe but charges of cavalry could make them lie even for a duck gun and cartridge; so, having no fleet horses to ride them down, I had no sport.

28th.—Attended church morning and evening, this being the day very properly appointed by our vicar to offer up our prayers for the cessation of the cholera, which has been raging almost everywhere, and our thanks for having as yet escaped this dreadful pestilence.

October 1st.—Kept up our old annual custom of a grand sally forth, and a 'blow-out' of cadgers in the hall; and had the great good luck to bring home the only 3 pheasants I saw. A very satisfactory day.

9th.—Up to London to take up my new model for punt gun; to see to the putting in hand my new ignition musket, which I've promised to show at the Ordnance early next month; and to do an innumerable lot of commissions.

10th.—Hard on again from daylight till midnight. My new model struck dumb the leading men. Wilkinson had just finished a stanchion gun with a boatload of iron, Lancaster ditto with a boatload of wood, while mine had nothing of weight except the large barrel.

11th.—The post brought a summons for Keyhaven, and a troublesome letter from the garrison chaplain, objecting to repairs or improvements in my record under ancestor's (Governor Hawker's) monument. Parsons always give ten times more trouble than any other set of men.

12th.—A splendid easterly wind, and all in a bustle to get free for the coast.

13th.—Started for Keyhaven, and before I got halfway there the beautiful easterly wind turned into a torrent of rain and southerly gale, that kept on all the evening and all night. Thus I emphatically kept up my charter this time of always bringing rain when I went to the coast. What birds had been here were all driven away, and but a very few couples had been killed by all the gunners put together.

15th.—The wet weather having left us, and the wind all yesterday and all last night having blown a gale from the north-east again, I this morning put afloat my small stanchion and light punt, in hopes that a few fowl may arrive on the coast; and, though suffering terribly, I sallied forth and cruised as far as a heavy sea would allow me to go, but, to my astonishment in such magnificent weather, not a single bird did I see. It is an absolute miracle that such a long series of easterly winds should have done nothing for gunners. Not above a dozen birds have this season been killed by all of them put together, and the popgun sportsmen complain that they never knew such a scarcity of snipes. The only way that I can account for this is that the incessant persecution of the few call birds that at first arrive and would call others down has banished all the birds from this place.

16th.—Old Read out all day, and never saw a fowl, though the weather was magnificent for gunning.

17th.—A total change of weather. Rain all night, and a strong south-wester all to-day. Wrapped up warm, and 'weathered it,' but not a bird could I see.

18th.—Out, and never got a chance even for the popgun. In the afternoon down came Sam Singer in his pretty little vessel, and we had such a 'yarn' for our mutual advantage as one seldom hears.

19th.—A fine warm south wind, and butterfly weather. Sam Singer sailed up for Leap and Cowes this morning, and I ill and a prisoner.

20th.—Better, and out to-day, and not a bird. At night Sam Singer returned from a fifty miles' cruise, and had got but 1 wigeon.

21st.—Mr. Wilkinson arrived from London at four o'clock P.M. for a general inspection of my arsenal and trials afloat to-morrow.

22nd.—Up very early, and went through everything, and showed Mr. Wilkinson the system of punt gunning, in order that he may learn all necessary for stanchion guns, as he is now the leading gunmaker of London. He returned to town not a little delighted with the lesson he had learned and the novelties I had shown him.

25th.—At Longparish, having returned yesterday from Keyhaven, from whence what few fowl had arrived were all driven away by the legions of tyro shooters both afloat and ashore.

27th.—An old cock pheasant came and dropped within ten yards of my window while I was writing. I threw down my pen and flew to my gun, but before I could get down stairs he ran away, and then flew off out of gunshot. I turned out 'all hands,' and though I beat the whole morning I never could make him out.

November 9th.—London. Much bother about my new Government musket, which Wilkinson undertook to get finished for me. But his myrmidons were so spread over the town that half the work was wrong, and must be done over again. These outskirt savages had spoiled all Greenfield's beautiful work, which will have to be altered over again at my expense. How can things be done right if a gun has to go east, west, north, and south, and the master is too busy with dandies to follow up his pack of artisans?

10th.—Having packed up all my models &c. I this day started for Birmingham. We left the terminus (the most splendid one in Europe) in Euston Square at ten, and arrived in Birmingham a quarter before two. The railway by far the most perfect of any I ever saw. To an item everything was perfection and first-rate. Great Western not to be named with it. Took up my quarters at the 'Stork' hotel, reputed to be the most comfortable one, and then sallied out in order to make the most of my time. After seeing my old friend Westley Richards for a short time, I proceeded to Clive's barrel-forging factory, a place more like the incantation scene in 'Der Freischütz' than anything else I can compare it to; and here I was happy to learn from Mr. Shardlow he would be all ready to forge for me early next week. I then went on gun business to Greener, the harpoon gunmaker. Dined at half-past six, and then 'cut off' for the evening to the new public 'Exposition of Manufactures,' a most interesting lounge, and brilliantly lit up as an evening promenade at *6d.*

admission. Went to bed as tired as a dog about eleven o'clock.

11*th.*—Sunday. Went with Mr. Westley Richards to his pew in St. Philip's Church. Service well performed, and a clever sermon from the Honourable Mr. Yorke. The evening service I reserved till half-past six, in order to see St. Martin's Church, and hear the celebrated Mr. Miller, the rector. He has great feeling, with most energetic eloquence, good logic, fine metaphor, and a most Christian-like manner. I am inclined to put him as No. 1 of all the preachers I have yet heard.

12*th.*—Went to Clive's barrel factory with my models of patent ignition for my new stanchion gun, preparative to the forging &c. Called on Mr. Parker, who makes the crested handles for my primers, and was interestingly amused by his showing me all the departments of his button and army accoutrement manufactory. I could see but little of Westley Richards, as he was the principal of the 'Exposition,' which Prince Albert came down to see this day. I explored many places, and was much pleased with the civility and industry of the people of Birmingham.

13*th.*—Nearly all day in Clive's factory, superintending the forging of my newly invented single stanchion gun. The noise and heat was terrific. The power of the beating hammer 3½ tons, and it was a service of danger to avoid being burned or knocked down. A majestic old fellow named Talbot was the 'Lamiel' of this infernal region, in which men and boys were running about just like so many devils. Mr. Shardlow, the foreman, as well as Mr. Clive, kindly attended and explained everything, and Mr. Wilkinson arrived from town soon after we had begun work. I then dressed, and took a fly to go out to Mr. Westley Richards's country house, where he gave us a most excellent dinner.

14*th.*—On from breakfast till near two trying my new ignition gun at Mr. Westley Richards's splendid factory.

The performance of the gun satisfied him that I had not exaggerated about its effect. I then went all over his factory, which surpasses all the gun establishments I ever saw or heard of. He has his whole army of workmen, as it were, in a barrack, with spacious ground to try his guns from the very windows of the workmen. To have seen as many departments of gunmaking in London, I must have gone over twenty miles of ground. After lunch I went all over the electro-plate manufactory, in the company of Sir Robert and Lady Peel and daughter, who had run over with four horses from Drayton (fifteen miles) to see this splendid establishment, also the 'Exposition of Manufactures' that had brought Prince Albert here on Monday. I then inspected the grand papier-mâché manufactory, which was even better worth seeing.

15*th*.—This being the day for a general thanksgiving, I went again to St. Philip's Church, in Mr. Richards's pew, and returned with him to his villa, where we lunched. In the evening I went once more to hear Mr. Miller, who preached with great energy on our delivery from cholera, but as he this evening held forth extempore and preached for nearly two hours, I was not so much delighted with him as on Sunday last.

16*th*.—Up early, and off to Wolverhampton to see Mr. Brazier, the great lockmaker of Britain, about the lock for my new stanchion. I had a terrible job to find the right man, as the name of 'Brazier' here was like 'Smith,' too universal to be distinguished. After an hour's tramp in mud and filthy streets, I got on the right scent, and found him at his little country seat, called 'The Ashes,' and ascertained that 'Joseph Brazier, Esq.' was the precise direction to catch him. I had to carry my models on my back to show the whole concern, and lucky it was that I did, as Wilkinson had directed him all wrong about the lock, which luckily he had not yet begun. I left the models by his particular request, and after a most hospitable blow-out of Staffordshire pork-pie, and such a glass of strong beer as I had not tasted for years, I shuffled off to a fine old church, built in the time of Ethelred, where I tried the organ, and inspected a superb ancient stone pulpit, and various other antiquities. I got back by four, and then drove to Clive's factory; and lucky was it that I went there, as my direction and correction were necessary. But I don't find fault, because it's expecting impossibilities to ask my gunmaker, or rather gun merchant, to understand a stanchion gun.

19*th.*—On again, as busy as a bee. Saw to rough boring of barrel. Went all over the Government factory, where Evans (an old friend of mine, formerly at Joe Manton's, and who had worked at my 'Champion double swivel gun' in 1824) showed me the whole process of musket making, of which he is the lord lieutenant at Birmingham. Had a long chatter with Westley Richards and his men, who were delighted with my plan, which the editor of the 'Birmingham Gazette' kindly noticed in a long article. In the evening I went to the weekly choral concert in the magnificent town hall, and not a little was I surprised at the performance. Some of the choruses went far better than on our stage in London (except when we had the Germans there), and the organ was splendid. A Miss Stephens (pupil of Sterndale Bennett) played extremely well Moscheles' lovely fantasia on 'Au Clair de la Lune;' and all this for sixpence in the spacious gallery, and only threepence *parterre.*

20*th.*—On again at Clive's, proceeding with the new gun. Saw Evans at the Government ordnance factory, and had a minute inspection and dissection of a nondescript piece of intricacy, called the Prussian musket, fifty of which are ordered by the wiseacres at headquarters. Called on Richards to show him a letter from Clayton of Lymington, proving the superiority of my new ignition.

21*st.*—On at Clive's, boring the first cylinder of the barrel, and at Evans's ordnance office, to show him my new musket-sized gun. Then off to see the manufacturing of cut glass at Osler's, and from there to the rolling mills of Mr. Muntz, M.P., whose brother kindly showed me all the process for making copper for the navy (which has in it an amalgamation of zinc), and the old 110 horse-power engine of the great Watt. Came home so tired I could hardly stand.

23rd.—This being the day for grinding the barrel of my new stanchion gun, I was off duty with the men, so resigned myself for a morning's pleasure. Got in the four-horse 'bus at ten and went to Dudley (ten and a half miles) and saw Dudley Castle, one of the finest ruins in England. There were two novelties on the road, near West Bromwich: the one, two bridges that we went under, one a viaduct for a railway, and the other an aqueduct for the canal, and close together; the other was the gasometer that supplies the enormous town of Birmingham with gas at about seven miles' distance (a cheaper plan than drawing the coals from the pits at this place to Birmingham). I had a regular wet day for my trip, as an incessant rain set in just before we entered Worcestershire, where I had never been before. Except Herefordshire I've now been in every county in England.

24th.—Down to Clive's the first thing. Grinding not enough, so left the men to grind away to-day. Being then adrift I overhauled the fine Catholic cathedral and the magnificent market place, 123 yards under cover and splendidly built.

27th.—Busy directing Mr. Aston's men at the lock and screws of the big gun. Then at Clive's, afterwards with Mr. Shardlow at the proof house, where I saw the barrel proved. The proof, however, is but little more than a double charge. Mr. Marsh, the principal there, kindly showed me all over the establishment.

28th.—Stood over Aston's man to direct him. Then at Clive's and on to Greener's, after seeing Evans about my stock &c. He sent me to Messrs. Hollis and Sheath, the large wholesale gun manufacturers in St. Mary's Square, to see a large gun they were doing with my new plan of ignition. They were working from a Burnett gun copied from my 'old Moll;' and when Mr. Sheath found out who I was, the scene was rather amusing. He came away with me to see my models, which, he said, should be his standard for all future guns, if not expressly ordered to the contrary. Mr. Sheath, it appears, makes these stanchion guns up for the leading gunmakers in London to put their names on, and almost all their work in the large way is packed off by rail to him; and he has a sad difficulty to interpret some of their foolish directions. Aston makes locks for him, and the cost of a common cheap lock is 11*d.*; 4*d.* the iron, 6*d.* the work, and a penny profit for Mr. Aston.

29*th.*—A letter from Read to say birds were at Keyhaven, and that he was ill from a fall. On from morning till dinner with all my divers workmen, and we had a grand council together, at which I explained all my plans so far that my imprisonment in Birmingham was no longer necessary, and that all could now go on without my daily attendance over the workmen. In the evening, though all in a fuss for leaving, I could not resist attending the clever lecture by Lieutenant Gale, R.N., and his plans for an exploring expedition in search of Sir J. Franklin.

30*th.*—Having been up till past twelve last evening, owing to Lieutenant Gale's lecture, I had to turn out at six this morning on gun business, and finally arrived in London to-day.

N.B.—I must not take leave of Birmingham without doing the justice to this town to say that I never met with a more civil and obliging set of people than the inhabitants of this place, which is a town of unrivalled industry and mechanical genius.

December 1*st.*—London. Up very early, and on with Greenfield, Wilkinson &c. about my new military musket, which was, of course, done wrong in my absence. Run off my legs in order to get away after an early dinner, to take down my little tablet, and see it placed myself in the garrison chapel at Portsmouth, and to interview Sam Singer. I much wanted to see his new punt that he brags about so much.

2nd.—Sunday. Portsmouth. Went to church at garrison chapel, and arranged all for tablet in morning. The Governor, Lord F. Fitzclarence, had moved five miles off (while his house was doing up), so I had to hire a sailor to take a note for him, in a deluge of rain and gale of wind, and after all his lordship had bolted to London.

3rd.—Up by candlelight, and got the tablet well fixed before the parson was about, and then returned to London.

5th.—London. Heard from Keyhaven that a few geese and a fair show of wigeon were come, and that old Read had recovered from his fall that had laid him up.

11th.—I had a holiday at last, and so went to see the lamented Queen Dowager's coffin, and other things that I had no time for before.

13th.—To-day was the poor Queen Dowager's funeral, when there was observed in town all that respect which her exemplary conduct was entitled to, and at three o'clock there were, as usual on such occasions, the royal salutes of the Park and Tower guns.

14th.—Busy from nine till eleven at night, and among other jobs about a gun that had burst in the hands of Sir Claude Scott, Bart., the great banker, on the demerits of which I gave him a certificate, he having applied to me, though an utter stranger, as the first authority on the subject of arms.

18th.—A wet day. Down to the proof house in Whitechapel, with Sir Claude Scott and 'Uncle' Bishop, to go before the committee (where we met Purdey, Old Nock, and other eminent gunmakers), to present the shattered remains of Sir Claude's gun, with the view of taking steps to a more stringent Act of Parliament, as a check upon ironmongers selling guns, as well as the danger of introducing light steel barrels. A gun in Birmingham can be finished up for 6*s.* 6*d.*, and a 'tidy' gun, as they call it, for 9*s.* 6*d.*, and thus, by making the lock to feel pleasant and high ornament, it may be passed off to a green young lord as a 20-guinea gun.

20*th.*—On ding-dong blowing the rascally steel barrels in the 'Times' and other papers.

24*th.*—Longparish. Up by candlelight and run off my legs to cut through business between the Sunday and Christmas Day. In the midst of jobs, accounts &c. I had to run down to the river for a foreign tufted duck, at which I made a most lucky long shot. I tipped his pinion precisely in the right place for cutting, and turned him a-going on the pond with 9 pinioned ones that I had bought. I then attended my distribution of beef to the poor; partook of my usual birth-day turkey, and got to bed, dead tired, about twelve o'clock.

25*th.*—Christmas Day. A torrent of letters, both private and in the papers, about my late war against the dangerous new-fashioned light steel gun barrels.

26*th.*—Got 1 duck and 1 mallard from the decoy hut, the only 2 birds on the river. Finished alterations in my 'Invisible' approach, and tried the 'Hornet' little stanchion in it, and it went beautifully. Erected a little tablet in the new-made island, and in short was all day 'as busy as a bee.'

27*th.*—Made up my mind for a holiday at last. But no. The post brought me in a batch of letters and papers that pinned me for nine hours to my writing desk.

28*th.*—There set in last night the most sudden intensity of bitter cold weather I ever experienced, with a heavy gale of snow from the north-west. This morning there set in a northerly gale of wind enough to perish one, and it froze hard all day. I got out with my gun, and was so cold even while fagging that I could hardly hold it. The country seemed destitute of every living creature. I worked all over the rivers, moors, and our wood, and had the great luck to bring home 1 jack snipe, or else should have had a blank day.

29th.—Got 1 wild duck that pitched in front of the house, where I had to crawl to her a long way in the snow. A bitter cold day, and everything freezing even in the house.

1850

January 1st.—Intense frost. Prepared for going down to Keyhaven. About four this afternoon I was sent for by my tenant, Mr. Goodall, who, poor man, was ill in bed, as he wished to shake hands with me before I went to the coast; and to my horror in a few hours afterwards, a message came to say he was dead.

2nd.—Went down to Keyhaven. On my arrival found that such an awful flood had taken place last week that Read has put all my guns &c. upstairs in my cottage, and this with a northerly wind which always keeps back the tide.

3rd.—We had all last night the most cruel white frost that ever bit a man's limbs. Up by candlelight, and got our fleet afloat before luncheon. Went off at half-past two, but never had a chance for a shot, and we had not been afloat half an hour before the wind flew to the south-west, and gave us a drizzling rain all the time we were out, so my charter of always turning the cock, and bringing rain when I set my foot in Keyhaven, was this new year most brilliantly kept up.

4th.—Up by candlelight, and hard on with Clayton, about his new stanchion on my plan for the Marquis of Hastings.

5th.—Up early and out all day, but saw nothing except 5 geese travelling in the air to the eastward, so I went up the creek and was in Lymington for some hours with Lord Hastings about his new stanchion on my plan, and again with Dagwell about the punt I prescribed for Mr. Wilkinson's gentleman gunner.

7th.—Up at six, and afloat at daylight, in the most intensely cold white frost I ever was bit by. Harbour frozen up in one night. Lots of boats off, but not a shot fired. Refused a fine shot of plover because a large company of wigeon was near, which two monkeys of boys put up with their sail boat, and in short I never pulled a trigger the whole day.

8th.—Up, breakfasted, and off by break of day. Harbour a sheet of ice, though a beastly white frost. Saw a company of about 1,500 wigeon, but so restless, owing to a fog, that they would not stay a minute in one place. Shifted my shot, and went at them, prepared for a huge distance. Blew off a barrel at near 300 yards, and got 4 wigeon.

9th.—Afloat at daylight, and saw nothing all day, though a good easterly wind.

10th.—Off early again, but not a fowl to be seen. Came back about ten o'clock.

About an hour after, who should land but my old and able satellite, Buckle, whom I had recommended for a gunning tutor to Sir John Carnac. But the Marquis, all hot of course, was gone off to try for birds, so I could not show the new gun to Buckle.

11th.—The beastly white frost burst itself into rain, of course, in the night, and this morning the harbour was released from the white ice and open again. Off early, as usual, but saw not so much as an ox-bird. In to lunch and off again, when the cock flew back to the east, and drove us home, by four o'clock, with a cold gale of wind and heavy snow. The coast appears to be destitute, and no wonder. There are ten stanchion guns within about ten miles of shore, besides amateurs and snobs innumerable. The fowl appear to be absolutely banished from Keyhaven coast.

12th.—Heavy snow and easterly gale. Very unwell, so sent out Read, who saw only a few geese out of shot. Went into Lymington in a shut-up fly to see Clayton about my new ignition guns that he is getting up for divers customers. Called on the Marchioness of Hastings, to make my excuse for not venturing out to-night for a concert to which she had kindly invited me, and just came in for a part of the rehearsal, which was a credit to amateurs.

14*th.*—Having been all yesterday a prisoner with illness, I got up this morning, feeling better, two hours before daylight, but to no purpose, as the tremendous easterly freezing gale embargoed every punt and boat. The sea was terrific, and I viewed with my glass acres of birds near the foaming surf on the Channel's edge. Snobs in every direction round shore, but not a fowl shot by anyone, as everything inland was a sheet of ice.

15*th.*—Tremendous easterly gale with biting frost all night, so despaired of getting afloat to-day. But about noon the wind abated, and we then 'shipped' our big gun and gear; but before we could get under way the tyros in every direction had scared away the army of fowl. We had one chance at a bank of birds, when a 'lubber' ran down on us and sprung them. So instead of a boatload of fowl, we came home without a pull of trigger.

16*th.*—Intense frost, but scarcely any wind. What was the consequence? The whole army of birds retired for safety to their old haunt at sea, and I never pulled a trigger all day except at a few geese flying past about two gunshots off. I by chance hit down 1 brent goose, and another fell off on tide.

17*th.*—Off early again, but not a chance, as a moderate and pleasant day brought out a boatload of snobs to every quarter of a mile of channel. A pretty pass our once splendid sport is come to. Not a bird got by anyone, of course.

18*th.*—Off as usual; channel so bombarded with boats full of bullet poppers, that I retreated about twelve and came home again. A white frost last night, which, of course, altered the weather, and soon after one o'clock the cock shifted to a determined south-wester, with a pour of heavy rain that never ceased all day. This drove in the wigeon and geese from sea to within a quarter of a mile of the quay, and we would have 'weathered it' and gone into them, but a snob in every furze bush kept popping off blank shots, and drove the fowl for miles away from the harbour, and to a distance that we dare not attempt to go in a heavy gale and torrents of rain. Keyhaven is now quite 'done for.'

19th.—Busy clearing tons of thick ice from our little harbour. Off in the afternoon, when a few geese came down; but the shore snobs drove them out to sea.

20th.—Sunday. Weathercock round again to north-east, with a black frost and breeze all day. How lucky that I badgered my men into clearing off the ice yesterday!

21st.—South-easterly breeze with small rain all day. The first good company of geese that I have seen this year pitched on our mud before tide was up. Went off and lay under them (and not out of shot); but as a fellow was after them also, I dare not wait for tide to flow, so made Read blow off the popgun in order to spring them above the bearings of the gun. But they skimmed away low till too far for small shot, and my barrel, which had large shot, missed fire through the cock catching in the lock cover; and I was thus at the loss of perhaps a dozen birds, as the company was about 700 strong. Was there ever such a run of bad luck as I've had this season? The birds went off towards Lymington creek. We went after them in a rainy day, but came home blank as usual, without any further chance.

22nd.—The grand company of geese came down again at low water. Lay under them, and a fellow opposite blew a ball into them at the risk of our being shot, and away they went. Sir John Carnac and Buckle came down in the yacht and were off to-day, but the snobs would not allow any gunner a chance. I blew off a mould-shot cartridge in despair, and hit down 2 geese at near 400 yards. What assassination of our harbour! With fair play 100 geese might have died this day.

23rd.—Up by candlelight us usual. Off all day. Isle of

Wight bullet poppers in every direction: no chance for anyone to get a shot. Out again in the evening, and brought in 2 brent geese by a mould-shot cartridge at above 300 yards.

24th.—Off early. A fair show of geese, but three boats to every company. A hard day's work for a blank.

25th.—Off at daybreak in fog and drizzling rain. A few geese in, but so wild they were off the moment we were in sight. We came home to lunch, and had a providential escape. Old Read, in cleaning up, accidentally fired the percussion barrel of the great gun, which blew a hole through both sides of the 'Feather' (my beautiful following punt); and singular enough I heard the report of this shot just as I had finished reading a letter from Mr. Guildford Onslow on a similar accident that had wounded him on the Lake of Como, from whence he had gone to Milan for surgical assistance. The chief object of his letter, however, was to report to me the extraordinary performance of the Austrian muskets with copper primers at 1,000 yards.

26th.—Off till two, not a chance for a shot.

28th.—Extraordinary weather. Yesterday a biting white frost, and then a day for ladies and butterflies. At night a south-west gale and rain; and to-day such a ferocious tempest that no boat could row on end. An army of birds swept in from the wild ocean, but no one could do more than view them with a spy-glass. Attempted to go off, but it was impossible.

29th.—Foggy rain, dead calm, and remarkably high tide. Off early. Fell in with a fine company of geese, but the opposition scoundrels kept popping on purpose to prevent my shooting, consequently the birds were driven to sea, and I never got a chance to shoot.

30th.—A light easterly breeze. Got 1 brent goose, and devoted the remainder of the day to experiments, as it was of no use to be afloat with a few very wild birds only to be seen, and lots of slug-shooting stanchion-gun shooters to make them, if possible, wilder.

31*st.*—Read crawled last night in his mud punt and got 3 wigeon; but the mud was so mobbed with 'snobs,' as well as mud crawlers, that the birds were all dispersed like blackbirds and thrushes instead of being in good companies, as in former years. I persevered to-day again in a south-wester and constant thick rain; but the only company I saw (geese) would not stay a minute in a place, and at ground ebb we were washed off by a gale and torrents of rain. Here ends (January) the most execrable month's sport that I ever saw or heard of since the hour I was born.

February 1*st.*—Extraordinary weather; a dense fog with a gale of wind from the west. Out early and came home blank.

2*nd.*—A heavy west gale and blue fog, as yesterday. Off early for chance of flight as geese travelled by; but 'done' by winkle-boys infesting Shore Head. Out again at two, and tried the inaccessible geese with sail at the rate of ten miles an hour. By this change we got nearer to them than we had done before (about 230 yards), and I brought in 8 brent geese; and coming home I got a flying shot with which I picked up 5 curlews, besides one that dropped off on the breakers. The first bit of sport this trip, so let us hope our luck is on the mend.

4*th.*—Out early, and in about midday. Never saw a chance. Decided on 'knocking off,' and turned to 'all hands' to get furbished and laid up before dark. Started off the royal basket for their Majesties; cleared off a torrent of letters; and was run off my legs, though far from well, in order to get emancipated for a start to-morrow.

5*th.*—Up by candlelight in order to complete my furbish and the storing of divers 'traps,' &c., and left by the morning rail train. Got to Longparish in the afternoon; and never was I more delighted to get away from any place than from my favourite quarter, Keyhaven, now that it affords nothing but provocation in lieu of the finest of all sport in existence.

Game &c. killed in the season to February 10th, 1850:

Game—115 partridges, 8 hares, 4 rabbits, 1 landrail (all I saw), 3 pheasants, 15 snipes. Total, 146. Wild fowl—3 ducks and mallards, 1 tufted duck, 1 teal, 12 wigeon, 12 brent geese. In all, only 29. Waders—5 curlews, 1 godwit, 6 plover, 41 dunlins, 1 peewit. Makes 54 head. Grand total, 229 head only. One of the worst seasons ever known.[1]

11*th.*—A letter from Keyhaven. Not a fowl has been shot since I left, though the young red-hot marquis had been slaving every day, and as furious as a Scotch terrier among mice when the farmers are taking down a wheat rick.

March 11*th.*—Down to Birmingham.

15*th.*—All in a fair way to go on without me after four days' slaving with gunmakers, so prepared for my return home, and packed up my models that were no longer wanted. Had a little job with Mr. Osborne; and the reason it was not ready proved to be the burglarious entrance of a gang of ruffians in the night, and the pillage of 700*l.* worth of silver articles and other valuable goods.

18*th.*—London. Met Captain Lautour at Greenfield's, to whom I had recommended him for a new stanchion gun on my improved plan. He told me the Poole coast was quite 'done for;' though for this last week we've had an intense black frost, and London swarming with wild fowl from our north coast and Scotland.

30*th.*—Longparish. Paid the last wages to Charles Grayston, the very best servant I ever had, who left me with views of a literary situation; and my poor old dog 'Viper,' that always greeted me with his welcome, was no more, as some villain had shot him. Never did I arrive at Longparish under more sad circumstances.

April 6*th.*—Had a narrow escape from a serious accident.

[1] A general complaint that this was a miserable game season, and the worst snipe season on record, in spite of five weeks' hard winter. Moreover I was absent on my new inventions all the best time, both for sea and land, though the coast shooting was no loss, as Keyhaven is now annihilated.

Being engaged to be with Mr. Earle before twelve to-day, I put my favourite mare into my gig and drove off for Andover soon after eleven o'clock. As the mare was as quiet as a lamb I required no servant. When about two and a quarter miles from Andover, the poor mare was suddenly seized with megrims, or mad staggers, and in all my life I never saw any animal in such an awfully horrid state. She suddenly stopped and shook her head, and then lay down; she then sprung furiously up again, and violently ran back so as to throw herself and the gig into a quickset hedge on the top of a rising bank. With a still more violent struggle she precipitated herself down into the road, falling on her back and twisting the gig to what a sailor would call 'keel uppermost;' by further struggles she then got on her side and there lay, kicking and plunging in a desolate turnpike road, where, for near half an hour, I had not a soul to come near me. At last a waggon and cart came by, and the men belonging to them helped me to extricate the mare. She then ran about like a mad bull and fell down and got up again repeatedly; at last she made one finishing fall, and I made sure she was dying, when I proceeded to Andover with the man in the cart, and hastened off the veterinary surgeon to bleed her as a last resource. On completing my business I went back and found that the mare had been saved by bleeding, and was actually led off for Longparish.

13*th.*—Engaged every day on the business of re-letting my farms &c.; of course to a great disadvantage and loss in these deplorably bad times.

July 8*th.*—Dragged the river in order to clear off promises of fish to friends. We had but two draws; the second we took 104 fish, including some thrown back as not in season. The best haul for many years, though not more than a quarter of what we took twenty or thirty years ago. This evening came the intelligence of the death of the poor old Duke of Cambridge, and on which sad news I had the minute bell tolled.

August 5*th*.—London. At Woolwich before ten this morning. My new military musket never failed, and, in fact, all three (Lancaster's, the Prussian, and mine) went as well as could be, owing to the very fine weather. They are, however, to be left with 300 rounds each, at the Arsenal, to be further tested in all weather, and kept out at night. This is as it should be. Other new arms are coming, and it may therefore be many months before the committee can decide as to their recommendation.

15*th*.—Birmingham. On from morning till night, like a cat after a mouse, stirring up engravers, finishers, &c., or they would have put my new grand stanchion gun on one side for the work of other parties, who were all eager to complete guns for the 1st of September.

16*th*.—Very unwell, so hired a car for the day and rode about in state. As soon as I had got several parts of my new stanchion gun from the workmen, by means of standing at their elbows, lest they should put my work aside for other pressing jobs for the London makers, I drove into the country to see a splendid Catholic church (with images from Munich) at a village called Erdington, three miles from Birmingham; and then on to Sutton Park, four miles farther, which is a celebrated place for the picnics or gipsy parties of all the pleasure people in Birmingham.

17*th*.—As my workmen to-day had to do only the hardening and polishing of the stanchion gun, which did not require the help of my suggestions, I treated myself to a holiday in order to see the country 'lions,' lest I might not have to come again to Birmingham. At nine o'clock I started by a heavily loaded omnibus, and soon after eleven got to Warwick, twenty miles, where I went all over that most splendid of all baronial residences, Warwick Castle. To my taste it surpasses all the *châteaux* I ever saw in my life. Went on to Leamington Spa, where I saw all that was to be seen. After this I proceeded to Kenilworth Castle, six miles, where I spent an hour; and then was driven on a lovely road, surrounded by the finest oaks, to Coventry. Here I saw St. Michael's Church, the ancient figure of 'peeping Tom,' &c., and got to the rail station about six, soon after which the train brought me (eighteen miles) back to Birmingham, having seen in ten hours what some people would have spent ten days in doing.

20th.—Up at six and on to London, and off immediately to Greenfield about rectifying my new military musket, which had got broken at Woolwich, and consequently lost the remainder of its trial.

27th.—To Keyhaven, where I arrived at six; I felt much at not seeing my faithful servant, old Peter Fifield, to greet me as usual, he having lately died; and there set in a gale of wind and rain, as there always is on my arrival here. But this was all right, as I was thereby enabled to give my new musket a bitter night's lodging in the thick of it, on board a boat off in harbour, and after putting the weapon in a bucket of fresh water for a finish, she fired as well as possible after breakfast on the next morning. If this is not a waterproof musket, I know not what one is.

CHAPTER XLIII

1850

September 2nd.—Longparish. Had a severely hard first day. Found a very good breed of birds, and all as large and strong as the old ones ; and as the country was cleared of the corn, the birds were wilder than I ever saw them in September. Not even the scattered birds would lie to the dogs, though driven into fine turnips, and moreover I never found the scent so bad. By sheer slavery, however, I contrived to bring home 22 partridges and 4 hares.

It was near three hours before I got my first shot; an extraordinary day on the whole. We had an army of volunteers, with a carriage full of grub, to follow us, and a stiff supper for 'all hands' at night.

4th.—Another severe day, and birds even wilder than on Monday. Came home to an eight o'clock dinner, with 21 partridges.

7th.—My bag was 12 partridges and 2 hares. Scent worse than ever, but no reason to complain, as I killed all that it was possible to kill, and took the lead of other parties.

8th.—I never knew the birds so wild, or the scent so bad. Shooting absolute slavery. Had to walk all day on dry, burning ground, and take snap shots, as the birds would not lie to my pointers even when dispersed.

N.B.—I have, however, every reason to be satisfied, when I hear how very little most other parties have yet done.

16*th*.—Not having been out since last Tuesday, from being too unwell to walk, I prepared for a quiet ride out with dogs and gun this morning, but was seized with such pain that I had to lie down instead of starting out. But in the afternoon I was a little better, and the sal volatile and camphor julep that I finished myself off with gave me such a fillip that I killed all I fired at, and not a shot but what was far beyond slow time or easy distance.

28*th*.—In want of some game, so went out, though not till past twelve, as I had no strength for a day's fag. I despaired of being well enough to shoot, though as things turned out I could not have shot better. I brought in 9 partridges, 2 hares, and 2 jack snipes, and lost also 1 bird, that I shot in a slovenly manner, for want of nerve to give him the bull's-eye. With this exception I bagged all I fired at.

Game &c. killed in September 1850: 71 partridges, 15 hares, 5 snipes, 1 teal. Total, 92 head.

October 1*st*.—The most brilliant 1st of October that my annihilated little beat has afforded for many years. I sallied forth, according to annual custom, with my army of beaters, expecting only about 4 head of game, and came in with 4 pheasants, 4 hares, 3 partridges, and 1 turtle dove, without missing a shot.

I bagged every pheasant I found except 1 old cock that I never saw. This splendid little bit of shooting was as usual wound up with a heavy blow-out in the servants' hall, and universal satisfaction over our home-brewed ale.

7*th*.—Availed myself of a furious gale of wind to accept of a day's fishing at Gavel acre. But such a failure did it prove that I only just saved my blank with 1 trout. There was scarcely a fish in the river. So I left the place in disgust and came home, after which I took my rod up my own river, where I picked out 4 brace of the largest trout, besides lots thrown in, as out of season. I took also my gun, and brought home 6 snipes in little more than two hours, having thus made ample amends for the time lost all the early part of the day.

9th.—Called away from my writing desk after an old cock pheasant that was actually seen flying across the meadow for our wood. Summoned all my myrmidons to the chase of him, and in spite of cavalry and infantry the old devil escaped, though we never failed to head him in advance and surround him in every way. We found him first about a quarter past eleven, and saw him last about a quarter before six, and he outwitted me and all my unrivalled army from morning till nightfall.

15th.—A fine day, so went off early to search for the artful old cock pheasant again; and in the very last field, as we were coming home at night, up he flew eight gunshots off, and mounted over our wood, but though we beat till dark, I never found him.

December 28th.—A holiday for me at last. Went off with Mr. Griesbach and three men and three dogs, and scoured the whole of our wood and inclosed country, and never set eyes on one single head of game. In my life I never saw such an utterly barren chase. But as I never had a blank day in all my life, I was determined to fight hard for the salvation of my character, so sallied off all the way to Furgo Farm. One bird happened to come towards me, a very long shot, and I knocked him down. So I came in happy with my blank saved by killing 1 partridge.

1851

January 9th.—Tried a gun of Moore and Gray, and nothing could be more satisfactory. It shot quite as well as my 'Old Joe' (Manton), that Lord Poulett once offered me 100 guineas for.

10th.—A letter from Keyhaven to announce the death of my old and faithful housekeeper for above a quarter of a century at my cottage, and also to say the coast was quite destitute of all wild fowl.

11*th.*—Sadly in want of brace of birds, so took out my duck gun, 'Big Joe,' at dusk, crawled up to 3 partridges that were feeding, and floored the whole trio at ninety-five yards with a 4-oz. Eley cartridge. This may be called poaching, but show me the gent who would not chuckle at such an extraordinary shot.

As the coast was so destitute of plover &c. as well as wild fowl, I never went to Keyhaven for any shooting this deplorable season.

Killed at Longparish.—150 game, 5 wild fowl. Grand total, 155 head only.

N.B.—The most destitute season for every kind of winter bird known in memory of man.

February 5*th.*—Keyhaven. Up long before daylight, and on till very late at night, in order to cut through the multitude of odd jobs I had to get quit of; amongst others to engage a *pro tem.* manager of my boathouse and garden, as poor old Read is nearly done for. Keyhaven has become overloaded with gunners, and not one of them has got enough in the whole season to make up a moderate shot for a common hand gun. In short the coast is literally destitute of fowl, as it is everywhere else; and it is sixty-two years since such a rotten and barren winter was known.

6*th to* 12*th.*—Bedridden and in agony. What with constant pain and incessant plague with fomentations, poultices, and medicine, I am almost worn out both in body and nerves.

20*th.*—Better; and I crawled out of doors after over a fortnight's imprisonment.

April 17*th.*—London. Better; but suffering in the place where I was wounded in 1809. Went to Mr. Grey's shooting ground at Kensal Green, where we all tried my first application of my new ignition to a dandy double sporting gun; and it even far exceeded my expectations. The conical breechings for large cannon powder shot quite as well as, or even better than, the usual patent breechings; and we made magnificent targets without one failure of the primers, and at forty yards put some of the shot through forty thicknesses of thick brown paper. Nothing could be more satisfactory; and all I wanted was the use of my limbs to be more active at the trial.

19th.—On all day at the Glass House putting on the crimson cloth to my counter, and unpacking and laying out on it all my things that came up some weeks ago (and luckily I took also my man-servant, for whom I had some difficulty in getting a pass), though I was too lame to help to lift the things myself. In short, I never met such an ill-regulated concern as this mighty Glass House called by many 'The Folly.'

24th.—Since Sunday I have taken no memoranda (through incessant bustle about my new military musket for the Great Exhibition) because on Sunday afternoon I lost the use of my right hand and could not even sign my name. To-day, thank God, I can write again, though very slowly; and I was on hard all this afternoon completing the arrangement of my things at the Glass House, with my servants.

30th.—Yesterday was the last day for exhibitors to uncover their articles for the exhibition; but I had the promise of a special entrée from Captain Westmacott, the director of our class, if I would send in my card to him. I therefore went to ask for the promised admission, but the doors were so fortified by a large body of police that I could not get near the entrance, and they refused to pass a card for anyone. After waiting above an hour, I chanced to see Captain Westmacott and holloaed out to him; and by his interceding with the committee he with difficulty got me in. But it was impossible that I could go back; so I had to borrow the few tools I wanted; and with the kind help of persons I knew, got all my things uncovered and set in proper ɔrder just before two o'clock, when a bell rang to clear out :very person from the building. Thus I had a narrow escape rom having my things roughly handled, and perhaps broken o pieces, by the rough hands of officials who would have orn off the cases and thrown them away. I never saw such ɩ bear garden in my life; and all the exhibitors were refused ɩdmission to meet the Queen on the opening to-morrow ɩnless they paid three guineas for a season ticket. They vere almost in a state of mutiny at this rascally injustice; ɩnd for my own part, as I am still an invalid, I did not regret hat I was emancipated from the awful crowd that there must ɔe on the grand opening to-morrow.

May 1st.—Opening, by the Queen, of the Grand Exɪibition.

Exhibitors, however, were not admitted but by three-ɡuinea ticket; and I was lucky in not having taken one, as ny exertions of yesterday had so crippled me that I could ɪot have gone.

6th.—Longparish. Obliged to have a poor valuable horse :illed owing to his accident, and we ordered him to be buried ɪear the other old favourite animals. I was so cut up with ɔne annoyance and the other, that I had no heart for any-hing all day. Having been for months a sufferer, I had ɪoped a little change of air would do me good.

14th.—London. All day at the Glass House, where, after ɔaying 5*s.* to get in, I had some hours' trouble to obtain an :xhibitor's ticket for future admission. My things were a ittle deranged, though I soon put them right again. Many oreign articles were not yet arrived. I stood this severe day ɔetter than I expected, but I was so weak I could hardly valk about the gigantic building.

16th.—Received an official letter from the Ordnance, with he Master-General's thanks for my exertions in small arms, ɔut inclosing a report from the committee as to some failures ɔf my primers. For this, however, I was fully prepared, as long illness had prevented my properly attending to the workmen, and I had consequently prepared another musket with superior primers on an improved plan, which I left in hand yesterday. I therefore wrote to Colonel Chalmer to state what I had since done.

29th.—London. A letter forwarded from Longparish, requiring my attendance at the Glass House every day till the jurors had passed my class. Went there for the whole day, and none of them came.

30th.—There again after breakfast, and kept an hour at the committee door till I could learn something as to the probable time of their inspection, which took place in about half an hour after I got to my counter. Nothing could be more flattering than the politeness I received and the compliments paid to my (original) productions; but, of course, I am not so sanguine as to suppose that such articles would be considered of such general utility as to justify the grant of a medal or any other premium. Other persons had copied my inventions and attempted to pass them off for their own; but here they were defeated by my luckily being present, and the jurors, therefore, were satisfied as to who was the inventor and who the imitators.

June 1st.—Longparish. Most unpleasantly situated. Just before we went to church I got a hasty summons from the Glass House to meet the Queen and Prince Albert at my counter there at nine to-morrow morning. Situated as I was I had no alternative but to fly off by the mail train after midnight; but I was so ill I was obliged to forego my attempt to get up to London to-night.

2nd.—London. The moment I arrived I hastened to Mr. Wilkinson, who told me I had 'missed the royal inspection,' of which he knew nothing beyond what concerned himself. I therefore proceeded, per 'bus,' to Glass House all anxiety about what had taken place, and the only person who could give me any information was the policeman belonging to my class. He said that Captain Inglefield, R.N. (our superintendent, who had learned all from me), had explained everything, and that the Queen and Prince had paid marked attention and given some time to see my counter, and appeared to be much pleased with my new musket for the army and what else I exhibited. So far so good ; and many thanks to the captain for his kind aid in my unfortunate absence. But still I would rather have lost one hundred pounds than not have been there myself.

3rd.—Went early to the Glass House. Found that most of our exhibitors had received their notices too late to attend the royal command for yesterday, so I acquitted myself and others by forwarding to Windsor Castle, for Prince Albert, a complaint against this shameful neglect of the authorities. I also posted this want of courtesy on their part in the newspapers.

5th.—I saw Captain Inglefield, who gave me an account of his explaining my inventions, and a flattering report of her Majesty's and Prince Albert's interrogations and approbation.

18th.—Got a holiday at last, and had a few hours' pleasure in hearing the six bands of the Household troops, added to that of the Artillery, at Chelsea Hospital, where a fête was given for a charity. The tremendous crescendos of 350 men playing together, and all the drums added, produced such an effect as I never before heard.

21st.—Busy at the Glass House cleaning up and repairing the articles exhibited at my counter, and then devoted myself to the lions of the exhibition for as long as I had strength to crawl about.

26th.—Keyhaven. Off behind the Isle of Wight all day in hopes that being at sea would do me good. Took my new musket to prove the ignition on salt water ; nothing could go better.

29th.—Scarcely able to breathe for the intense heat, and so weak I could hardly get about. Lost my charter at Keyhaven. The first time for thirty years that I visited this plac without having a drop of rain.

July 19th.—London. Busy all the past week, every day about the finishing of my new ignition double sporting gun for which I got an order of admission to the Glass House; bu at the same time a letter from Mr. Digby Wyatt to say tha 'the jurors were all dismissed from their labours,' and, conse quently, there was no more chance for any more prizes being awarded. The Prince Albert started yesterday for Osborne so I had not even the chance of showing the gun to his Roya Highness, unless he should have time to see me on his return to London, previously to the Court leaving for Scotland.

26th.—Run off my legs the whole week, and at last got my new double gun this morning into the Glass House, and had to work all day with the press to proclaim it by circulars and articles.

31st.—Indefatigable every day pushing my new plan, which the brutes of gunmakers tried all they could to sup-press while I was ill and a cripple.

August 9th.—On from eight in the morning till a seven o'clock dinner every day in the past week at a multiplicity of callings on different subjects by the press. This morning, at nine o'clock, I was in attendance at my counter in the Glass House, by recommendation of Mr. Dilke, the Queen's factotum and cicerone, prepared to show my new double gun to Prince Albert, whom I had apprised of its completion, and who, I believe, would have made a point of seeing it, but her Majesty had been induced to stay so long over other articles in the transept that no time was left to go up to our gallery, and the royal party 'bolted' soon after ten o'clock, and went off direct from the Glass House *en route* for Osborne.

After giving long explanations of all my 'lions' (in my French) to a leading man of Madrid, and then a great man from Liège, I left the building, and was busy the rest of the day about my models for altering the disgraceful blunders of the new double carbines for the Cape service, and doing my best towards proclaiming a reform in the wretched arms of the Government.

16th.—On, for the last week, from morning till night every day, jobbing, writing for the press, &c.

23rd.—Not an hour's rest from Monday morning till this (Saturday) night. No time to take a journal. To-day hard on at Glass House and in City.

CHAPTER XLIV

1851.

September 25*th.*—Longparish. Unable to put pen to paper till this day from severe illness, and now scarcely able to write, and consequently could make no daily memoranda; the use of my hand so gone that I had to be dressed and fed like a child. No great loss of shooting, as there is such a miserable breed of birds.

October 9*th.*—I removed to Keyhaven in order that I might try change of air. I was taken twice across to the Isle of Wight, and managed to get on the hills, as my legs are far less weak than my hands and head.

13*th and* 14*th.*—London. All day at the Glass House. On the 14th I was honoured with a special interview on the subject of my new gun, not only with Prince Albert, but with her Majesty also; and their affability was not a little flattering to a veteran amateur in gunmaking.

15*th.*—Attended the grand finale of the exhibition, which will be the leading subject of every newspaper in the world. And this evening my servants rescued all my property from the building.

16*th.*—There was one pour of incessant rain all yesterday, and then a white frost at night, which produced a lovely morning for the removal of goods, for which no packing cases were allowed till after the 20th, when the confusion was expected to be dreadful. I therefore went off about eight this morning with six assistants, and by means of having the great double champion duck gun carried across Hyde Park, and all the brittle articles taken in a large cab, I had housed everything that had been exhibited a few minutes before twelve in Dorset Place, and at three o'clock the bright sun had 'shut up shop,' and there was a return of wet weather. Nothing could have been better managed, all at no expense, except the mere fare for the cab, and I had therefore every reason to be truly thankful for this extreme good fortune.

25th.—My portrait and sketch of my life &c. appeared, by desire of the commissioners, and at the request of the editor, with other leading exhibitors, in the 'Illustrated London News' of this day.

December 1st.—As all other remedies had failed to make me warm, I had this day recourse to a desperate one, that cured a cold for me many years ago, and that was to sally forth in great heavy water boots, and slave in the river from island to island in search of snipes, and this, instead of the 1st of September, was my first sortie with a gun this season. I was too weak and unwell to shoot as I always had done, and consequently missed four shots that I ought to have killed; but I managed to bag 2 teal and 6 snipes. The full snipes were extremely wild, as they always are in white frosts.

N.B.—While fagging hard I got circulation, which I had not felt for the last fortnight; but when in the house I felt cold again.

3rd.—Started with Charles Heath and a cry of dogs and beaters, and scoured our wood, and all the home inclosures; and except getting a glimpse of two rabbits, I never set eyes on one single head of game. Determined not to lose my charter as to never yet having made a blank day, I proceeded to the river, and got 6 snipes and 1 teal without missing a shot.

6th.—Went out again to circulate my chilly limbs, and in spite of such a severe cold that made my eyes weak and dim, I killed all I shot at, and all very long quick shots, viz. 6 snipes and 1 teal.

22nd.—Got 2 mallards from my decoy hut at midnight.

1852

January 5th.—Went round the home beat, but never saw a head of game. Went to the river at three o'clock to save my blank. All I saw was 3 snipes and 2 jack snipes, all of which I killed dead and bagged, and I also made two very long shots at a wild duck and a water rail. I discharged my gun seven times, and killed my 7 head all quite dead. A satisfactory little bit of sport for one in bad trim and with damaged eyes.

8th.—Received the report of the death on November 6 of my friend Colonel Fordyce, who was killed in action by one of the savage Caffres. This was a sad blow to me, not only a subject of deep regret, but a circumstance of provocation, because my son, had he not retired on half-pay, would now, to an almost certainty, have come in for the lieutenant-colonelcy of the 74th. His junior, Major Seton, is now senior major, in command of the depot, where Peter would have been in safety; and his services would, no question, have gained for him this splendid promotion.

17th.—London. Had the mortification to see the appointment of my son's junior, Major Seton, to the lieutenant-colonelcy and command of the gallant 74th Highlanders on the death vacancy of the lamented Colonel Fordyce. Persons say, 'But your son might have been killed.' Not at all; Seton was snug in command of the depot, and by the time he gets to the Cape, the reinforcements now gone out, and the new constitution granted, will most likely render the war there now of infinitely less danger. While I was off in the City on a torrent of further business, who should call but Signor Vercellini from Liverpool. I had heard he was dead, and he heard I was dead. Old Sola also called, and him I had long lost sight of. A singular coincidence this visit of my Italian singers of olden time.

19th.—To-day Peter's birthday, which brings him to the age of forty. I had an interview with Lord Clarence Paget, and then with his excellent father, the Marquis of Anglesea, to present my new double carbine for the Cape, as an amendment to the ridiculous ignitions that have been just sent out there, ordered by the leather-headed people in office from young Lancaster, who objected to the construction of them, but dare not remonstrate, lest he should lose the order and the patronage.

24th.—Busy at the Ordnance for the last few days, in hopes of preventing further blunders in the new arms that are ordered for the Cape.

31st.—Much engaged all the past week about firearms &c., though so weak and unwell that I had scarcely strength to get about. Much to do with printers, editors &c. to prevent my being robbed of the credit of my inventions.

February 3rd.—After seeing the Queen's procession to open Parliament, I went to the club, where I saw conspicuously in the 'Times,' 'Herald,' &c. a notice of my advice on the Cape rifles and other arms quoted from the 'Birmingham Gazette,' so if my plans be adopted, the Government superficials cannot pass them off as their own suggestions, as is their custom.

6th.—Got a private admission to see the Crystal Palace, now that it is quite clear of all partitions &c., and no tongue can describe its symmetrical beauties. The building itself is even a greater 'lion' than all the valuables it had contained.

I omitted to state that I received my splendid prize medal several days ago.

10th.—Attended by command the select committee at the Ordnance, who, among many other things, sat on my new military carbine, which was decided *nem. con.* as 'by far the best that had been invented.' I took also a very clever French musket, to show how ours ought to be ignited, and had to hear much nonsense from Mr. Lovell, the inspector of small arms, who attempted to show that his was the best, and was absolutely uncivil when he met his match in meeting me. Other troublesome jobs, and a levee of lookers-in all at the same time, so that I could only compare myself to a cat thrown by the tail among all the cur dogs of Marylebone.

19th.—Had a long and most agreeable interview with Prince Albert, in order to explain to his Royal Highness my new primer and my carbine, that was approved by the Ordnance committee. I was honoured with the highest approbation, and the Prince was, as usual, most kind and affable, and entered, *con amore*, into all particulars.

20th and 21st.—On like a mad dog from morning till night with Captain Shrapnel, my old friend the General's son, with gunmakers, projectilists, general officers, Ordnance authorities, engineers, &c., on the subject of arms and national defence.

23rd.—Ran down to Keyhaven. Sorry reports; not one tolerable shot in the whole season. Universal complaints as to the scarcity of all kinds of birds on the coast.

24th.—A hard black frost, with a cutting north-east gale, but far too late to bring over fowl, though it may drive in the very few geese that have been about, as they rarely go home till April. Serenaded by Milford ringers and band, on my recovery from a winter's illness, and my arrival after getting the prize medal for big 'guns.'

26th.—Went with Buckle, Read, Parker, and Shuttler over the mud, from my leak to another one that I had nicknamed 'Molesworth's Spreader,' after an enthusiastic amateur that used almost to live in it with his punt, and we all agreed that to cut a channel across would be an incalculable advantage to Keyhaven gunners and boatmen by shortening the distance and avoiding heavy seas to the eastward. I therefore drew out and headed a subscription paper with 2*l.* on my own part, which I thought enough for me, after I had expended near 50*l.* on my large creek, which has proved such a universal convenience and accommodation, not only to gunners, but to the public at large. There were a few geese seen this morning near my creek, so I mustered three stanchions, as I had promised some geese to Prince Albert if they could be got. The birds, however, were all gone to the eastward before we had turned out, and it blew a heavy gale, so I left my small set-out afloat all night for the chance of a shot to-morrow.

27th.—Gale abated, and not a bird to be seen on the coast except 2 burrough ducks, both of which I brought home. I got well on board them, though the wildest of birds, by washing my punt with umber and water, as the tyros had so ill-used the white punts that even the ox-birds had become awake to them, insomuch that anything white had become a signal for every living fowl to be off. Furbished up and put all in store, preparative to leaving to-morrow.

All the birds I killed up to March 1852 were: Game, never shot at. 3 rabbits and 24 snipes. Total, 27. Wild fowl.—4 teal, 8 ducks and mallards, 2 sheldrakes. Total, 27 + 14. Grand total, only 41 head.

Illness nearly the whole season prevented my shooting, and at one time I was in danger.

March 3rd.—London. Attended the Queen's Levee, which was a very full one, owing to the numerous presentations on the happy change of Government, and our riddance from the Cobden-bullied ministers.

4th.—On with Captain Shrapnel, Uncle Bishop,[1] Mr. Elmslie, Lancaster and Grey, all more or less on experiments for the new engines of war.

13th.—Out again, and had a long, flattering, and interesting interview with Lord Hardinge, the newly appointed Master-General of the Ordnance under Lord Derby's Government, on the disgraceful apathy and monopoly of the officials, who have long had the control of the small arms department, and left with his lordship a wooden model of my suggestion for several improvements in the stock, ignition, ramrod &c. of the

[1] The head man and manager for 'Westley Richards.'

army musket, and found that the exertions of myself and others would be taken up and tried fairly.

Busy every day with Lord Hardinge, Colonel Chalmer, Purdey, Grey, Lancaster and Wilkinson up to end of March, and with divers other gunmakers on experiments, &c.

April 3rd.—A grand trial on Purdey's shooting ground, near Starch Green. Purdey went off in the morning, and at half-past twelve we had a meeting at Purdey's shop, of Lord Hardinge, the Master-General, Sir Howard Douglas, Colonel Chalmer, Colonel Gordon, Mr. Purdey, jun., and myself, with Sergeant Baker, the crack shot at Woolwich Arsenal, and then started off to try the Frenchman's Minié ball against a new conical ball of old Purdey's invention, and had the satisfaction to prove that we were no longer to be beat and laughed at by foreigners. Purdey's ball proved to be the best. We were hard at work till near five o'clock, and the result was this :

Through hard elm boards

Line musket (with four drams of powder and ball) through boards	9
Ditto with Minié	11
Purdey's 20 bore (with his ball and three drams of powder)	12
Purdey's 1 oz. 32 bore (with only two drams of powder)	14

We then tried for accuracy of range, and the Purdey 32 beat all others out of the field, so that on further trials there is every reason to hope that the Minié will no longer be the idol of the Woolwich authorities.

5th.—On from the time I got up till bedtime with all parties. Heard a flaming report of Lancaster at Woolwich, so between all my constituents I hope to see the Minié snuffed out, no matter by whom so long as he is an honest Englishman.

6th.—Heard of the awful wreck of the 'Birkenhead' troop ship off the Cape, where nearly 500 persons were launched into eternity, and among them poor Colonel Seton, who was on passage to command the 74th. Here would have been my son had he not retired on half-pay, so that all my regret at his losing this grand promotion was cancelled by his providential escape.

28th.—Had an interview with Lord Hardinge, with some models, &c., and among them a large model of my wheel-barrow stanchion gun artillery, with wool battery, for raking a close column of infantry with a pound mould shot goose cartridge. His lordship was pleased with my idea, and approved of introducing stanchion guns in future warfare.

May 6th.—Attended a grand meeting of gunmakers and riflemen, at the villa, Mulgrave House, Putney, of Lord Ranelagh, who deserves the thanks of the whole country for his zealous endeavours to encourage the art of projectiles, and who will have future meetings on a larger scale which will stimulate all the gunmakers to come forward in fair competition. This is what was long wanted, but hitherto no one has had the spirit for such an undertaking.

18th.—To Longparish for a day's business. Took down in my hand the dandy exhibition gun, in order to try that and the cannon powder at the rooks, which are now the only game of which our poor country will afford a rapid succession of shots. Got 125 rooks without cleaning the gun, so proved the humbug of this powder being too dirty to stand a hard day's shooting, and moreover proved that it shot much stronger than the fine powder. The only real fault of the former is, that it is bad for trade, being only 1*s.* per lb.

June 1st.—London. Went down with Mr. Lancaster, by desire of Lord Hardinge, to Mr. Lancaster's shooting ground, at Wormwood Scrubbs, to try the relative qualities of best fine powder and 'T.P.L.G.' cannon powder. Lancaster's new ground afforded quite a treat, and we had some fine sport shooting at his iron stags that fly up and down a railway similar to the 'Montagne Russe' in Paris.

21st.—Took the barrel and my new models to Mr. Lacy, 21 Great St. Helen's, near the India House, who does almost everything for Lancaster.

22nd.—The barrel was proved this morning, and then I set the foreman upon my job, which was to produce my style of musket for the Ordnance committee agreeably to an official letter that I had received.

July 1st.—Had a sad disappointment by missing a full-dress admission to hear the Queen's Speech in the Lords on a ticket from the Lord Great Chamberlain.

3rd.—Kept prisoner here in the dog days about this botheration musket of mine, having to go every day to the City, to prevent blunders and misunderstanding.

7th.—Much worry with the musket, owing to my directions being given by a middleman, and therefore I was obliged to see the workmen myself and correct divers mistakes. Had to go to Lord Hardinge's room, and bring away my perfect carbine as a guide to prevent more blunders. General Bacon caught me up and wished me to meet him and Prince George of Cambridge, to try Deane's five-barrel revolving carbine. Prisoner in the Palace from half-past two till a quarter past three. No one came, and no message left, so took a cab and returned to the City; first to Deane's and then to Lacy's, where I left the carbine in charge of Jones, a very clever 'screwer together,' after having waited an hour and a quarter in durance vile till he had returned from his tea. And all this in the hottest weather that had been known in England for many years. The thermometer about 112, and everything broiling, and all this too in the bustling nuisance of the City election. Did not get home till seven o'clock, and then completely knocked up. All this I go through from my anxiety to do good to the service, by superseding the vile rubbish that is served out to the army. But were a hundred guineas offered me, I would refuse it, rather than go through the worry I've had for this last month, and particularly this day.

8th.—On all day again about my musket, and did not get home to dinner till nine o'clock at night, as I was determined not to leave the factory till I could rescue the musket and all my models. The latter I left with Mr. Adams, in order to pit Deane & Co. versus Lancaster, on my way home to dinner, in a flying hansom cab, which cut along almost at railway speed. Thus, after eighteen days of perpetual pother, I got rid of Lacy's factory. The double carbine I left to have engraved on it the inscription which I had merely written and pasted on the butt, as to its being approved by the Ordnance committee last February.

13*th.*—Longparish. Went over to Andover on a multiplicity of business, and soon after one o'clock there set in the most awful storm of thunder, lightning, and enormous hailstones that I have ever seen. In one hour the town of Andover was in an absolute river. About four o'clock the storm abated and I started back for Longparish, but when I got about halfway home this dreadful weather set in again. My man and I were at one time in a stroke of lightning that passed between us and the splashboard of the gig, but, thanks to God's mercy, we just escaped this danger. The hail, larger than pigeons' eggs, continued to pour upon us, as it were, one incessant vertical volley of musketry, which the poor pony weathered as not one horse in 1,000 would have done. On our arrival home, drenched to the skin and with tattered umbrella, we found things in a sad state, and all the men we had clearing the parapets, lest the ceilings should burst in with the deluge of water that had overflowed the pipes, and, of course, windows out of number smashed to pieces. The storm did not cease till near six, when I went out and found the garden, greenhouse, and everything else in one absolute state of wreck. Fruit and vegetables beat level with the ground and scarcely a pane of glass left whole on the premises, the trees half stripped of their leaves, and branches blown off by the gale. The hail lay on the ground like a fall of snow, and we shovelled up as much as we wanted to make some ice, which was excellent and refreshing after our excitement. In short, no such a storm was ever known to old men of over ninety in our neighbourhood, and the consequence to crops and other property must be a severe loss to both the rich and the poor.

Dreadful reports from all parts as to damage to corn &c.

Broken panes in house	94
" " " greenhouse	286
Broken in all	380

19th.—Ran up to London to vote at the Middlesex election, and lucky that I did, as the fellows had put aside my musket to do rough work (for India), which I made them put aside by a little *douceur.*

20th.—Went to my district, Bethnal Green, and gave a plumper for the Marquis of Blandford, whose party was, of course, hooted at by the scum and rads at this dirty end of the town.

24th.—Up very early and down to Keyhaven, to clear off my bills &c. (after five months' absence from the place), to see to my new creek, and other work done, overhaul my flotilla, great guns and gear, after five months of such extremes of weather as had rarely been known before; and with a new man (Shuttler) to trust to, since poor old Fifield dead, and old Read retired and gone away to live the other side of Lymington. Found all things even better than I could expect.

A regular set in of wet weather at last, so I failed not to keep up my charter of bringing rain whenever I came to Keyhaven.

31st.—Intense heat up to this day, when I got a letter to say my musket was gone on with all wrong in my absence, so I flew at once up to town.

August 4th.—London. Saw Lord Hardinge for a few minutes, and gave a hasty explanation of the musket, which I then took away to be either made right or mended with a new one; and much regretted I had not gone to Birmingham, instead of being handed over to the barbarous gun butchers in the City.

7th.—Up very early, and went down to Waltham to the Government factory for small arms. Was received by Colonel Gordon in command, from whom I received the kindest ttention and hospitality. Though my trip was a visit f demi-official business, it repaid me well as an excursion of leasure, by seeing all the manufactory, splendid shooting round &c. Here the machinery is worked by water as well s by steam engines, and 5,000 Miniés are being made from he forged, or rather rolled, tubes from Birmingham.

13*th.*—Up soon after four, and at Waterloo Station by alf-past six to go down for the lord lieutenant's meeting at Winchester this morning. The Duke of Wellington had rrived when I got to the station office. This meeting of the ieutenancy of the county was relative to raising the militia, bout which the old Duke is most active and energetic. The proceedings commenced before twelve, and ended soon fter two; after which I had a fine opportunity to speak to is Grace about the muskets, and show him my models; and, what's more, tell him about the failure of the arms at the Cape, which he told me he had never before heard of, so it's high ime he did.

19*th.*—London. Went early to Deane's factory, as the percussion hole was to be drilled to-day, and on that depends the well-going of my new musket. Captain Shrapnel's musket has ust failed from this delicate job being blundered, and I had o throw away Lancaster's City job for the same reason. I hen went to inspect Sydenham and the site for the new glass palace; it is to stand on twenty-one acres, surrounded by 300 acres, with a magnificent view from a lofty hill.

23*rd to* 26*th.*—Every day and all day at the factory over London Bridge, and after all my trouble had to order another musket to be got up, in consequence of the blunders of the City workmen. The scramble in preparing for the 1st of September put the whole factory in such a drive, that the men had no brains for any new and out-of-the-way job, and I was determined nothing should be sent to he board in my name with faults that were open to criticism.

CHAPTER XLV

1852

September 1*st.*—A wonderful day, considering the bad reports of game and the unusual wildness of the birds. Came home to an eight o'clock dinner, with 30 partridges, 1 rabbit, 1 curlew and 1 hedgehog. Made four double shots and missed but twice. Hardly credible after my being pronounced this time last year as never likely to survive another season. Thank God, however, the doctors were out in their judgment.

4*th.*—A sorry show of wild birds, and yet had another extraordinary day, bagging all that it was possible to kill, as the behaviour of the dogs, the marking and the shooting, were perfection. My bag was 21 partridges, 1 hare, 1 landrail, and 1 quail.

7*th.*—Out for a hard day again, but was so unwell that I missed three shots, and two of them very fair ones. The bag was 17 partridges and 2 hares, and should have been sure of a third hare, a most easy shot; but both my barrels missed fire, a mishap that never occurred to me in all my life, unless in wet weather.

13*th.*—An extraordinary day's good luck, and first-rate shooting. I could not get away till twelve o'clock, but came home to a seven-o'clock dinner, with 15 partridges, 3 quails, and 2 landrails; I only fired 21 shots.

16*th.*—This morning's paper in deep mourning announced the almost sudden death of the Duke of Wellington at Walmer Castle on the 14th. The event quite cut me up, as it was only on the 13th of August that I had such an affable interview with his Grace at Winchester on the subjects of the militia and my improvements in firearms. An immense flight of snipes having been seen by Lovelock while watching the fishery, I went up the river to try for them; but they were so extremely wild for want of wind, that though I saw above 20 couple, I could only bring in 4 snipes. Being thus engaged, I sent Siney off with my new exhibition gun, as I wanted game for the farmers; and he had the splendid luck to get 5 hares, 5 partridges, and 1 wood pigeon.

29th.—At Longparish House. List of game brought in up to Michaelmas: 125 partridges, 27 hares, 1 rabbit, 4 quails, 4 landrails, 7 snipes (and 3 caught in wires), 1 wood pigeon. Total, 172 head.

N.B.—The most extraordinary list on record, considering the bad breed of birds, and that last year I was too ill to shoot, and was pronounced as 'never likely to take the field again.' Thank God for my unexpected recovery.

30th.—Attended a large meeting with deputy-lieutenants at Romsey; and so much there was to do that I did not get home to a meal till about half-past nine at night. While waiting for arrival of parties, I had just time to inspect the celebrated old Abbey Church, the greatest curiosities of which were the ancient monument of the daughter of King Stephen, and a female human skull with long plaited hair, in a most perfect state and resting on a block of oak, 1500 years old.

October 1st.—Kept up my old charter of scouring our wood and hedgerows, and 'blowing out' my myrmidons in the hall. One old cock was the only pheasant seen or heard of on the estate. I had the luck to bag this said pheasant, with 7 partridges, 2 hares, and 1 rabbit; which performance, under all circumstances, I considered an excellent day's sport.

20th.—Keyhaven. Busy all the morning, and then afloat till dark to explore the coast; but saw nothing, though heard that a company of wigeon had been seen within a day or two.

Well repaid for a long day's cruise, by the delightful change to healthy sea air.

21*st.*—Off at six for anything to try a stanchion gun that I had made after my prize medal gun for the late young Marquis of Hastings, whose family gave it to Shuttler who now goes with me; but the gun missed fire every shot but one, and then it hung fire at a cormorant, which, however, I bagged, after near an hour's chase in the channel. He regularly dived at about fifty yards; just twenty yards too far for the stripe of shot to catch his head in time. After several blank rounds most accurately fired, I tried him by firing enough before him for the cartridge to meet his head at right angles when in the act of 'shutting his port.' What was the result? He turned up as dead as a log of wood. Here then is a recipe for stopping a crippled 'parson.' Never too late to learn something.

November 4th.—London. Up at seven and on till night: First, with Lord Winchester on militia concerns; second, with Westley Richards on my new plan for a cripple gun; third, at Ordnance about committee; fourth, with Wilkinson on firearms; fifth, with Dingwall about my rents and leases; sixth, at Deane's factory on military arms and experiments; seventh, with Purdey and Brazier on locks and revolvers; besides doing a long list of commissions at West End and in City.

10*th.*—In a crowd and bustle getting tickets from Lord Chamberlain for the Duke lying in state at Chelsea on the 12th, and for getting into the House of Lords to-morrow.

11*th.*—I had the closest possible stare at the *cortége.* An incessant pour of rain all day; but it was fun to see the silk-stocking flunkeys (for whom nothing is good enough) obliged to trample through the mud like a brood of young ducks.

12*th.*—An awful gale from south-east, and torrents of heavy rain all day. Started at nine for Chelsea, where the lying in state of the Duke was the most magnificent spectacle I ever saw; and on this occasion the whole concern of carriage regulations &c. &c. was conducted as well as in Paris. This regularity, it appears, was but of short duration; so it's lucky I went early in the morning. In the afternoon the confusion was such that one-half of the select people could not get in at all; and the next day, Saturday, the first day for public admission, the crowd was awful. Two females carried off dead, and no one can tell how many cripples. Much damage done by the overflowing of Thames to-day. Such tides as had rarely been known.

15*th to* 17*th*.—Hard on at Deane's factory, as the Ordnance had sent word that they wished Captain Shrapnel and myself to prepare some specimens of arms, they not having yet had any on which they had not a difference of opinion. The City was like a field of battle, preparing for the monster 'black job' of the 18th, to-morrow.

18*th*.—The Duke's funeral. Up before four o'clock. Our retired part of town already in a roar with carriages. Got to the Club at half-past six, and had about the best place in all the house. To describe the magnificence of this, the most glorious of all funerals ever before heard of in the world, is superfluous because impossible, and every newspaper will feed on it for weeks to come. But I cannot help recording how much my feelings were excited at the last sight of the coffin, which was placed open to view upon such a car as eyes never yet beheld, and the poor old Duke's favourite horse following in the rear. The procession was above two hours long.

25*th*.—Went on private view to see all the orders, bâtons, swords &c. of the late Duke by permission of Mr. Garrard. A sight well worth seeing, as no man on earth ever held so many honours.

26*th*.—Went by tickets to the last view of the Duke's pageant—the interior of St. Paul's Cathedral, lit up with gas, and hung with black, precisely as it appeared at the funeral. Here ends what may be considered the last 'lion' of the grand and mournful exhibition of 1852.

December 6th.—At the factory again to-day, and to my great relief got my new military musket finished, all but polishing and other trumpery, which will be done by midday to-morrow.

7th.—Wet weather and a stiff day's work. 1. Went to the factory, where I had to wait till the rifle musket was finished. 2. To work it to the West End and then to the Horse Guards. 3. To wait till the Commander-in-Chief's levee of eighty officers was over, and then to show him the arm, with which he was much pleased, and directed me to proceed, officially, with it to the Ordnance Office. Here I left it, and then wrote from the Club an application for a committee. Several general officers saw the arm, and pronounced it to be the 'best yet produced.' A most satisfactory day.

8th.—Another wet day. Had an interview with Lord Raglan, the new Master-General at the Ordnance, and explained to him the advantages of my new arm. Nothing could be more satisfactory than my interview; but, unfortunately, the last committee had sat yesterday morning, when some very inferior arms were passed. Lord Raglan, however, wished me to see Sir George Berkeley; but he having left the office, I had to await the interview.

N.B.—While alone in the ante-room, I passed a good hour in overhauling every arm that has ever been sent in. I never set eyes on a worse heap of rubbish; not a new idea among all the gunmakers or Government officials.

9th.—After waiting an hour and a half among all the lot of firearms, which I overhauled again, I got my interview with Sir George Berkeley, who had only just arrived at the office. I explained to him my new arm, in juxtaposition with the 'Enfield' one that had been approved. He desired me to leave it with him, took down my address, and hinted about having another committee.

23rd.—Attended the Ordnance committee on my new arm. I produced and explained its advantages over those that had hitherto been brought before the board, and here the matter ended, till I received an official letter to my address in the country.

27th.—Longparish. The most terrific tempest ever known, all last night and till about three this afternoon. About fifty of my trees blown down, and among them the old lofty poplars in front of the house.

30th.—An answer to my letter of inquiry about Keyhaven. Thank God! the Cottage just escaped the awful flood and gale, in which, by help of old Payne, Shuttler, and others, all my heavy guns and property were removed upstairs. The damage done to boats on the quay &c. was extensive, as the raging sea came over all the walls and up to the houses. To-day I went out and viewed the awful wrecks of trees in my wood here, and finished with an afternoon's shooting, though expecting almost a blank. Had the luck, however, to come home with 3 rabbits, 1 snipe, and 3 partridges.

31st.—Proceeded to order labourers, sawyers, bricklayers &c. to clear the mischief done by the late ferocious hurricane. The number of trees blown down here proved to be seventy-six, besides those on the other side of the river, and on my estate at Bullington. Thus it appears that both in the summer hailstorm and in this winter tempest I was the greatest sufferer in the neighbourhood. While too busy to try for game, I espied that ever-intruding scamp-keeper of Mr. Coles going to his constant beat on my farm, and was just in time to have the ground well scoured before him, and gloriously finished the old year with 3 hares, 2 partridges, and 2 rabbits.

1853

January 5th.—Too busy to shoot, and wanting a head or two of game I sent my keeper Siney out for the whole day, and after slaving over all my best ground, he came home at night with (what I never yet had) a blank. I therefore exulted at my escape.

10th.—Received yesterday an official from Ordnance,

stating that a portion of my improvements in military arms would be adopted for the service, but, most unwisely, declining to adopt all my suggestions.

13*th*.—London. On from morning to night, and this day left my improved musket with Mr. Purdey, who was delighted with it, and kindly agreed to show it to everyone, in order to let the world see how superior this (my arm for 1853) was to the Enfield one of 1852, that the committee had obstinately fixed on, and had the impudence to send to Prince Albert. Captain Shrapnel was not even allowed a committee after his some hundreds of pounds expense. He is writing these people down; I merely advertise in the papers.

List of game brought in up to February 1853: 164 partridges, 39 hares, 9 rabbits, 4 quails, 4 landrails, 1 pheasant, 1 wood pigeon, 20 snipes. Total, 242 head.

N.B.—Not a shot at a wild fowl as yet this season. I beat all the neighbours for game this autumn, but the floods annihilated all winter shooting for coast or inland.

February 25th.—Bitter cold weather. Very unwell. (Tantalising reports of the sport at Keyhaven.)

April 23rd.—Longparish. I feebly take up the pen, which I've been unable to use ever since the 9th of March. I've had an awful illness, and been in agony for forty-two days; repeated consultations with Sir Ben. Brodie, Dr. Bright, Dr. Pope, and Dr. Badger, and in very serious danger; almost at the point of death more than once. Prayed for at Longparish and Milford churches. My son, telegraphed for from Scotland, came to my bedside before daylight on the 14th of March.[1] As all remedies proved ineffectual, Sir Ben. advised as a last

[1] He came from Inverary, N.B., sixteen miles by coach to Aberdeen, and from Aberdeen to London, 551 miles, in twenty-one hours. Coach fare, 2*s*. 6*d*.; 2nd class train, 2*l*. 19*s*. 6*d*., say 3 guineas, with 1*s*. to coachman. This cheap and quick record I made him write down for me to copy here. On April 21 a remarkable circumstance, a woodpecker came in shot of the window, and, a gun being loaded, I killed it; and Mrs. Hawker sent it off to Leadbeater as a companion to the woodcock that I shot out of the parlour window (on Jan. 25, 1810) when on crutches with my Talavera wound.

resource, I should get removed from London to country air without loss of time. Being too ill to exist in an inn, or at any place without a nurse and all other attendants (in addition to my dear wife, who has never left me, day or night, since my first illness on the 14th of January), I, on the 9th of this month, April, got down to Longparish House, and, by the mercy of Almighty God, bore the journey better than I expected, and found my almost departed breath somewhat restored by total removal to a clear atmosphere.

10*th.*—My complaint is a violent affection of the heart, from having worked for years too hard, and had such a series of painful excitement on divers affairs.

20*th.*—I may venture to say that I am getting on (though of course very, very slowly) towards the chance of recovery, for which prospect I have to thank Sir B. Brodie and an All-wise Providence.

Another remarkable circumstance—and a lucky one for me, who could eat nothing more nourishing than fish—the trout in our river, which were not even eatable when broiled till near July, have come in many months before their time, and ate better than I have known them to be for these last twenty years. One of my fishery tenants, Mr. Macleod, in the first week of March, had killed, in a severe winter's day, 15 brace with a fly, and he kindly sent me a few as red and as good as salmon. This phenomenon is accounted for by the continued rains flooding all the low lands, and washing down constant winter food for the fish, which, notwithstanding the severe winter that afterwards cut up everything in March and April, never lost their high condition.

23*rd.*—I have been taken out for the last few days, for short drives in the carriage; but I am now a figure of skin and bone.

24*th.*—Another circumstance to record—Captain Duff and his friend came to my river to fish, and, in spite of the adverse weather, had a few days' good sport; and, what is a miracle, every trout was better in season (though in April) than, for these twenty years, I have seen them—even than in June and July, the only time they have hitherto been fit to eat. They were quite red, firm, and full of curd—in short, delicious. Thus my lamentable illness has 'cut me out of' the best angling season on record, as well as the use of my new ignition punt gun at Keyhaven, in the finest hard weather we have had there since 1838.

May 4th.—Winter again; bitter cold gale of wind east by north. As I made but slow progress in the low and water-meadow situation of Longparish, I had made up my mind to forego all the comforts of the mansion for the more healthy air of my dear little cottage on the coast, and therefore I left Longparish for Keyhaven this day, after having passed twenty-five days and nights at the former place, without strength or appetite. We arrived at Keyhaven Cottage about six in the evening, after my very long absence from the 26th of October, 1852, up to this 4th of May, 1853. My good people were all delighted to see me, which they had made up their minds they should never do any more.

5th.—Keyhaven. Stephen Shuttler has done me justice in every possible way in my long absence, and kept everything in the very best order, in spite of awful floods; and then a north-pole winter in spring.

N.B.—Found the air here far pleasanter than at the other places. Thanks to God for all blessings up to this Holy Thursday—or Ascension Day—for 1853.

7th.—A total change of weather to south by west, and a pouring fall of rain all day; in the afternoon the cock flew round again to the north-east with the most furious increase of cold rain, and a heavy fall of snow—lamentable weather for my poor eyes and limbs. Instead of having a fair chance to breathe the good air here, I've been, ever since I entered the cottage, a close prisoner; could not even step into the garden.

12th.—Anniversary of my Douro affair, forty-four years ago. Cold and piercing north-easter, which is comparative luxury to the deadly poison of a white frost, insomuch that I suffered far less to-day, and my eyes got better.

13*th and* 14*th.*—Bitter white frosts again. But two hours' fine weather on the 14th, when I got the sea air for the first time by being rowed down to Hurst and back. I came home refreshed, but much exhausted; and, on landing, who should be here but old Buckle, just arrived from Scotland? I was, however, not man enough to enjoy his 'yarn' as of old.

18*th.*—A beautiful day. Crossed to Yarmouth, and got driven to Freshwater for the fine sea air, but too weak to walk along the cliffs. Lots of 'gents' popping at rock birds and rifling the cormorants, and rookeries being stormed inland. All to tantalise me, like the gents having good sport angling the other day in view of my windows at Longparish, and I too ill to go out.

26*th.*—I sailed to Yarmouth, and got Butler's excellent phaeton to the high lighthouse, and returned by Groves's Hotel; but was so weak I could not enjoy my old paradise, Alum Bay, as before. The lighthouse is now kept by a Mr. Henderson, *vice* Coleraine, and the dangerous occupation of taking the eggs of rock birds is performed by a man named Lane, of the village below, called Weston, whose brother was lately killed in this awful pursuit.

29*th.*—Sunday. Being too weak to walk, I went in a donkey chaise to morning church at Milford (where, as well as at Longparish, Mrs. Hawker had me prayed for when expected not to recover), to return thanks to God for my escape from death in my long and dangerous illness, through which I had not been in church since the early part of last January, and never expected to be in church again, except on my way to the grave.

July.—Longparish. From the 1st I have been so dreadfully ill that I could do nothing. My nights have been as awful as before.

7*th.*—The thunder and lightning all night caused such

oppressive heat that no one could rest in bed. My sufferings could scarcely be conceived.

8th to 14th.—Too ill to get about save by quiet easy drives in the carriage, and to crawl out to look at all the grand repairs outside the house, which are now done. Attended by Dr. Hempsted twice a day, as my sufferings are alarming. We have had incessant wet weather ever since I returned to Longparish, and consequently the heavy water-meadow fogs oppressed me even more than those of London, from which I had retreated on the score of health. To-day, the 14th, Dr. Hempsted went from me to his other patient, the Earl of Portsmouth, for whom he had no hope, and who died this day at one o'clock. Peace to his soul!

[Colonel Hawker died shortly after the last entry (on August 7th) at 2 Dorset Place, London.—ED.]

SUMMARY OF THE BAGS OF GAME AND WILD FOWL RECORDED IN COLONEL HAWKER'S DIARY, 1802–1853.

GAME.

Partridges	7,035	Wood pigeons	20
Pheasants	575	Turtle doves	7
Blackcock	11	Stock dove	1
Grouse	16	Hares	631
Landrails	56	Rabbits	318
Quails	58	Total	8,728

Wild Fowl (Swans, Ducks and Geese).

Wild swans (hoopers)	38	Pochard (dunbirds)	64
Brent geese	1,327	Golden-eye ducks	21
Barnacle geese	3	Eider duck	1
White-fronted laughing geese	20	Scoters	2
Grey geese	3	Velvet scoters	4
Wild ducks	441	Curres (scaup ducks)	112
Wigeon	2,211	Shell ducks	37
Pintails	39	Mergansers	3
Teal	135		
Tufted ducks	27	Total	4,488

Riverside and Seashore Birds.

Curlews	118	Green sandpipers (ox-eyes)	8
Godwits	87	Sanderlings	2
Ox-birds (dunlins)	1,329	Oyster catchers (olives)	15
Redshanks	4	Avocet	1
Water rails	50	Moorhens	64
Spotted crakes	3	Coots	48
Sandpipers (stone runners and summer snipe)	13	Dabchicks	9
Stone curlews	5	Herons	18
Ring dotterels	28	Bitterns	3
Whimbrels (curlew jacks)	12	Phalaropes	2
Reeves	2	Total	1,821

Woodcock	68	Snipes	2 116

Plover, grey, green, and golden 351

Various.

Including great northern and red-throated divers		Night jars	5
Cormorants		Goshawks	2
Cliff birds—terns		Hoopoe	1
besides Grebes	3	And deer	3
		Total	181

Grand Total 17,753

SEASON 1

1802–1803.

Sept. 1 *to Sept.* 1.

(N.B.—Æt. 16½ years. Gun, Single-barrel flint.)

Partridges	198	Peewits	7
Pheasants	12	Stone curlews	3
Hares	17	Reeve	1
Rabbits	10	Nightjar	2
Quails	4	Black-headed terns	3
Snipes	99	Black tern	1
Wild ducks	2	Common terns	12
Diving duck (dunbird)	1	Black-headed gull	1
Woodcock	1	Cobb gull (great blackbacked)	3
Turtle dove	1	Kipps[1]	5
Wood pigeons	2	Ring dotterels	6
Moorhens	15	Sanderlings	
Water rails	10	Cuckoo	1
Heron	1	Redwings	2
Sea-gulls (common)	4	Brown owl	1
Dunlin	4	Woodpecker	1
Dabchicks	6	Missel thrush	1
Baldcoot	1	Fieldfares	8
Summer snipes (sandpipers)	7		
Ox-eye (green sandpiper)	1	Total	456

SEASON 2

1803–1804.

Sept. 1 *to Sept.* 1.

Partridges	38	Golden plover	2
Pheasants	8	Grey plover	5
Hares	8	Ring dotterel	12
Quails	4	Dunlins	30
Landrails	12	Windar (i.e. wigeon diver or dunbird)	1
Olives (oyster catchers)	4		
Woodpecker	1	Peewits	3
Stockdove	1	Godwit	1
Woodcock	1	Stone runners (sandpipers)	5
Snipes	32	Baldcoot	1
Water rail	1	Avocet	1
Curlew	1	Reeve	1
Curlew jacks (whimbrels)	12	Total	185

[1] A kipp is a genus of tern peculiar to the vicinity of Romney.

SEASON 3

1804–1805.

Sept. 1 *to Sept.* 1.

Partridges	55	Green plover	3
Pheasants	5	Dunlins	12
Hares	14	Olives (oyster catchers)	3
Rabbits	9	Diving wigeon (dunbird)	12
Landrails	3	Black duck (scoter)	1
Quails	1	Bittern	1
Snipes	35	Ox-eye (green sandpiper)	1
Stone plover	1	Coot	1
Turtle doves	2	Moorhens	10
Godwits	2	Turtle dove	2
Water rails	4	Nightjar	1
Golden plover	3		
Grey plover	1	Total	182

SEASON 4

1805–1806.

Sept. 1 *to Sept.* 1.

Partridges	93	Moorhens	11
Pheasants	8	Quail	1
Hares	24	Dabchick	1
Rabbits	16	Heron	2
Snipes	48	Green sandpipers (i.e. ox-eyes)	2
Wild duck	1	Peewit	
Teal	2	Summer snipe (sandpiper)	1
Landrails	2	Hoopoe	1
Water rails	8	Total	222

SEASON 5

1806–1807.

Sept. 1 *to Sept.* 1.

Partridges	182	Woodcocks	16
Pheasants	33	Landrails	2
Hares	43	Water rails	2
Rabbits	31	Quails	2
Wild duck	4	Moorhens	5
Teal	9	Heron	1
Golden-eye duck	1	Wood pigeons	2
Snipes	77	Total	410

SEASON 6

1807–1808.

Sept. 1 *to Sept.* 1.

Partridges	217	Moorhens	9
Pheasants	11	Dabchick	1
Hares	31	Dunlins	3
Rabbits	14	Ring dotterel	7
Wild ducks	5	Peewits	2
Woodcock	6	Redshanks	2
Snipes	72	Nightjar	1
Water rails	15	Total	396

SEASON 7

1808–1809.

Sept. 1 *to Sept.* 1.

Partridges	235	Snipes	22
French red-legged ditto	9	Turtle doves	2
Pheasants	33	Redshank	1
Hares	9		
Rabbits	5	Total	316

Left for Spain November 17, 1808, and returned September 28, 1809.

SEASON 8

1809–1810.

Sept. 1 *to Sept.* 1.

Woodcock	1	Peewits	4
Snipes	11	Wood pigeon	1
Hare	1		
Moorhen	1	Total	19

Only returned from Spain September 28, and had very little shooting this season, owing to severe wound received at Talavera last July 28.

SEASON 9

1810–1811.

Sept. 1 *to Sept.* 1.

Partridges	253	Bald coots	14
Hares	16	Water rails	5
Pheasants	24	Pochard	1
Rabbits	9	Dabchick	1
Woodcocks	6	Heron	1
Snipes	71	Wood pigeons	2
Quails	4	Peewits	2
Landrails	3		
Wild ducks	16	Total	428

Left on January 7 for Portugal, and returned home May 30.

SEASON 10
1811–1812.
Sept. 1 *to Sept.* 1.

Partridges	119	Snipes	65
Hares	36	Peewits	4
Quails	3	Heron	1
Landrail	1	Wood pigeons	2
Pheasants	41	Water rails	2
Rabbits	14	Ox-eye (green sandpiper)	1
Woodcocks	2	Nightjar	1
Wild ducks	9		
Teal	1	Total	303
Wigeon	1		

SEASON 11
1812–1813.
Sept. 1 *to Sept.* 1.

Partridges	119	Wild duck	16
Pheasants	41	Plover	5
Hares	18	Stone curlew	1
Blackcock	1	Wood pigeons	2
Grouse	16	Moorhen	1
Rabbits	11	Deer	1
Snipes	37		
Woodcocks	8	Total	277

SEASON 12
1813–1814.
Sept. 1 *to Sept.* 1.

Partridges	158	Coots	3
Pheasants	50	Dusky grebe (a kind of black and white sea dabchick)	2
Hares	19	Green sandpiper (ox-eye)	1
Rabbits	23	Ringed dotterel	1
Woodcocks	3	Dunlins (ox-birds)	32
Snipes	103	Curlews	4
Wild ducks	24	Grey plover	3
Brent geese	14	Peewits	2
Curres (scaup ducks)	7	Cormorants	2
Pochard	4	Wood pigeons	2
Teal	3	Goshawk	1
Wigeon	6	Heron	1
Golden-eye duck	1	Deer	1
Sheldrake	4		
Great northern speckled divers	3	Total	478
Water rail	1		

SEASON 13

1814–1815.

Sept. 1 *to Sept.* 1.

Partridges	126	Dunbirds	18
Hares	21	Curres (scaup ducks)	14
Pheasants	48	Brent goose	1
Snipes	63	Coots	8
Rabbits	11	Cormorant	1
Quails	3	Tippet grebe	3
Wild ducks	12	Deer	1
Wigeon	14		
		Total	342

SEASON 14

1815–1816.

Sept. 1 *to Sept.* 1.

Partridges	164	Teal	2
Pheasants	106	Woodcock	1
Hares	31	Godwit	1
Rabbits	15	Redshank	1
Quails	2	Heron	1
Snipes	40	Dunlin	15
Wild ducks	25		
Wigeon	4	Total	408

SEASON 15

1816–1817.

Sept. 1 *to Sept.* 1.

Partridges	308	Brent geese	6
Pheasants	40	Plover (golden)	3
Quail	1	Woodcocks	10
Hares	17	Peewits	6
Rabbits	9	Heron	1
Snipes	99	Grey plover	2
Wild duck	9	Knot	1
Wigeon	3		
Teal	1	Total	516

SEASON 16

1817–1818.

Sept. 1 *to Sept.* 1.

Partridges	178	Wild duck	15
Pheasants	20	Teal	2
Hares	12	Brent goose	1
Rabbits	8	Bitterns	2
Woodcocks	7	Heron	3
Snipes	230	Spotted crake	1
Quail	1	Water rail	1
Landrail	1	Total	482

SEASON 17

1818–1819.

Sept. 1 *to Sept.* 1.

Partridges	125	Wood pigeon	1
Pheasants	3	Heron	2
Hares	11	Peewits	4
Rabbits	3	Goshawk	1
Snipes	92	Landrails	5
Wild duck	27	Moorhens	8
Wigeon	1	Greenshank	1
Brent goose	1	Coots	2
Teal	2	Total	289

SEASON 18

1819–1820.

Sept. 1 *to Sept.* 1.

Partridges	216	Brent geese	7
Hares	10	Wigeon	1
Pheasants	2	Teal	3
Rabbits	3	Sheldrake	1
Landrails	4	Curlew	4
Snipes	90		
Wild ducks	17	Total	358

SEASON 19

1820–1821.

Sept. 1 *to Sept.* 1.

Partridges	103	Tufted ducks	2
Hares	7	Golden-eyes	2
Rabbits	3	Teal	1
Pheasants	2	Wigeon	6
Snipes	100	Brent geese	26
Wild ducks	8	Curlews	2
Curres (scaup ducks)	6	Total	268

SEASON 20

1821–1822.

Sept. 1 *to Sept.* 1.

Partridges	164	Teal	8
Hares	13	Wigeon	44
Snipes	8	Brent geese	9
Pheasant	1		
Wild ducks	6	Total	253

Illness and other matters prevented my shooting but very little this season.

SEASON 21

1822–1823.

Sept. 1 *to Sept.* 1.

Partridges	132	Wigeon	97
Quail	1	Brent geese	180
Hares	6	Wild swans	4
Rabbits	3	Peewit	1
Pheasants	4	Spotted crake	1
Snipes	43	Curlews	5
Wild duck	22	Godwits	5
Curres (scaup ducks)	5	Golden plover	1
Teal	5		
Pintails	3	Total	518

SEASON 22

1823–1824.

Sept. 1 *to Sept.* 1.

Partridges	216	Wild ducks	8
Hares	7	Wigeon	1
Quail	1	Curres (scaup ducks)	3
Rabbits	3	Teal	4
Pheasants	2	Grey plover	2
Snipes	46		
Brent geese	2	Total	295

SEASON 23

1824–1825.

Sept. 1 *to Sept.* 1.

Partridges	160	Wild ducks	4
Hares	8	Tufted duck	1
Pheasant	1	Teal	9
Rabbit	1	Blackgame	10
Landrails	2	Stone curlew	1
Quail	1	Coots	7
Snipes	42	Total	247

Very little shooting this and last season owing to illness.

SEASON 24

1825–1826.

Sept. 1 *to Sept.* 1.

Partridges	184	Pintails	3
Hares	8	Dunbirds	10
Rabbit	1	Curres (scaup ducks)	9
Wood pigeons	2	Grey plover	4
Landrails	3	Godwits	4
Quails	2	Coots	3
Snipes	46	Cormorant	1
Brent geese	2	Dunlins	120
Wild ducks	7		
Wigeon	64	Total	475
Teal	2		

SEASON 25

1826–1827.

Sept. 1 *to Sept.* 1.

Partridges	122	Pintail	1
Hares	8	Teal	3
Pheasant	1	Curlews	5
Woodcock	1	Coots	4
Rabbits	3	Godwits	16
Brent geese[1]	8	Plover	9
Wigeon	209	Dunlins[2]	146
Wild duck	12	Olives (oyster catchers)	2
Sheldrake	1	Herons	3
Curres (scaup ducks)	11	Total	565

[1] The most killed this winter by anyone.

[2] In three shots.

SEASON 26

1827–1828.

Sept. 1 *to Sept.* 1.

Partridges	375	Brent geese	4
Hares	15	Black duck	1
Rabbits	12	Tufted duck	1
Pheasants	12	Curlews	2
Landrail	1	Olive (oyster catcher)	1
Snipes	22	Heron	1
Wild duck	3	Moorhen	1
Wigeon	80	Grey plover	2
Pintails	2		
Teal	2	Total	537

Besides many shore birds not here given.

SEASON 27

1828–1829.

Sept. 1 *to Sept.* 1.

Partridges	388	Wigeon	433
Hares	7	Teal	4
Quail	1	Curres (scaup ducks)	15
Rabbits	2	Great or velvet scoters	2
Pheasants	8	Dunbirds (pochards)	2
Woodcock	1	Plover	10
Snipes	70	Curlews	14
Wild swans	5	Coots	4
Barnacle goose	1	Olive (oyster catcher)	1
Brent geese	96	Moorhens	3
Wild ducks	25		
Pintail	1	Total	1,093

SEASON 28

1829–1830.

Sept. 1 *to Sept.* 1.

Partridges	122	Dunbirds (pochards)	2
Hares	14	Golden-eye ducks	3
Landrail	1	Pintails	2
Quail	1	Tufted duck	1
Pheasants	3	Scoter	1
Rabbits	3	Sheldrakes	12
Snipes	38	Brent geese	154
Wild ducks	11	Laughing geese	20
Wigeon	149	Wild swans	9
Teal	2	Plover	29
Curres (scaup ducks)	21		
		Total	598

Besides curlews, dunlins, coots, &c.

SEASON 29

1830–1831.

Sept. 1 *to Sept.* 1.

Partridges	173	Teal	3
Quails	7	Wigeon	103
Landrail	1	Curres (scaup ducks)	12
Hares	17	Brent geese	9
Rabbits	5	Pintails	2
Pheasants	10	Scoter	1
Woodcocks	2	Golden plover	4
Snipes	23		
Wild ducks	11	Total	383

No account kept of curlews, coots, dunlins, &c., shot.

SEASON 30

1831–1832.

Sept. 1 *to Sept.* 1.

Partridges	56	Dunbirds (pochards)	3
Hare[1]	1	Tufted ducks	10
Rabbit[1]	1	Pintail	1
Pheasants[1]	2	Wild ducks	7
Snipes	13	Teal	3
Wigeon	95	Curlews	2
Brent geese	38		
Curres (scaup ducks)	5	Total	237

Very little shooting this season, owing to an almost annihilation of game, and my own pressure of business.

SEASON 31

1832–1833.

Sept. 1 *to Sept.* 1.

Partridges	149	Wild duck	4
Hares	7	Wigeon	19
Quails	4	Brent geese	4
Landrail	1	Merganser	1
Rabbits	4	Tufted duck	1
Pheasants	3		
Snipes	7	Total	204

[1] All I saw.

SEASON 32

1833–1834.

Sept. 1 *to Sept.* 1.

Partridges	107	Snipe	1
Hares	5	Grey goose	1
Rabbits	2		
Pheasant	1	Total	117

Owing to trouble and business, only a few days' shooting this season.

SEASON 33

1834–1835.

Sept. 1 *to Sept.* 1.

Partridges	118	Wigeon	10
Hares	8	Teal	7
Pheasants	4	Spotted crake	1
Snipes	29	Grey plover	1
Wild ducks	7	Woodcock	1
Brent geese	2	Total	188

Illness prevented my shooting but very little this season.

SEASON 34

1835–1836.

Sept. 1 *to Sept.* 1.

Partridges	130	Pintails	6
Hare	1	Teal	6
Rabbits	3	Golden-eye ducks	2
Pheasants	3	Brent geese	8
Snipes	21	Plover	13
Wild ducks	20		
Wigeon	24	Total	337

I had but little shooting, and the scarcity of wild fowl lamentable; a general failure of all sport on the coast, and the geese appear to have been banished therefrom altogether.

SEASON 35

1836–1837.

Sept. 1 *to Sept.* 1.

Partridges	136	Shell duck	1
Pheasant	1	Curre (scaup duck)	1
Quail	1	Wigeon	81
Hares	5	Brent geese	33
Rabbits	5	Godwits	15
Snipes	24	Plover	3
Wild ducks	5		
		Total	311

As poor a season as ever was known. The coast is ruined, and we have now no game shooting after September.

SEASON 36

1837–1838.

Sept. 1 *to Sept.* 1.

Partridges[1]	106	Pintails	3
Hares	5	Tufted duck	1
Landrail	1	Pochards	4
Rabbits	4	Golden-eye ducks	8
Snipes	9	Shell ducks	6
Brent geese	310	Plover	56
Wild swans	19	Curlews	34
Eider duck	1	Godwits	5
Wild ducks	5	Dunlins	95
Wigeon	220		
Teal	2	Total	894

SEASON 37

1838–1839.

Sept. 1 *to Sept.* 1.

Partridges	58	Wigeon	5
Hares	6	Teal	1
Pheasants	7	Curlew	1
Rabbits	8	Godwits	2
Woodcock	1	Plover	4
Snipes	4		
		Total	97

The worst season in the memory of man, both on the coast for wild fowl, and inland for game. I never even launched a punt (it was not worth while) this winter, and did not fire a shot after November 26.

[1] Not a shot even at a pheasant this season.

SEASON 38

1839–1840.

Sept. 1 *to Sept.* 1.

Partridges	42	Wild ducks	2
Pheasants	4	Wigeon	30
Landrail	1	Velvet scoters	4
Hares	3	Curlews	7
Rabbits	3	Godwits	4
Snipes	11	Plovers	11
Brent geese [1]	5		
		Total	127

The game season was so bad I gave it up early as hopeless. The coast destitute of wild fowl.

SEASON 39

1840–1841.

Sept. 1 *to Sept.* 1.

Partridges [2]	80	Pintails	4
Pheasants	2	Shell ducks	6
Hare	1	Golden-eye duck	1
Rabbits	4	Grey geese	2
Wild ducks	19	Merganser	1
Brent geese	145	Plover	23
Teal	14	Godwits	13
Curres (scaup ducks)	2	Olive (oyster catcher)	1
Dunbird	1	Dunlins	179
Wigeon	185		
		Total	683

SEASON 40

1841–1842.

Sept. 1 *to Sept.* 1.

Partridges	53	Tufted ducks	2
Pheasant	1	Brent geese	20
Hares	7	Shell duck	1
Rabbits	8	Merganser	1
Landrail	1	Dunbirds (pochard)	3
Snipes	13	Curlews	4
Wild ducks	5	Plover	7
Wigeon	22	Dunlins	48
Pintails	4		
Golden-eye ducks	3	Total	203

Great scarcity of both game and wild fowl this season.

[1] Most killed by anyone at Keyhaven this winter.

[2] Owing to illness and business, I was only out five times game shooting.

SEASON 41

1842–1843.

Sept. 1 *to Sept.* 1.

Partridges	26	Wigeon	8
Pheasant[1]	1	Tufted duck	2
Landrail[1]	1	Teal	6
Hares[1]	2	Curlews	10
Rabbit[1]	1	Godwit	1
Snipes	31	Plovers	4
Brent geese	2	Total	95

No shooting for anyone on the coast this winter, and out only a few days in September, my health being very bad.

SEASON 42

1843–1844.

Sept. 1 *to Sept.* 1.

Partridges[2]	50	Teal	4
Hares[2]	2	Brent geese	3
Rabbits[2]	3	Plover	14
Landrail[2]	1	Godwits	4
Snipes	17	Grey plover	2
Wild duck	1	Dunlins	85
Wigeon	7	Total	193

Scarcely a gunner on the coast killed a dozen wild fowl all this cruel bad season.

SEASON 43

1844–1845.

Sept. 1 *to Sept.* 1.

Partridges[3]	10	Tufted ducks	3
Pheasant[3]	1	Teal	10
Hares[3]	3	Shell ducks	3
Rabbits[3]	5	Plover	37
Snipes	17	Godwits	14
Wild swan	1	Curlews	4
Brent geese	94	Olive (oyster catcher)	1
Barnacle geese	2	Ring dotterels	2
Wild ducks	6	Dunlins	196
Wigeon	206		
Pintails	6	Total	621

A very long and yet not a brilliant season at Keyhaven.

[1] All I set eyes on. [2] No time for game shooting in September.

[3] Had very little time for game shooting this season.

SEASON 44

1845–1846.

Sept. 1 *to Sept.* 1.

Partridges [1]	157	Rabbits [3]	4
Pheasants [2]	2	Snipes	21
Hares [3]	18		
		Total	202

Such an unprecedented scarcity of wild fowl at Keyhaven on the coast that I would not disgrace myself by putting a great gun afloat. A general complaint all over England that there were no wild fowl, woodcocks, snipes, and other winter birds this season.

SEASON 45

1846–1847.

Sept. 1 *to Sept.* 1.

Partridges [1]	87	Wigeon	31
Pheasants [5]	3	Pintail	1
Hares [5]	16	Teal	2
Rabbits	6	Shell duck	1
Wood pigeons	3	Phalaropes	2
Snipes	40	Plovers	39
Brent geese	28	Dunlins	313
Wild ducks	39		
		Total	611

Keyhaven ruined for coast shooting.

SEASON 46

1847–1848.

Sept. 1 *to Sept.* 1.

Partridges [6]	173	Teal	3
Pheasant [7]	1	Pochard	2
Landrail	1	Curre (scaup duck)	1
Quail	8	Spotted crake	1
Hares	5	Green sandpiper (ox-eye)	1
Snipes	22	Golden plover	2
Brent geese	76	Olives (oyster catchers)	2
Wild ducks	5	Curlews	5
Wigeon	12		
		Total	320

[1] I was out but eleven half-days, and then too weak and unwell to fag as usual.
[2] All I saw.
[3] All I shot at.
[4] No game shooting after September.
[5] All I saw.
[6] All in September.
[7] All I saw.

SEASON 47

1848–1849.

Sept. 1 *to Sept.* 1.

Partridges	191	Wigeon	26
Pheasants [1]	2	Tufted duck	1
Landrails [1]	3	Teal	3
Quail [1]	1	Curlews	9
Hares	14	Godwit	1
Rabbits	11	Plovers	3
Snipes	32	Dunlins	2
Brent geese	27		
Wild ducks	5	Total	331

A wretched season on the coast at Keyhaven.

SEASON 48

1849–1850.

Sept. 1 *to Sept.* 1.

Partridges	115	Wigeon	12
Pheasants [1]	3	Tufted duck	1
Landrail	1	Teal	1
Hares	8	Curlews	5
Rabbits	4	Godwit	1
Snipes	15	Plover	7
Brent geese	12	Dunlins	41
Wild ducks	3		
		Total	229

The coast shooting now at Keyhaven is annihilated, and we have had a miserable game season, and the worst snipe shooting on record in spite of five weeks of hard winter weather.

SEASON 49

1850–1851.

Sept. 1 *to Sept.* 1.

Partridges	95	Wild duck	1
Pheasants [1]	4	Tufted duck	1
Hares [2]	27	Wigeon	2
Rabbits	3	Teal	1
Snipes	21		
		Total	155

As the coast was destitute of every kind of winter bird, I never went to Keyhaven this season.

[1] All I saw.

[2] With the help of 'Siney' and 'Charles Heath' we made up to 53 hares this season, the most ever killed here for many years.

SEASON 50

1851–1852.

Sept. 1 *to Sept.* 1.

Partridges [1]	0	Wild ducks	8
Pheasants [1]	0	Shell ducks	2
Rabbits	3	Teal	4
Snipes	24	Total	41

Illness nearly the whole season prevented my shooting, and at one time my life was in danger.

SEASON 51

1852–1853.

Sept. 1 *to Aug.* 7.[2]

Partridges	164	Rabbits	9
Pheasant [3]	1	Wood pigeon	1
Landrails [3]	4	Snipes	20
Quails [3]	4	Dunlins	8
Hares	39	Total	250

Not a shot at a wild fowl this season, but I beat all the neighbours at partridge shooting in September.

The foregoing lists are epitomised from the original Diary of Colonel Peter Hawker, but they do not include many hundred shore birds that were, besides those given, killed by him, and, as stated in his Diary, unrecorded at the time. The wild fowl and marsh birds that were killed by the Colonel in his visits to Norfolk are also omitted in his Diary, though alluded to as having been numerous.

The bags of trout caught by Colonel Hawker in the river 'Test' at Longparish are only recorded occasionally, and the entries that are to be found under this head but roughly indicate the numbers taken by his rod. The trout killed in the fifty years of the Colonel's sporting life could not (from the allusions to angling in his Diary), at a low estimate, have been less than twelve thousand.

[1] None; never fired a shot. [2] Colonel Hawker died this day. [3] All I saw.

INDEX

THE END.